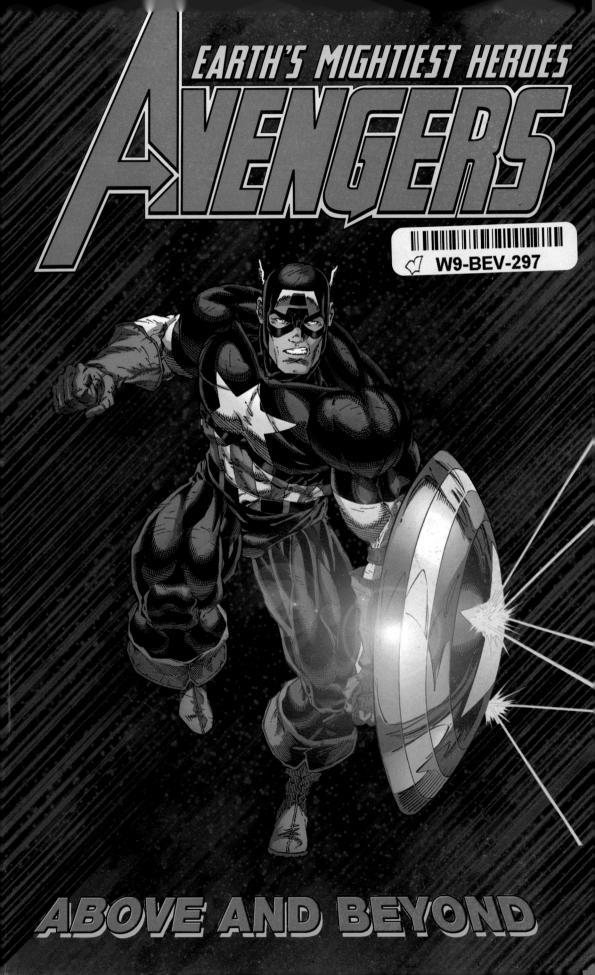

EARTH'S MIGHTIEST HEROES

AVENGERS

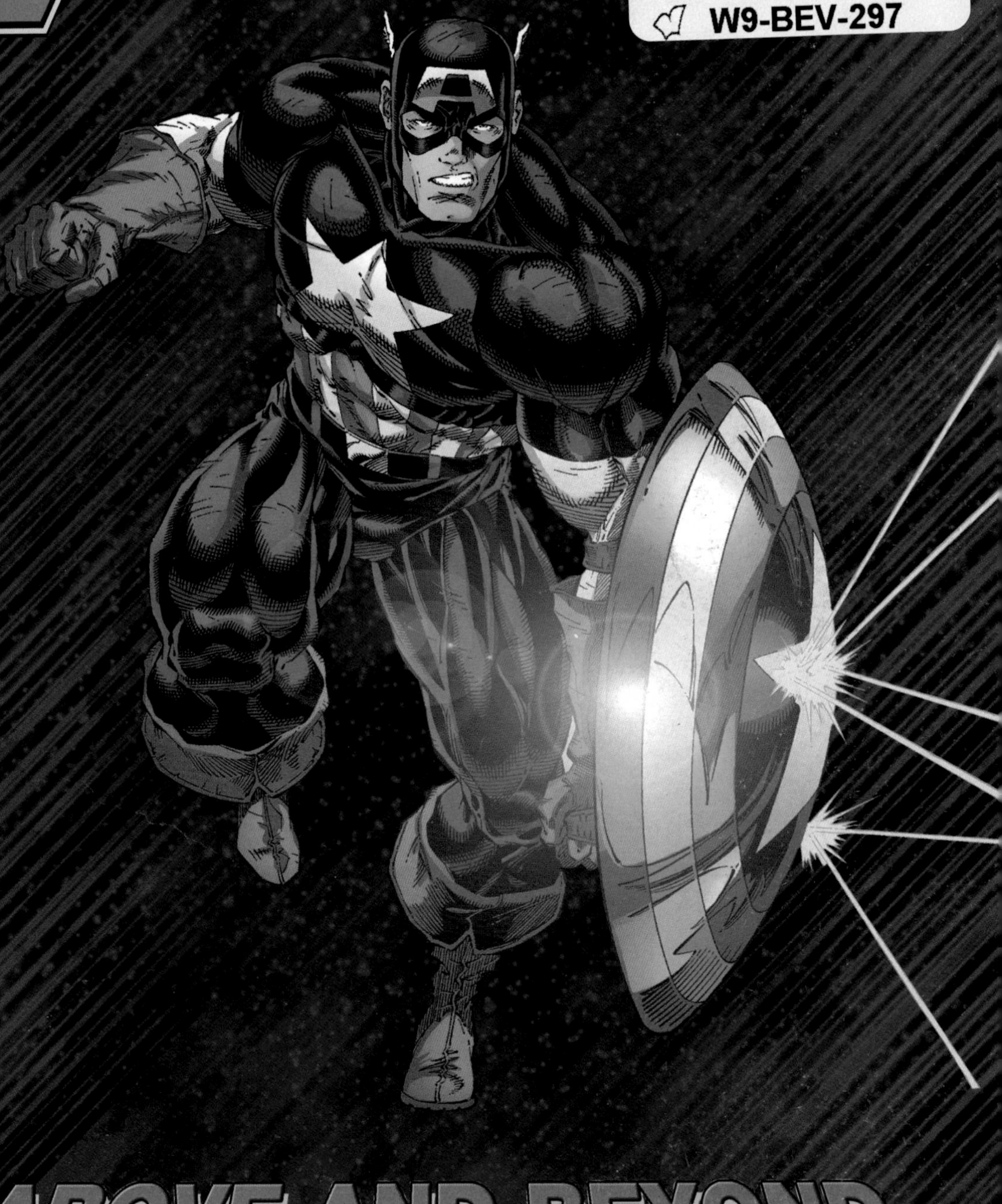

ABOVE AND BEYOND

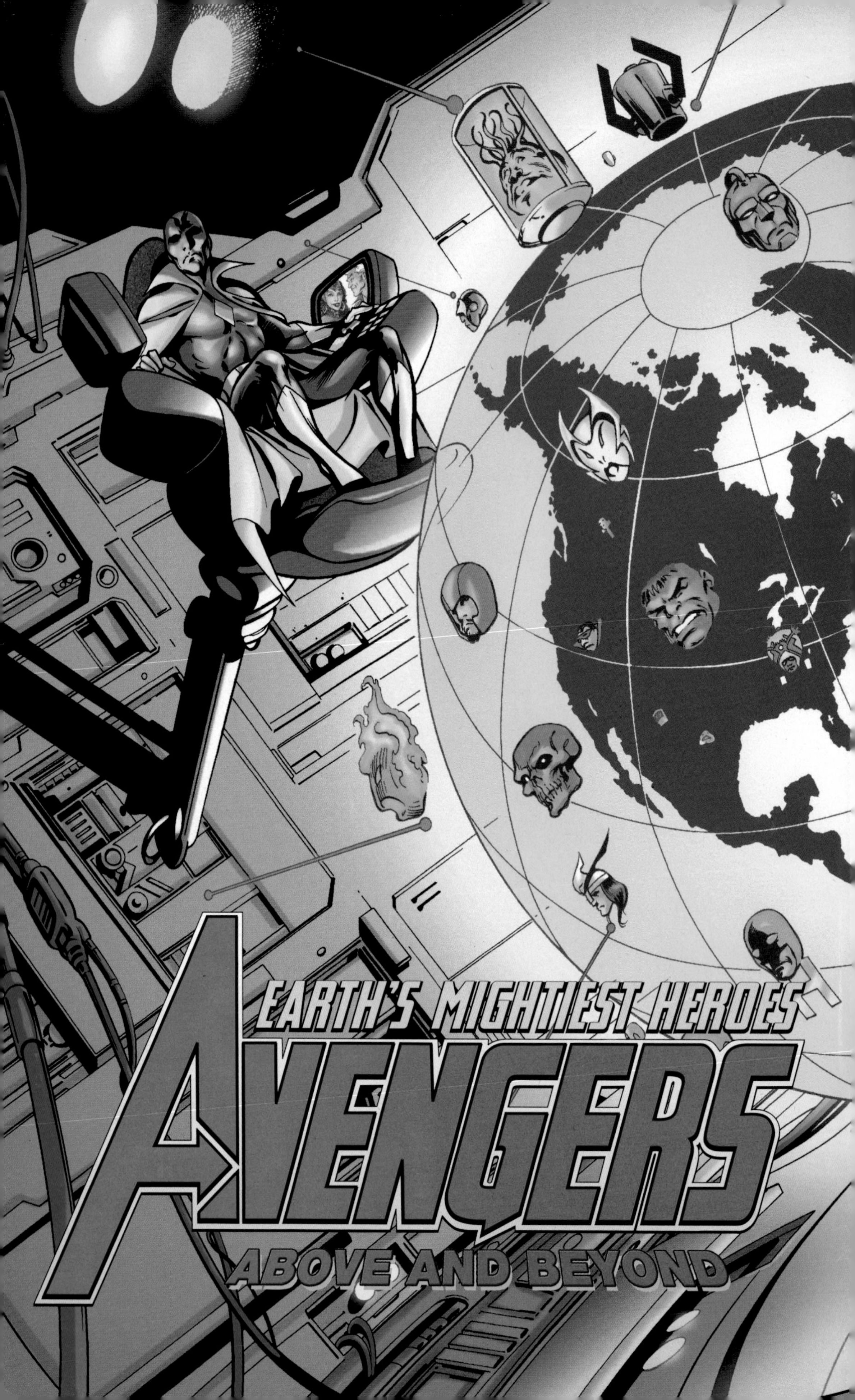
EARTH'S MIGHTIEST HEROES
AVENGERS
ABOVE AND BEYOND

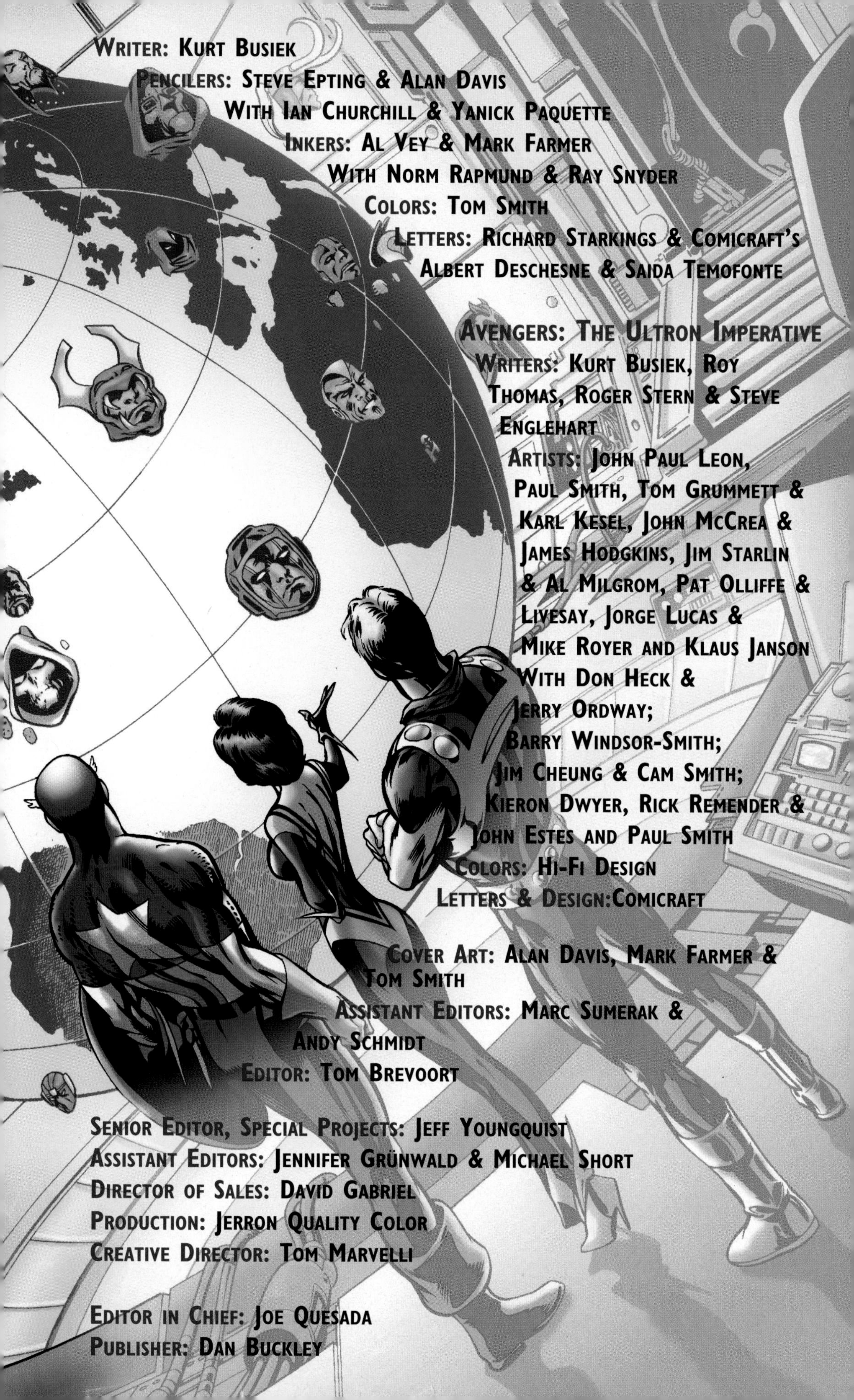

Writer: Kurt Busiek
Pencilers: Steve Epting & Alan Davis
With Ian Churchill & Yanick Paquette
Inkers: Al Vey & Mark Farmer
With Norm Rapmund & Ray Snyder
Colors: Tom Smith
Letters: Richard Starkings & Comicraft's
Albert Deschesne & Saida Temofonte

Avengers: The Ultron Imperative
Writers: Kurt Busiek, Roy Thomas, Roger Stern & Steve Englehart
Artists: John Paul Leon, Paul Smith, Tom Grummett & Karl Kesel, John McCrea & James Hodgkins, Jim Starlin & Al Milgrom, Pat Olliffe & Livesay, Jorge Lucas & Mike Royer and Klaus Janson With Don Heck & Jerry Ordway; Barry Windsor-Smith; Jim Cheung & Cam Smith; Kieron Dwyer, Rick Remender & John Estes and Paul Smith
Colors: Hi-Fi Design
Letters & Design: Comicraft

Cover Art: Alan Davis, Mark Farmer & Tom Smith
Assistant Editors: Marc Sumerak & Andy Schmidt
Editor: Tom Brevoort

Senior Editor, Special Projects: Jeff Youngquist
Assistant Editors: Jennifer Grünwald & Michael Short
Director of Sales: David Gabriel
Production: Jerron Quality Color
Creative Director: Tom Marvelli

Editor in Chief: Joe Quesada
Publisher: Dan Buckley

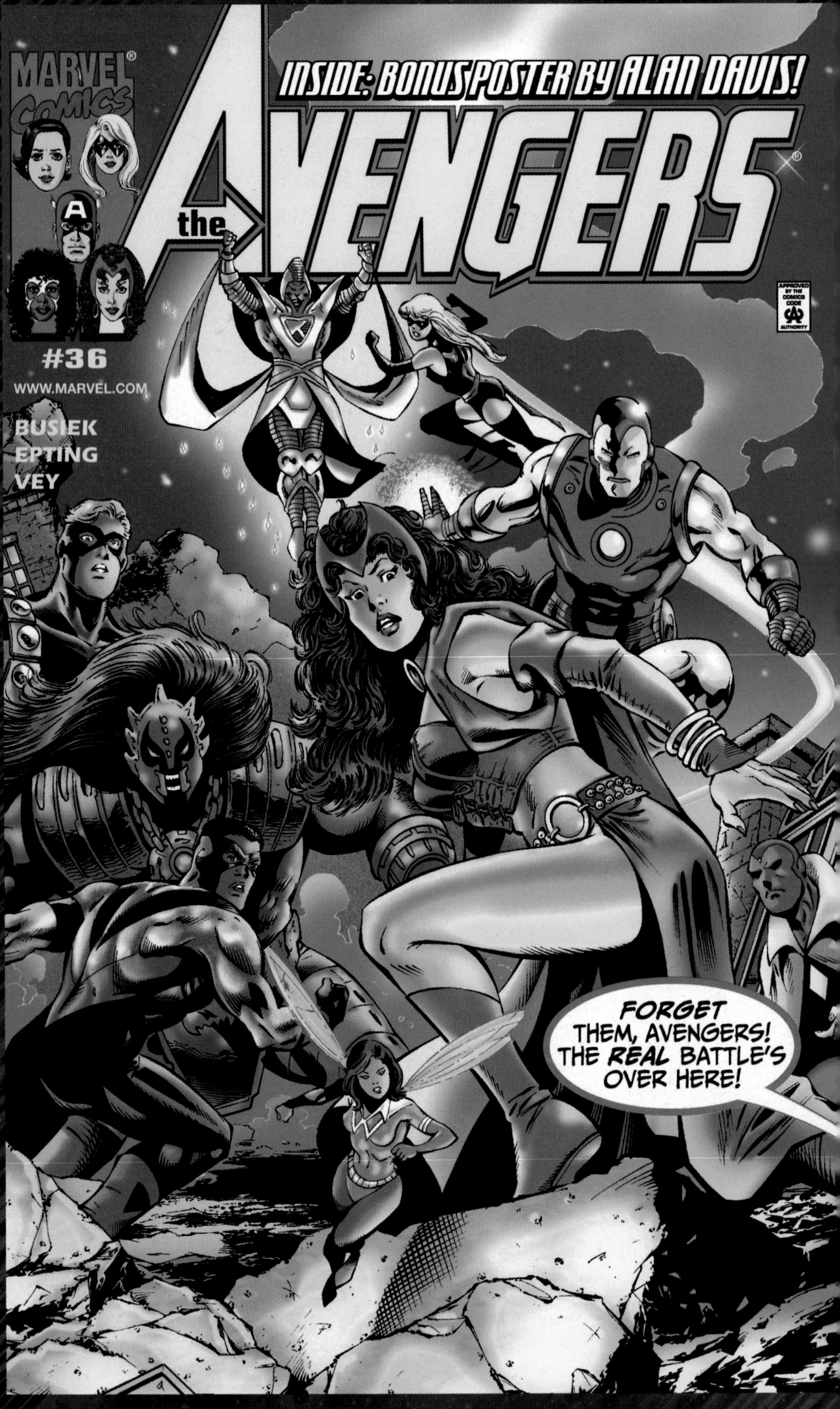
MARVEL COMICS
INSIDE: BONUS POSTER BY ALAN DAVIS!
the AVENGERS
#36
WWW.MARVEL.COM
BUSIEK
EPTING
VEY
FORGET THEM, AVENGERS! THE REAL BATTLE'S OVER HERE!

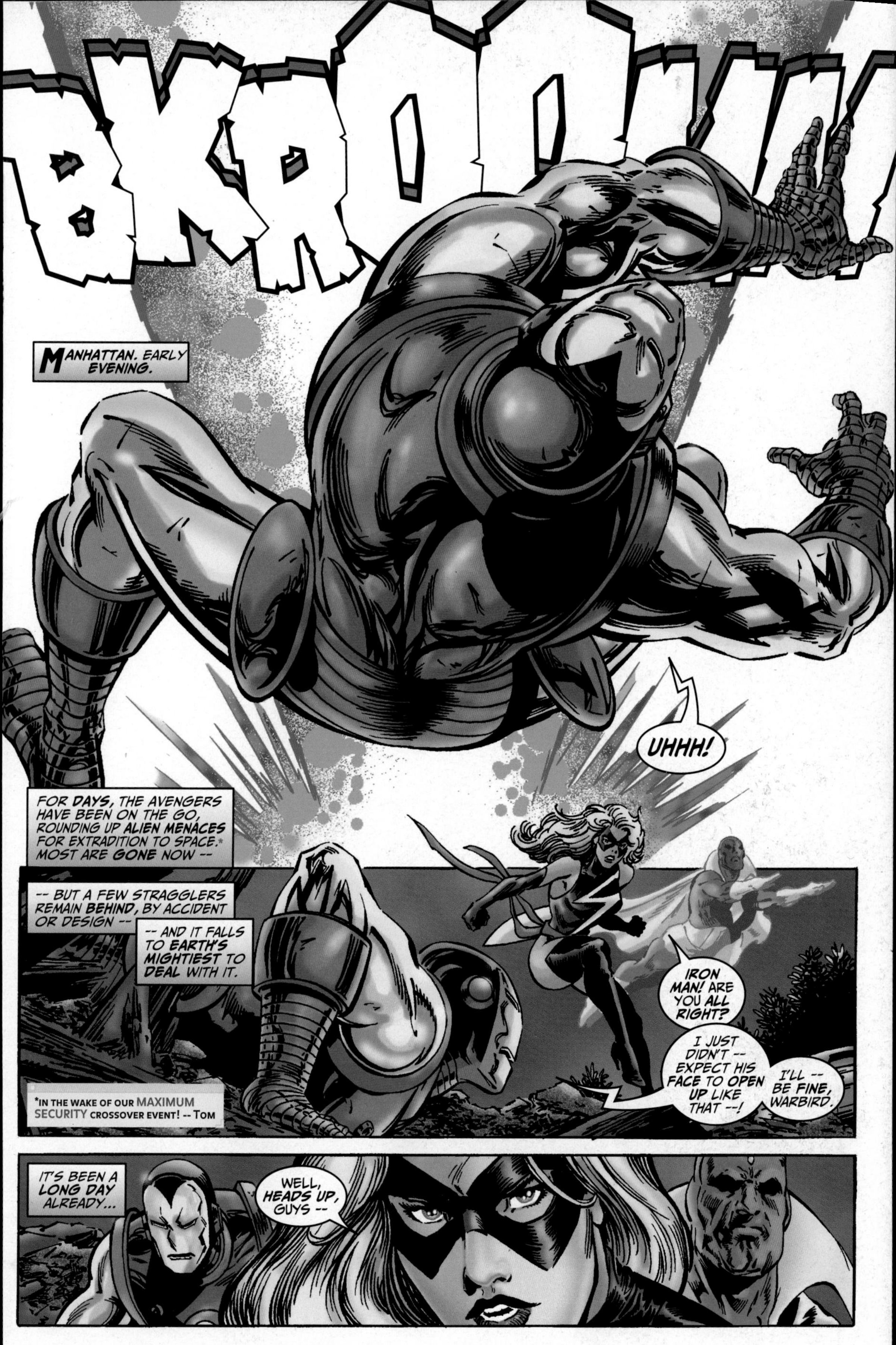
BKROOOM!
MANHATTAN. EARLY EVENING.
UHHH!
FOR DAYS, THE AVENGERS HAVE BEEN ON THE GO, ROUNDING UP ALIEN MENACES FOR EXTRADITION TO SPACE.* MOST ARE GONE NOW --
-- BUT A FEW STRAGGLERS REMAIN BEHIND, BY ACCIDENT OR DESIGN --
-- AND IT FALLS TO EARTH'S MIGHTIEST TO DEAL WITH IT.
IRON MAN! ARE YOU ALL RIGHT?
I JUST DIDN'T -- EXPECT HIS FACE TO OPEN UP LIKE THAT --!
I'LL -- BE FINE, WARBIRD.
*IN THE WAKE OF OUR MAXIMUM SECURITY CROSSOVER EVENT! -- TOM
IT'S BEEN A LONG DAY ALREADY...
WELL, HEADS UP, GUYS --

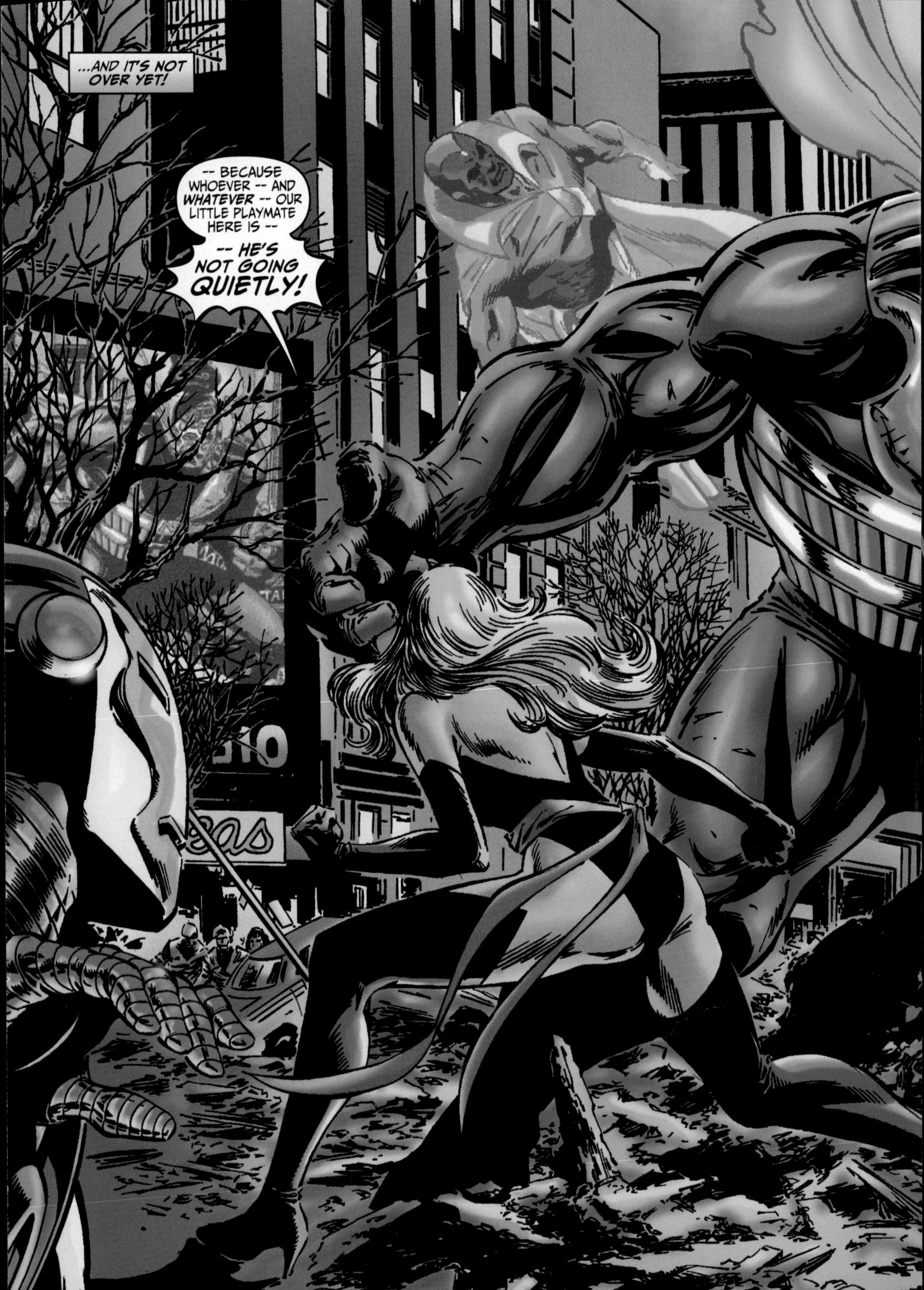
...AND IT'S NOT OVER YET!
-- BECAUSE WHOEVER -- AND WHATEVER -- OUR LITTLE PLAYMATE HERE IS --
-- HE'S NOT GOING QUIETLY!

AND THERE CAME A DAY UNLIKE ANY OTHER, WHEN EARTH'S MIGHTIEST HEROES FOUND THEMSELVES UNITED AGAINST A COMMON THREAT! ON THAT DAY, THE AVENGERS WERE BORN - TO FIGHT THE FOES NO SINGLE SUPER HERO COULD WITHSTAND! STAN LEE PRESENTS:

NO REST FOR THE

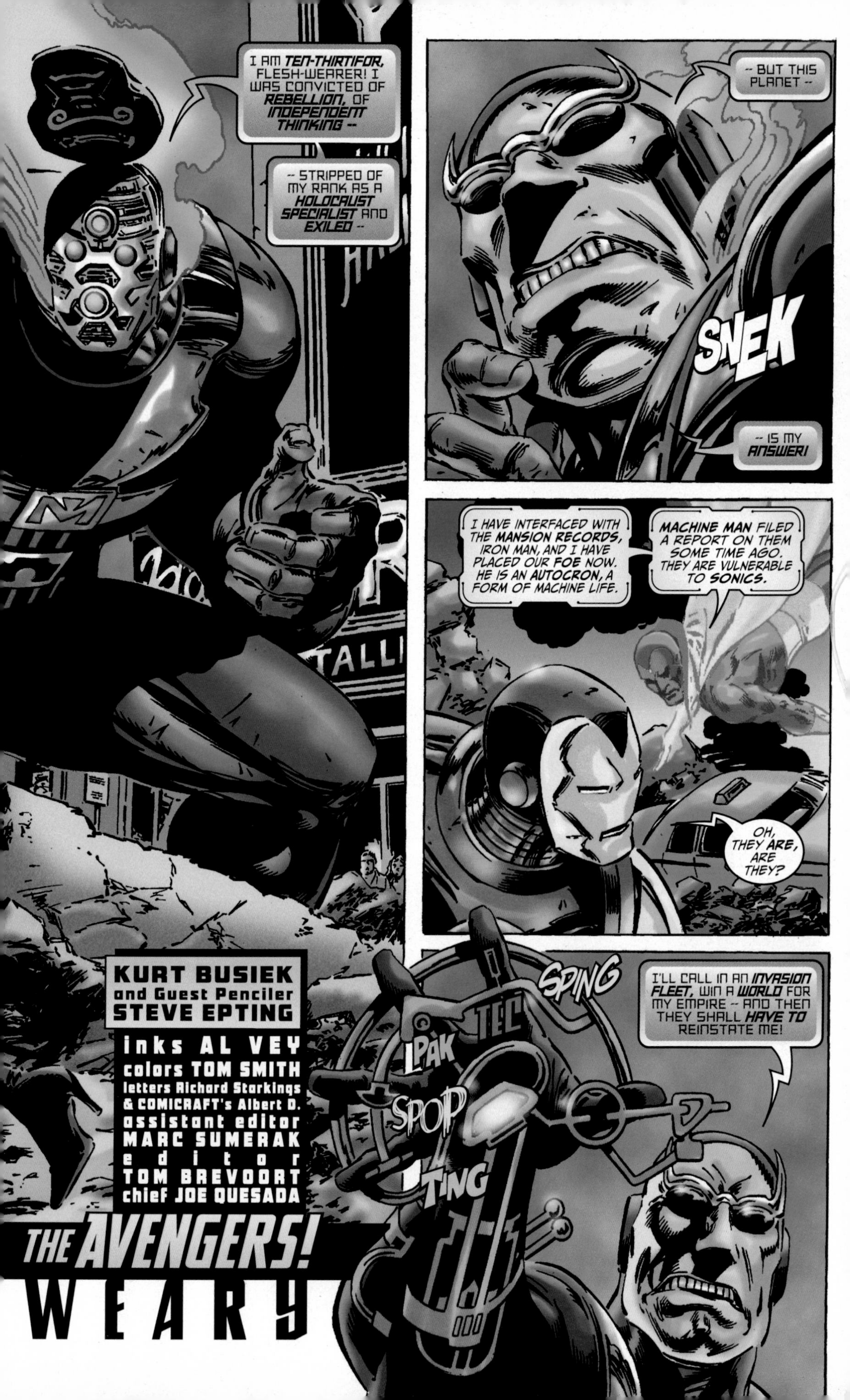
I AM TEN-THIRTIFOR, FLESH-WEARER! I WAS CONVICTED OF REBELLION, OF INDEPENDENT THINKING --
-- STRIPPED OF MY RANK AS A HOLOCAUST SPECIALIST AND EXILED --
-- BUT THIS PLANET --
SNEK
-- IS MY ANSWER!
I HAVE INTERFACED WITH THE MANSION RECORDS, IRON MAN, AND I HAVE PLACED OUR FOE NOW. HE IS AN AUTOCRON, A FORM OF MACHINE LIFE.
MACHINE MAN FILED A REPORT ON THEM SOME TIME AGO. THEY ARE VULNERABLE TO SONICS.
OH, THEY ARE, ARE THEY?
SPING
TEC
LPAK
SPOP
TING
I'LL CALL IN AN INVASION FLEET, WIN A WORLD FOR MY EMPIRE -- AND THEN THEY SHALL HAVE TO REINSTATE ME!
KURT BUSIEK
and Guest Penciler
STEVE EPTING
inks AL VEY
colors TOM SMITH
letters Richard Starkings
& COMICRAFT's Albert D.
assistant editor
MARC SUMERAK
editor
TOM BREVOORT
chief JOE QUESADA
THE AVENGERS!
WEARY

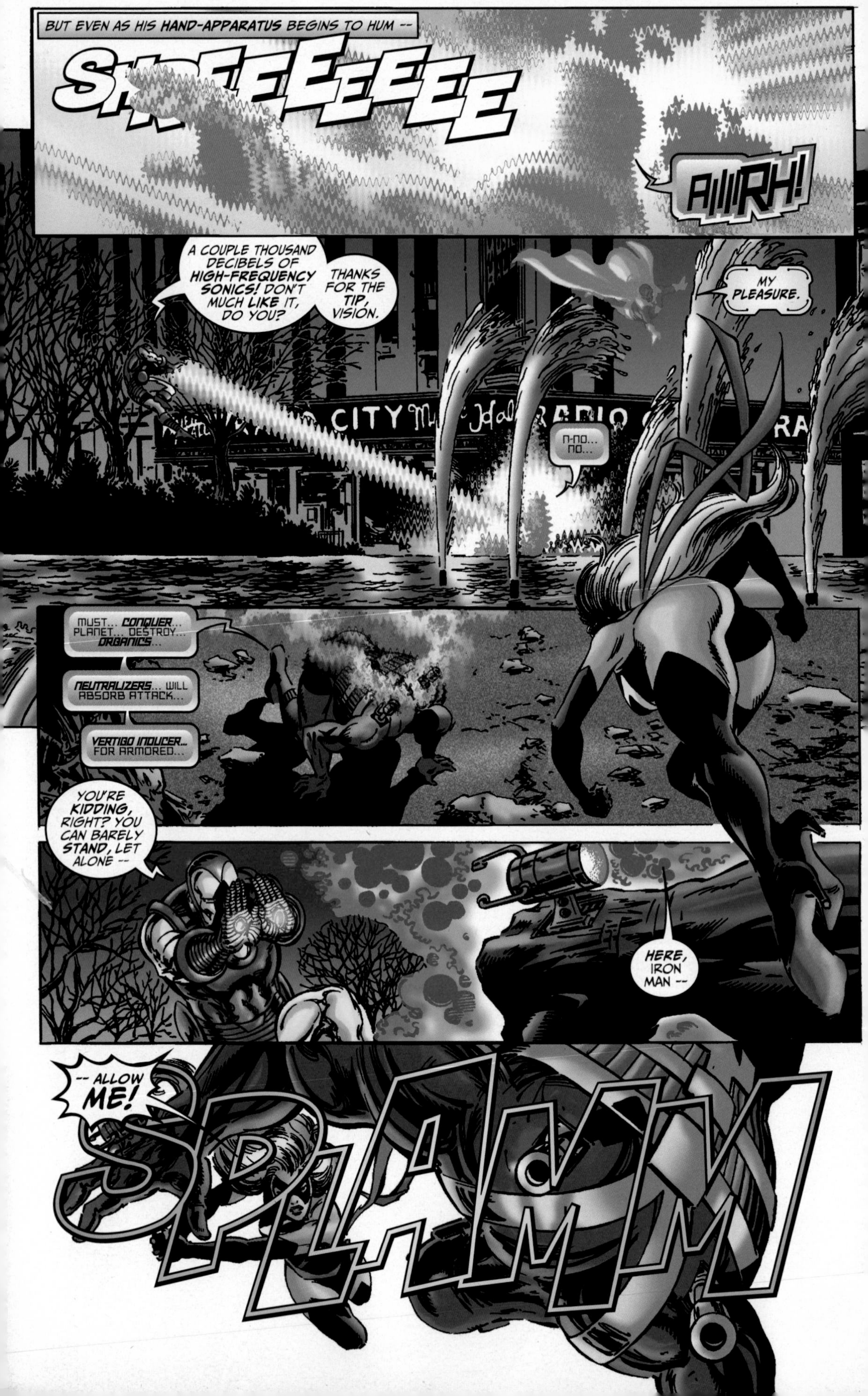
BUT EVEN AS HIS HAND-APPARATUS BEGINS TO HUM --
AIIIRH!
A COUPLE THOUSAND DECIBELS OF HIGH-FREQUENCY SONICS! DON'T MUCH LIKE IT, DO YOU?
THANKS FOR THE TIP, VISION.
MY PLEASURE.
CITY
RADIO
N-NO... NO...
MUST... CONQUER... PLANET... DESTROY... ORGANICS...
NEUTRALIZERS... WILL ABSORB ATTACK...
VERTIGO INDUCER... FOR ARMORED...
YOU'RE KIDDING, RIGHT? YOU CAN BARELY STAND, LET ALONE --
HERE, IRON MAN --
-- ALLOW ME!

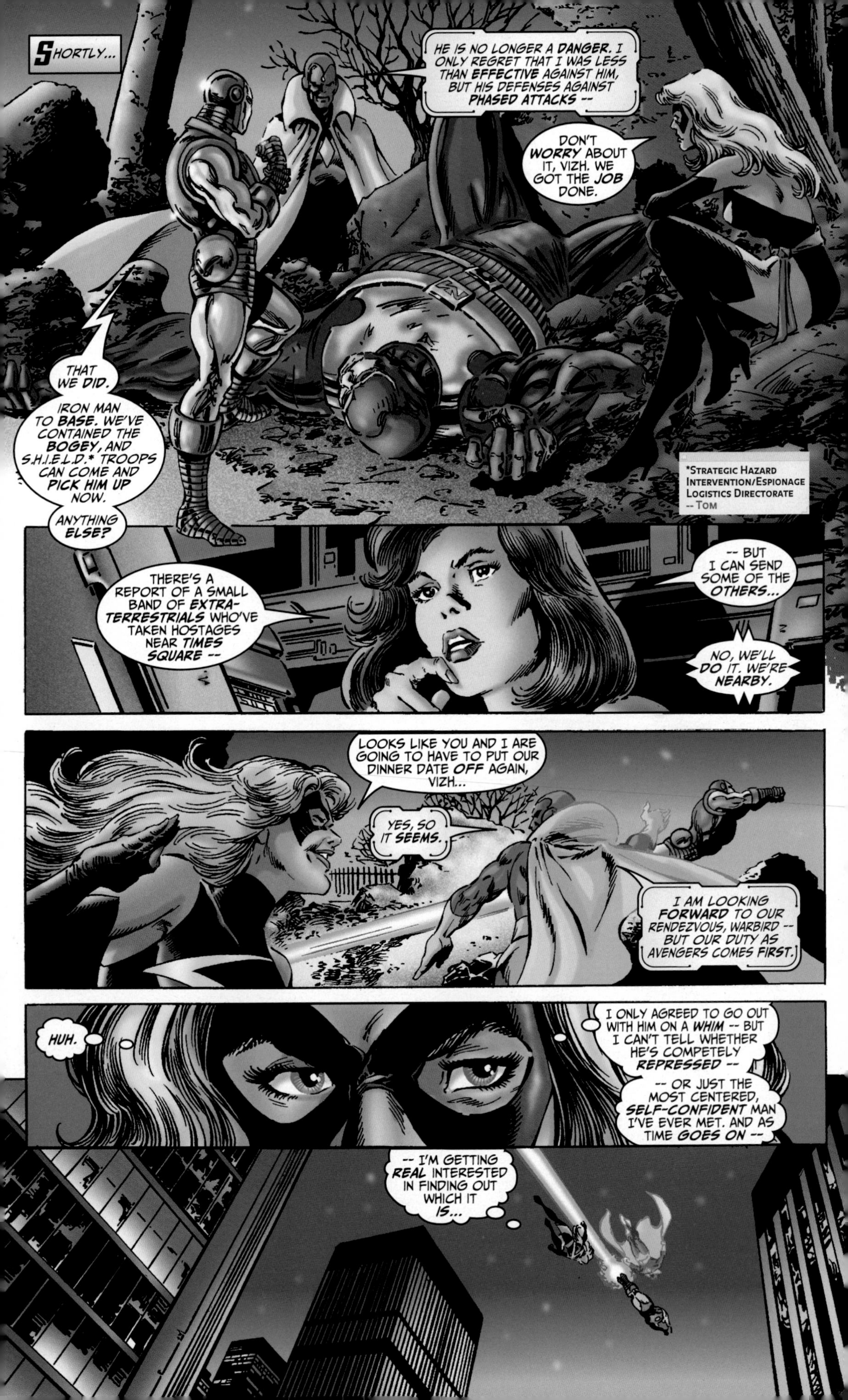
SHORTLY...
HE IS NO LONGER A DANGER. I ONLY REGRET THAT I WAS LESS THAN EFFECTIVE AGAINST HIM, BUT HIS DEFENSES AGAINST PHASED ATTACKS --
DON'T WORRY ABOUT IT, VIZH. WE GOT THE JOB DONE.
THAT WE DID.
IRON MAN TO BASE. WE'VE CONTAINED THE BOGEY, AND S.H.I.E.L.D.* TROOPS CAN COME AND PICK HIM UP NOW.
ANYTHING ELSE?
*STRATEGIC HAZARD INTERVENTION/ESPIONAGE LOGISTICS DIRECTORATE -- TOM
THERE'S A REPORT OF A SMALL BAND OF EXTRA-TERRESTRIALS WHO'VE TAKEN HOSTAGES NEAR TIMES SQUARE --
-- BUT I CAN SEND SOME OF THE OTHERS...
NO, WE'LL DO IT. WE'RE NEARBY.
LOOKS LIKE YOU AND I ARE GOING TO HAVE TO PUT OUR DINNER DATE OFF AGAIN, VIZH...
YES, SO IT SEEMS.
I AM LOOKING FORWARD TO OUR RENDEZVOUS, WARBIRD -- BUT OUR DUTY AS AVENGERS COMES FIRST.
HUH.
I ONLY AGREED TO GO OUT WITH HIM ON A WHIM -- BUT I CAN'T TELL WHETHER HE'S COMPETELY REPRESSED --
-- OR JUST THE MOST CENTERED, SELF-CONFIDENT MAN I'VE EVER MET. AND AS TIME GOES ON --
-- I'M GETTING REAL INTERESTED IN FINDING OUT WHICH IT IS...

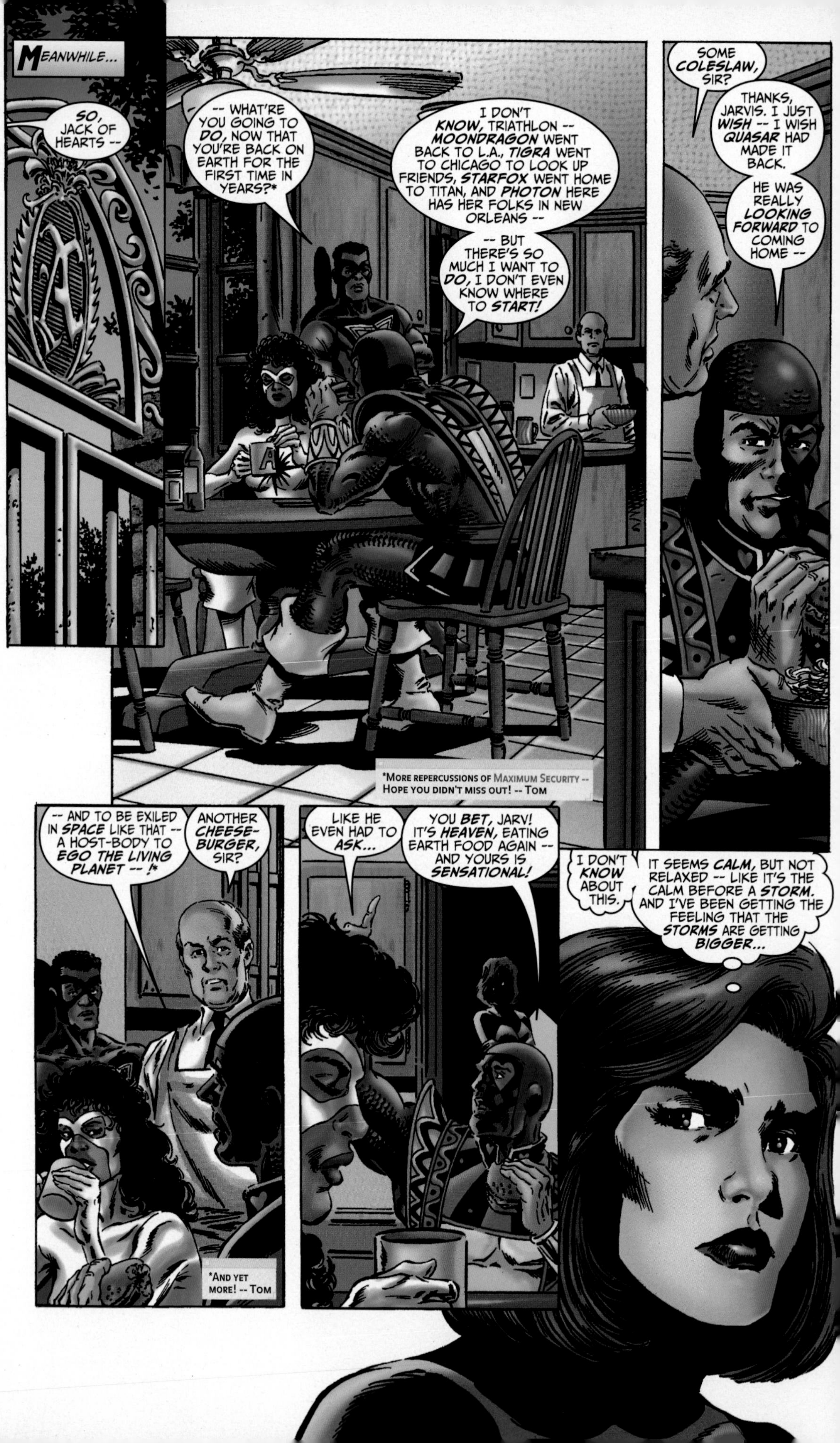
MEANWHILE...
SO, JACK OF HEARTS --
-- WHAT'RE YOU GOING TO DO, NOW THAT YOU'RE BACK ON EARTH FOR THE FIRST TIME IN YEARS?*
I DON'T KNOW, TRIATHLON -- MOONDRAGON WENT BACK TO L.A., TIGRA WENT TO CHICAGO TO LOOK UP FRIENDS, STARFOX WENT HOME TO TITAN, AND PHOTON HERE HAS HER FOLKS IN NEW ORLEANS --
-- BUT THERE'S SO MUCH I WANT TO DO, I DON'T EVEN KNOW WHERE TO START!
*MORE REPERCUSSIONS OF MAXIMUM SECURITY -- HOPE YOU DIDN'T MISS OUT! -- TOM
SOME COLESLAW, SIR?
THANKS, JARVIS. I JUST WISH -- I WISH QUASAR HAD MADE IT BACK.
HE WAS REALLY LOOKING FORWARD TO COMING HOME --
-- AND TO BE EXILED IN SPACE LIKE THAT -- A HOST-BODY TO EGO THE LIVING PLANET -- !*
ANOTHER CHEESE-BURGER, SIR?
*AND YET MORE! -- TOM
LIKE HE EVEN HAD TO ASK...
YOU BET, JARV! IT'S HEAVEN, EATING EARTH FOOD AGAIN -- AND YOURS IS SENSATIONAL!
I DON'T KNOW ABOUT THIS.
IT SEEMS CALM, BUT NOT RELAXED -- LIKE IT'S THE CALM BEFORE A STORM. AND I'VE BEEN GETTING THE FEELING THAT THE STORMS ARE GETTING BIGGER...

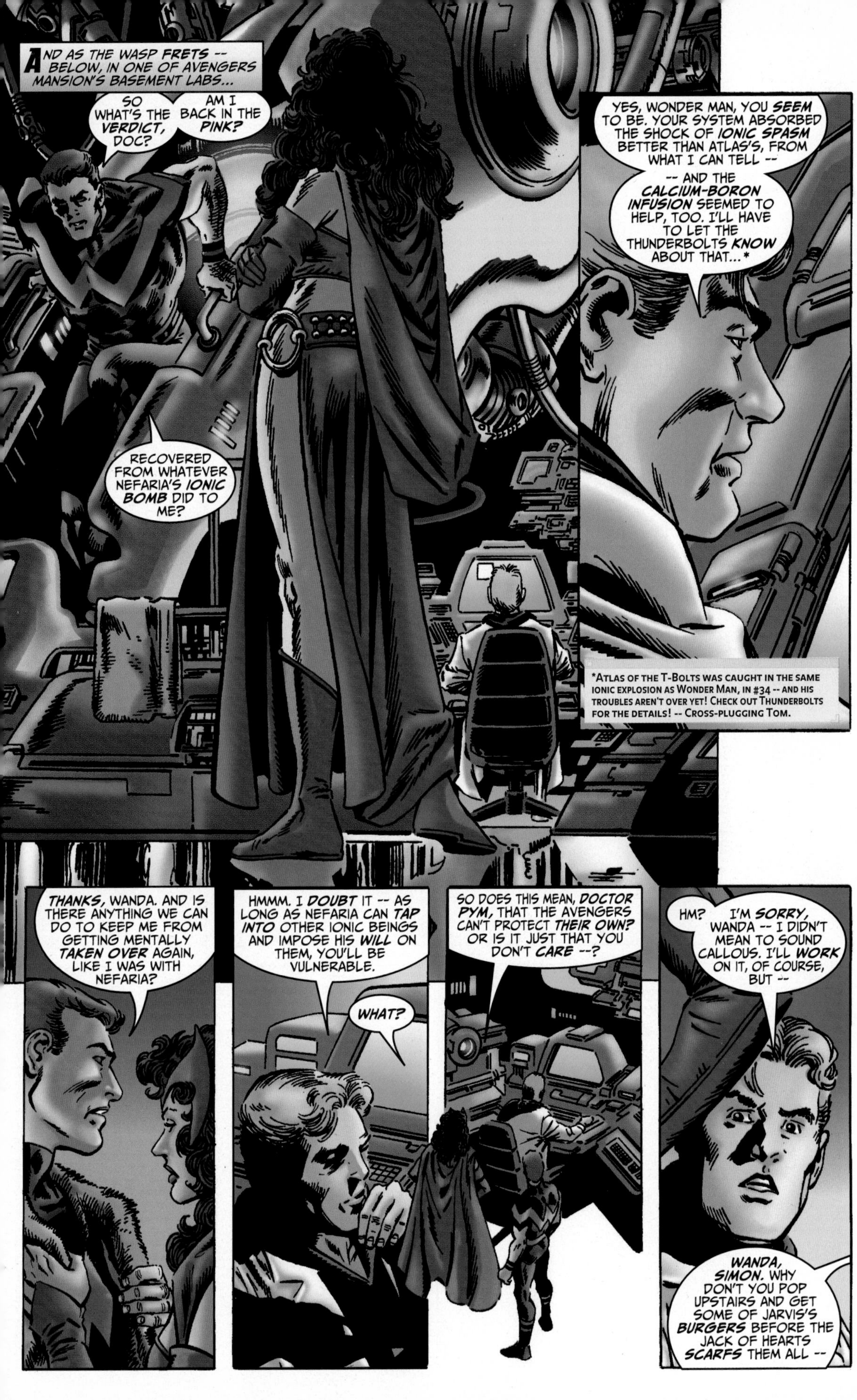
AND AS THE WASP FRETS -- BELOW, IN ONE OF AVENGERS MANSION'S BASEMENT LABS...
SO WHAT'S THE VERDICT, DOC?
AM I BACK IN THE PINK?
RECOVERED FROM WHATEVER NEFARIA'S IONIC BOMB DID TO ME?
YES, WONDER MAN, YOU SEEM TO BE. YOUR SYSTEM ABSORBED THE SHOCK OF IONIC SPASM BETTER THAN ATLAS'S, FROM WHAT I CAN TELL --
-- AND THE CALCIUM-BORON INFUSION SEEMED TO HELP, TOO. I'LL HAVE TO LET THE THUNDERBOLTS KNOW ABOUT THAT...*
*ATLAS OF THE T-BOLTS WAS CAUGHT IN THE SAME IONIC EXPLOSION AS WONDER MAN, IN #34 -- AND HIS TROUBLES AREN'T OVER YET! CHECK OUT THUNDERBOLTS FOR THE DETAILS! -- CROSS-PLUGGING TOM.
THANKS, WANDA. AND IS THERE ANYTHING WE CAN DO TO KEEP ME FROM GETTING MENTALLY TAKEN OVER AGAIN, LIKE I WAS WITH NEFARIA?
HMMM. I DOUBT IT -- AS LONG AS NEFARIA CAN TAP INTO OTHER IONIC BEINGS AND IMPOSE HIS WILL ON THEM, YOU'LL BE VULNERABLE.
WHAT?
SO DOES THIS MEAN, DOCTOR PYM, THAT THE AVENGERS CAN'T PROTECT THEIR OWN? OR IS IT JUST THAT YOU DON'T CARE --?
HM?
I'M SORRY, WANDA -- I DIDN'T MEAN TO SOUND CALLOUS. I'LL WORK ON IT, OF COURSE, BUT --
WANDA, SIMON. WHY DON'T YOU POP UPSTAIRS AND GET SOME OF JARVIS'S BURGERS BEFORE THE JACK OF HEARTS SCARFS THEM ALL --

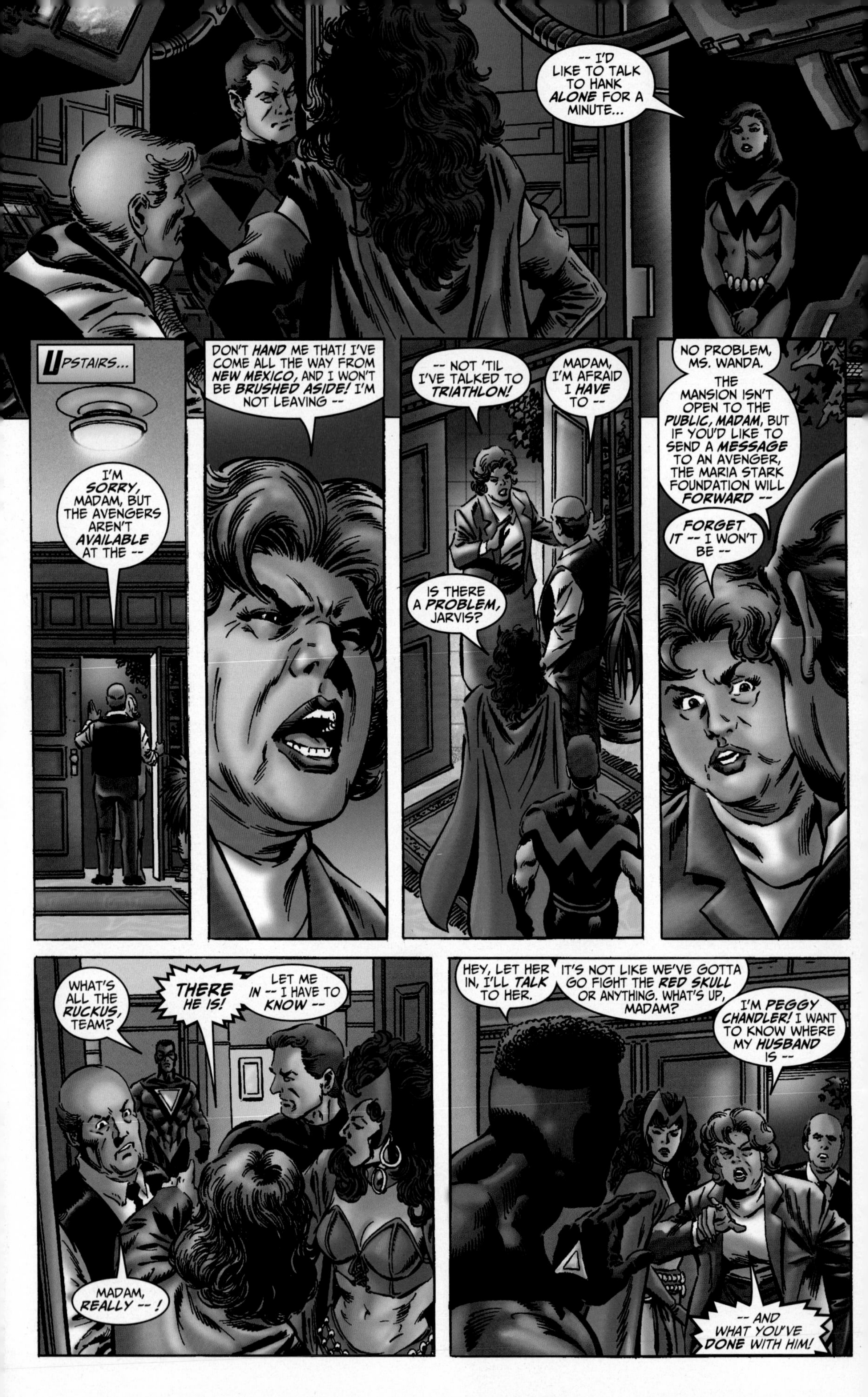
-- I'D LIKE TO TALK TO HANK ALONE FOR A MINUTE...
UPSTAIRS...
I'M SORRY, MADAM, BUT THE AVENGERS AREN'T AVAILABLE AT THE --
DON'T HAND ME THAT! I'VE COME ALL THE WAY FROM NEW MEXICO, AND I WON'T BE BRUSHED ASIDE! I'M NOT LEAVING --
-- NOT 'TIL I'VE TALKED TO TRIATHLON!
MADAM, I'M AFRAID I HAVE TO --
IS THERE A PROBLEM, JARVIS?
NO PROBLEM, MS. WANDA.
THE MANSION ISN'T OPEN TO THE PUBLIC, MADAM, BUT IF YOU'D LIKE TO SEND A MESSAGE TO AN AVENGER, THE MARIA STARK FOUNDATION WILL FORWARD --
FORGET IT -- I WON'T BE --
WHAT'S ALL THE RUCKUS, TEAM?
THERE HE IS!
LET ME IN -- I HAVE TO KNOW --
MADAM, REALLY -- !
HEY, LET HER IN, I'LL TALK TO HER.
IT'S NOT LIKE WE'VE GOTTA GO FIGHT THE RED SKULL OR ANYTHING. WHAT'S UP, MADAM?
I'M PEGGY CHANDLER! I WANT TO KNOW WHERE MY HUSBAND IS --
-- AND WHAT YOU'VE DONE WITH HIM!

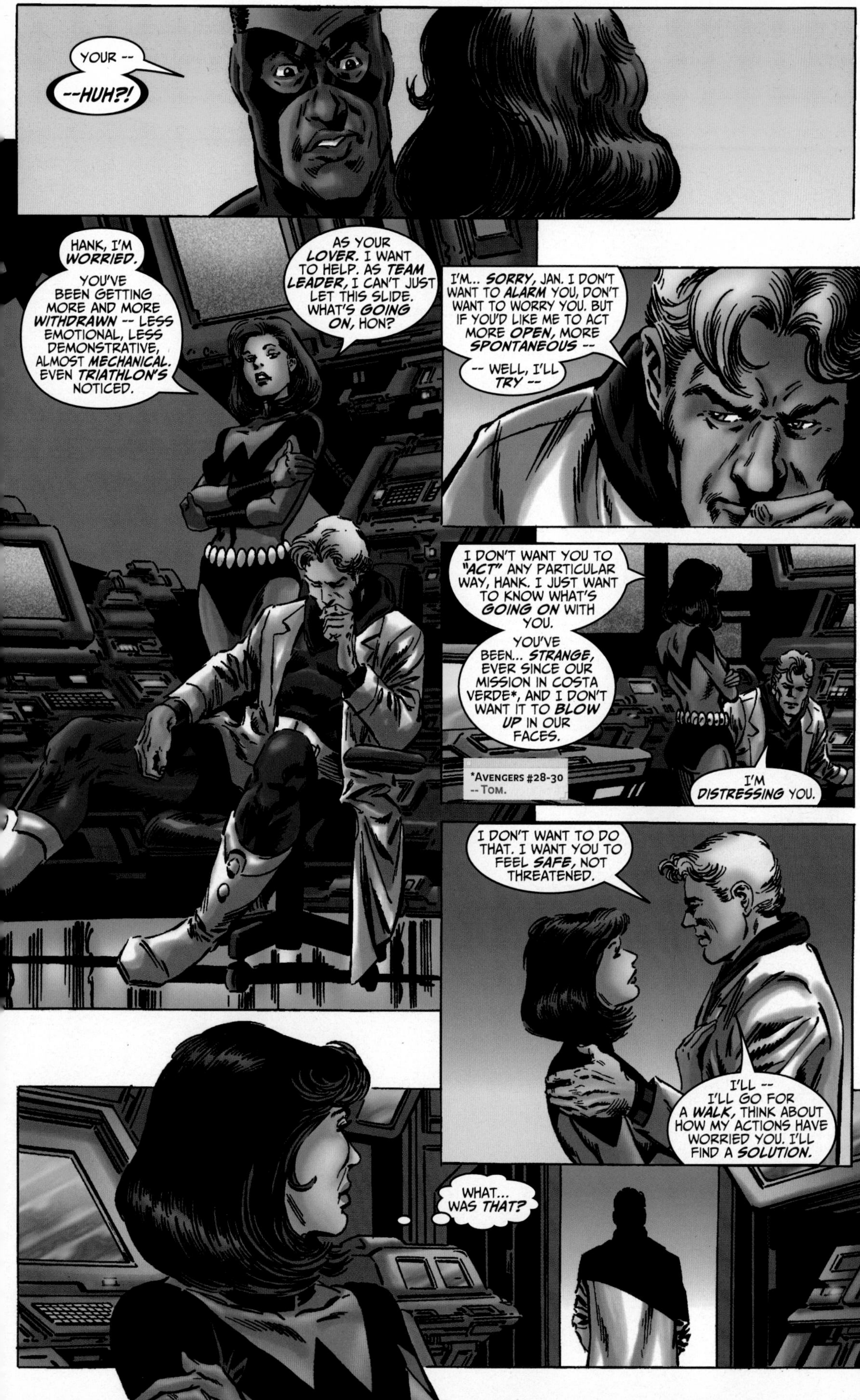

YOUR --
--HUH?!
HANK, I'M WORRIED.
YOU'VE BEEN GETTING MORE AND MORE WITHDRAWN -- LESS EMOTIONAL, LESS DEMONSTRATIVE, ALMOST MECHANICAL. EVEN TRIATHLON'S NOTICED.
AS YOUR LOVER, I WANT TO HELP. AS TEAM LEADER, I CAN'T JUST LET THIS SLIDE. WHAT'S GOING ON, HON?
I'M... SORRY, JAN. I DON'T WANT TO ALARM YOU, DON'T WANT TO WORRY YOU. BUT IF YOU'D LIKE ME TO ACT MORE OPEN, MORE SPONTANEOUS --
-- WELL, I'LL TRY --
I DON'T WANT YOU TO "ACT" ANY PARTICULAR WAY, HANK. I JUST WANT TO KNOW WHAT'S GOING ON WITH YOU.
YOU'VE BEEN... STRANGE, EVER SINCE OUR MISSION IN COSTA VERDE*, AND I DON'T WANT IT TO BLOW UP IN OUR FACES.
*AVENGERS #28-30 -- TOM.
I'M DISTRESSING YOU.
I DON'T WANT TO DO THAT. I WANT YOU TO FEEL SAFE, NOT THREATENED.
I'LL -- I'LL GO FOR A WALK, THINK ABOUT HOW MY ACTIONS HAVE WORRIED YOU. I'LL FIND A SOLUTION.
WHAT... WAS THAT?

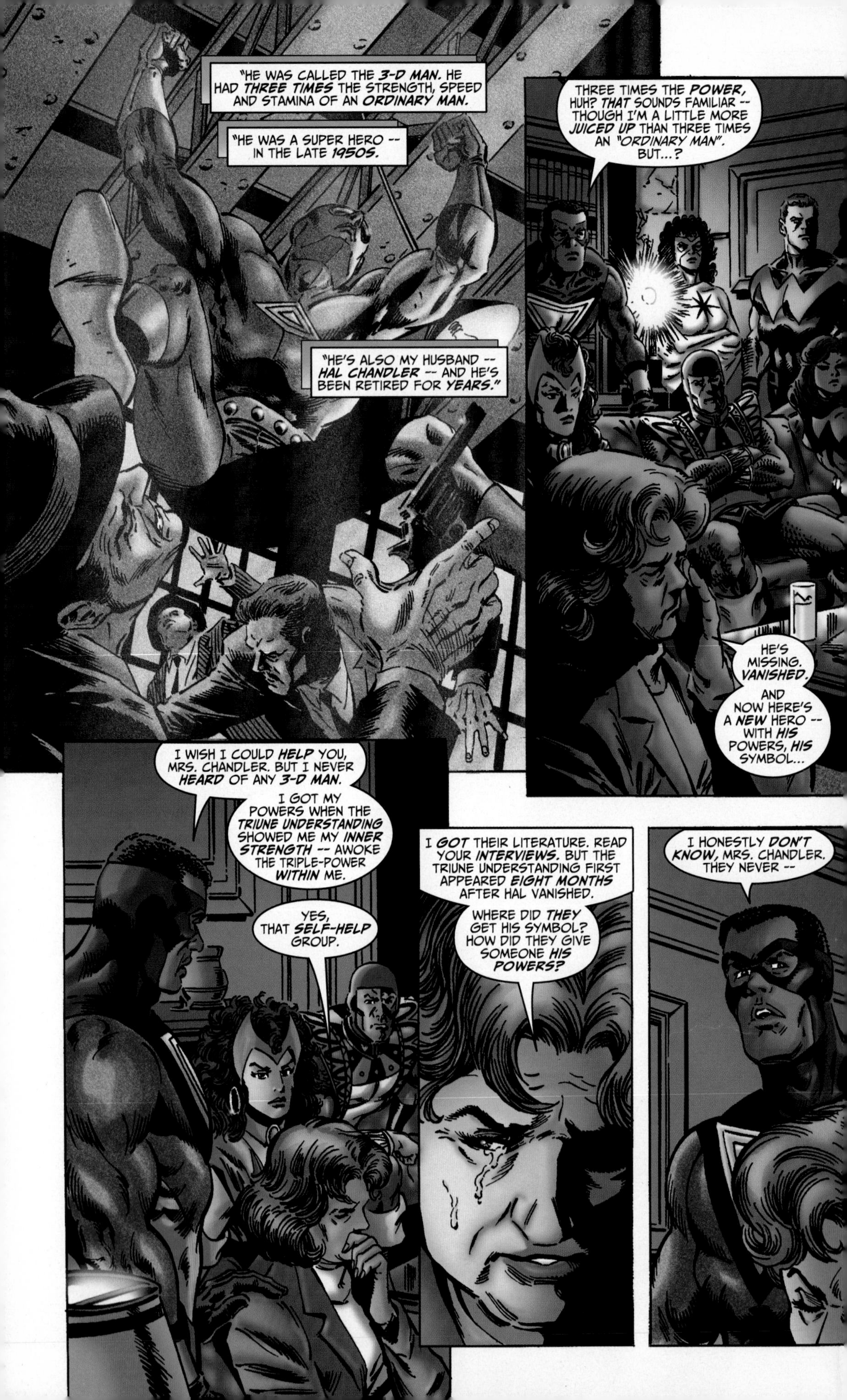
"HE WAS CALLED THE 3-D MAN. HE HAD THREE TIMES THE STRENGTH, SPEED AND STAMINA OF AN ORDINARY MAN.
"HE WAS A SUPER HERO -- IN THE LATE 1950S.
"HE'S ALSO MY HUSBAND -- HAL CHANDLER -- AND HE'S BEEN RETIRED FOR YEARS."
THREE TIMES THE POWER, HUH? THAT SOUNDS FAMILIAR -- THOUGH I'M A LITTLE MORE JUICED UP THAN THREE TIMES AN "ORDINARY MAN". BUT...?
HE'S MISSING. VANISHED.
AND NOW HERE'S A NEW HERO -- WITH HIS POWERS, HIS SYMBOL...
I WISH I COULD HELP YOU, MRS. CHANDLER. BUT I NEVER HEARD OF ANY 3-D MAN.
I GOT MY POWERS WHEN THE TRIUNE UNDERSTANDING SHOWED ME MY INNER STRENGTH -- AWOKE THE TRIPLE-POWER WITHIN ME.
YES, THAT SELF-HELP GROUP.
I GOT THEIR LITERATURE. READ YOUR INTERVIEWS. BUT THE TRIUNE UNDERSTANDING FIRST APPEARED EIGHT MONTHS AFTER HAL VANISHED.
WHERE DID THEY GET HIS SYMBOL? HOW DID THEY GIVE SOMEONE HIS POWERS?
I HONESTLY DON'T KNOW, MRS. CHANDLER. THEY NEVER --

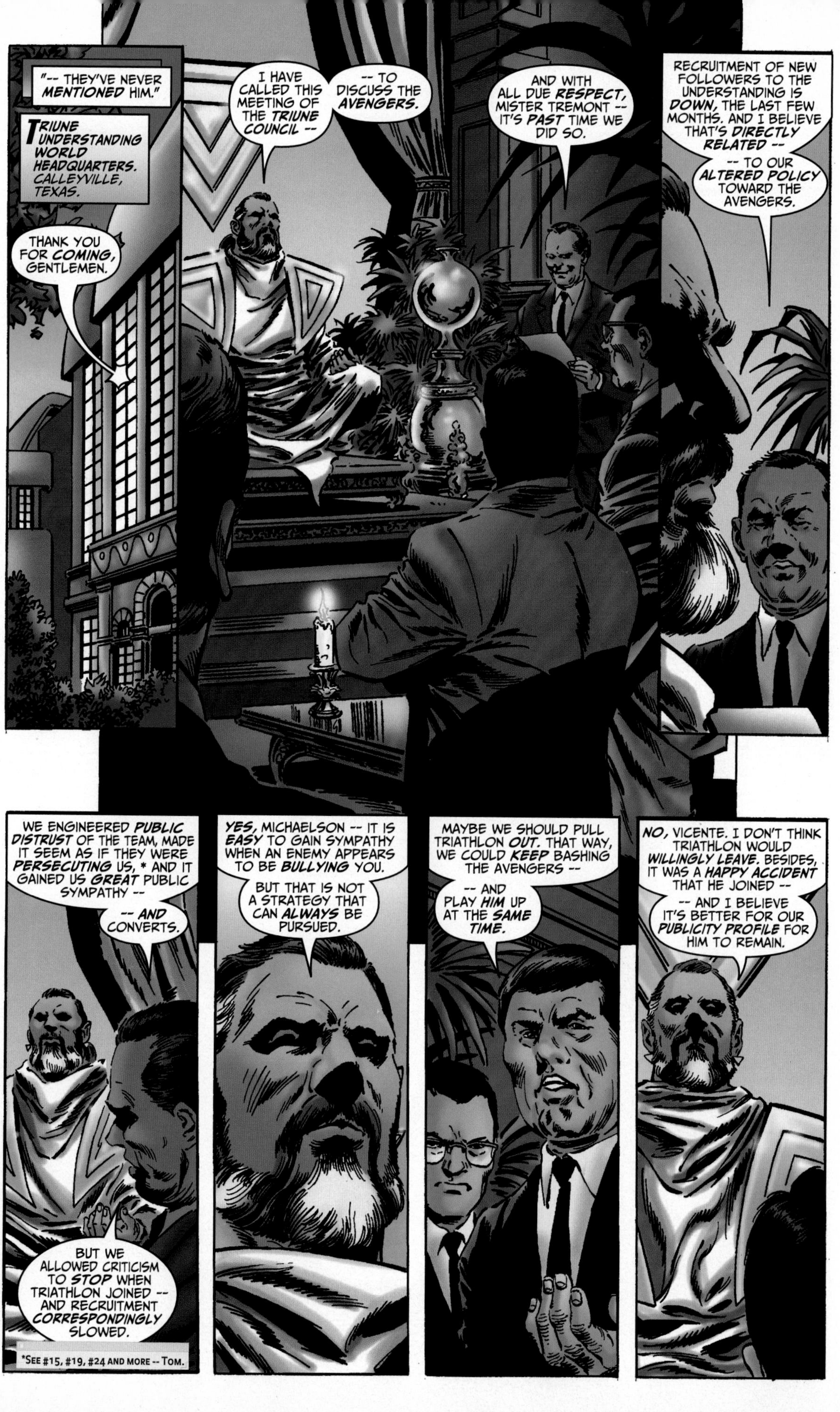
"-- THEY'VE NEVER MENTIONED HIM."
TRIUNE UNDERSTANDING WORLD HEADQUARTERS. CALLEYVILLE, TEXAS.
THANK YOU FOR COMING, GENTLEMEN.
I HAVE CALLED THIS MEETING OF THE TRIUNE COUNCIL --
-- TO DISCUSS THE AVENGERS.
AND WITH ALL DUE RESPECT, MISTER TREMONT -- IT'S PAST TIME WE DID SO.
RECRUITMENT OF NEW FOLLOWERS TO THE UNDERSTANDING IS DOWN, THE LAST FEW MONTHS. AND I BELIEVE THAT'S DIRECTLY RELATED --
-- TO OUR ALTERED POLICY TOWARD THE AVENGERS.
WE ENGINEERED PUBLIC DISTRUST OF THE TEAM, MADE IT SEEM AS IF THEY WERE PERSECUTING US, * AND IT GAINED US GREAT PUBLIC SYMPATHY --
-- AND CONVERTS.
BUT WE ALLOWED CRITICISM TO STOP WHEN TRIATHLON JOINED -- AND RECRUITMENT CORRESPONDINGLY SLOWED.
*SEE #15, #19, #24 AND MORE -- TOM.
YES, MICHAELSON -- IT IS EASY TO GAIN SYMPATHY WHEN AN ENEMY APPEARS TO BE BULLYING YOU.
BUT THAT IS NOT A STRATEGY THAT CAN ALWAYS BE PURSUED.
MAYBE WE SHOULD PULL TRIATHLON OUT. THAT WAY, WE COULD KEEP BASHING THE AVENGERS --
-- AND PLAY HIM UP AT THE SAME TIME.
NO, VICENTE. I DON'T THINK TRIATHLON WOULD WILLINGLY LEAVE. BESIDES, IT WAS A HAPPY ACCIDENT THAT HE JOINED --
-- AND I BELIEVE IT'S BETTER FOR OUR PUBLICITY PROFILE FOR HIM TO REMAIN.

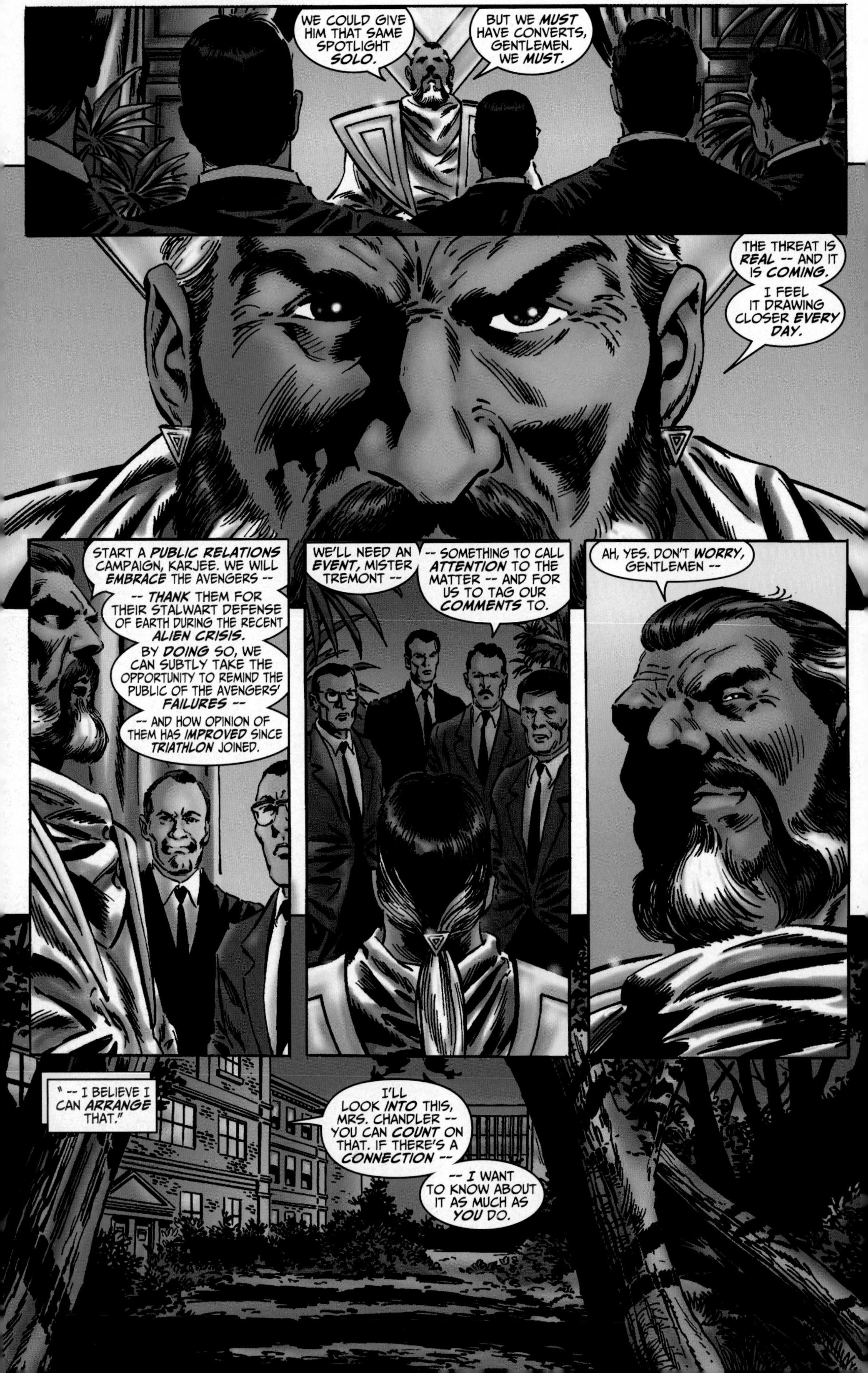
WE COULD GIVE HIM THAT SAME SPOTLIGHT SOLO.
BUT WE MUST HAVE CONVERTS, GENTLEMEN. WE MUST.
THE THREAT IS REAL -- AND IT IS COMING.
I FEEL IT DRAWING CLOSER EVERY DAY.
START A PUBLIC RELATIONS CAMPAIGN, KARJEE. WE WILL EMBRACE THE AVENGERS --
-- THANK THEM FOR THEIR STALWART DEFENSE OF EARTH DURING THE RECENT ALIEN CRISIS.
BY DOING SO, WE CAN SUBTLY TAKE THE OPPORTUNITY TO REMIND THE PUBLIC OF THE AVENGERS' FAILURES --
-- AND HOW OPINION OF THEM HAS IMPROVED SINCE TRIATHLON JOINED.
WE'LL NEED AN EVENT, MISTER TREMONT --
-- SOMETHING TO CALL ATTENTION TO THE MATTER -- AND FOR US TO TAG OUR COMMENTS TO.
AH, YES. DON'T WORRY, GENTLEMEN --
" -- I BELIEVE I CAN ARRANGE THAT."
I'LL LOOK INTO THIS, MRS. CHANDLER -- YOU CAN COUNT ON THAT. IF THERE'S A CONNECTION --
-- I WANT TO KNOW ABOUT IT AS MUCH AS YOU DO.

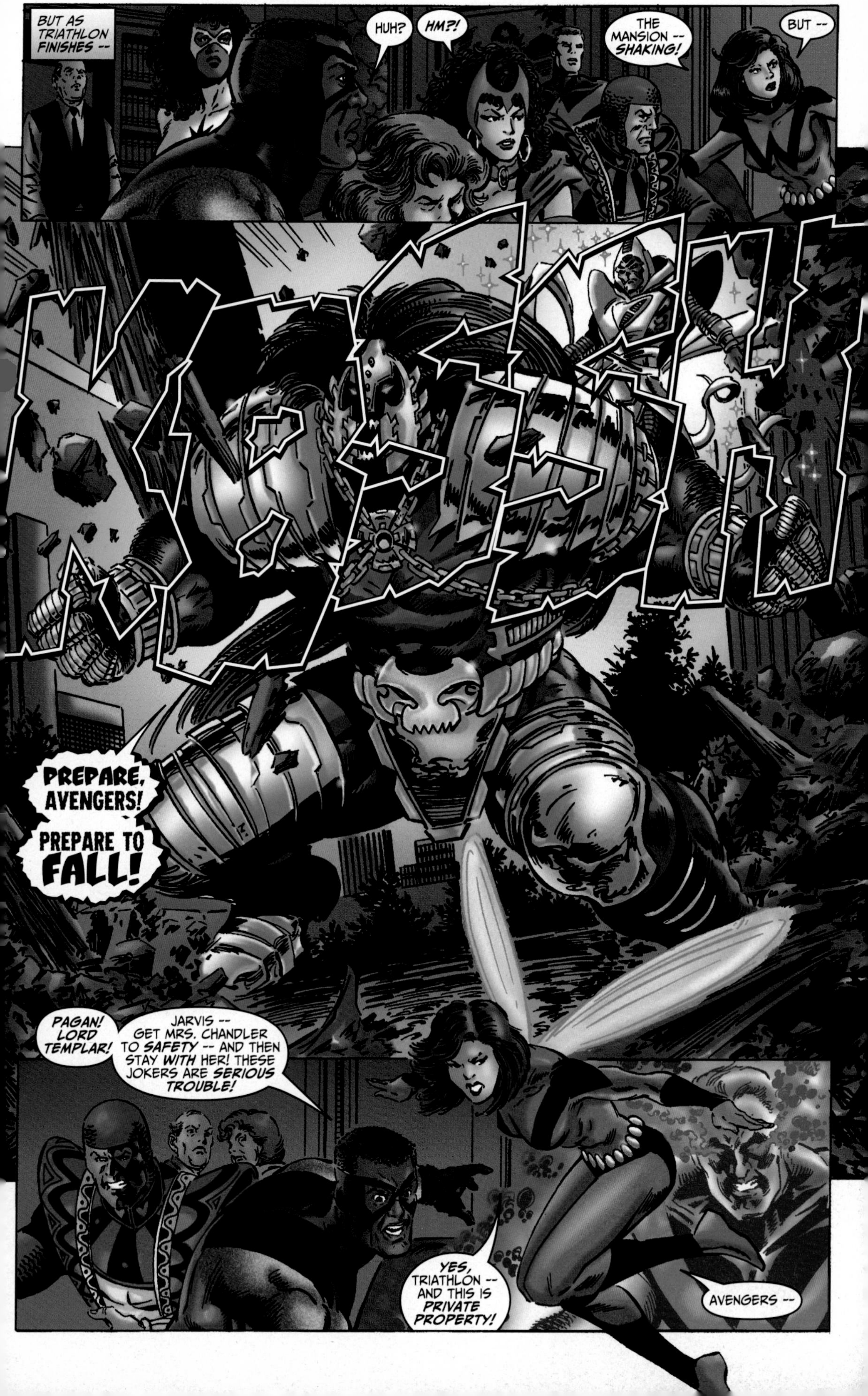
BUT AS TRIATHLON FINISHES --
HUH?
HM?!
THE MANSION -- SHAKING!
BUT --
PREPARE, AVENGERS!
PREPARE TO FALL!
PAGAN! LORD TEMPLAR!
JARVIS -- GET MRS. CHANDLER TO SAFETY -- AND THEN STAY WITH HER! THESE JOKERS ARE SERIOUS TROUBLE!
YES, TRIATHLON -- AND THIS IS PRIVATE PROPERTY!
AVENGERS --

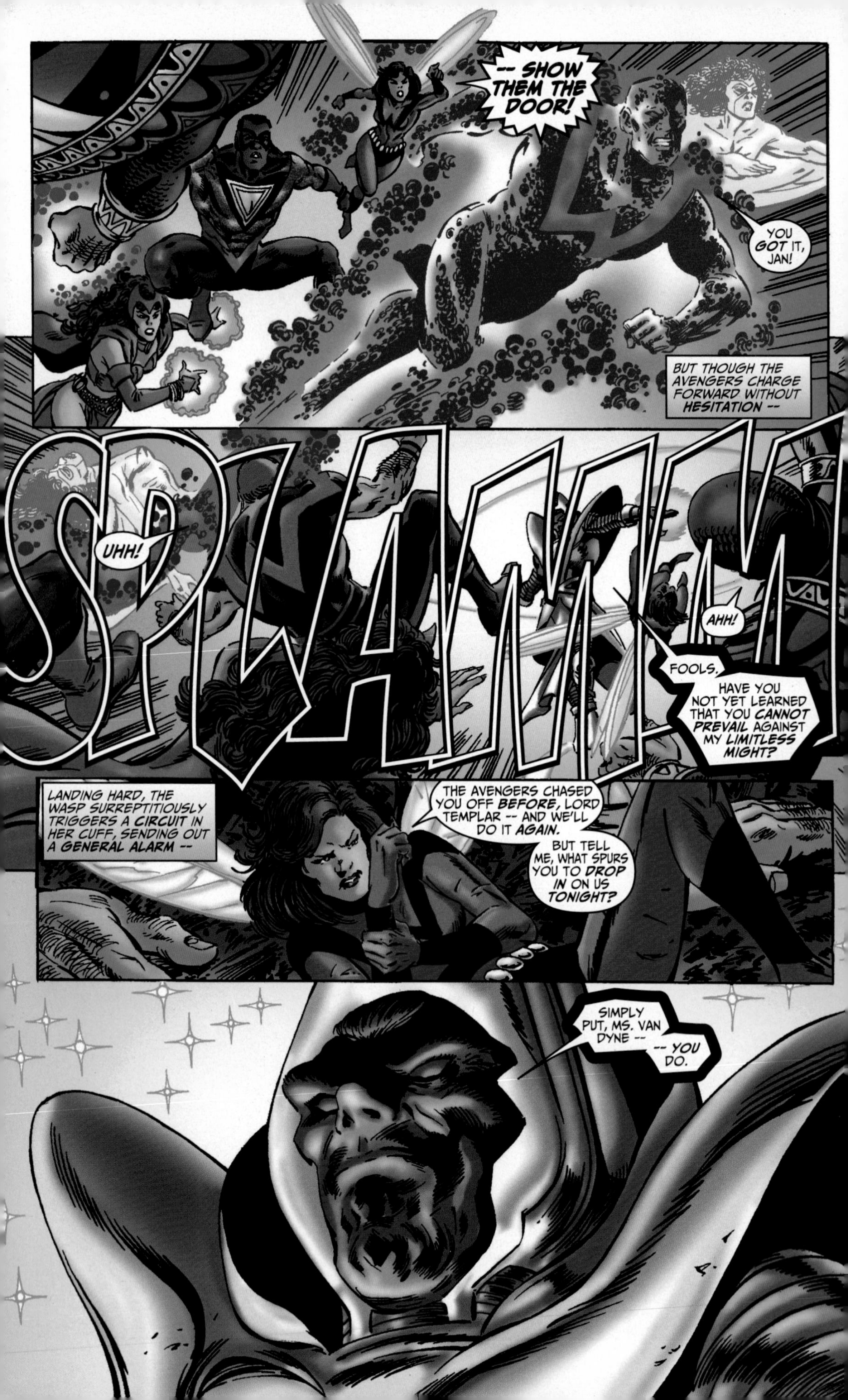
-- SHOW THEM THE DOOR!
YOU GOT IT, JAN!
BUT THOUGH THE AVENGERS CHARGE FORWARD WITHOUT HESITATION --
SPLAMMM
UHH!
AHH!
FOOLS.
HAVE YOU NOT YET LEARNED THAT YOU CANNOT PREVAIL AGAINST MY LIMITLESS MIGHT?
LANDING HARD, THE WASP SURREPTITIOUSLY TRIGGERS A CIRCUIT IN HER CUFF, SENDING OUT A GENERAL ALARM --
THE AVENGERS CHASED YOU OFF BEFORE, LORD TEMPLAR -- AND WE'LL DO IT AGAIN.
BUT TELL ME, WHAT SPURS YOU TO DROP IN ON US TONIGHT?
SIMPLY PUT, MS. VAN DYNE --
-- YOU DO.

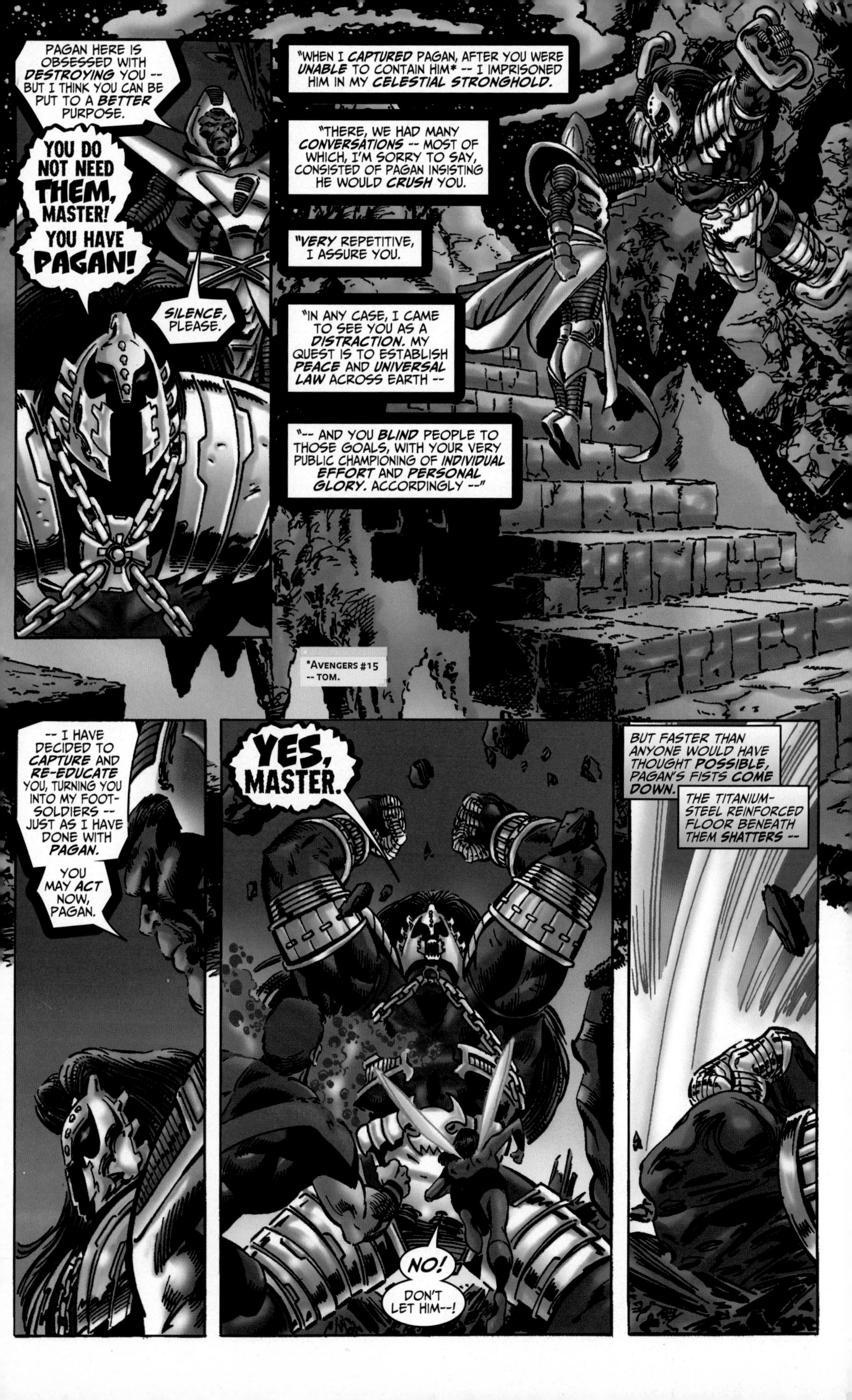
PAGAN HERE IS OBSESSED WITH DESTROYING YOU -- BUT I THINK YOU CAN BE PUT TO A BETTER PURPOSE.
YOU DO NOT NEED THEM, MASTER! YOU HAVE PAGAN!
SILENCE, PLEASE.
"WHEN I CAPTURED PAGAN, AFTER YOU WERE UNABLE TO CONTAIN HIM* -- I IMPRISONED HIM IN MY CELESTIAL STRONGHOLD.
"THERE, WE HAD MANY CONVERSATIONS -- MOST OF WHICH, I'M SORRY TO SAY, CONSISTED OF PAGAN INSISTING HE WOULD CRUSH YOU.
"VERY REPETITIVE, I ASSURE YOU.
"IN ANY CASE, I CAME TO SEE YOU AS A DISTRACTION. MY QUEST IS TO ESTABLISH PEACE AND UNIVERSAL LAW ACROSS EARTH --
"-- AND YOU BLIND PEOPLE TO THOSE GOALS, WITH YOUR VERY PUBLIC CHAMPIONING OF INDIVIDUAL EFFORT AND PERSONAL GLORY. ACCORDINGLY --"
*AVENGERS #15 -- TOM.
-- I HAVE DECIDED TO CAPTURE AND RE-EDUCATE YOU, TURNING YOU INTO MY FOOT-SOLDIERS -- JUST AS I HAVE DONE WITH PAGAN.
YOU MAY ACT NOW, PAGAN.
YES, MASTER.
NO! DON'T LET HIM--!
BUT FASTER THAN ANYONE WOULD HAVE THOUGHT POSSIBLE, PAGAN'S FISTS COME DOWN.
THE TITANIUM-STEEL REINFORCED FLOOR BENEATH THEM SHATTERS --

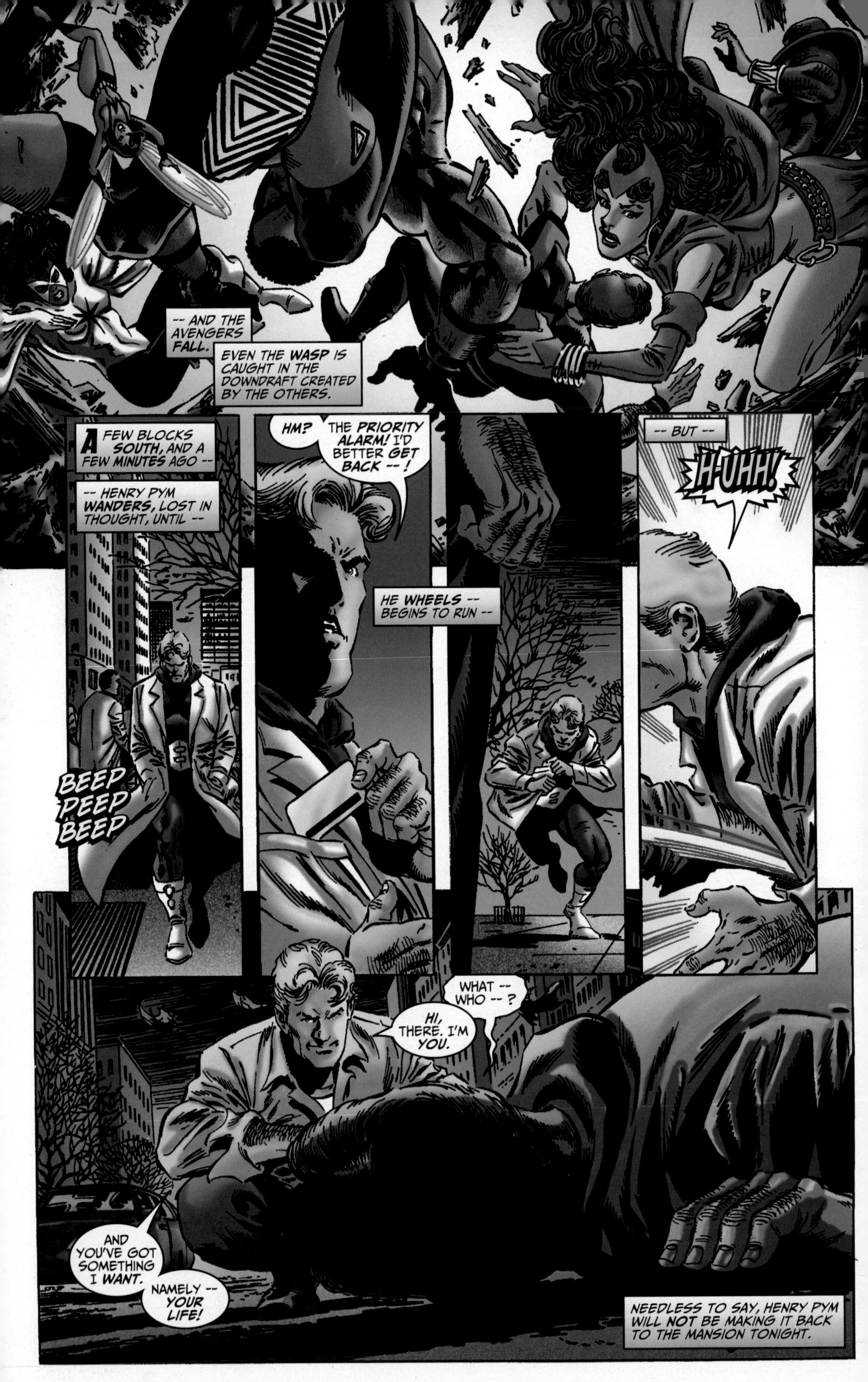
-- AND THE AVENGERS FALL.
EVEN THE WASP IS CAUGHT IN THE DOWNDRAFT CREATED BY THE OTHERS.
A FEW BLOCKS SOUTH, AND A FEW MINUTES AGO --
-- HENRY PYM WANDERS, LOST IN THOUGHT, UNTIL --
BEEP PEEP BEEP
HM?
THE PRIORITY ALARM! I'D BETTER GET BACK -- !
HE WHEELS -- BEGINS TO RUN --
-- BUT --
H-UHH!
WHAT -- WHO -- ?
HI, THERE. I'M YOU.
AND YOU'VE GOT SOMETHING I WANT.
NAMELY -- YOUR LIFE!
NEEDLESS TO SAY, HENRY PYM WILL NOT BE MAKING IT BACK TO THE MANSION TONIGHT.

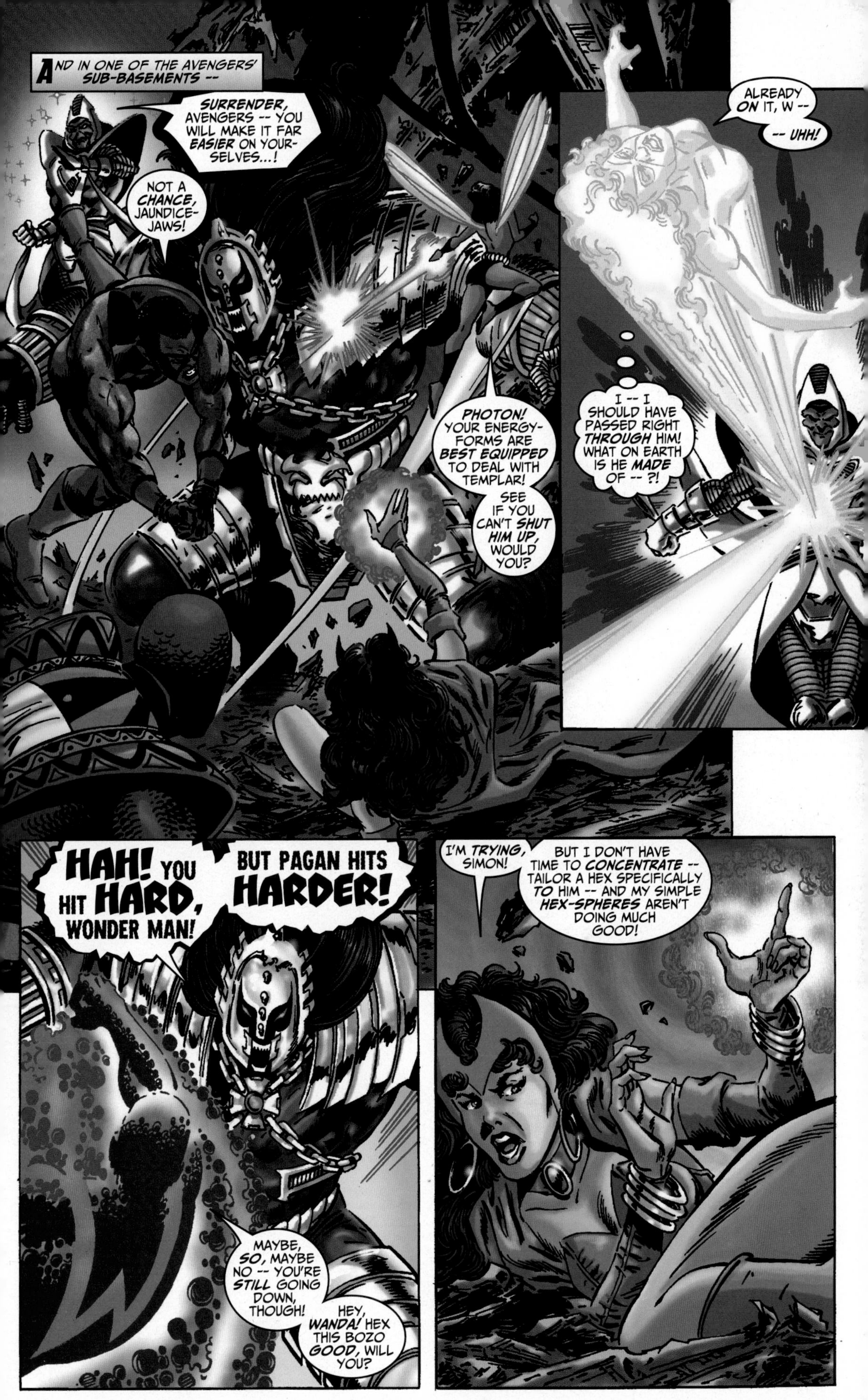
AND IN ONE OF THE AVENGERS' SUB-BASEMENTS --
SURRENDER, AVENGERS -- YOU WILL MAKE IT FAR EASIER ON YOURSELVES...!
NOT A CHANCE, JAUNDICE-JAWS!
PHOTON! YOUR ENERGY-FORMS ARE BEST EQUIPPED TO DEAL WITH TEMPLAR!
SEE IF YOU CAN'T SHUT HIM UP, WOULD YOU?
ALREADY ON IT, W --
-- UHH!
I -- I SHOULD HAVE PASSED RIGHT THROUGH HIM! WHAT ON EARTH IS HE MADE OF -- ?!
HAH! YOU HIT HARD, WONDER MAN!
BUT PAGAN HITS HARDER!
MAYBE, SO, MAYBE NO -- YOU'RE STILL GOING DOWN, THOUGH!
HEY, WANDA! HEX THIS BOZO GOOD, WILL YOU?
I'M TRYING, SIMON!
BUT I DON'T HAVE TIME TO CONCENTRATE -- TAILOR A HEX SPECIFICALLY TO HIM -- AND MY SIMPLE HEX-SPHERES AREN'T DOING MUCH GOOD!

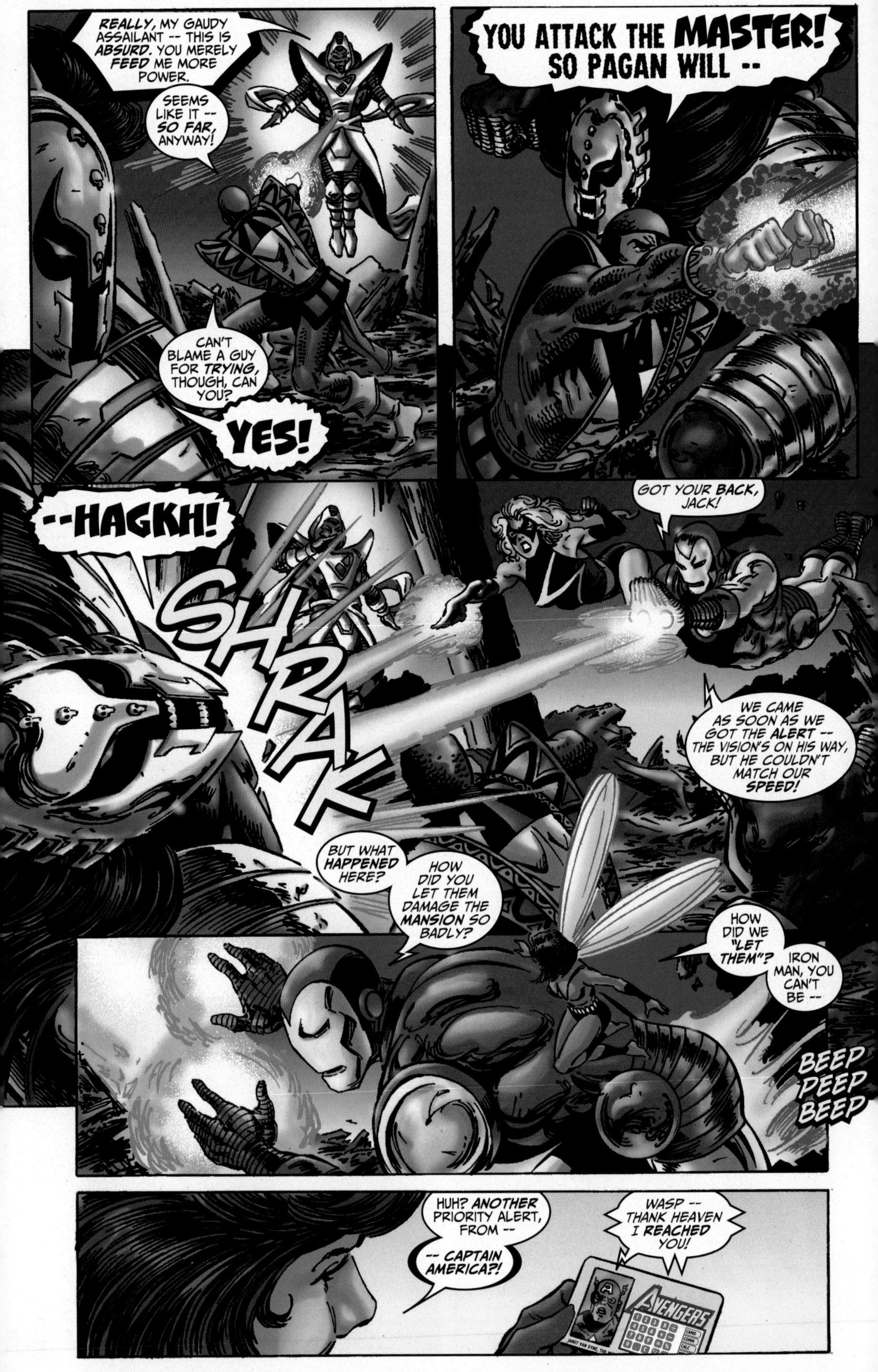
REALLY, MY GAUDY ASSAILANT -- THIS IS ABSURD. YOU MERELY FEED ME MORE POWER.
SEEMS LIKE IT -- SO FAR, ANYWAY!
CAN'T BLAME A GUY FOR TRYING, THOUGH, CAN YOU?
YES!
YOU ATTACK THE MASTER! SO PAGAN WILL --
--HAGKH!
SHRAK
GOT YOUR BACK, JACK!
WE CAME AS SOON AS WE GOT THE ALERT -- THE VISION'S ON HIS WAY, BUT HE COULDN'T MATCH OUR SPEED!
BUT WHAT HAPPENED HERE?
HOW DID YOU LET THEM DAMAGE THE MANSION SO BADLY?
HOW DID WE "LET THEM"?
IRON MAN, YOU CAN'T BE --
BEEP PEEP BEEP
HUH? ANOTHER PRIORITY ALERT, FROM --
-- CAPTAIN AMERICA?!
WASP -- THANK HEAVEN I REACHED YOU!
AVENGERS

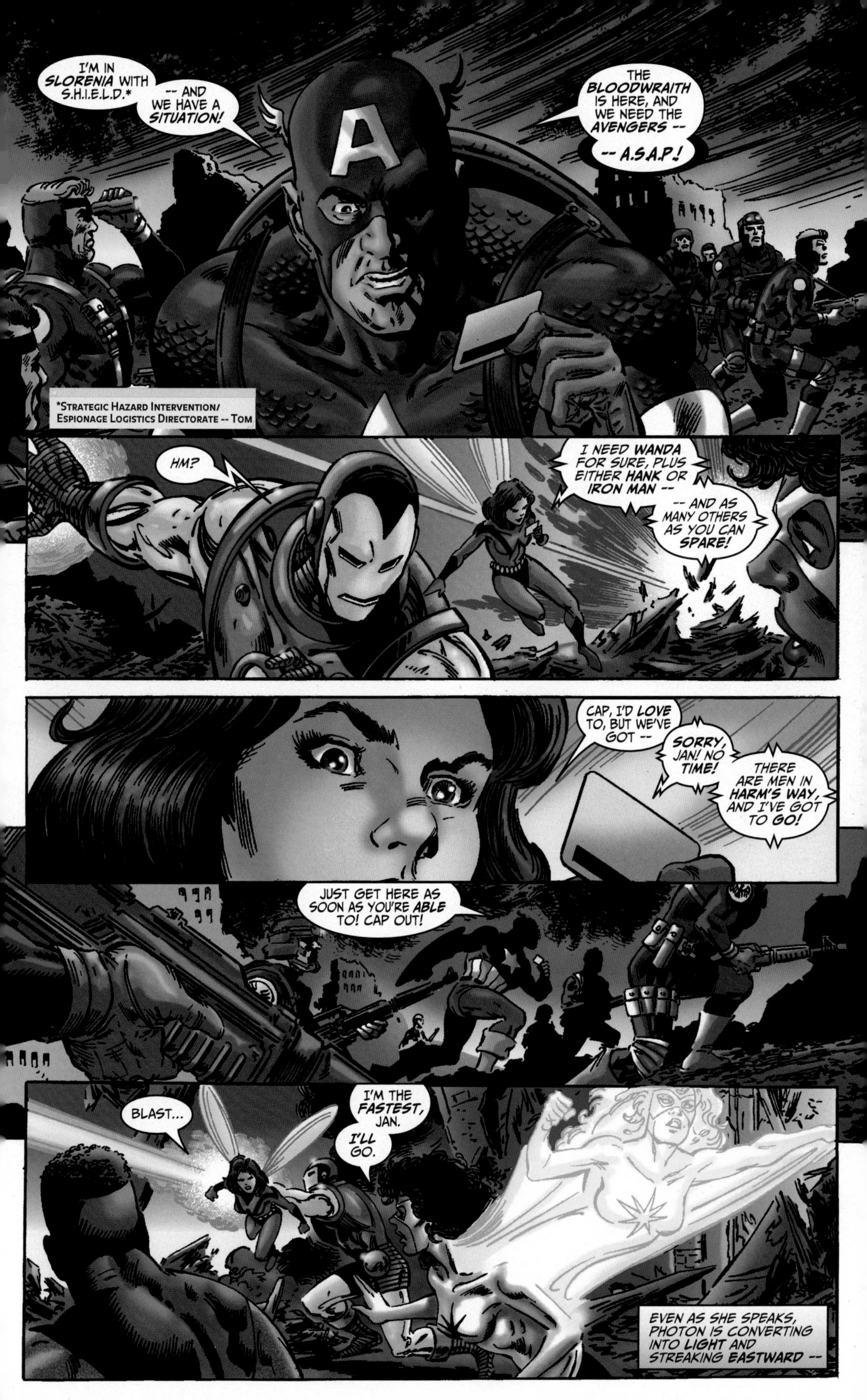
I'M IN SLORENIA WITH S.H.I.E.L.D.*
-- AND WE HAVE A SITUATION!
THE BLOODWRAITH IS HERE, AND WE NEED THE AVENGERS --
-- A.S.A.P.!
*Strategic Hazard Intervention/ Espionage Logistics Directorate -- Tom
HM?
I NEED WANDA FOR SURE, PLUS EITHER HANK OR IRON MAN --
-- AND AS MANY OTHERS AS YOU CAN SPARE!
CAP, I'D LOVE TO, BUT WE'VE GOT --
SORRY, JAN! NO TIME!
THERE ARE MEN IN HARM'S WAY, AND I'VE GOT TO GO!
JUST GET HERE AS SOON AS YOU'RE ABLE TO! CAP OUT!
BLAST...
I'M THE FASTEST, JAN.
I'LL GO.
EVEN AS SHE SPEAKS, PHOTON IS CONVERTING INTO LIGHT AND STREAKING EASTWARD --

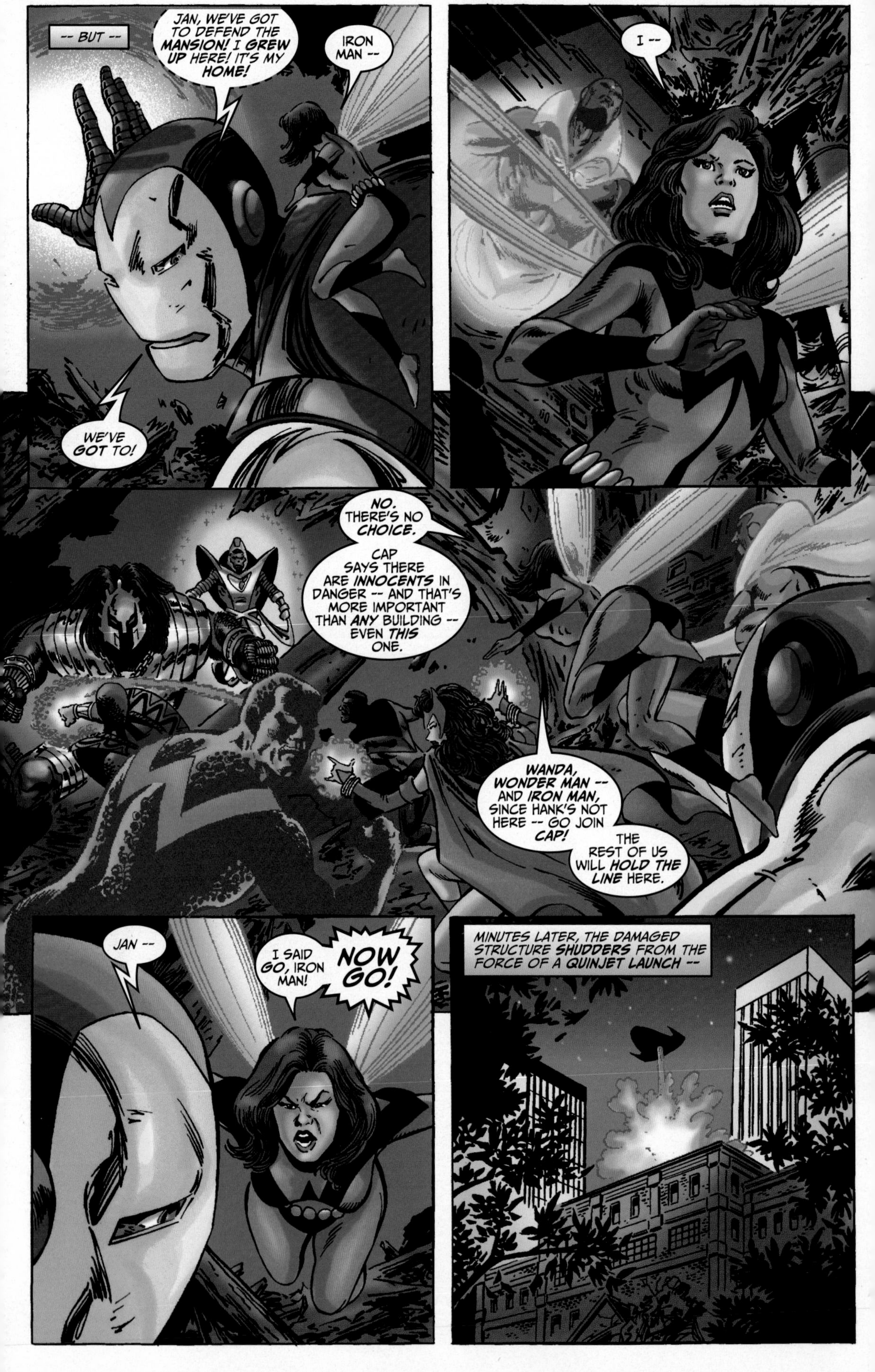
-- BUT --
JAN, WE'VE GOT TO DEFEND THE MANSION! I GREW UP HERE! IT'S MY HOME!
IRON MAN --
WE'VE GOT TO!
I --
NO. THERE'S NO CHOICE.
CAP SAYS THERE ARE INNOCENTS IN DANGER -- AND THAT'S MORE IMPORTANT THAN ANY BUILDING -- EVEN THIS ONE.
WANDA, WONDER MAN -- AND IRON MAN, SINCE HANK'S NOT HERE -- GO JOIN CAP!
THE REST OF US WILL HOLD THE LINE HERE.
JAN --
I SAID GO, IRON MAN!
NOW GO!
MINUTES LATER, THE DAMAGED STRUCTURE SHUDDERS FROM THE FORCE OF A QUINJET LAUNCH --

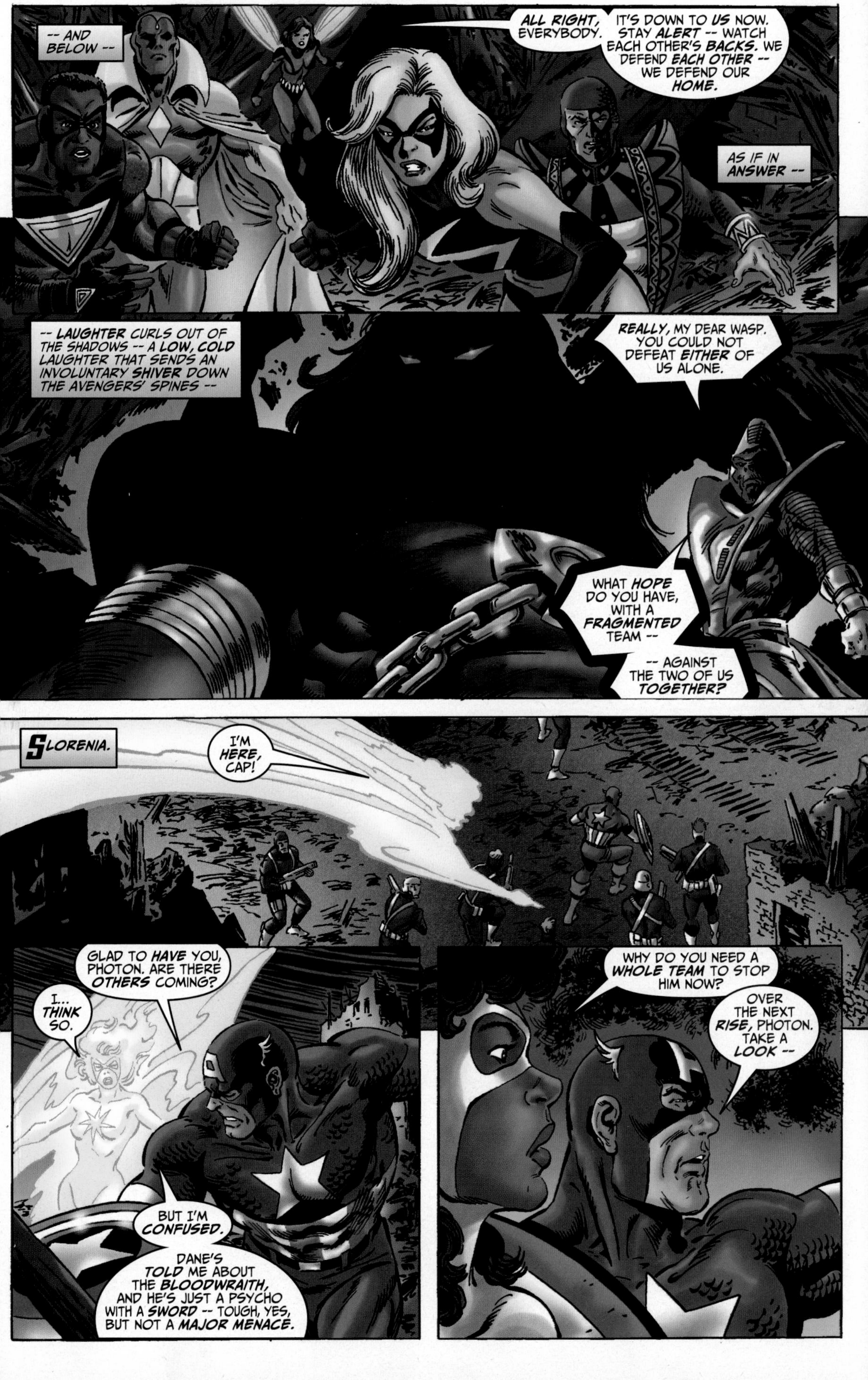

-- AND BELOW --
ALL RIGHT, EVERYBODY.
IT'S DOWN TO US NOW. STAY ALERT -- WATCH EACH OTHER'S BACKS. WE DEFEND EACH OTHER -- WE DEFEND OUR HOME.
AS IF IN ANSWER --
-- LAUGHTER CURLS OUT OF THE SHADOWS -- A LOW, COLD LAUGHTER THAT SENDS AN INVOLUNTARY SHIVER DOWN THE AVENGERS' SPINES --
REALLY, MY DEAR WASP. YOU COULD NOT DEFEAT EITHER OF US ALONE.
WHAT HOPE DO YOU HAVE, WITH A FRAGMENTED TEAM --
-- AGAINST THE TWO OF US TOGETHER?
SLORENIA.
I'M HERE, CAP!
GLAD TO HAVE YOU, PHOTON. ARE THERE OTHERS COMING?
I... THINK SO.
BUT I'M CONFUSED.
DANE'S TOLD ME ABOUT THE BLOODWRAITH, AND HE'S JUST A PSYCHO WITH A SWORD -- TOUGH, YES, BUT NOT A MAJOR MENACE.
WHY DO YOU NEED A WHOLE TEAM TO STOP HIM NOW?
OVER THE NEXT RISE, PHOTON. TAKE A LOOK --

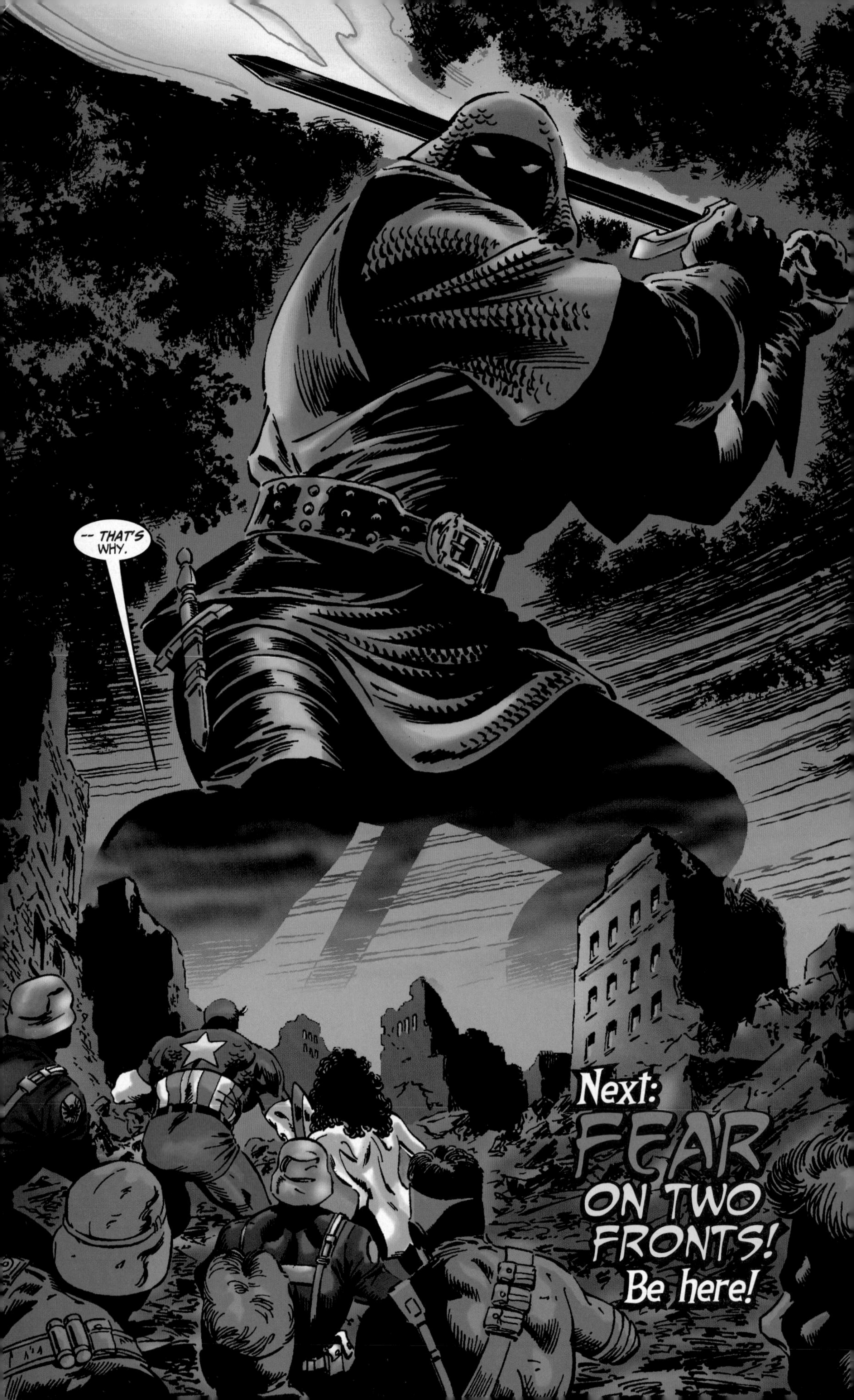
-- THAT'S WHY.
Next:
FEAR ON TWO FRONTS!
Be here!

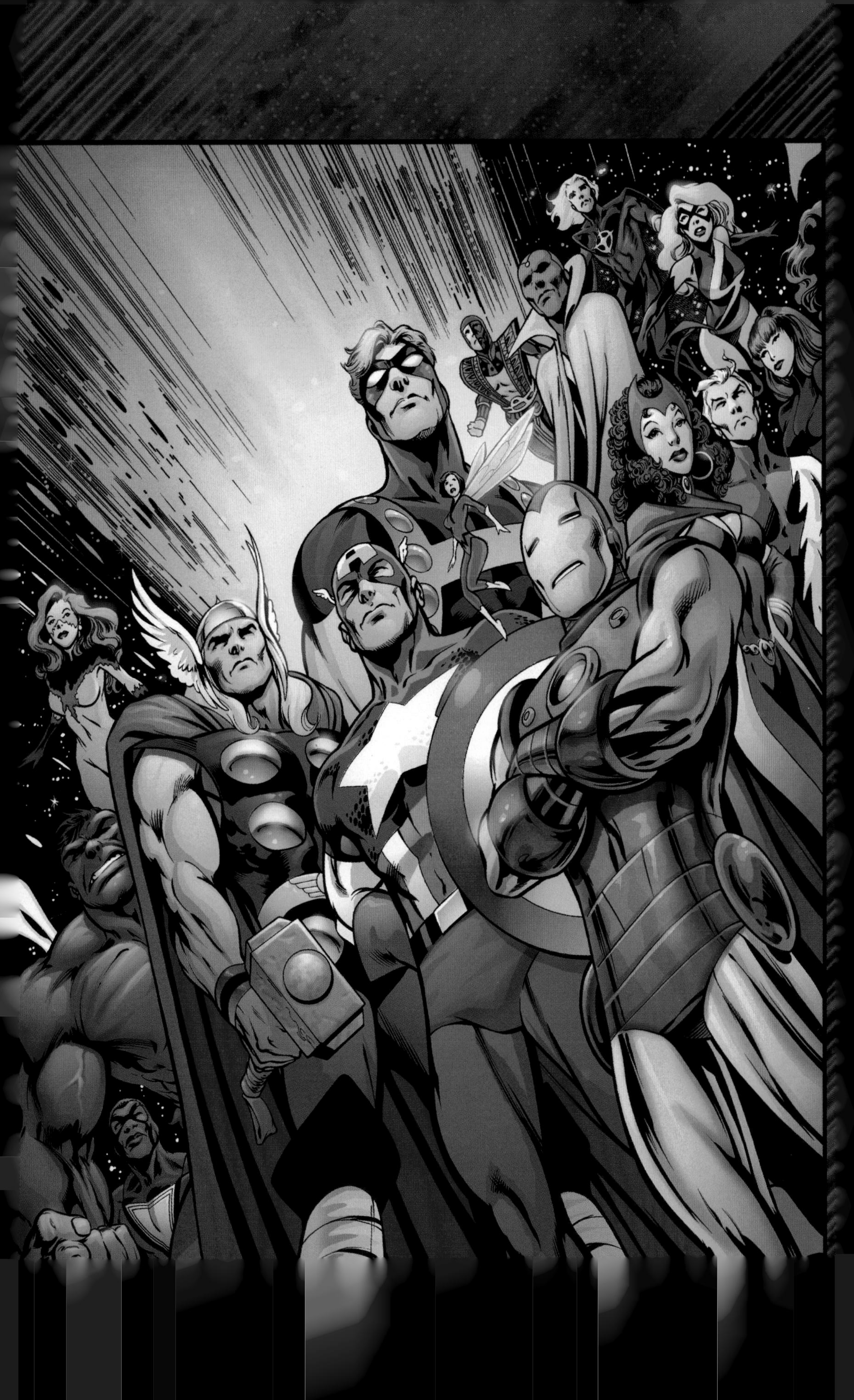

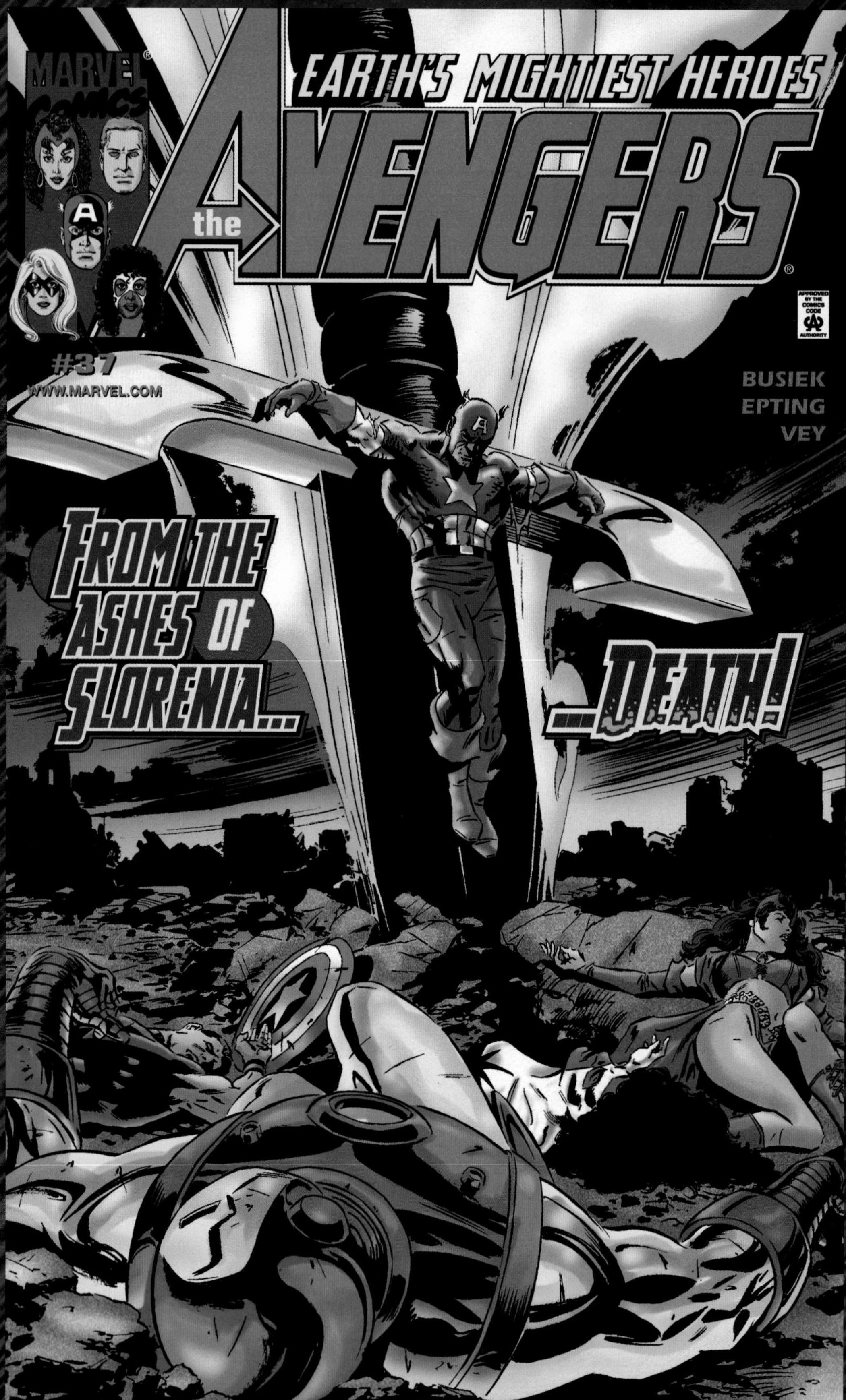

MARVEL COMICS
EARTH'S MIGHTIEST HEROES
the AVENGERS
#37
WWW.MARVEL.COM
APPROVED BY THE COMICS CODE AUTHORITY
BUSIEK
EPTING
VEY
FROM THE ASHES OF SLORENIA...
...DEATH!

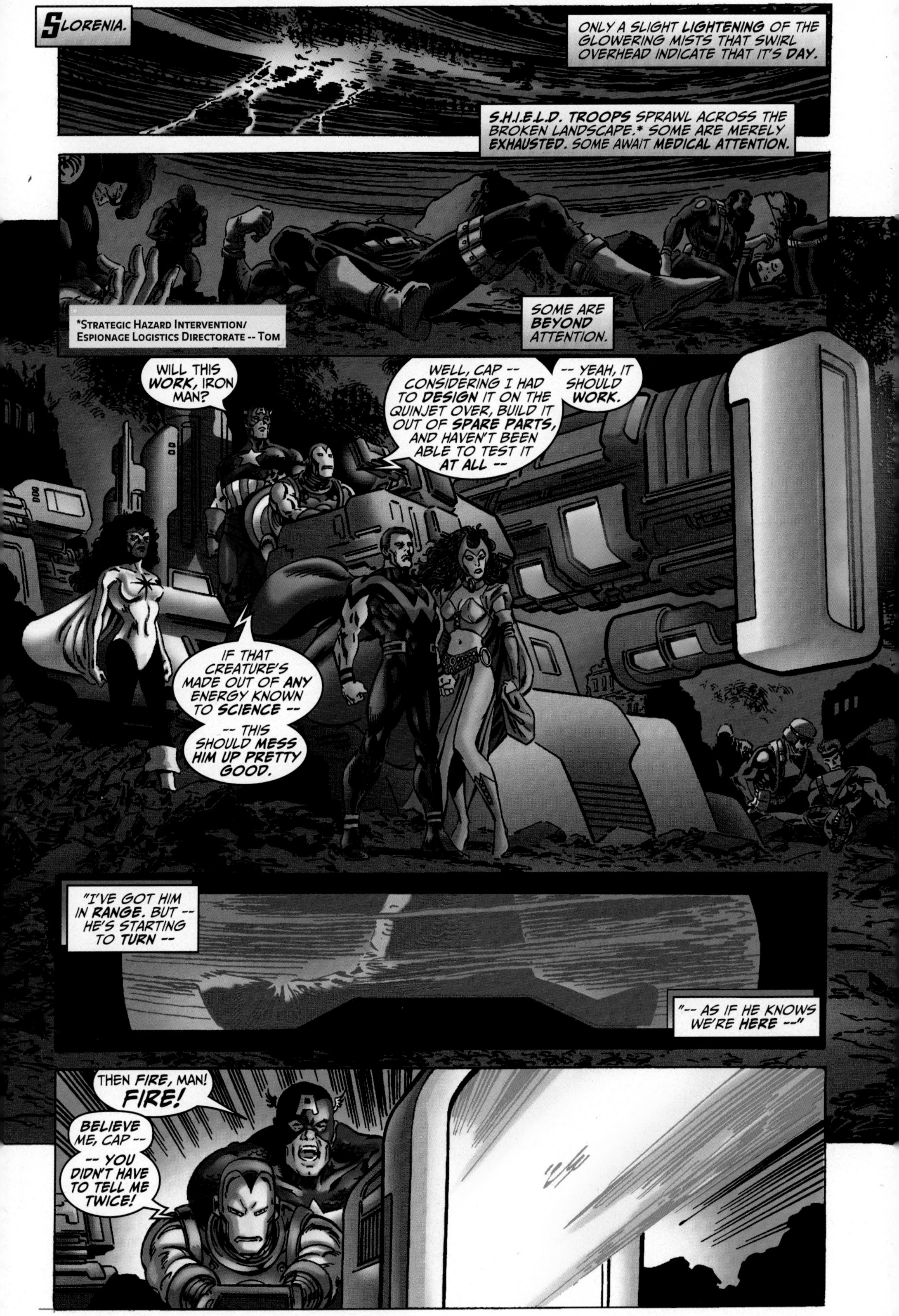
SLORENIA.
ONLY A SLIGHT LIGHTENING OF THE GLOWERING MISTS THAT SWIRL OVERHEAD INDICATE THAT IT'S DAY.
S.H.I.E.L.D. TROOPS SPRAWL ACROSS THE BROKEN LANDSCAPE.* SOME ARE MERELY EXHAUSTED. SOME AWAIT MEDICAL ATTENTION.
SOME ARE BEYOND ATTENTION.
*STRATEGIC HAZARD INTERVENTION/ ESPIONAGE LOGISTICS DIRECTORATE -- TOM
WILL THIS WORK, IRON MAN?
WELL, CAP -- CONSIDERING I HAD TO DESIGN IT ON THE QUINJET OVER, BUILD IT OUT OF SPARE PARTS, AND HAVEN'T BEEN ABLE TO TEST IT AT ALL --
-- YEAH, IT SHOULD WORK.
IF THAT CREATURE'S MADE OUT OF ANY ENERGY KNOWN TO SCIENCE --
-- THIS SHOULD MESS HIM UP PRETTY GOOD.
"I'VE GOT HIM IN RANGE. BUT -- HE'S STARTING TO TURN --
"-- AS IF HE KNOWS WE'RE HERE --"
THEN FIRE, MAN! FIRE!
BELIEVE ME, CAP --
-- YOU DIDN'T HAVE TO TELL ME TWICE!

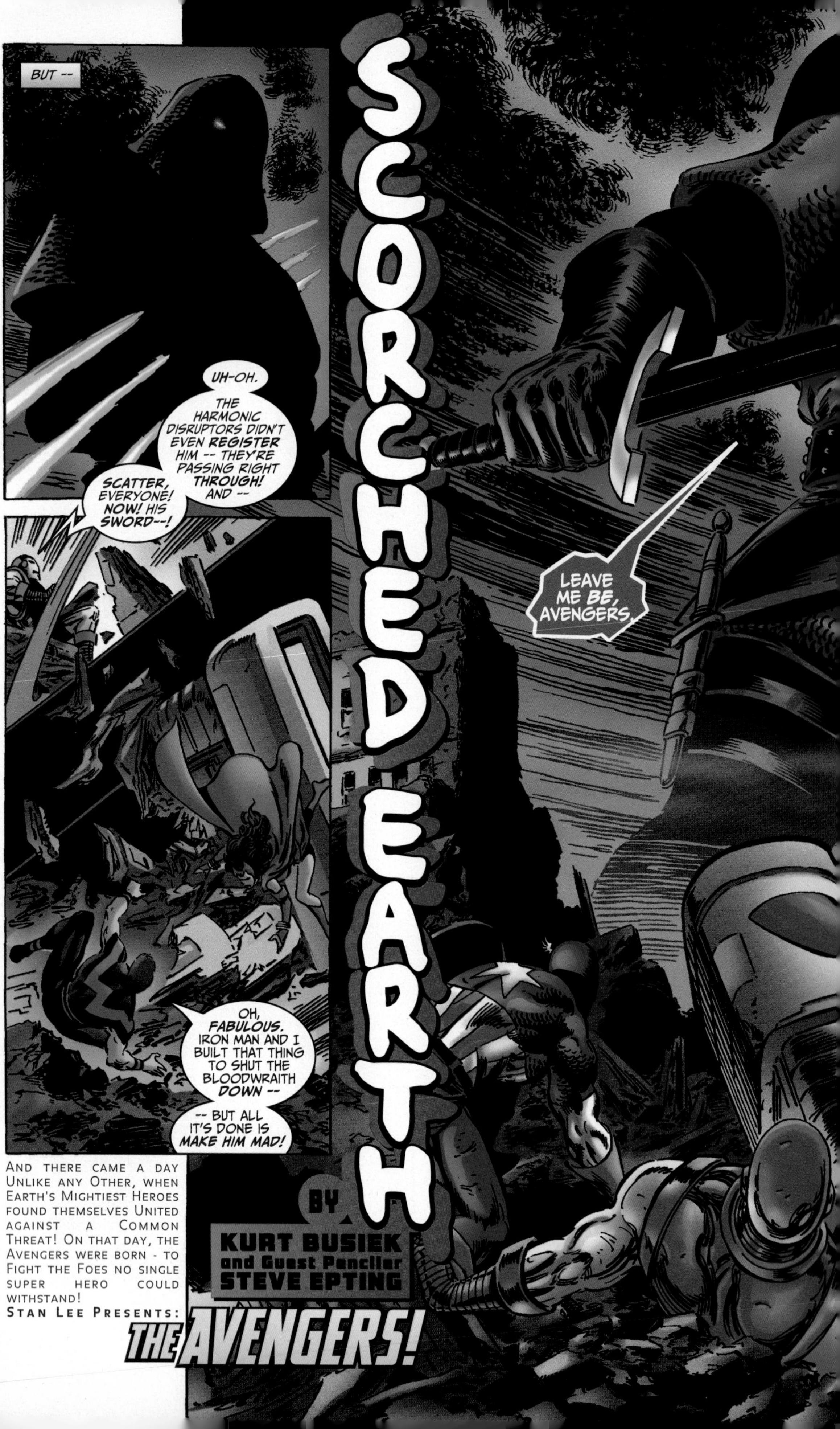
BUT --
UH-OH.
THE HARMONIC DISRUPTORS DIDN'T EVEN REGISTER HIM -- THEY'RE PASSING RIGHT THROUGH! AND --
SCATTER, EVERYONE! NOW! HIS SWORD--!
LEAVE ME BE, AVENGERS.
OH, FABULOUS. IRON MAN AND I BUILT THAT THING TO SHUT THE BLOODWRAITH DOWN --
-- BUT ALL IT'S DONE IS MAKE HIM MAD!
SCORCHED EARTH
BY
KURT BUSIEK
and Guest Penciler
STEVE EPTING
AND THERE CAME A DAY UNLIKE ANY OTHER, WHEN EARTH'S MIGHTIEST HEROES FOUND THEMSELVES UNITED AGAINST A COMMON THREAT! ON THAT DAY, THE AVENGERS WERE BORN - TO FIGHT THE FOES NO SINGLE SUPER HERO COULD WITHSTAND!
STAN LEE PRESENTS:
THE AVENGERS!

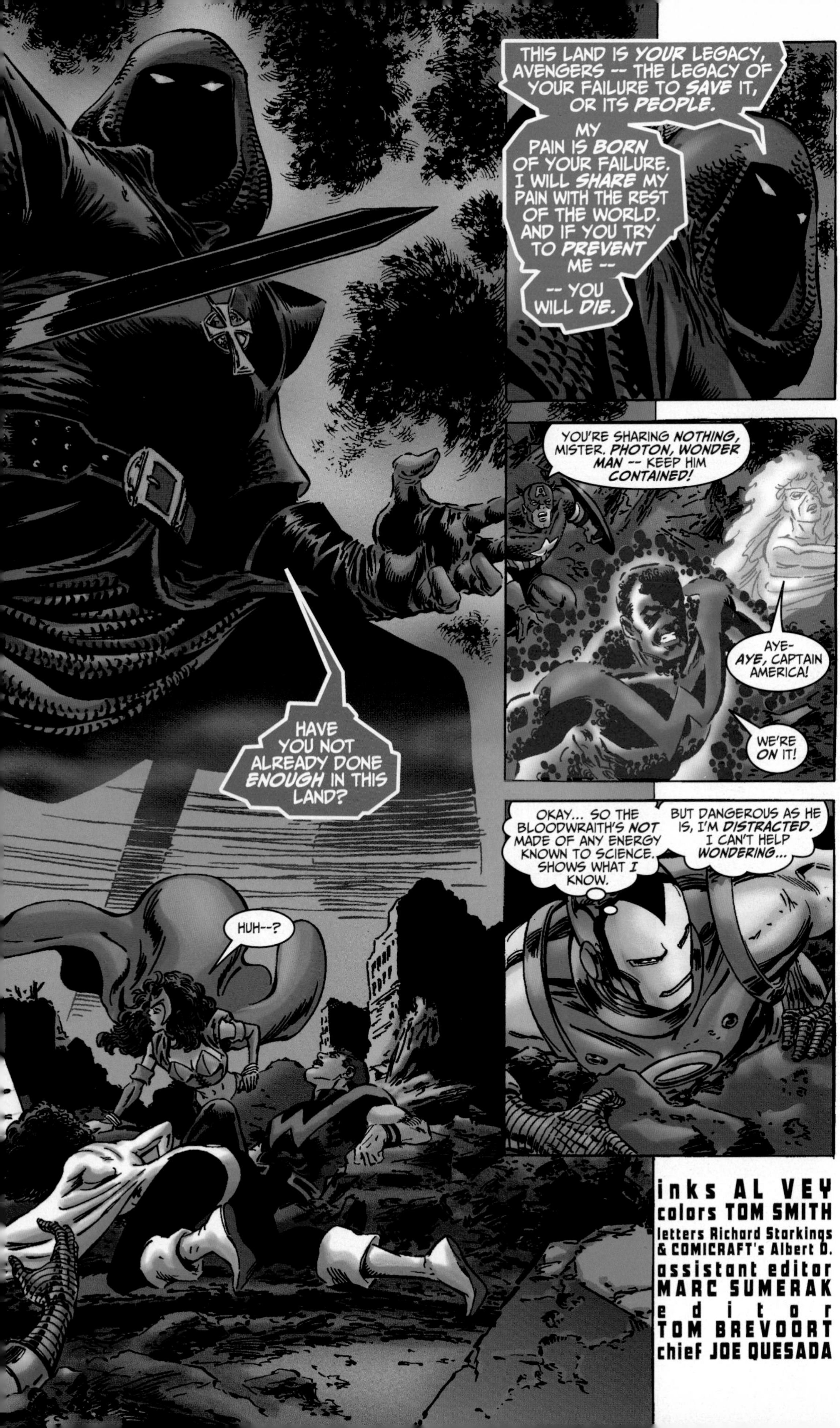
HAVE YOU NOT ALREADY DONE ENOUGH IN THIS LAND?
HUH--?
THIS LAND IS YOUR LEGACY, AVENGERS -- THE LEGACY OF YOUR FAILURE TO SAVE IT, OR ITS PEOPLE.
MY PAIN IS BORN OF YOUR FAILURE. I WILL SHARE MY PAIN WITH THE REST OF THE WORLD. AND IF YOU TRY TO PREVENT ME --
-- YOU WILL DIE.
YOU'RE SHARING NOTHING, MISTER. PHOTON, WONDER MAN -- KEEP HIM CONTAINED!
AYE-AYE, CAPTAIN AMERICA!
WE'RE ON IT!
OKAY... SO THE BLOODWRAITH'S NOT MADE OF ANY ENERGY KNOWN TO SCIENCE. SHOWS WHAT I KNOW.
BUT DANGEROUS AS HE IS, I'M DISTRACTED. I CAN'T HELP WONDERING...

inks AL VEY
colors TOM SMITH
letters Richard Starkings & COMICRAFT's Albert D.
assistant editor MARC SUMERAK
editor TOM BREVOORT
chief JOE QUESADA

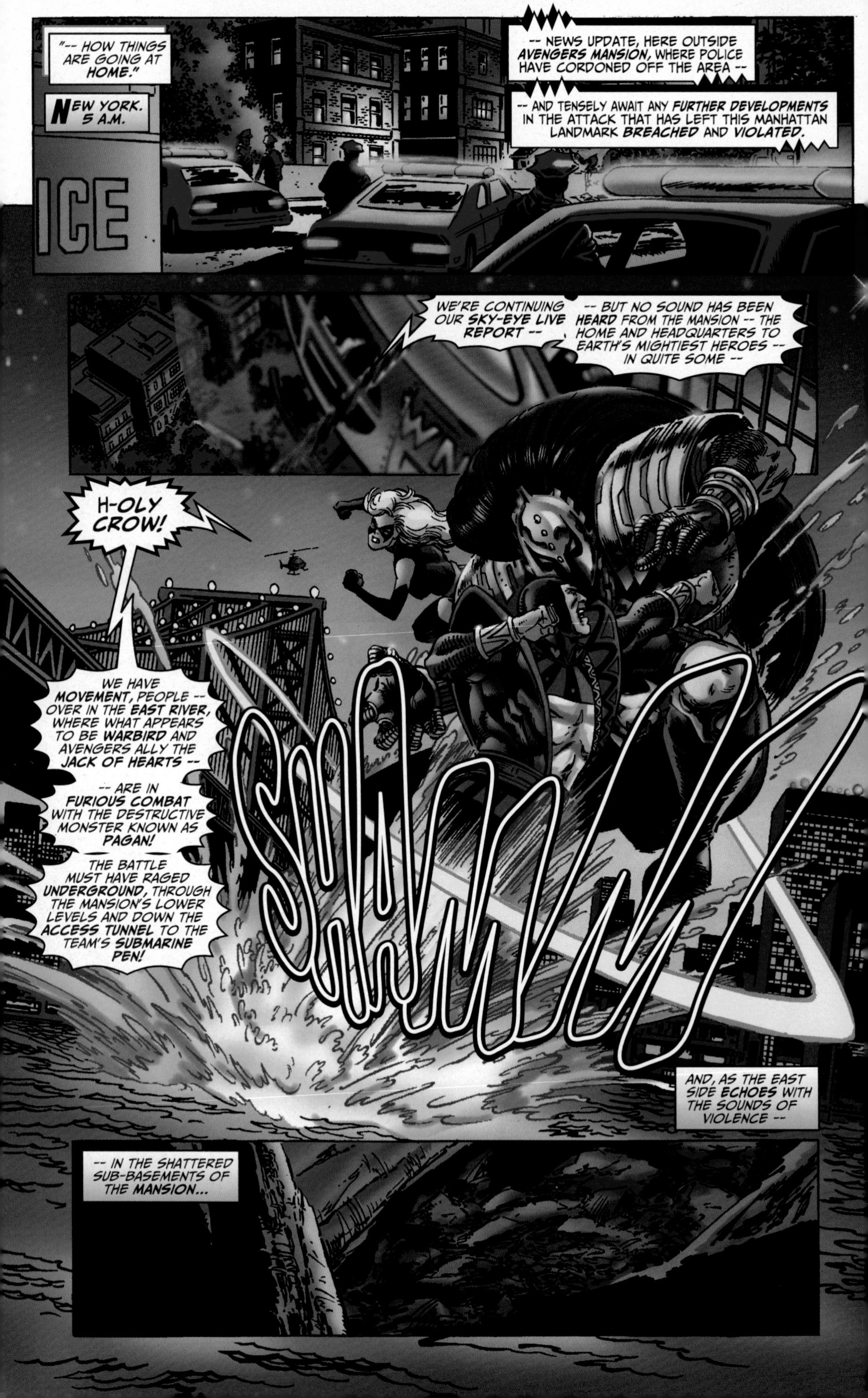
"-- HOW THINGS ARE GOING AT HOME."
NEW YORK. 5 A.M.
-- NEWS UPDATE, HERE OUTSIDE AVENGERS MANSION, WHERE POLICE HAVE CORDONED OFF THE AREA --
-- AND TENSELY AWAIT ANY FURTHER DEVELOPMENTS IN THE ATTACK THAT HAS LEFT THIS MANHATTAN LANDMARK BREACHED AND VIOLATED.
ICE
WE'RE CONTINUING OUR SKY-EYE LIVE REPORT --
-- BUT NO SOUND HAS BEEN HEARD FROM THE MANSION -- THE HOME AND HEADQUARTERS TO EARTH'S MIGHTIEST HEROES -- IN QUITE SOME --
H-OLY CROW!
WE HAVE MOVEMENT, PEOPLE -- OVER IN THE EAST RIVER, WHERE WHAT APPEARS TO BE WARBIRD AND AVENGERS ALLY THE JACK OF HEARTS --
-- ARE IN FURIOUS COMBAT WITH THE DESTRUCTIVE MONSTER KNOWN AS PAGAN!
THE BATTLE MUST HAVE RAGED UNDERGROUND, THROUGH THE MANSION'S LOWER LEVELS AND DOWN THE ACCESS TUNNEL TO THE TEAM'S SUBMARINE PEN!
SHWOOM
AND, AS THE EAST SIDE ECHOES WITH THE SOUNDS OF VIOLENCE --
-- IN THE SHATTERED SUB-BASEMENTS OF THE MANSION...

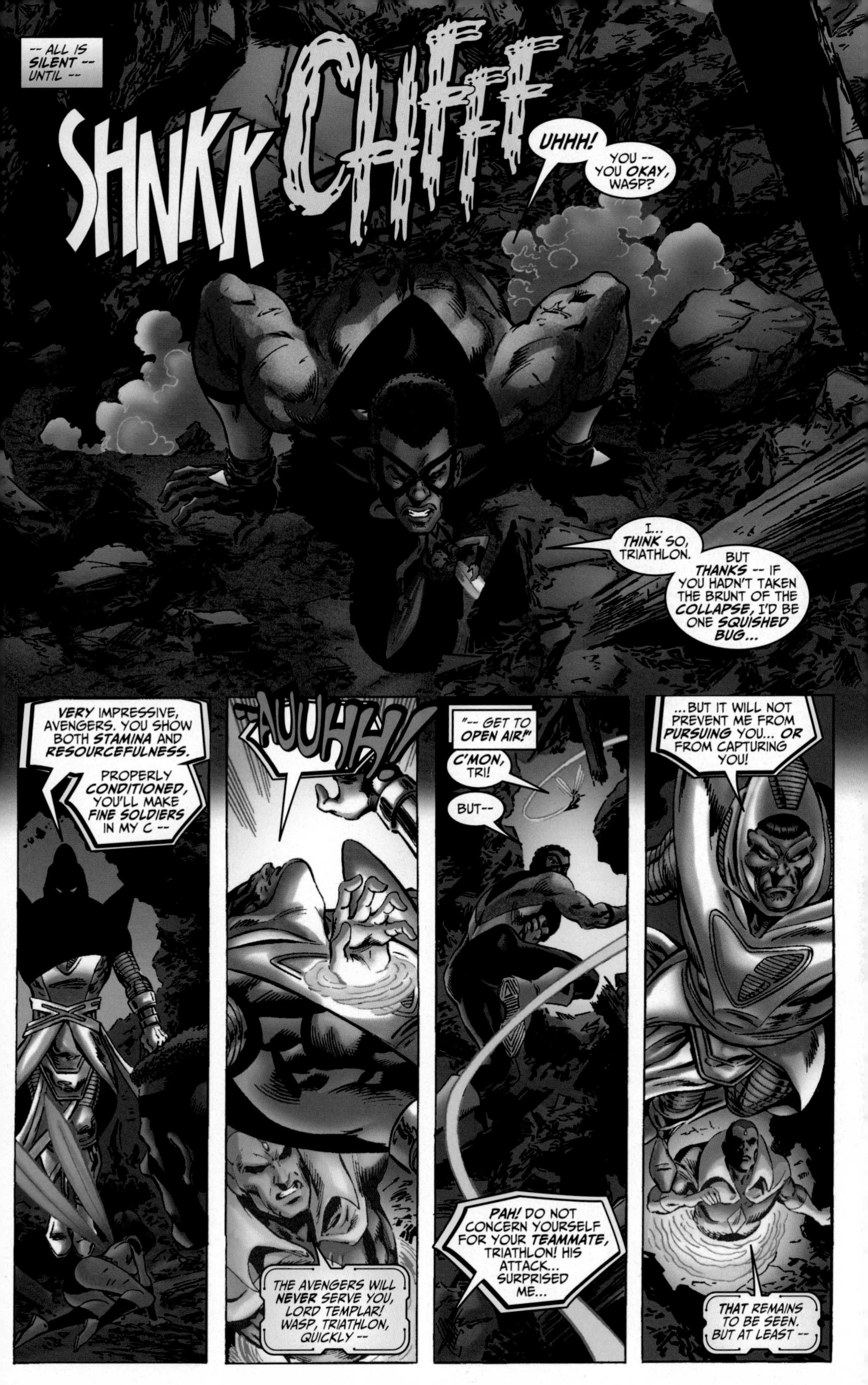

-- ALL IS SILENT -- UNTIL --
SHNKK
CHFFF
UHHH!
YOU -- YOU OKAY, WASP?
I... THINK SO, TRIATHLON.
BUT THANKS -- IF YOU HADN'T TAKEN THE BRUNT OF THE COLLAPSE, I'D BE ONE SQUISHED BUG...
VERY IMPRESSIVE, AVENGERS. YOU SHOW BOTH STAMINA AND RESOURCEFULNESS.
PROPERLY CONDITIONED, YOU'LL MAKE FINE SOLDIERS IN MY C --
AUUHH!
THE AVENGERS WILL NEVER SERVE YOU, LORD TEMPLAR! WASP, TRIATHLON, QUICKLY --
"-- GET TO OPEN AIR!"
C'MON, TRI!
BUT--
PAH! DO NOT CONCERN YOURSELF FOR YOUR TEAMMATE, TRIATHLON! HIS ATTACK... SURPRISED ME...
...BUT IT WILL NOT PREVENT ME FROM PURSUING YOU... OR FROM CAPTURING YOU!
THAT REMAINS TO BE SEEN. BUT AT LEAST --

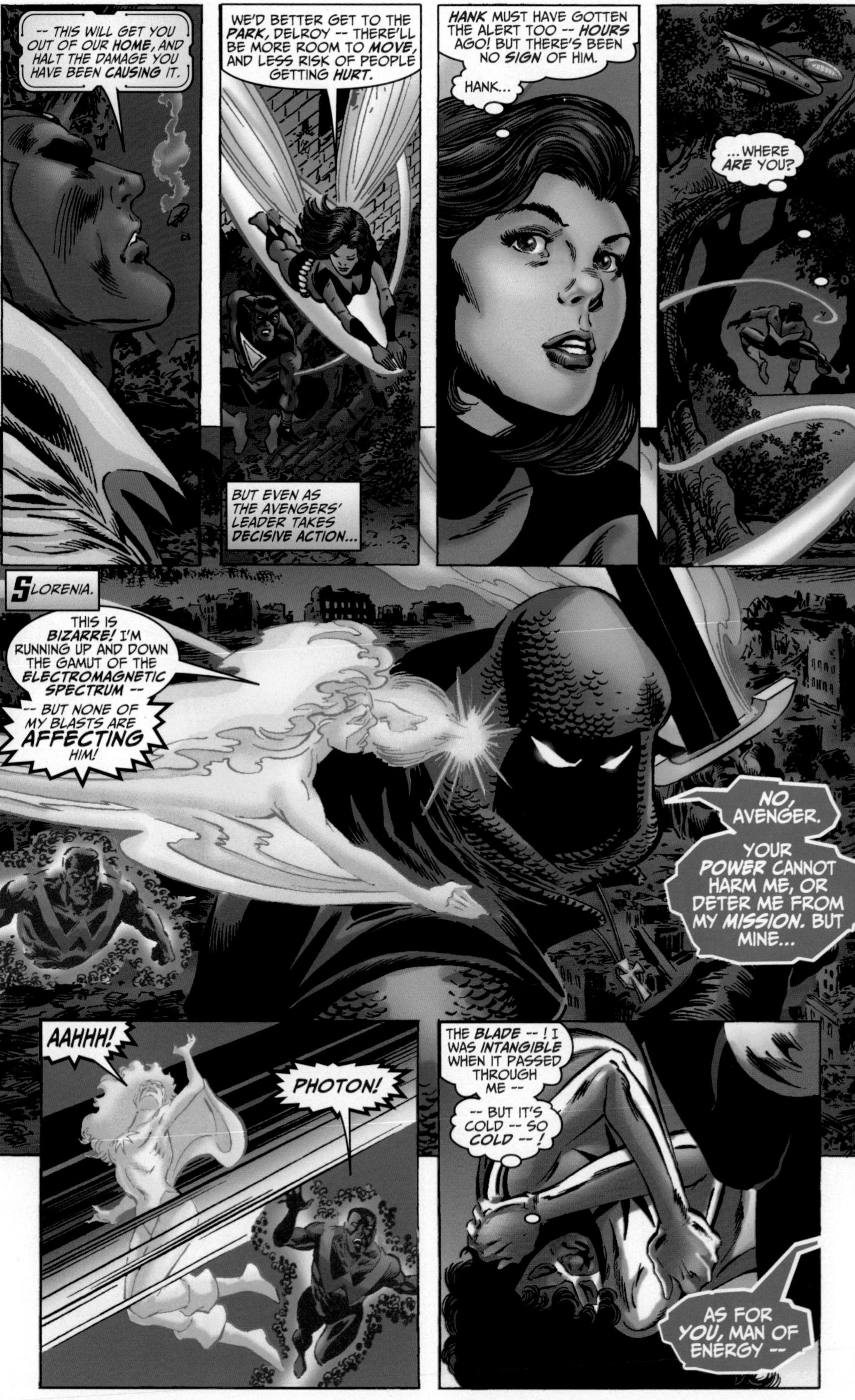
-- THIS WILL GET YOU OUT OF OUR HOME, AND HALT THE DAMAGE YOU HAVE BEEN CAUSING IT.
WE'D BETTER GET TO THE PARK, DELROY -- THERE'LL BE MORE ROOM TO MOVE, AND LESS RISK OF PEOPLE GETTING HURT.
BUT EVEN AS THE AVENGERS' LEADER TAKES DECISIVE ACTION...
HANK MUST HAVE GOTTEN THE ALERT TOO -- HOURS AGO! BUT THERE'S BEEN NO SIGN OF HIM.
HANK...
...WHERE ARE YOU?
SLORENIA.
THIS IS BIZARRE! I'M RUNNING UP AND DOWN THE GAMUT OF THE ELECTROMAGNETIC SPECTRUM --
-- BUT NONE OF MY BLASTS ARE AFFECTING HIM!
NO, AVENGER.
YOUR POWER CANNOT HARM ME, OR DETER ME FROM MY MISSION. BUT MINE...
AAHHH!
PHOTON!
THE BLADE -- ! I WAS INTANGIBLE WHEN IT PASSED THROUGH ME --
-- BUT IT'S COLD -- SO COLD -- !
AS FOR YOU, MAN OF ENERGY --

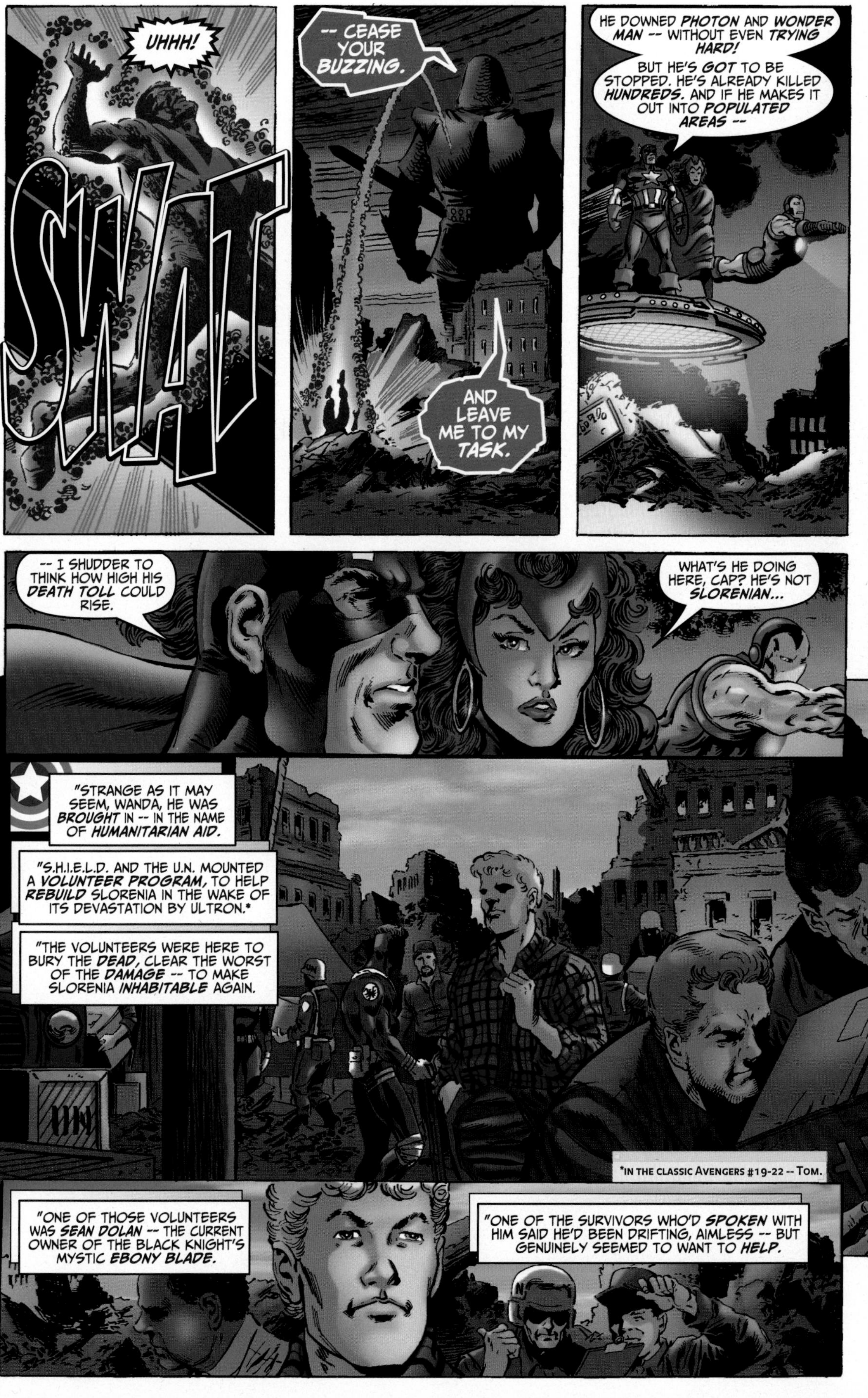
UHHH!
SWAT
-- CEASE YOUR BUZZING.
AND LEAVE ME TO MY TASK.
HE DOWNED PHOTON AND WONDER MAN -- WITHOUT EVEN TRYING HARD!
BUT HE'S GOT TO BE STOPPED. HE'S ALREADY KILLED HUNDREDS. AND IF HE MAKES IT OUT INTO POPULATED AREAS --
-- I SHUDDER TO THINK HOW HIGH HIS DEATH TOLL COULD RISE.
WHAT'S HE DOING HERE, CAP? HE'S NOT SLORENIAN...
"STRANGE AS IT MAY SEEM, WANDA, HE WAS BROUGHT IN -- IN THE NAME OF HUMANITARIAN AID.
"S.H.I.E.L.D. AND THE U.N. MOUNTED A VOLUNTEER PROGRAM, TO HELP REBUILD SLORENIA IN THE WAKE OF ITS DEVASTATION BY ULTRON.*
"THE VOLUNTEERS WERE HERE TO BURY THE DEAD, CLEAR THE WORST OF THE DAMAGE -- TO MAKE SLORENIA INHABITABLE AGAIN.
*IN THE CLASSIC AVENGERS #19-22 -- TOM.
"ONE OF THOSE VOLUNTEERS WAS SEAN DOLAN -- THE CURRENT OWNER OF THE BLACK KNIGHT'S MYSTIC EBONY BLADE.
"ONE OF THE SURVIVORS WHO'D SPOKEN WITH HIM SAID HE'D BEEN DRIFTING, AIMLESS -- BUT GENUINELY SEEMED TO WANT TO HELP.

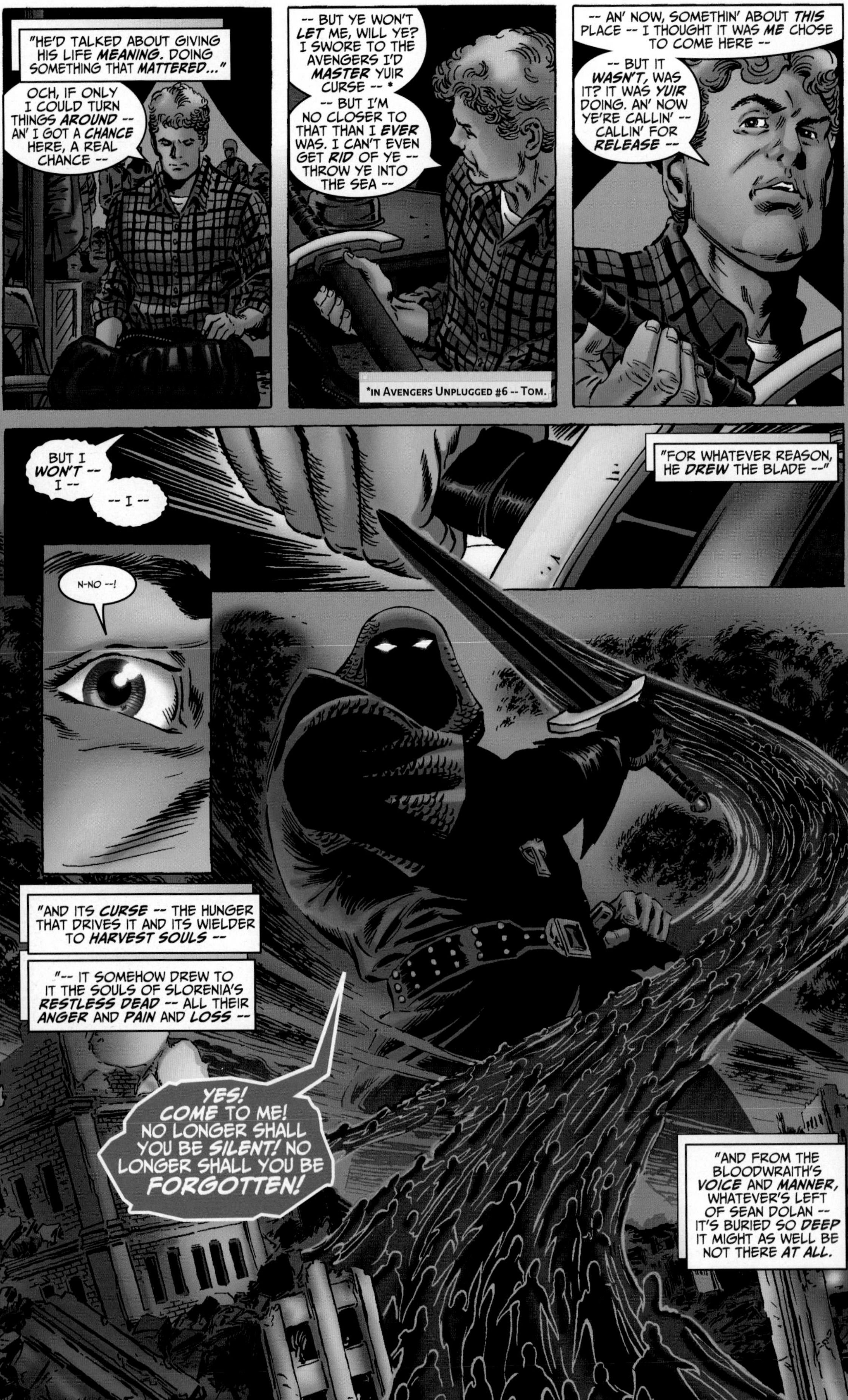
"HE'D TALKED ABOUT GIVING HIS LIFE MEANING. DOING SOMETHING THAT MATTERED..."
OCH, IF ONLY I COULD TURN THINGS AROUND -- AN' I GOT A CHANCE HERE, A REAL CHANCE --
-- BUT YE WON'T LET ME, WILL YE? I SWORE TO THE AVENGERS I'D MASTER YUIR CURSE -- *
-- BUT I'M NO CLOSER TO THAT THAN I EVER WAS. I CAN'T EVEN GET RID OF YE -- THROW YE INTO THE SEA --
*IN AVENGERS UNPLUGGED #6 -- TOM.
-- AN' NOW, SOMETHIN' ABOUT THIS PLACE -- I THOUGHT IT WAS ME CHOSE TO COME HERE --
-- BUT IT WASN'T, WAS IT? IT WAS YUIR DOING. AN' NOW YE'RE CALLIN' -- CALLIN' FOR RELEASE --
BUT I WON'T -- I --
-- I --
"FOR WHATEVER REASON, HE DREW THE BLADE --"
N-NO --!
"AND ITS CURSE -- THE HUNGER THAT DRIVES IT AND ITS WIELDER TO HARVEST SOULS --
"-- IT SOMEHOW DREW TO IT THE SOULS OF SLORENIA'S RESTLESS DEAD -- ALL THEIR ANGER AND PAIN AND LOSS --
YES! COME TO ME! NO LONGER SHALL YOU BE SILENT! NO LONGER SHALL YOU BE FORGOTTEN!
"AND FROM THE BLOODWRAITH'S VOICE AND MANNER, WHATEVER'S LEFT OF SEAN DOLAN -- IT'S BURIED SO DEEP IT MIGHT AS WELL BE NOT THERE AT ALL.

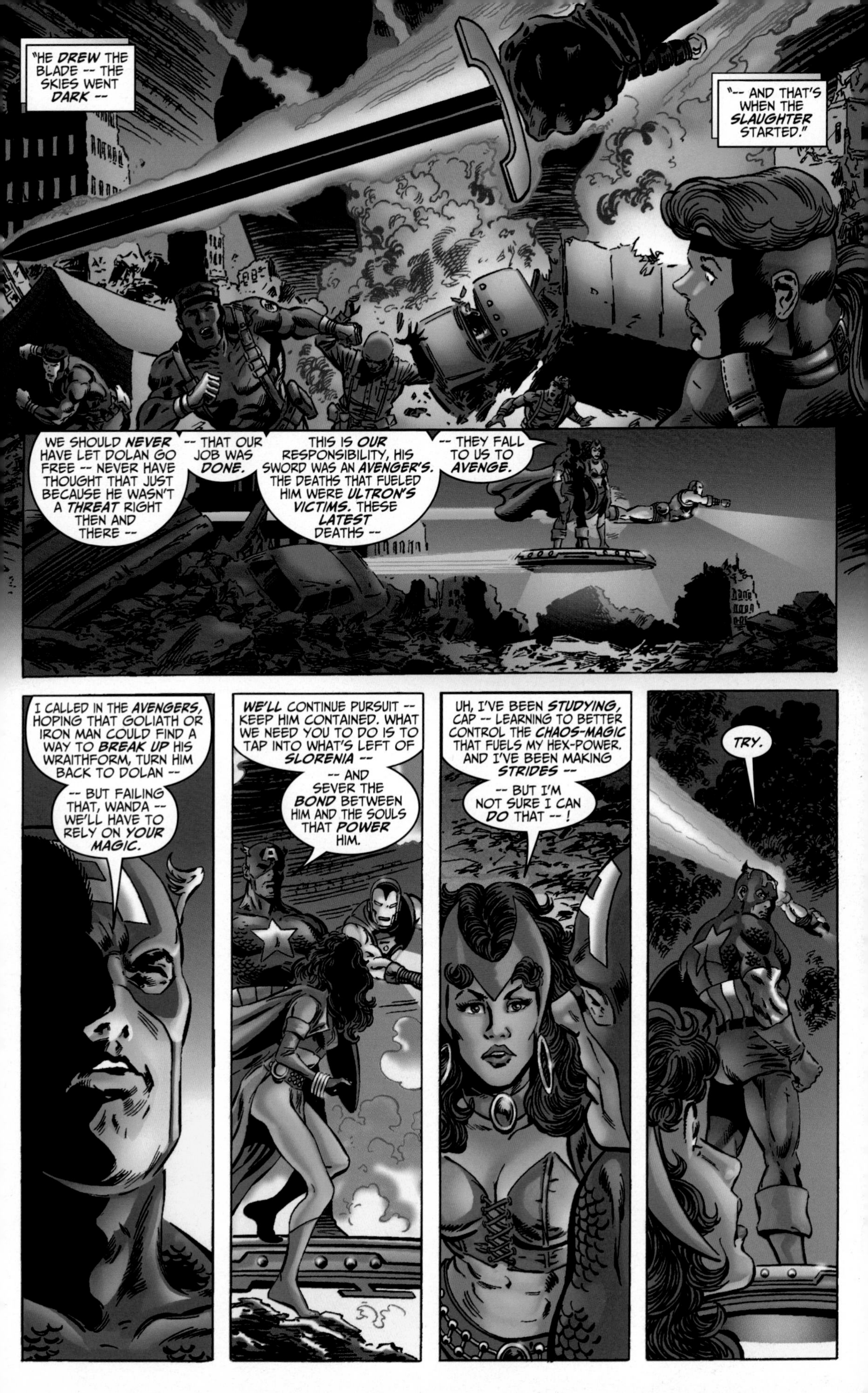
"HE DREW THE BLADE -- THE SKIES WENT DARK --
"-- AND THAT'S WHEN THE SLAUGHTER STARTED."
WE SHOULD NEVER HAVE LET DOLAN GO FREE -- NEVER HAVE THOUGHT THAT JUST BECAUSE HE WASN'T A THREAT RIGHT THEN AND THERE --
-- THAT OUR JOB WAS DONE.
THIS IS OUR RESPONSIBILITY, HIS SWORD WAS AN AVENGER'S. THE DEATHS THAT FUELED HIM WERE ULTRON'S VICTIMS. THESE LATEST DEATHS --
-- THEY FALL TO US TO AVENGE.
I CALLED IN THE AVENGERS, HOPING THAT GOLIATH OR IRON MAN COULD FIND A WAY TO BREAK UP HIS WRAITHFORM, TURN HIM BACK TO DOLAN --
-- BUT FAILING THAT, WANDA -- WE'LL HAVE TO RELY ON YOUR MAGIC.
WE'LL CONTINUE PURSUIT -- KEEP HIM CONTAINED. WHAT WE NEED YOU TO DO IS TO TAP INTO WHAT'S LEFT OF SLORENIA --
-- AND SEVER THE BOND BETWEEN HIM AND THE SOULS THAT POWER HIM.
UH, I'VE BEEN STUDYING, CAP -- LEARNING TO BETTER CONTROL THE CHAOS-MAGIC THAT FUELS MY HEX-POWER. AND I'VE BEEN MAKING STRIDES --
-- BUT I'M NOT SURE I CAN DO THAT -- !
TRY.

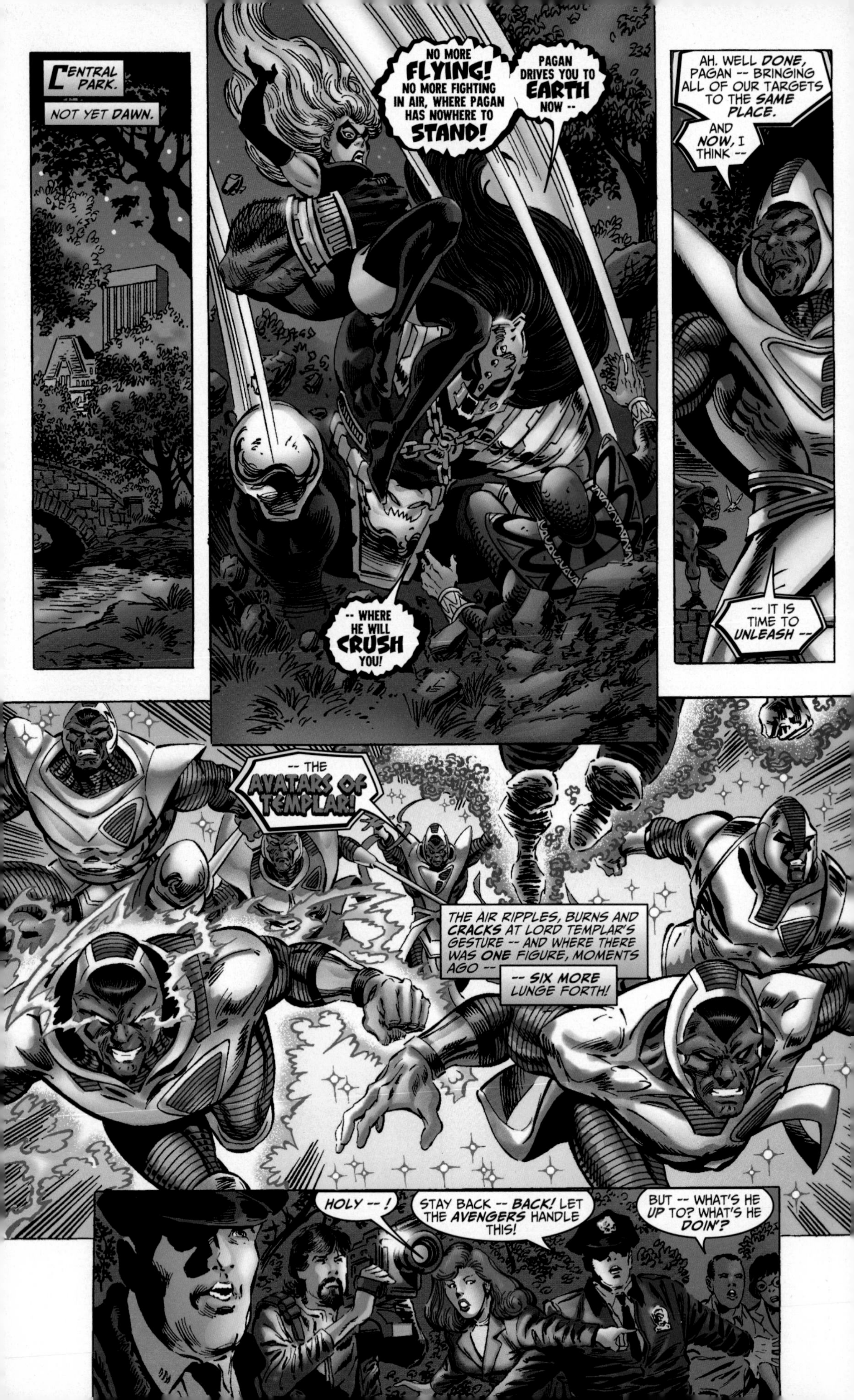
CENTRAL PARK.
NOT YET DAWN.
NO MORE FLYING! NO MORE FIGHTING IN AIR, WHERE PAGAN HAS NOWHERE TO STAND!
PAGAN DRIVES YOU TO EARTH NOW --
-- WHERE HE WILL CRUSH YOU!
AH, WELL DONE, PAGAN -- BRINGING ALL OF OUR TARGETS TO THE SAME PLACE.
AND NOW, I THINK --
-- IT IS TIME TO UNLEASH --
-- THE AVATARS OF TEMPLAR!
THE AIR RIPPLES, BURNS AND CRACKS AT LORD TEMPLAR'S GESTURE -- AND WHERE THERE WAS ONE FIGURE, MOMENTS AGO --
-- SIX MORE LUNGE FORTH!
HOLY -- !
STAY BACK -- BACK! LET THE AVENGERS HANDLE THIS!
BUT -- WHAT'S HE UP TO? WHAT'S HE DOIN'?

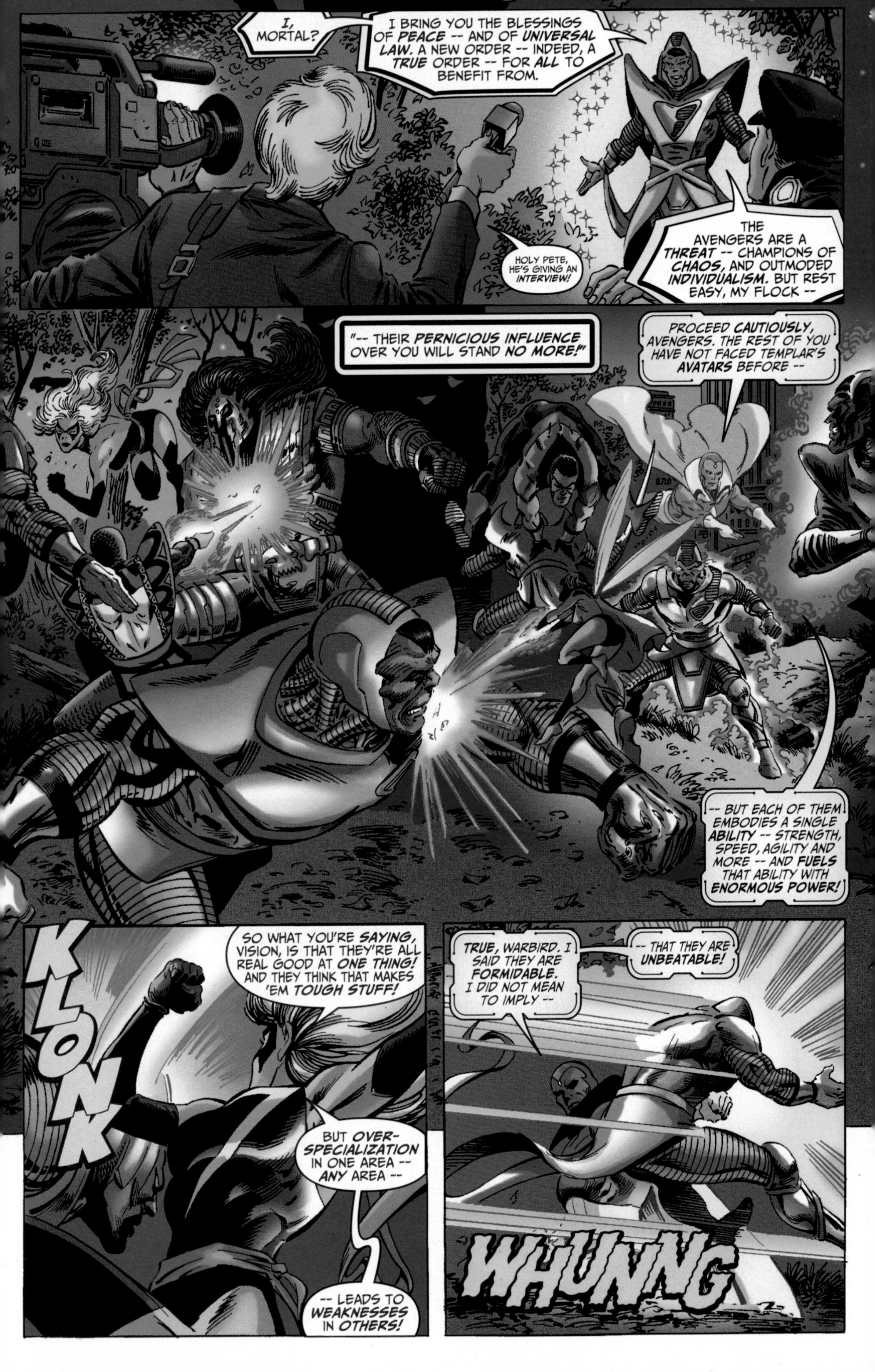
I, MORTAL?
I BRING YOU THE BLESSINGS OF PEACE -- AND OF UNIVERSAL LAW. A NEW ORDER -- INDEED, A TRUE ORDER -- FOR ALL TO BENEFIT FROM.
HOLY PETE, HE'S GIVING AN INTERVIEW!
THE AVENGERS ARE A THREAT -- CHAMPIONS OF CHAOS, AND OUTMODED INDIVIDUALISM. BUT REST EASY, MY FLOCK --
"-- THEIR PERNICIOUS INFLUENCE OVER YOU WILL STAND NO MORE!"
PROCEED CAUTIOUSLY, AVENGERS. THE REST OF YOU HAVE NOT FACED TEMPLAR'S AVATARS BEFORE --
-- BUT EACH OF THEM EMBODIES A SINGLE ABILITY -- STRENGTH, SPEED, AGILITY AND MORE -- AND FUELS THAT ABILITY WITH ENORMOUS POWER!
KLONK
SO WHAT YOU'RE SAYING, VISION, IS THAT THEY'RE ALL REAL GOOD AT ONE THING! AND THEY THINK THAT MAKES 'EM TOUGH STUFF!
BUT OVER-SPECIALIZATION IN ONE AREA -- ANY AREA --
-- LEADS TO WEAKNESSES IN OTHERS!
TRUE, WARBIRD. I SAID THEY ARE FORMIDABLE. I DID NOT MEAN TO IMPLY --
-- THAT THEY ARE UNBEATABLE!
WHUNNG

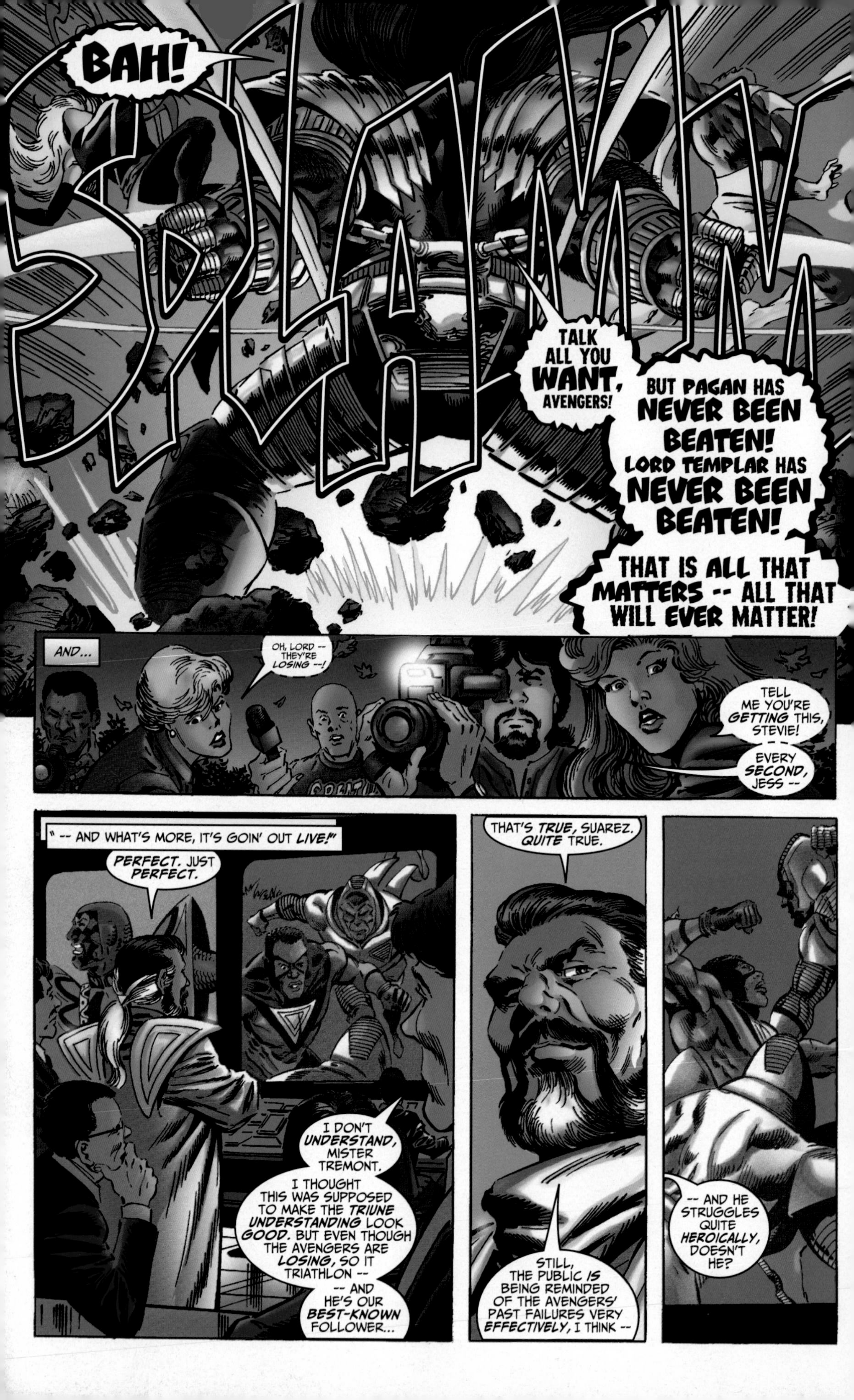
BAH!
SPLAMMM
TALK ALL YOU WANT, AVENGERS!
BUT PAGAN HAS NEVER BEEN BEATEN! LORD TEMPLAR HAS NEVER BEEN BEATEN!
THAT IS ALL THAT MATTERS -- ALL THAT WILL EVER MATTER!
AND...
OH, LORD -- THEY'RE LOSING --!
TELL ME YOU'RE GETTING THIS, STEVIE!
EVERY SECOND, JESS --
" -- AND WHAT'S MORE, IT'S GOIN' OUT LIVE!"
PERFECT. JUST PERFECT.
I DON'T UNDERSTAND, MISTER TREMONT.
I THOUGHT THIS WAS SUPPOSED TO MAKE THE TRIUNE UNDERSTANDING LOOK GOOD. BUT EVEN THOUGH THE AVENGERS ARE LOSING, SO IT TRIATHLON --
-- AND HE'S OUR BEST-KNOWN FOLLOWER...
THAT'S TRUE, SUAREZ. QUITE TRUE.
STILL, THE PUBLIC IS BEING REMINDED OF THE AVENGERS' PAST FAILURES VERY EFFECTIVELY, I THINK --
-- AND HE STRUGGLES QUITE HEROICALLY, DOESN'T HE?

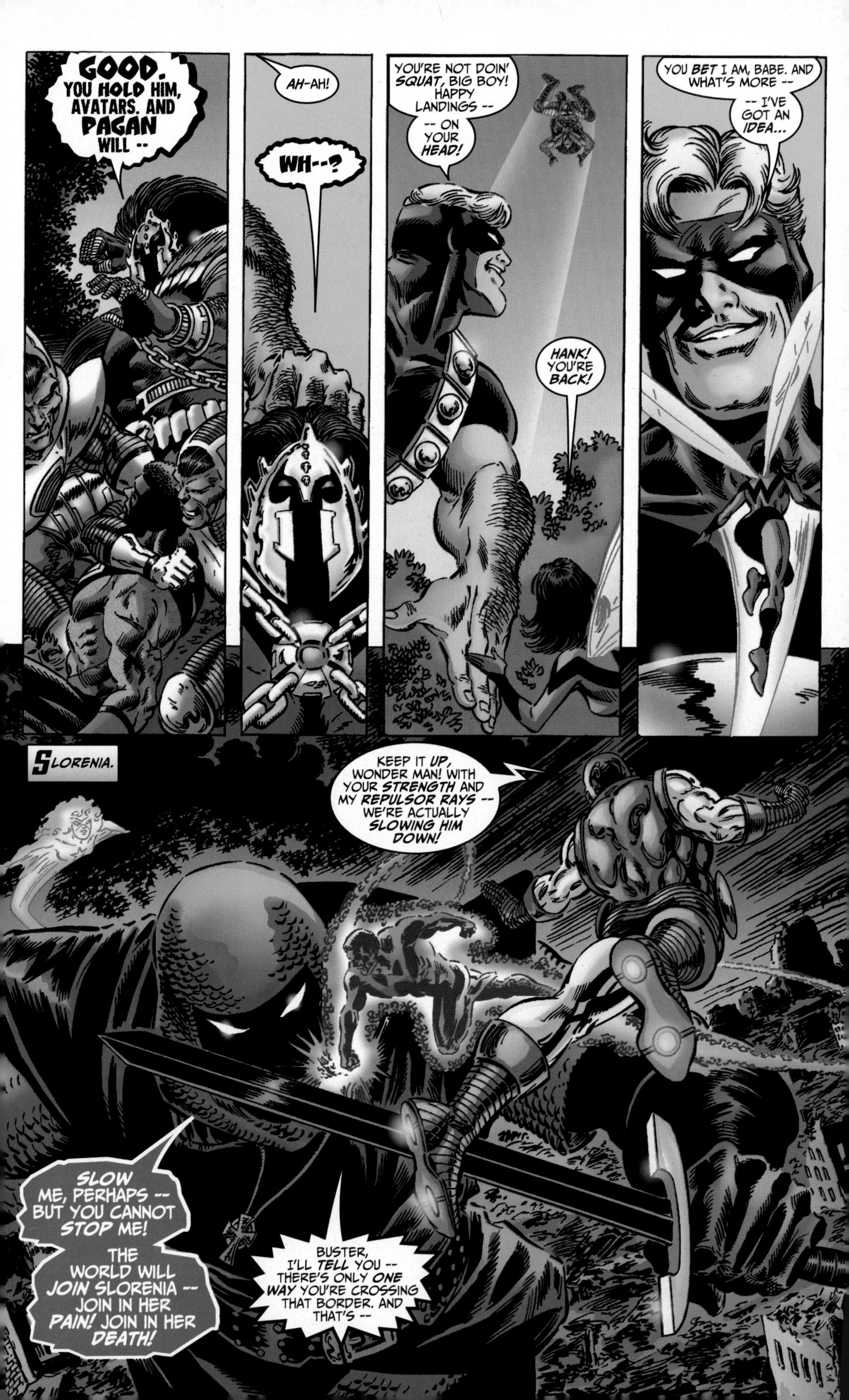
GOOD. YOU HOLD HIM, AVATARS. AND PAGAN WILL --
AH-AH!
WH--?
YOU'RE NOT DOIN' SQUAT, BIG BOY! HAPPY LANDINGS --
-- ON YOUR HEAD!
HANK! YOU'RE BACK!
YOU BET I AM, BABE. AND WHAT'S MORE --
-- I'VE GOT AN IDEA...
SLORENIA.
KEEP IT UP, WONDER MAN! WITH YOUR STRENGTH AND MY REPULSOR RAYS -- WE'RE ACTUALLY SLOWING HIM DOWN!
SLOW ME, PERHAPS -- BUT YOU CANNOT STOP ME!
THE WORLD WILL JOIN SLORENIA -- JOIN IN HER PAIN! JOIN IN HER DEATH!
BUSTER, I'LL TELL YOU -- THERE'S ONLY ONE WAY YOU'RE CROSSING THAT BORDER. AND THAT'S --

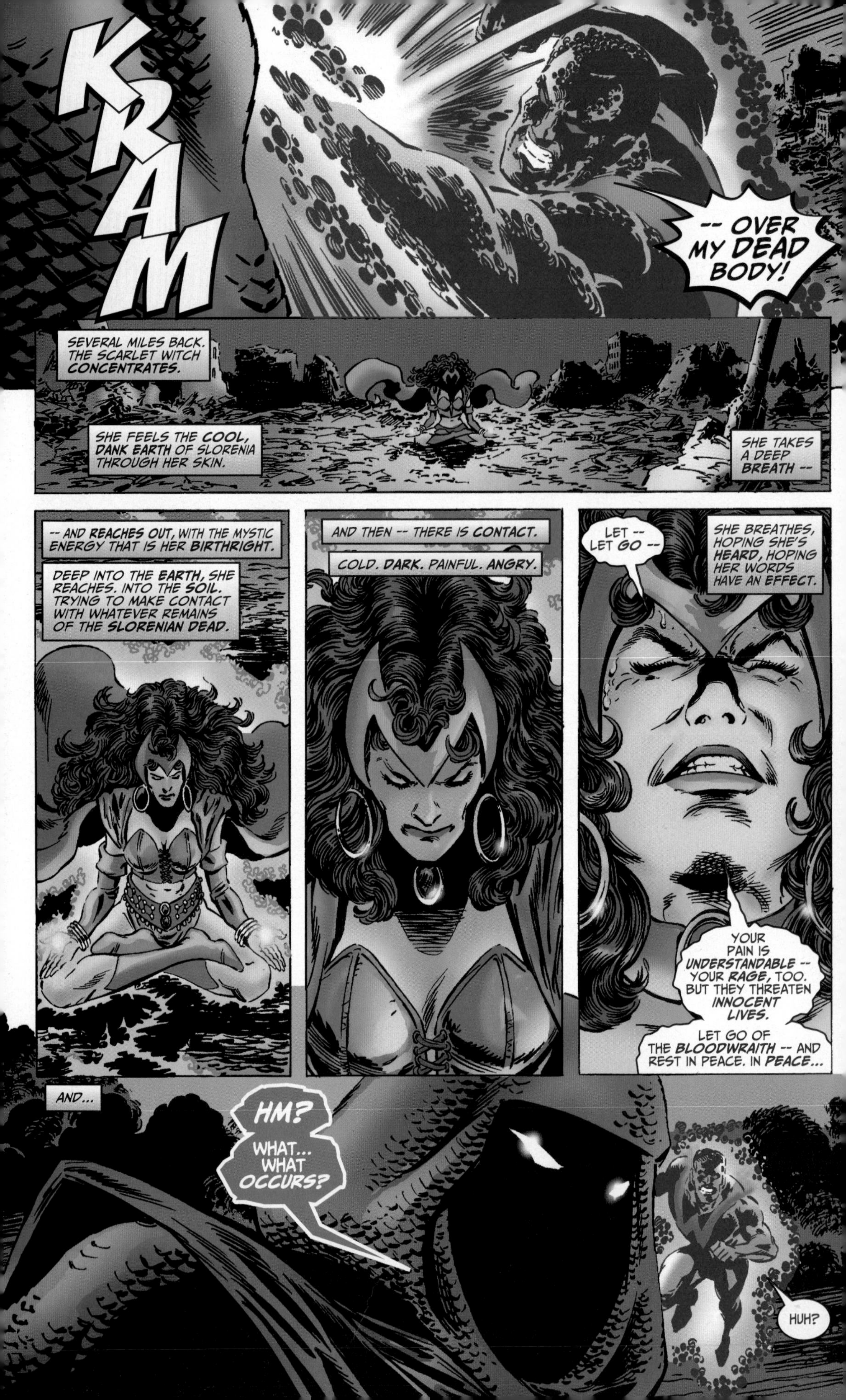
KRAM
-- OVER MY DEAD BODY!
SEVERAL MILES BACK. THE SCARLET WITCH CONCENTRATES.
SHE FEELS THE COOL, DANK EARTH OF SLORENIA THROUGH HER SKIN.
SHE TAKES A DEEP BREATH --
-- AND REACHES OUT, WITH THE MYSTIC ENERGY THAT IS HER BIRTHRIGHT.
DEEP INTO THE EARTH, SHE REACHES. INTO THE SOIL. TRYING TO MAKE CONTACT WITH WHATEVER REMAINS OF THE SLORENIAN DEAD.
AND THEN -- THERE IS CONTACT.
COLD. DARK. PAINFUL. ANGRY.
LET -- LET GO --
SHE BREATHES, HOPING SHE'S HEARD, HOPING HER WORDS HAVE AN EFFECT.
YOUR PAIN IS UNDERSTANDABLE -- YOUR RAGE, TOO. BUT THEY THREATEN INNOCENT LIVES.
LET GO OF THE BLOODWRAITH -- AND REST IN PEACE. IN PEACE...
AND...
HM? WHAT... WHAT OCCURS?
HUH?

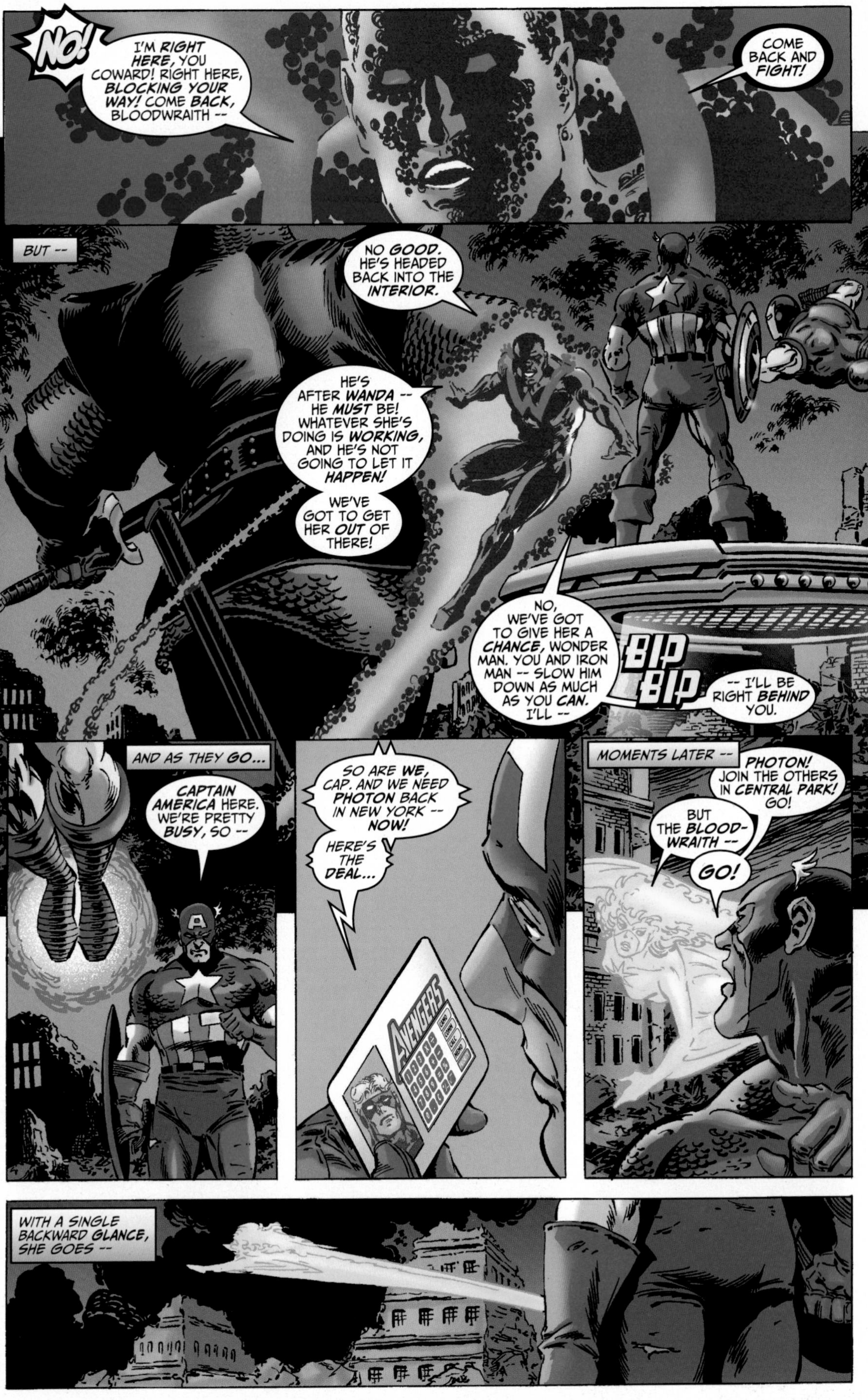
NO!
I'M RIGHT HERE, YOU COWARD! RIGHT HERE, BLOCKING YOUR WAY! COME BACK, BLOODWRAITH --
COME BACK AND FIGHT!
BUT --
NO GOOD. HE'S HEADED BACK INTO THE INTERIOR.
HE'S AFTER WANDA -- HE MUST BE! WHATEVER SHE'S DOING IS WORKING, AND HE'S NOT GOING TO LET IT HAPPEN!
WE'VE GOT TO GET HER OUT OF THERE!
NO, WE'VE GOT TO GIVE HER A CHANCE, WONDER MAN. YOU AND IRON MAN -- SLOW HIM DOWN AS MUCH AS YOU CAN. I'LL --
BIP BIP
-- I'LL BE RIGHT BEHIND YOU.
AND AS THEY GO...
CAPTAIN AMERICA HERE. WE'RE PRETTY BUSY, SO --
SO ARE WE, CAP. AND WE NEED PHOTON BACK IN NEW YORK -- NOW!
HERE'S THE DEAL...
AVENGERS
MOMENTS LATER --
PHOTON! JOIN THE OTHERS IN CENTRAL PARK! GO!
BUT THE BLOOD-WRAITH --
GO!
WITH A SINGLE BACKWARD GLANCE, SHE GOES --

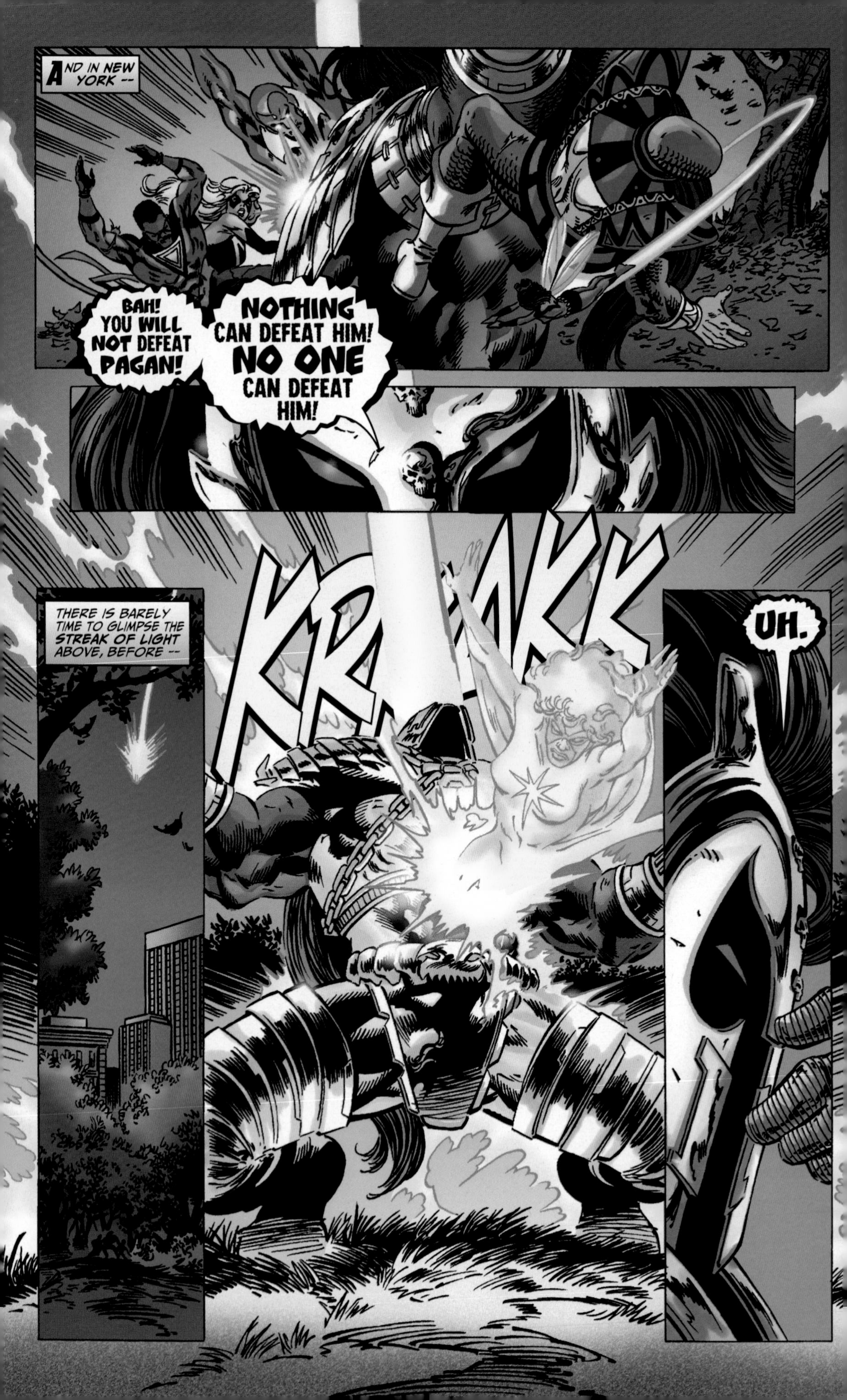
AND IN NEW YORK --
BAH! YOU WILL NOT DEFEAT PAGAN!
NOTHING CAN DEFEAT HIM! NO ONE CAN DEFEAT HIM!
THERE IS BARELY TIME TO GLIMPSE THE STREAK OF LIGHT ABOVE, BEFORE --
UH.

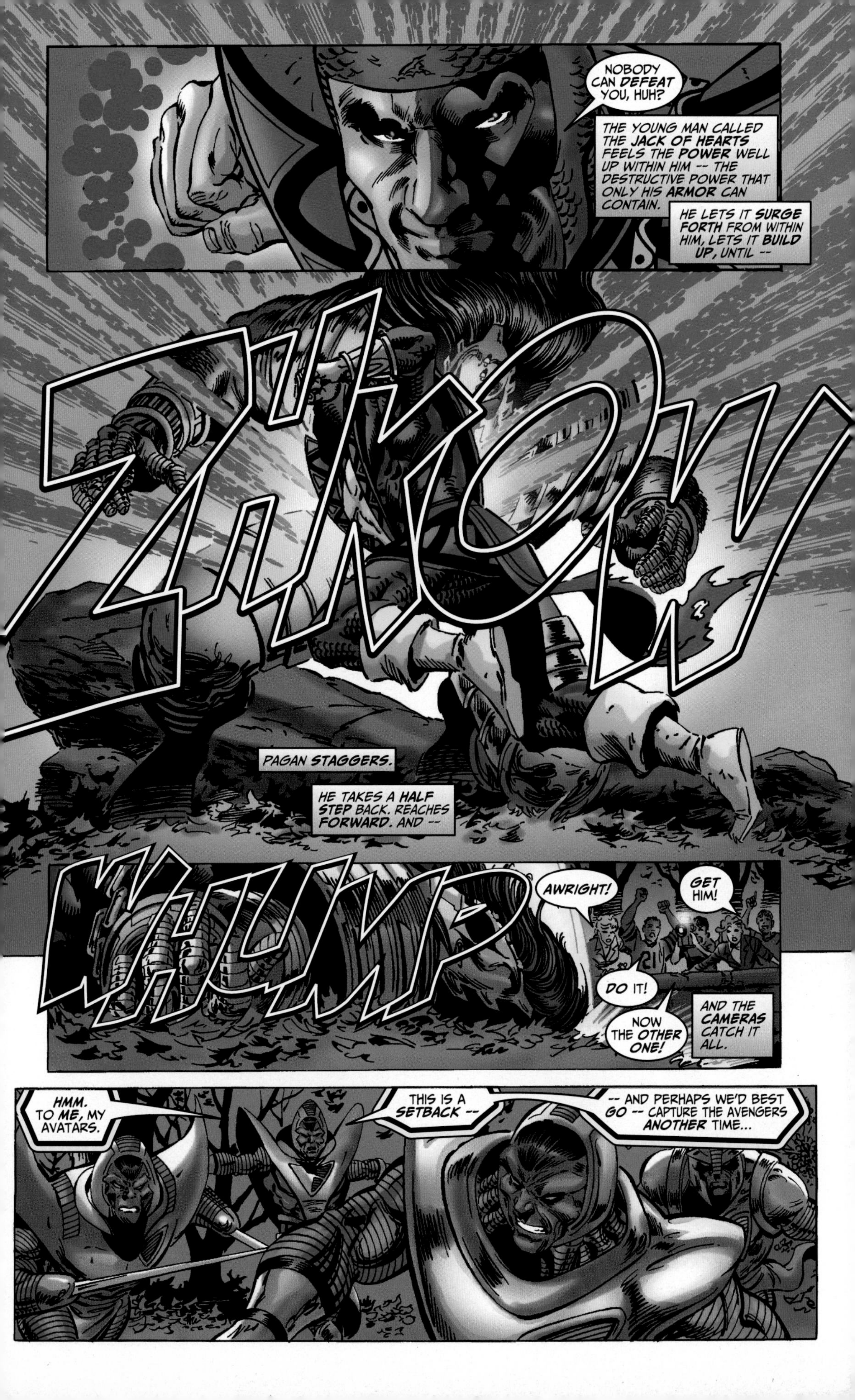
NOBODY CAN DEFEAT YOU, HUH?
THE YOUNG MAN CALLED THE JACK OF HEARTS FEELS THE POWER WELL UP WITHIN HIM -- THE DESTRUCTIVE POWER THAT ONLY HIS ARMOR CAN CONTAIN.
HE LETS IT SURGE FORTH FROM WITHIN HIM, LETS IT BUILD UP, UNTIL --
ZAKOW
PAGAN STAGGERS.
HE TAKES A HALF STEP BACK. REACHES FORWARD. AND --
WHUMP
AWRIGHT!
GET HIM!
DO IT!
NOW THE OTHER ONE!
AND THE CAMERAS CATCH IT ALL.
HMM. TO ME, MY AVATARS.
THIS IS A SETBACK --
-- AND PERHAPS WE'D BEST GO -- CAPTURE THE AVENGERS ANOTHER TIME...

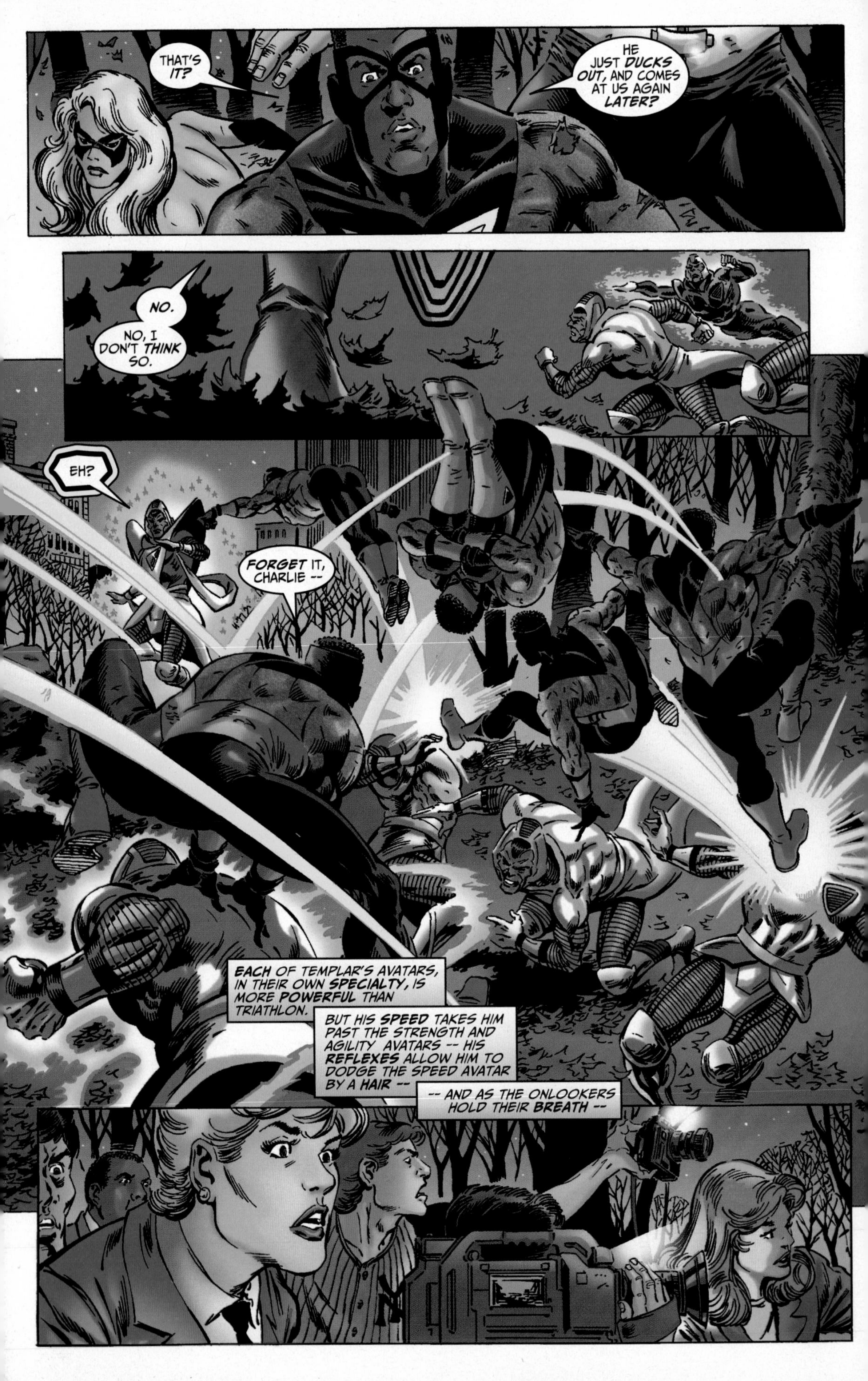

THAT'S IT?
HE JUST DUCKS OUT, AND COMES AT US AGAIN LATER?
NO.
NO, I DON'T THINK SO.
EH?
FORGET IT, CHARLIE --
EACH OF TEMPLAR'S AVATARS, IN THEIR OWN SPECIALTY, IS MORE POWERFUL THAN TRIATHLON.
BUT HIS SPEED TAKES HIM PAST THE STRENGTH AND AGILITY AVATARS -- HIS REFLEXES ALLOW HIM TO DODGE THE SPEED AVATAR BY A HAIR --
-- AND AS THE ONLOOKERS HOLD THEIR BREATH --

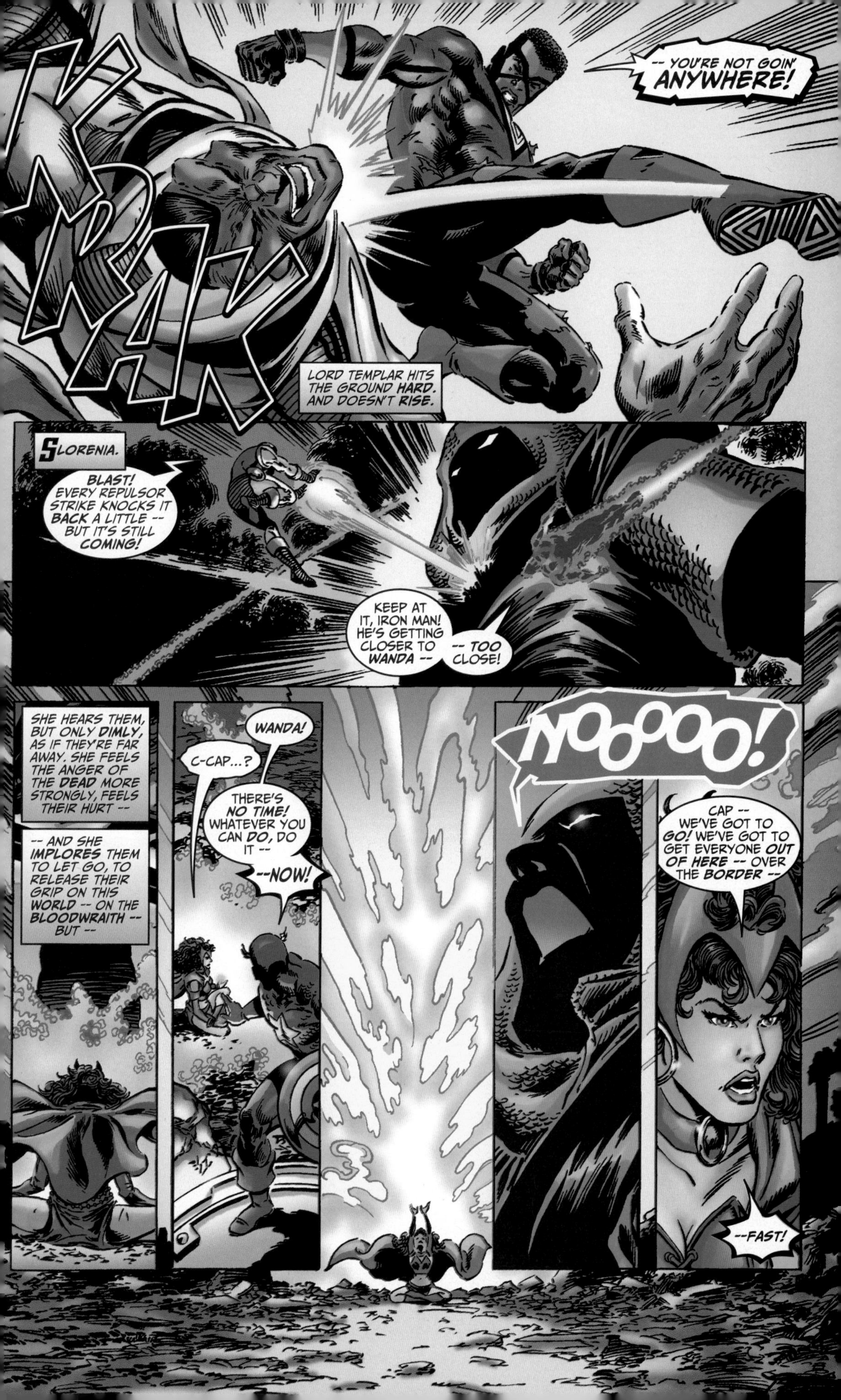

KRAKK
-- YOU'RE NOT GOIN' ANYWHERE!
LORD TEMPLAR HITS THE GROUND HARD. AND DOESN'T RISE.
SLORENIA.
BLAST! EVERY REPULSOR STRIKE KNOCKS IT BACK A LITTLE -- BUT IT'S STILL COMING!
KEEP AT IT, IRON MAN! HE'S GETTING CLOSER TO WANDA --
-- TOO CLOSE!
SHE HEARS THEM, BUT ONLY DIMLY, AS IF THEY'RE FAR AWAY. SHE FEELS THE ANGER OF THE DEAD MORE STRONGLY, FEELS THEIR HURT --
-- AND SHE IMPLORES THEM TO LET GO, TO RELEASE THEIR GRIP ON THIS WORLD -- ON THE BLOODWRAITH -- BUT --
WANDA!
C-CAP...?
THERE'S NO TIME! WHATEVER YOU CAN DO, DO IT --
--NOW!
NOOOOO!
CAP -- WE'VE GOT TO GO! WE'VE GOT TO GET EVERYONE OUT OF HERE -- OVER THE BORDER --
--FAST!

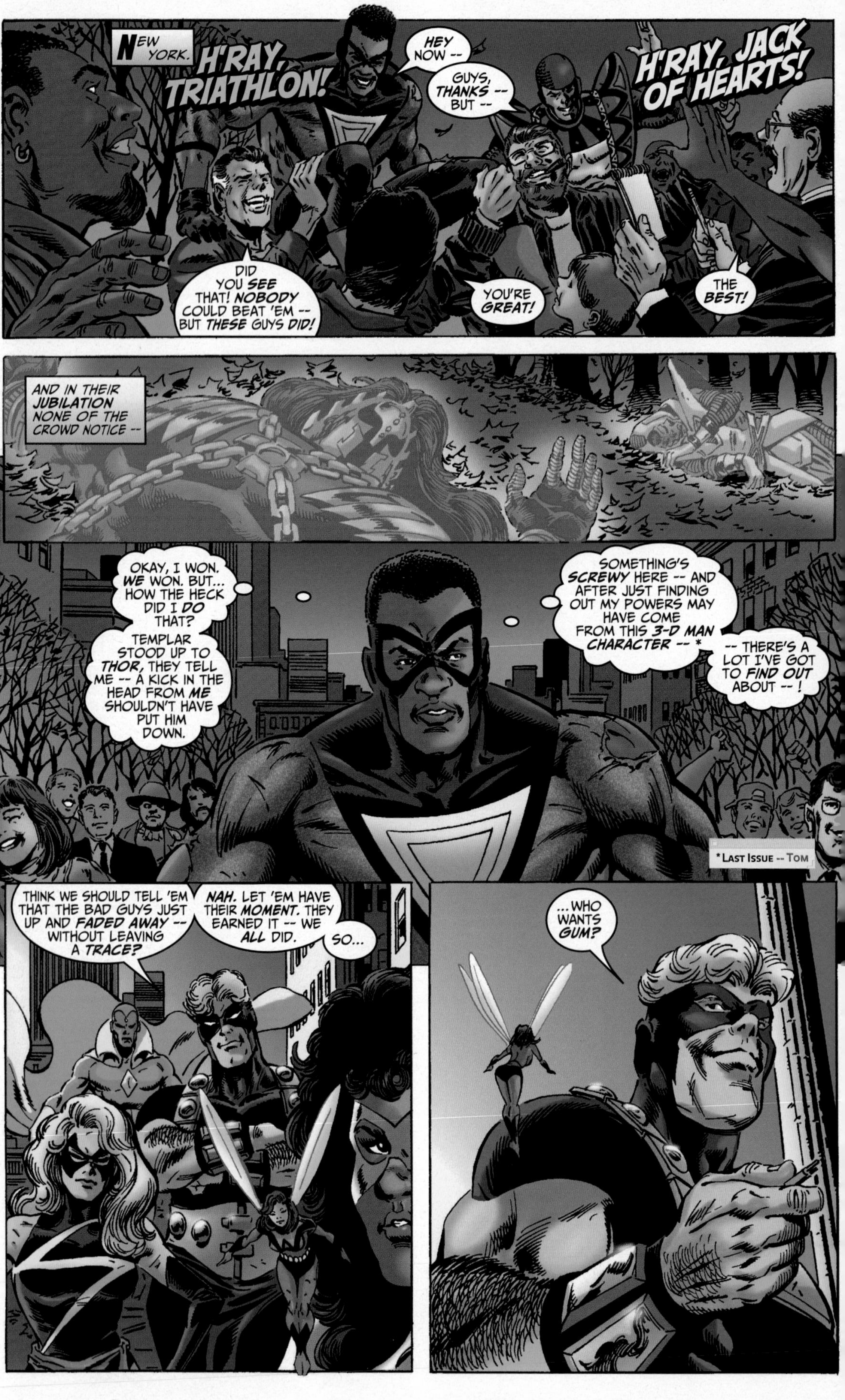
NEW YORK.
H'RAY, TRIATHLON!
HEY NOW --
GUSE, THANKS -- BUT --
H'RAY, JACK OF HEARTS!
DID YOU SEE THAT! NOBODY COULD BEAT 'EM -- BUT THESE GUYS DID!
YOU'RE GREAT!
THE BEST!
AND IN THEIR JUBILATION NONE OF THE CROWD NOTICE --
OKAY, I WON. WE WON. BUT... HOW THE HECK DID I DO THAT?
TEMPLAR STOOD UP TO THOR, THEY TELL ME -- A KICK IN THE HEAD FROM ME SHOULDN'T HAVE PUT HIM DOWN.
SOMETHING'S SCREWY HERE -- AND AFTER JUST FINDING OUT MY POWERS MAY HAVE COME FROM THIS 3-D MAN CHARACTER -- *
-- THERE'S A LOT I'VE GOT TO FIND OUT ABOUT -- !
*LAST ISSUE -- TOM
THINK WE SHOULD TELL 'EM THAT THE BAD GUYS JUST UP AND FADED AWAY -- WITHOUT LEAVING A TRACE?
NAH. LET 'EM HAVE THEIR MOMENT. THEY EARNED IT -- WE ALL DID.
SO...
...WHO WANTS GUM?

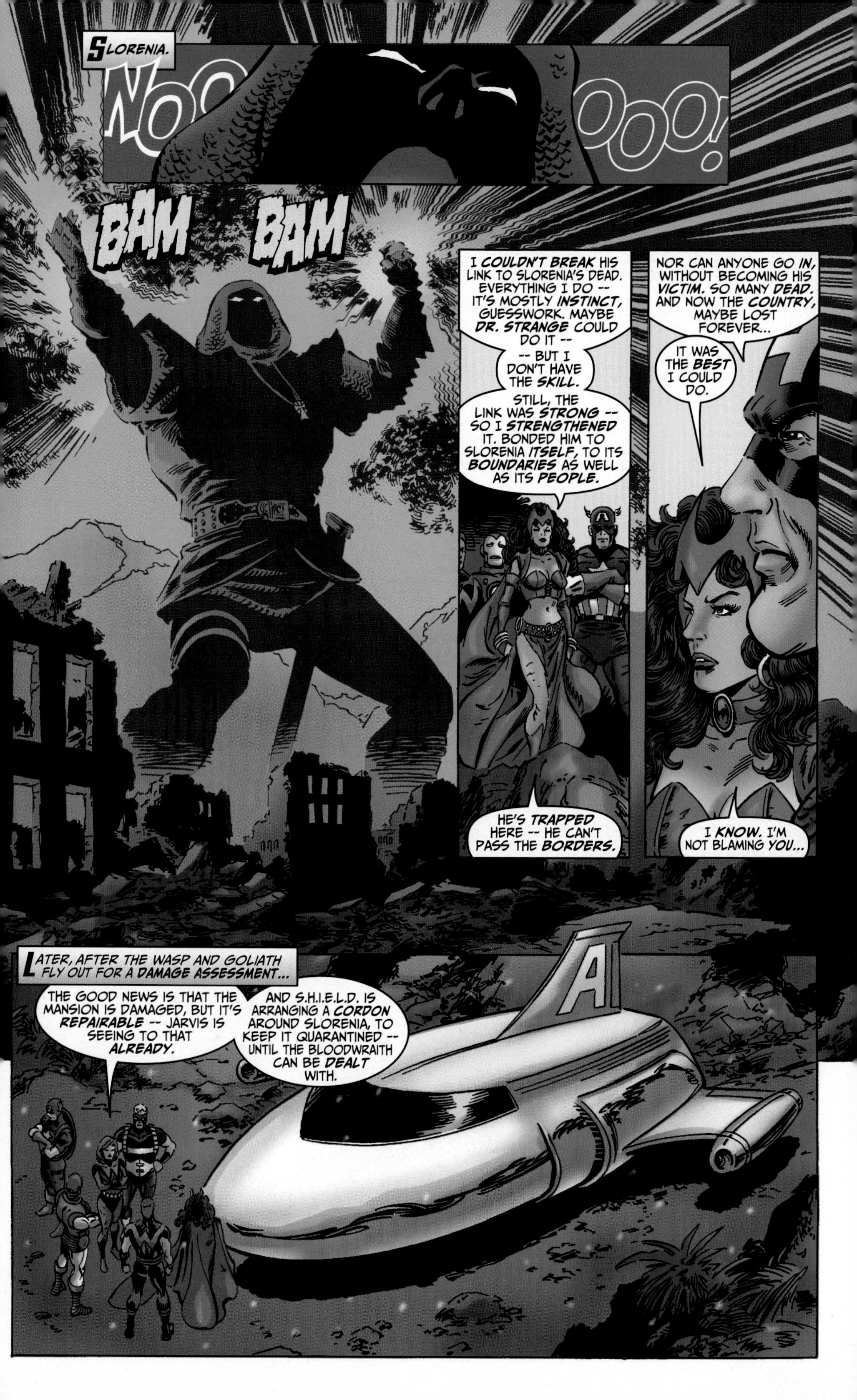
SLORENIA.
NOOOOOOO!
BAM
BAM
I COULDN'T BREAK HIS LINK TO SLORENIA'S DEAD. EVERYTHING I DO -- IT'S MOSTLY INSTINCT, GUESSWORK. MAYBE DR. STRANGE COULD DO IT --
-- BUT I DON'T HAVE THE SKILL.
STILL, THE LINK WAS STRONG -- SO I STRENGTHENED IT. BONDED HIM TO SLORENIA ITSELF, TO ITS BOUNDARIES AS WELL AS ITS PEOPLE.
HE'S TRAPPED HERE -- HE CAN'T PASS THE BORDERS.
NOR CAN ANYONE GO IN, WITHOUT BECOMING HIS VICTIM. SO MANY DEAD. AND NOW THE COUNTRY, MAYBE LOST FOREVER...
IT WAS THE BEST I COULD DO.
I KNOW. I'M NOT BLAMING YOU...
LATER, AFTER THE WASP AND GOLIATH FLY OUT FOR A DAMAGE ASSESSMENT...
THE GOOD NEWS IS THAT THE MANSION IS DAMAGED, BUT IT'S REPAIRABLE -- JARVIS IS SEEING TO THAT ALREADY.
AND S.H.I.E.L.D. IS ARRANGING A CORDON AROUND SLORENIA, TO KEEP IT QUARANTINED -- UNTIL THE BLOODWRAITH CAN BE DEALT WITH.
A

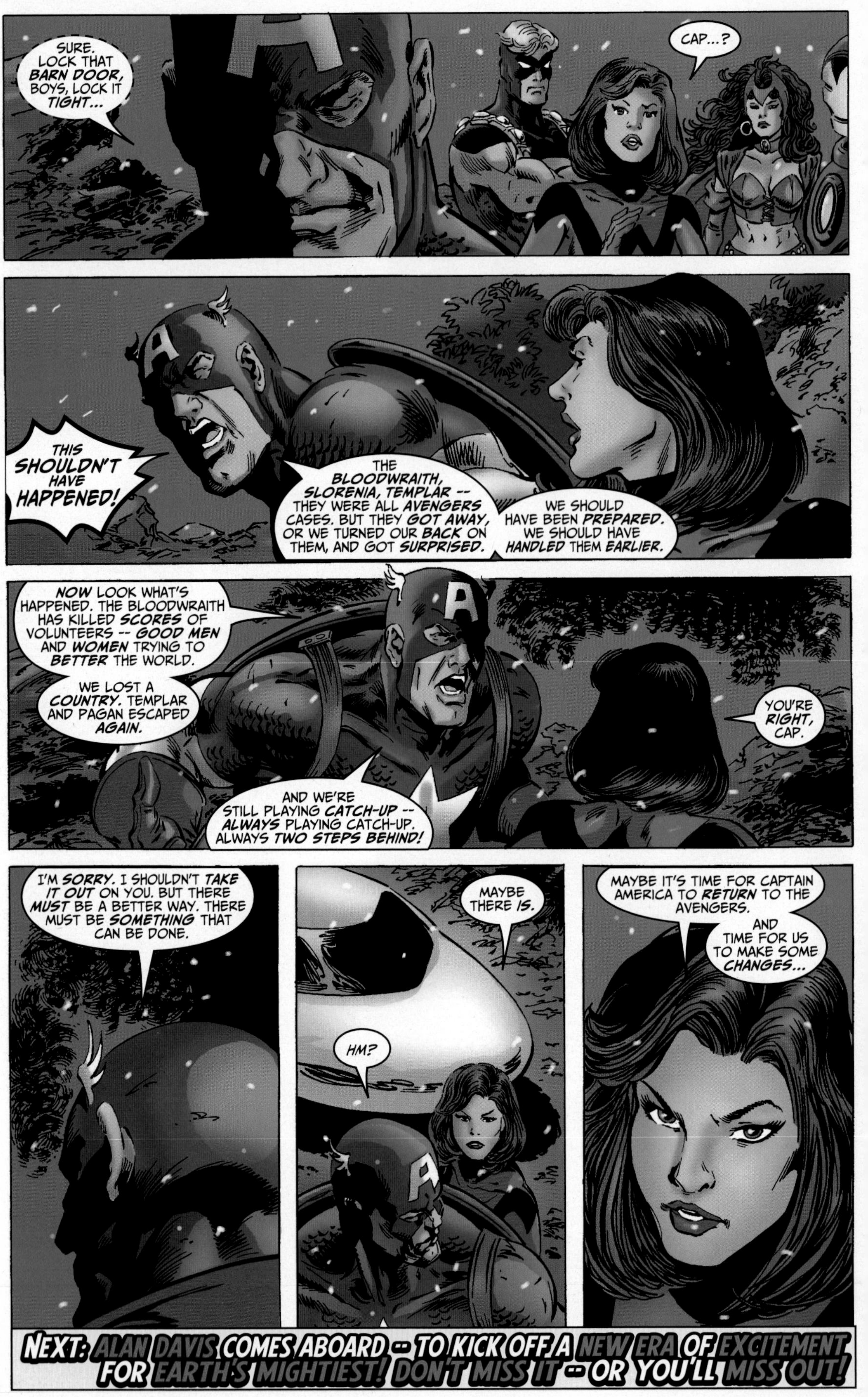
SURE. LOCK THAT BARN DOOR, BOYS, LOCK IT TIGHT...
CAP...?
THIS SHOULDN'T HAVE HAPPENED!
THE BLOODWRAITH, SLORENIA, TEMPLAR -- THEY WERE ALL AVENGERS CASES. BUT THEY GOT AWAY, OR WE TURNED OUR BACK ON THEM, AND GOT SURPRISED.
WE SHOULD HAVE BEEN PREPARED. WE SHOULD HAVE HANDLED THEM EARLIER.
NOW LOOK WHAT'S HAPPENED. THE BLOODWRAITH HAS KILLED SCORES OF VOLUNTEERS -- GOOD MEN AND WOMEN TRYING TO BETTER THE WORLD.
WE LOST A COUNTRY. TEMPLAR AND PAGAN ESCAPED AGAIN.
AND WE'RE STILL PLAYING CATCH-UP -- ALWAYS PLAYING CATCH-UP. ALWAYS TWO STEPS BEHIND!
YOU'RE RIGHT, CAP.
I'M SORRY. I SHOULDN'T TAKE IT OUT ON YOU. BUT THERE MUST BE A BETTER WAY. THERE MUST BE SOMETHING THAT CAN BE DONE.
MAYBE THERE IS.
HM?
MAYBE IT'S TIME FOR CAPTAIN AMERICA TO RETURN TO THE AVENGERS.
AND TIME FOR US TO MAKE SOME CHANGES...

NEXT: ALAN DAVIS COMES ABOARD -- TO KICK OFF A NEW ERA OF EXCITEMENT FOR EARTH'S MIGHTIEST! DON'T MISS IT -- OR YOU'LL MISS OUT!

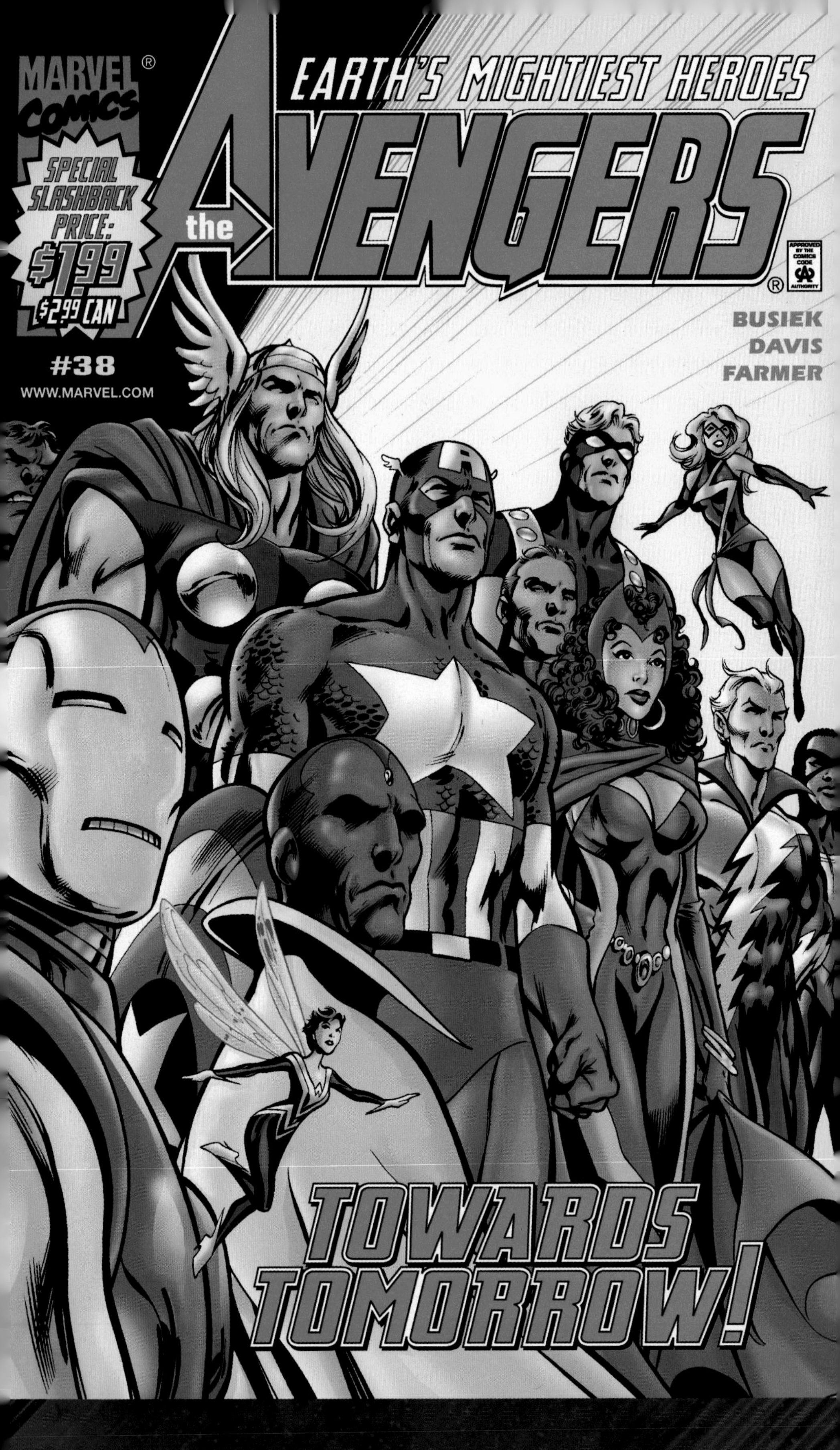
MARVEL COMICS
SPECIAL SLASHBACK PRICE: $1.99 $2.99 CAN
#38
WWW.MARVEL.COM
EARTH'S MIGHTIEST HEROES
the AVENGERS
APPROVED BY THE COMICS CODE AUTHORITY
BUSIEK
DAVIS
FARMER
TOWARDS TOMORROW!

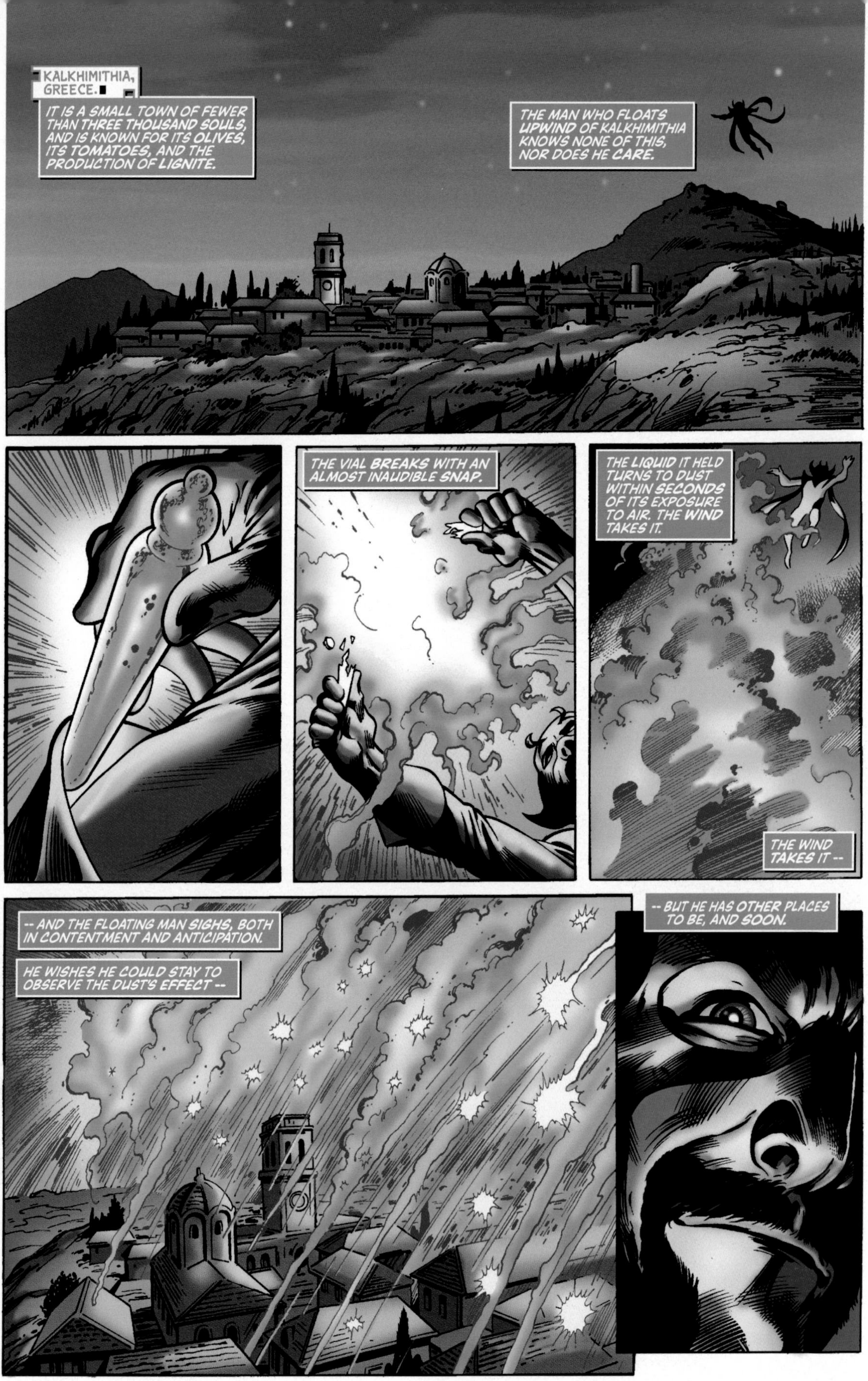
KALKHIMITHIA, GREECE.
IT IS A SMALL TOWN OF FEWER THAN THREE THOUSAND SOULS, AND IS KNOWN FOR ITS OLIVES, ITS TOMATOES, AND THE PRODUCTION OF LIGNITE.
THE MAN WHO FLOATS UPWIND OF KALKHIMITHIA KNOWS NONE OF THIS, NOR DOES HE CARE.
THE VIAL BREAKS WITH AN ALMOST INAUDIBLE SNAP.
THE LIQUID IT HELD TURNS TO DUST WITHIN SECONDS OF ITS EXPOSURE TO AIR. THE WIND TAKES IT.
THE WIND TAKES IT --
-- AND THE FLOATING MAN SIGHS, BOTH IN CONTENTMENT AND ANTICIPATION.
HE WISHES HE COULD STAY TO OBSERVE THE DUST'S EFFECT --
-- BUT HE HAS OTHER PLACES TO BE, AND SOON.

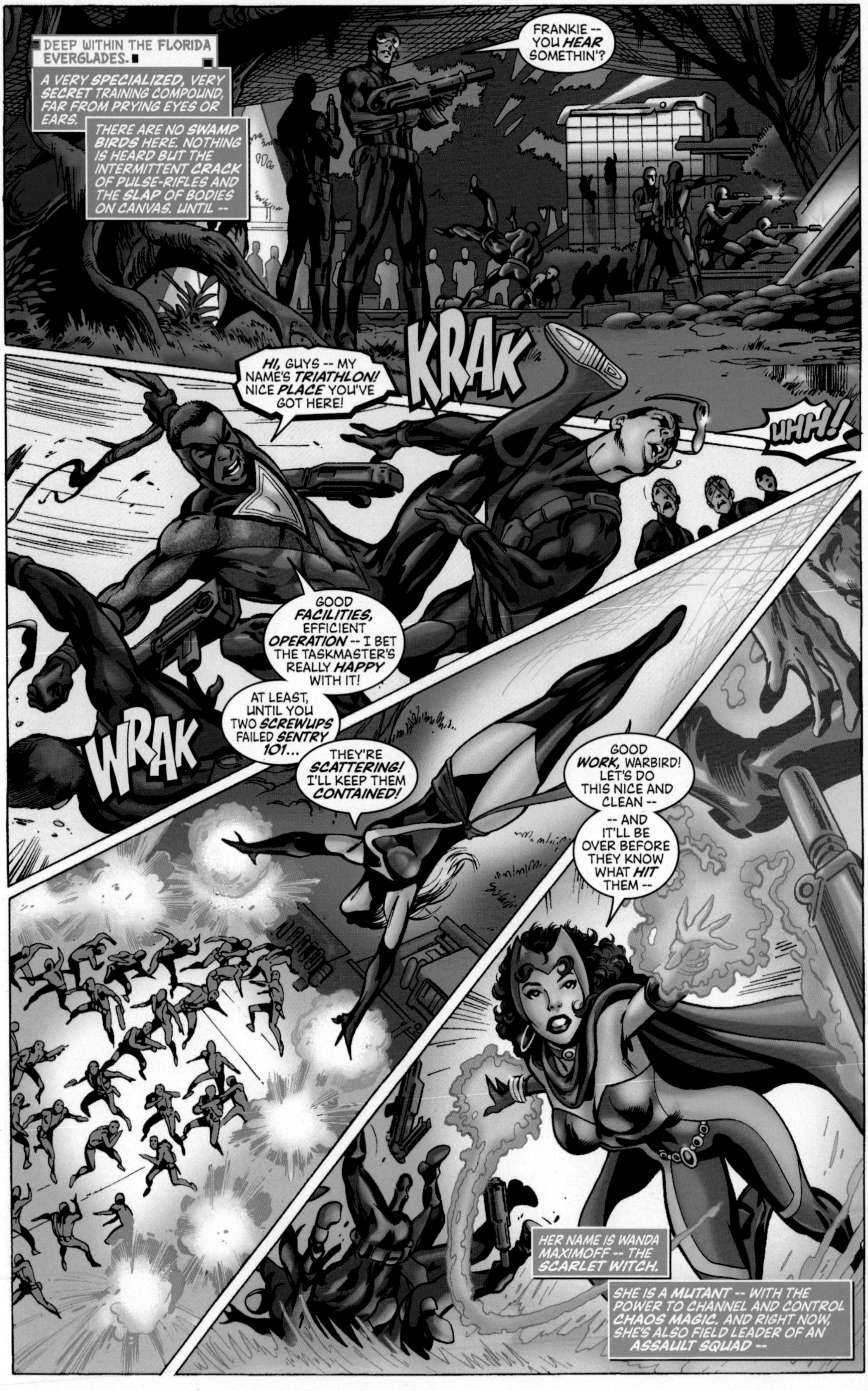
DEEP WITHIN THE FLORIDA EVERGLADES.
A VERY SPECIALIZED, VERY SECRET TRAINING COMPOUND, FAR FROM PRYING EYES OR EARS.
THERE ARE NO SWAMP BIRDS HERE. NOTHING IS HEARD BUT THE INTERMITTENT CRACK OF PULSE-RIFLES AND THE SLAP OF BODIES ON CANVAS. UNTIL --
FRANKIE -- YOU HEAR SOMETHIN'?
KRAK
HI, GUYS -- MY NAME'S TRIATHLON! NICE PLACE YOU'VE GOT HERE!
UHH!
GOOD FACILITIES, EFFICIENT OPERATION -- I BET THE TASKMASTER'S REALLY HAPPY WITH IT!
AT LEAST, UNTIL YOU TWO SCREWUPS FAILED SENTRY 101...
WRAK
THEY'RE SCATTERING! I'LL KEEP THEM CONTAINED!
GOOD WORK, WARBIRD! LET'S DO THIS NICE AND CLEAN --
-- AND IT'LL BE OVER BEFORE THEY KNOW WHAT HIT THEM --
HER NAME IS WANDA MAXIMOFF -- THE SCARLET WITCH.
SHE IS A MUTANT -- WITH THE POWER TO CHANNEL AND CONTROL CHAOS MAGIC. AND RIGHT NOW, SHE'S ALSO FIELD LEADER OF AN ASSAULT SQUAD --

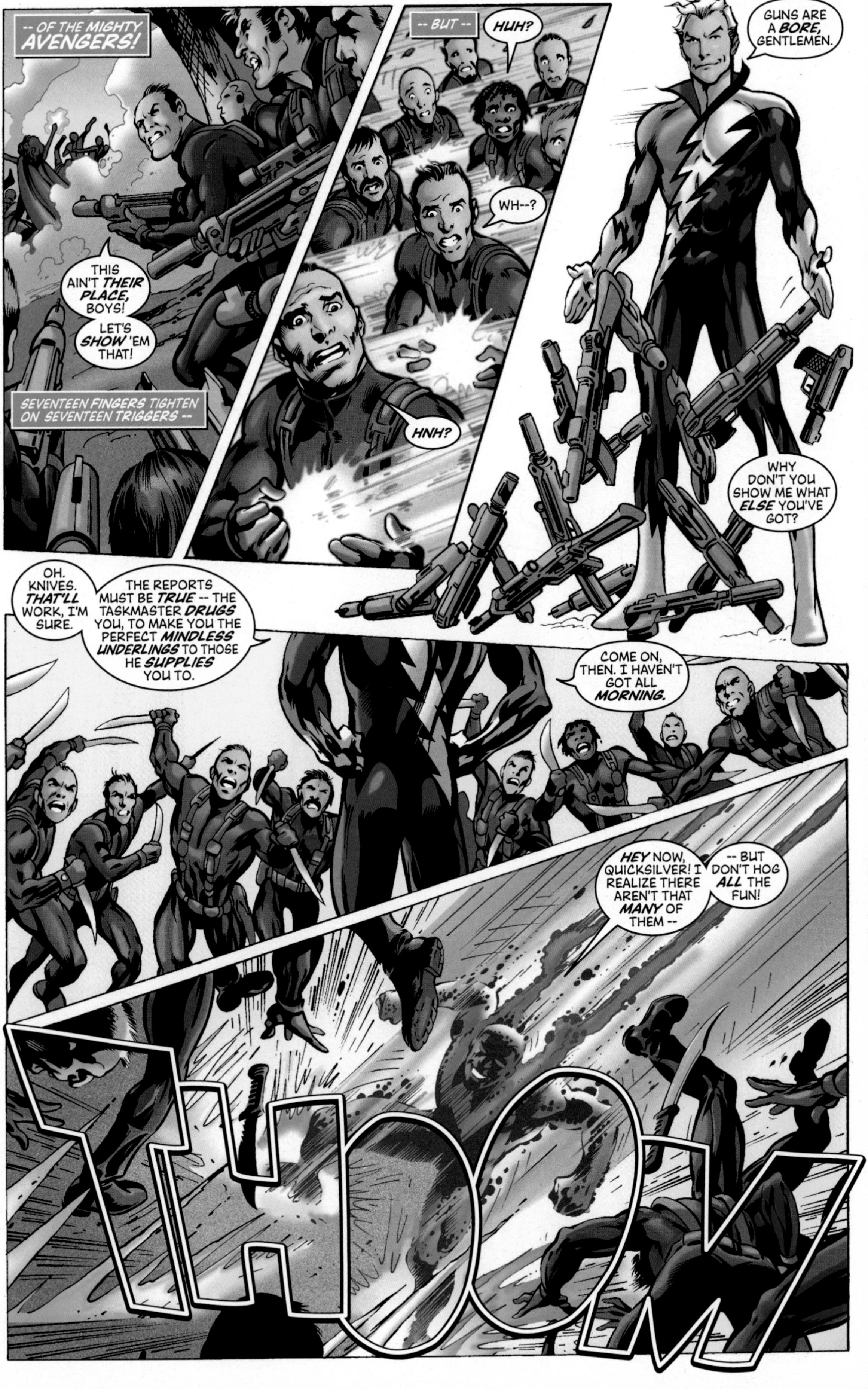
-- OF THE MIGHTY AVENGERS!
THIS AIN'T THEIR PLACE, BOYS!
LET'S SHOW 'EM THAT!
SEVENTEEN FINGERS TIGHTEN ON SEVENTEEN TRIGGERS --
-- BUT --
HUH?
WH--?
HNH?
GUNS ARE A BORE, GENTLEMEN.
WHY DON'T YOU SHOW ME WHAT ELSE YOU'VE GOT?
OH. KNIVES. THAT'LL WORK, I'M SURE.
THE REPORTS MUST BE TRUE -- THE TASKMASTER DRUGS YOU, TO MAKE YOU THE PERFECT MINDLESS UNDERLINGS TO THOSE HE SUPPLIES YOU TO.
COME ON, THEN. I HAVEN'T GOT ALL MORNING.
HEY NOW, QUICKSILVER! I REALIZE THERE AREN'T THAT MANY OF THEM --
-- BUT DON'T HOG ALL THE FUN!
THOOM

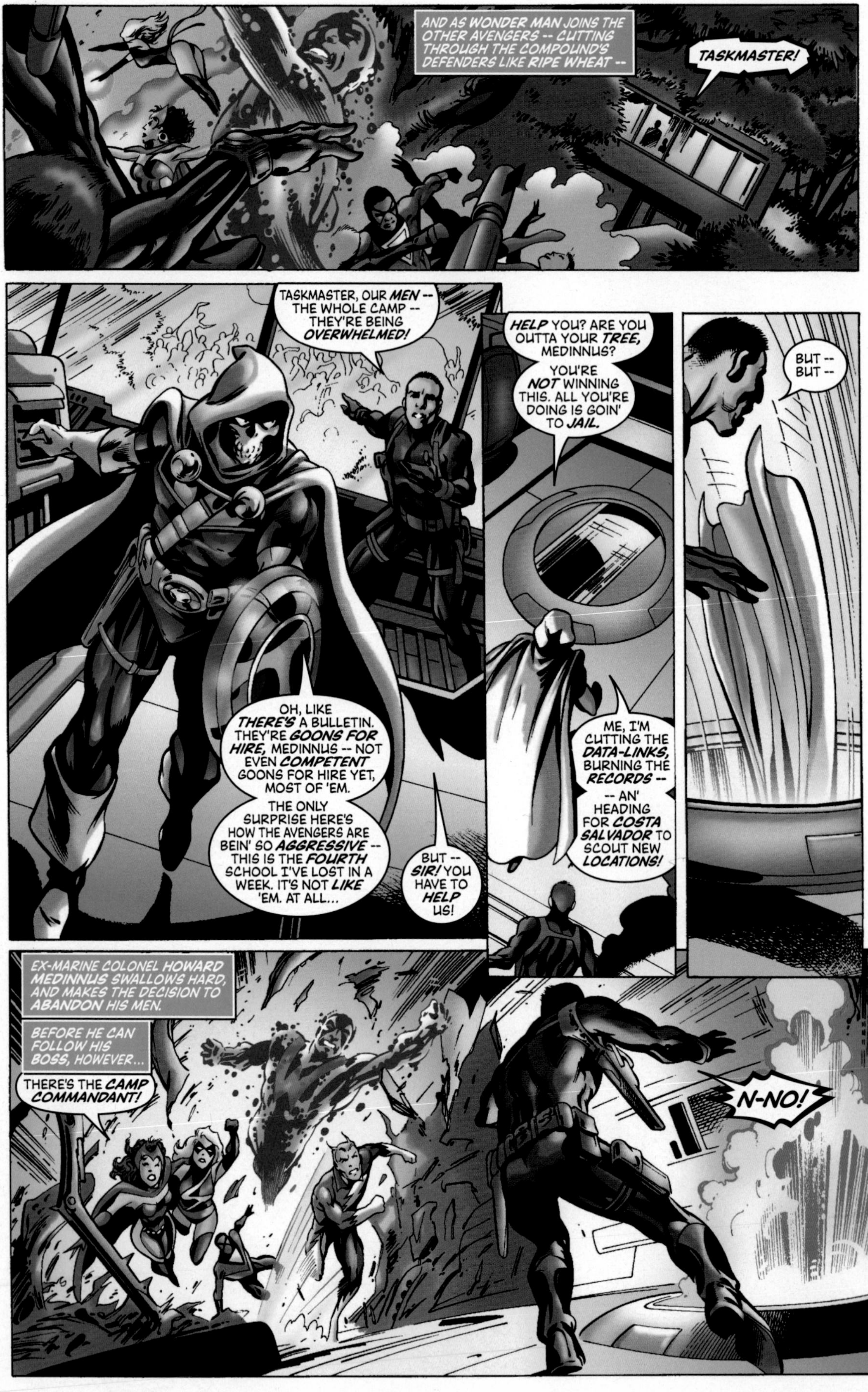
AND AS WONDER MAN JOINS THE OTHER AVENGERS -- CUTTING THROUGH THE COMPOUND'S DEFENDERS LIKE RIPE WHEAT --
TASKMASTER!
TASKMASTER, OUR MEN -- THE WHOLE CAMP -- THEY'RE BEING OVERWHELMED!
OH, LIKE THERE'S A BULLETIN. THEY'RE GOONS FOR HIRE, MEDINNUS -- NOT EVEN COMPETENT GOONS FOR HIRE YET, MOST OF 'EM.
THE ONLY SURPRISE HERE'S HOW THE AVENGERS ARE BEIN' SO AGGRESSIVE -- THIS IS THE FOURTH SCHOOL I'VE LOST IN A WEEK. IT'S NOT LIKE 'EM. AT ALL...
BUT -- SIR! YOU HAVE TO HELP US!
HELP YOU? ARE YOU OUTTA YOUR TREE, MEDINNUS?
YOU'RE NOT WINNING THIS. ALL YOU'RE DOING IS GOIN' TO JAIL.
ME, I'M CUTTING THE DATA-LINKS, BURNING THE RECORDS --
-- AN' HEADING FOR COSTA SALVADOR TO SCOUT NEW LOCATIONS!
BUT -- BUT --
EX-MARINE COLONEL HOWARD MEDINNUS SWALLOWS HARD, AND MAKES THE DECISION TO ABANDON HIS MEN.
BEFORE HE CAN FOLLOW HIS BOSS, HOWEVER...
THERE'S THE CAMP COMMANDANT!
N-NO!

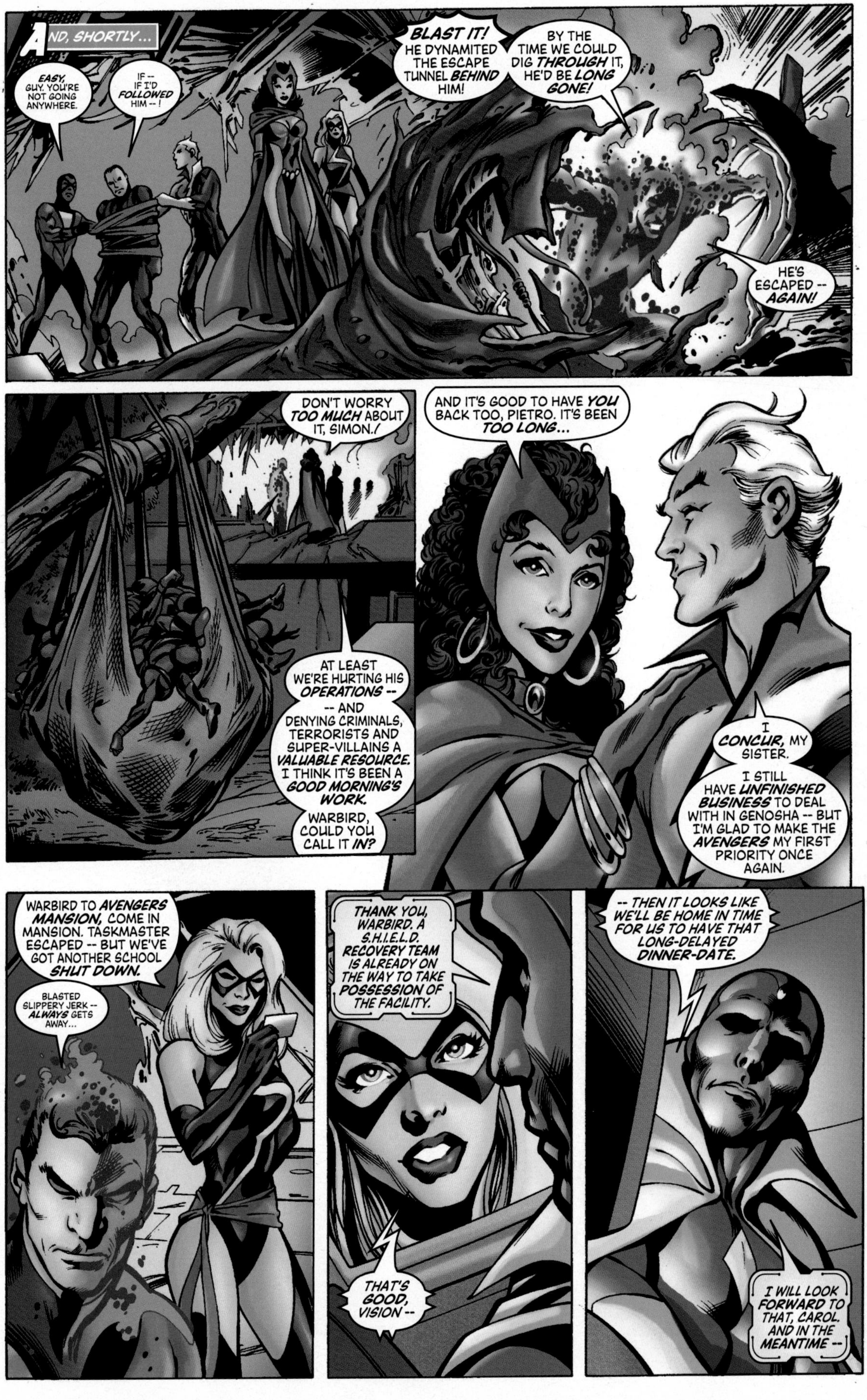
AND, SHORTLY...
EASY, GUY. YOU'RE NOT GOING ANYWHERE.
IF -- IF I'D FOLLOWED HIM -- !
BLAST IT! HE DYNAMITED THE ESCAPE TUNNEL BEHIND HIM!
BY THE TIME WE COULD DIG THROUGH IT, HE'D BE LONG GONE!
HE'S ESCAPED -- AGAIN!
DON'T WORRY TOO MUCH ABOUT IT, SIMON.!
AT LEAST WE'RE HURTING HIS OPERATIONS --
-- AND DENYING CRIMINALS, TERRORISTS AND SUPER-VILLAINS A VALUABLE RESOURCE. I THINK IT'S BEEN A GOOD MORNING'S WORK.
WARBIRD, COULD YOU CALL IT IN?
AND IT'S GOOD TO HAVE YOU BACK TOO, PIETRO. IT'S BEEN TOO LONG...
I CONCUR, MY SISTER.
I STILL HAVE UNFINISHED BUSINESS TO DEAL WITH IN GENOSHA -- BUT I'M GLAD TO MAKE THE AVENGERS MY FIRST PRIORITY ONCE AGAIN.
WARBIRD TO AVENGERS MANSION, COME IN MANSION. TASKMASTER ESCAPED -- BUT WE'VE GOT ANOTHER SCHOOL SHUT DOWN.
BLASTED SLIPPERY JERK -- ALWAYS GETS AWAY...
THANK YOU, WARBIRD. A S.H.I.E.L.D. RECOVERY TEAM IS ALREADY ON THE WAY TO TAKE POSSESSION OF THE FACILITY.
THAT'S GOOD, VISION --
-- THEN IT LOOKS LIKE WE'LL BE HOME IN TIME FOR US TO HAVE THAT LONG-DELAYED DINNER-DATE.
I WILL LOOK FORWARD TO THAT, CAROL. AND IN THE MEANTIME --

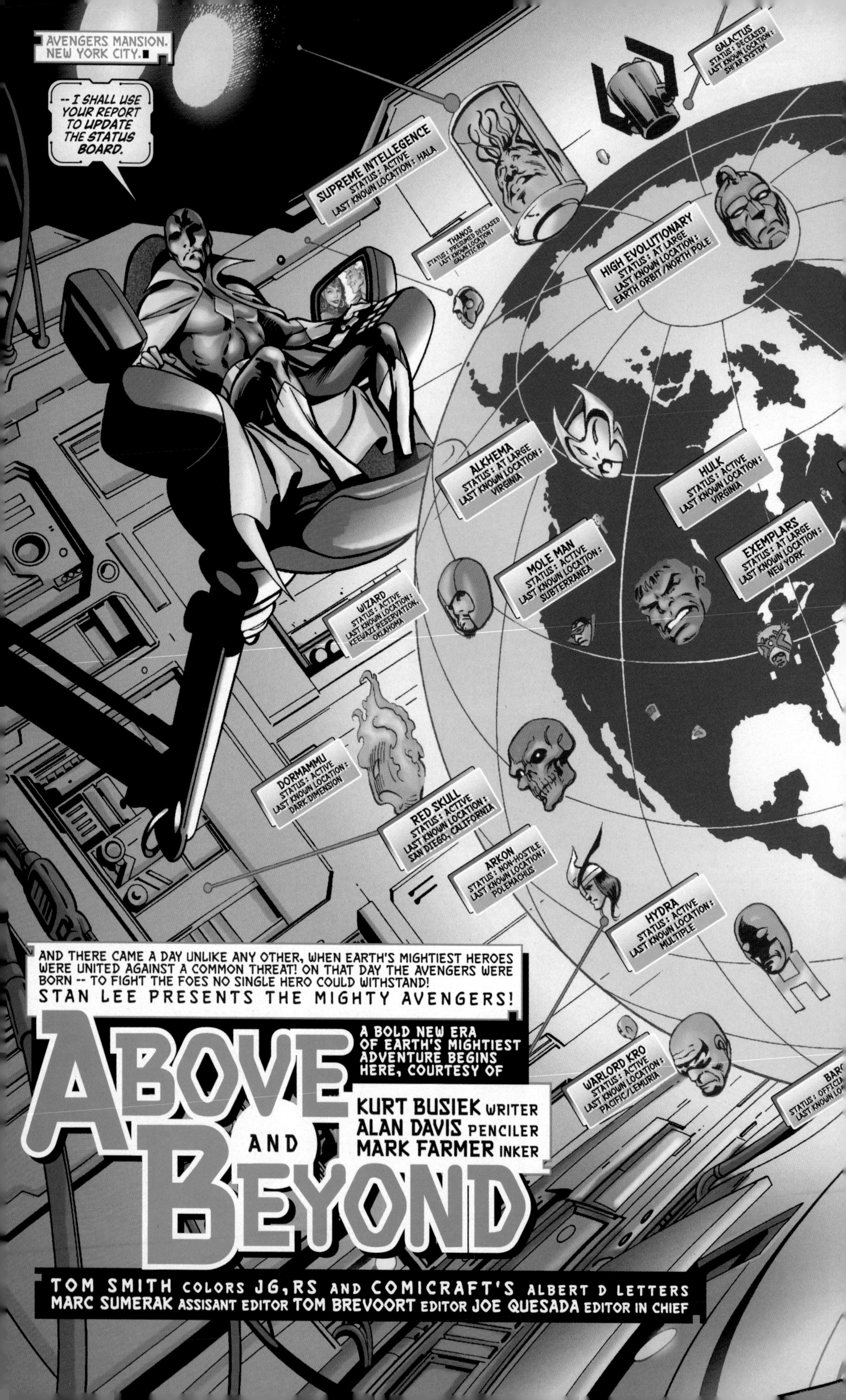
AVENGERS MANSION. NEW YORK CITY.
-- I SHALL USE YOUR REPORT TO UPDATE THE STATUS BOARD.
SUPREME INTELLEGENCE STATUS: ACTIVE LAST KNOWN LOCATION: HALA
THANOS STATUS: PRESUMED DECEASED LAST KNOWN LOCATION: GALACTIC RIM
GALACTUS STATUS: DECEASED LAST KNOWN LOCATION: SHI'AR SYSTEM
HIGH EVOLUTIONARY STATUS: AT LARGE LAST KNOWN LOCATION: EARTH ORBIT/NORTH POLE
ALKHEMA STATUS: AT LARGE LAST KNOWN LOCATION: VIRGINIA
HULK STATUS: ACTIVE LAST KNOWN LOCATION: VIRGINIA
EXEMPLARS STATUS: AT LARGE LAST KNOWN LOCATION: NEW YORK
MOLE MAN STATUS: ACTIVE LAST KNOWN LOCATION: SUBTERRANEA
WIZARD STATUS: ACTIVE LAST KNOWN LOCATION: KEEWAZI RESERVATION, OKLAHOMA
DORMAMMU STATUS: ACTIVE LAST KNOWN LOCATION: DARK DIMENSION
RED SKULL STATUS: ACTIVE LAST KNOWN LOCATION: SAN DIEGO, CALIFORNIA
ARKON STATUS: NON-HOSTILE LAST KNOWN LOCATION: POLEMACHUS
HYDRA STATUS: ACTIVE LAST KNOWN LOCATION: MULTIPLE
WARLORD KRO STATUS: ACTIVE LAST KNOWN LOCATION: PACIFIC/LEMURIA
AND THERE CAME A DAY UNLIKE ANY OTHER, WHEN EARTH'S MIGHTIEST HEROES WERE UNITED AGAINST A COMMON THREAT! ON THAT DAY THE AVENGERS WERE BORN -- TO FIGHT THE FOES NO SINGLE HERO COULD WITHSTAND!
STAN LEE PRESENTS THE MIGHTY AVENGERS!
ABOVE AND BEYOND
A BOLD NEW ERA OF EARTH'S MIGHTIEST ADVENTURE BEGINS HERE, COURTESY OF
KURT BUSIEK WRITER
ALAN DAVIS PENCILER
MARK FARMER INKER
TOM SMITH COLORS JG, RS AND COMICRAFT'S ALBERT D LETTERS
MARC SUMERAK ASSISANT EDITOR TOM BREVOORT EDITOR JOE QUESADA EDITOR IN CHIEF

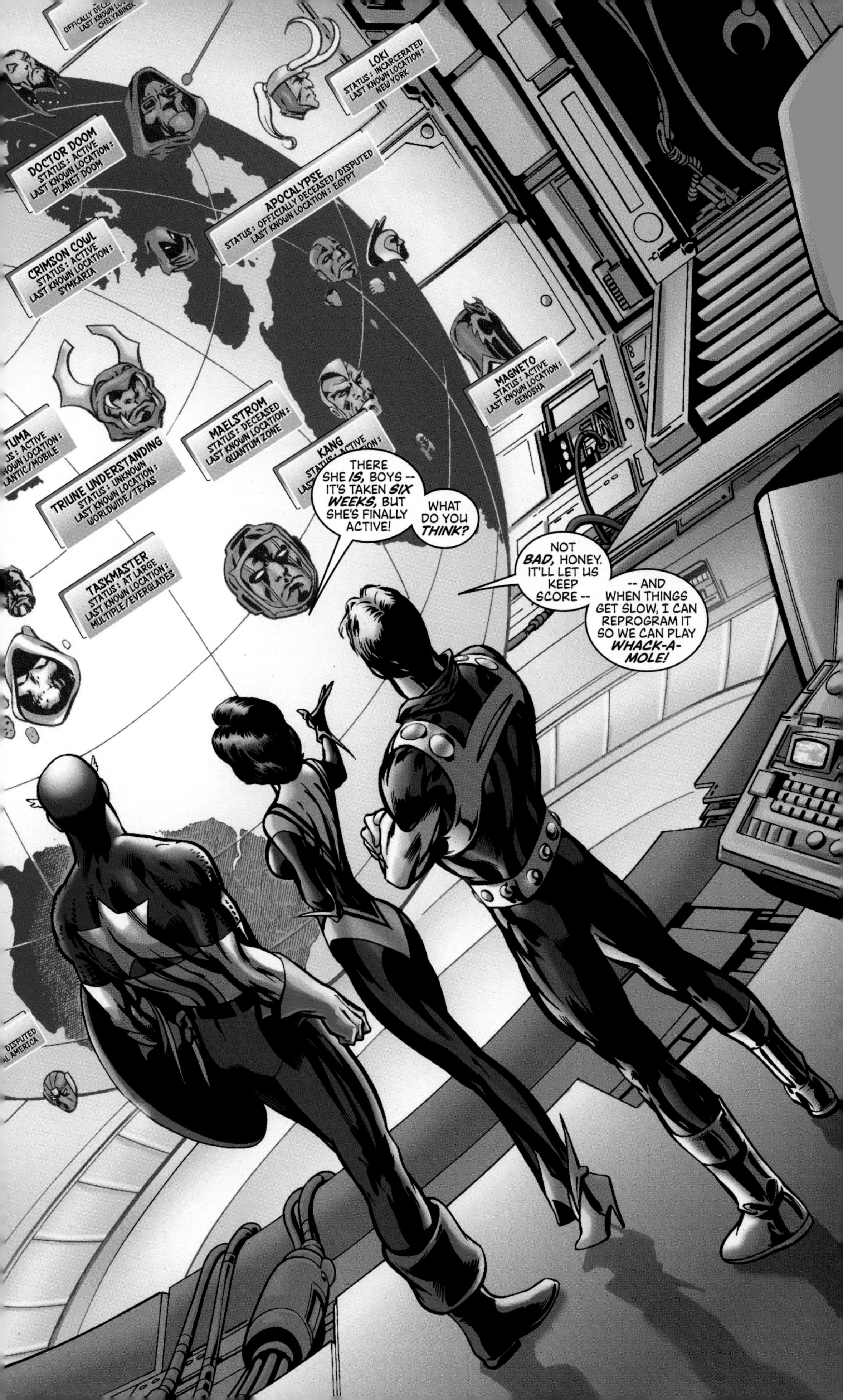
LOKI
STATUS : INCARCERATED
LAST KNOWN LOCATION :
NEW YORK
DOCTOR DOOM
STATUS : ACTIVE
LAST KNOWN LOCATION :
PLANET DOOM
APOCALYPSE
STATUS : OFFICIALLY DECEASED/DISPUTED
LAST KNOWN LOCATION : EGYPT
CRIMSON COWL
STATUS : ACTIVE
LAST KNOWN LOCATION :
SYMKARIA
MAGNETO
STATUS : ACTIVE
LAST KNOWN LOCATION :
GENOSHA
MAELSTROM
STATUS : DECEASED
LAST KNOWN LOCATION :
QUANTUM ZONE
KANG
TRIUNE UNDERSTANDING
STATUS : UNKNOWN
LAST KNOWN LOCATION :
WORLDWIDE/TEXAS
TASKMASTER
STATUS : AT LARGE
LAST KNOWN LOCATION :
MULTIPLE/EVERGLADES
THERE SHE *IS,* BOYS -- IT'S TAKEN ***SIX WEEKS,*** BUT SHE'S FINALLY ACTIVE!
WHAT DO YOU ***THINK?***
NOT ***BAD,*** HONEY. IT'LL LET US KEEP SCORE --
-- AND WHEN THINGS GET SLOW, I CAN REPROGRAM IT SO WE CAN PLAY ***WHACK-A-MOLE!***

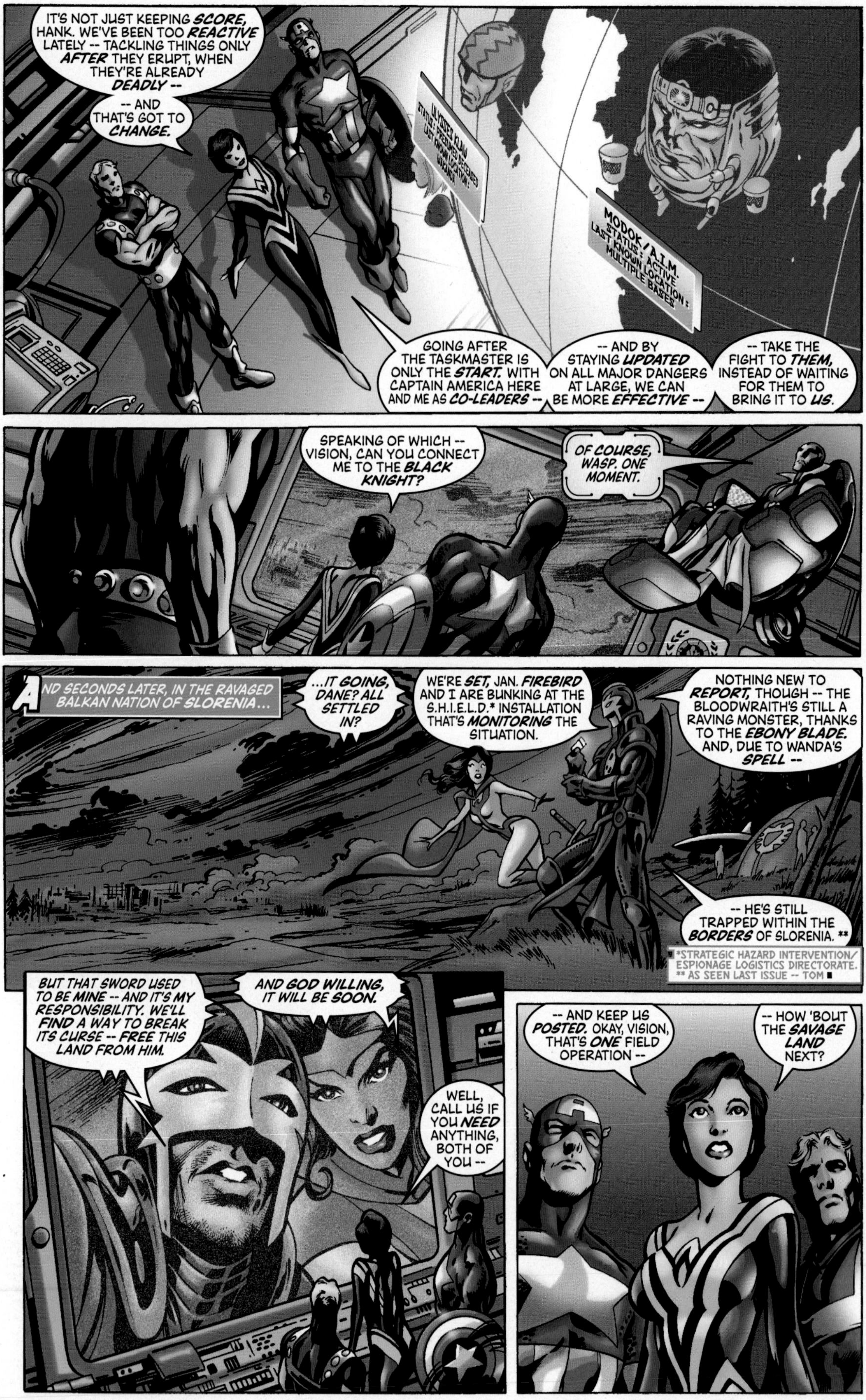

IT'S NOT JUST KEEPING SCORE, HANK. WE'VE BEEN TOO REACTIVE LATELY -- TACKLING THINGS ONLY AFTER THEY ERUPT, WHEN THEY'RE ALREADY DEADLY --
-- AND THAT'S GOT TO CHANGE.
ULYSSES KLAW STATUS: PRESUMED DECEASED LAST KNOWN LOCATION: WAKANDA
MODOK / A.I.M. STATUS: ACTIVE LAST KNOWN LOCATION: MULTIPLE BASES
GOING AFTER THE TASKMASTER IS ONLY THE START. WITH CAPTAIN AMERICA HERE AND ME AS CO-LEADERS --
-- AND BY STAYING UPDATED ON ALL MAJOR DANGERS AT LARGE, WE CAN BE MORE EFFECTIVE --
-- TAKE THE FIGHT TO THEM, INSTEAD OF WAITING FOR THEM TO BRING IT TO US.
SPEAKING OF WHICH -- VISION, CAN YOU CONNECT ME TO THE BLACK KNIGHT?
OF COURSE, WASP. ONE MOMENT.
AND SECONDS LATER, IN THE RAVAGED BALKAN NATION OF SLORENIA...
...IT GOING, DANE? ALL SETTLED IN?
WE'RE SET, JAN. FIREBIRD AND I ARE BUNKING AT THE S.H.I.E.L.D.* INSTALLATION THAT'S MONITORING THE SITUATION.
NOTHING NEW TO REPORT, THOUGH -- THE BLOODWRAITH'S STILL A RAVING MONSTER, THANKS TO THE EBONY BLADE. AND, DUE TO WANDA'S SPELL --
-- HE'S STILL TRAPPED WITHIN THE BORDERS OF SLORENIA.**
*STRATEGIC HAZARD INTERVENTION/ ESPIONAGE LOGISTICS DIRECTORATE. ** AS SEEN LAST ISSUE -- TOM
BUT THAT SWORD USED TO BE MINE -- AND IT'S MY RESPONSIBILITY. WE'LL FIND A WAY TO BREAK ITS CURSE -- FREE THIS LAND FROM HIM.
AND GOD WILLING, IT WILL BE SOON.
WELL, CALL US IF YOU NEED ANYTHING, BOTH OF YOU --
-- AND KEEP US POSTED. OKAY, VISION, THAT'S ONE FIELD OPERATION --
-- HOW 'BOUT THE SAVAGE LAND NEXT?

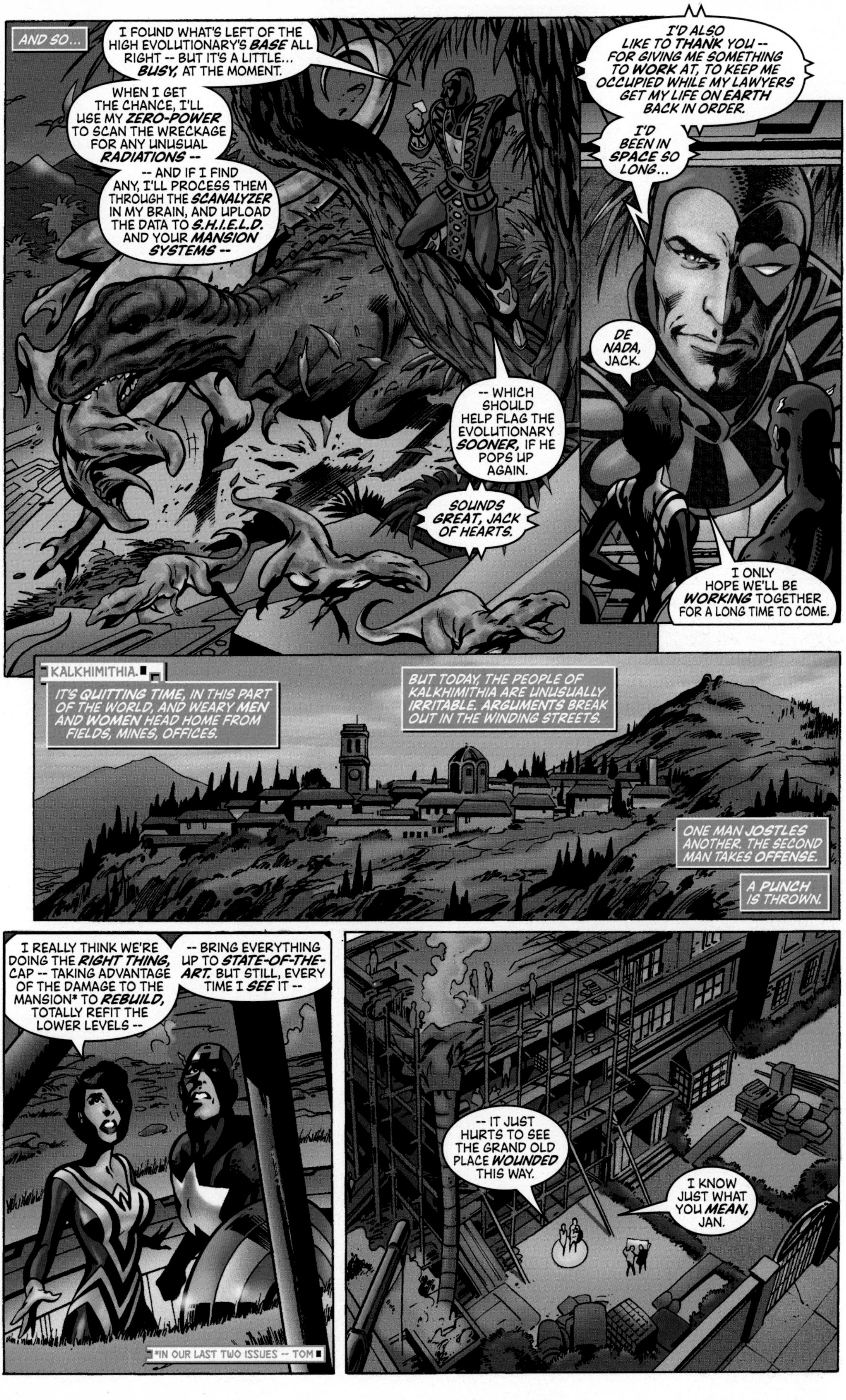
AND SO...
I FOUND WHAT'S LEFT OF THE HIGH EVOLUTIONARY'S BASE ALL RIGHT -- BUT IT'S A LITTLE... BUSY, AT THE MOMENT.
WHEN I GET THE CHANCE, I'LL USE MY ZERO-POWER TO SCAN THE WRECKAGE FOR ANY UNUSUAL RADIATIONS --
-- AND IF I FIND ANY, I'LL PROCESS THEM THROUGH THE SCANALYZER IN MY BRAIN, AND UPLOAD THE DATA TO S.H.I.E.L.D. AND YOUR MANSION SYSTEMS --
-- WHICH SHOULD HELP FLAG THE EVOLUTIONARY SOONER, IF HE POPS UP AGAIN.
SOUNDS GREAT, JACK OF HEARTS.
I'D ALSO LIKE TO THANK YOU -- FOR GIVING ME SOMETHING TO WORK AT, TO KEEP ME OCCUPIED WHILE MY LAWYERS GET MY LIFE ON EARTH BACK IN ORDER.
I'D BEEN IN SPACE SO LONG...
DE NADA, JACK.
I ONLY HOPE WE'LL BE WORKING TOGETHER FOR A LONG TIME TO COME.
KALKHIMITHIA.
IT'S QUITTING TIME, IN THIS PART OF THE WORLD, AND WEARY MEN AND WOMEN HEAD HOME FROM FIELDS, MINES, OFFICES.
BUT TODAY, THE PEOPLE OF KALKHIMITHIA ARE UNUSUALLY IRRITABLE. ARGUMENTS BREAK OUT IN THE WINDING STREETS.
ONE MAN JOSTLES ANOTHER. THE SECOND MAN TAKES OFFENSE.
A PUNCH IS THROWN.
I REALLY THINK WE'RE DOING THE RIGHT THING, CAP -- TAKING ADVANTAGE OF THE DAMAGE TO THE MANSION* TO REBUILD, TOTALLY REFIT THE LOWER LEVELS --
-- BRING EVERYTHING UP TO STATE-OF-THE-ART. BUT STILL, EVERY TIME I SEE IT --
*IN OUR LAST TWO ISSUES -- TOM
-- IT JUST HURTS TO SEE THE GRAND OLD PLACE WOUNDED THIS WAY.
I KNOW JUST WHAT YOU MEAN, JAN.

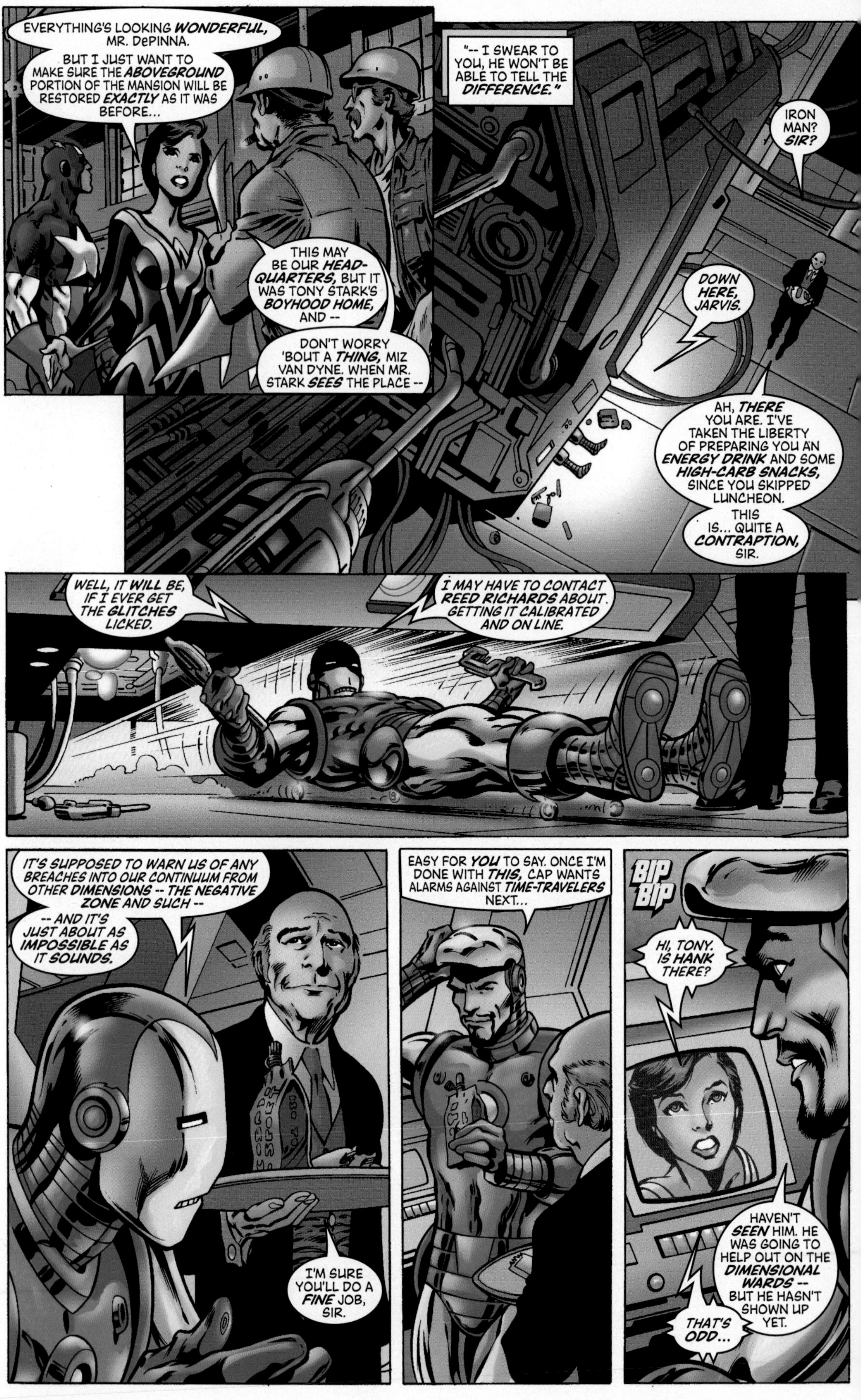
EVERYTHING'S LOOKING WONDERFUL, MR. DePINNA.
BUT I JUST WANT TO MAKE SURE THE ABOVEGROUND PORTION OF THE MANSION WILL BE RESTORED EXACTLY AS IT WAS BEFORE...
THIS MAY BE OUR HEAD-QUARTERS, BUT IT WAS TONY STARK'S BOYHOOD HOME, AND --
DON'T WORRY 'BOUT A THING, MIZ VAN DYNE. WHEN MR. STARK SEES THE PLACE --
"-- I SWEAR TO YOU, HE WON'T BE ABLE TO TELL THE DIFFERENCE."
IRON MAN? SIR?
DOWN HERE, JARVIS.
AH, THERE YOU ARE. I'VE TAKEN THE LIBERTY OF PREPARING YOU AN ENERGY DRINK AND SOME HIGH-CARB SNACKS, SINCE YOU SKIPPED LUNCHEON.
THIS IS... QUITE A CONTRAPTION, SIR.
WELL, IT WILL BE, IF I EVER GET THE GLITCHES LICKED.
I MAY HAVE TO CONTACT REED RICHARDS ABOUT GETTING IT CALIBRATED AND ON LINE.
IT'S SUPPOSED TO WARN US OF ANY BREACHES INTO OUR CONTINUUM FROM OTHER DIMENSIONS -- THE NEGATIVE ZONE AND SUCH --
-- AND IT'S JUST ABOUT AS IMPOSSIBLE AS IT SOUNDS.
I'M SURE YOU'LL DO A FINE JOB, SIR.
EASY FOR YOU TO SAY. ONCE I'M DONE WITH THIS, CAP WANTS ALARMS AGAINST TIME-TRAVELERS NEXT...
BIP BIP
HI, TONY. IS HANK THERE?
HAVEN'T SEEN HIM. HE WAS GOING TO HELP OUT ON THE DIMENSIONAL WARDS -- BUT HE HASN'T SHOWN UP YET.
THAT'S ODD...

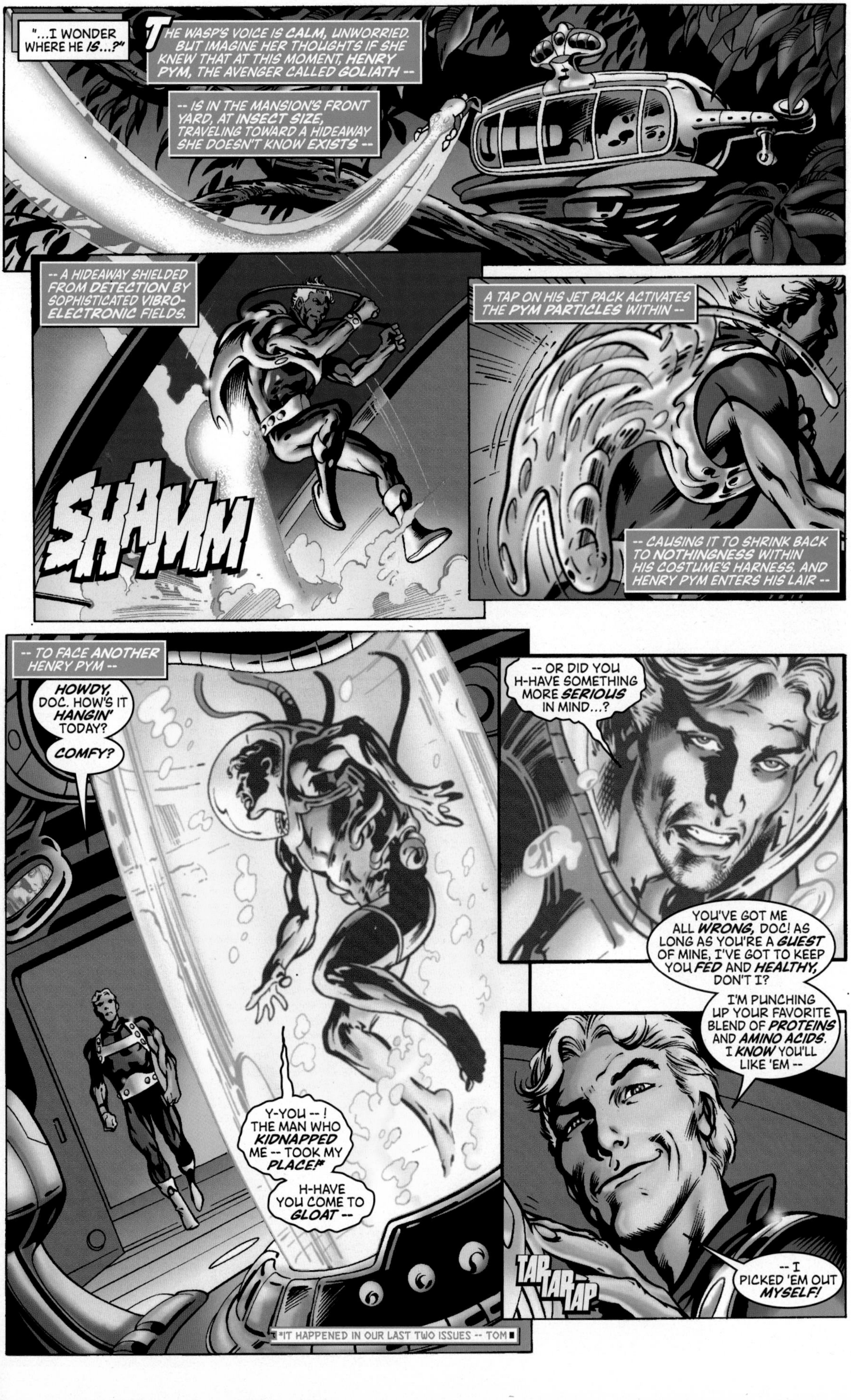
"...I WONDER WHERE HE IS...?"
THE WASP'S VOICE IS CALM, UNWORRIED. BUT IMAGINE HER THOUGHTS IF SHE KNEW THAT AT THIS MOMENT, HENRY PYM, THE AVENGER CALLED GOLIATH --
-- IS IN THE MANSION'S FRONT YARD, AT INSECT SIZE, TRAVELING TOWARD A HIDEAWAY SHE DOESN'T KNOW EXISTS --
-- A HIDEAWAY SHIELDED FROM DETECTION BY SOPHISTICATED VIBRO-ELECTRONIC FIELDS.
SHAMM
A TAP ON HIS JET PACK ACTIVATES THE PYM PARTICLES WITHIN --
-- CAUSING IT TO SHRINK BACK TO NOTHINGNESS WITHIN HIS COSTUME'S HARNESS. AND HENRY PYM ENTERS HIS LAIR --
-- TO FACE ANOTHER HENRY PYM --
HOWDY, DOC. HOW'S IT HANGIN' TODAY?
COMFY?
Y-YOU -- ! THE MAN WHO KIDNAPPED ME -- TOOK MY PLACE!*
H-HAVE YOU COME TO GLOAT --
-- OR DID YOU H-HAVE SOMETHING MORE SERIOUS IN MIND...?
YOU'VE GOT ME ALL WRONG, DOC! AS LONG AS YOU'RE A GUEST OF MINE, I'VE GOT TO KEEP YOU FED AND HEALTHY, DON'T I?
I'M PUNCHING UP YOUR FAVORITE BLEND OF PROTEINS AND AMINO ACIDS. I KNOW YOU'LL LIKE 'EM --
TAP TAP TAP
-- I PICKED 'EM OUT MYSELF!
*IT HAPPENED IN OUR LAST TWO ISSUES -- TOM

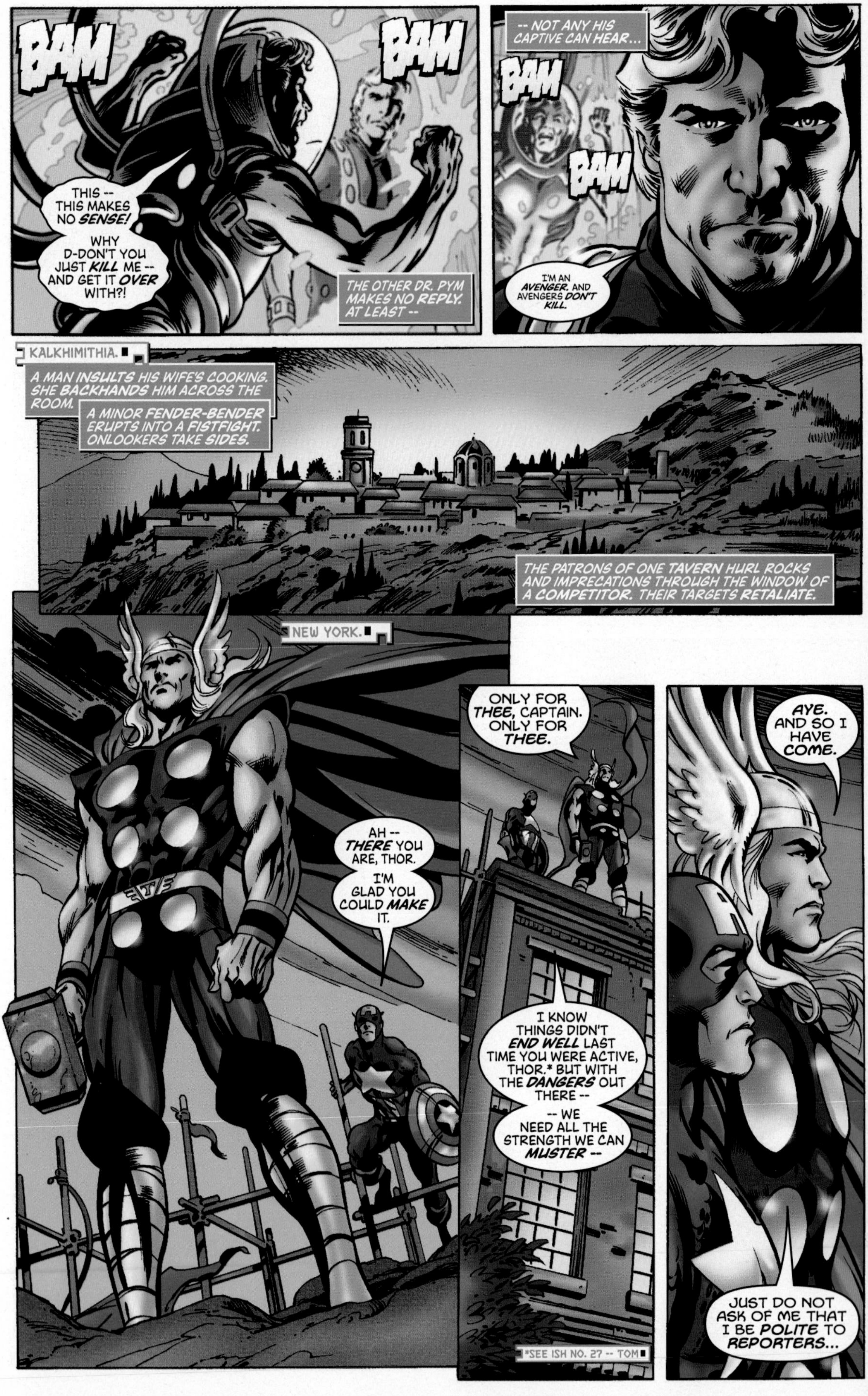
BAM
BAM
THIS -- THIS MAKES NO SENSE!
WHY D-DON'T YOU JUST KILL ME -- AND GET IT OVER WITH?!
THE OTHER DR. PYM MAKES NO REPLY. AT LEAST --
-- NOT ANY HIS CAPTIVE CAN HEAR...
BAM
BAM
I'M AN AVENGER. AND AVENGERS DON'T KILL.
KALKHIMITHIA.
A MAN INSULTS HIS WIFE'S COOKING. SHE BACKHANDS HIM ACROSS THE ROOM.
A MINOR FENDER-BENDER ERUPTS INTO A FISTFIGHT. ONLOOKERS TAKE SIDES.
THE PATRONS OF ONE TAVERN HURL ROCKS AND IMPRECATIONS THROUGH THE WINDOW OF A COMPETITOR. THEIR TARGETS RETALIATE.
NEW YORK.
AH -- THERE YOU ARE, THOR.
I'M GLAD YOU COULD MAKE IT.
ONLY FOR THEE, CAPTAIN. ONLY FOR THEE.
I KNOW THINGS DIDN'T END WELL LAST TIME YOU WERE ACTIVE, THOR.* BUT WITH THE DANGERS OUT THERE --
-- WE NEED ALL THE STRENGTH WE CAN MUSTER --
*SEE ISH NO. 27 -- TOM
AYE. AND SO I HAVE COME.
JUST DO NOT ASK OF ME THAT I BE POLITE TO REPORTERS...

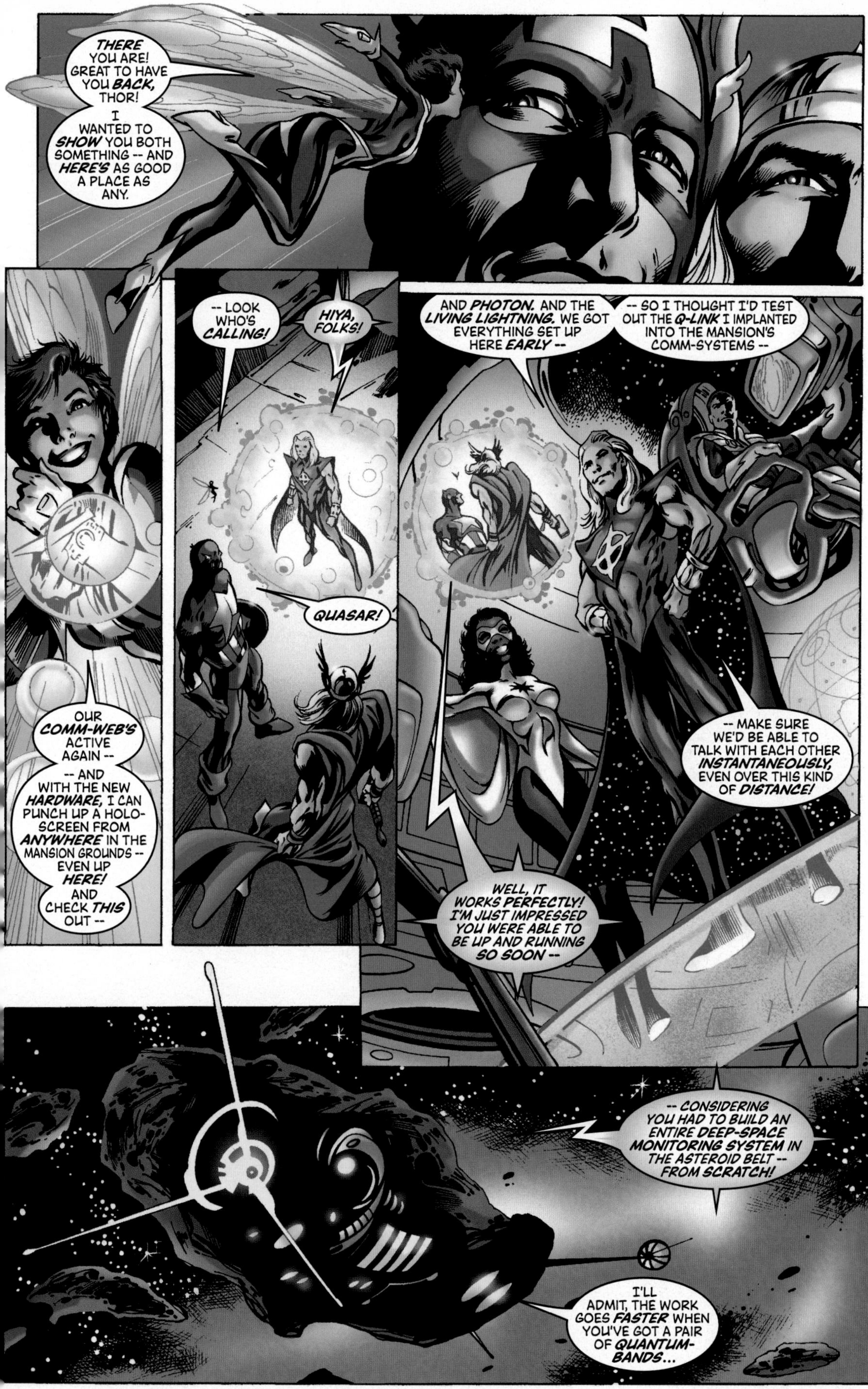
THERE YOU ARE! GREAT TO HAVE YOU BACK, THOR!
I WANTED TO SHOW YOU BOTH SOMETHING -- AND HERE'S AS GOOD A PLACE AS ANY.
OUR COMM-WEB'S ACTIVE AGAIN --
-- AND WITH THE NEW HARDWARE, I CAN PUNCH UP A HOLO-SCREEN FROM ANYWHERE IN THE MANSION GROUNDS -- EVEN UP HERE!
AND CHECK THIS OUT --
-- LOOK WHO'S CALLING!
HIYA, FOLKS!
QUASAR!
AND PHOTON. AND THE LIVING LIGHTNING. WE GOT EVERYTHING SET UP HERE EARLY --
-- SO I THOUGHT I'D TEST OUT THE Q-LINK I IMPLANTED INTO THE MANSION'S COMM-SYSTEMS --
-- MAKE SURE WE'D BE ABLE TO TALK WITH EACH OTHER INSTANTANEOUSLY, EVEN OVER THIS KIND OF DISTANCE!
WELL, IT WORKS PERFECTLY! I'M JUST IMPRESSED YOU WERE ABLE TO BE UP AND RUNNING SO SOON --
-- CONSIDERING YOU HAD TO BUILD AN ENTIRE DEEP-SPACE MONITORING SYSTEM IN THE ASTEROID BELT -- FROM SCRATCH!
I'LL ADMIT, THE WORK GOES FASTER WHEN YOU'VE GOT A PAIR OF QUANTUM-BANDS...

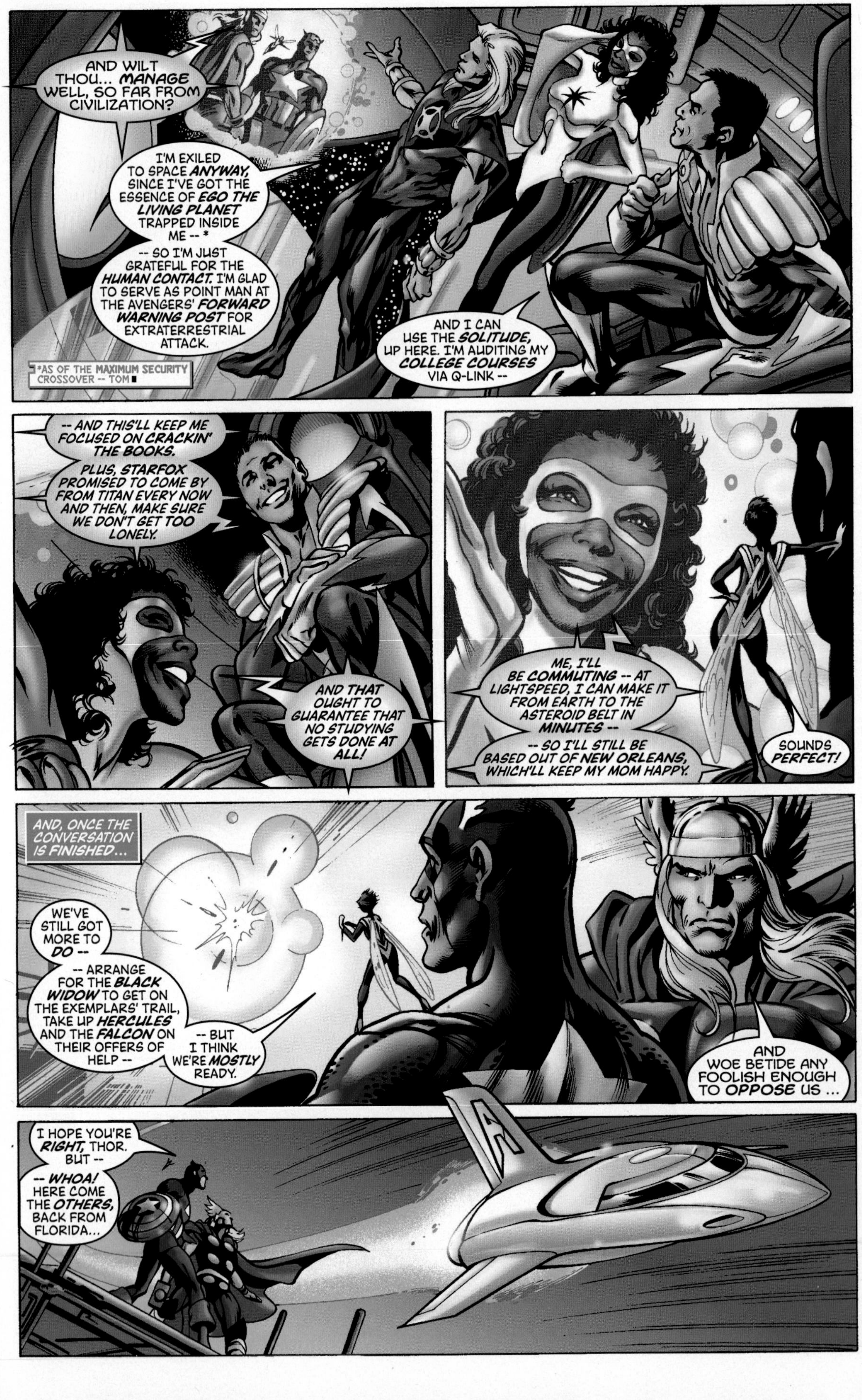
AND WILT THOU... MANAGE WELL, SO FAR FROM CIVILIZATION?
I'M EXILED TO SPACE ANYWAY, SINCE I'VE GOT THE ESSENCE OF EGO THE LIVING PLANET TRAPPED INSIDE ME -- *
-- SO I'M JUST GRATEFUL FOR THE HUMAN CONTACT. I'M GLAD TO SERVE AS POINT MAN AT THE AVENGERS' FORWARD WARNING POST FOR EXTRATERRESTRIAL ATTACK.
*AS OF THE MAXIMUM SECURITY CROSSOVER -- TOM
AND I CAN USE THE SOLITUDE, UP HERE. I'M AUDITING MY COLLEGE COURSES VIA Q-LINK --
-- AND THIS'LL KEEP ME FOCUSED ON CRACKIN' THE BOOKS.
PLUS, STARFOX PROMISED TO COME BY FROM TITAN EVERY NOW AND THEN, MAKE SURE WE DON'T GET TOO LONELY.
AND THAT OUGHT TO GUARANTEE THAT NO STUDYING GETS DONE AT ALL!
ME, I'LL BE COMMUTING -- AT LIGHTSPEED, I CAN MAKE IT FROM EARTH TO THE ASTEROID BELT IN MINUTES --
-- SO I'LL STILL BE BASED OUT OF NEW ORLEANS, WHICH'LL KEEP MY MOM HAPPY.
SOUNDS PERFECT!
AND, ONCE THE CONVERSATION IS FINISHED...
WE'VE STILL GOT MORE TO DO --
-- ARRANGE FOR THE BLACK WIDOW TO GET ON THE EXEMPLARS' TRAIL, TAKE UP HERCULES AND THE FALCON ON THEIR OFFERS OF HELP --
-- BUT I THINK WE'RE MOSTLY READY.
AND WOE BETIDE ANY FOOLISH ENOUGH TO OPPOSE US ...
I HOPE YOU'RE RIGHT, THOR. BUT --
-- WHOA! HERE COME THE OTHERS, BACK FROM FLORIDA...

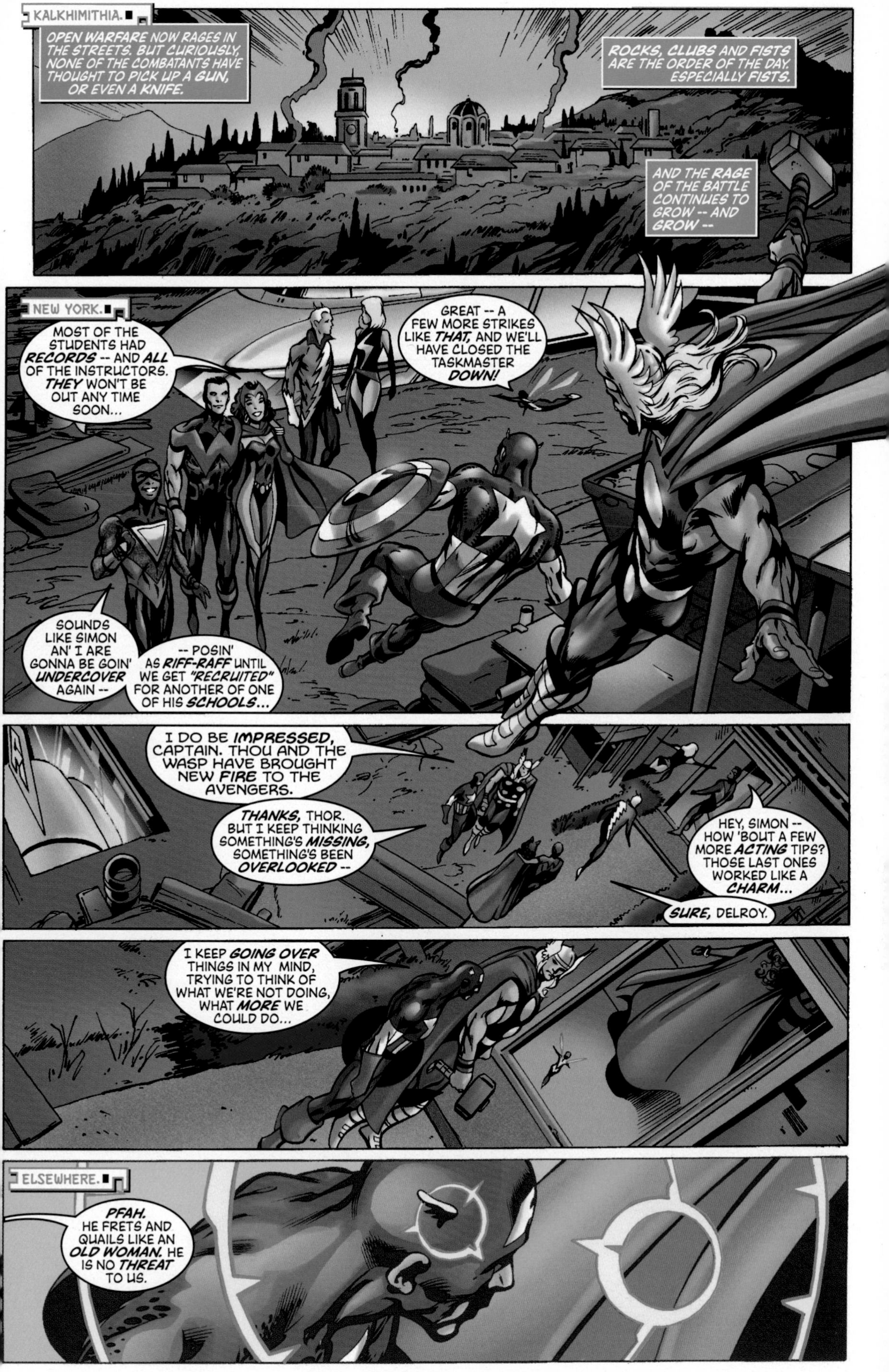
KALKHIMITHIA.
OPEN WARFARE NOW RAGES IN THE STREETS. BUT CURIOUSLY, NONE OF THE COMBATANTS HAVE THOUGHT TO PICK UP A GUN, OR EVEN A KNIFE.
ROCKS, CLUBS AND FISTS ARE THE ORDER OF THE DAY. ESPECIALLY FISTS.
AND THE RAGE OF THE BATTLE CONTINUES TO GROW -- AND GROW --
NEW YORK.
MOST OF THE STUDENTS HAD RECORDS -- AND ALL OF THE INSTRUCTORS. THEY WON'T BE OUT ANY TIME SOON...
GREAT -- A FEW MORE STRIKES LIKE THAT, AND WE'LL HAVE CLOSED THE TASKMASTER DOWN!
SOUNDS LIKE SIMON AN' I ARE GONNA BE GOIN' UNDERCOVER AGAIN --
-- POSIN' AS RIFF-RAFF UNTIL WE GET "RECRUITED" FOR ANOTHER OF ONE OF HIS SCHOOLS...
I DO BE IMPRESSED, CAPTAIN. THOU AND THE WASP HAVE BROUGHT NEW FIRE TO THE AVENGERS.
THANKS, THOR. BUT I KEEP THINKING SOMETHING'S MISSING, SOMETHING'S BEEN OVERLOOKED --
HEY, SIMON -- HOW 'BOUT A FEW MORE ACTING TIPS? THOSE LAST ONES WORKED LIKE A CHARM...
SURE, DELROY.
I KEEP GOING OVER THINGS IN MY MIND, TRYING TO THINK OF WHAT WE'RE NOT DOING, WHAT MORE WE COULD DO...
ELSEWHERE.
PFAH. HE FRETS AND QUAILS LIKE AN OLD WOMAN. HE IS NO THREAT TO US.

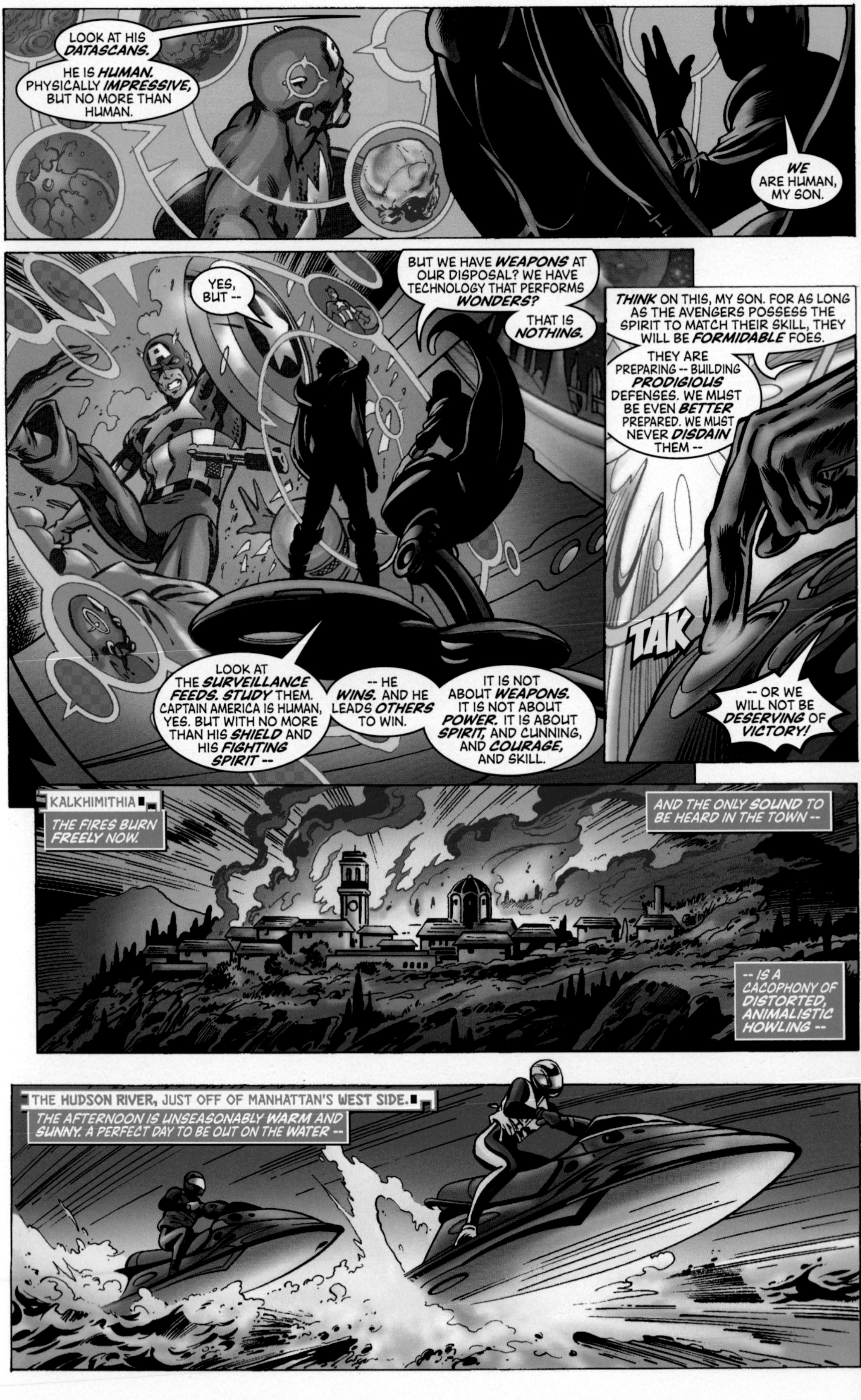
LOOK AT HIS DATASCANS.
HE IS HUMAN. PHYSICALLY IMPRESSIVE, BUT NO MORE THAN HUMAN.
WE ARE HUMAN, MY SON.
YES, BUT --
BUT WE HAVE WEAPONS AT OUR DISPOSAL? WE HAVE TECHNOLOGY THAT PERFORMS WONDERS?
THAT IS NOTHING.
LOOK AT THE SURVEILLANCE FEEDS. STUDY THEM. CAPTAIN AMERICA IS HUMAN, YES. BUT WITH NO MORE THAN HIS SHIELD AND HIS FIGHTING SPIRIT --
-- HE WINS. AND HE LEADS OTHERS TO WIN.
IT IS NOT ABOUT WEAPONS. IT IS NOT ABOUT POWER. IT IS ABOUT SPIRIT, AND CUNNING, AND COURAGE, AND SKILL.
THINK ON THIS, MY SON. FOR AS LONG AS THE AVENGERS POSSESS THE SPIRIT TO MATCH THEIR SKILL, THEY WILL BE FORMIDABLE FOES.
THEY ARE PREPARING -- BUILDING PRODIGIOUS DEFENSES. WE MUST BE EVEN BETTER PREPARED. WE MUST NEVER DISDAIN THEM --
TAK
-- OR WE WILL NOT BE DESERVING OF VICTORY!
KALKHIMITHIA
THE FIRES BURN FREELY NOW.
AND THE ONLY SOUND TO BE HEARD IN THE TOWN --
-- IS A CACOPHONY OF DISTORTED, ANIMALISTIC HOWLING --
THE HUDSON RIVER, JUST OFF OF MANHATTAN'S WEST SIDE.
THE AFTERNOON IS UNSEASONABLY WARM AND SUNNY. A PERFECT DAY TO BE OUT ON THE WATER --

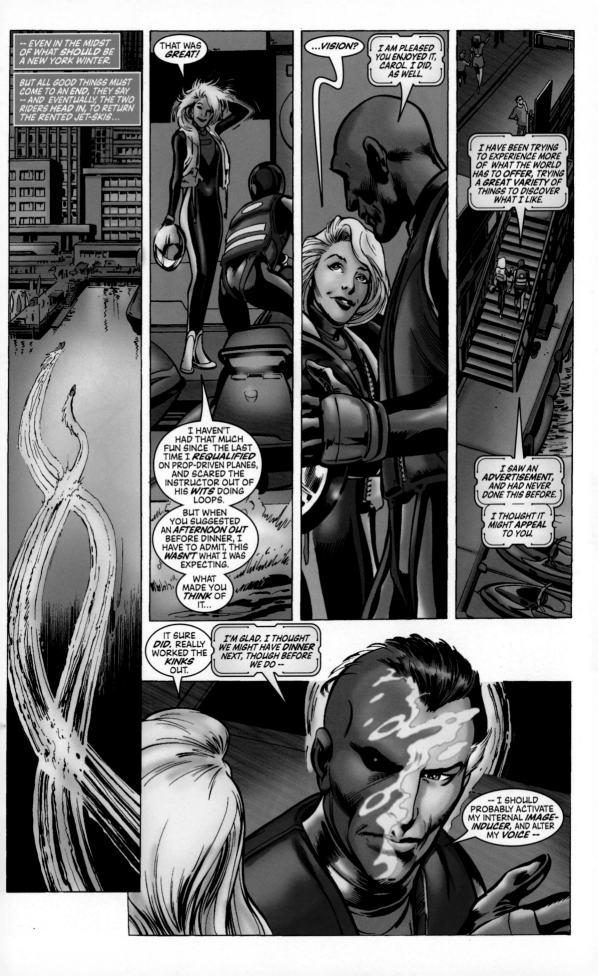

-- EVEN IN THE MIDST OF WHAT **SHOULD** BE A NEW YORK WINTER.

BUT ALL GOOD THINGS MUST COME TO AN END, THEY SAY -- AND EVENTUALLY, THE TWO RIDERS HEAD IN, TO RETURN THE RENTED JET-SKIS...

THAT WAS **GREAT!**

...**VISION?**

I AM PLEASED YOU ENJOYED IT, CAROL. I DID, AS WELL.

I HAVE BEEN TRYING TO EXPERIENCE MORE OF WHAT THE WORLD HAS TO OFFER, TRYING A GREAT VARIETY OF THINGS TO DISCOVER WHAT I LIKE.

I HAVEN'T HAD THAT MUCH FUN SINCE THE LAST TIME I **REQUALIFIED** ON PROP-DRIVEN PLANES, AND SCARED THE INSTRUCTOR OUT OF HIS **WITS** DOING LOOPS.

BUT WHEN YOU SUGGESTED AN **AFTERNOON OUT** BEFORE DINNER, I HAVE TO ADMIT, THIS **WASN'T** WHAT I WAS EXPECTING.

WHAT MADE YOU **THINK** OF IT...

I SAW AN **ADVERTISEMENT,** AND HAD NEVER DONE THIS BEFORE.

I THOUGHT IT MIGHT **APPEAL** TO YOU.

IT SURE **DID.** REALLY WORKED THE **KINKS** OUT.

I'M GLAD. I THOUGHT WE MIGHT HAVE **DINNER** NEXT, THOUGH BEFORE WE DO --

-- I SHOULD PROBABLY ACTIVATE MY INTERNAL **IMAGE-INDUCER,** AND ALTER MY **VOICE** --

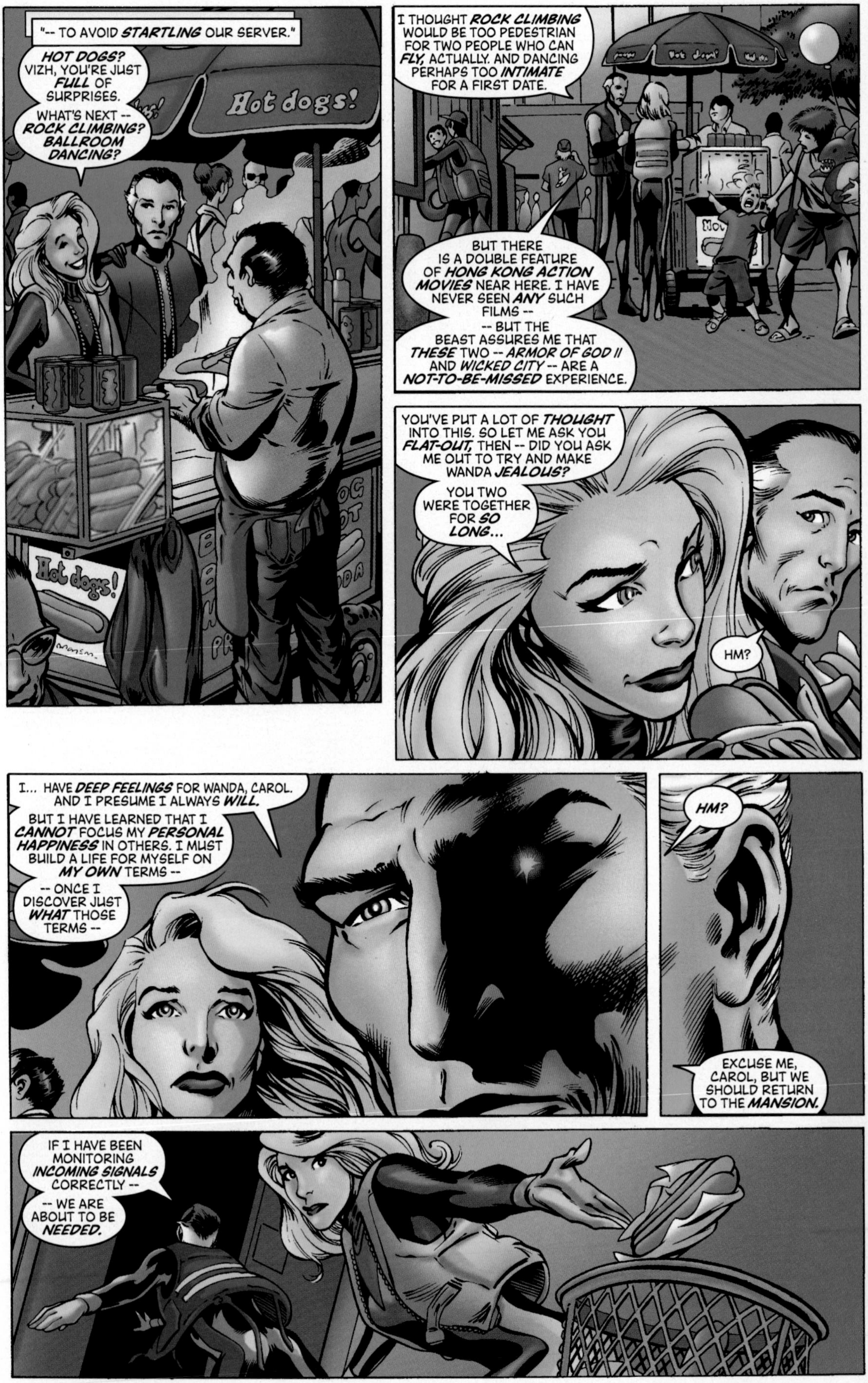
"-- TO AVOID STARTLING OUR SERVER."
HOT DOGS? VIZH, YOU'RE JUST FULL OF SURPRISES.
WHAT'S NEXT -- ROCK CLIMBING? BALLROOM DANCING?
Hot dogs!
Hot dogs!
I THOUGHT ROCK CLIMBING WOULD BE TOO PEDESTRIAN FOR TWO PEOPLE WHO CAN FLY, ACTUALLY. AND DANCING PERHAPS TOO INTIMATE FOR A FIRST DATE.
BUT THERE IS A DOUBLE FEATURE OF HONG KONG ACTION MOVIES NEAR HERE. I HAVE NEVER SEEN ANY SUCH FILMS --
-- BUT THE BEAST ASSURES ME THAT THESE TWO -- ARMOR OF GOD II AND WICKED CITY -- ARE A NOT-TO-BE-MISSED EXPERIENCE.
YOU'VE PUT A LOT OF THOUGHT INTO THIS. SO LET ME ASK YOU FLAT-OUT, THEN -- DID YOU ASK ME OUT TO TRY AND MAKE WANDA JEALOUS?
YOU TWO WERE TOGETHER FOR SO LONG...
HM?
I... HAVE DEEP FEELINGS FOR WANDA, CAROL. AND I PRESUME I ALWAYS WILL.
BUT I HAVE LEARNED THAT I CANNOT FOCUS MY PERSONAL HAPPINESS IN OTHERS. I MUST BUILD A LIFE FOR MYSELF ON MY OWN TERMS --
-- ONCE I DISCOVER JUST WHAT THOSE TERMS --
HM?
EXCUSE ME, CAROL, BUT WE SHOULD RETURN TO THE MANSION.
IF I HAVE BEEN MONITORING INCOMING SIGNALS CORRECTLY --
-- WE ARE ABOUT TO BE NEEDED.

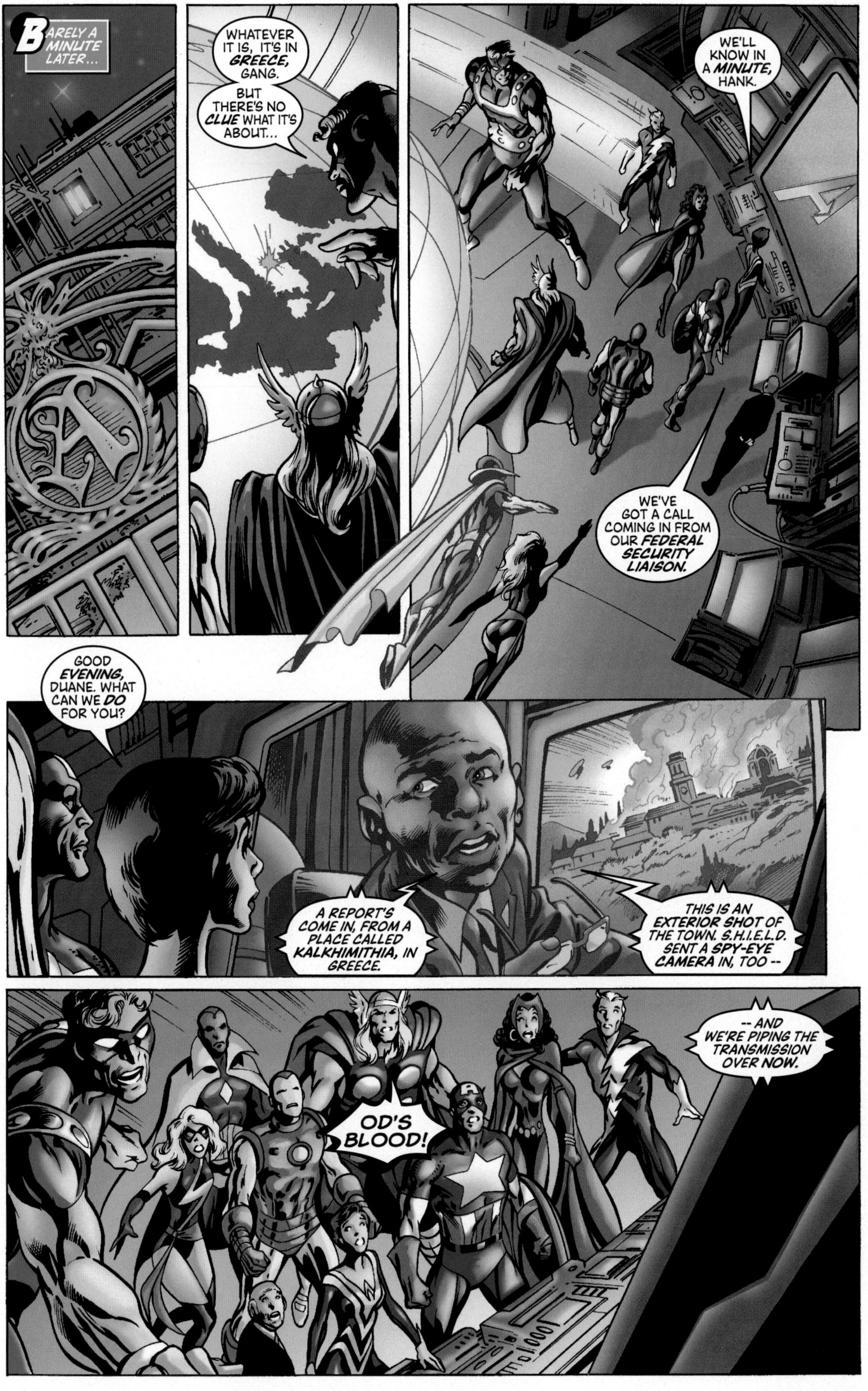
BARELY A MINUTE LATER...
WHATEVER IT IS, IT'S IN GREECE, GANG.
BUT THERE'S NO CLUE WHAT IT'S ABOUT...
WE'LL KNOW IN A MINUTE, HANK.
WE'VE GOT A CALL COMING IN FROM OUR FEDERAL SECURITY LIAISON.
GOOD EVENING, DUANE. WHAT CAN WE DO FOR YOU?
A REPORT'S COME IN, FROM A PLACE CALLED KALKHIMITHIA, IN GREECE.
THIS IS AN EXTERIOR SHOT OF THE TOWN. S.H.I.E.L.D. SENT A SPY-EYE CAMERA IN, TOO --
-- AND WE'RE PIPING THE TRANSMISSION OVER NOW.
OD'S BLOOD!

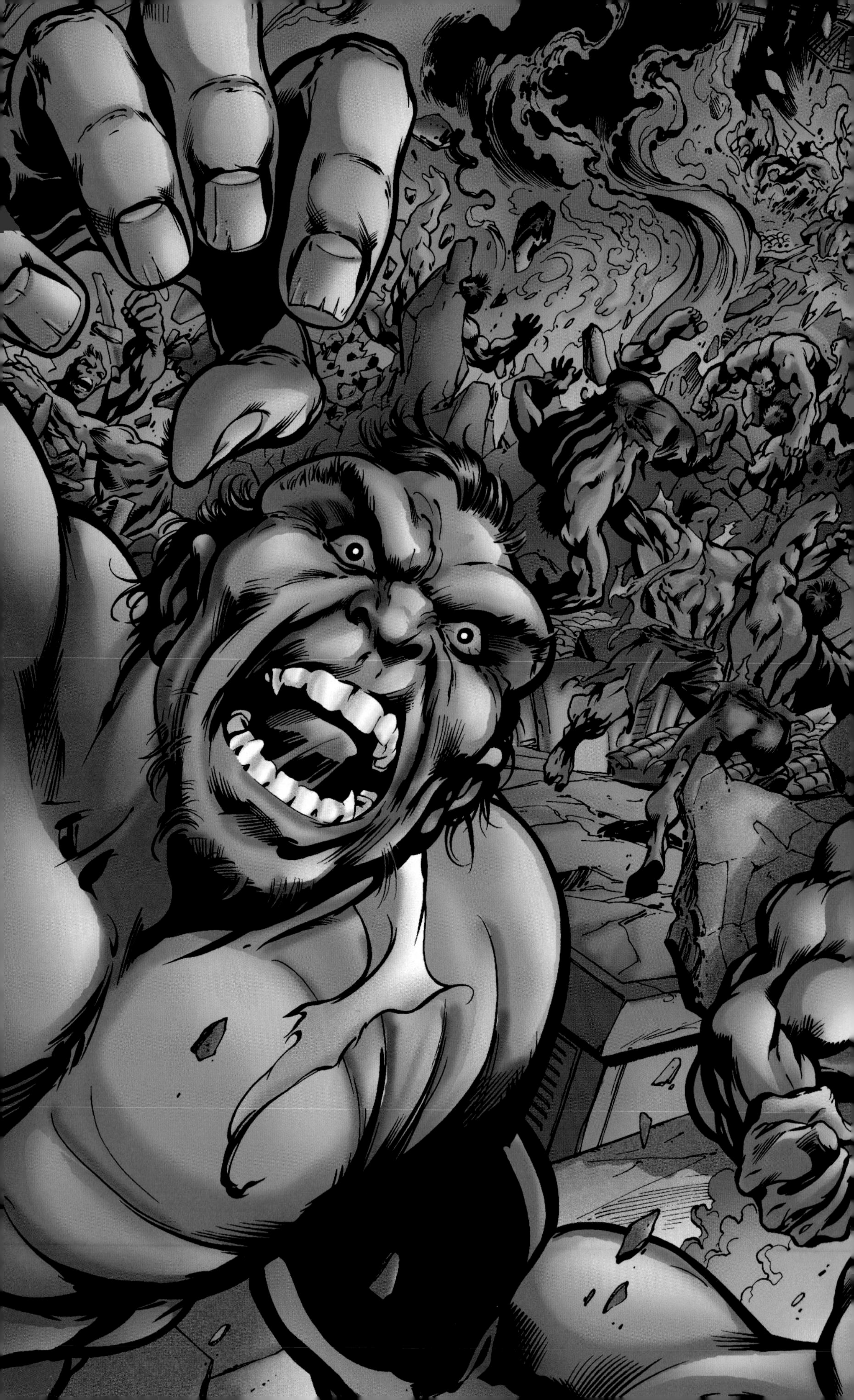

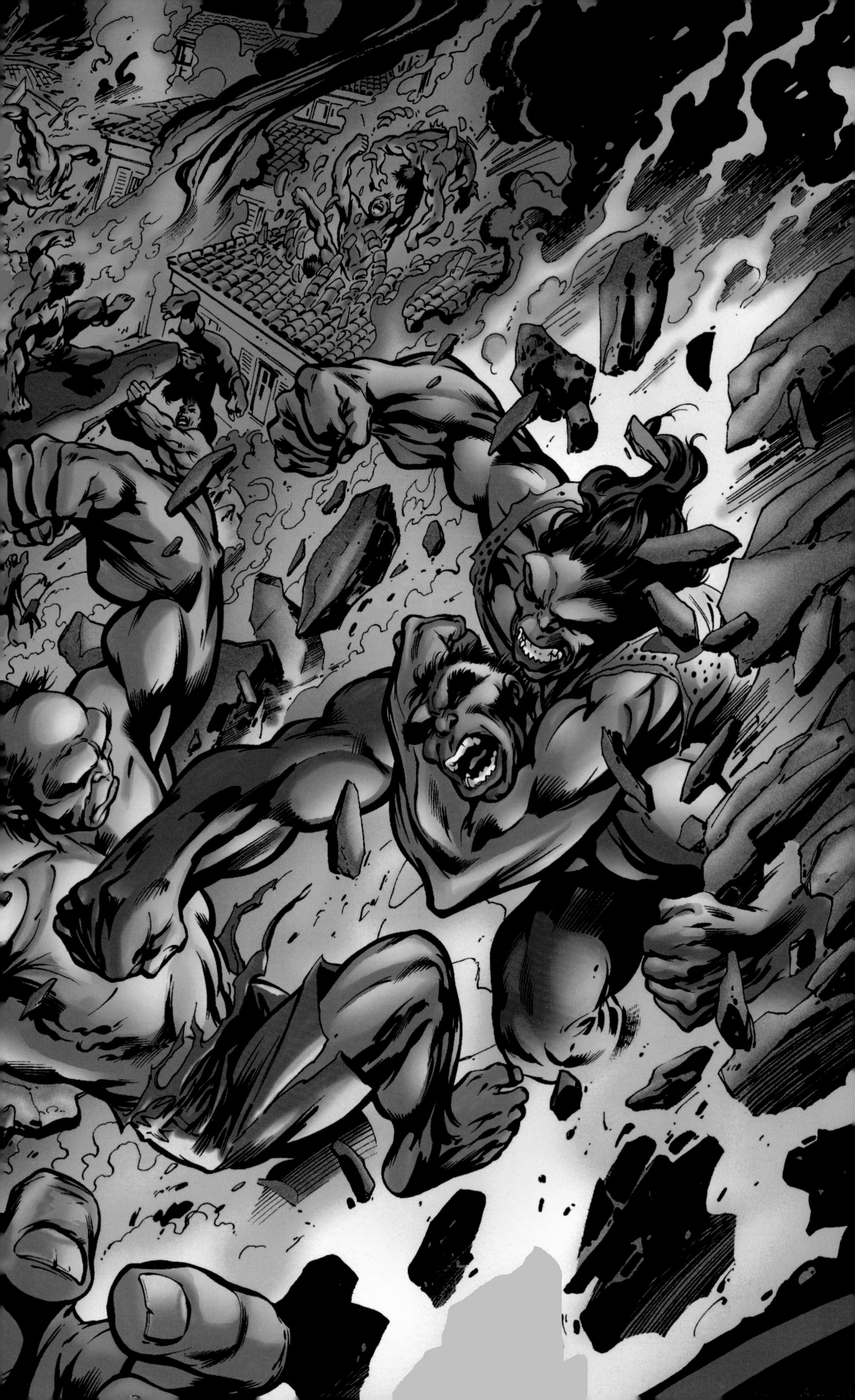

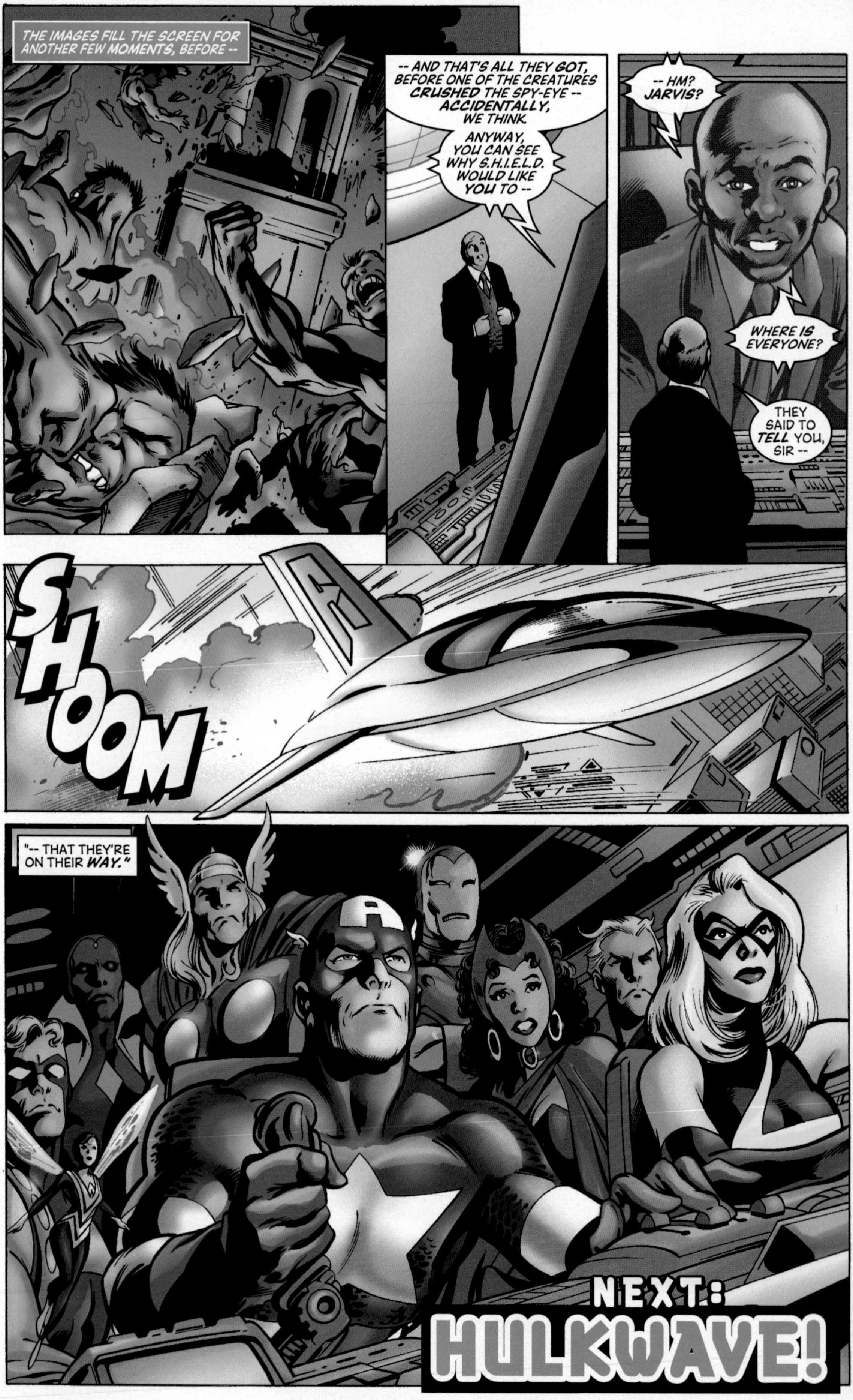
THE IMAGES FILL THE SCREEN FOR ANOTHER FEW MOMENTS, BEFORE --
-- AND THAT'S ALL THEY GOT, BEFORE ONE OF THE CREATURES CRUSHED THE SPY-EYE -- ACCIDENTALLY, WE THINK.
ANYWAY, YOU CAN SEE WHY S.H.I.E.L.D. WOULD LIKE YOU TO --
-- HM? JARVIS?
WHERE IS EVERYONE?
THEY SAID TO TELL YOU, SIR --
SHOOM
"-- THAT THEY'RE ON THEIR WAY."
NEXT:
HULKWAVE!

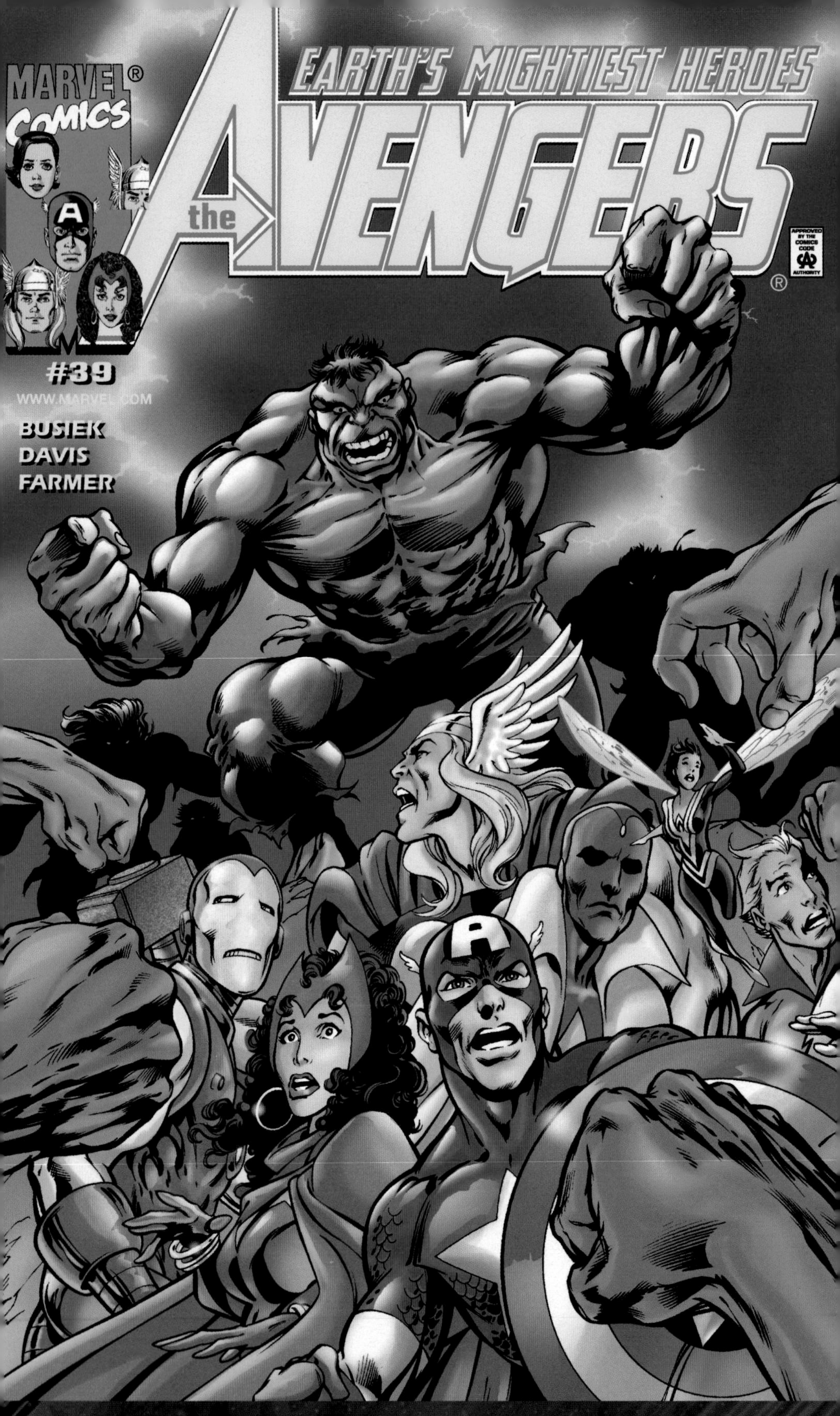
MARVEL COMICS
EARTH'S MIGHTIEST HEROES
the AVENGERS
APPROVED BY THE COMICS CODE AUTHORITY
#39
WWW.MARVEL.COM
BUSIEK
DAVIS
FARMER

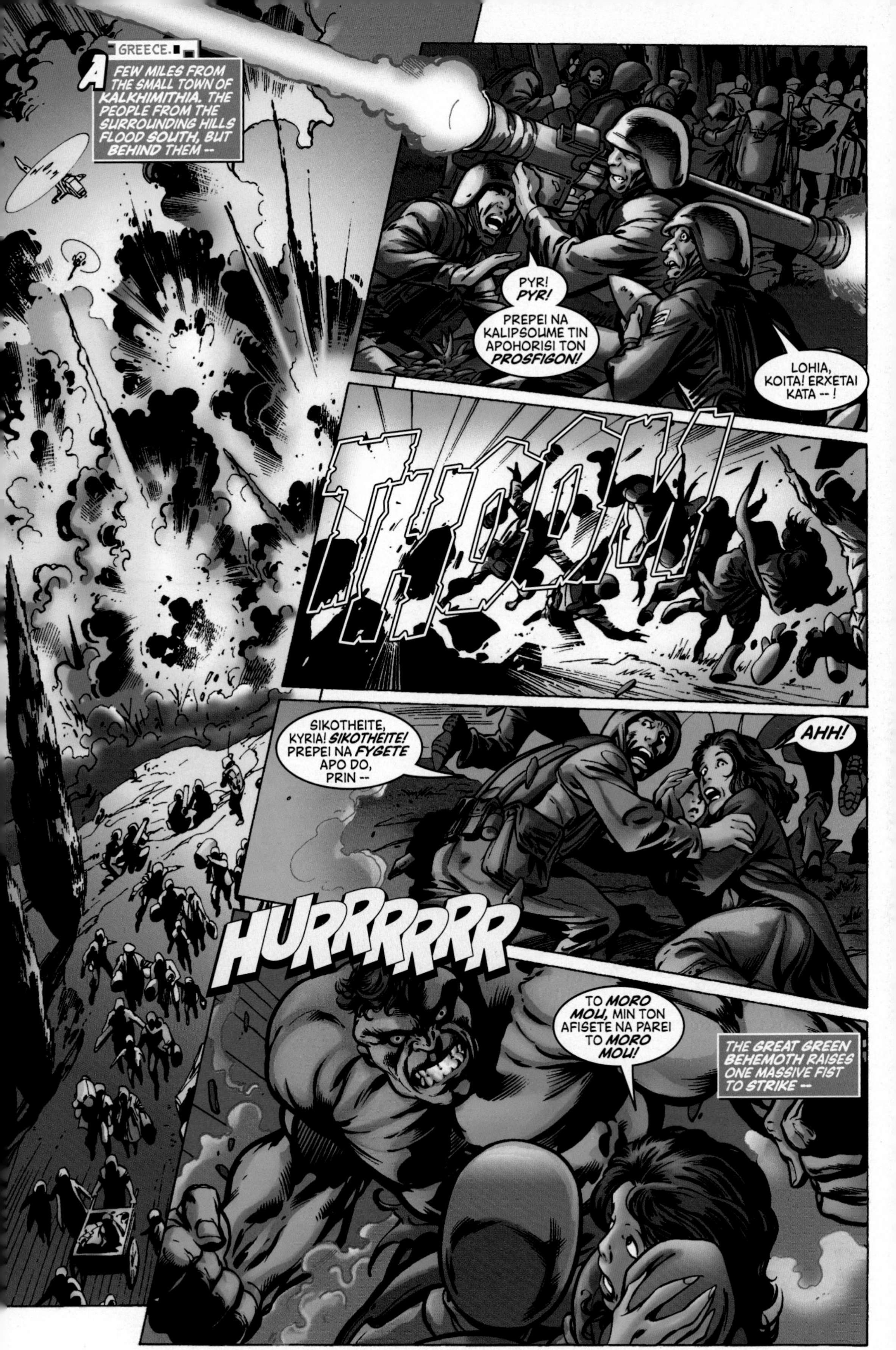
GREECE.
A FEW MILES FROM THE SMALL TOWN OF KALKHIMITHIA. THE PEOPLE FROM THE SURROUNDING HILLS FLOOD SOUTH, BUT BEHIND THEM --
PYR! PYR!
PREPEI NA KALIPSOUME TIN APOHORISI TON PROSFIGON!
LOHIA, KOITA! ERXETAI KATA -- !
THOOM
SIKOTHEITE, KYRIA! SIKOTHEITE! PREPEI NA FYGETE APO DO, PRIN --
AHH!
HURRRRRR
TO MORO MOU, MIN TON AFISETE NA PAREI TO MORO MOU!
THE GREAT GREEN BEHEMOTH RAISES ONE MASSIVE FIST TO STRIKE --

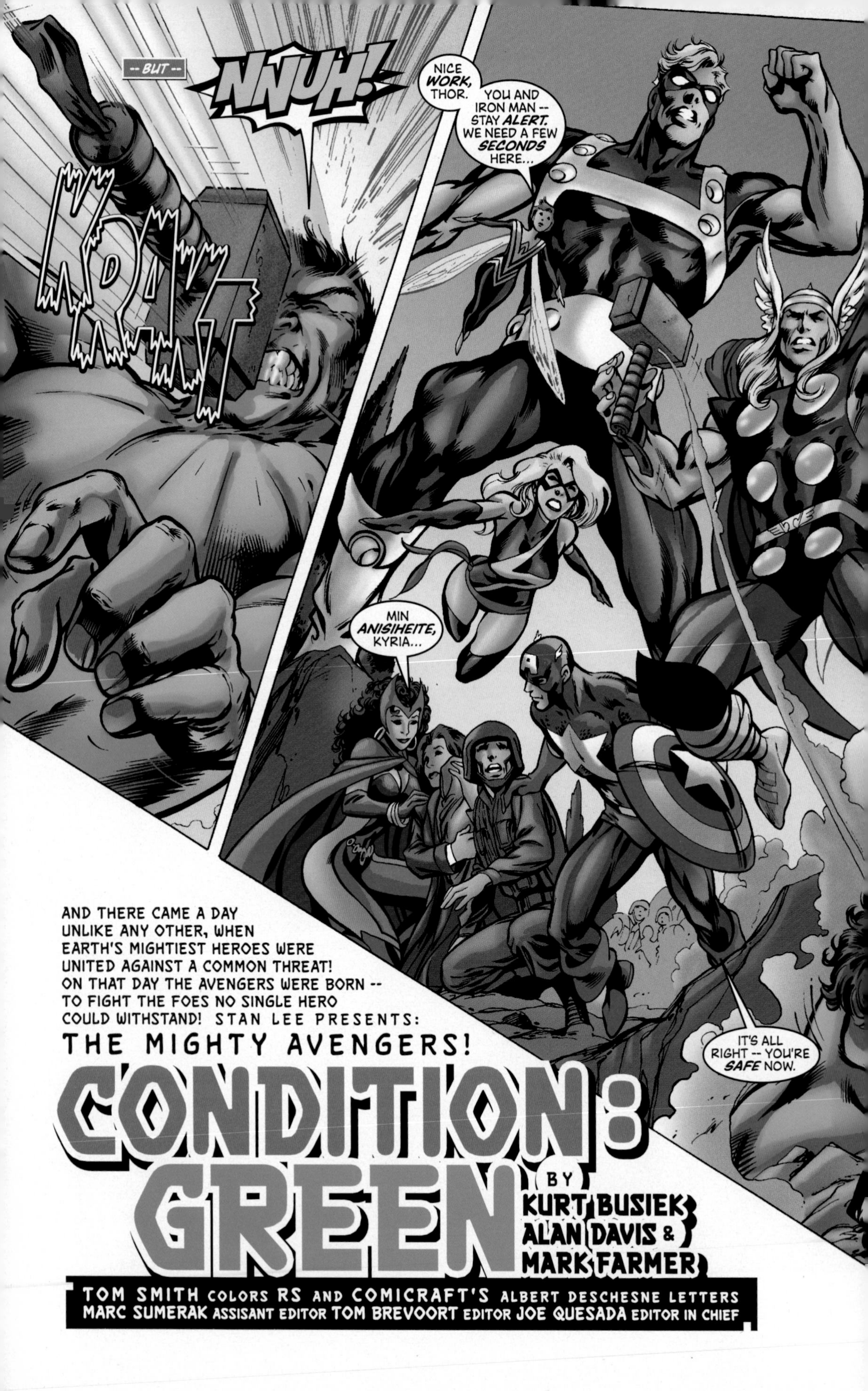
-- BUT --
NNUH!
KRAKT
NICE WORK, THOR.
YOU AND IRON MAN -- STAY ALERT. WE NEED A FEW SECONDS HERE...
MIN ANISIHEITE, KYRIA...
IT'S ALL RIGHT -- YOU'RE SAFE NOW.
AND THERE CAME A DAY UNLIKE ANY OTHER, WHEN EARTH'S MIGHTIEST HEROES WERE UNITED AGAINST A COMMON THREAT! ON THAT DAY THE AVENGERS WERE BORN -- TO FIGHT THE FOES NO SINGLE HERO COULD WITHSTAND! STAN LEE PRESENTS:
THE MIGHTY AVENGERS!
CONDITION: GREEN
BY KURT BUSIEK ALAN DAVIS & MARK FARMER
TOM SMITH COLORS RS AND COMICRAFT'S ALBERT DESCHESNE LETTERS
MARC SUMERAK ASSISANT EDITOR TOM BREVOORT EDITOR JOE QUESADA EDITOR IN CHIEF

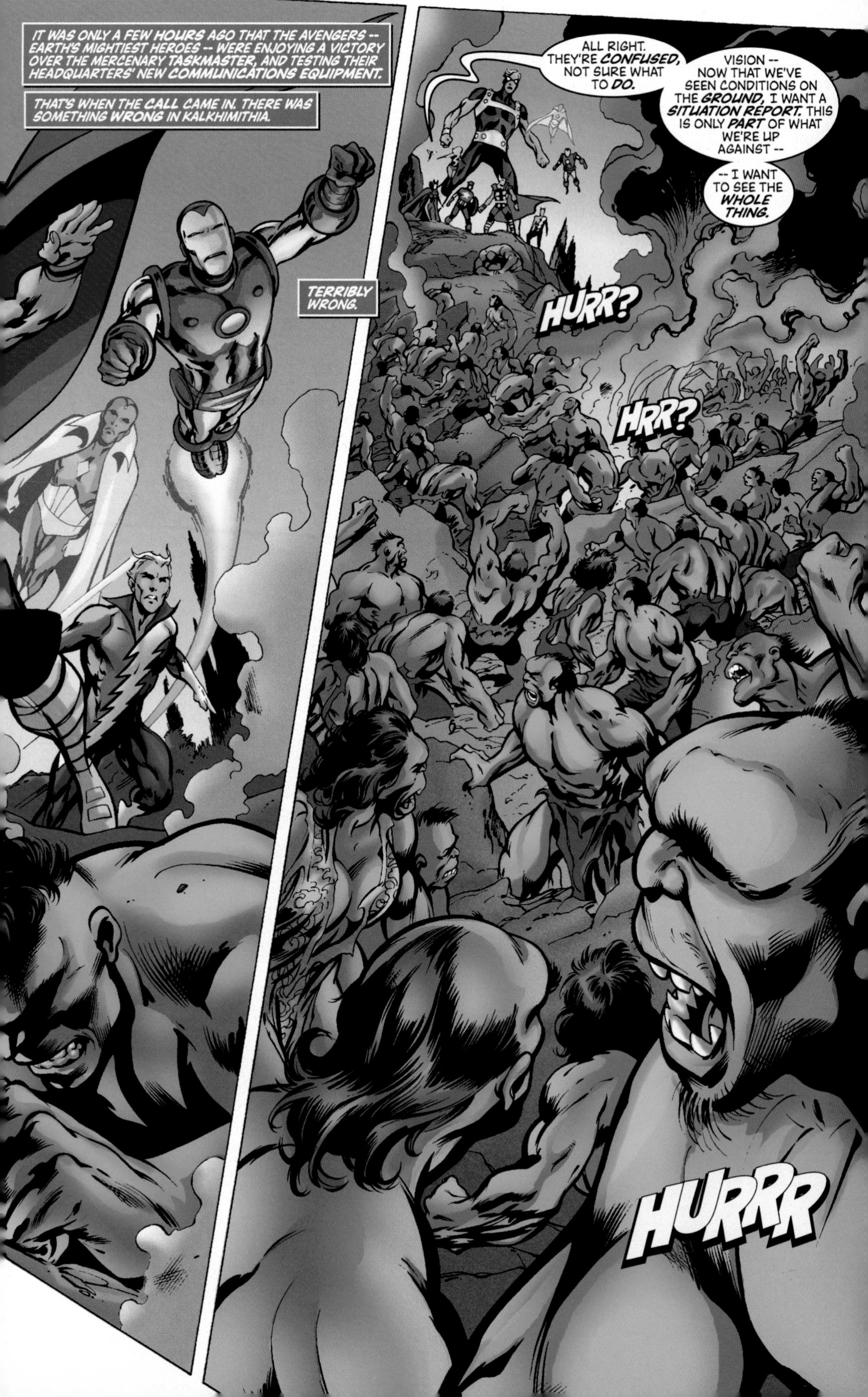
IT WAS ONLY A FEW HOURS AGO THAT THE AVENGERS -- EARTH'S MIGHTIEST HEROES -- WERE ENJOYING A VICTORY OVER THE MERCENARY TASKMASTER, AND TESTING THEIR HEADQUARTERS' NEW COMMUNICATIONS EQUIPMENT.
THAT'S WHEN THE CALL CAME IN. THERE WAS SOMETHING WRONG IN KALKHIMITHIA.
TERRIBLY WRONG.
ALL RIGHT. THEY'RE CONFUSED, NOT SURE WHAT TO DO.
VISION -- NOW THAT WE'VE SEEN CONDITIONS ON THE GROUND, I WANT A SITUATION REPORT. THIS IS ONLY PART OF WHAT WE'RE UP AGAINST --
-- I WANT TO SEE THE WHOLE THING.
HURR?
HRR?
HURRR

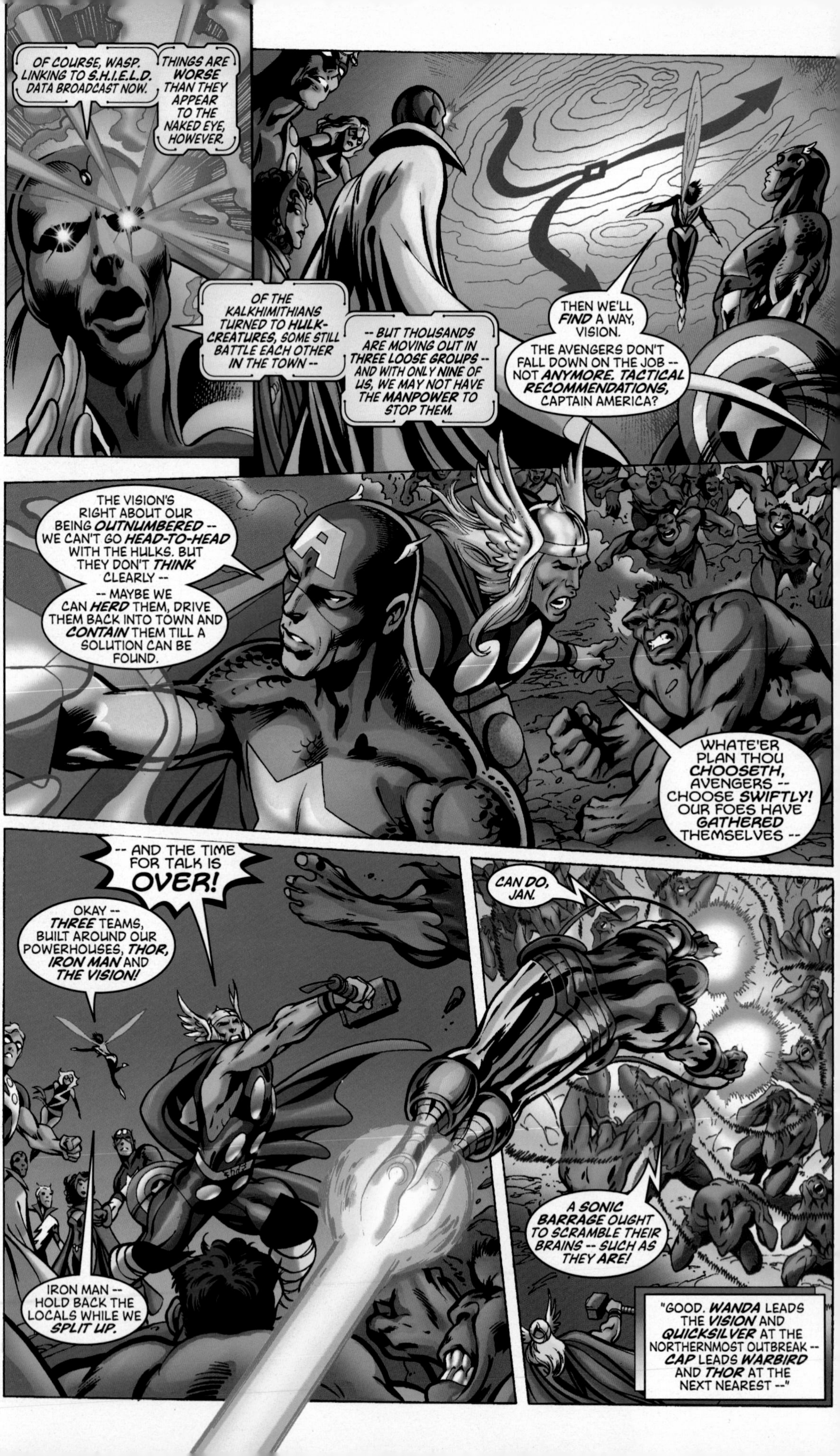
OF COURSE, WASP. LINKING TO S.H.I.E.L.D. DATA BROADCAST NOW.
THINGS ARE WORSE THAN THEY APPEAR TO THE NAKED EYE, HOWEVER.
OF THE KALKHIMITHIANS TURNED TO HULK-CREATURES, SOME STILL BATTLE EACH OTHER IN THE TOWN --
-- BUT THOUSANDS ARE MOVING OUT IN THREE LOOSE GROUPS -- AND WITH ONLY NINE OF US, WE MAY NOT HAVE THE MANPOWER TO STOP THEM.
THEN WE'LL FIND A WAY, VISION.
THE AVENGERS DON'T FALL DOWN ON THE JOB -- NOT ANYMORE. TACTICAL RECOMMENDATIONS, CAPTAIN AMERICA?
THE VISION'S RIGHT ABOUT OUR BEING OUTNUMBERED -- WE CAN'T GO HEAD-TO-HEAD WITH THE HULKS. BUT THEY DON'T THINK CLEARLY --
-- MAYBE WE CAN HERD THEM, DRIVE THEM BACK INTO TOWN AND CONTAIN THEM TILL A SOLUTION CAN BE FOUND.
WHATE'ER PLAN THOU CHOOSETH, AVENGERS -- CHOOSE SWIFTLY! OUR FOES HAVE GATHERED THEMSELVES --
-- AND THE TIME FOR TALK IS OVER!
OKAY -- THREE TEAMS, BUILT AROUND OUR POWERHOUSES, THOR, IRON MAN AND THE VISION!
IRON MAN -- HOLD BACK THE LOCALS WHILE WE SPLIT UP.
CAN DO, JAN.
A SONIC BARRAGE OUGHT TO SCRAMBLE THEIR BRAINS -- SUCH AS THEY ARE!
"GOOD. WANDA LEADS THE VISION AND QUICKSILVER AT THE NORTHERNMOST OUTBREAK -- CAP LEADS WARBIRD AND THOR AT THE NEXT NEAREST --"

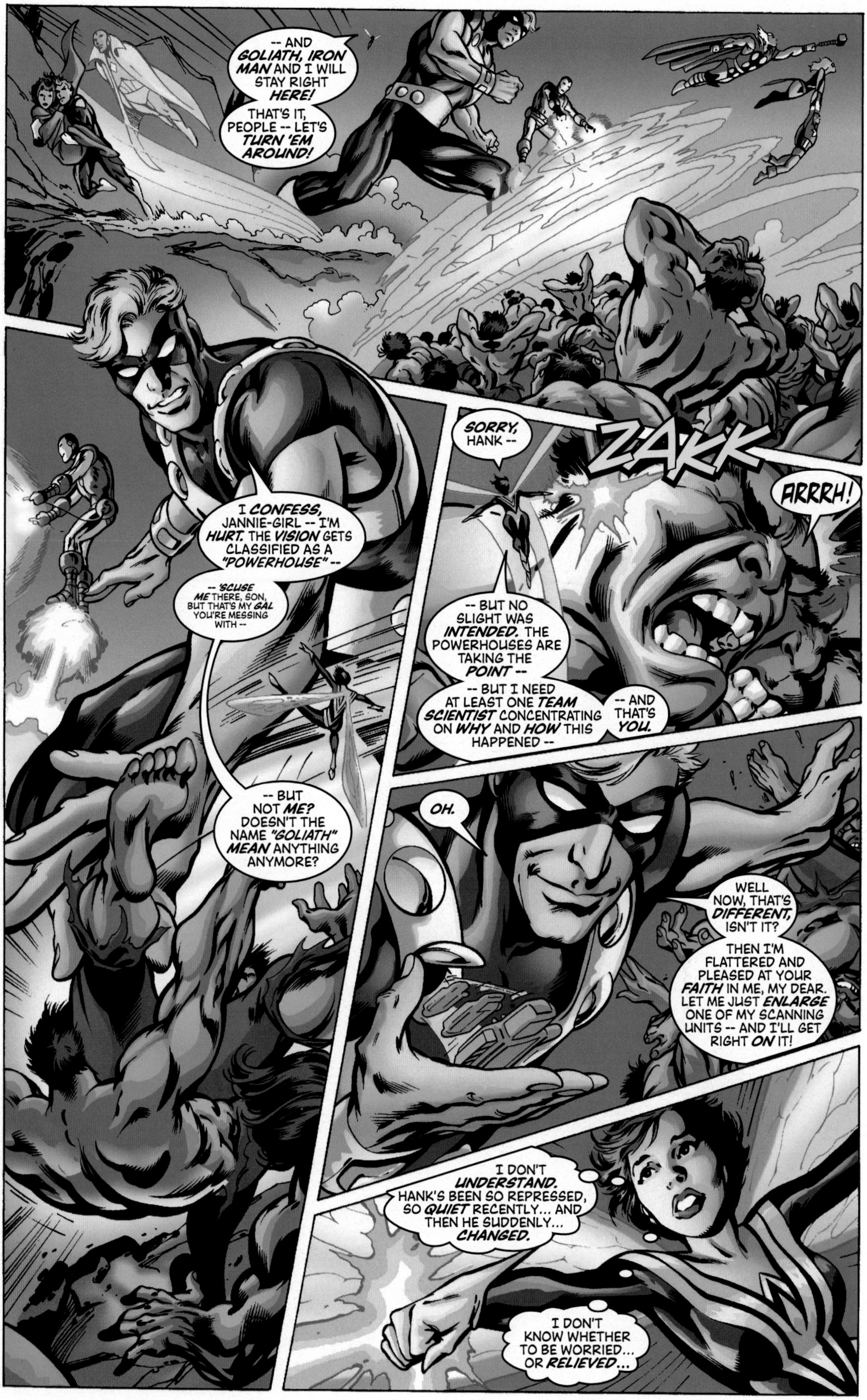
-- AND GOLIATH, IRON MAN AND I WILL STAY RIGHT HERE!
THAT'S IT, PEOPLE -- LET'S TURN 'EM AROUND!
I CONFESS, JANNIE-GIRL -- I'M HURT. THE VISION GETS CLASSIFIED AS A "POWERHOUSE" --
-- 'SCUSE ME THERE, SON, BUT THAT'S MY GAL YOU'RE MESSING WITH --
-- BUT NOT ME? DOESN'T THE NAME "GOLIATH" MEAN ANYTHING ANYMORE?
SORRY, HANK --
ZAKK
ARRRH!
-- BUT NO SLIGHT WAS INTENDED. THE POWERHOUSES ARE TAKING THE POINT --
-- BUT I NEED AT LEAST ONE TEAM SCIENTIST CONCENTRATING ON WHY AND HOW THIS HAPPENED --
-- AND THAT'S YOU.
OH.
WELL NOW, THAT'S DIFFERENT, ISN'T IT?
THEN I'M FLATTERED AND PLEASED AT YOUR FAITH IN ME, MY DEAR. LET ME JUST ENLARGE ONE OF MY SCANNING UNITS -- AND I'LL GET RIGHT ON IT!
I DON'T UNDERSTAND. HANK'S BEEN SO REPRESSED, SO QUIET RECENTLY... AND THEN HE SUDDENLY... CHANGED.
I DON'T KNOW WHETHER TO BE WORRIED... OR RELIEVED...

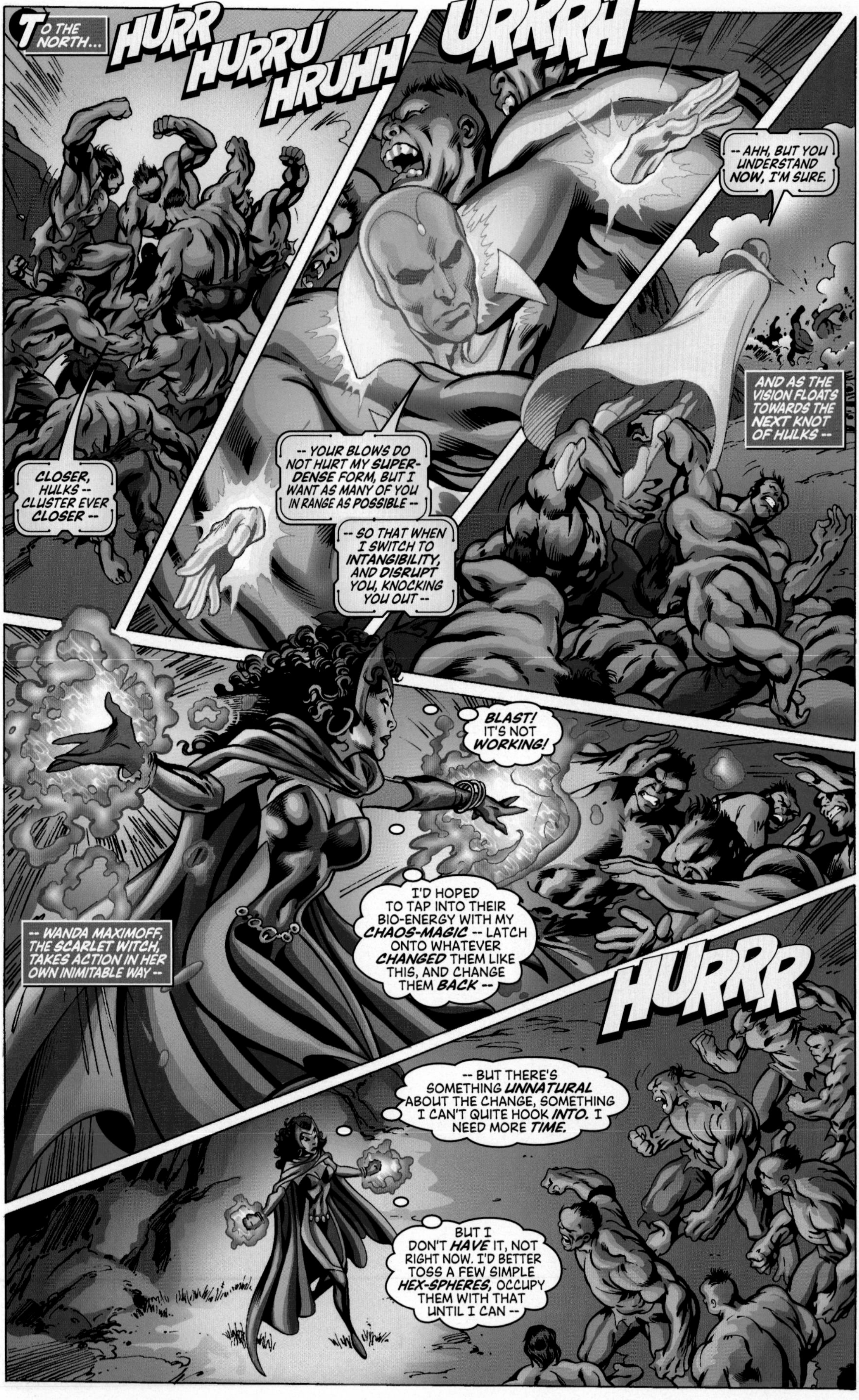
TO THE NORTH...
HURR HURRU HRUHH
CLOSER, HULKS -- CLUSTER EVER CLOSER --
URRRH
-- YOUR BLOWS DO NOT HURT MY SUPER-DENSE FORM, BUT I WANT AS MANY OF YOU IN RANGE AS POSSIBLE --
-- SO THAT WHEN I SWITCH TO INTANGIBILITY, AND DISRUPT YOU, KNOCKING YOU OUT --
-- AHH, BUT YOU UNDERSTAND NOW, I'M SURE.
AND AS THE VISION FLOATS TOWARDS THE NEXT KNOT OF HULKS --
-- WANDA MAXIMOFF, THE SCARLET WITCH, TAKES ACTION IN HER OWN INIMITABLE WAY --
BLAST! IT'S NOT WORKING!
I'D HOPED TO TAP INTO THEIR BIO-ENERGY WITH MY CHAOS-MAGIC -- LATCH ONTO WHATEVER CHANGED THEM LIKE THIS, AND CHANGE THEM BACK --
HURRR
-- BUT THERE'S SOMETHING UNNATURAL ABOUT THE CHANGE, SOMETHING I CAN'T QUITE HOOK INTO. I NEED MORE TIME.
BUT I DON'T HAVE IT, NOT RIGHT NOW. I'D BETTER TOSS A FEW SIMPLE HEX-SPHERES, OCCUPY THEM WITH THAT UNTIL I CAN --

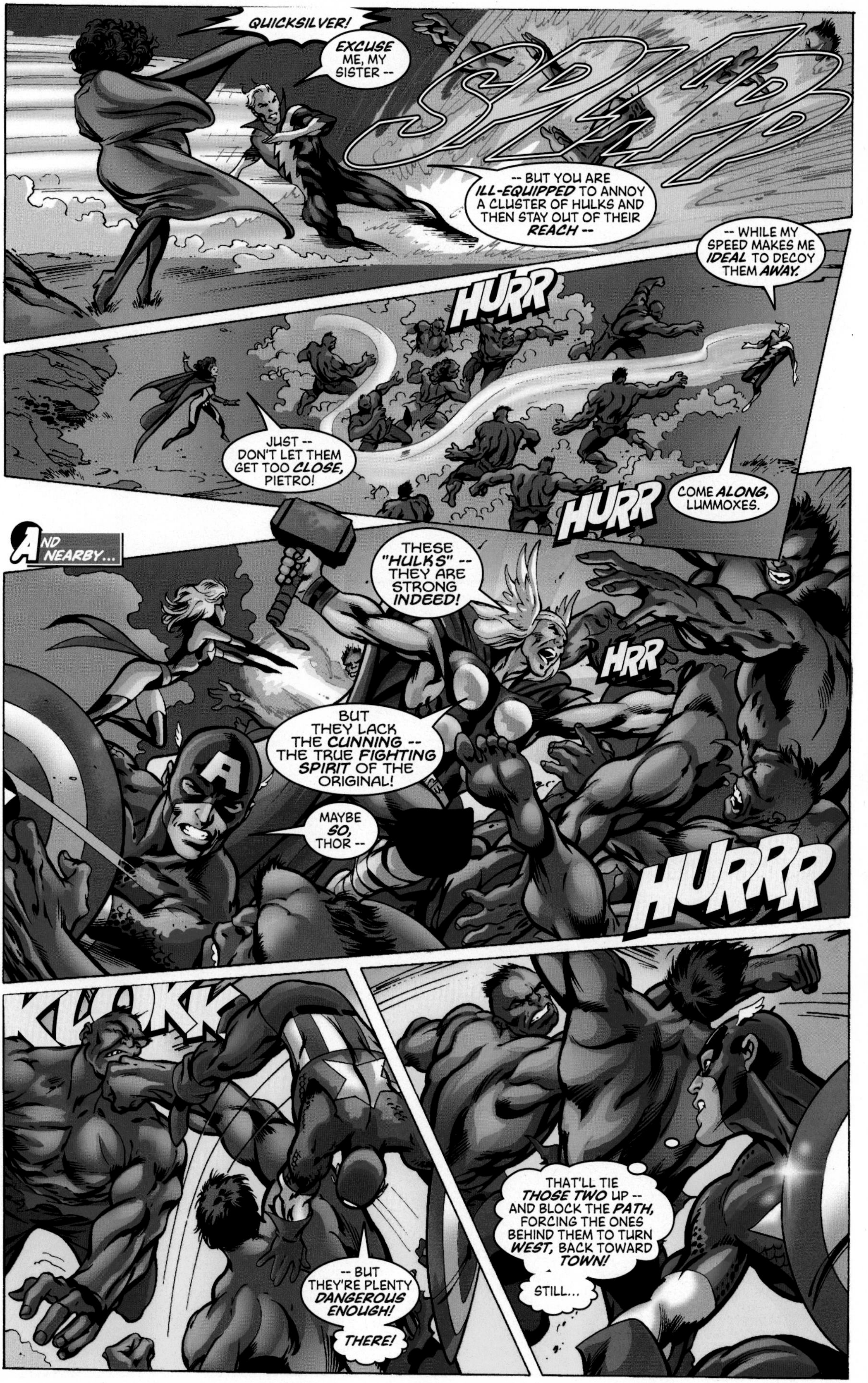
QUICKSILVER!
EXCUSE ME, MY SISTER --
SPLIP
-- BUT YOU ARE ILL-EQUIPPED TO ANNOY A CLUSTER OF HULKS AND THEN STAY OUT OF THEIR REACH --
-- WHILE MY SPEED MAKES ME IDEAL TO DECOY THEM AWAY.
HURR
JUST -- DON'T LET THEM GET TOO CLOSE, PIETRO!
HURR
COME ALONG, LUMMOXES.
AND NEARBY...
THESE "HULKS" -- THEY ARE STRONG INDEED!
HRR
BUT THEY LACK THE CUNNING -- THE TRUE FIGHTING SPIRIT OF THE ORIGINAL!
MAYBE SO, THOR --
HURRR
KLOKK
-- BUT THEY'RE PLENTY DANGEROUS ENOUGH!
THERE!
THAT'LL TIE THOSE TWO UP -- AND BLOCK THE PATH, FORCING THE ONES BEHIND THEM TO TURN WEST, BACK TOWARD TOWN!
STILL...

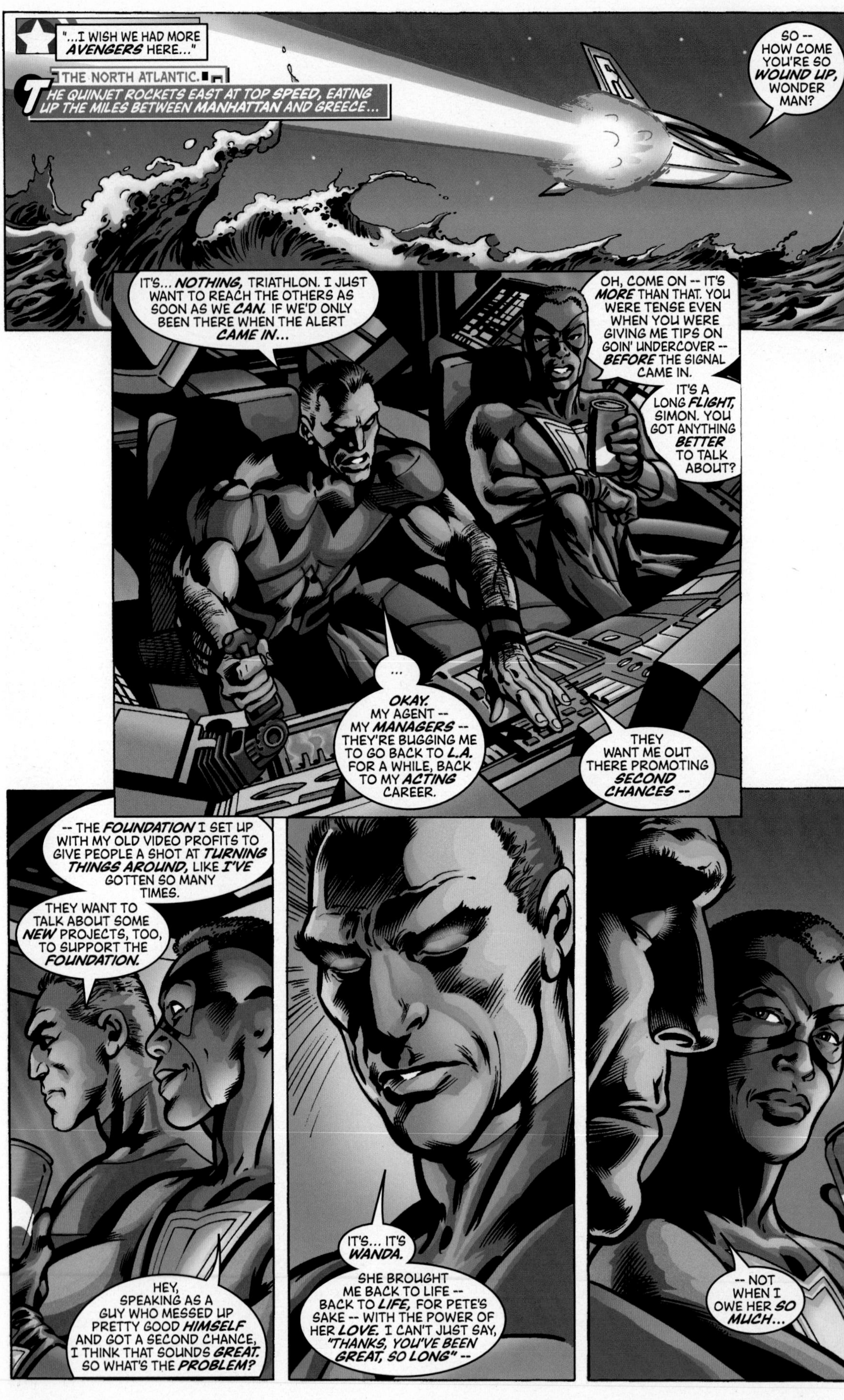
"...I WISH WE HAD MORE AVENGERS HERE..."
THE NORTH ATLANTIC.
THE QUINJET ROCKETS EAST AT TOP SPEED, EATING UP THE MILES BETWEEN MANHATTAN AND GREECE...
SO -- HOW COME YOU'RE SO WOUND UP, WONDER MAN?
IT'S... NOTHING, TRIATHLON. I JUST WANT TO REACH THE OTHERS AS SOON AS WE CAN. IF WE'D ONLY BEEN THERE WHEN THE ALERT CAME IN...
OH, COME ON -- IT'S MORE THAN THAT. YOU WERE TENSE EVEN WHEN YOU WERE GIVING ME TIPS ON GOIN' UNDERCOVER -- BEFORE THE SIGNAL CAME IN.
IT'S A LONG FLIGHT, SIMON. YOU GOT ANYTHING BETTER TO TALK ABOUT?
...
OKAY. MY AGENT -- MY MANAGERS -- THEY'RE BUGGING ME TO GO BACK TO L.A. FOR A WHILE, BACK TO MY ACTING CAREER.
THEY WANT ME OUT THERE PROMOTING SECOND CHANCES --
-- THE FOUNDATION I SET UP WITH MY OLD VIDEO PROFITS TO GIVE PEOPLE A SHOT AT TURNING THINGS AROUND, LIKE I'VE GOTTEN SO MANY TIMES.
THEY WANT TO TALK ABOUT SOME NEW PROJECTS, TOO, TO SUPPORT THE FOUNDATION.
HEY, SPEAKING AS A GUY WHO MESSED UP PRETTY GOOD HIMSELF AND GOT A SECOND CHANCE, I THINK THAT SOUNDS GREAT. SO WHAT'S THE PROBLEM?
IT'S... IT'S WANDA.
SHE BROUGHT ME BACK TO LIFE -- BACK TO LIFE, FOR PETE'S SAKE -- WITH THE POWER OF HER LOVE. I CAN'T JUST SAY, "THANKS, YOU'VE BEEN GREAT, SO LONG" --
-- NOT WHEN I OWE HER SO MUCH...

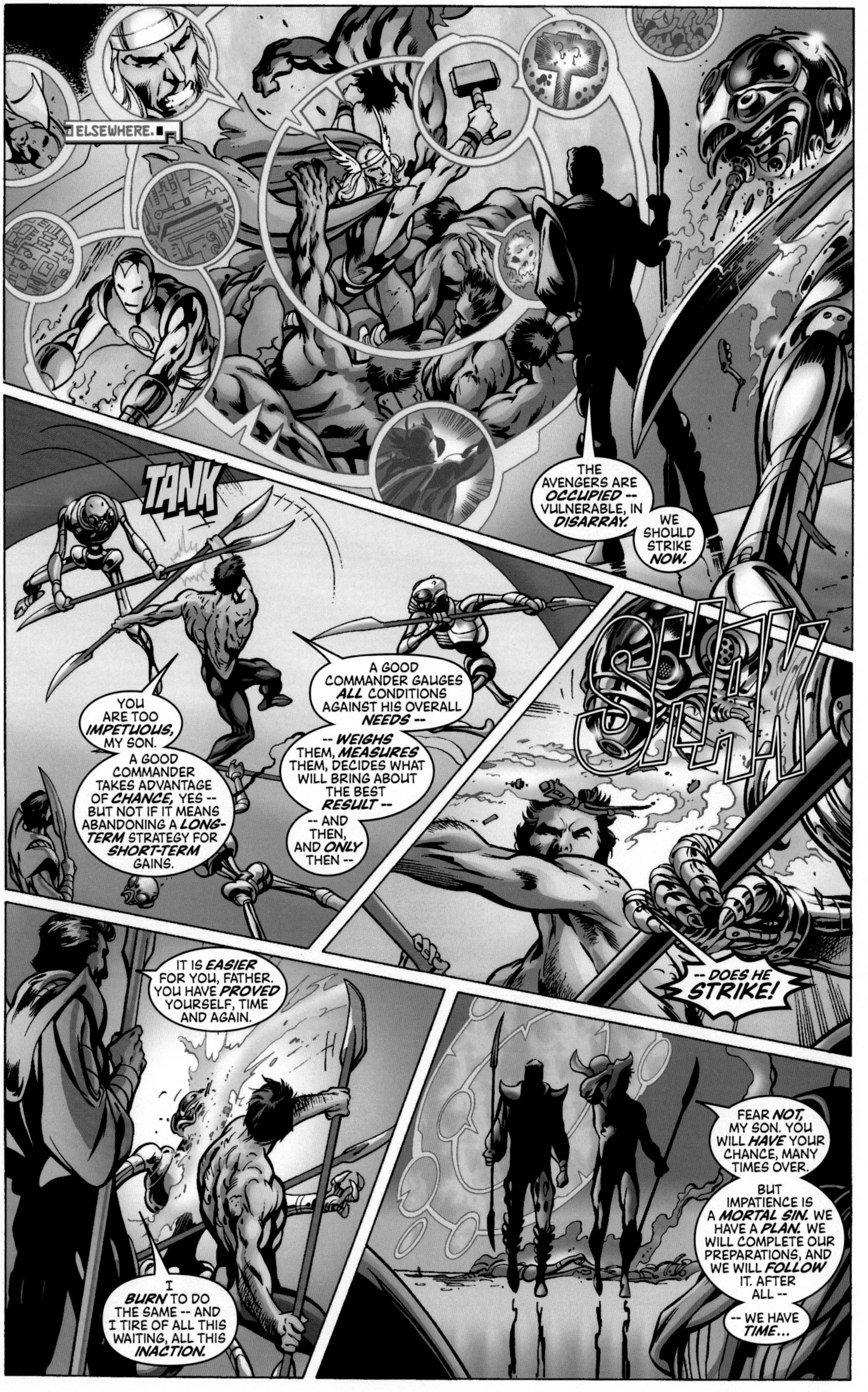
ELSEWHERE.
THE AVENGERS ARE OCCUPIED -- VULNERABLE, IN DISARRAY.
WE SHOULD STRIKE NOW.
TANK
YOU ARE TOO IMPETUOUS, MY SON.
A GOOD COMMANDER TAKES ADVANTAGE OF CHANCE, YES -- BUT NOT IF IT MEANS ABANDONING A LONG-TERM STRATEGY FOR SHORT-TERM GAINS.
A GOOD COMMANDER GAUGES ALL CONDITIONS AGAINST HIS OVERALL NEEDS --
-- WEIGHS THEM, MEASURES THEM, DECIDES WHAT WILL BRING ABOUT THE BEST RESULT --
-- AND THEN, AND ONLY THEN --
SHAKK
-- DOES HE STRIKE!
IT IS EASIER FOR YOU, FATHER. YOU HAVE PROVED YOURSELF, TIME AND AGAIN.
I BURN TO DO THE SAME -- AND I TIRE OF ALL THIS WAITING, ALL THIS INACTION.
FEAR NOT, MY SON. YOU WILL HAVE YOUR CHANCE, MANY TIMES OVER.
BUT IMPATIENCE IS A MORTAL SIN. WE HAVE A PLAN. WE WILL COMPLETE OUR PREPARATIONS, AND WE WILL FOLLOW IT. AFTER ALL --
-- WE HAVE TIME...

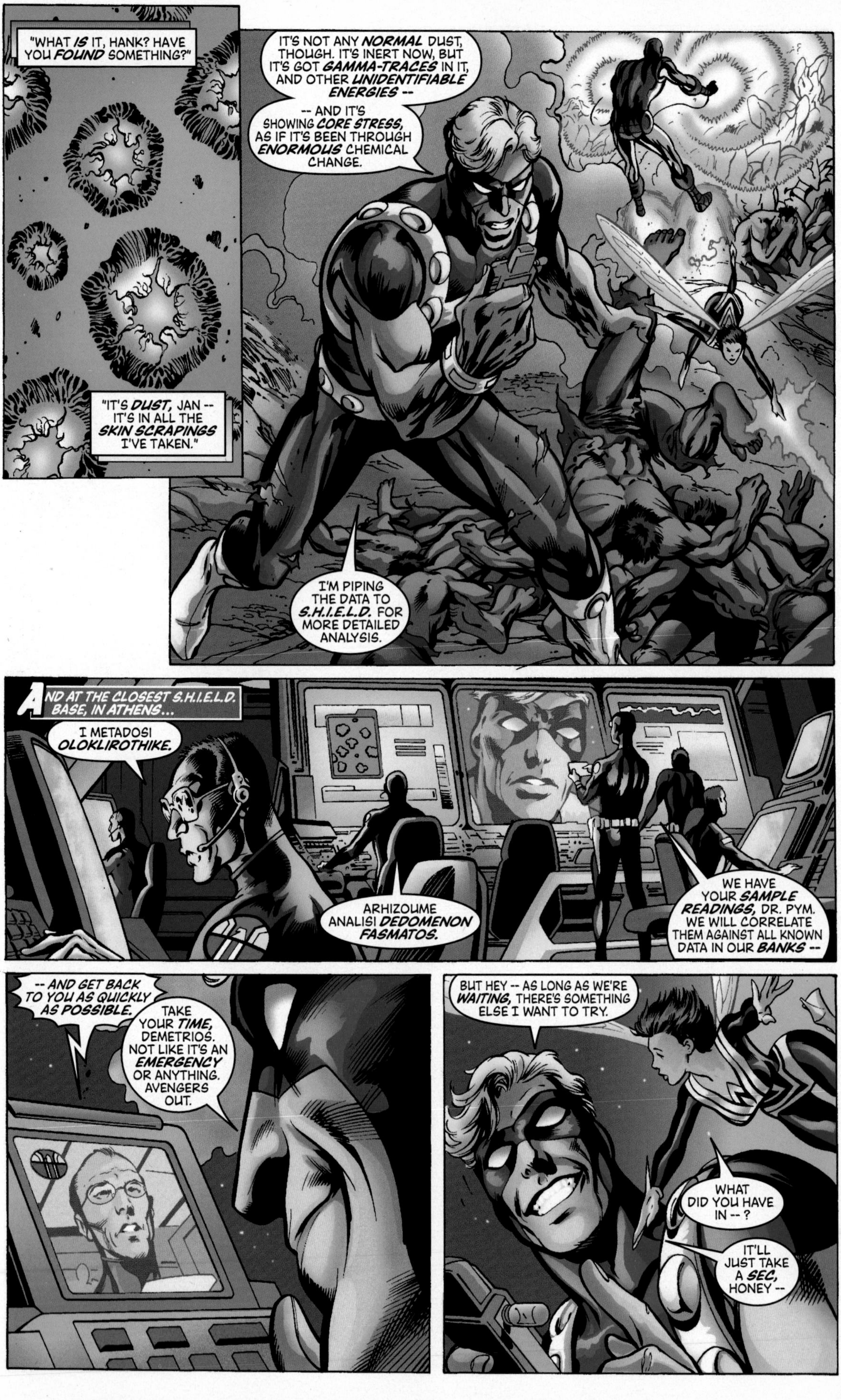
"WHAT IS IT, HANK? HAVE YOU FOUND SOMETHING?"
"IT'S DUST, JAN -- IT'S IN ALL THE SKIN SCRAPINGS I'VE TAKEN."
IT'S NOT ANY NORMAL DUST, THOUGH. IT'S INERT NOW, BUT IT'S GOT GAMMA-TRACES IN IT, AND OTHER UNIDENTIFIABLE ENERGIES --
-- AND IT'S SHOWING CORE STRESS, AS IF IT'S BEEN THROUGH ENORMOUS CHEMICAL CHANGE.
I'M PIPING THE DATA TO S.H.I.E.L.D. FOR MORE DETAILED ANALYSIS.
AND AT THE CLOSEST S.H.I.E.L.D. BASE, IN ATHENS...
I METADOSI OLOKLIROTHIKE.
ARHIZOUME ANALISI DEDOMENON FASMATOS.
WE HAVE YOUR SAMPLE READINGS, DR. PYM. WE WILL CORRELATE THEM AGAINST ALL KNOWN DATA IN OUR BANKS --
-- AND GET BACK TO YOU AS QUICKLY AS POSSIBLE.
TAKE YOUR TIME, DEMETRIOS. NOT LIKE IT'S AN EMERGENCY OR ANYTHING. AVENGERS OUT.
BUT HEY -- AS LONG AS WE'RE WAITING, THERE'S SOMETHING ELSE I WANT TO TRY.
WHAT DID YOU HAVE IN -- ?
IT'LL JUST TAKE A SEC, HONEY --

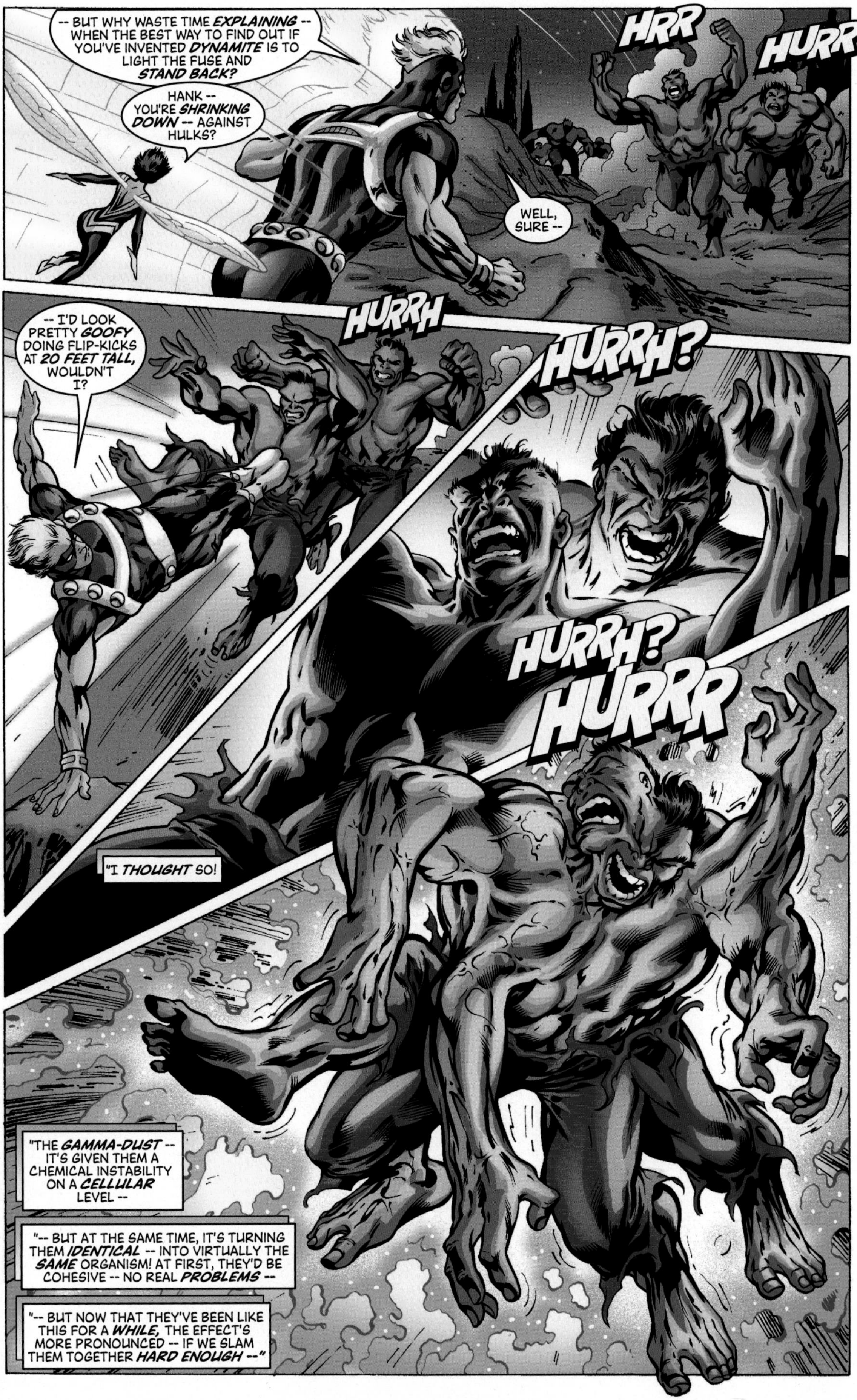
-- BUT WHY WASTE TIME EXPLAINING -- WHEN THE BEST WAY TO FIND OUT IF YOU'VE INVENTED DYNAMITE IS TO LIGHT THE FUSE AND STAND BACK?
HRR
HURR
HANK -- YOU'RE SHRINKING DOWN -- AGAINST HULKS?
WELL, SURE --
-- I'D LOOK PRETTY GOOFY DOING FLIP-KICKS AT 20 FEET TALL, WOULDN'T I?
HURRH
HURRH?
HURRH?
HURRR
"I THOUGHT SO!
"THE GAMMA-DUST -- IT'S GIVEN THEM A CHEMICAL INSTABILITY ON A CELLULAR LEVEL --
"-- BUT AT THE SAME TIME, IT'S TURNING THEM IDENTICAL -- INTO VIRTUALLY THE SAME ORGANISM! AT FIRST, THEY'D BE COHESIVE -- NO REAL PROBLEMS --
"-- BUT NOW THAT THEY'VE BEEN LIKE THIS FOR A WHILE, THE EFFECT'S MORE PRONOUNCED -- IF WE SLAM THEM TOGETHER HARD ENOUGH --"

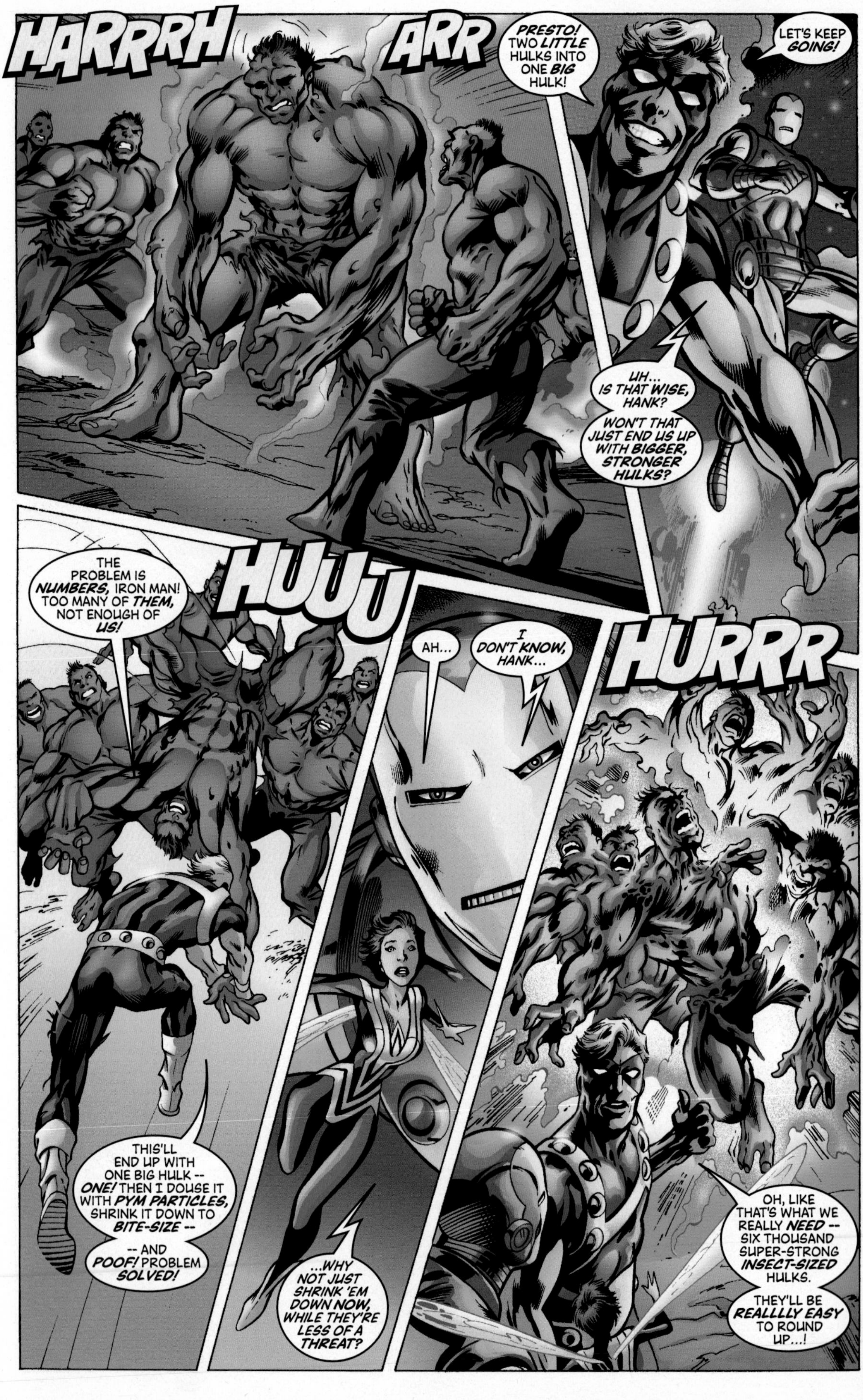
HARRRH
ARR
PRESTO! TWO LITTLE HULKS INTO ONE BIG HULK!
LET'S KEEP GOING!
UH... IS THAT WISE, HANK?
WON'T THAT JUST END US UP WITH BIGGER, STRONGER HULKS?
HUUU
THE PROBLEM IS NUMBERS, IRON MAN! TOO MANY OF THEM, NOT ENOUGH OF US!
THIS'LL END UP WITH ONE BIG HULK -- ONE! THEN I DOUSE IT WITH PYM PARTICLES, SHRINK IT DOWN TO BITE-SIZE --
-- AND POOF! PROBLEM SOLVED!
AH...
I DON'T KNOW, HANK...
...WHY NOT JUST SHRINK 'EM DOWN NOW, WHILE THEY'RE LESS OF A THREAT?
HURRR
OH, LIKE THAT'S WHAT WE REALLY NEED -- SIX THOUSAND SUPER-STRONG INSECT-SIZED HULKS.
THEY'LL BE REALLLLY EASY TO ROUND UP...!

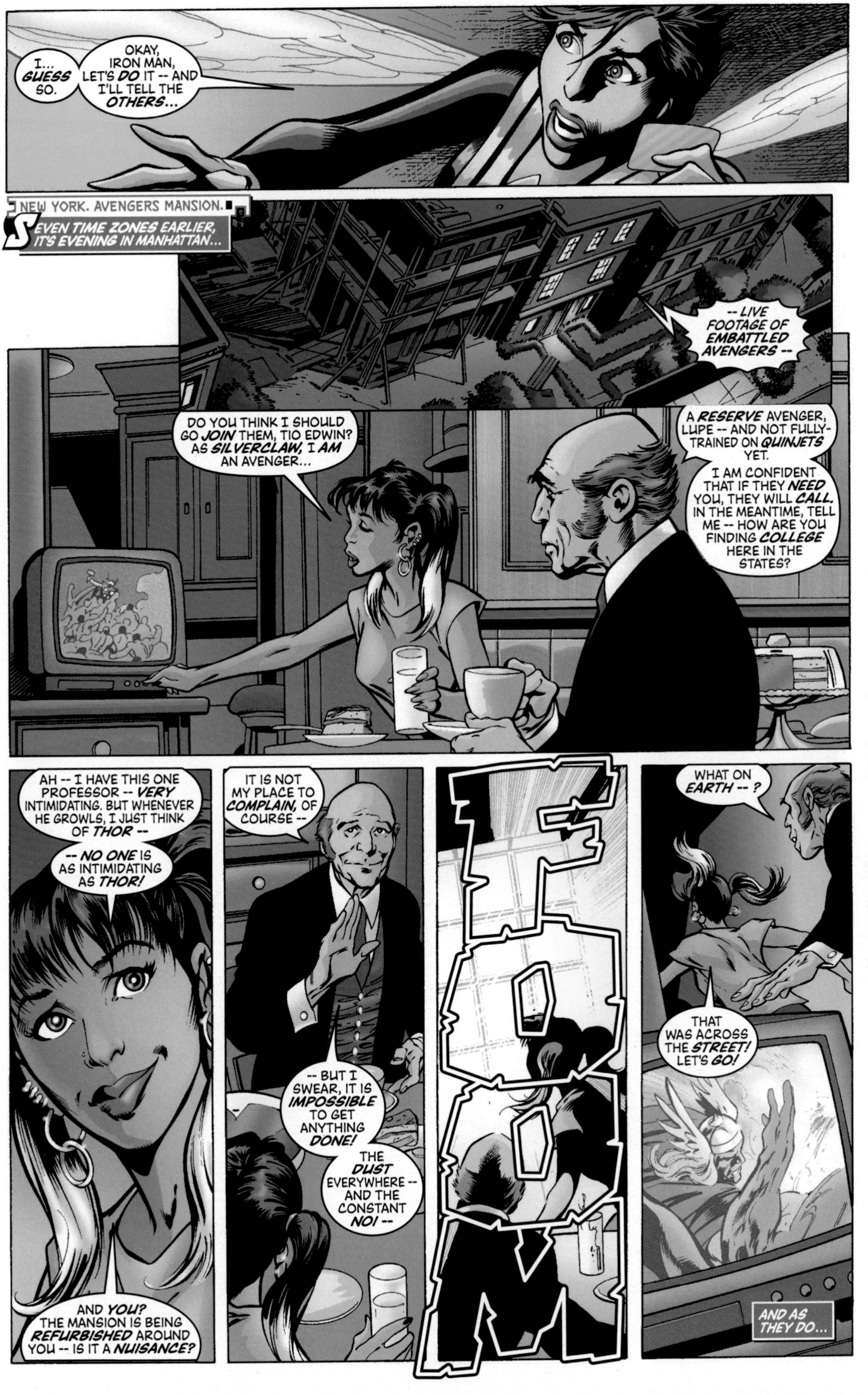

I... GUESS SO.
OKAY, IRON MAN, LET'S DO IT -- AND I'LL TELL THE OTHERS...
NEW YORK. AVENGERS MANSION.
SEVEN TIME ZONES EARLIER, IT'S EVENING IN MANHATTAN...
-- LIVE FOOTAGE OF EMBATTLED AVENGERS --
DO YOU THINK I SHOULD GO JOIN THEM, TIO EDWIN? AS SILVERCLAW, I AM AN AVENGER...
A RESERVE AVENGER, LUPE -- AND NOT FULLY-TRAINED ON QUINJETS YET.
I AM CONFIDENT THAT IF THEY NEED YOU, THEY WILL CALL. IN THE MEANTIME, TELL ME -- HOW ARE YOU FINDING COLLEGE HERE IN THE STATES?
AH -- I HAVE THIS ONE PROFESSOR -- VERY INTIMIDATING. BUT WHENEVER HE GROWLS, I JUST THINK OF THOR --
-- NO ONE IS AS INTIMIDATING AS THOR!
AND YOU? THE MANSION IS BEING REFURBISHED AROUND YOU -- IS IT A NUISANCE?
IT IS NOT MY PLACE TO COMPLAIN, OF COURSE --
-- BUT I SWEAR, IT IS IMPOSSIBLE TO GET ANYTHING DONE!
THE DUST EVERYWHERE -- AND THE CONSTANT NOI --
FOOM
WHAT ON EARTH -- ?
THAT WAS ACROSS THE STREET! LET'S GO!
AND AS THEY DO...

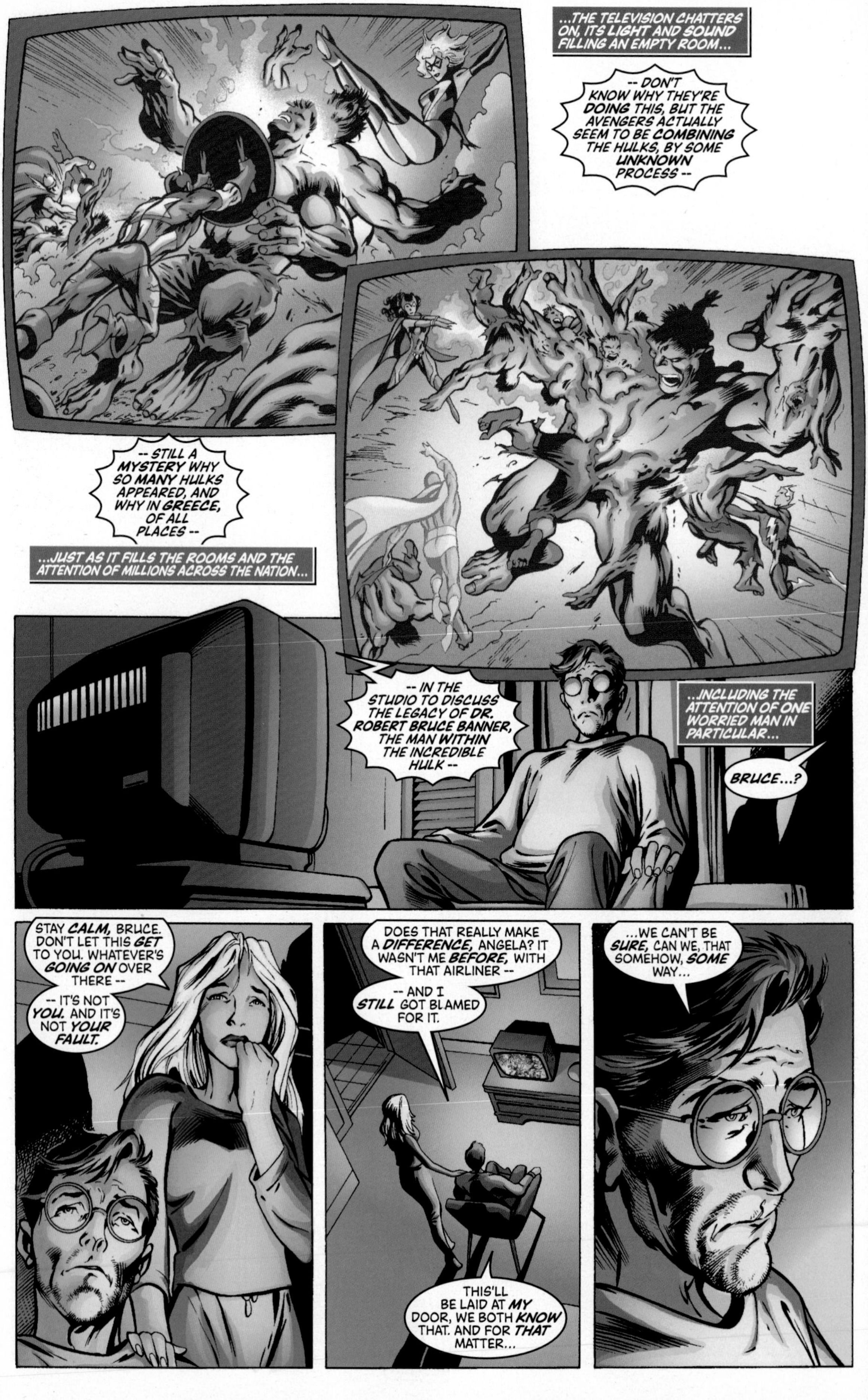
...THE TELEVISION CHATTERS ON, ITS LIGHT AND SOUND FILLING AN EMPTY ROOM...
-- DON'T KNOW WHY THEY'RE DOING THIS, BUT THE AVENGERS ACTUALLY SEEM TO BE COMBINING THE HULKS, BY SOME UNKNOWN PROCESS --
-- STILL A MYSTERY WHY SO MANY HULKS APPEARED, AND WHY IN GREECE, OF ALL PLACES --
...JUST AS IT FILLS THE ROOMS AND THE ATTENTION OF MILLIONS ACROSS THE NATION...
-- IN THE STUDIO TO DISCUSS THE LEGACY OF DR. ROBERT BRUCE BANNER, THE MAN WITHIN THE INCREDIBLE HULK --
...INCLUDING THE ATTENTION OF ONE WORRIED MAN IN PARTICULAR...
BRUCE...?
STAY CALM, BRUCE. DON'T LET THIS GET TO YOU. WHATEVER'S GOING ON OVER THERE --
-- IT'S NOT YOU. AND IT'S NOT YOUR FAULT.
DOES THAT REALLY MAKE A DIFFERENCE, ANGELA? IT WASN'T ME BEFORE, WITH THAT AIRLINER --
-- AND I STILL GOT BLAMED FOR IT.
THIS'LL BE LAID AT MY DOOR, WE BOTH KNOW THAT. AND FOR THAT MATTER...
...WE CAN'T BE SURE, CAN WE, THAT SOMEHOW, SOME WAY...

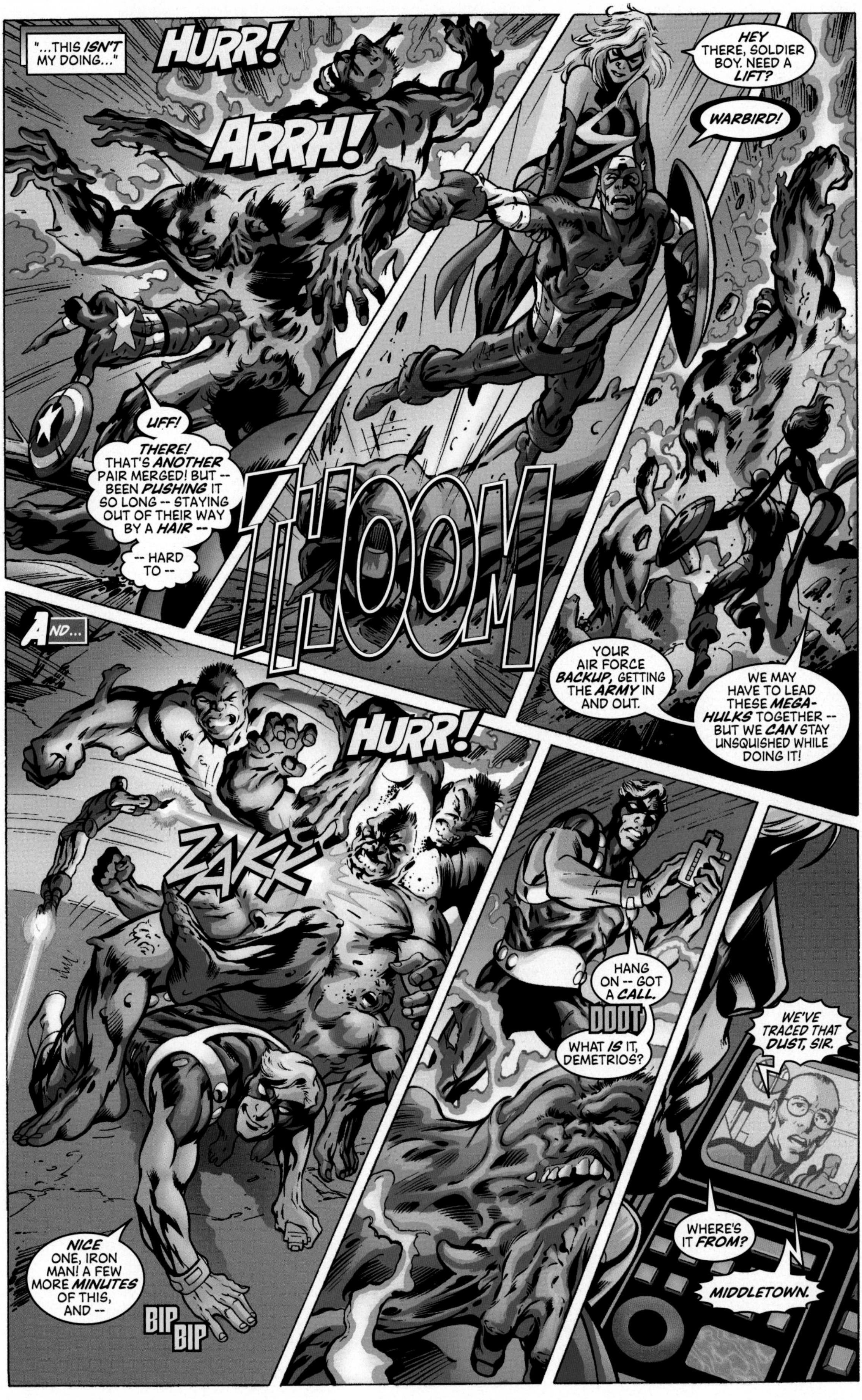
"...THIS ISN'T MY DOING..."
HURR!
ARRH!
UFF!
THERE! THAT'S ANOTHER PAIR MERGED! BUT -- BEEN PUSHING IT SO LONG -- STAYING OUT OF THEIR WAY BY A HAIR --
-- HARD TO --
THOOM
HEY THERE, SOLDIER BOY. NEED A LIFT?
WARBIRD!
YOUR AIR FORCE BACKUP, GETTING THE ARMY IN AND OUT.
WE MAY HAVE TO LEAD THESE MEGA-HULKS TOGETHER -- BUT WE CAN STAY UNSQUISHED WHILE DOING IT!
AND...
HURR!
ZAKK
NICE ONE, IRON MAN! A FEW MORE MINUTES OF THIS, AND --
BIP BIP
HANG ON -- GOT A CALL.
DOOT
WHAT IS IT, DEMETRIOS?
WE'VE TRACED THAT DUST, SIR.
WHERE'S IT FROM?
MIDDLETOWN.

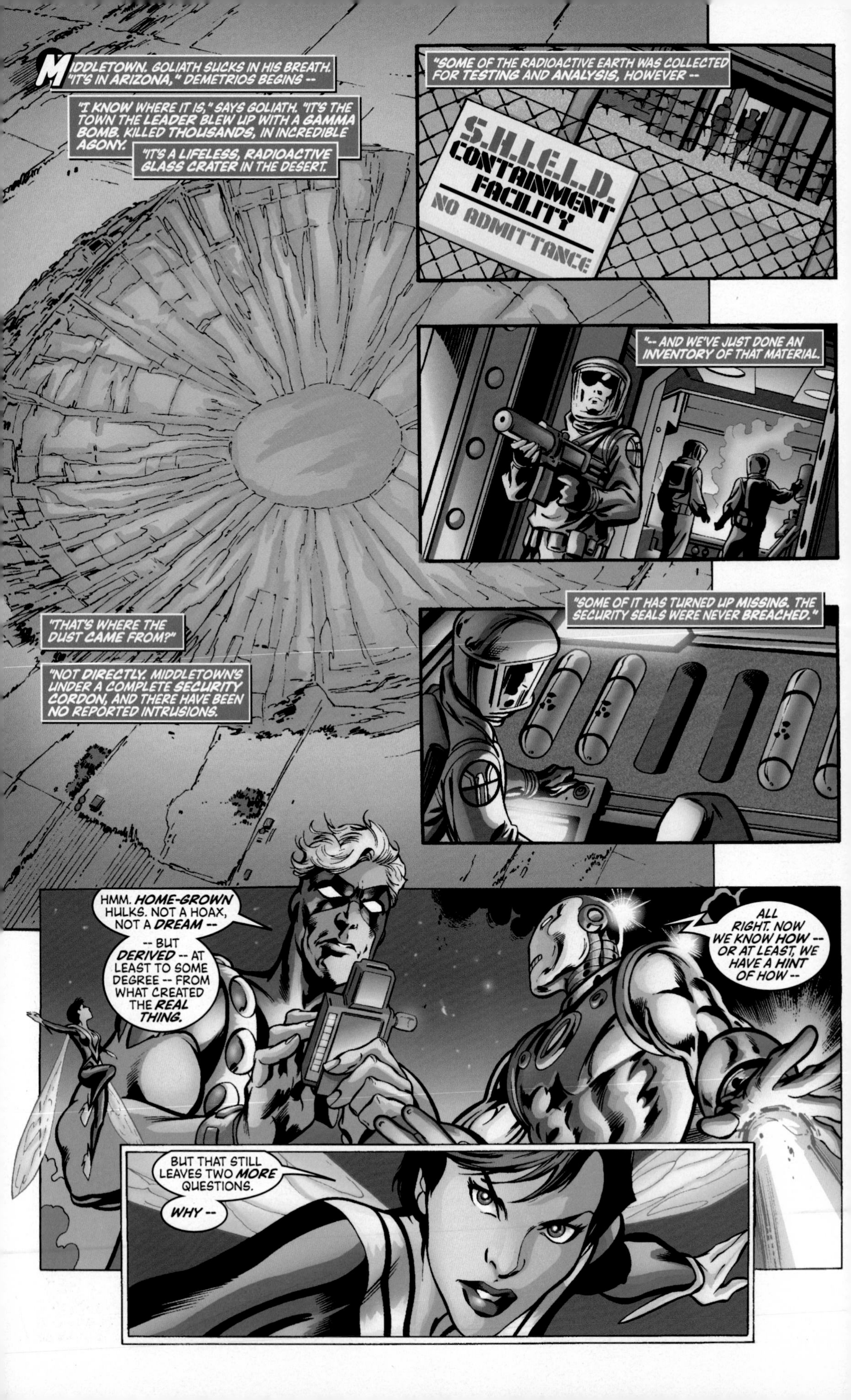
MIDDLETOWN. GOLIATH SUCKS IN HIS BREATH. "IT'S IN ARIZONA," DEMETRIOS BEGINS --
"I KNOW WHERE IT IS," SAYS GOLIATH. "IT'S THE TOWN THE LEADER BLEW UP WITH A GAMMA BOMB. KILLED THOUSANDS, IN INCREDIBLE AGONY.
"IT'S A LIFELESS, RADIOACTIVE GLASS CRATER IN THE DESERT.
"SOME OF THE RADIOACTIVE EARTH WAS COLLECTED FOR TESTING AND ANALYSIS, HOWEVER --
S.H.I.E.L.D. CONTAINMENT FACILITY
NO ADMITTANCE
"-- AND WE'VE JUST DONE AN INVENTORY OF THAT MATERIAL.
"THAT'S WHERE THE DUST CAME FROM?"
"NOT DIRECTLY. MIDDLETOWN'S UNDER A COMPLETE SECURITY CORDON, AND THERE HAVE BEEN NO REPORTED INTRUSIONS.
"SOME OF IT HAS TURNED UP MISSING. THE SECURITY SEALS WERE NEVER BREACHED."
HMM. HOME-GROWN HULKS. NOT A HOAX, NOT A DREAM --
-- BUT DERIVED -- AT LEAST TO SOME DEGREE -- FROM WHAT CREATED THE REAL THING.
ALL RIGHT. NOW WE KNOW HOW -- OR AT LEAST, WE HAVE A HINT OF HOW --
BUT THAT STILL LEAVES TWO MORE QUESTIONS.
WHY --

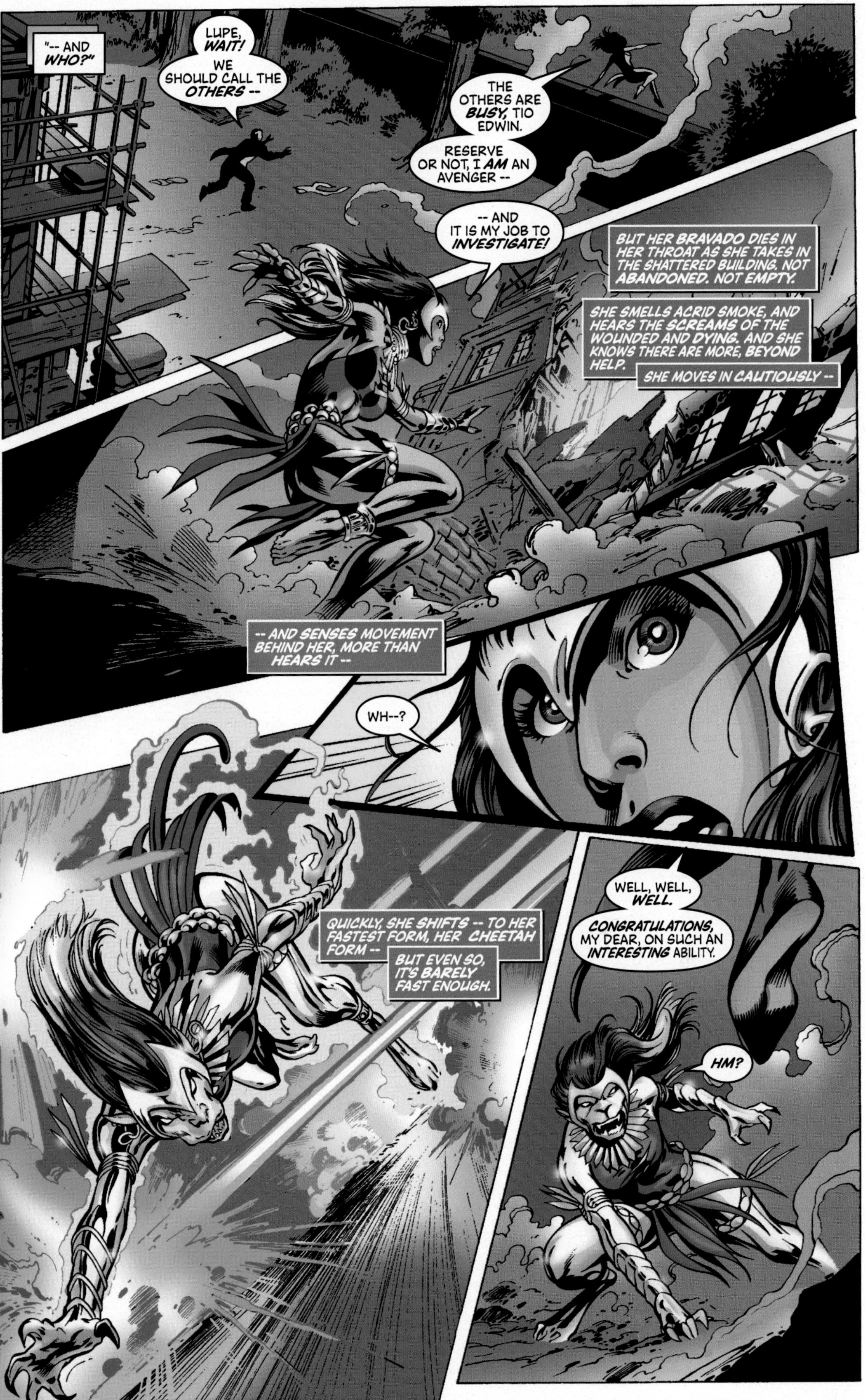

"-- AND WHO?"
LUPE, WAIT! WE SHOULD CALL THE OTHERS --
THE OTHERS ARE BUSY, TIO EDWIN.
RESERVE OR NOT, I AM AN AVENGER --
-- AND IT IS MY JOB TO INVESTIGATE!
BUT HER BRAVADO DIES IN HER THROAT AS SHE TAKES IN THE SHATTERED BUILDING. NOT ABANDONED. NOT EMPTY.
SHE SMELLS ACRID SMOKE, AND HEARS THE SCREAMS OF THE WOUNDED AND DYING. AND SHE KNOWS THERE ARE MORE, BEYOND HELP.
SHE MOVES IN CAUTIOUSLY --
-- AND SENSES MOVEMENT BEHIND HER, MORE THAN HEARS IT --
WH--?
QUICKLY, SHE SHIFTS -- TO HER FASTEST FORM, HER CHEETAH FORM --
BUT EVEN SO, IT'S BARELY FAST ENOUGH.
WELL, WELL, WELL.
CONGRATULATIONS, MY DEAR, ON SUCH AN INTERESTING ABILITY.
HM?

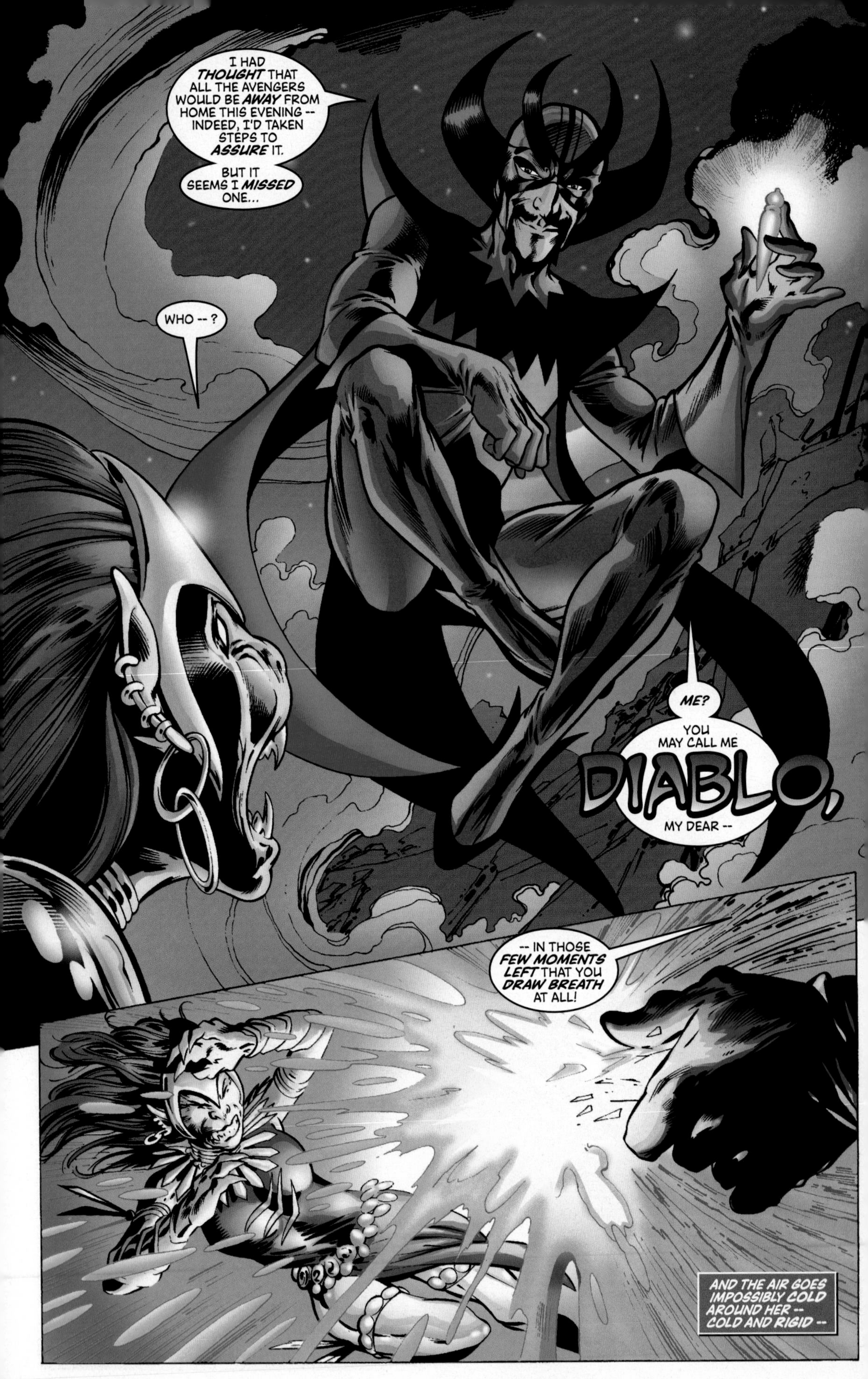
I HAD THOUGHT THAT ALL THE AVENGERS WOULD BE AWAY FROM HOME THIS EVENING -- INDEED, I'D TAKEN STEPS TO ASSURE IT.
BUT IT SEEMS I MISSED ONE...
WHO -- ?
ME?
YOU MAY CALL ME DIABLO, MY DEAR --
-- IN THOSE FEW MOMENTS LEFT THAT YOU DRAW BREATH AT ALL!
AND THE AIR GOES IMPOSSIBLY COLD AROUND HER -- COLD AND RIGID --

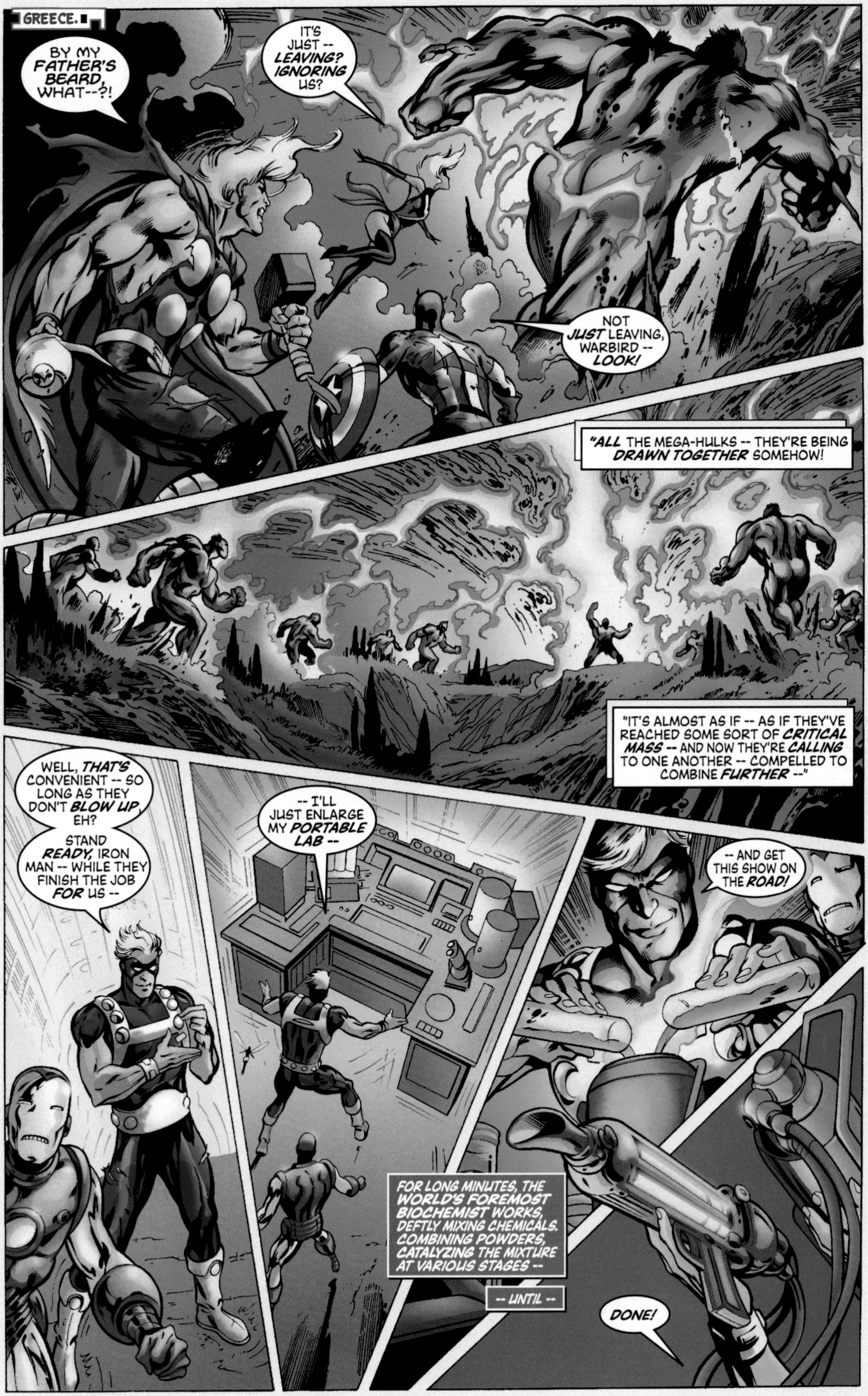
GREECE.
BY MY FATHER'S BEARD, WHAT--?!
IT'S JUST -- LEAVING? IGNORING US?
NOT JUST LEAVING, WARBIRD -- LOOK!
"ALL THE MEGA-HULKS -- THEY'RE BEING DRAWN TOGETHER SOMEHOW!
"IT'S ALMOST AS IF -- AS IF THEY'VE REACHED SOME SORT OF CRITICAL MASS -- AND NOW THEY'RE CALLING TO ONE ANOTHER -- COMPELLED TO COMBINE FURTHER --"
WELL, THAT'S CONVENIENT -- SO LONG AS THEY DON'T BLOW UP, EH?
STAND READY, IRON MAN -- WHILE THEY FINISH THE JOB FOR US --
-- I'LL JUST ENLARGE MY PORTABLE LAB --
-- AND GET THIS SHOW ON THE ROAD!
FOR LONG MINUTES, THE WORLD'S FOREMOST BIOCHEMIST WORKS, DEFTLY MIXING CHEMICALS. COMBINING POWDERS, CATALYZING THE MIXTURE AT VARIOUS STAGES --
-- UNTIL --
DONE!

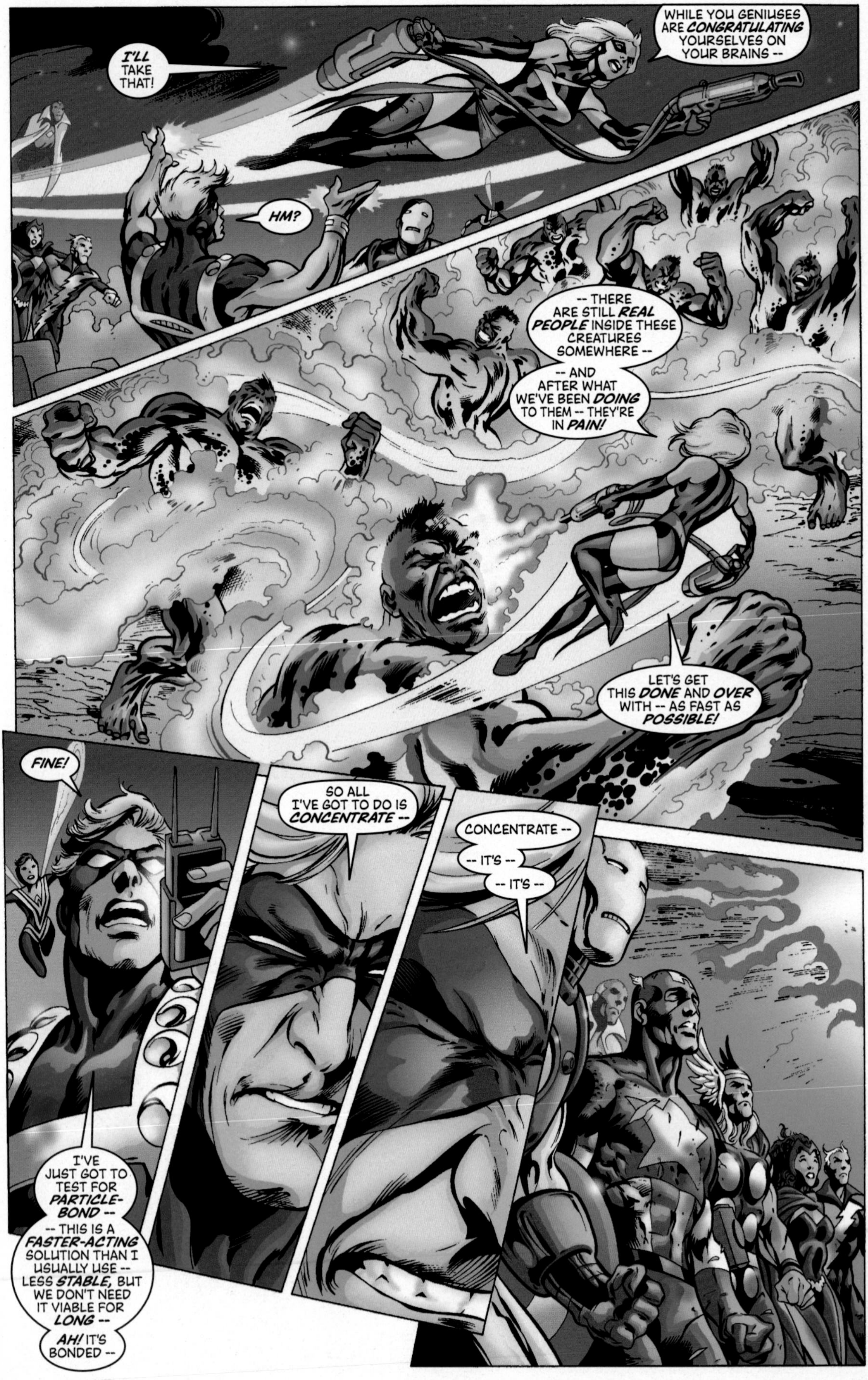
WHILE YOU GENIUSES ARE *CONGRATULATING* YOURSELVES ON YOUR BRAINS --
I'LL TAKE THAT!
HM?
-- THERE ARE STILL *REAL PEOPLE* INSIDE THESE CREATURES SOMEWHERE --
-- AND AFTER WHAT WE'VE BEEN *DOING* TO THEM -- THEY'RE IN *PAIN!*
LET'S GET THIS *DONE* AND *OVER* WITH -- AS FAST AS *POSSIBLE!*
FINE!
I'VE JUST GOT TO TEST FOR *PARTICLE-BOND* --
-- THIS IS A *FASTER-ACTING* SOLUTION THAN I USUALLY USE -- LESS *STABLE*, BUT WE DON'T NEED IT VIABLE FOR *LONG* --
AH! IT'S BONDED --
SO ALL I'VE GOT TO DO IS *CONCENTRATE* --
CONCENTRATE --
-- IT'S --
-- IT'S --

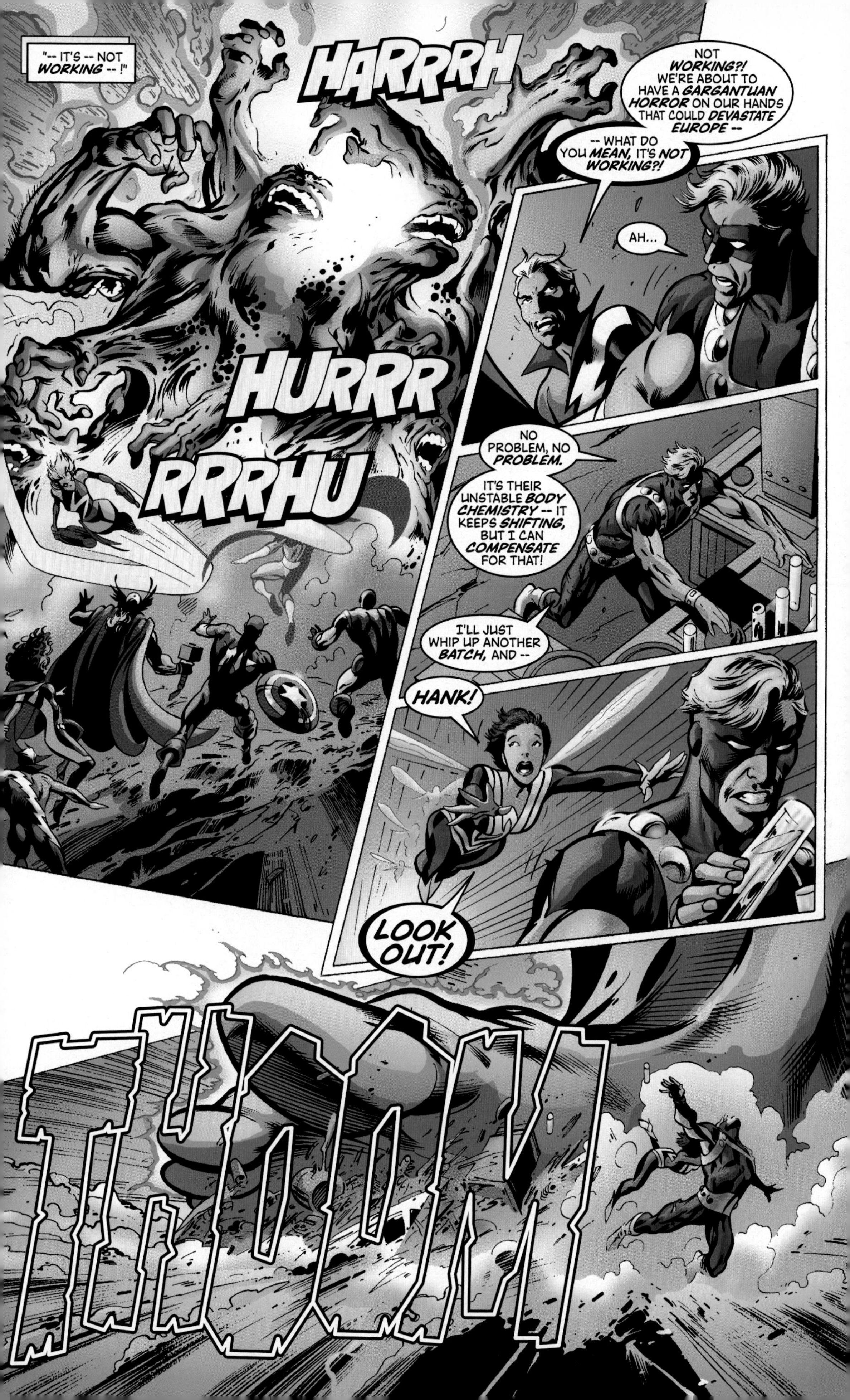
"-- IT'S -- NOT WORKING -- !"
HARRRH
NOT WORKING?! WE'RE ABOUT TO HAVE A GARGANTUAN HORROR ON OUR HANDS THAT COULD DEVASTATE EUROPE --
-- WHAT DO YOU MEAN, IT'S NOT WORKING?!
AH...
HURRR
RRRHU
NO PROBLEM, NO PROBLEM.
IT'S THEIR UNSTABLE BODY CHEMISTRY -- IT KEEPS SHIFTING, BUT I CAN COMPENSATE FOR THAT!
I'LL JUST WHIP UP ANOTHER BATCH, AND --
HANK!
LOOK OUT!
THOOOM

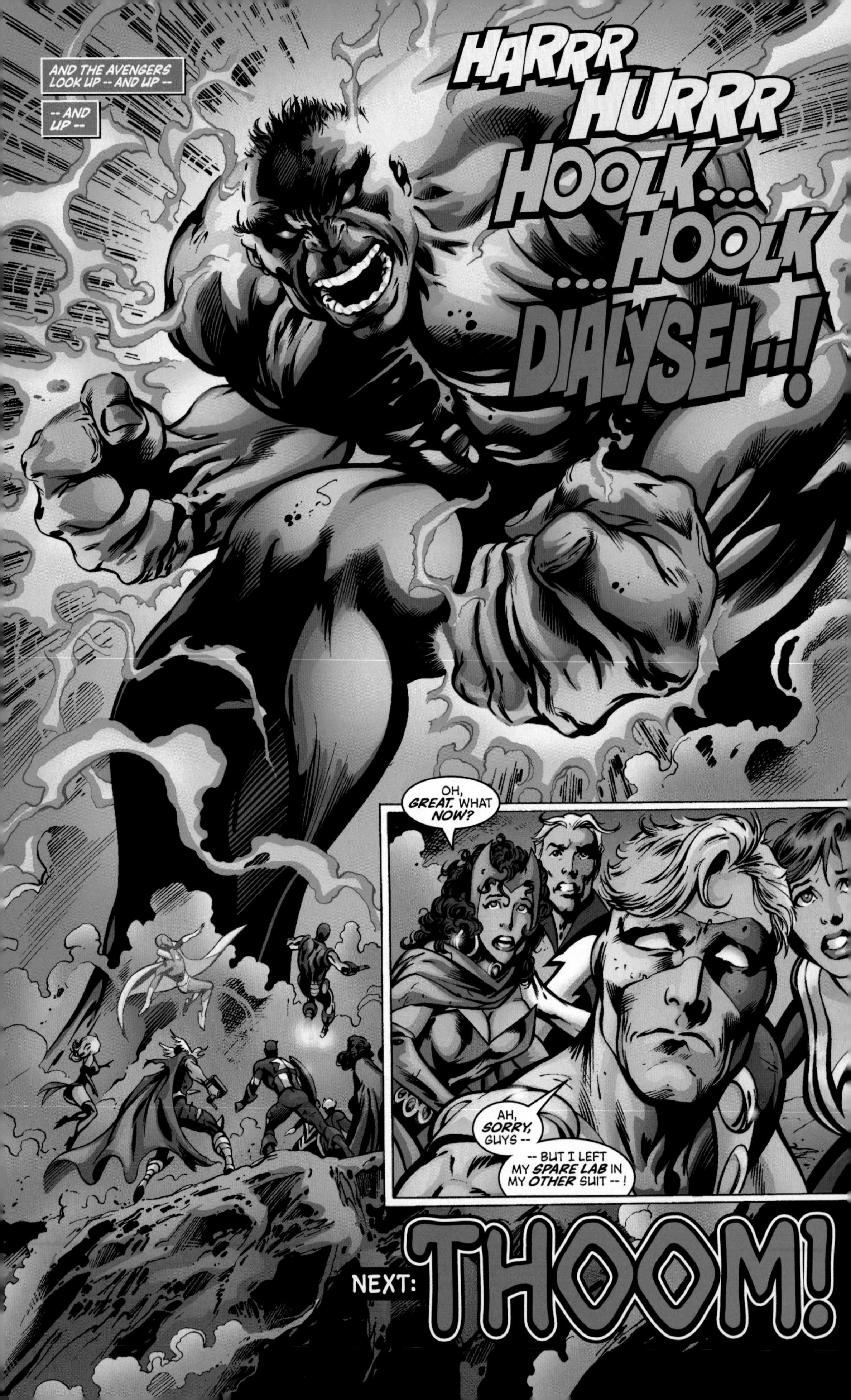
AND THE AVENGERS LOOK UP -- AND UP --
-- AND UP --
HARRR HURRR HOOLK... HOOLK ...DIALYSEI..!
OH, GREAT. WHAT NOW?
AH, SORRY, GUYS --
-- BUT I LEFT MY SPARE LAB IN MY OTHER SUIT -- !
NEXT: THOOM!

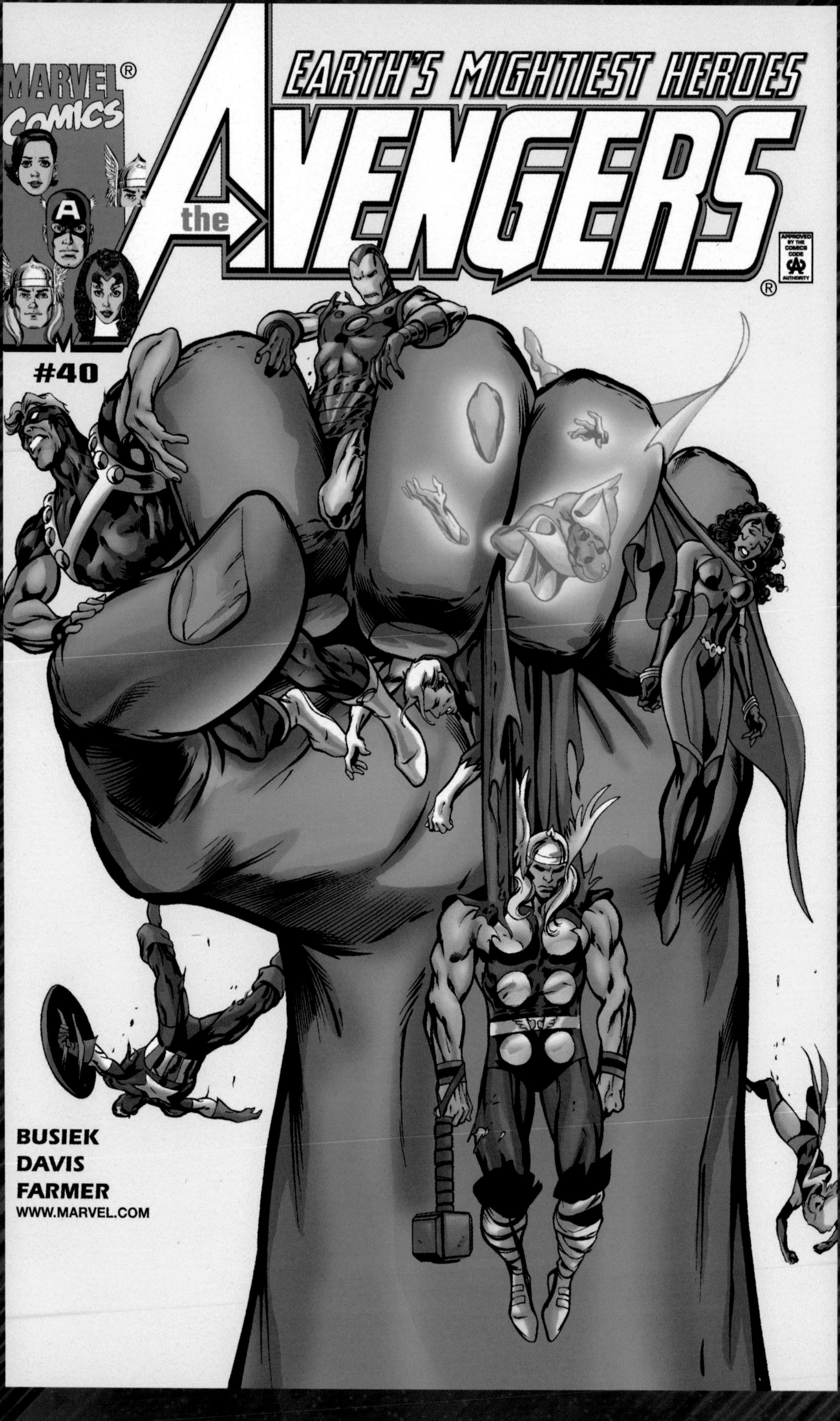
MARVEL COMICS
EARTH'S MIGHTIEST HEROES
the AVENGERS
APPROVED BY THE COMICS CODE AUTHORITY
#40
BUSIEK
DAVIS
FARMER
WWW.MARVEL.COM

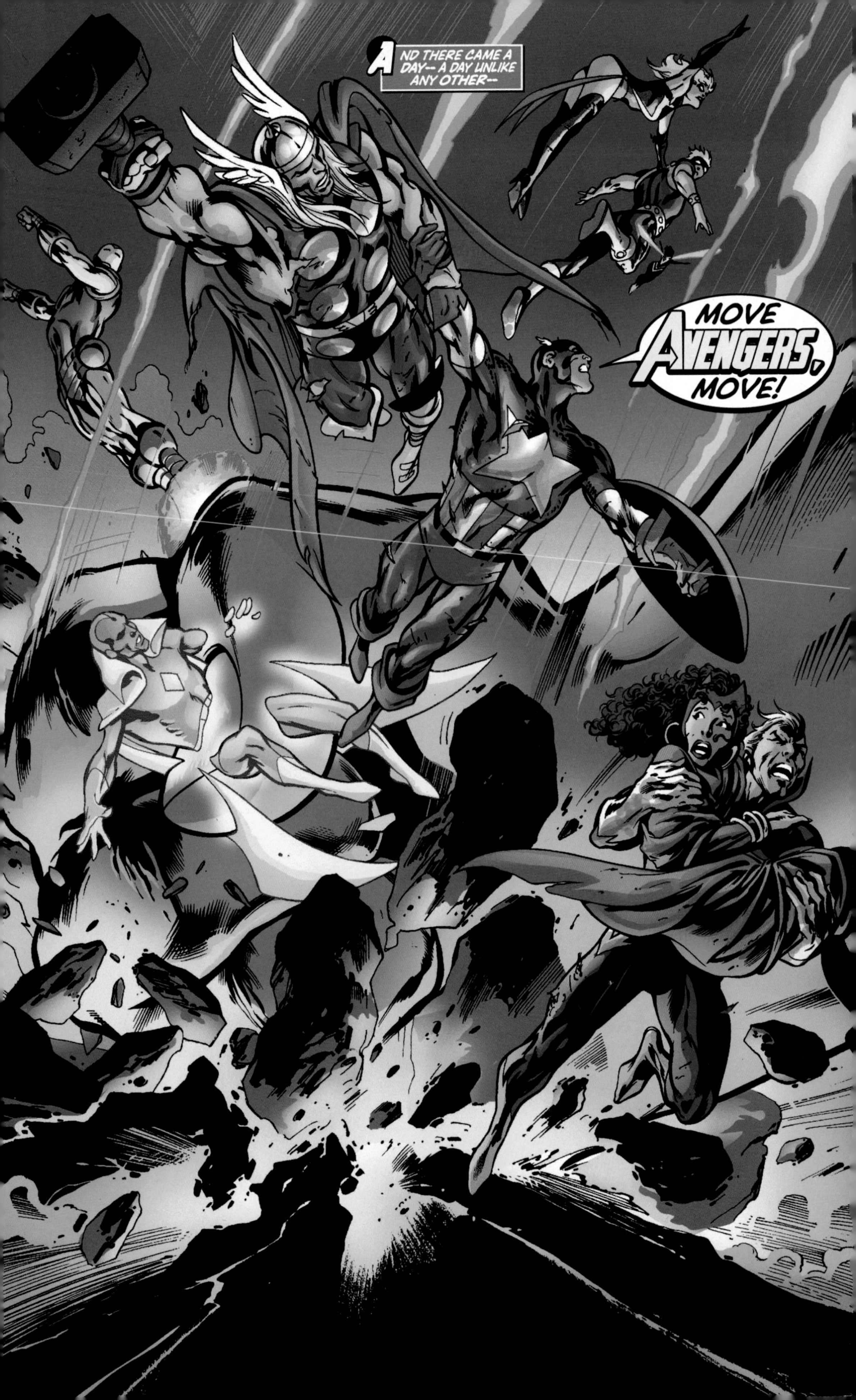
AND THERE CAME A DAY-- A DAY UNLIKE ANY OTHER--
MOVE AVENGERS, MOVE!

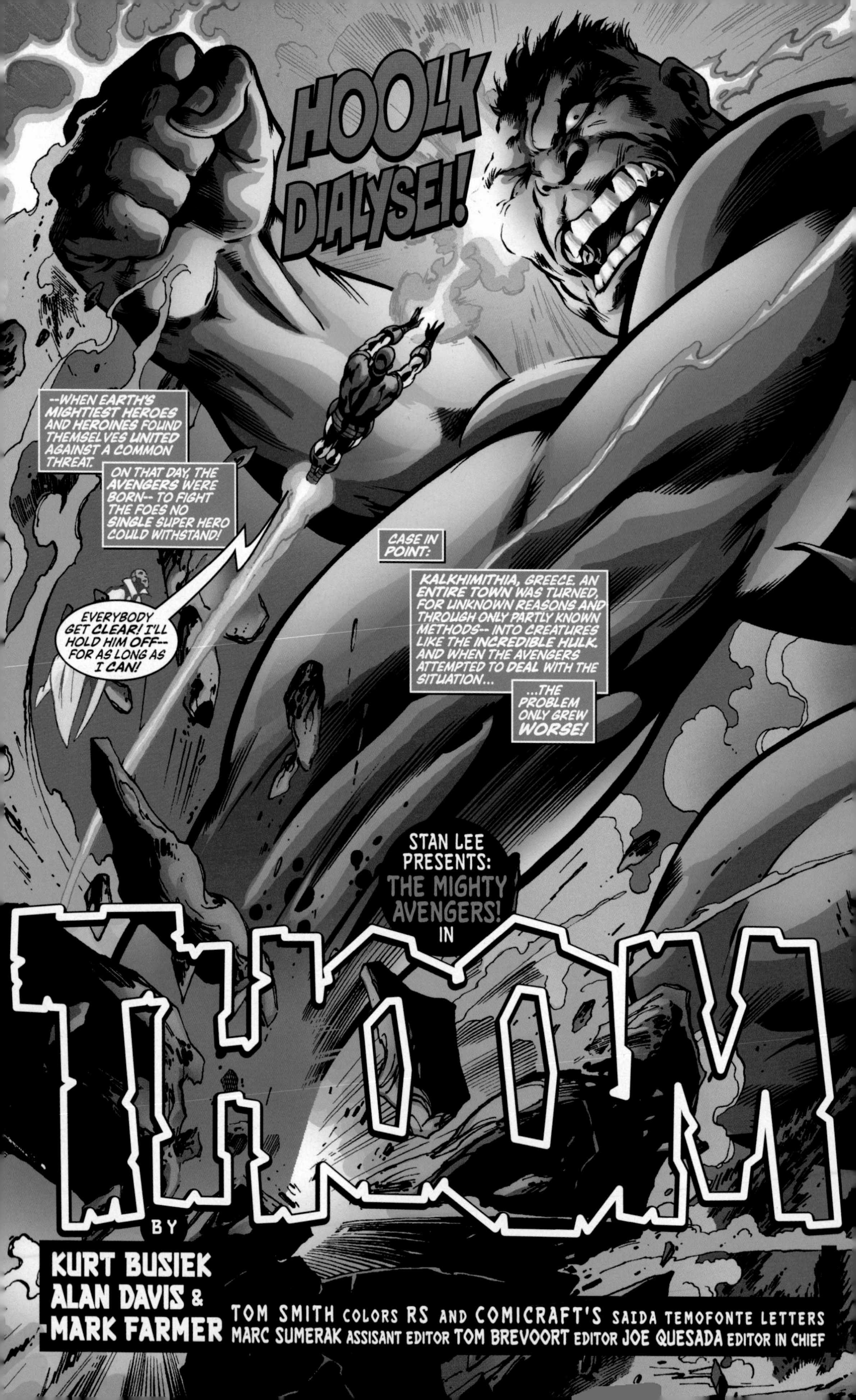
HOOLK DIALYSEI!
--WHEN EARTH'S MIGHTIEST HEROES AND HEROINES FOUND THEMSELVES UNITED AGAINST A COMMON THREAT.
ON THAT DAY, THE AVENGERS WERE BORN-- TO FIGHT THE FOES NO SINGLE SUPER HERO COULD WITHSTAND!
EVERYBODY GET CLEAR! I'LL HOLD HIM OFF-- FOR AS LONG AS I CAN!
CASE IN POINT:
KALKHIMITHIA, GREECE. AN ENTIRE TOWN WAS TURNED, FOR UNKNOWN REASONS AND THROUGH ONLY PARTLY KNOWN METHODS-- INTO CREATURES LIKE THE INCREDIBLE HULK. AND WHEN THE AVENGERS ATTEMPTED TO DEAL WITH THE SITUATION...
...THE PROBLEM ONLY GREW WORSE!
STAN LEE PRESENTS: THE MIGHTY AVENGERS! IN
THOOM
BY
KURT BUSIEK
ALAN DAVIS &
MARK FARMER
TOM SMITH COLORS RS AND COMICRAFT'S SAIDA TEMOFONTE LETTERS
MARC SUMERAK ASSISANT EDITOR TOM BREVOORT EDITOR JOE QUESADA EDITOR IN CHIEF

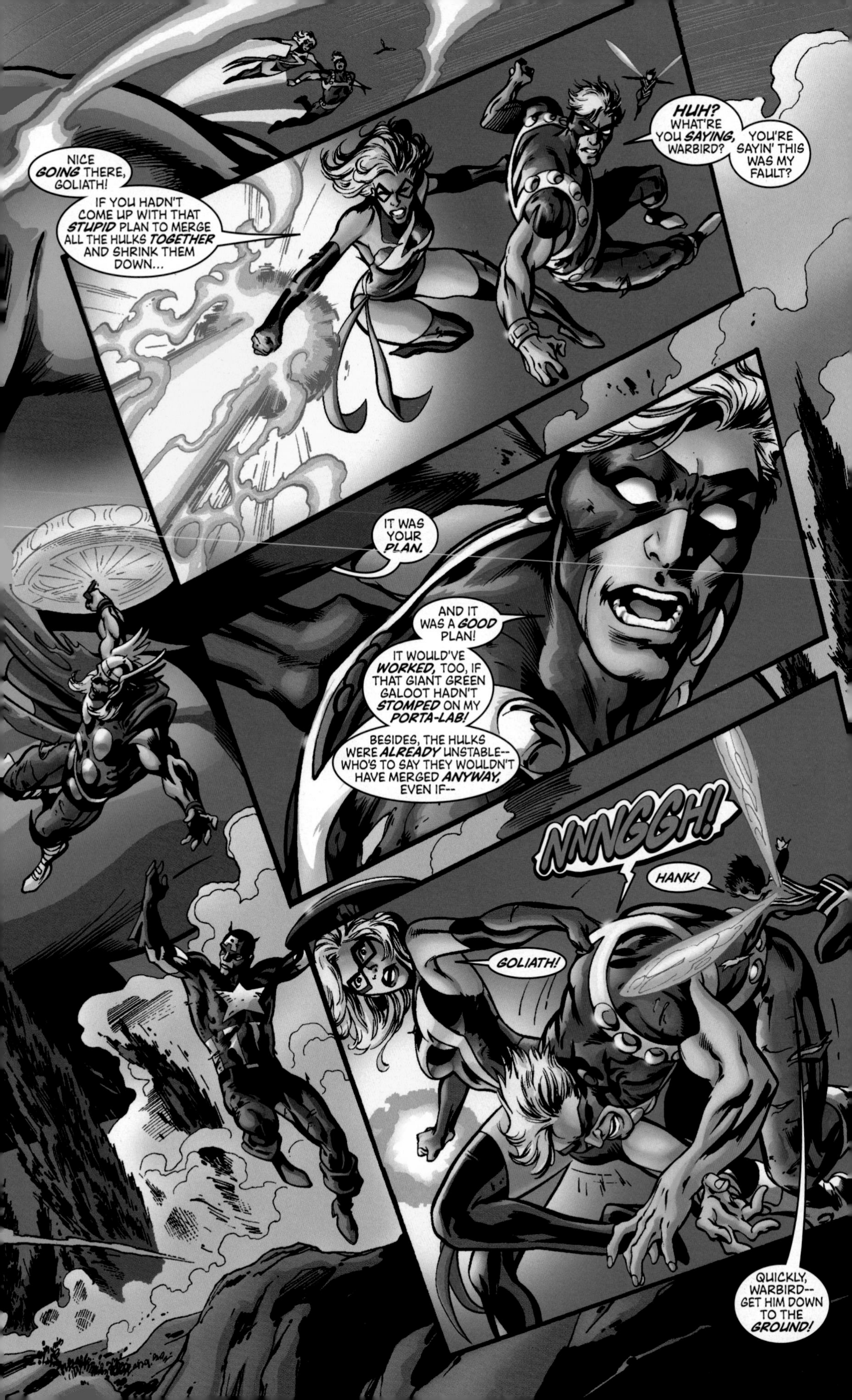
NICE GOING THERE, GOLIATH!
IF YOU HADN'T COME UP WITH THAT STUPID PLAN TO MERGE ALL THE HULKS TOGETHER AND SHRINK THEM DOWN...
HUH? WHAT'RE YOU SAYING, WARBIRD?
YOU'RE SAYIN' THIS WAS MY FAULT?
IT WAS YOUR PLAN.
AND IT WAS A GOOD PLAN!
IT WOULD'VE WORKED, TOO, IF THAT GIANT GREEN GALOOT HADN'T STOMPED ON MY PORTA-LAB!
BESIDES, THE HULKS WERE ALREADY UNSTABLE-- WHO'S TO SAY THEY WOULDN'T HAVE MERGED ANYWAY, EVEN IF--
NNNGGH!
HANK!
GOLIATH!
QUICKLY, WARBIRD-- GET HIM DOWN TO THE GROUND!

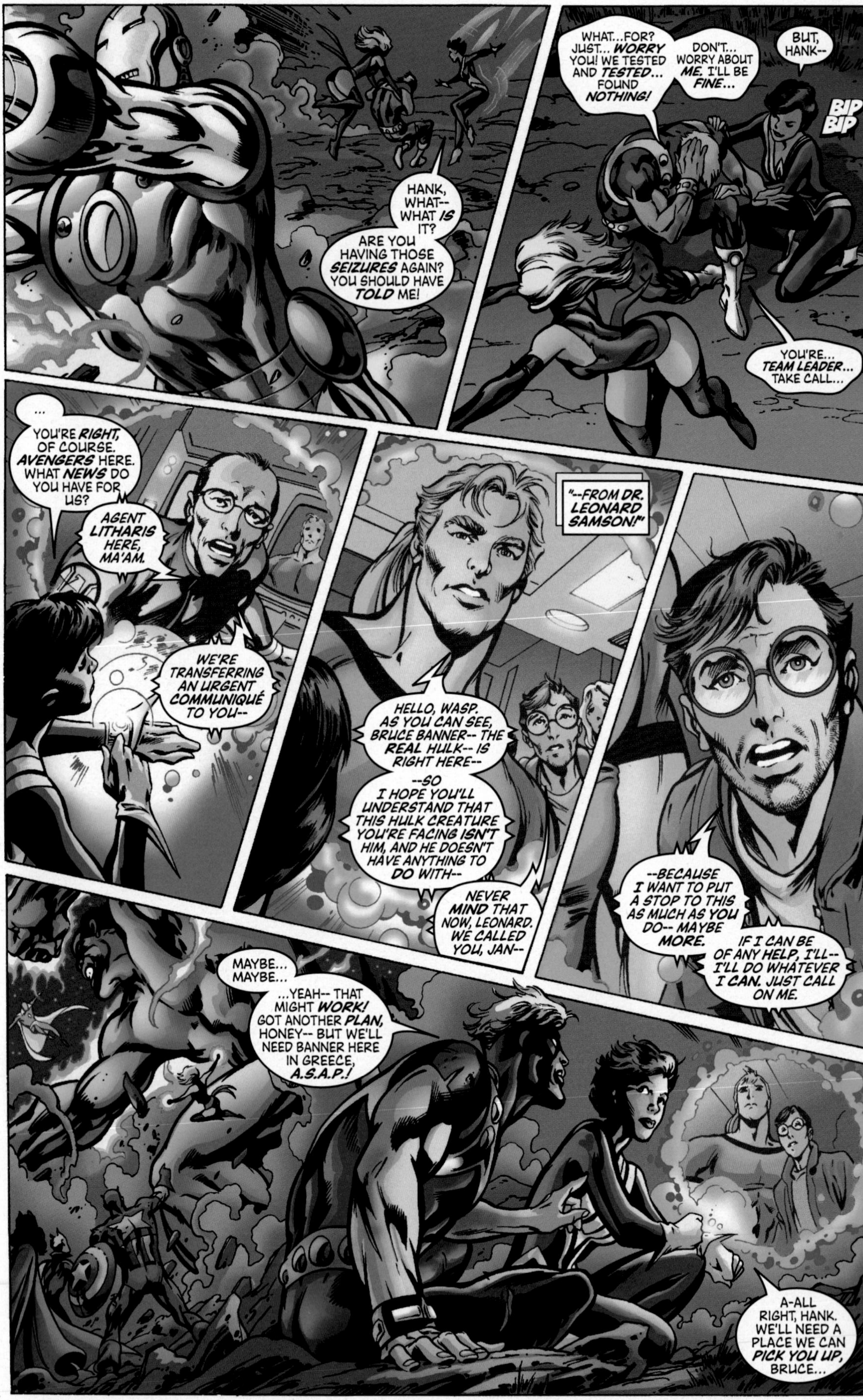
HANK, WHAT-- WHAT IS IT?
ARE YOU HAVING THOSE SEIZURES AGAIN? YOU SHOULD HAVE TOLD ME!
WHAT...FOR? JUST... WORRY YOU! WE TESTED AND TESTED... FOUND NOTHING!
DON'T... WORRY ABOUT ME. I'LL BE FINE...
BUT, HANK--
BIP BIP
YOU'RE... TEAM LEADER... TAKE CALL...
... YOU'RE RIGHT, OF COURSE. AVENGERS HERE. WHAT NEWS DO YOU HAVE FOR US?
AGENT LITHARIS HERE, MA'AM.
WE'RE TRANSFERRING AN URGENT COMMUNIQUÉ TO YOU--
"--FROM DR. LEONARD SAMSON!"
HELLO, WASP. AS YOU CAN SEE, BRUCE BANNER-- THE REAL HULK-- IS RIGHT HERE--
--SO I HOPE YOU'LL UNDERSTAND THAT THIS HULK CREATURE YOU'RE FACING ISN'T HIM, AND HE DOESN'T HAVE ANYTHING TO DO WITH--
NEVER MIND THAT NOW, LEONARD. WE CALLED YOU, JAN--
--BECAUSE I WANT TO PUT A STOP TO THIS AS MUCH AS YOU DO-- MAYBE MORE.
IF I CAN BE OF ANY HELP, I'LL-- I'LL DO WHATEVER I CAN. JUST CALL ON ME.
MAYBE... MAYBE...
...YEAH-- THAT MIGHT WORK! GOT ANOTHER PLAN, HONEY-- BUT WE'LL NEED BANNER HERE IN GREECE, A.S.A.P.!
A-ALL RIGHT, HANK. WE'LL NEED A PLACE WE CAN PICK YOU UP, BRUCE...

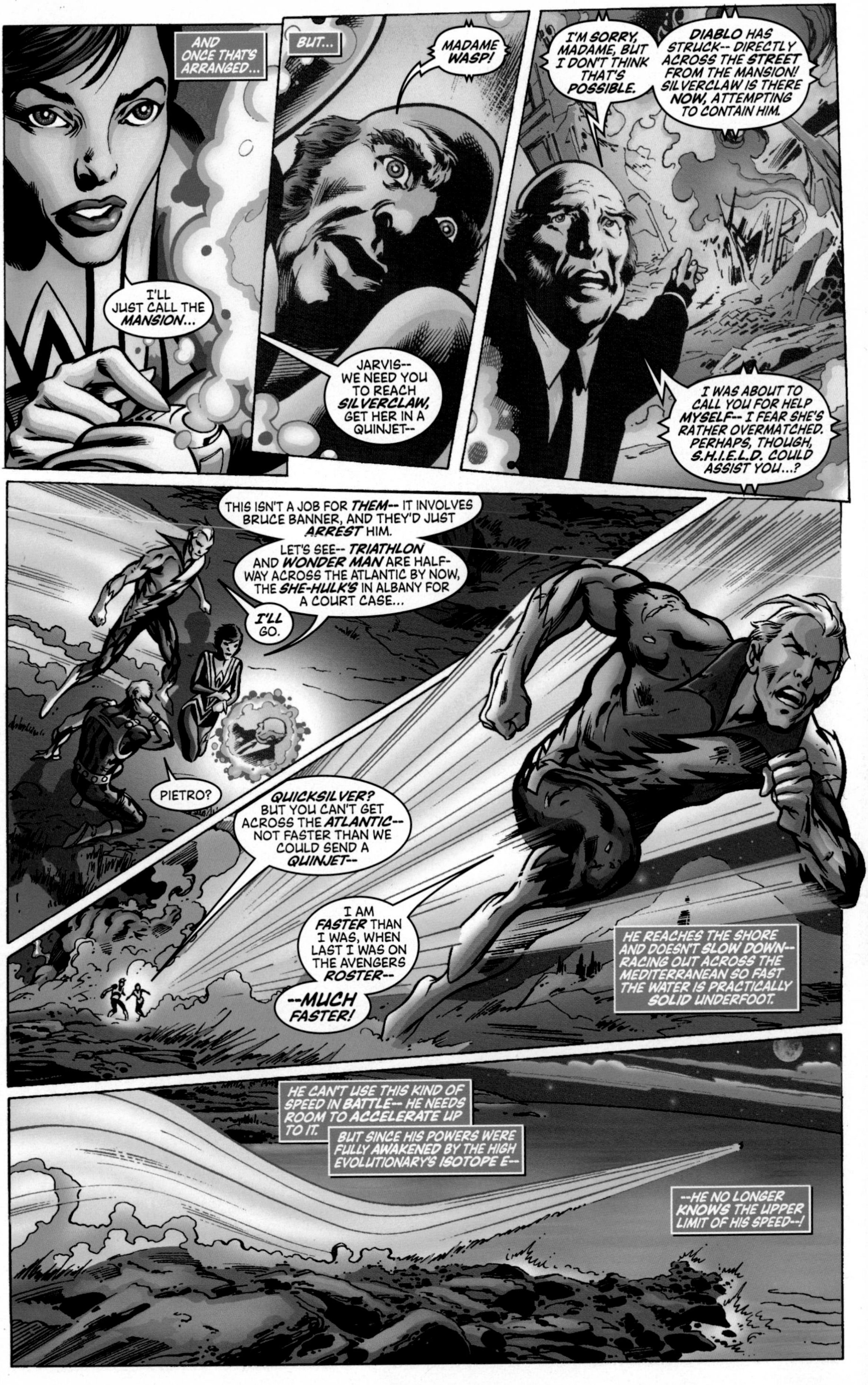
AND ONCE THAT'S ARRANGED...
I'LL JUST CALL THE MANSION...
BUT...
MADAME WASP!
JARVIS-- WE NEED YOU TO REACH SILVERCLAW, GET HER IN A QUINJET--
I'M SORRY, MADAME, BUT I DON'T THINK THAT'S POSSIBLE.
DIABLO HAS STRUCK-- DIRECTLY ACROSS THE STREET FROM THE MANSION! SILVERCLAW IS THERE NOW, ATTEMPTING TO CONTAIN HIM.
I WAS ABOUT TO CALL YOU FOR HELP MYSELF-- I FEAR SHE'S RATHER OVERMATCHED. PERHAPS, THOUGH, S.H.I.E.L.D. COULD ASSIST YOU...?
THIS ISN'T A JOB FOR THEM-- IT INVOLVES BRUCE BANNER, AND THEY'D JUST ARREST HIM.
LET'S SEE-- TRIATHLON AND WONDER MAN ARE HALF-WAY ACROSS THE ATLANTIC BY NOW, THE SHE-HULK'S IN ALBANY FOR A COURT CASE...
I'LL GO.
PIETRO?
QUICKSILVER? BUT YOU CAN'T GET ACROSS THE ATLANTIC-- NOT FASTER THAN WE COULD SEND A QUINJET--
I AM FASTER THAN I WAS, WHEN LAST I WAS ON THE AVENGERS ROSTER--
--MUCH FASTER!
HE REACHES THE SHORE AND DOESN'T SLOW DOWN-- RACING OUT ACROSS THE MEDITERRANEAN SO FAST THE WATER IS PRACTICALLY SOLID UNDERFOOT.
HE CAN'T USE THIS KIND OF SPEED IN BATTLE-- HE NEEDS ROOM TO ACCELERATE UP TO IT.
BUT SINCE HIS POWERS WERE FULLY AWAKENED BY THE HIGH EVOLUTIONARY'S ISOTOPE E--
--HE NO LONGER KNOWS THE UPPER LIMIT OF HIS SPEED--!

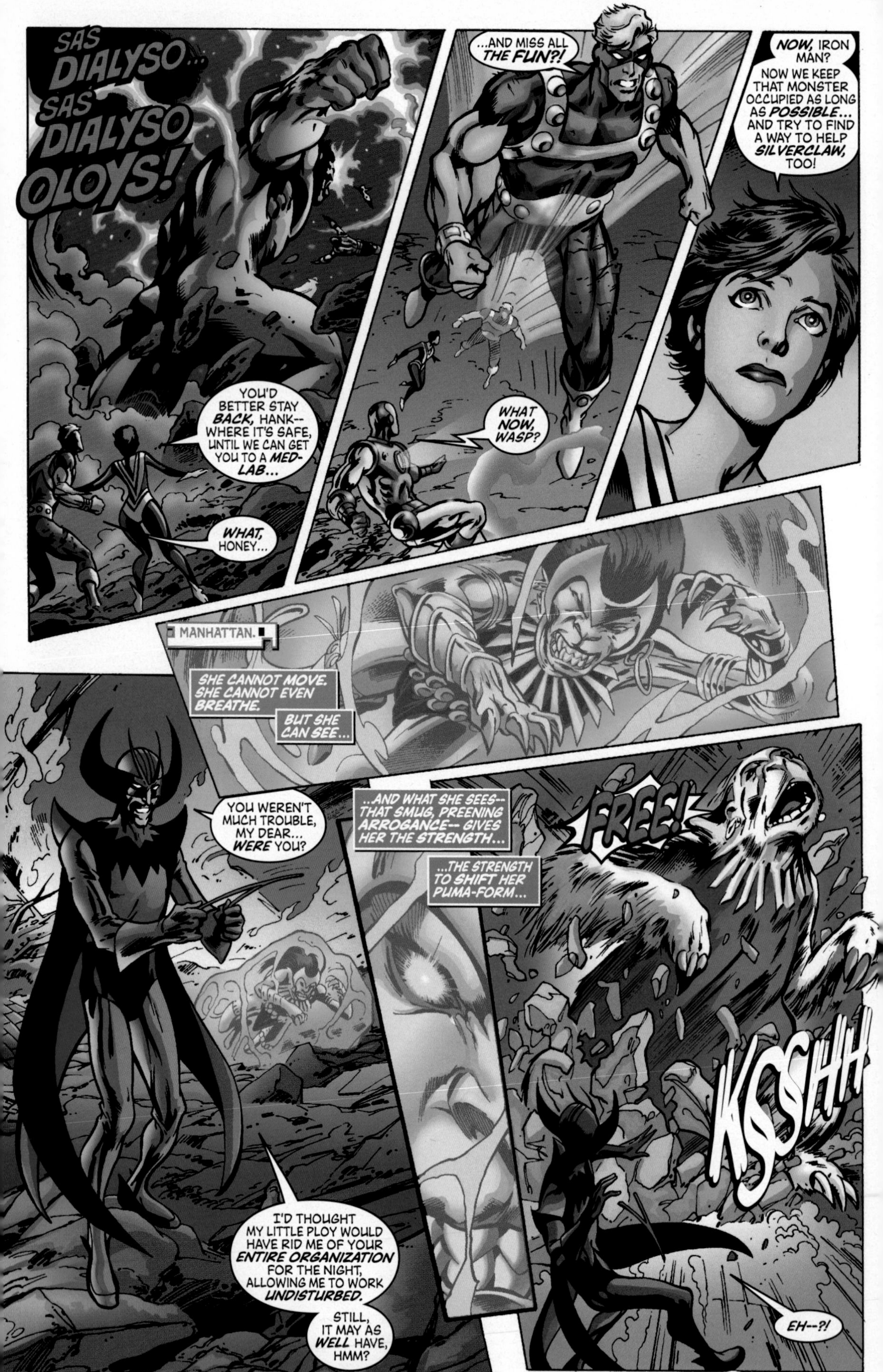

SAS DIALYSO... SAS DIALYSO OLOYS!
YOU'D BETTER STAY BACK, HANK-- WHERE IT'S SAFE, UNTIL WE CAN GET YOU TO A MED-LAB...
WHAT, HONEY...
...AND MISS ALL THE FUN?!
WHAT NOW, WASP?
NOW, IRON MAN? NOW WE KEEP THAT MONSTER OCCUPIED AS LONG AS POSSIBLE... AND TRY TO FIND A WAY TO HELP SILVERCLAW, TOO!
MANHATTAN.
SHE CANNOT MOVE. SHE CANNOT EVEN BREATHE.
BUT SHE CAN SEE...
YOU WEREN'T MUCH TROUBLE, MY DEAR... WERE YOU?
I'D THOUGHT MY LITTLE PLOY WOULD HAVE RID ME OF YOUR ENTIRE ORGANIZATION FOR THE NIGHT, ALLOWING ME TO WORK UNDISTURBED.
STILL, IT MAY AS WELL HAVE, HMM?
...AND WHAT SHE SEES-- THAT SMUG, PREENING ARROGANCE-- GIVES HER THE STRENGTH...
...THE STRENGTH TO SHIFT HER PUMA-FORM...
FREE!
KSSHH
EH--?!

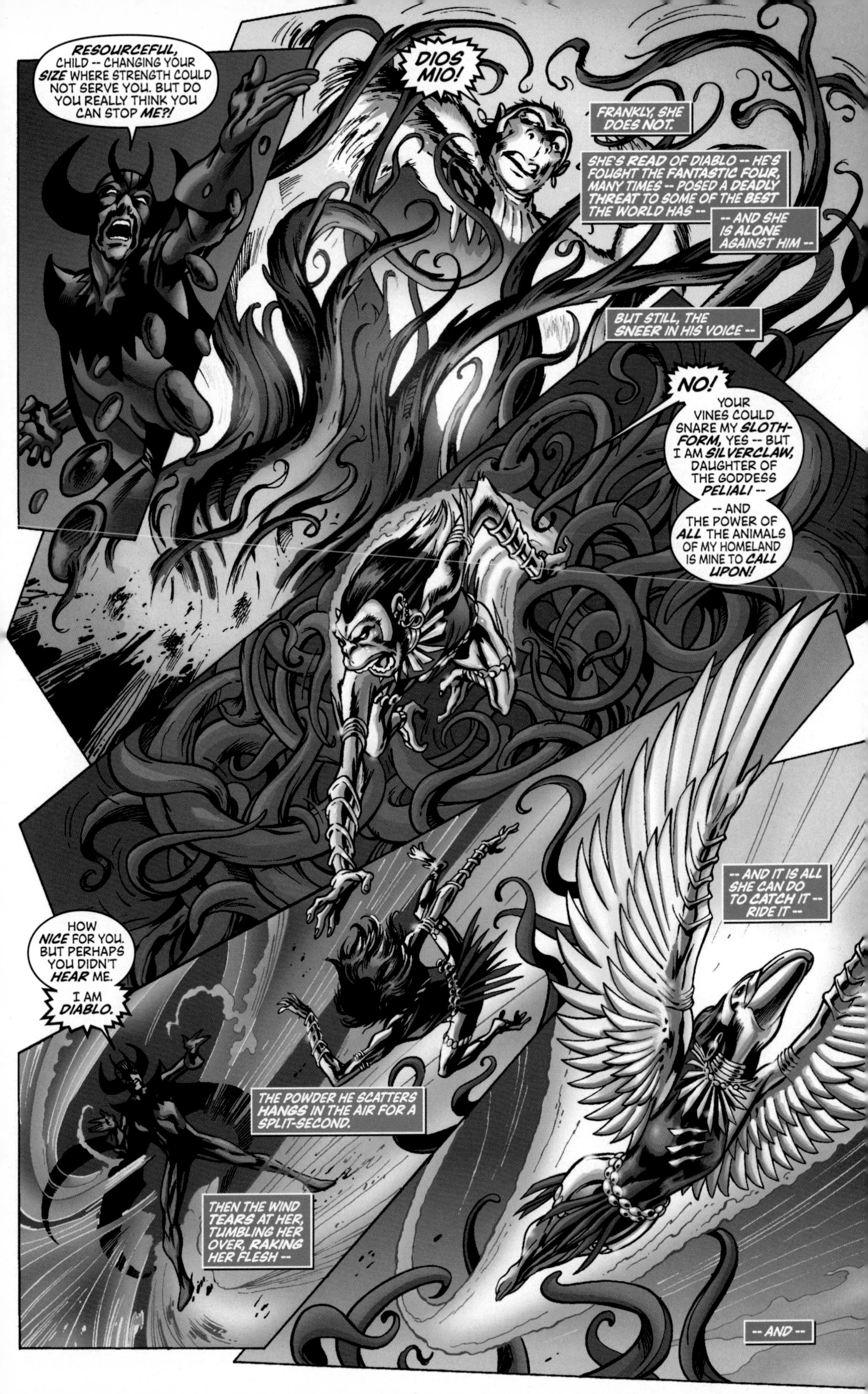

RESOURCEFUL, CHILD -- CHANGING YOUR SIZE WHERE STRENGTH COULD NOT SERVE YOU. BUT DO YOU REALLY THINK YOU CAN STOP ME?!
DIOS MIO!
FRANKLY, SHE DOES NOT.
SHE'S READ OF DIABLO -- HE'S FOUGHT THE FANTASTIC FOUR, MANY TIMES -- POSED A DEADLY THREAT TO SOME OF THE BEST THE WORLD HAS --
-- AND SHE IS ALONE AGAINST HIM --
BUT STILL, THE SNEER IN HIS VOICE --
NO!
YOUR VINES COULD SNARE MY SLOTH-FORM, YES -- BUT I AM SILVERCLAW, DAUGHTER OF THE GODDESS PELIALI --
-- AND THE POWER OF ALL THE ANIMALS OF MY HOMELAND IS MINE TO CALL UPON!
HOW NICE FOR YOU. BUT PERHAPS YOU DIDN'T HEAR ME.
I AM DIABLO.
-- AND IT IS ALL SHE CAN DO TO CATCH IT -- RIDE IT --
THE POWDER HE SCATTERS HANGS IN THE AIR FOR A SPLIT-SECOND.
THEN THE WIND TEARS AT HER, TUMBLING HER OVER, RAKING HER FLESH --
-- AND --

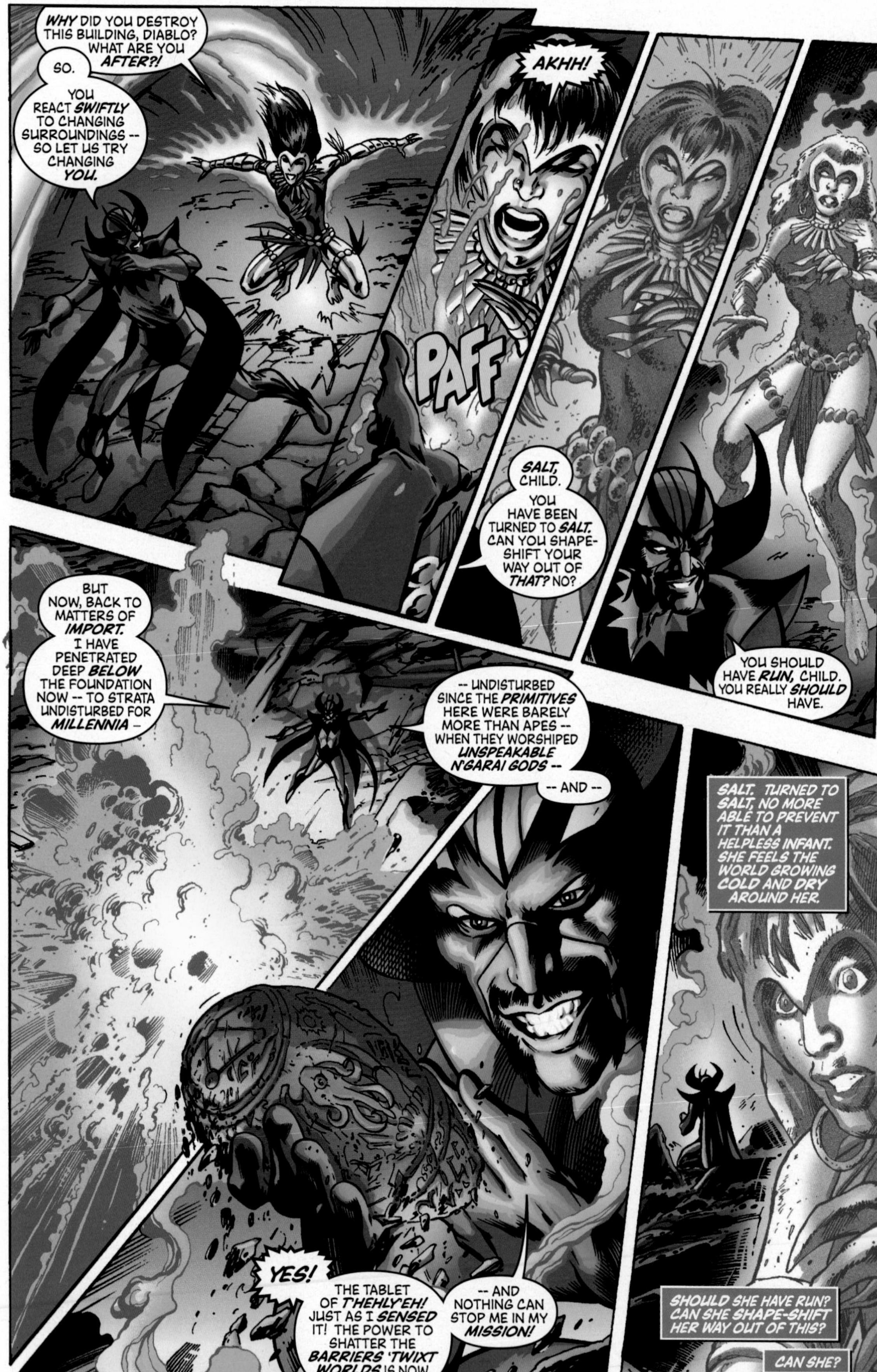
WHY DID YOU DESTROY THIS BUILDING, DIABLO? WHAT ARE YOU AFTER?!
SO.
YOU REACT SWIFTLY TO CHANGING SURROUNDINGS -- SO LET US TRY CHANGING YOU.
AKHH!
PAFF
SALT, CHILD.
YOU HAVE BEEN TURNED TO SALT. CAN YOU SHAPE-SHIFT YOUR WAY OUT OF THAT? NO?
YOU SHOULD HAVE RUN, CHILD. YOU REALLY SHOULD HAVE.
BUT NOW, BACK TO MATTERS OF IMPORT. I HAVE PENETRATED DEEP BELOW THE FOUNDATION NOW -- TO STRATA UNDISTURBED FOR MILLENNIA --
-- UNDISTURBED SINCE THE PRIMITIVES HERE WERE BARELY MORE THAN APES -- WHEN THEY WORSHIPED UNSPEAKABLE N'GARAI GODS --
-- AND --
YES!
THE TABLET OF T'HEHLY'EH! JUST AS I SENSED IT! THE POWER TO SHATTER THE BARRIERS 'TWIXT WORLDS IS NOW MINE --
-- AND NOTHING CAN STOP ME IN MY MISSION!
SALT. TURNED TO SALT, NO MORE ABLE TO PREVENT IT THAN A HELPLESS INFANT. SHE FEELS THE WORLD GROWING COLD AND DRY AROUND HER.
SHOULD SHE HAVE RUN? CAN SHE SHAPE-SHIFT HER WAY OUT OF THIS?
CAN SHE?

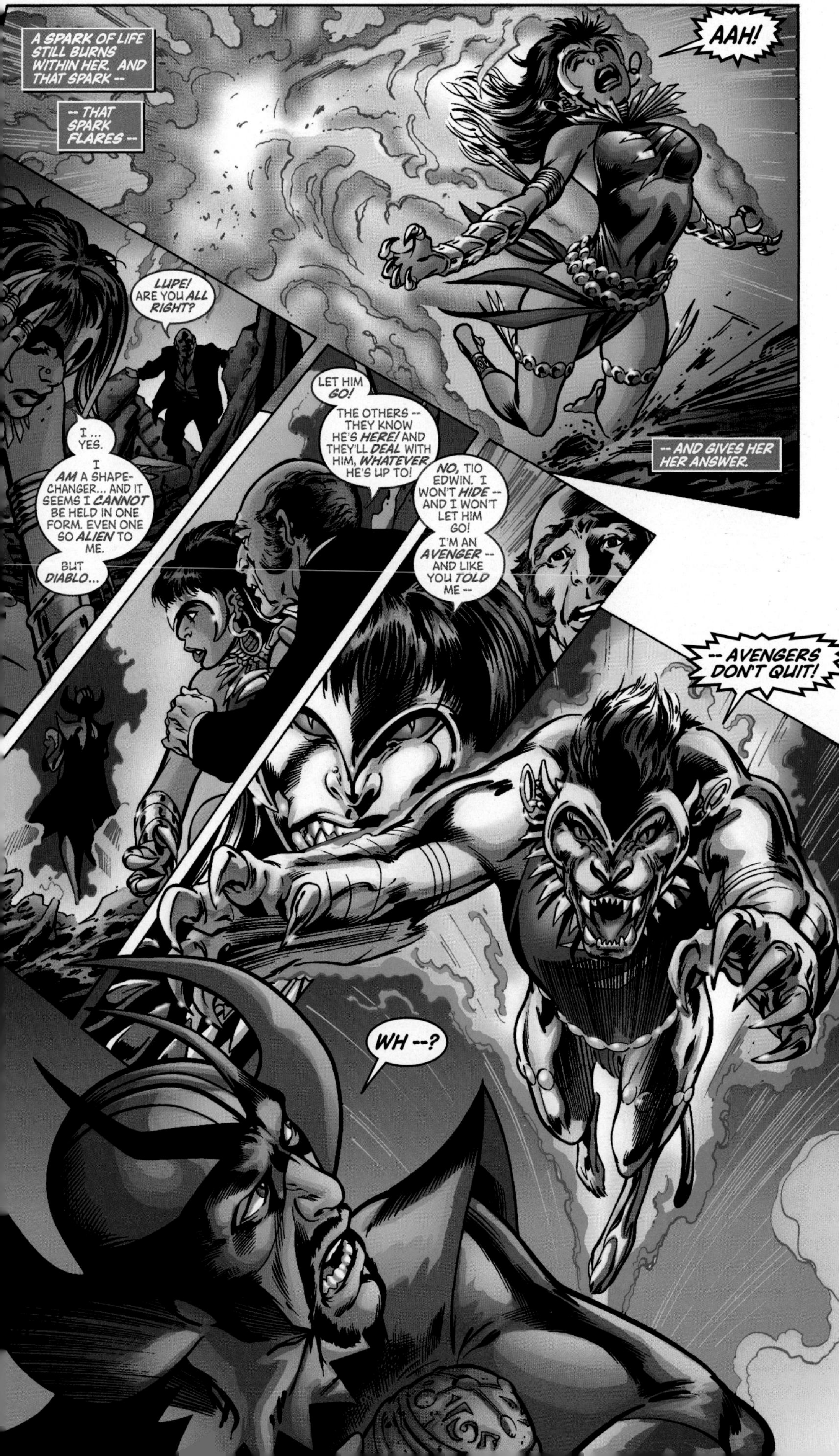
A SPARK OF LIFE STILL BURNS WITHIN HER. AND THAT SPARK --
-- THAT SPARK FLARES --
AAH!
-- AND GIVES HER HER ANSWER.
LUPE! ARE YOU ALL RIGHT?
I ... YES.
I AM A SHAPE-CHANGER... AND IT SEEMS I CANNOT BE HELD IN ONE FORM. EVEN ONE SO ALIEN TO ME.
BUT DIABLO...
LET HIM GO!
THE OTHERS -- THEY KNOW HE'S HERE! AND THEY'LL DEAL WITH HIM, WHATEVER HE'S UP TO!
NO, TIO EDWIN. I WON'T HIDE -- AND I WON'T LET HIM GO!
I'M AN AVENGER -- AND LIKE YOU TOLD ME --
-- AVENGERS DON'T QUIT!
WH --?

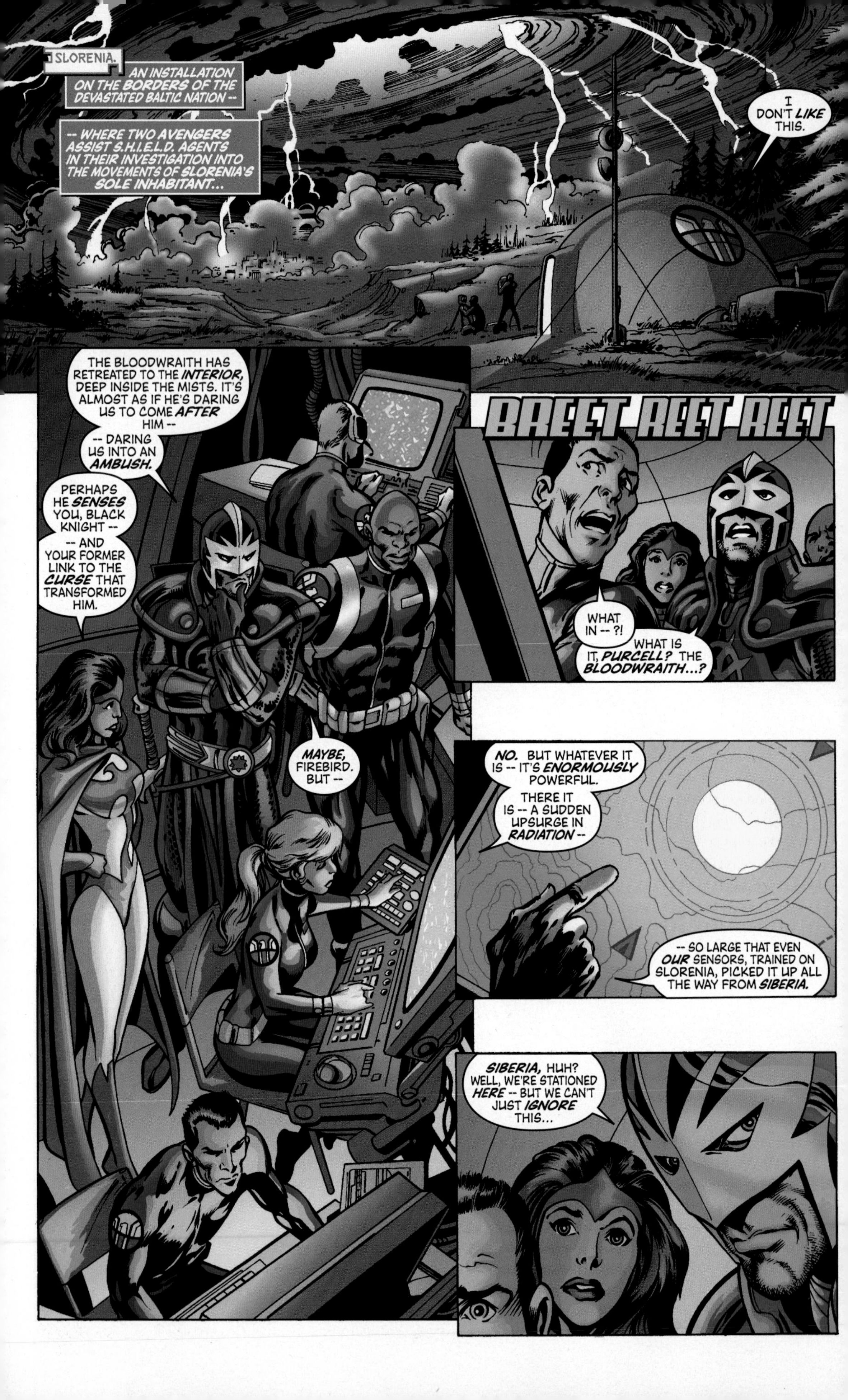
SLORENIA.
AN INSTALLATION ON THE BORDERS OF THE DEVASTATED BALTIC NATION --
-- WHERE TWO AVENGERS ASSIST S.H.I.E.L.D. AGENTS IN THEIR INVESTIGATION INTO THE MOVEMENTS OF SLORENIA'S SOLE INHABITANT...
I DON'T LIKE THIS.
THE BLOODWRAITH HAS RETREATED TO THE INTERIOR, DEEP INSIDE THE MISTS. IT'S ALMOST AS IF HE'S DARING US TO COME AFTER HIM --
-- DARING US INTO AN AMBUSH.
PERHAPS HE SENSES YOU, BLACK KNIGHT --
-- AND YOUR FORMER LINK TO THE CURSE THAT TRANSFORMED HIM.
MAYBE, FIREBIRD. BUT --
BREET REET REET
WHAT IN -- ?!
WHAT IS IT, PURCELL? THE BLOODWRAITH...?
NO. BUT WHATEVER IT IS -- IT'S ENORMOUSLY POWERFUL.
THERE IT IS -- A SUDDEN UPSURGE IN RADIATION --
-- SO LARGE THAT EVEN OUR SENSORS, TRAINED ON SLORENIA, PICKED IT UP ALL THE WAY FROM SIBERIA.
SIBERIA, HUH? WELL, WE'RE STATIONED HERE -- BUT WE CAN'T JUST IGNORE THIS...

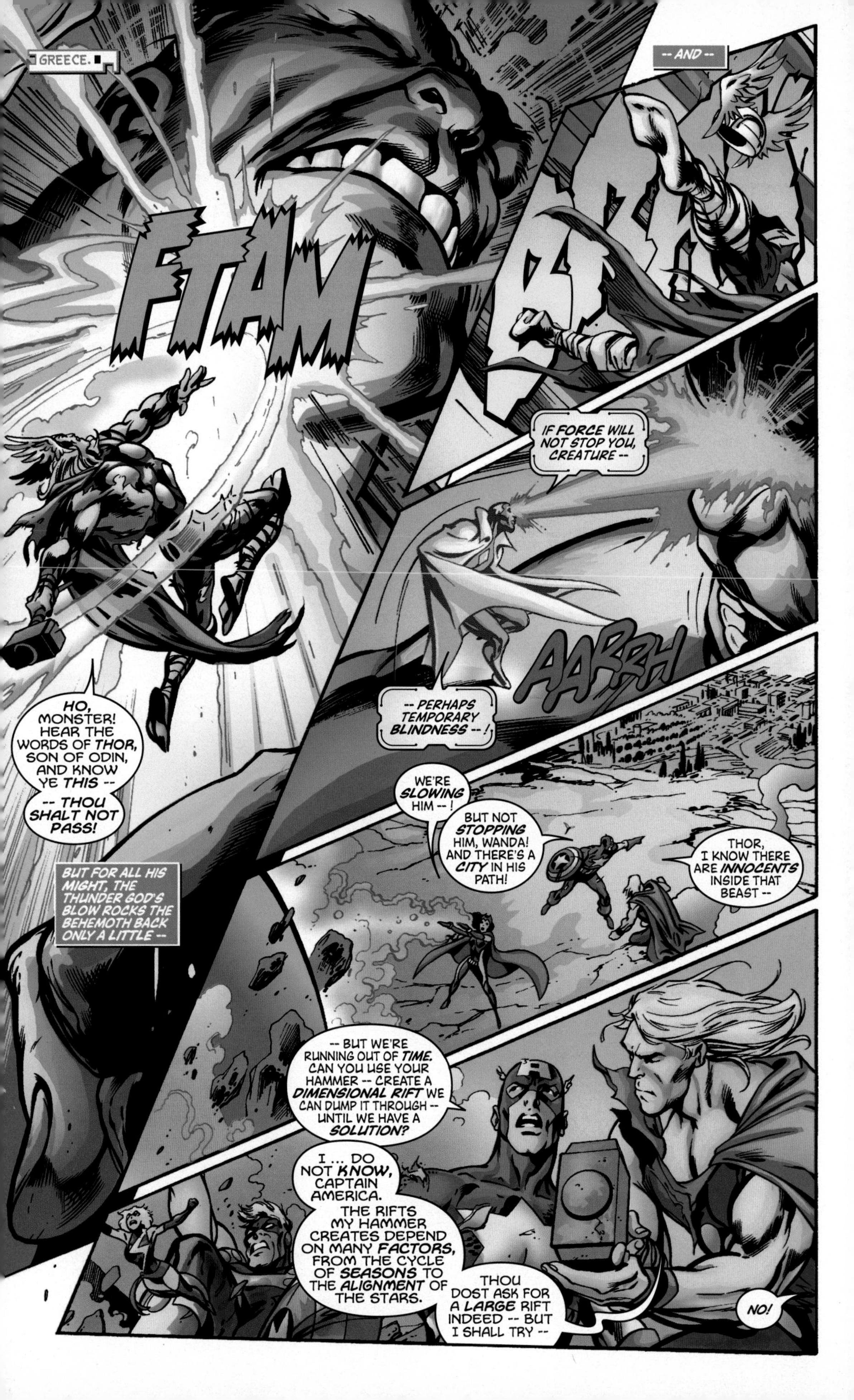
GREECE.
FTAM
-- AND --
HO, MONSTER! HEAR THE WORDS OF THOR, SON OF ODIN, AND KNOW YE THIS --
-- THOU SHALT NOT PASS!
BUT FOR ALL HIS MIGHT, THE THUNDER GOD'S BLOW ROCKS THE BEHEMOTH BACK ONLY A LITTLE --
IF FORCE WILL NOT STOP YOU, CREATURE --
-- PERHAPS TEMPORARY BLINDNESS -- !
AARRH
WE'RE SLOWING HIM -- !
BUT NOT STOPPING HIM, WANDA! AND THERE'S A CITY IN HIS PATH!
THOR, I KNOW THERE ARE INNOCENTS INSIDE THAT BEAST --
-- BUT WE'RE RUNNING OUT OF TIME. CAN YOU USE YOUR HAMMER -- CREATE A DIMENSIONAL RIFT WE CAN DUMP IT THROUGH -- UNTIL WE HAVE A SOLUTION?
I ... DO NOT KNOW, CAPTAIN AMERICA.
THE RIFTS MY HAMMER CREATES DEPEND ON MANY FACTORS, FROM THE CYCLE OF SEASONS TO THE ALIGNMENT OF THE STARS.
THOU DOST ASK FOR A LARGE RIFT INDEED -- BUT I SHALL TRY --
NO!

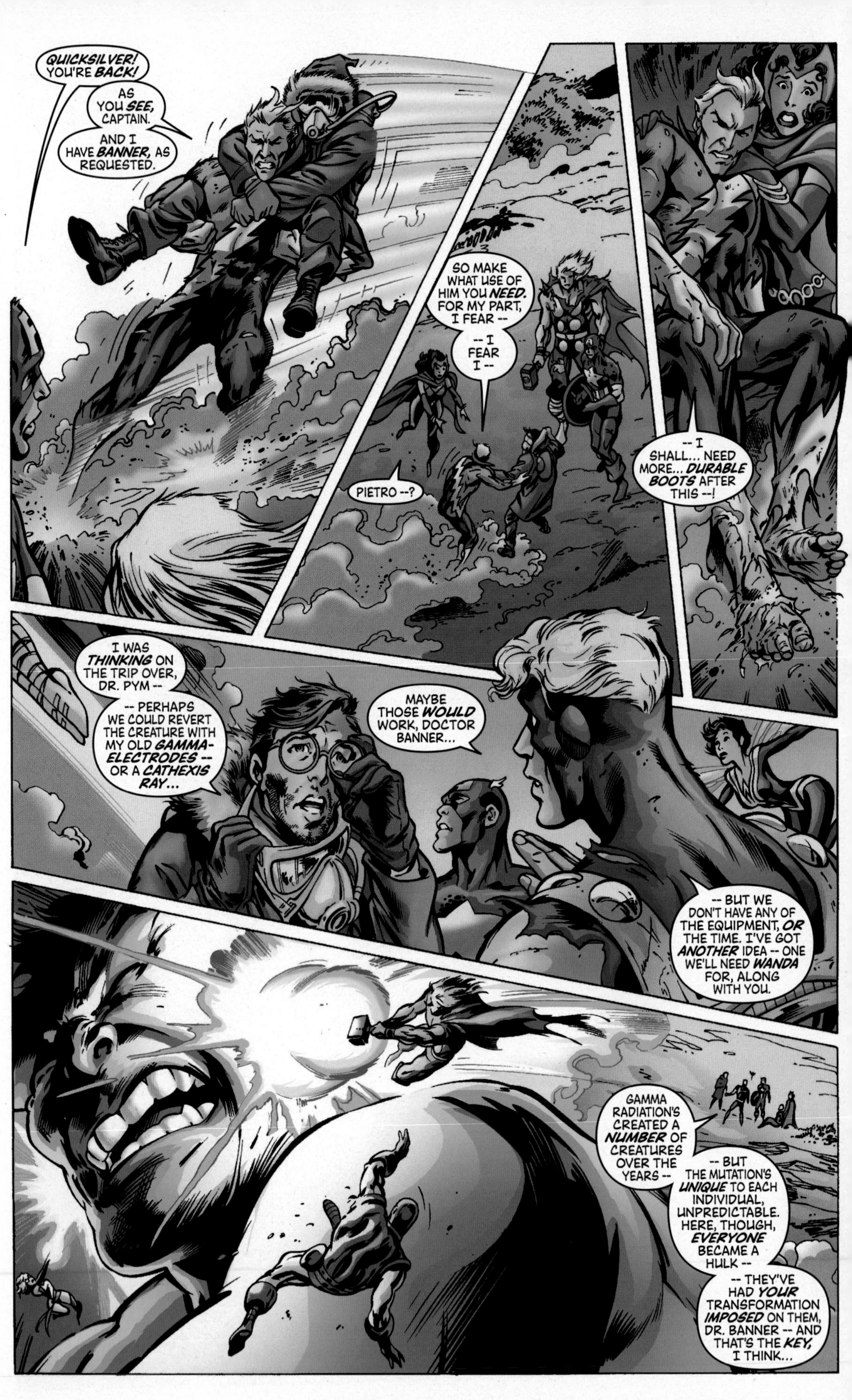

QUICKSILVER! YOU'RE BACK!
AS YOU SEE, CAPTAIN.
AND I HAVE BANNER, AS REQUESTED.
SO MAKE WHAT USE OF HIM YOU NEED. FOR MY PART, I FEAR --
-- I FEAR I --
PIETRO --?
-- I SHALL... NEED MORE... DURABLE BOOTS AFTER THIS --!
I WAS THINKING ON THE TRIP OVER, DR. PYM --
-- PERHAPS WE COULD REVERT THE CREATURE WITH MY OLD GAMMA-ELECTRODES -- OR A CATHEXIS RAY...
MAYBE THOSE WOULD WORK, DOCTOR BANNER...
-- BUT WE DON'T HAVE ANY OF THE EQUIPMENT, OR THE TIME. I'VE GOT ANOTHER IDEA -- ONE WE'LL NEED WANDA FOR, ALONG WITH YOU.
GAMMA RADIATION'S CREATED A NUMBER OF CREATURES OVER THE YEARS --
-- BUT THE MUTATION'S UNIQUE TO EACH INDIVIDUAL, UNPREDICTABLE. HERE, THOUGH, EVERYONE BECAME A HULK --
-- THEY'VE HAD YOUR TRANSFORMATION IMPOSED ON THEM, DR. BANNER -- AND THAT'S THE KEY, I THINK...

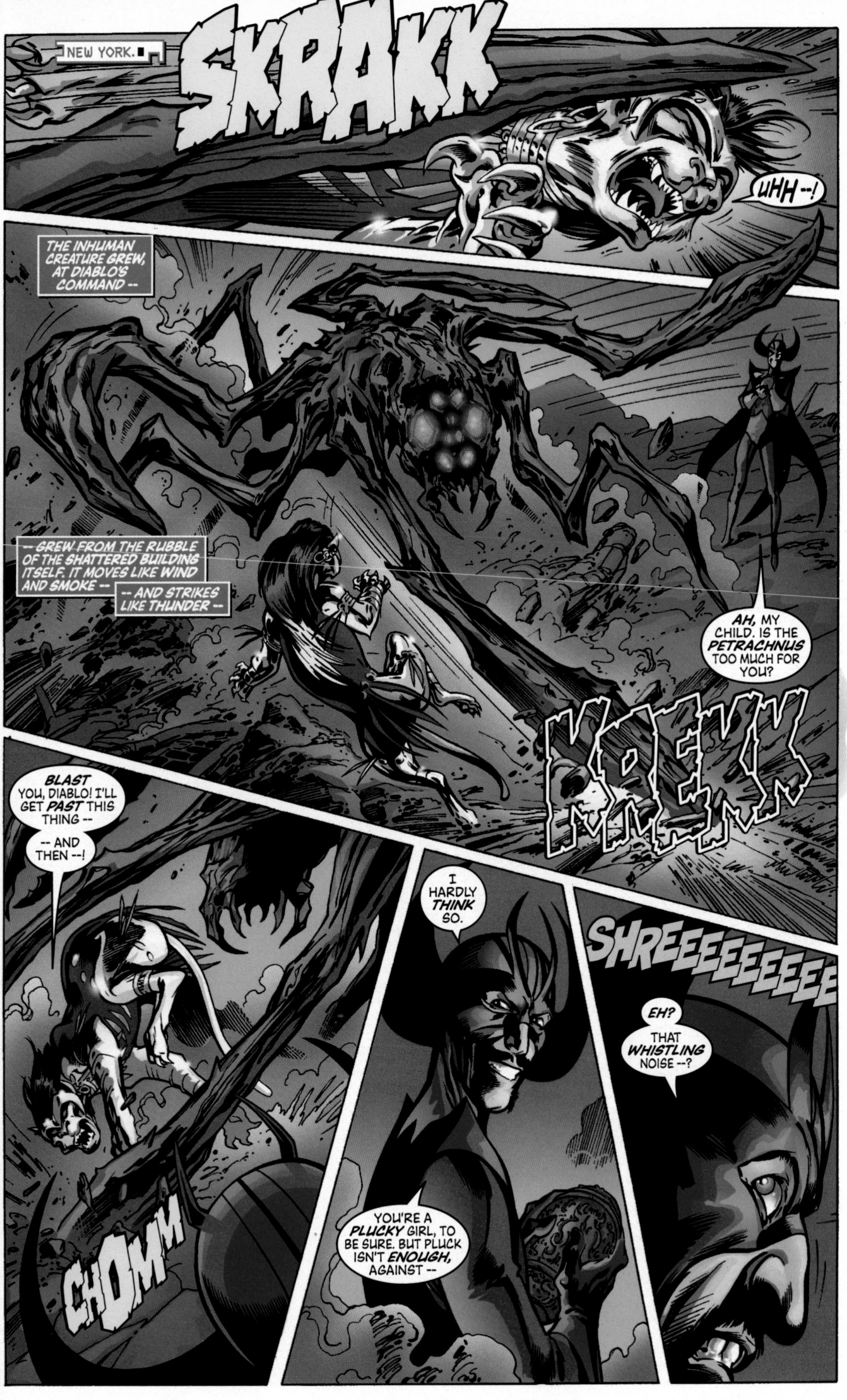

NEW YORK.
SKRAKK
UHH --!
THE INHUMAN CREATURE GREW, AT DIABLO'S COMMAND --
-- GREW FROM THE RUBBLE OF THE SHATTERED BUILDING ITSELF. IT MOVES LIKE WIND AND SMOKE --
-- AND STRIKES LIKE THUNDER --
AH, MY CHILD. IS THE PETRACHNUS TOO MUCH FOR YOU?
KRAKK
BLAST YOU, DIABLO! I'LL GET PAST THIS THING --
-- AND THEN --!
CHOMM
I HARDLY THINK SO.
YOU'RE A PLUCKY GIRL, TO BE SURE. BUT PLUCK ISN'T ENOUGH, AGAINST --
SHREEEEEEEEEE
EH? THAT WHISTLING NOISE --?

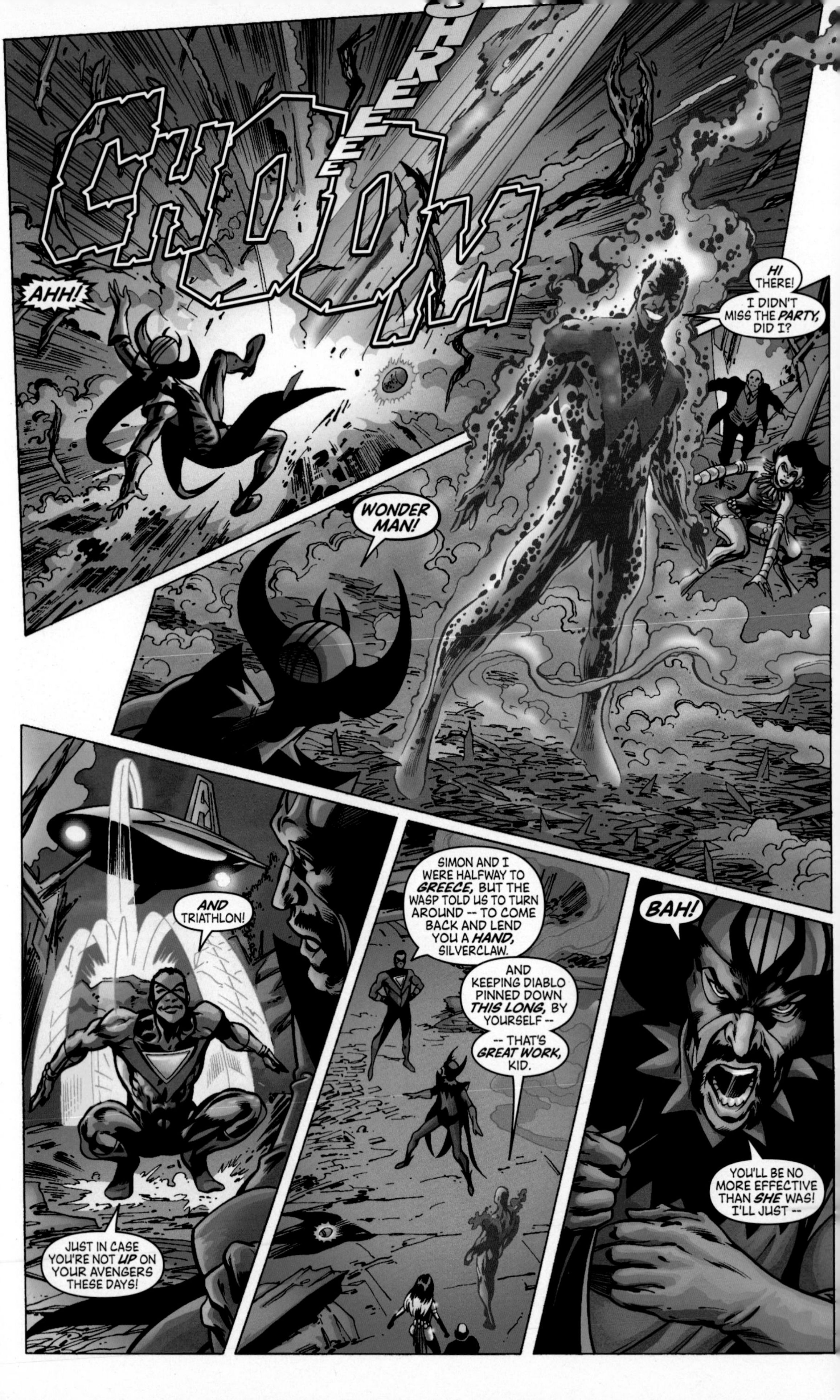
SHREEEEE
CHOOOM
AHH!
HI THERE! I DIDN'T MISS THE PARTY, DID I?
WONDER MAN!
AND TRIATHLON!
JUST IN CASE YOU'RE NOT UP ON YOUR AVENGERS THESE DAYS!
SIMON AND I WERE HALFWAY TO GREECE, BUT THE WASP TOLD US TO TURN AROUND -- TO COME BACK AND LEND YOU A HAND, SILVERCLAW.
AND KEEPING DIABLO PINNED DOWN THIS LONG, BY YOURSELF --
-- THAT'S GREAT WORK, KID.
BAH!
YOU'LL BE NO MORE EFFECTIVE THAN SHE WAS! I'LL JUST --

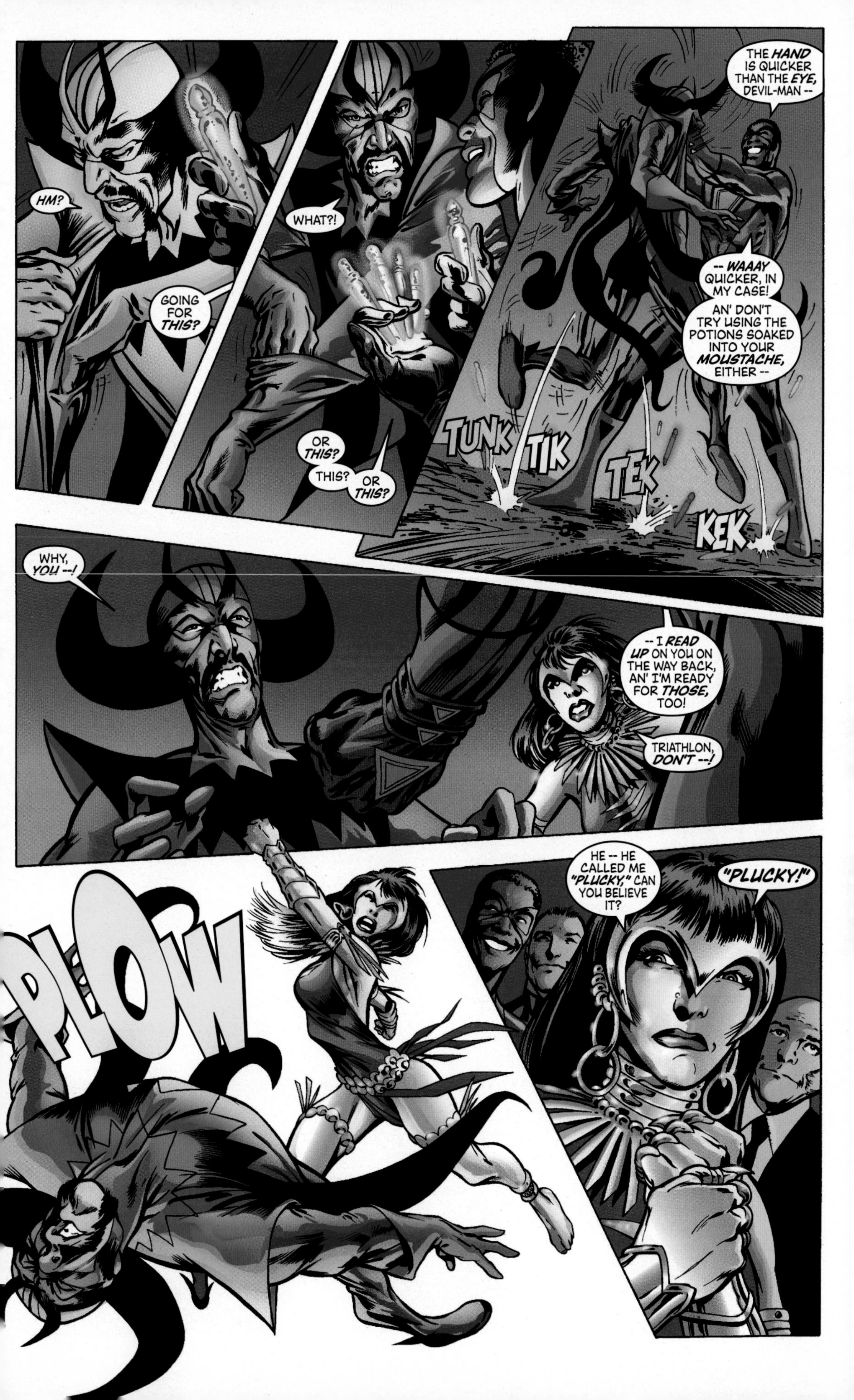
HM?
GOING FOR THIS?
WHAT?!
OR THIS?
THIS?
OR THIS?
THE HAND IS QUICKER THAN THE EYE, DEVIL-MAN --
-- WAAAY QUICKER, IN MY CASE!
AN' DON'T TRY USING THE POTIONS SOAKED INTO YOUR MOUSTACHE, EITHER --
TUNK
TIK
TEK
KEK
WHY, YOU --!
-- I READ UP ON YOU ON THE WAY BACK, AN' I'M READY FOR THOSE, TOO!
TRIATHLON, DON'T --!
PLOW
HE -- HE CALLED ME "PLUCKY," CAN YOU BELIEVE IT?
"PLUCKY!"

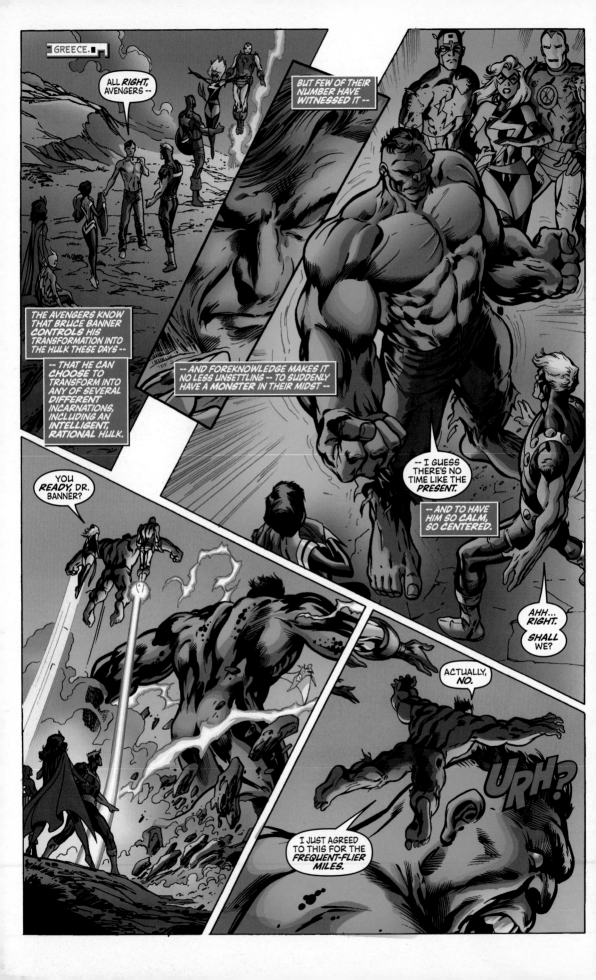

GREECE.

ALL *RIGHT,* AVENGERS --

BUT FEW OF THEIR *NUMBER* HAVE *WITNESSED* IT --

THE AVENGERS KNOW THAT BRUCE BANNER *CONTROLS* HIS *TRANSFORMATION* INTO THE HULK THESE DAYS --

-- THAT HE CAN *CHOOSE* TO TRANSFORM INTO ANY OF SEVERAL *DIFFERENT* INCARNATIONS, INCLUDING AN *INTELLIGENT,* *RATIONAL* HULK.

-- AND FOREKNOWLEDGE MAKES IT NO LESS UNSETTLING -- TO SUDDENLY HAVE A *MONSTER* IN THEIR MIDST --

-- I GUESS THERE'S NO TIME LIKE THE *PRESENT.*

-- AND TO HAVE HIM SO *CALM,* SO *CENTERED.*

YOU *READY,* DR. BANNER?

AHH... *RIGHT.* SHALL WE?

ACTUALLY, *NO.*

URH?

I JUST AGREED TO THIS FOR THE *FREQUENT-FLIER MILES.*

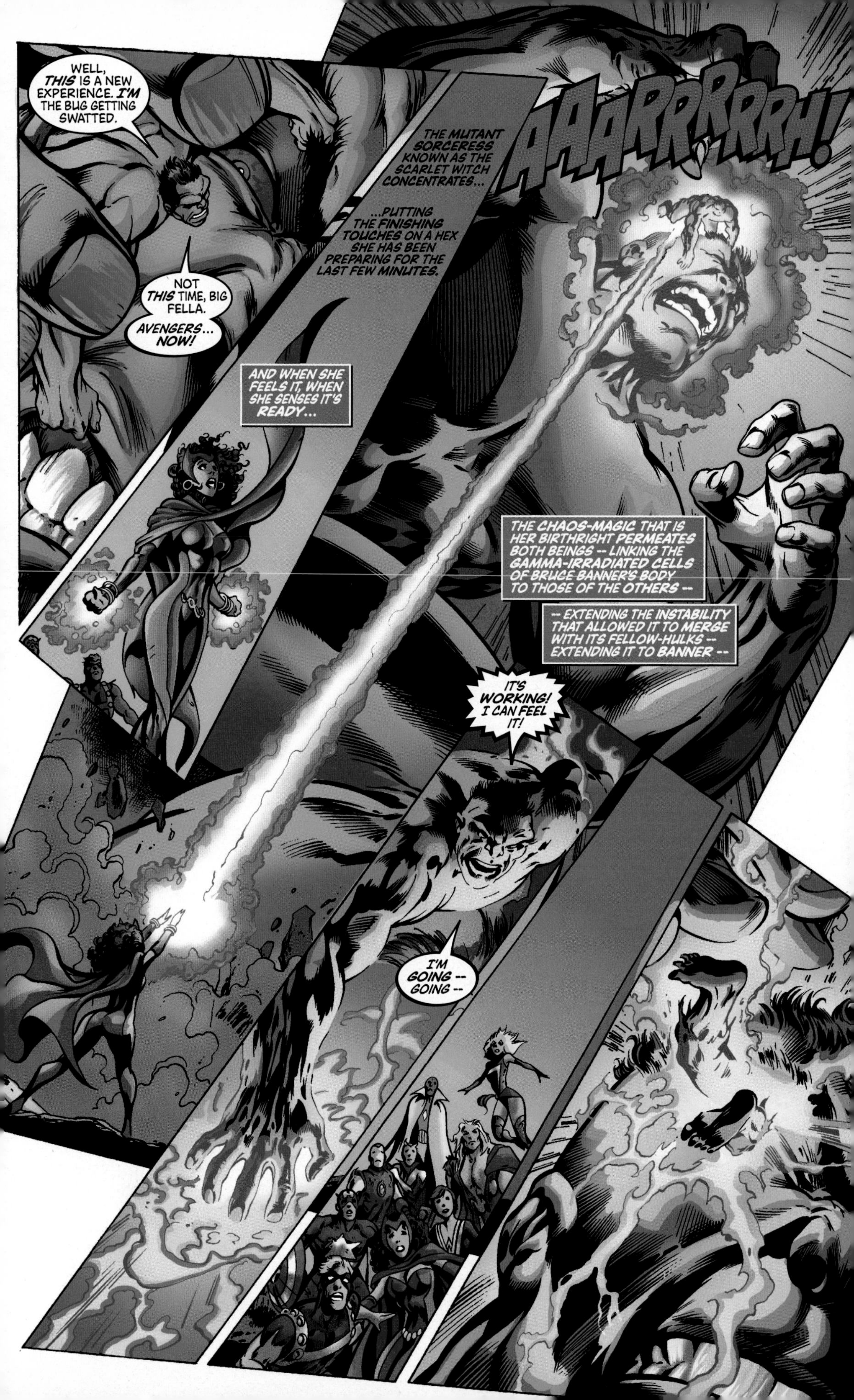
WELL, THIS IS A NEW EXPERIENCE. I'M THE BUG GETTING SWATTED.
NOT THIS TIME, BIG FELLA.
AVENGERS... NOW!
THE MUTANT SORCERESS KNOWN AS THE SCARLET WITCH CONCENTRATES...
...PUTTING THE FINISHING TOUCHES ON A HEX SHE HAS BEEN PREPARING FOR THE LAST FEW MINUTES.
AAAARRRRRRH!
AND WHEN SHE FEELS IT, WHEN SHE SENSES IT'S READY...
THE CHAOS-MAGIC THAT IS HER BIRTHRIGHT PERMEATES BOTH BEINGS -- LINKING THE GAMMA-IRRADIATED CELLS OF BRUCE BANNER'S BODY TO THOSE OF THE OTHERS --
-- EXTENDING THE INSTABILITY THAT ALLOWED IT TO MERGE WITH ITS FELLOW-HULKS -- EXTENDING IT TO BANNER --
IT'S WORKING! I CAN FEEL IT!
I'M GOING -- GOING --

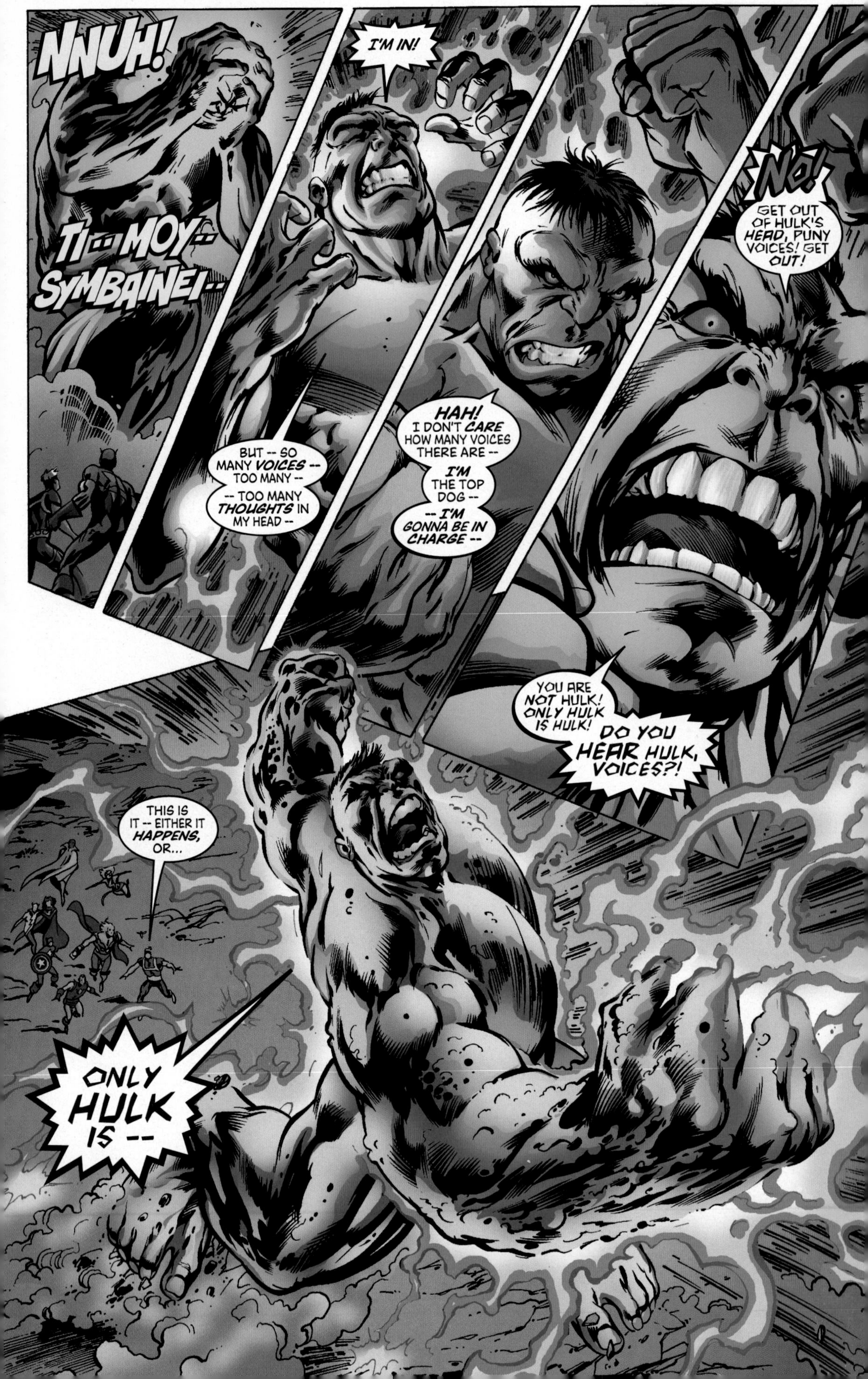
NNUH!
TI -- MOY -- SYMBAINEI --
I'M IN!
BUT -- SO MANY VOICES -- TOO MANY --
-- TOO MANY THOUGHTS IN MY HEAD --
HAH! I DON'T CARE HOW MANY VOICES THERE ARE --
I'M THE TOP DOG --
-- I'M GONNA BE IN CHARGE --
NO!
GET OUT OF HULK'S HEAD, PUNY VOICES! GET OUT!
YOU ARE NOT HULK! ONLY HULK IS HULK!
DO YOU HEAR HULK, VOICES?!
THIS IS IT -- EITHER IT HAPPENS, OR...
ONLY HULK IS --

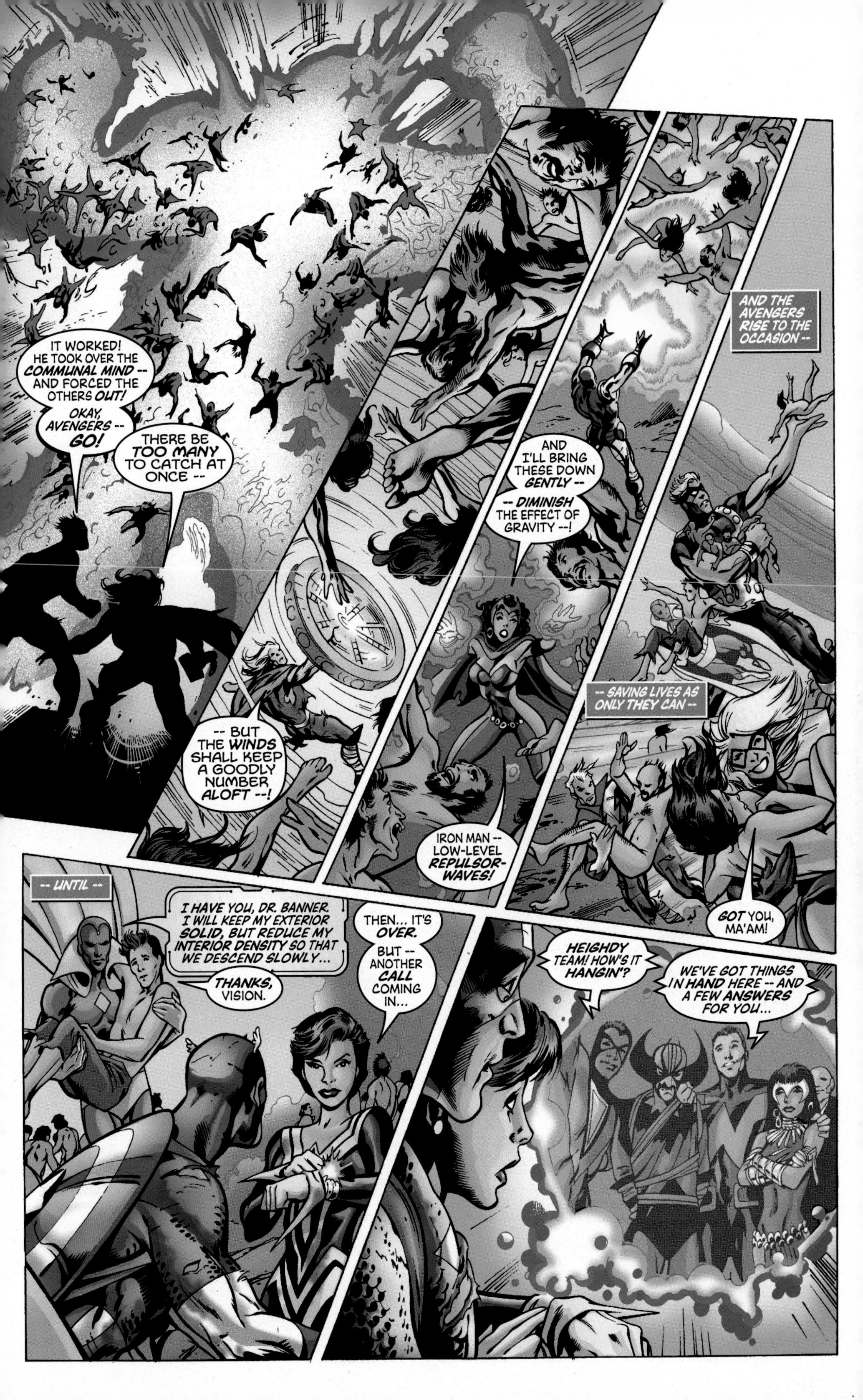

IT WORKED! HE TOOK OVER THE COMMUNAL MIND -- AND FORCED THE OTHERS OUT!
OKAY, AVENGERS -- GO!
THERE BE TOO MANY TO CATCH AT ONCE --
-- BUT THE WINDS SHALL KEEP A GOODLY NUMBER ALOFT --!
AND I'LL BRING THESE DOWN GENTLY --
-- DIMINISH THE EFFECT OF GRAVITY --!
IRON MAN -- LOW-LEVEL REPULSOR-WAVES!
AND THE AVENGERS RISE TO THE OCCASION --
-- SAVING LIVES AS ONLY THEY CAN --
GOT YOU, MA'AM!
-- UNTIL --
I HAVE YOU, DR. BANNER. I WILL KEEP MY EXTERIOR SOLID, BUT REDUCE MY INTERIOR DENSITY SO THAT WE DESCEND SLOWLY...
THANKS, VISION.
THEN... IT'S OVER.
BUT -- ANOTHER CALL COMING IN...
HEIGHDY TEAM! HOW'S IT HANGIN'?
WE'VE GOT THINGS IN HAND HERE -- AND A FEW ANSWERS FOR YOU...

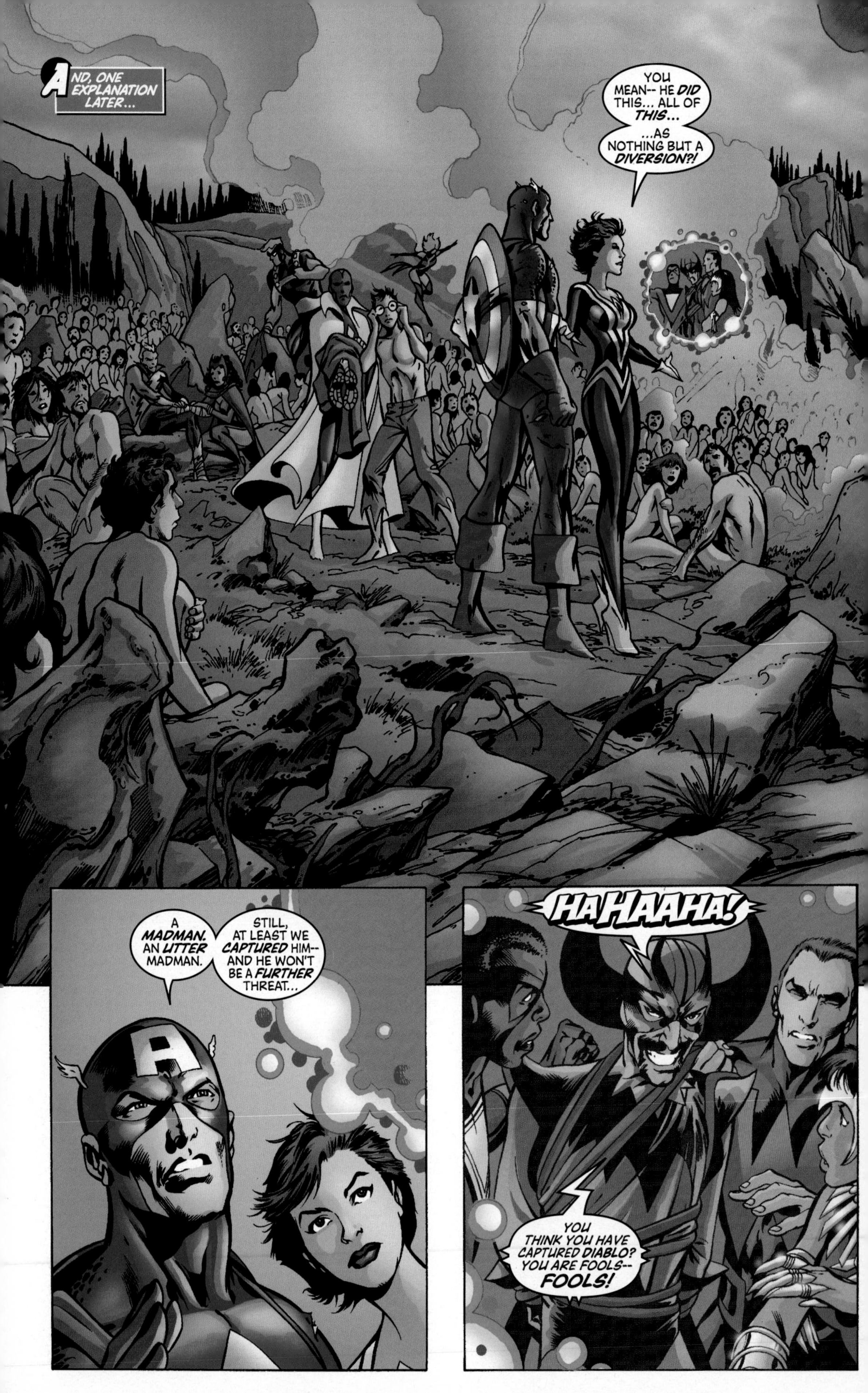
AND, ONE EXPLANATION LATER...
YOU MEAN-- HE DID THIS... ALL OF THIS...
...AS NOTHING BUT A DIVERSION?!
A MADMAN. AN UTTER MADMAN.
STILL, AT LEAST WE CAPTURED HIM-- AND HE WON'T BE A FURTHER THREAT...
HAHAAAHA!
YOU THINK YOU HAVE CAPTURED DIABLO? YOU ARE FOOLS-- FOOLS!

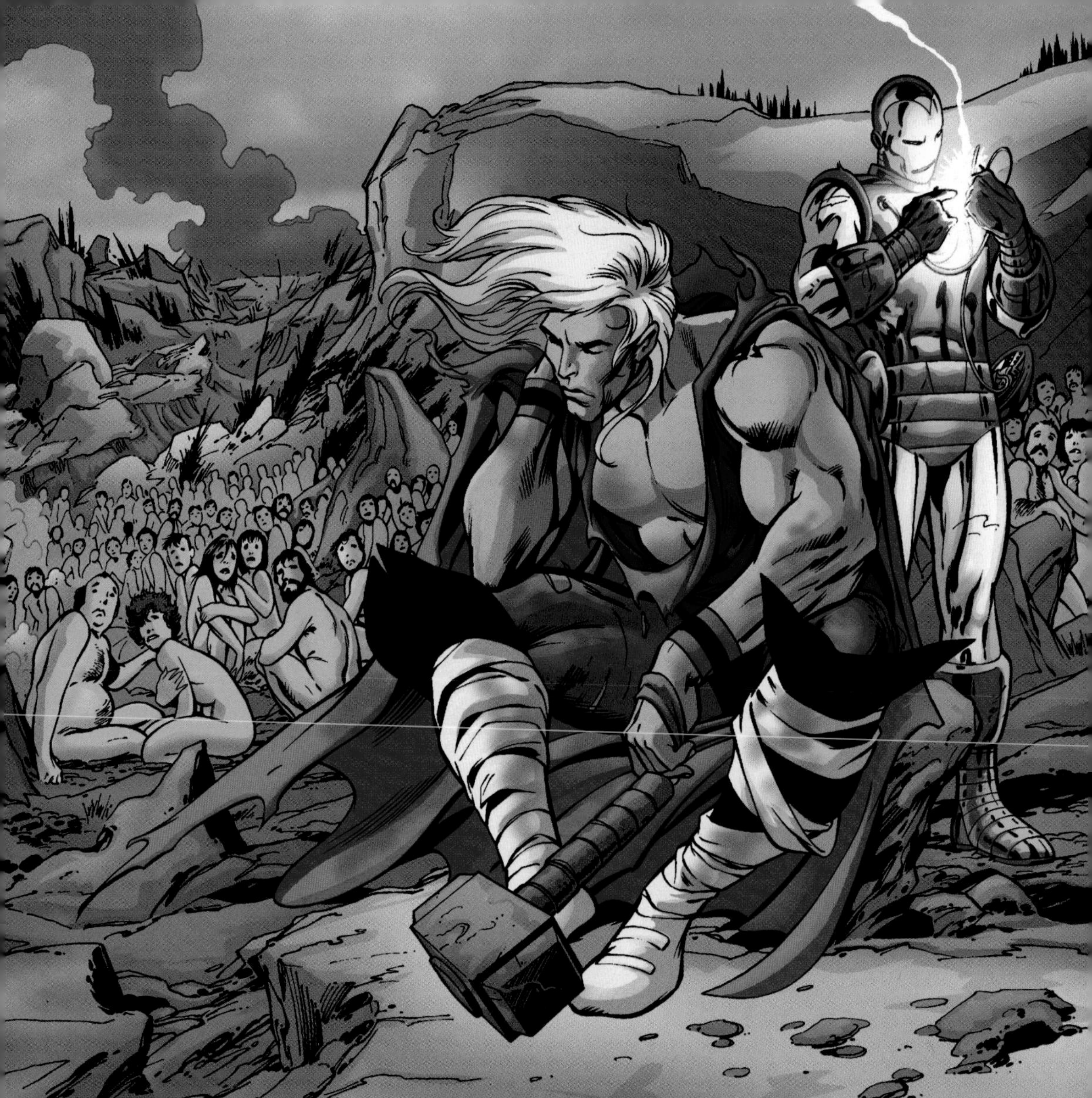

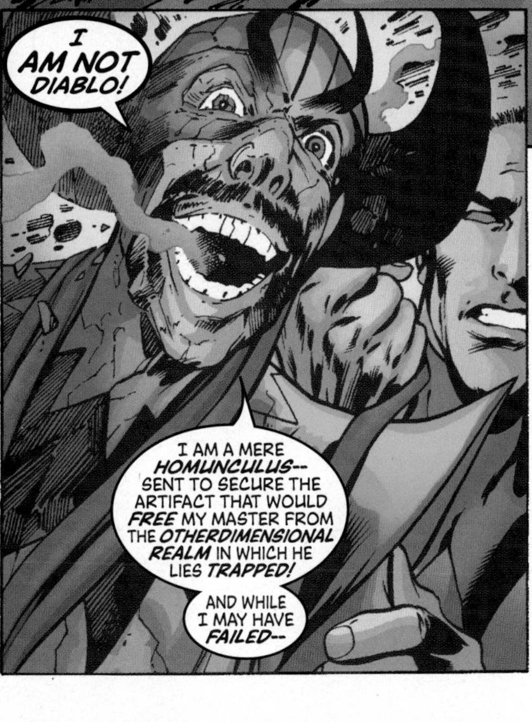
I AM NOT DIABLO!
I AM A MERE HOMUNCULUS-- SENT TO SECURE THE ARTIFACT THAT WOULD FREE MY MASTER FROM THE OTHERDIMENSIONAL REALM IN WHICH HE LIES TRAPPED!
AND WHILE I MAY HAVE FAILED--

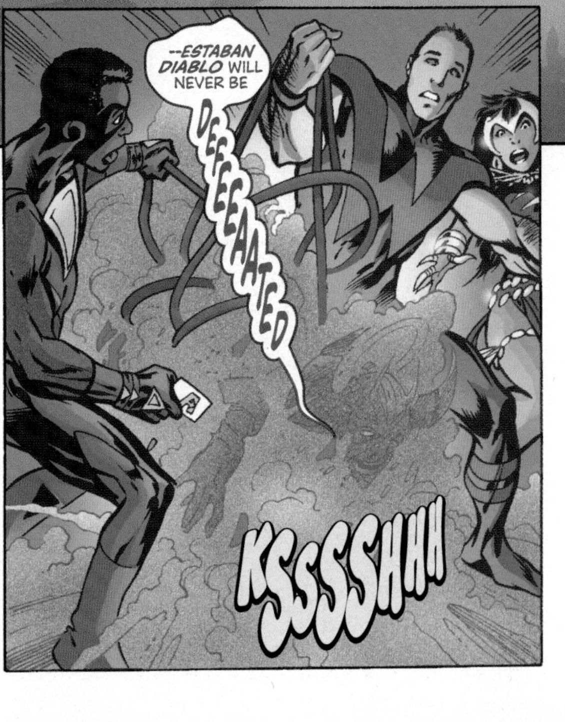
--ESTABAN DIABLO WILL NEVER BE DEFEEEAATED
KSSSSHHH

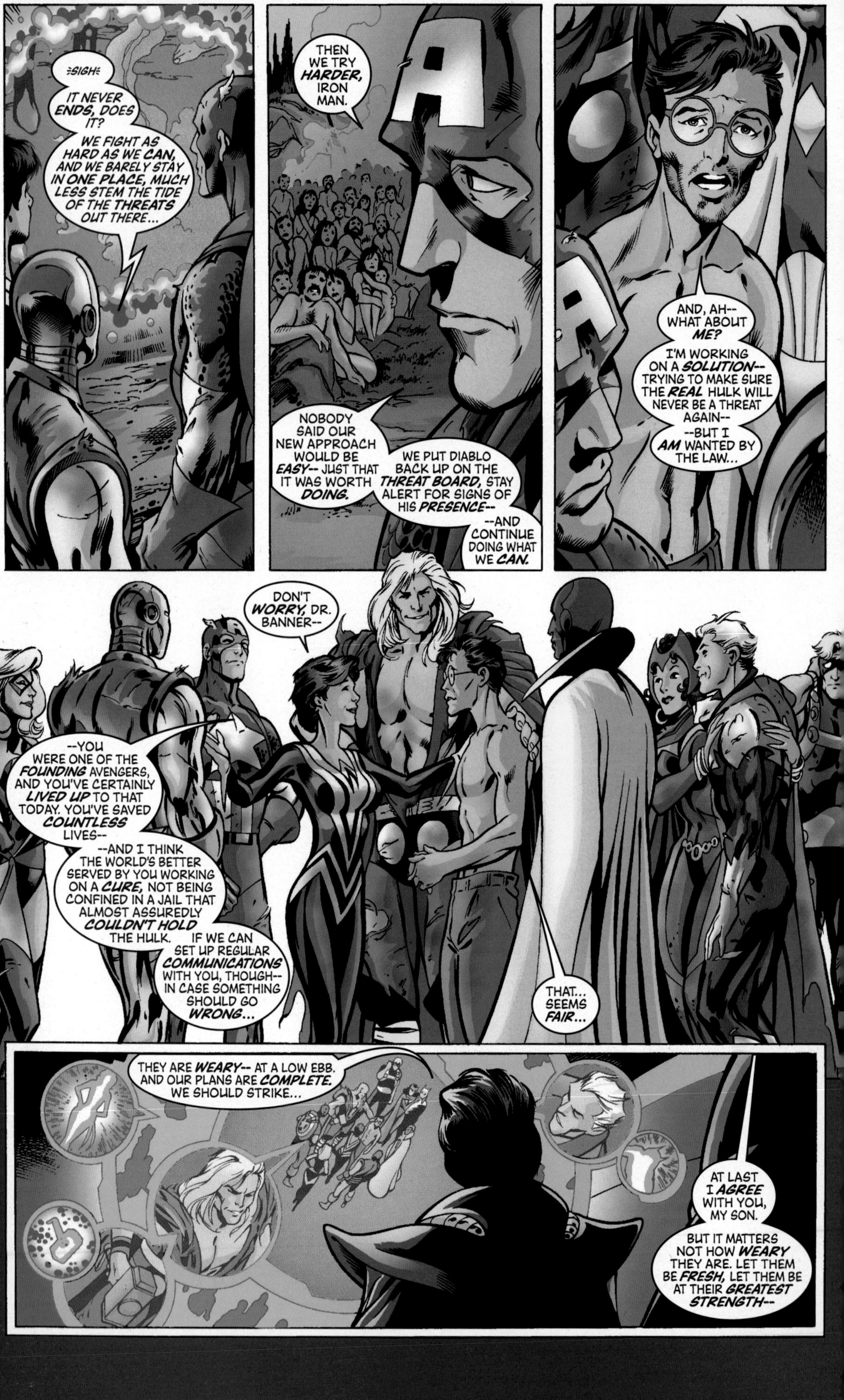

SIGH
IT NEVER ENDS, DOES IT?
WE FIGHT AS HARD AS WE CAN, AND WE BARELY STAY IN ONE PLACE, MUCH LESS STEM THE TIDE OF THE THREATS OUT THERE...
THEN WE TRY HARDER, IRON MAN.
NOBODY SAID OUR NEW APPROACH WOULD BE EASY-- JUST THAT IT WAS WORTH DOING.
WE PUT DIABLO BACK UP ON THE THREAT BOARD, STAY ALERT FOR SIGNS OF HIS PRESENCE--
--AND CONTINUE DOING WHAT WE CAN.
AND, AH-- WHAT ABOUT ME?
I'M WORKING ON A SOLUTION-- TRYING TO MAKE SURE THE REAL HULK WILL NEVER BE A THREAT AGAIN--
--BUT I AM WANTED BY THE LAW...
DON'T WORRY, DR. BANNER--
--YOU WERE ONE OF THE FOUNDING AVENGERS, AND YOU'VE CERTAINLY LIVED UP TO THAT TODAY. YOU'VE SAVED COUNTLESS LIVES--
--AND I THINK THE WORLD'S BETTER SERVED BY YOU WORKING ON A CURE, NOT BEING CONFINED IN A JAIL THAT ALMOST ASSUREDLY COULDN'T HOLD THE HULK.
IF WE CAN SET UP REGULAR COMMUNICATIONS WITH YOU, THOUGH-- IN CASE SOMETHING SHOULD GO WRONG...
THAT... SEEMS FAIR...
THEY ARE WEARY-- AT A LOW EBB. AND OUR PLANS ARE COMPLETE. WE SHOULD STRIKE...
AT LAST I AGREE WITH YOU, MY SON.
BUT IT MATTERS NOT HOW WEARY THEY ARE. LET THEM BE FRESH, LET THEM BE AT THEIR GREATEST STRENGTH--

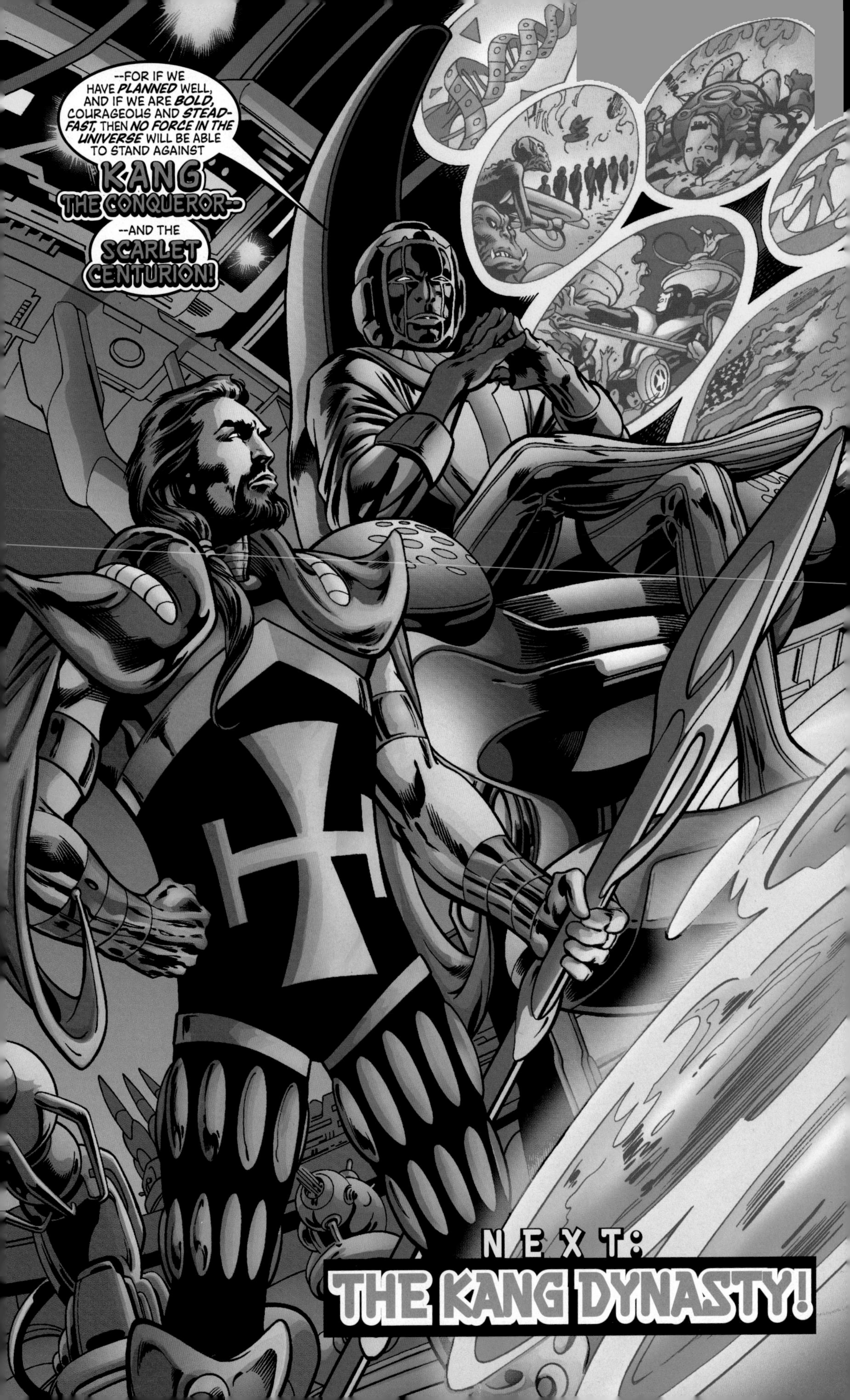
--FOR IF WE HAVE PLANNED WELL, AND IF WE ARE BOLD, COURAGEOUS AND STEAD-FAST, THEN NO FORCE IN THE UNIVERSE WILL BE ABLE TO STAND AGAINST KANG THE CONQUEROR--
--AND THE SCARLET CENTURION!
NEXT:
THE KANG DYNASTY!

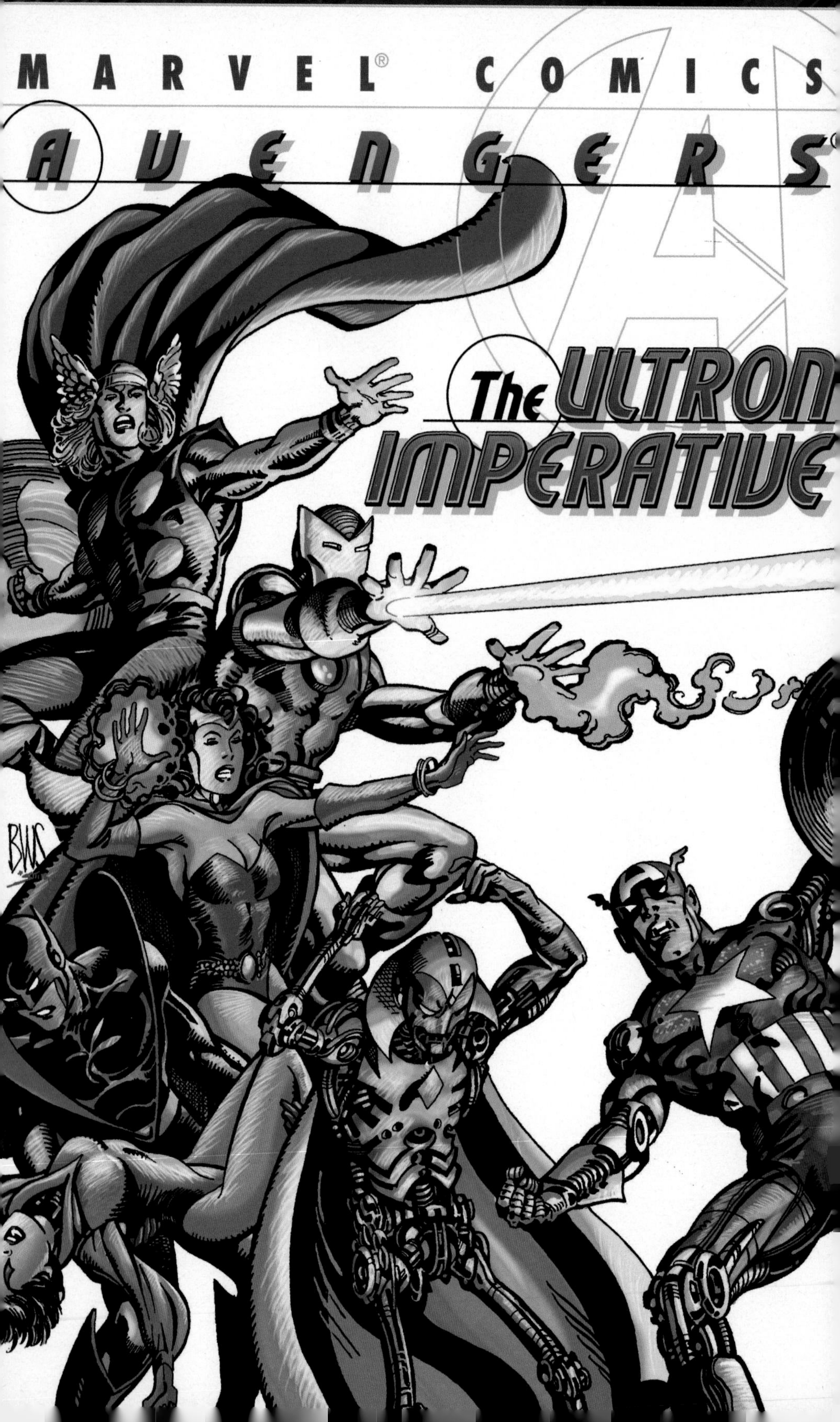
MARVEL® COMICS
AVENGERS®
The ULTRON IMPERATIVE
BWS

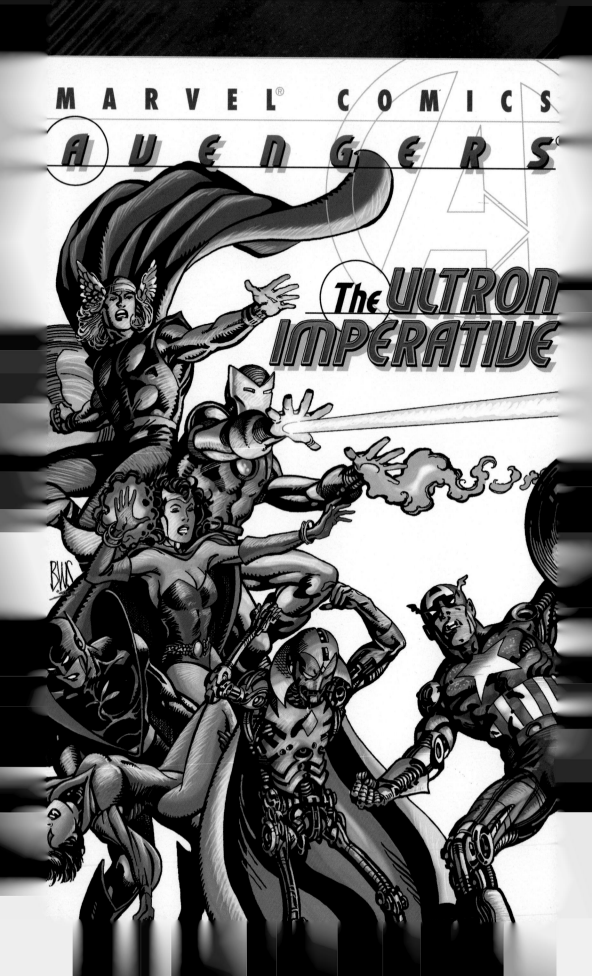

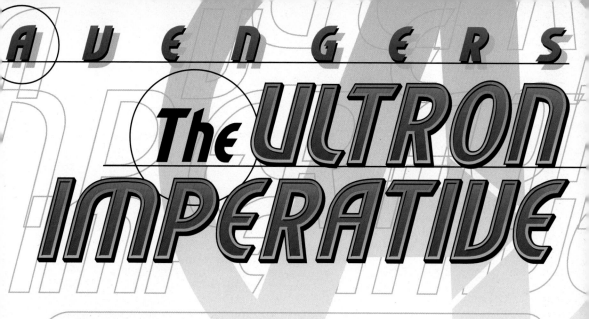

AVENGERS
The ULTRON IMPERATIVE

KURT BUSIEK
architect, co-plotter, script pages 23-25

ROY THOMAS
co-plotter, script pages 1-8, 26-35, 62-64
ROGER STERN
script pages 9-22
STEVE ENGLEHART
script pages 36-61

JOHN PAUL LEON
art, pages 1-8
PAUL SMITH
art, pages 9-22
TOM GRUMMETT & KARL KESEL
art, pages 23-25
JOHN McCREA & JAMES HODGKINS
art, pages 26-31
JIM STARLIN & AL MILGROM
art, pages 32-35
PAT OLLIFFE & JOHN LIVESAY
art, pages 36-47
JORGE LUCAS & MIKE ROYER
art, pages 48-61
KLAUS JANSON
art, pages 62-64

HI-FI DESIGN - coloring
COMICRAFT - lettering & design
BARRY WINDSOR-SMITH - cover
MARC SUMERAK - assistant editor
TOM BREVOORT - editor
JOE QUESADA - editor in chief
BILL JEMAS - president

SPECIAL GALLERY SECTION:

Unused Avengers promotional drawing by DON HECK & JERRY ORDWAY
Unused cover to AVENGERS v.1 #66 by BARRY WINDSOR-SMITH
Unused cover to the aborted AVENGERS: THE LEGEND by JIM CHEUNG & CAM SMITH
A preview of things to come by the new AVENGERS art team of
KIERON DWYER, RICK REMENDER & JOHN ESTES
A mock AVENGERS cover of yesteryear by PAUL SMITH

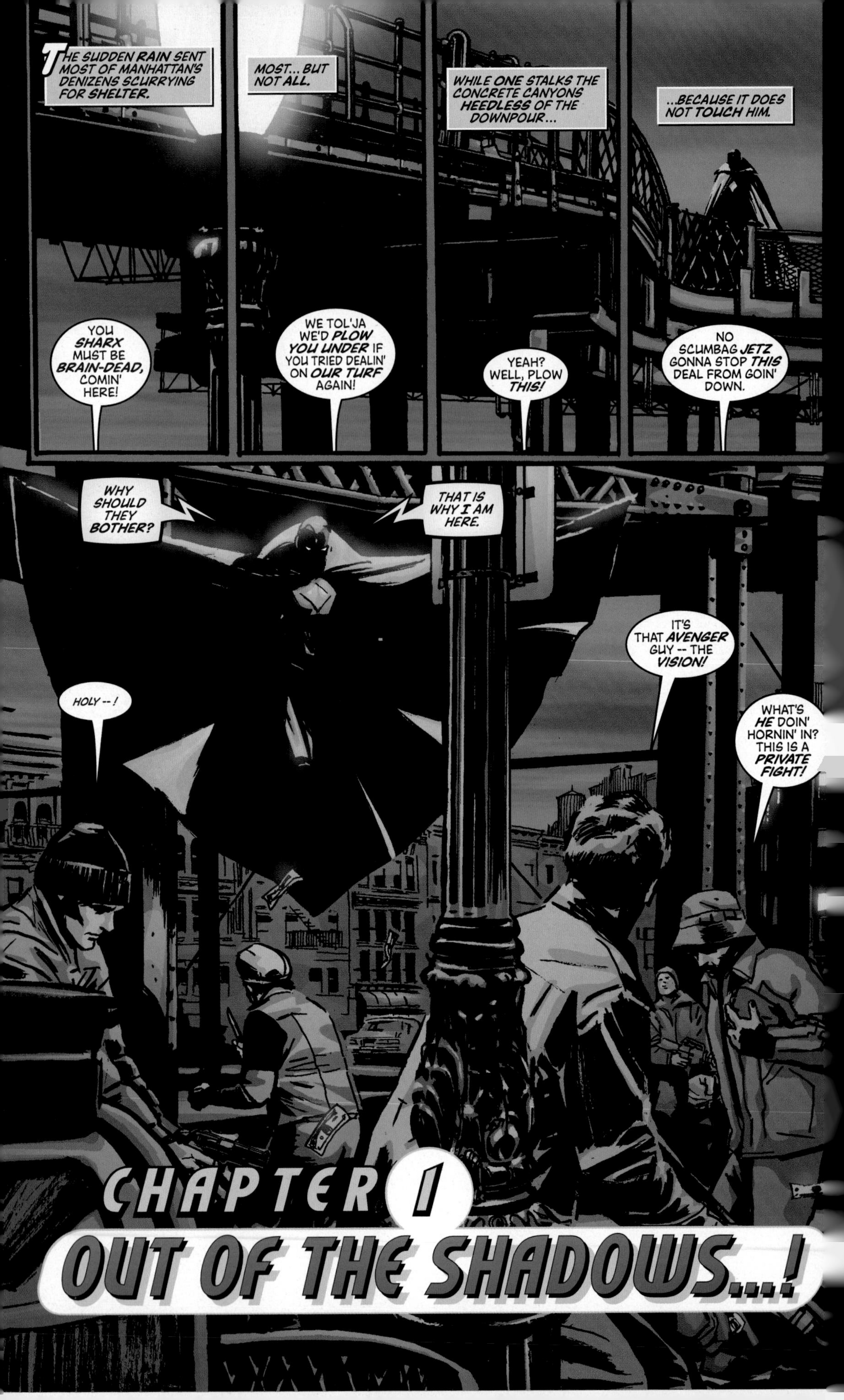
THE SUDDEN RAIN SENT MOST OF MANHATTAN'S DENIZENS SCURRYING FOR SHELTER.
MOST... BUT NOT ALL.
WHILE ONE STALKS THE CONCRETE CANYONS HEEDLESS OF THE DOWNPOUR...
...BECAUSE IT DOES NOT TOUCH HIM.
YOU SHARX MUST BE BRAIN-DEAD, COMIN' HERE!
WE TOL'JA WE'D PLOW YOU UNDER IF YOU TRIED DEALIN' ON OUR TURF AGAIN!
YEAH? WELL, PLOW THIS!
NO SCUMBAG JETZ GONNA STOP THIS DEAL FROM GOIN' DOWN.
WHY SHOULD THEY BOTHER?
THAT IS WHY I AM HERE.
IT'S THAT AVENGER GUY -- THE VISION!
HOLY -- !
WHAT'S HE DOIN' HORNIN' IN? THIS IS A PRIVATE FIGHT!
CHAPTER 1
OUT OF THE SHADOWS...!

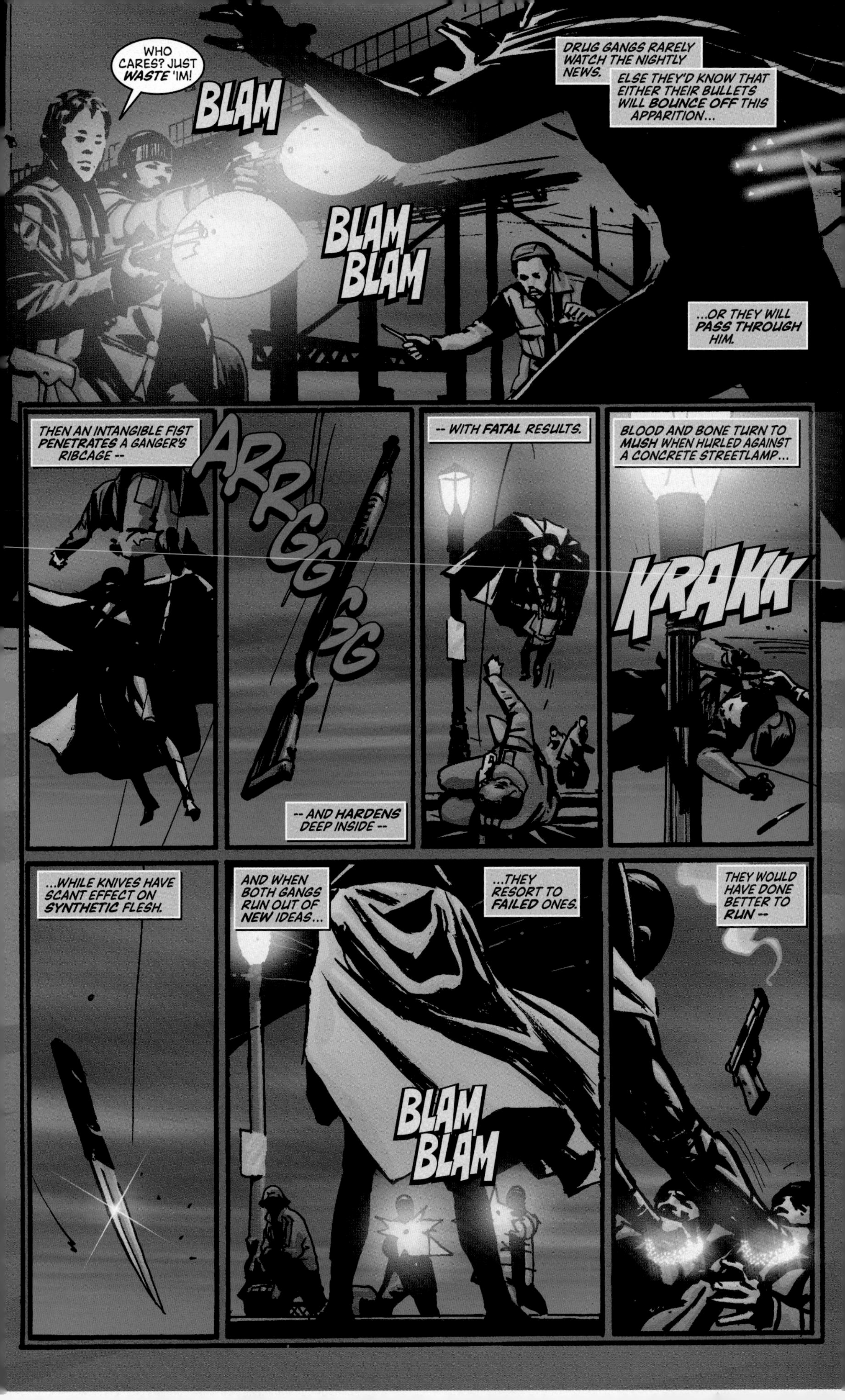
WHO CARES? JUST WASTE 'IM!
BLAM
DRUG GANGS RARELY WATCH THE NIGHTLY NEWS.
ELSE THEY'D KNOW THAT EITHER THEIR BULLETS WILL BOUNCE OFF THIS APPARITION...
BLAM BLAM
...OR THEY WILL PASS THROUGH HIM.
THEN AN INTANGIBLE FIST PENETRATES A GANGER'S RIBCAGE --
ARRGGGG
-- AND HARDENS DEEP INSIDE --
-- WITH FATAL RESULTS.
BLOOD AND BONE TURN TO MUSH WHEN HURLED AGAINST A CONCRETE STREETLAMP...
KRAKK
...WHILE KNIVES HAVE SCANT EFFECT ON SYNTHETIC FLESH.
AND WHEN BOTH GANGS RUN OUT OF NEW IDEAS...
...THEY RESORT TO FAILED ONES.
BLAM BLAM
THEY WOULD HAVE DONE BETTER TO RUN --

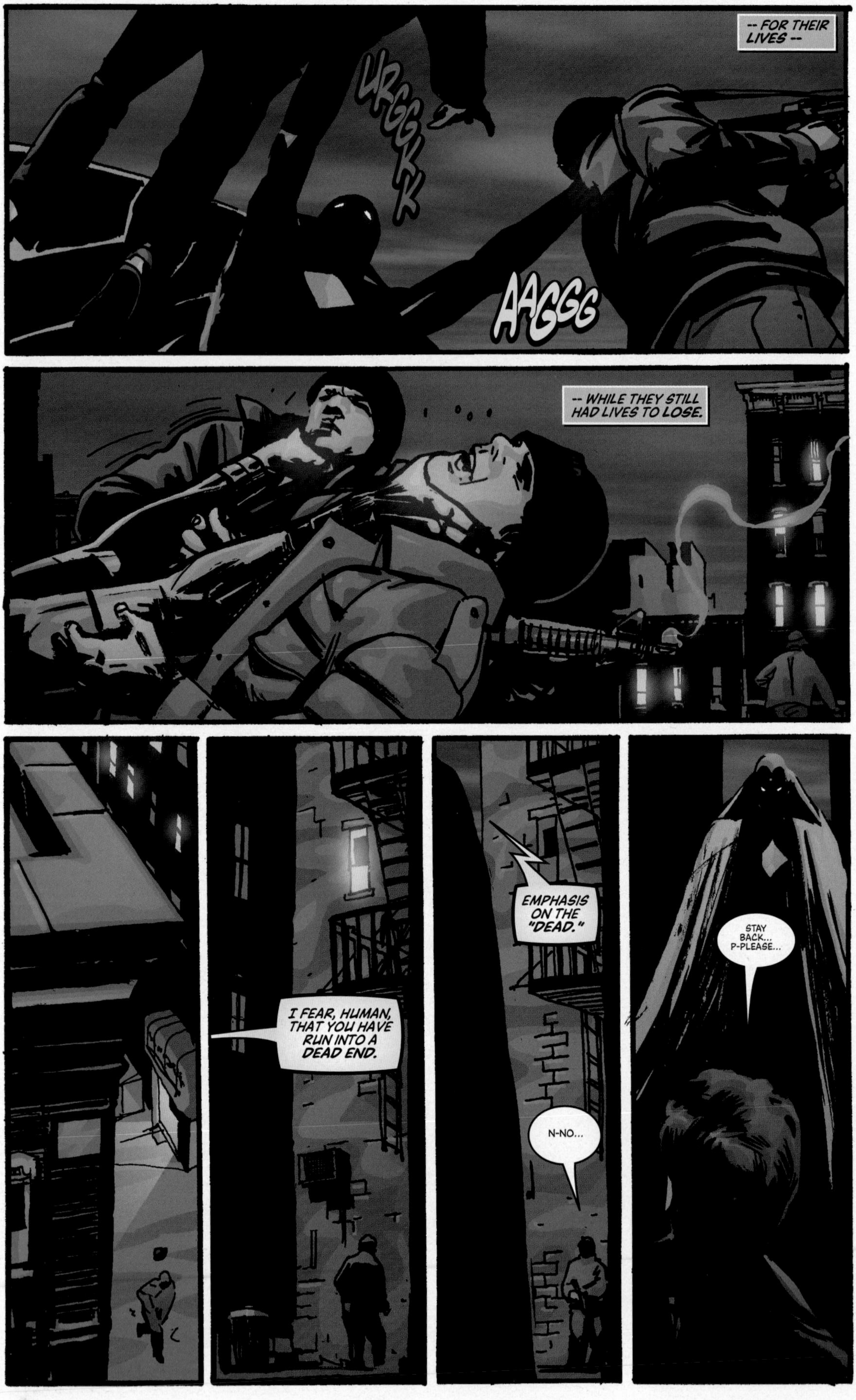
-- FOR THEIR LIVES --
URGGKK
AAGGG
-- WHILE THEY STILL HAD LIVES TO LOSE.
I FEAR, HUMAN, THAT YOU HAVE RUN INTO A DEAD END.
EMPHASIS ON THE "DEAD."
N-NO...
STAY BACK... P-PLEASE...

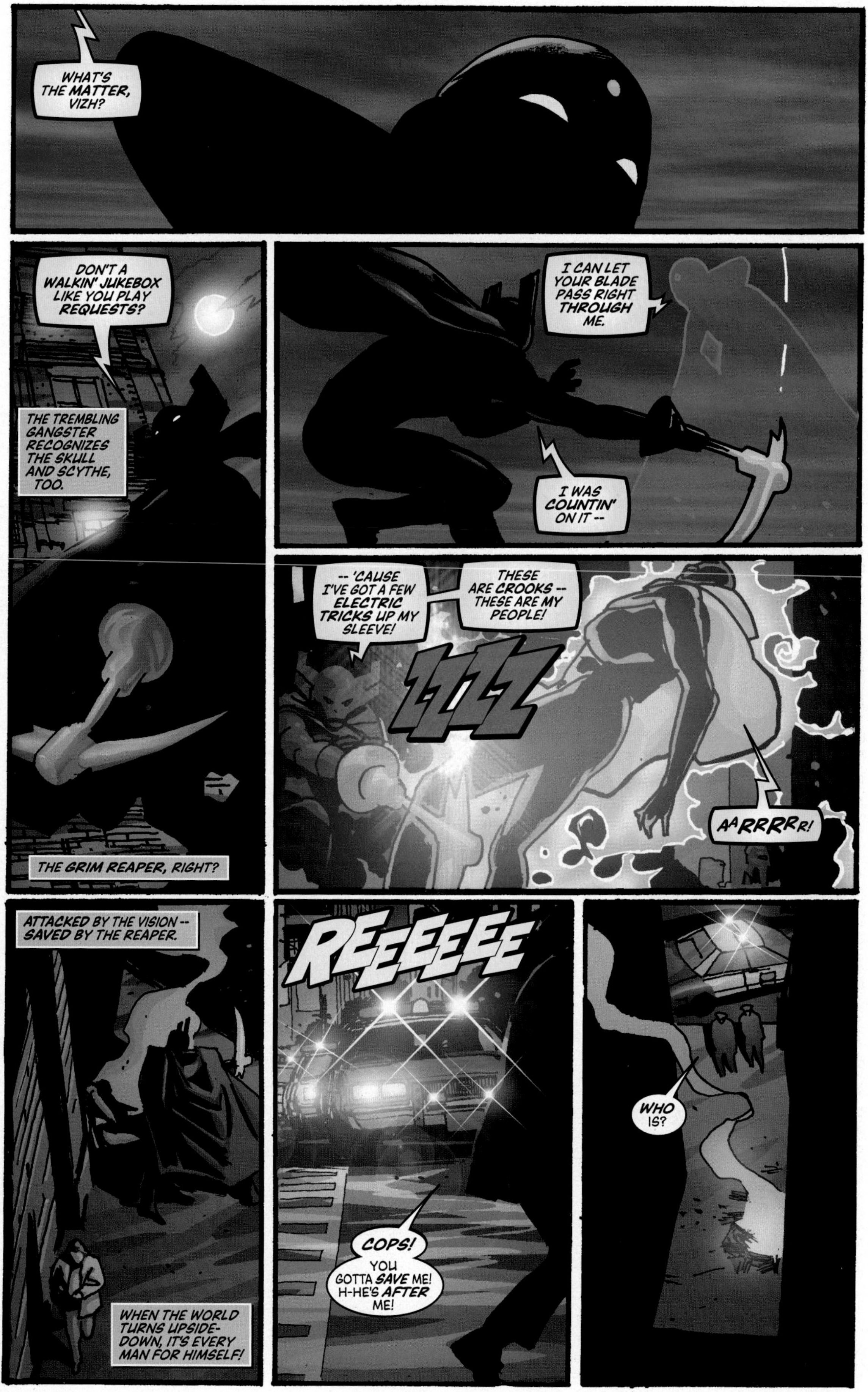
WHAT'S THE MATTER, VIZH?
DON'T A WALKIN' JUKEBOX LIKE YOU PLAY REQUESTS?
THE TREMBLING GANGSTER RECOGNIZES THE SKULL AND SCYTHE, TOO.
I CAN LET YOUR BLADE PASS RIGHT THROUGH ME.
I WAS COUNTIN' ON IT --
THE GRIM REAPER, RIGHT?
-- 'CAUSE I'VE GOT A FEW ELECTRIC TRICKS UP MY SLEEVE!
THESE ARE CROOKS -- THESE ARE MY PEOPLE!
ZZZZ
AARRRRR!
ATTACKED BY THE VISION -- SAVED BY THE REAPER.
WHEN THE WORLD TURNS UPSIDE-DOWN, IT'S EVERY MAN FOR HIMSELF!
REEEEEE
COPS!
YOU GOTTA SAVE ME! H-HE'S AFTER ME!
WHO IS?

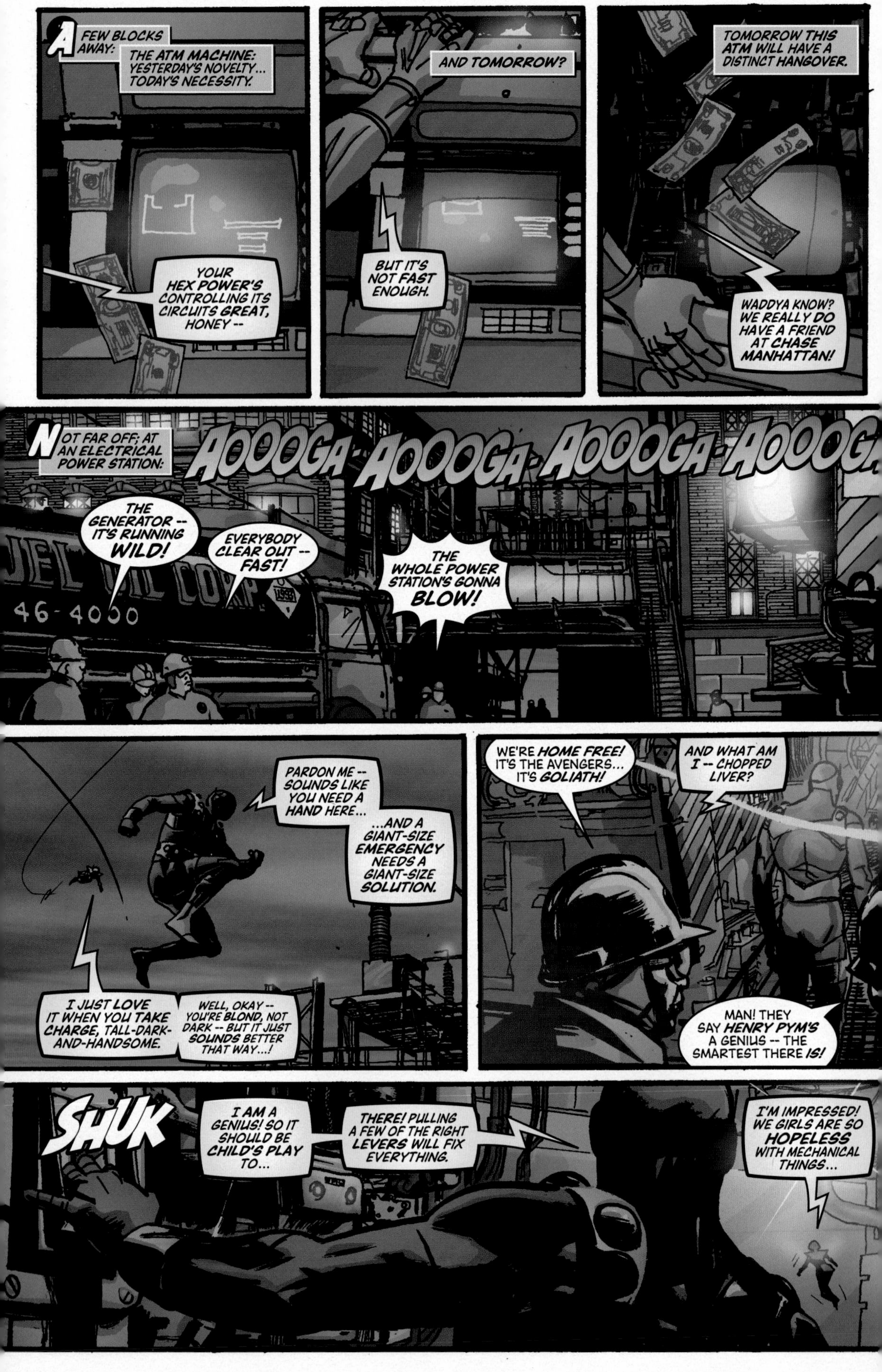
A FEW BLOCKS AWAY:
THE ATM MACHINE: YESTERDAY'S NOVELTY... TODAY'S NECESSITY.
YOUR HEX POWER'S CONTROLLING ITS CIRCUITS GREAT, HONEY --
AND TOMORROW?
BUT IT'S NOT FAST ENOUGH.
TOMORROW THIS ATM WILL HAVE A DISTINCT HANGOVER.
WADDYA KNOW? WE REALLY DO HAVE A FRIEND AT CHASE MANHATTAN!
NOT FAR OFF; AT AN ELECTRICAL POWER STATION:
AOOOGA AOOOGA AOOOGA AOOOG
THE GENERATOR -- IT'S RUNNING WILD!
EVERYBODY CLEAR OUT -- FAST!
THE WHOLE POWER STATION'S GONNA BLOW!
46-4000
PARDON ME -- SOUNDS LIKE YOU NEED A HAND HERE...
...AND A GIANT-SIZE EMERGENCY NEEDS A GIANT-SIZE SOLUTION.
I JUST LOVE IT WHEN YOU TAKE CHARGE, TALL-DARK-AND-HANDSOME.
WELL, OKAY -- YOU'RE BLOND, NOT DARK -- BUT IT JUST SOUNDS BETTER THAT WAY...!
WE'RE HOME FREE! IT'S THE AVENGERS... IT'S GOLIATH!
AND WHAT AM I -- CHOPPED LIVER?
MAN! THEY SAY HENRY PYM'S A GENIUS -- THE SMARTEST THERE IS!
SHUK
I AM A GENIUS! SO IT SHOULD BE CHILD'S PLAY TO...
THERE! PULLING A FEW OF THE RIGHT LEVERS WILL FIX EVERYTHING.
I'M IMPRESSED! WE GIRLS ARE SO HOPELESS WITH MECHANICAL THINGS...

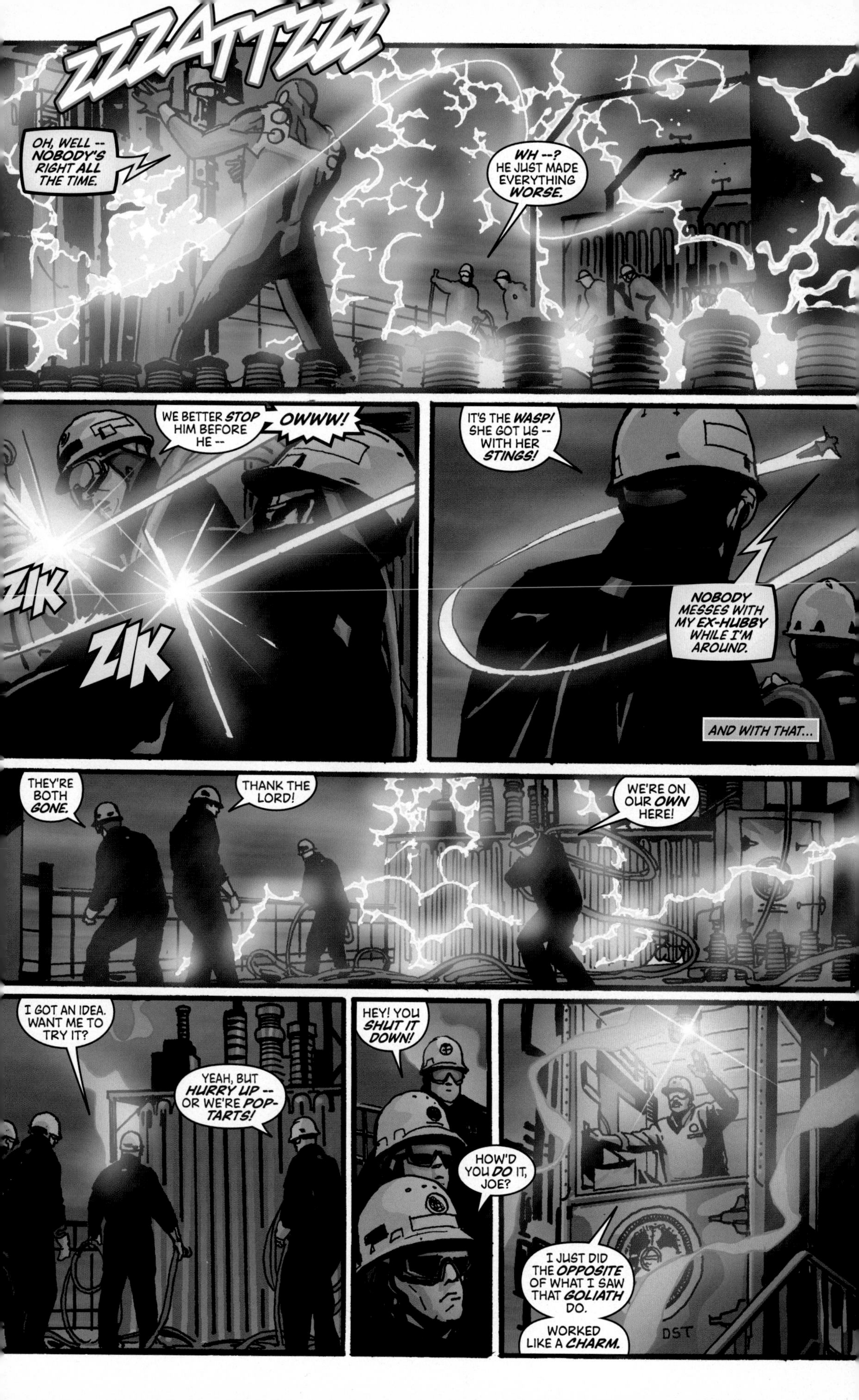

ZZZATTZZZ
OH, WELL -- NOBODY'S RIGHT ALL THE TIME.
WH --? HE JUST MADE EVERYTHING WORSE.
WE BETTER STOP HIM BEFORE HE --
OWWW!
ZIK
ZIK
IT'S THE WASP! SHE GOT US -- WITH HER STINGS!
NOBODY MESSES WITH MY EX-HUBBY WHILE I'M AROUND.
AND WITH THAT...
THEY'RE BOTH GONE.
THANK THE LORD!
WE'RE ON OUR OWN HERE!
I GOT AN IDEA. WANT ME TO TRY IT?
YEAH, BUT HURRY UP -- OR WE'RE POP-TARTS!
HEY! YOU SHUT IT DOWN!
HOW'D YOU DO IT, JOE?
I JUST DID THE OPPOSITE OF WHAT I SAW THAT GOLIATH DO.
WORKED LIKE A CHARM.
DST

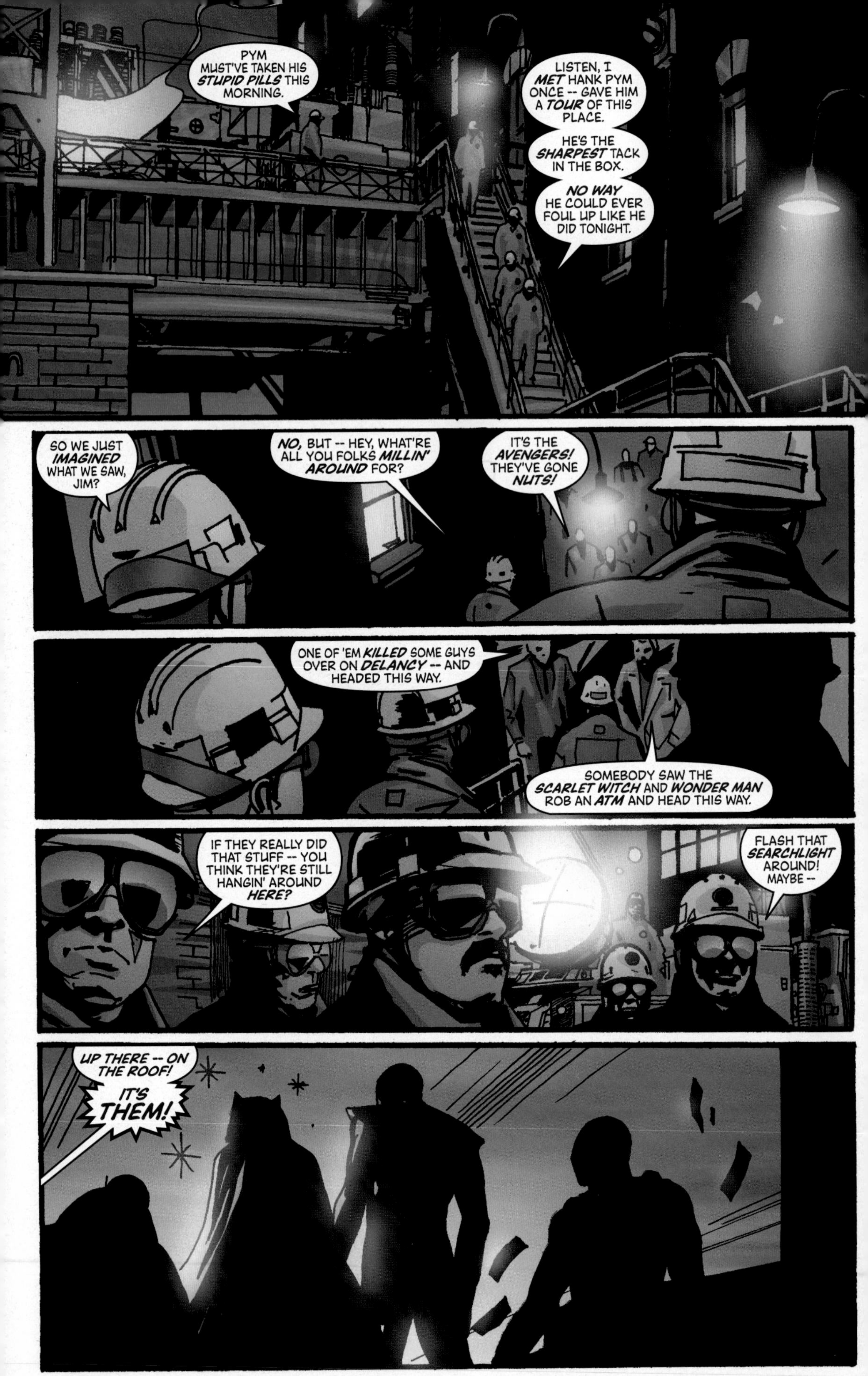
PYM MUST'VE TAKEN HIS STUPID PILLS THIS MORNING.
LISTEN, I MET HANK PYM ONCE -- GAVE HIM A TOUR OF THIS PLACE.
HE'S THE SHARPEST TACK IN THE BOX.
NO WAY HE COULD EVER FOUL UP LIKE HE DID TONIGHT.
SO WE JUST IMAGINED WHAT WE SAW, JIM?
NO, BUT -- HEY, WHAT'RE ALL YOU FOLKS MILLIN' AROUND FOR?
IT'S THE AVENGERS! THEY'VE GONE NUTS!
ONE OF 'EM KILLED SOME GUYS OVER ON DELANCY -- AND HEADED THIS WAY.
SOMEBODY SAW THE SCARLET WITCH AND WONDER MAN ROB AN ATM AND HEAD THIS WAY.
IF THEY REALLY DID THAT STUFF -- YOU THINK THEY'RE STILL HANGIN' AROUND HERE?
FLASH THAT SEARCHLIGHT AROUND! MAYBE --
UP THERE -- ON THE ROOF!
IT'S THEM!

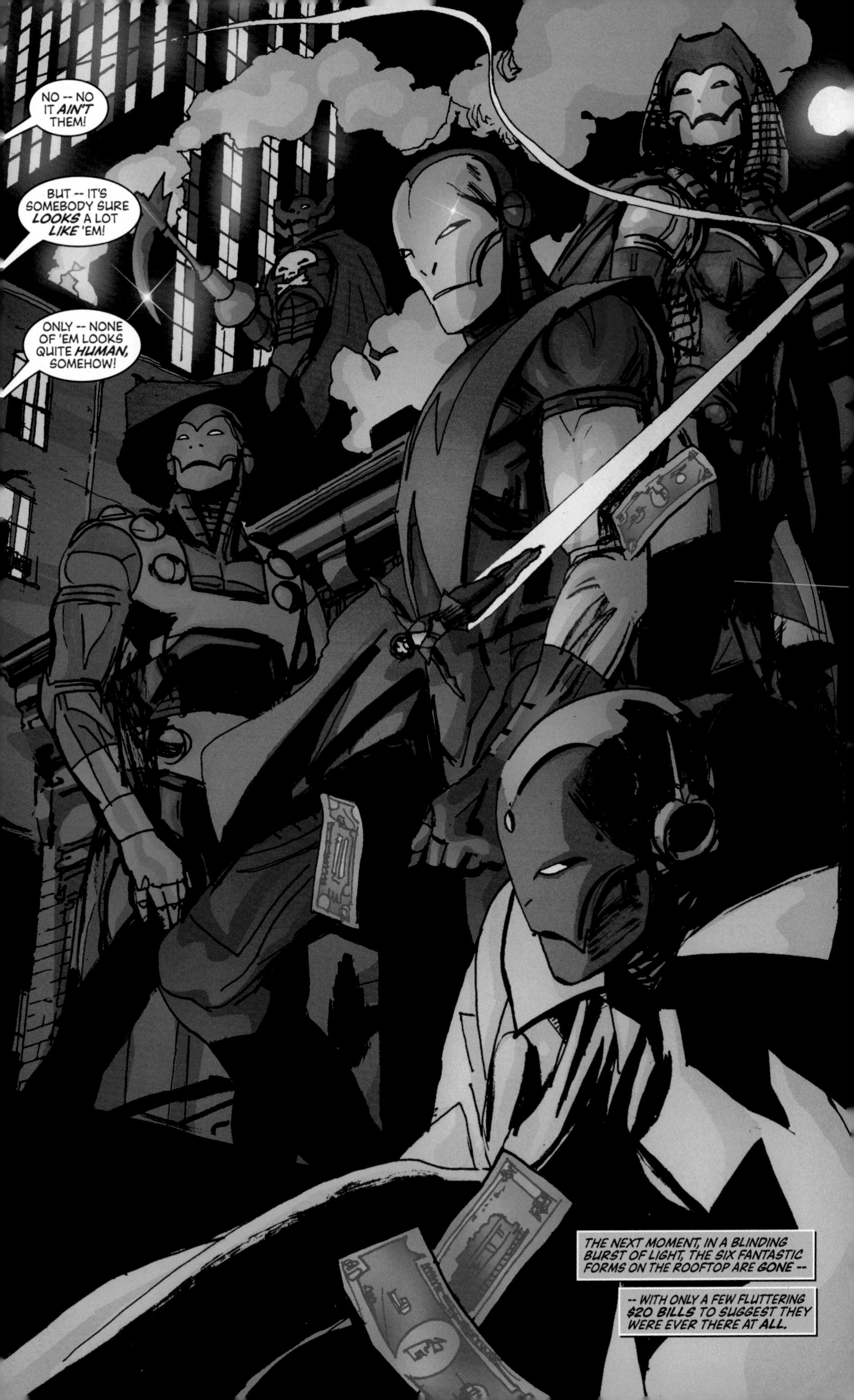
NO -- NO IT AIN'T THEM!
BUT -- IT'S SOMEBODY SURE LOOKS A LOT LIKE 'EM!
ONLY -- NONE OF 'EM LOOKS QUITE HUMAN, SOMEHOW!
THE NEXT MOMENT, IN A BLINDING BURST OF LIGHT, THE SIX FANTASTIC FORMS ON THE ROOFTOP ARE GONE --
-- WITH ONLY A FEW FLUTTERING $20 BILLS TO SUGGEST THEY WERE EVER THERE AT ALL.

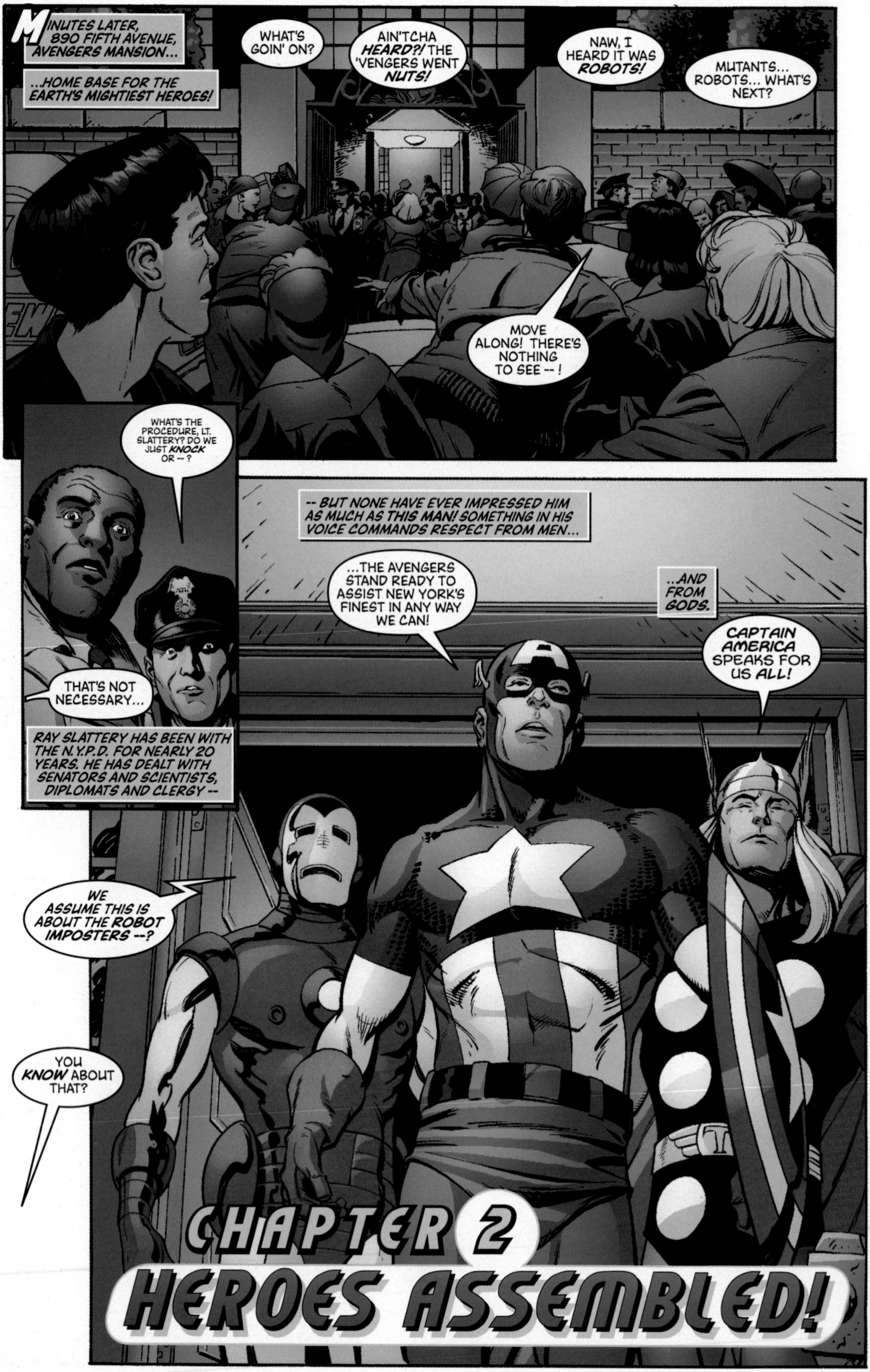
MINUTES LATER, 890 FIFTH AVENUE, AVENGERS MANSION...
...HOME BASE FOR THE EARTH'S MIGHTIEST HEROES!
WHAT'S GOIN' ON?
AIN'TCHA HEARD?! THE 'VENGERS WENT NUTS!
NAW, I HEARD IT WAS ROBOTS!
MUTANTS... ROBOTS... WHAT'S NEXT?
MOVE ALONG! THERE'S NOTHING TO SEE -- !
WHAT'S THE PROCEDURE, LT. SLATTERY? DO WE JUST KNOCK OR -- ?
THAT'S NOT NECESSARY...
RAY SLATTERY HAS BEEN WITH THE N.Y.P.D. FOR NEARLY 20 YEARS. HE HAS DEALT WITH SENATORS AND SCIENTISTS, DIPLOMATS AND CLERGY --
-- BUT NONE HAVE EVER IMPRESSED HIM AS MUCH AS THIS MAN! SOMETHING IN HIS VOICE COMMANDS RESPECT FROM MEN...
...THE AVENGERS STAND READY TO ASSIST NEW YORK'S FINEST IN ANY WAY WE CAN!
...AND FROM GODS.
CAPTAIN AMERICA SPEAKS FOR US ALL!
WE ASSUME THIS IS ABOUT THE ROBOT IMPOSTERS --?
YOU KNOW ABOUT THAT?
CHAPTER 2
HEROES ASSEMBLED!

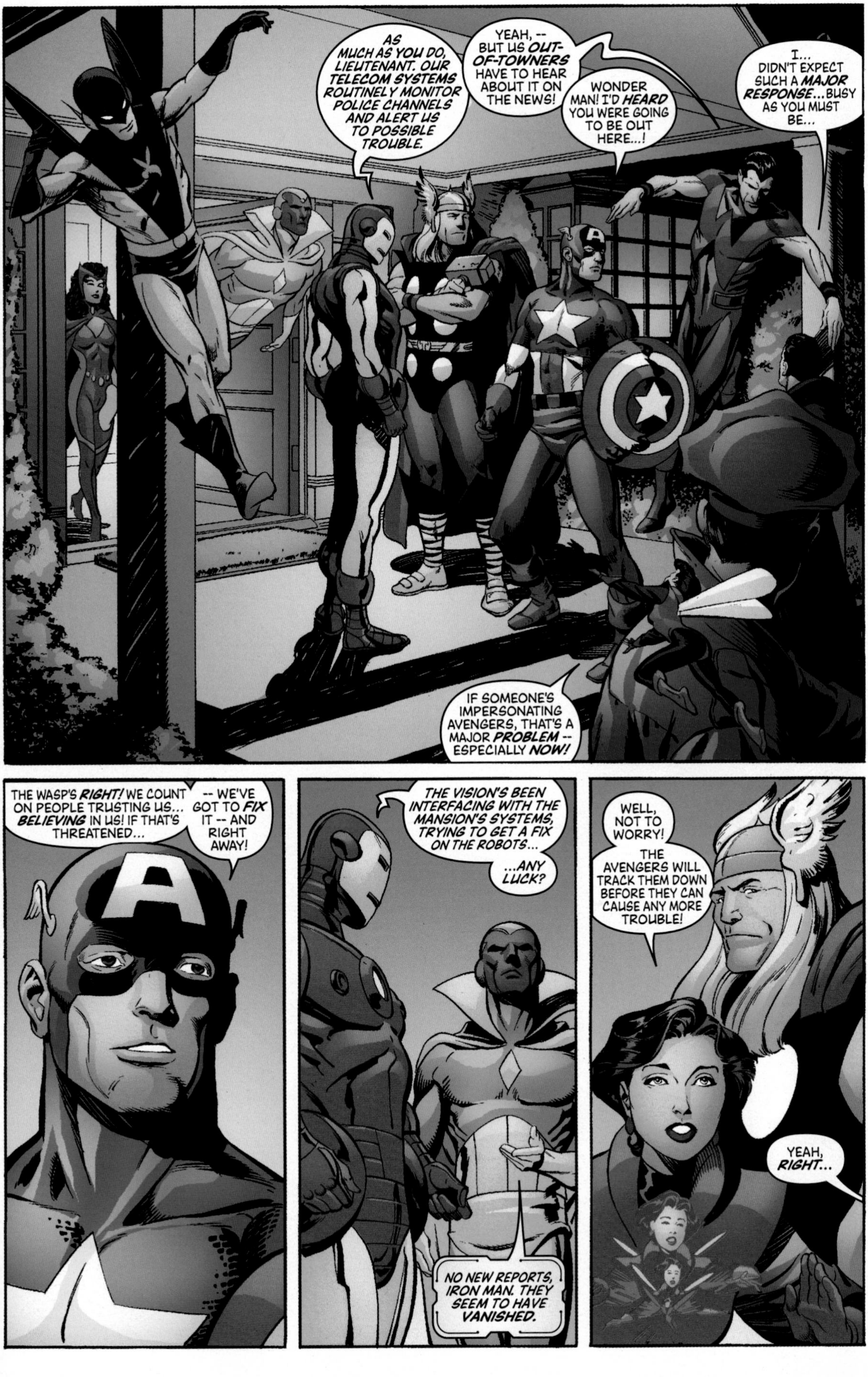
AS MUCH AS YOU DO, LIEUTENANT. OUR TELECOM SYSTEMS ROUTINELY MONITOR POLICE CHANNELS AND ALERT US TO POSSIBLE TROUBLE.
YEAH, -- BUT US OUT-OF-TOWNERS HAVE TO HEAR ABOUT IT ON THE NEWS!
WONDER MAN! I'D HEARD YOU WERE GOING TO BE OUT HERE...!
I... DIDN'T EXPECT SUCH A MAJOR RESPONSE... BUSY AS YOU MUST BE...
IF SOMEONE'S IMPERSONATING AVENGERS, THAT'S A MAJOR PROBLEM -- ESPECIALLY NOW!
THE WASP'S RIGHT! WE COUNT ON PEOPLE TRUSTING US... BELIEVING IN US! IF THAT'S THREATENED...
-- WE'VE GOT TO FIX IT -- AND RIGHT AWAY!
THE VISION'S BEEN INTERFACING WITH THE MANSION'S SYSTEMS, TRYING TO GET A FIX ON THE ROBOTS...
...ANY LUCK?
NO NEW REPORTS, IRON MAN. THEY SEEM TO HAVE VANISHED.
WELL, NOT TO WORRY!
THE AVENGERS WILL TRACK THEM DOWN BEFORE THEY CAN CAUSE ANY MORE TROUBLE!
YEAH, RIGHT...

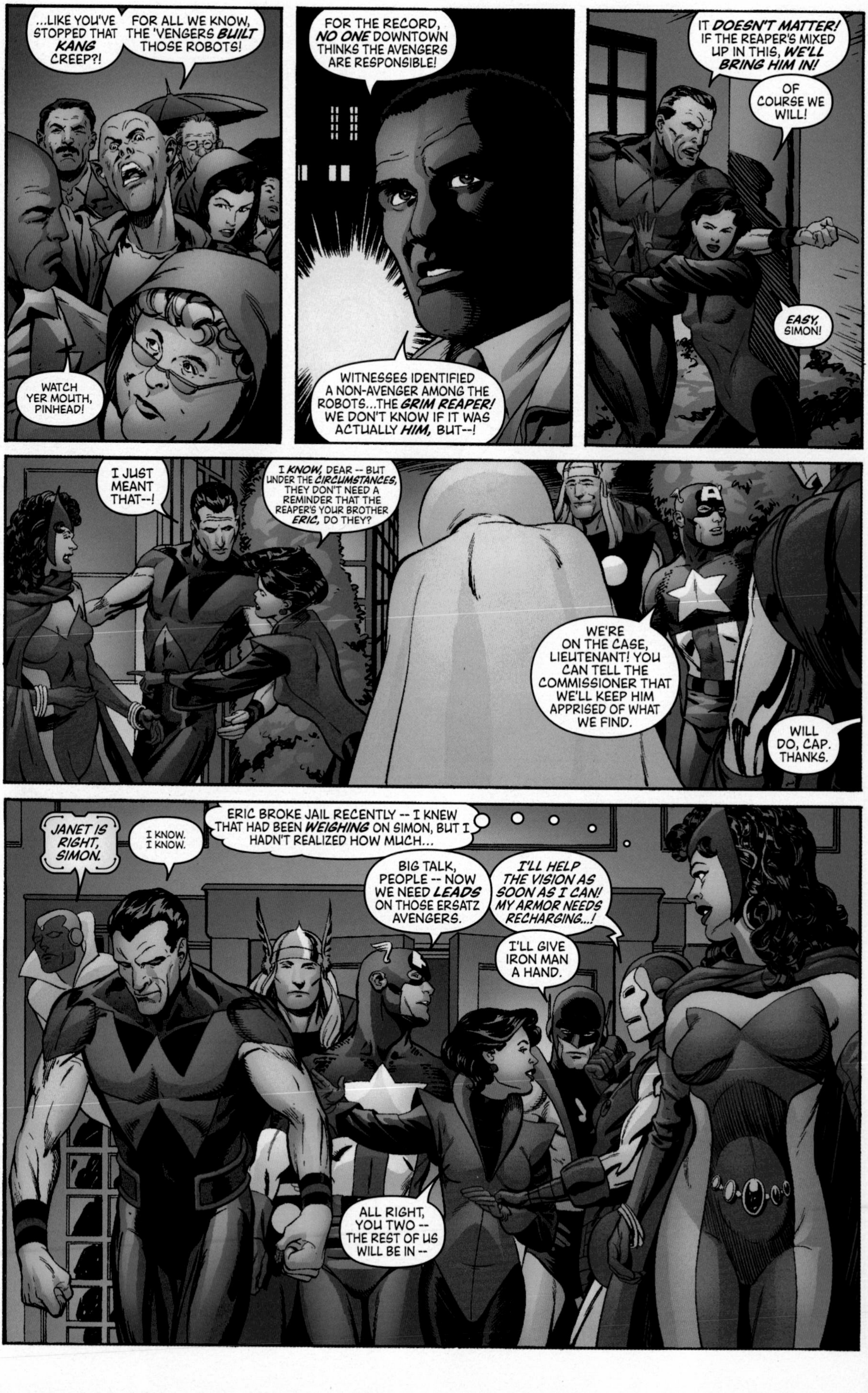

...LIKE YOU'VE STOPPED THAT KANG CREEP?!
FOR ALL WE KNOW, THE 'VENGERS BUILT THOSE ROBOTS!
WATCH YER MOUTH, PINHEAD!
FOR THE RECORD, NO ONE DOWNTOWN THINKS THE AVENGERS ARE RESPONSIBLE!
WITNESSES IDENTIFIED A NON-AVENGER AMONG THE ROBOTS...THE GRIM REAPER! WE DON'T KNOW IF IT WAS ACTUALLY HIM, BUT--!
IT DOESN'T MATTER! IF THE REAPER'S MIXED UP IN THIS, WE'LL BRING HIM IN!
OF COURSE WE WILL!
EASY, SIMON!
I JUST MEANT THAT--!
I KNOW, DEAR -- BUT UNDER THE CIRCUMSTANCES, THEY DON'T NEED A REMINDER THAT THE REAPER'S YOUR BROTHER ERIC, DO THEY?
WE'RE ON THE CASE, LIEUTENANT! YOU CAN TELL THE COMMISSIONER THAT WE'LL KEEP HIM APPRISED OF WHAT WE FIND.
WILL DO, CAP. THANKS.
JANET IS RIGHT, SIMON.
I KNOW. I KNOW.
ERIC BROKE JAIL RECENTLY -- I KNEW THAT HAD BEEN WEIGHING ON SIMON, BUT I HADN'T REALIZED HOW MUCH...
BIG TALK, PEOPLE -- NOW WE NEED LEADS ON THOSE ERSATZ AVENGERS.
I'LL HELP THE VISION AS SOON AS I CAN! MY ARMOR NEEDS RECHARGING...!
I'LL GIVE IRON MAN A HAND.
ALL RIGHT, YOU TWO -- THE REST OF US WILL BE IN --

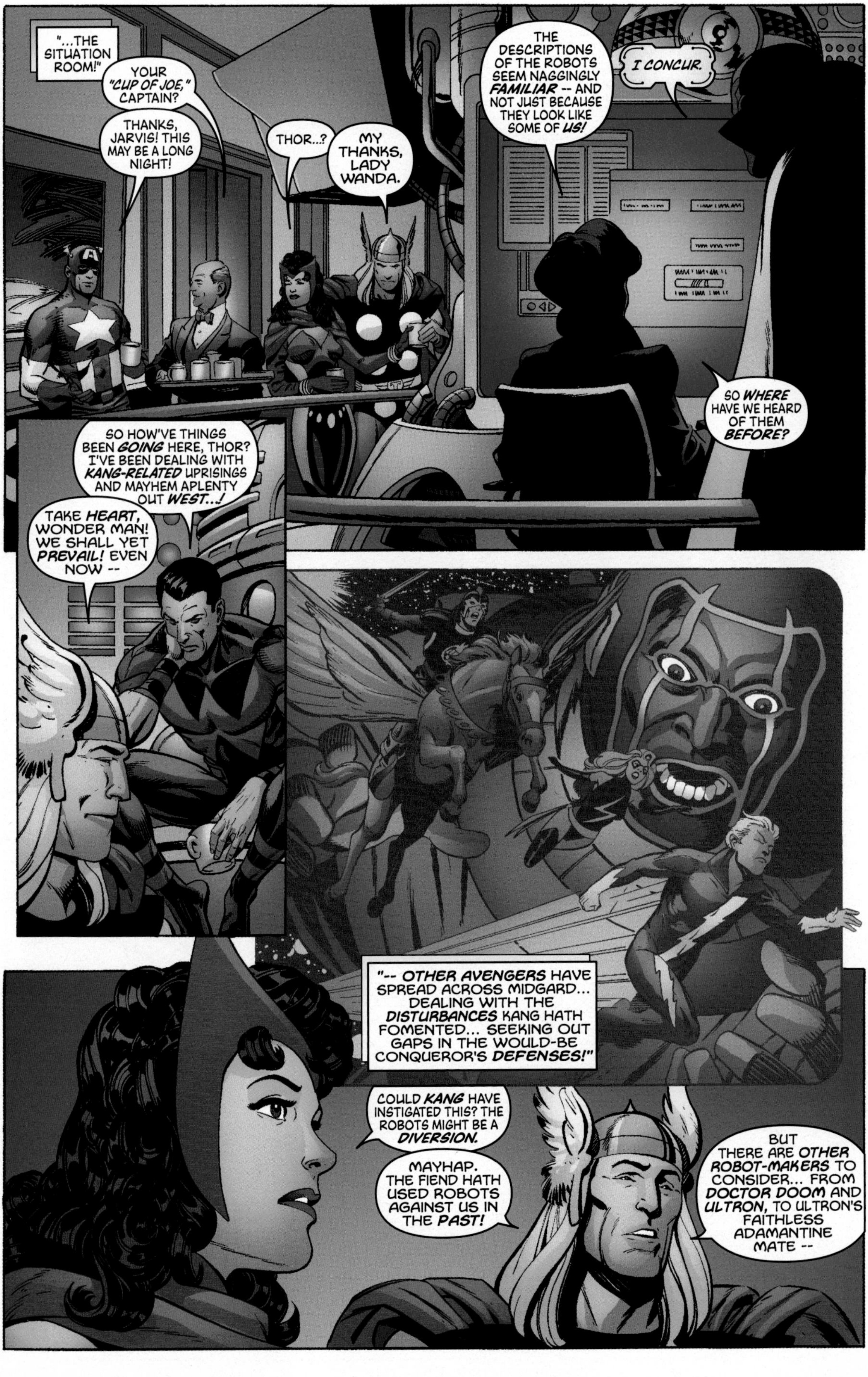
"...THE SITUATION ROOM!"
YOUR "CUP OF JOE," CAPTAIN?
THANKS, JARVIS! THIS MAY BE A LONG NIGHT!
THOR...?
MY THANKS, LADY WANDA.
THE DESCRIPTIONS OF THE ROBOTS SEEM NAGGINGLY FAMILIAR -- AND NOT JUST BECAUSE THEY LOOK LIKE SOME OF US!
I CONCUR.
SO WHERE HAVE WE HEARD OF THEM BEFORE?
SO HOW'VE THINGS BEEN GOING HERE, THOR? I'VE BEEN DEALING WITH KANG-RELATED UPRISINGS AND MAYHEM APLENTY OUT WEST...!
TAKE HEART, WONDER MAN! WE SHALL YET PREVAIL! EVEN NOW --
"-- OTHER AVENGERS HAVE SPREAD ACROSS MIDGARD... DEALING WITH THE DISTURBANCES KANG HATH FOMENTED... SEEKING OUT GAPS IN THE WOULD-BE CONQUEROR'S DEFENSES!"
COULD KANG HAVE INSTIGATED THIS? THE ROBOTS MIGHT BE A DIVERSION.
MAYHAP. THE FIEND HATH USED ROBOTS AGAINST US IN THE PAST!
BUT THERE ARE OTHER ROBOT-MAKERS TO CONSIDER... FROM DOCTOR DOOM AND ULTRON, TO ULTRON'S FAITHLESS ADAMANTINE MATE --

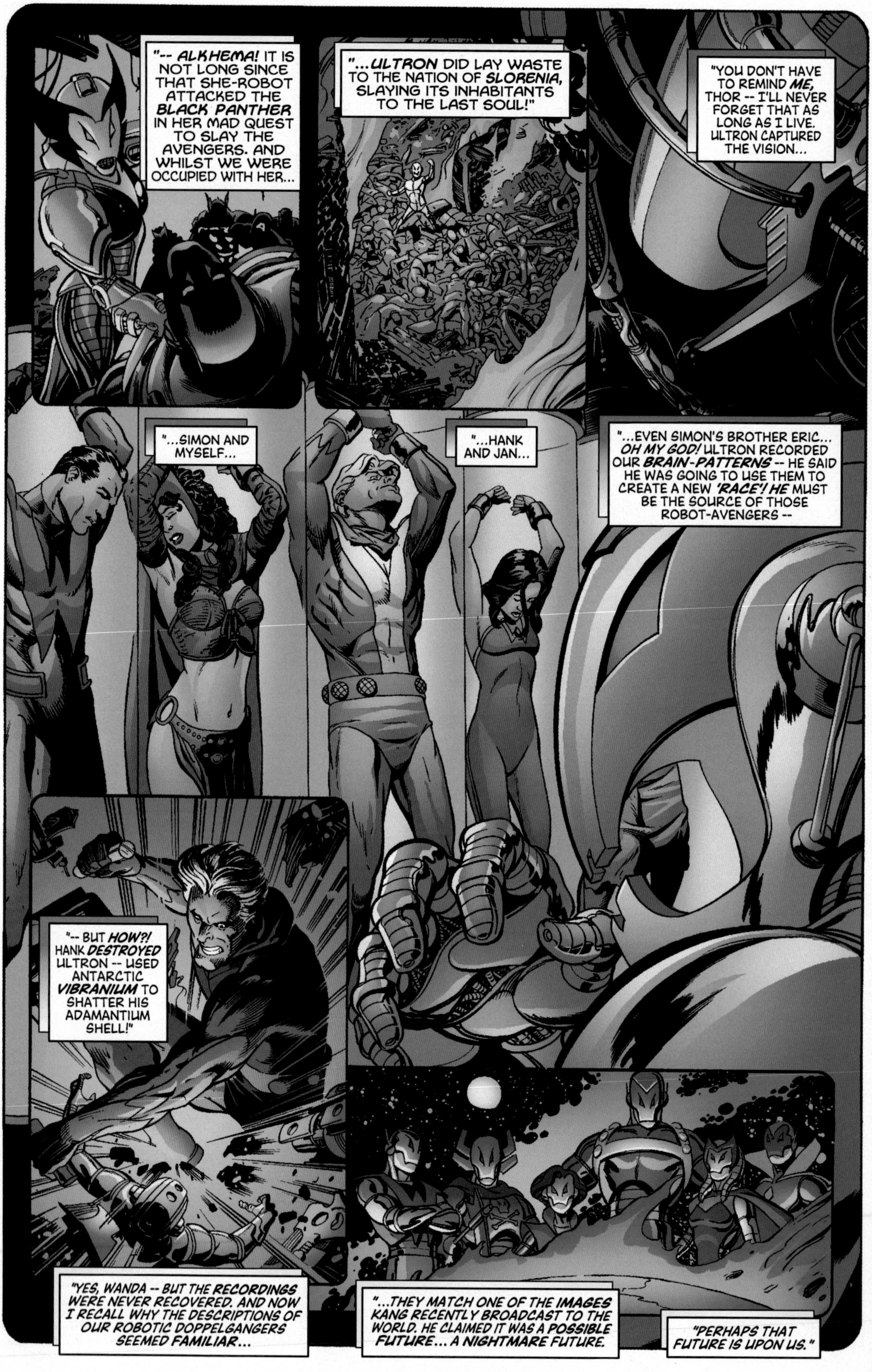
"-- ALKHEMA! IT IS NOT LONG SINCE THAT SHE-ROBOT ATTACKED THE BLACK PANTHER IN HER MAD QUEST TO SLAY THE AVENGERS. AND WHILST WE WERE OCCUPIED WITH HER...
"...ULTRON DID LAY WASTE TO THE NATION OF SLORENIA, SLAYING ITS INHABITANTS TO THE LAST SOUL!"
"YOU DON'T HAVE TO REMIND ME, THOR -- I'LL NEVER FORGET THAT AS LONG AS I LIVE. ULTRON CAPTURED THE VISION...
"...SIMON AND MYSELF...
"...HANK AND JAN...
"...EVEN SIMON'S BROTHER ERIC... OH MY GOD! ULTRON RECORDED OUR BRAIN-PATTERNS -- HE SAID HE WAS GOING TO USE THEM TO CREATE A NEW 'RACE'! HE MUST BE THE SOURCE OF THOSE ROBOT-AVENGERS --
"-- BUT HOW?! HANK DESTROYED ULTRON -- USED ANTARCTIC VIBRANIUM TO SHATTER HIS ADAMANTIUM SHELL!"
"YES, WANDA -- BUT THE RECORDINGS WERE NEVER RECOVERED. AND NOW I RECALL WHY THE DESCRIPTIONS OF OUR ROBOTIC DOPPELGANGERS SEEMED FAMILIAR...
"...THEY MATCH ONE OF THE IMAGES KANG RECENTLY BROADCAST TO THE WORLD. HE CLAIMED IT WAS A POSSIBLE FUTURE... A NIGHTMARE FUTURE.
"PERHAPS THAT FUTURE IS UPON US."

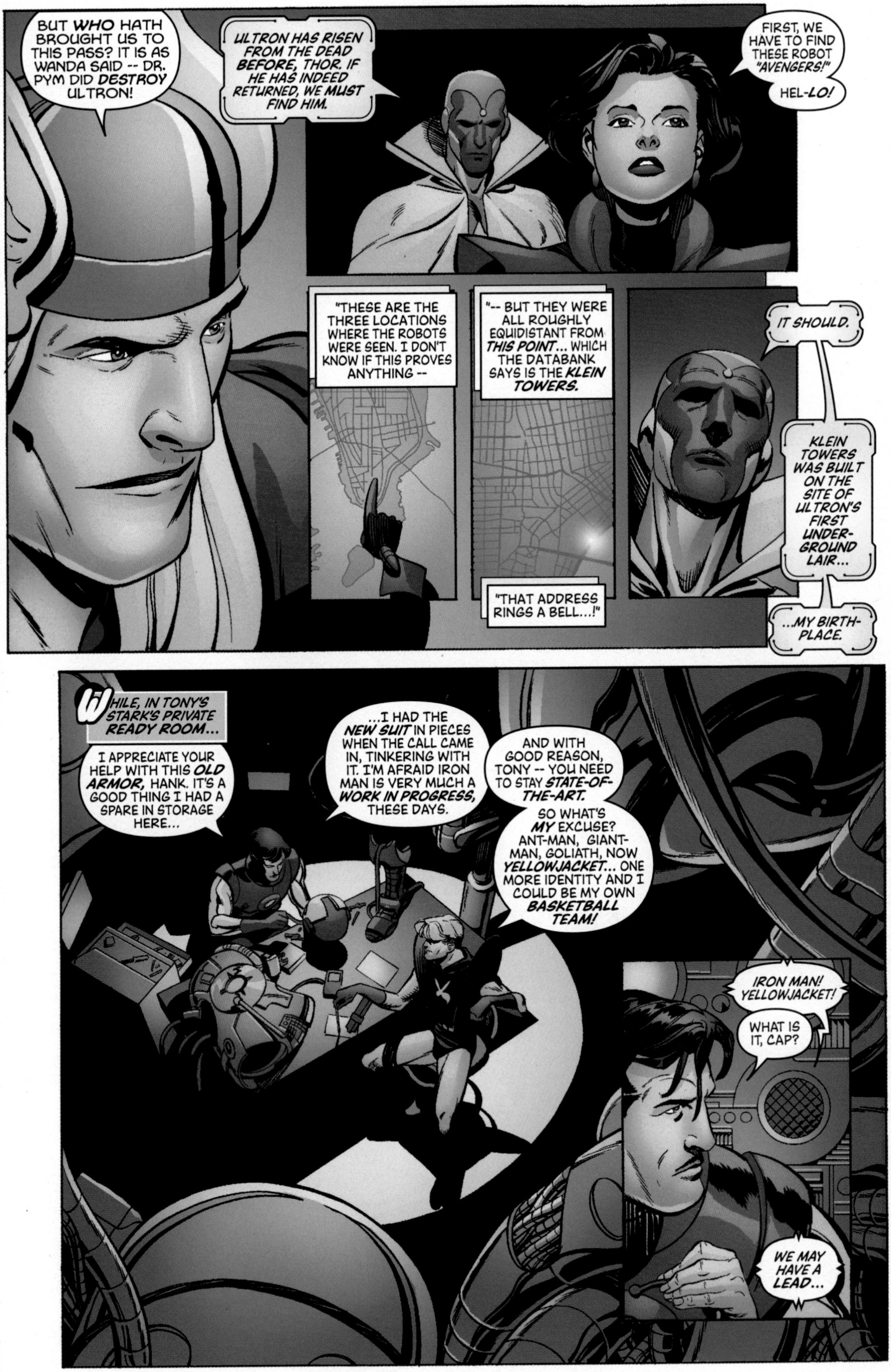
BUT WHO HATH BROUGHT US TO THIS PASS? IT IS AS WANDA SAID -- DR. PYM DID DESTROY ULTRON!
ULTRON HAS RISEN FROM THE DEAD BEFORE, THOR. IF HE HAS INDEED RETURNED, WE MUST FIND HIM.
FIRST, WE HAVE TO FIND THESE ROBOT "AVENGERS!"
HEL-LO!
"THESE ARE THE THREE LOCATIONS WHERE THE ROBOTS WERE SEEN. I DON'T KNOW IF THIS PROVES ANYTHING --
"-- BUT THEY WERE ALL ROUGHLY EQUIDISTANT FROM THIS POINT... WHICH THE DATABANK SAYS IS THE KLEIN TOWERS.
"THAT ADDRESS RINGS A BELL...!"
IT SHOULD.
KLEIN TOWERS WAS BUILT ON THE SITE OF ULTRON'S FIRST UNDER-GROUND LAIR...
...MY BIRTH-PLACE.
WHILE, IN TONY'S STARK'S PRIVATE READY ROOM...
I APPRECIATE YOUR HELP WITH THIS OLD ARMOR, HANK. IT'S A GOOD THING I HAD A SPARE IN STORAGE HERE...
...I HAD THE NEW SUIT IN PIECES WHEN THE CALL CAME IN, TINKERING WITH IT. I'M AFRAID IRON MAN IS VERY MUCH A WORK IN PROGRESS, THESE DAYS.
AND WITH GOOD REASON, TONY -- YOU NEED TO STAY STATE-OF-THE-ART.
SO WHAT'S MY EXCUSE? ANT-MAN, GIANT-MAN, GOLIATH, NOW YELLOWJACKET... ONE MORE IDENTITY AND I COULD BE MY OWN BASKETBALL TEAM!
IRON MAN! YELLOWJACKET!
WHAT IS IT, CAP?
WE MAY HAVE A LEAD...

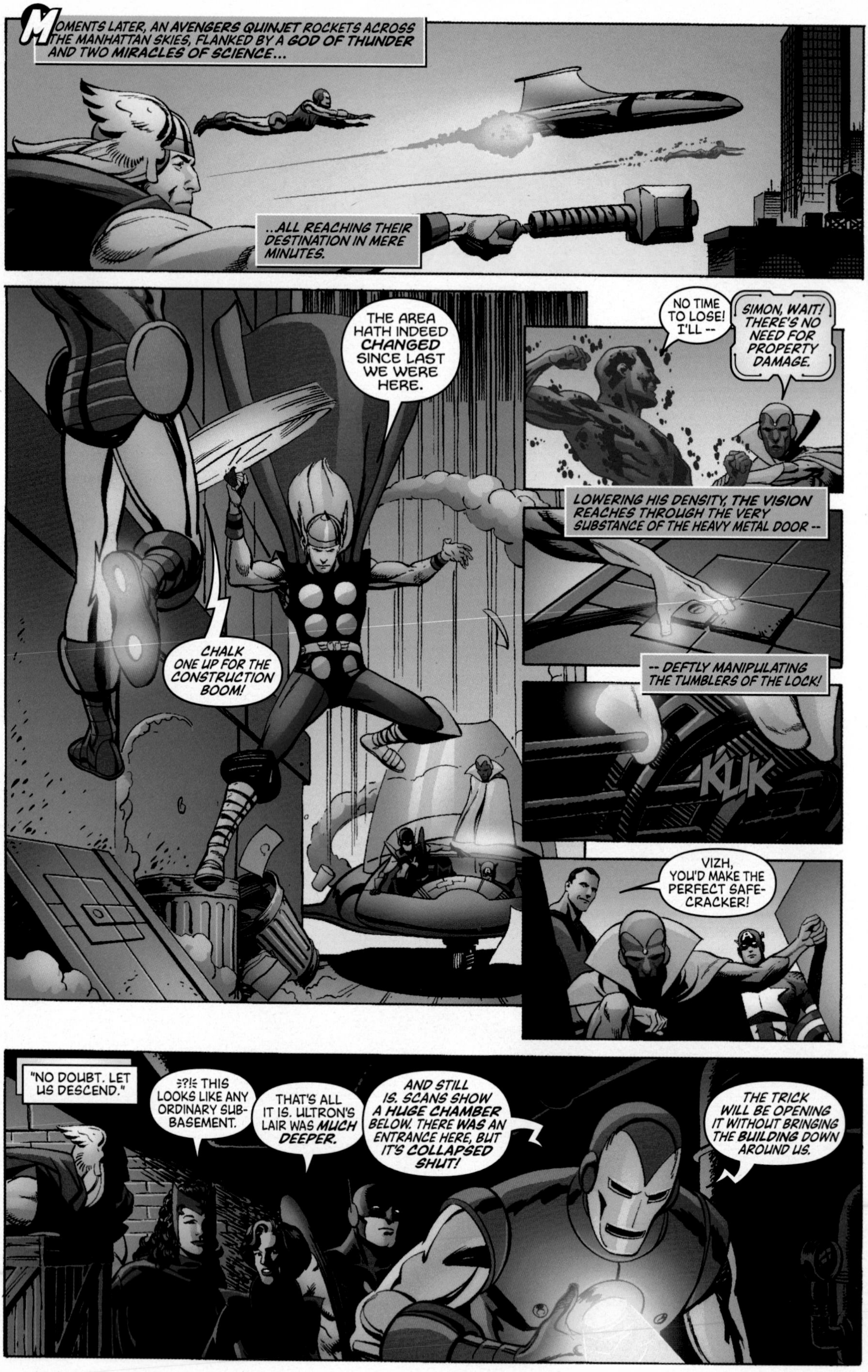
MOMENTS LATER, AN AVENGERS QUINJET ROCKETS ACROSS THE MANHATTAN SKIES, FLANKED BY A GOD OF THUNDER AND TWO MIRACLES OF SCIENCE...
...ALL REACHING THEIR DESTINATION IN MERE MINUTES.
THE AREA HATH INDEED CHANGED SINCE LAST WE WERE HERE.
CHALK ONE UP FOR THE CONSTRUCTION BOOM!
NO TIME TO LOSE! I'LL --
SIMON, WAIT! THERE'S NO NEED FOR PROPERTY DAMAGE.
LOWERING HIS DENSITY, THE VISION REACHES THROUGH THE VERY SUBSTANCE OF THE HEAVY METAL DOOR --
-- DEFTLY MANIPULATING THE TUMBLERS OF THE LOCK!
KLIK
VIZH, YOU'D MAKE THE PERFECT SAFE-CRACKER!
"NO DOUBT. LET US DESCEND."
THIS LOOKS LIKE ANY ORDINARY SUB-BASEMENT.
THAT'S ALL IT IS. ULTRON'S LAIR WAS MUCH DEEPER.
AND STILL IS. SCANS SHOW A HUGE CHAMBER BELOW. THERE WAS AN ENTRANCE HERE, BUT IT'S COLLAPSED SHUT!
THE TRICK WILL BE OPENING IT WITHOUT BRINGING THE BUILDING DOWN AROUND US.

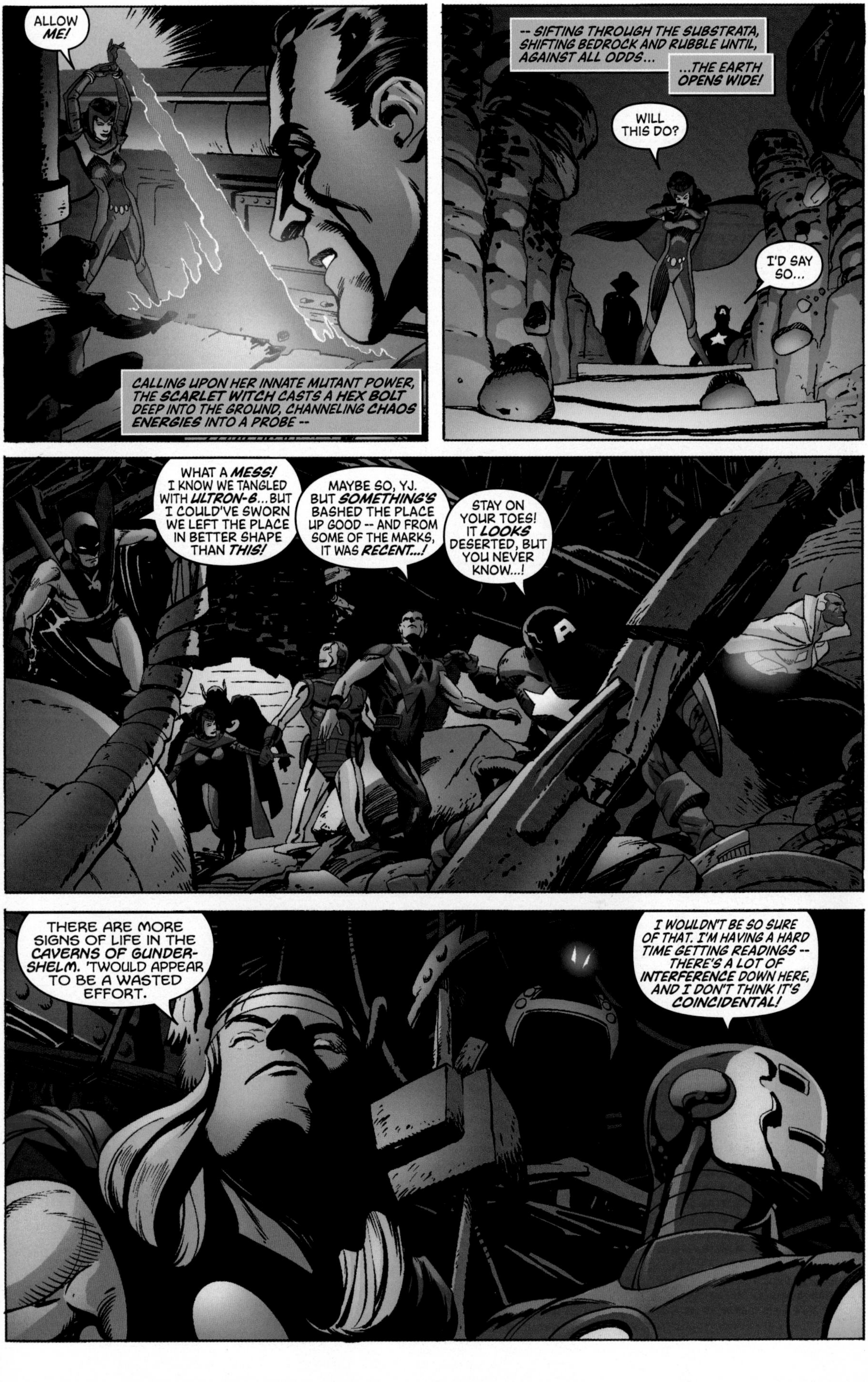
ALLOW ME!
CALLING UPON HER INNATE MUTANT POWER, THE SCARLET WITCH CASTS A HEX BOLT DEEP INTO THE GROUND, CHANNELING CHAOS ENERGIES INTO A PROBE --
-- SIFTING THROUGH THE SUBSTRATA, SHIFTING BEDROCK AND RUBBLE UNTIL, AGAINST ALL ODDS...
...THE EARTH OPENS WIDE!
WILL THIS DO?
I'D SAY SO...
WHAT A MESS! I KNOW WE TANGLED WITH ULTRON-6... BUT I COULD'VE SWORN WE LEFT THE PLACE IN BETTER SHAPE THAN THIS!
MAYBE SO, YJ. BUT SOMETHING'S BASHED THE PLACE UP GOOD -- AND FROM SOME OF THE MARKS, IT WAS RECENT...!
STAY ON YOUR TOES! IT LOOKS DESERTED, BUT YOU NEVER KNOW...!
THERE ARE MORE SIGNS OF LIFE IN THE CAVERNS OF GUNDERSHELM. 'TWOULD APPEAR TO BE A WASTED EFFORT.
I WOULDN'T BE SO SURE OF THAT. I'M HAVING A HARD TIME GETTING READINGS -- THERE'S A LOT OF INTERFERENCE DOWN HERE, AND I DON'T THINK IT'S COINCIDENTAL!

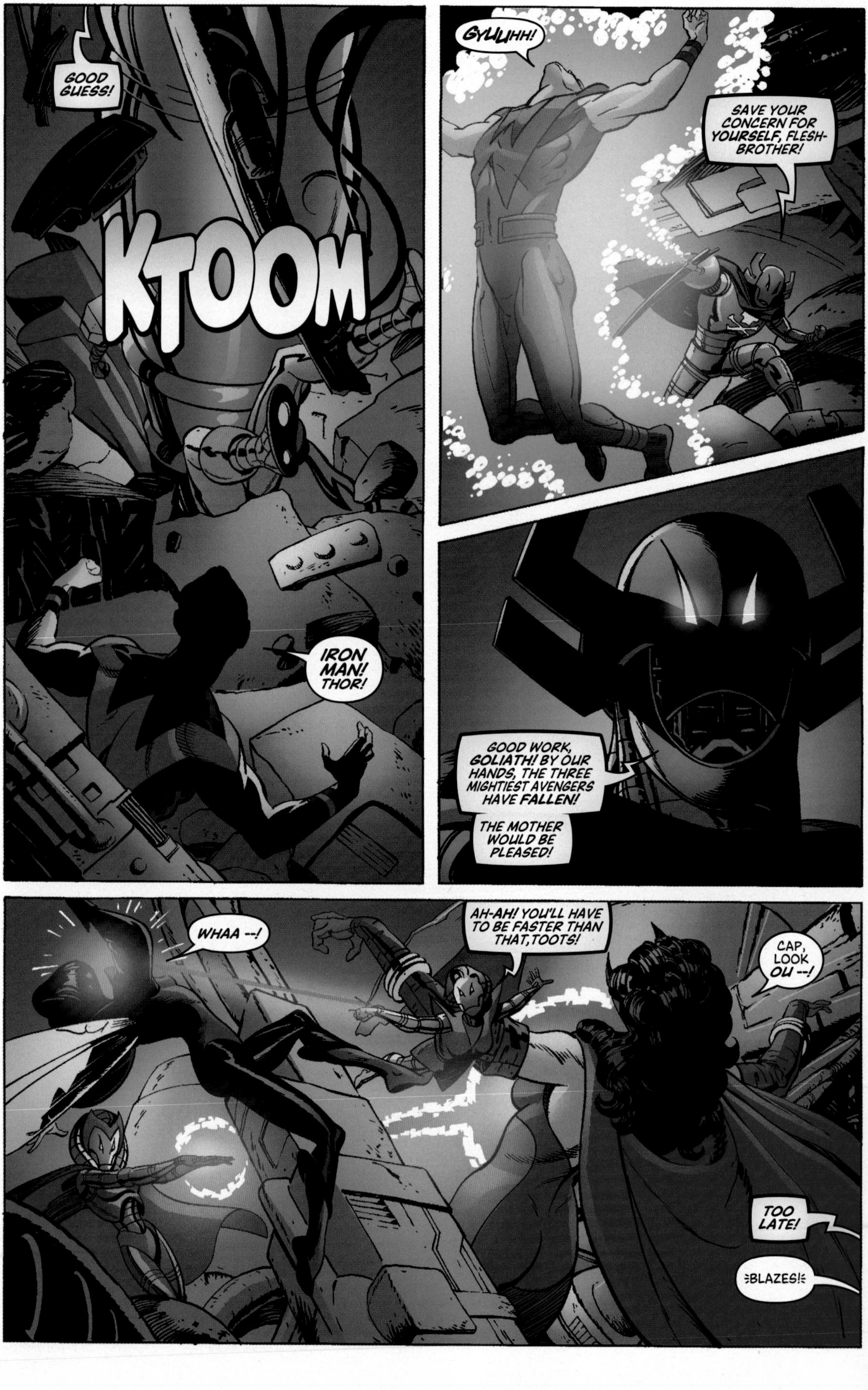
GOOD GUESS!
KTOOM
IRON MAN! THOR!
GYUHH!
SAVE YOUR CONCERN FOR YOURSELF, FLESH-BROTHER!
GOOD WORK, GOLIATH! BY OUR HANDS, THE THREE MIGHTIEST AVENGERS HAVE FALLEN!
THE MOTHER WOULD BE PLEASED!
WHAA --!
AH-AH! YOU'LL HAVE TO BE FASTER THAN THAT,TOOTS!
CAP, LOOK OU --!
TOO LATE!
BLAZES!

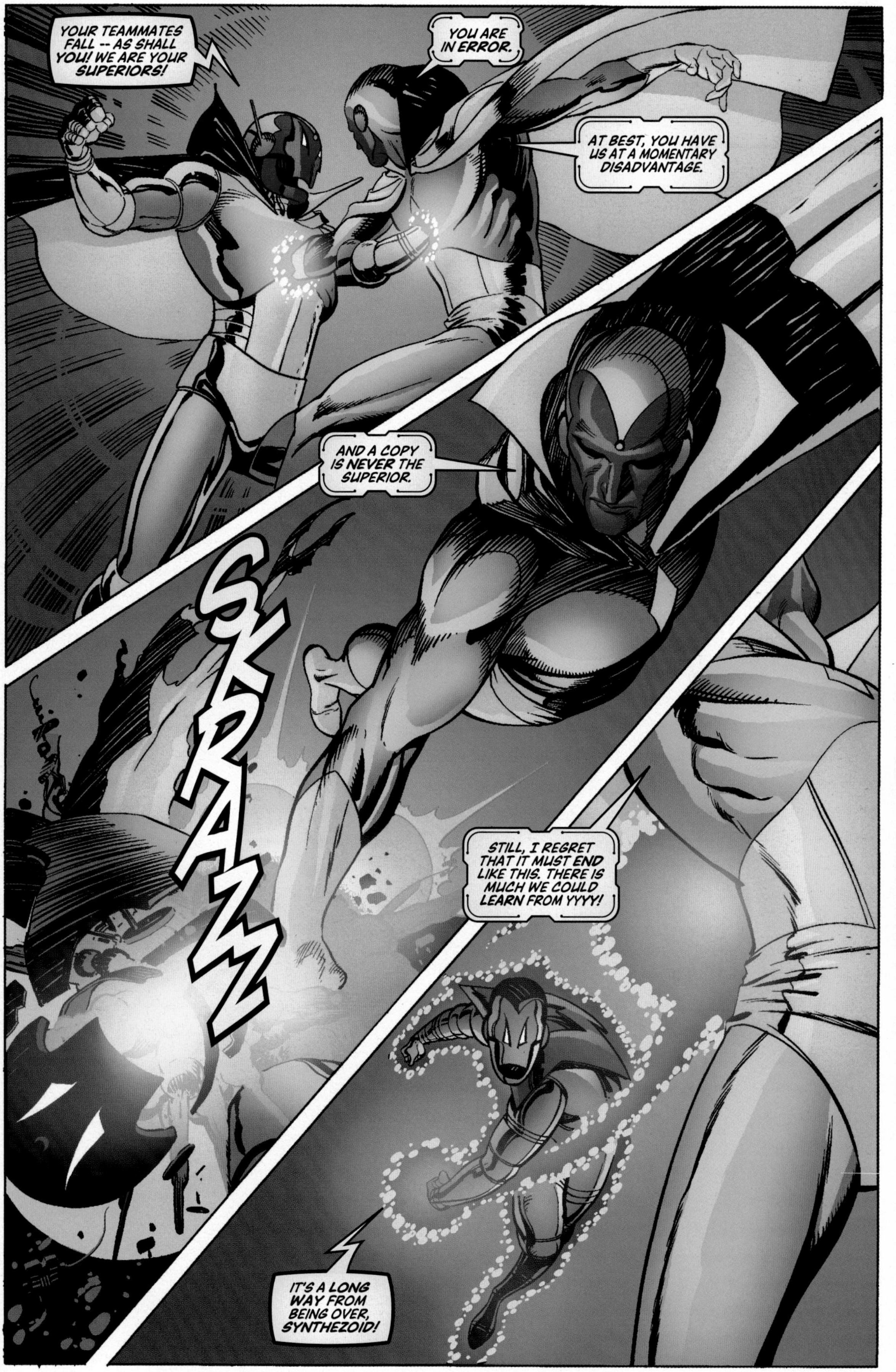
YOUR TEAMMATES FALL -- AS SHALL YOU! WE ARE YOUR SUPERIORS!
YOU ARE IN ERROR.
AT BEST, YOU HAVE US AT A MOMENTARY DISADVANTAGE.
AND A COPY IS NEVER THE SUPERIOR.
SKRAM
STILL, I REGRET THAT IT MUST END LIKE THIS. THERE IS MUCH WE COULD LEARN FROM YYYY!
IT'S A LONG WAY FROM BEING OVER, SYNTHEZOID!

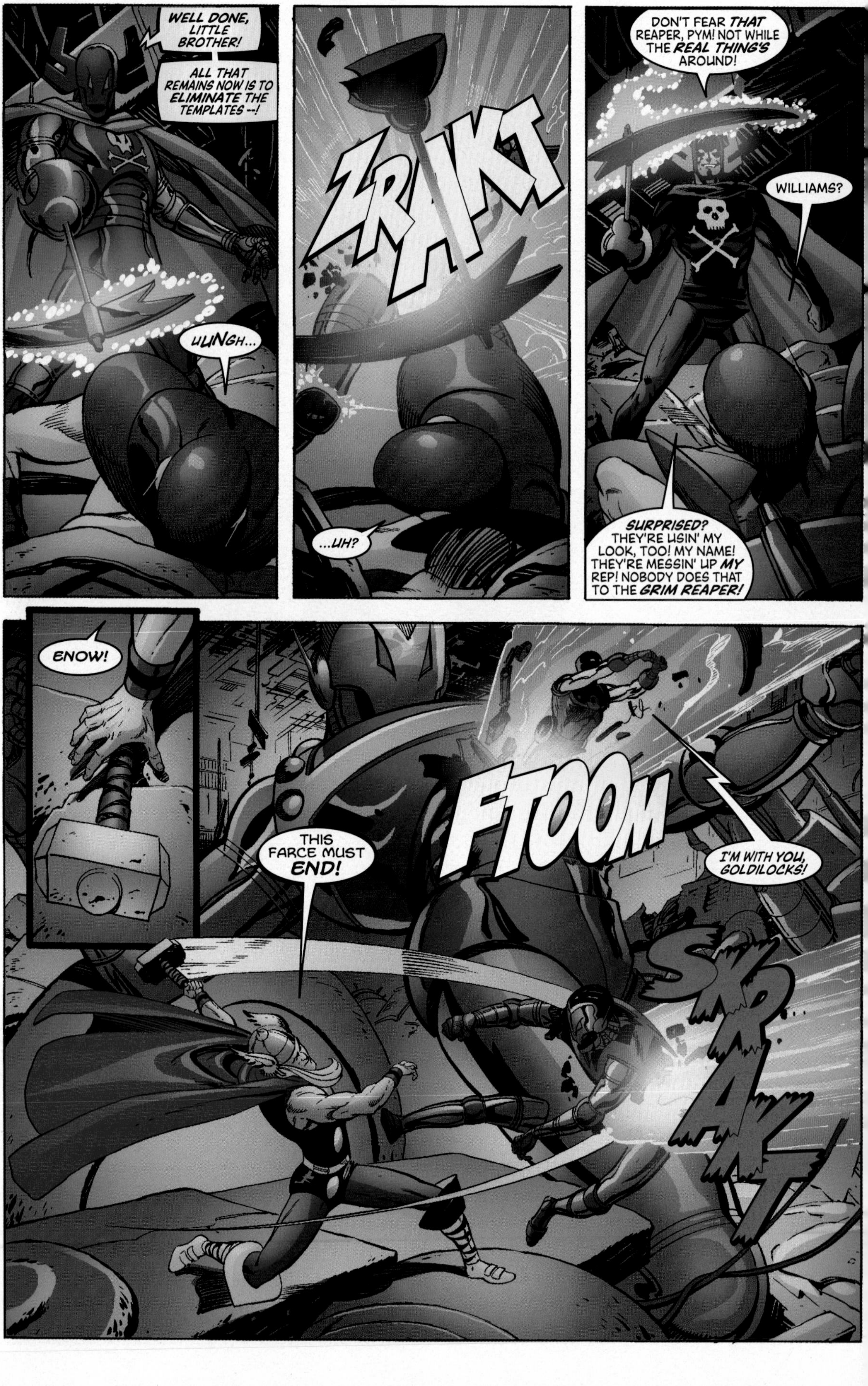

WELL DONE, LITTLE BROTHER!
ALL THAT REMAINS NOW IS TO ELIMINATE THE TEMPLATES --!
UUNGH...
ZRAKT
...UH?
DON'T FEAR THAT REAPER, PYM! NOT WHILE THE REAL THING'S AROUND!
WILLIAMS?
SURPRISED? THEY'RE USIN' MY LOOK, TOO! MY NAME! THEY'RE MESSIN' UP MY REP! NOBODY DOES THAT TO THE GRIM REAPER!
ENOW!
THIS FARCE MUST END!
FTOOM
I'M WITH YOU, GOLDILOCKS!
SKRAKT

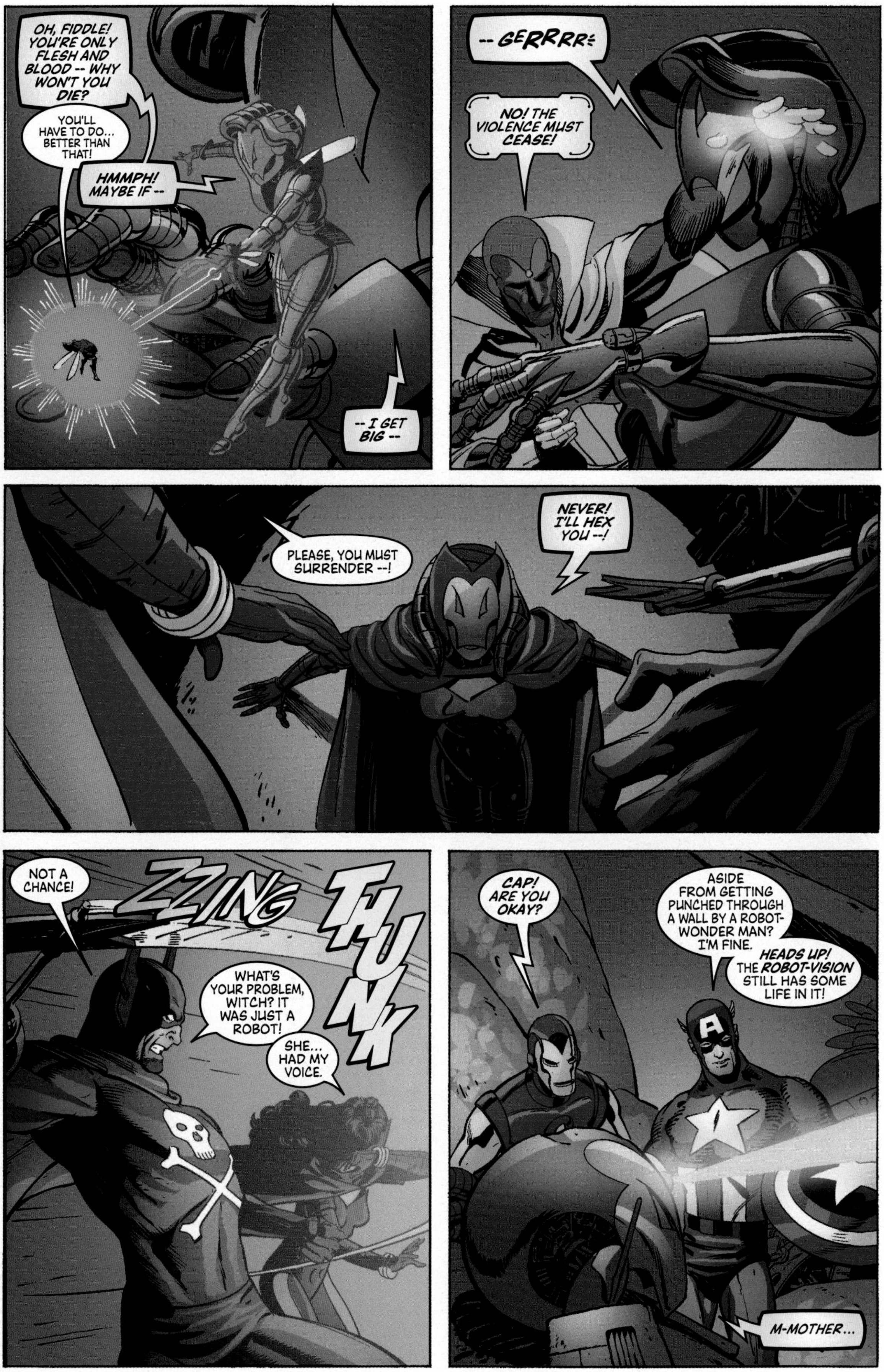
OH, FIDDLE! YOU'RE ONLY FLESH AND BLOOD -- WHY WON'T YOU DIE?
YOU'LL HAVE TO DO... BETTER THAN THAT!
HMMPH! MAYBE IF --
-- I GET BIG --
-- GERRRR--
NO! THE VIOLENCE MUST CEASE!
PLEASE, YOU MUST SURRENDER --!
NEVER! I'LL HEX YOU --!
NOT A CHANCE!
ZZING
THUNK
WHAT'S YOUR PROBLEM, WITCH? IT WAS JUST A ROBOT!
SHE... HAD MY VOICE.
CAP! ARE YOU OKAY?
ASIDE FROM GETTING PUNCHED THROUGH A WALL BY A ROBOT-WONDER MAN? I'M FINE.
HEADS UP! THE ROBOT-VISION STILL HAS SOME LIFE IN IT!
M-MOTHER...

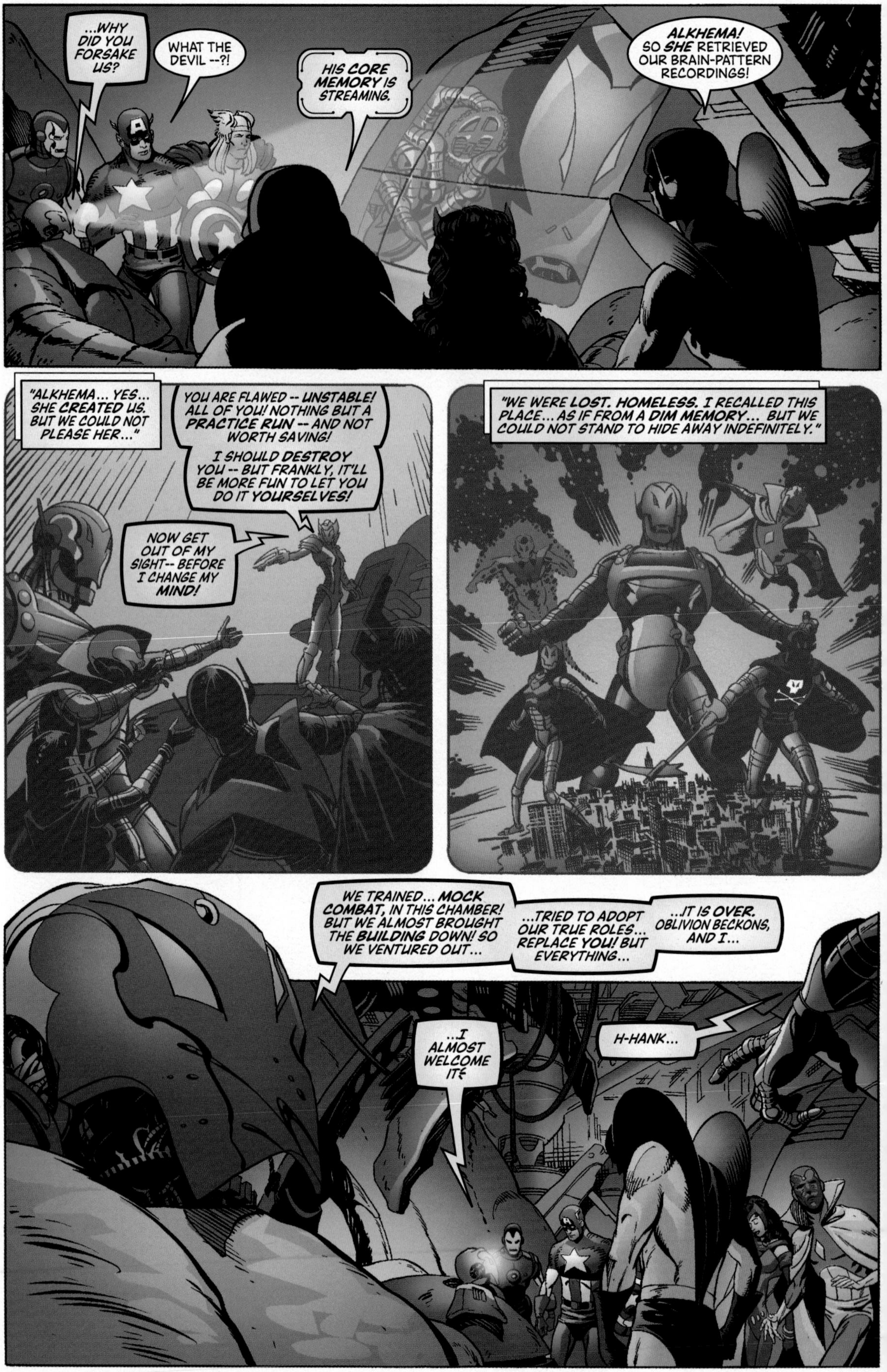
...WHY DID YOU FORSAKE US?
WHAT THE DEVIL --?!
HIS CORE MEMORY IS STREAMING.
ALKHEMA! SO SHE RETRIEVED OUR BRAIN-PATTERN RECORDINGS!
"ALKHEMA... YES... SHE CREATED US. BUT WE COULD NOT PLEASE HER..."
YOU ARE FLAWED -- UNSTABLE! ALL OF YOU! NOTHING BUT A PRACTICE RUN -- AND NOT WORTH SAVING!
I SHOULD DESTROY YOU -- BUT FRANKLY, IT'LL BE MORE FUN TO LET YOU DO IT YOURSELVES!
NOW GET OUT OF MY SIGHT-- BEFORE I CHANGE MY MIND!
"WE WERE LOST. HOMELESS. I RECALLED THIS PLACE... AS IF FROM A DIM MEMORY... BUT WE COULD NOT STAND TO HIDE AWAY INDEFINITELY."
WE TRAINED... MOCK COMBAT, IN THIS CHAMBER! BUT WE ALMOST BROUGHT THE BUILDING DOWN! SO WE VENTURED OUT...
...TRIED TO ADOPT OUR TRUE ROLES... REPLACE YOU! BUT EVERYTHING...
...IT IS OVER. OBLIVION BECKONS, AND I...
...I ALMOST WELCOME IT.
H-HANK...

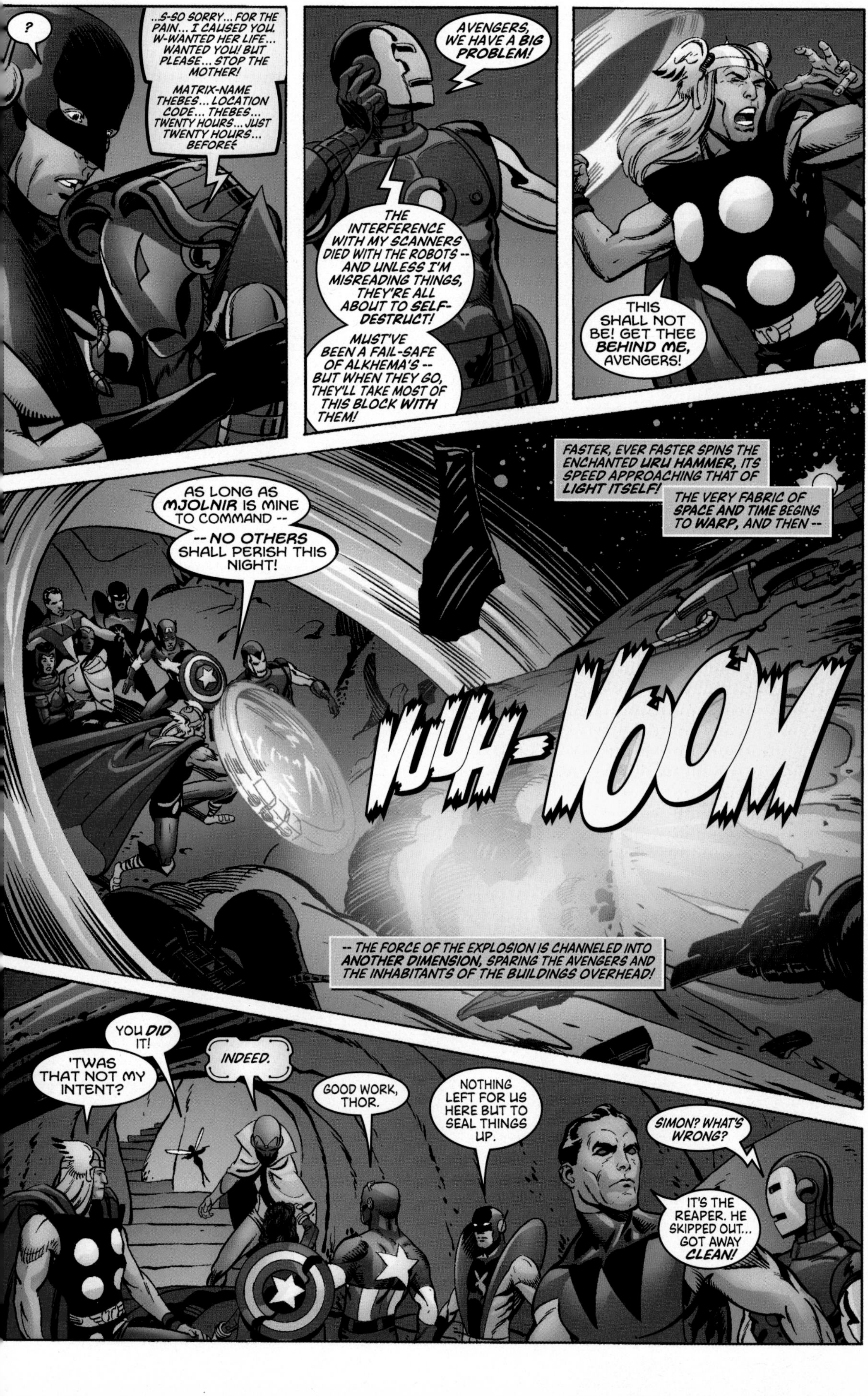
?
...S-SO SORRY... FOR THE PAIN... I CAUSED YOU. W-WANTED HER LIFE... WANTED YOU! BUT PLEASE... STOP THE MOTHER!
MATRIX-NAME THEBES... LOCATION CODE... THEBES... TWENTY HOURS... JUST TWENTY HOURS... BEFORE¿
AVENGERS, WE HAVE A BIG PROBLEM!
THE INTERFERENCE WITH MY SCANNERS DIED WITH THE ROBOTS -- AND UNLESS I'M MISREADING THINGS, THEY'RE ALL ABOUT TO SELF-DESTRUCT!
MUST'VE BEEN A FAIL-SAFE OF ALKHEMA'S -- BUT WHEN THEY GO, THEY'LL TAKE MOST OF THIS BLOCK WITH THEM!
THIS SHALL NOT BE! GET THEE BEHIND ME, AVENGERS!
FASTER, EVER FASTER SPINS THE ENCHANTED URU HAMMER, ITS SPEED APPROACHING THAT OF LIGHT ITSELF!
THE VERY FABRIC OF SPACE AND TIME BEGINS TO WARP, AND THEN --
AS LONG AS MJOLNIR IS MINE TO COMMAND --
-- NO OTHERS SHALL PERISH THIS NIGHT!
VUUH-VOOM
-- THE FORCE OF THE EXPLOSION IS CHANNELED INTO ANOTHER DIMENSION, SPARING THE AVENGERS AND THE INHABITANTS OF THE BUILDINGS OVERHEAD!
YOU DID IT!
'TWAS THAT NOT MY INTENT?
INDEED.
GOOD WORK, THOR.
NOTHING LEFT FOR US HERE BUT TO SEAL THINGS UP.
SIMON? WHAT'S WRONG?
IT'S THE REAPER. HE SKIPPED OUT... GOT AWAY CLEAN!

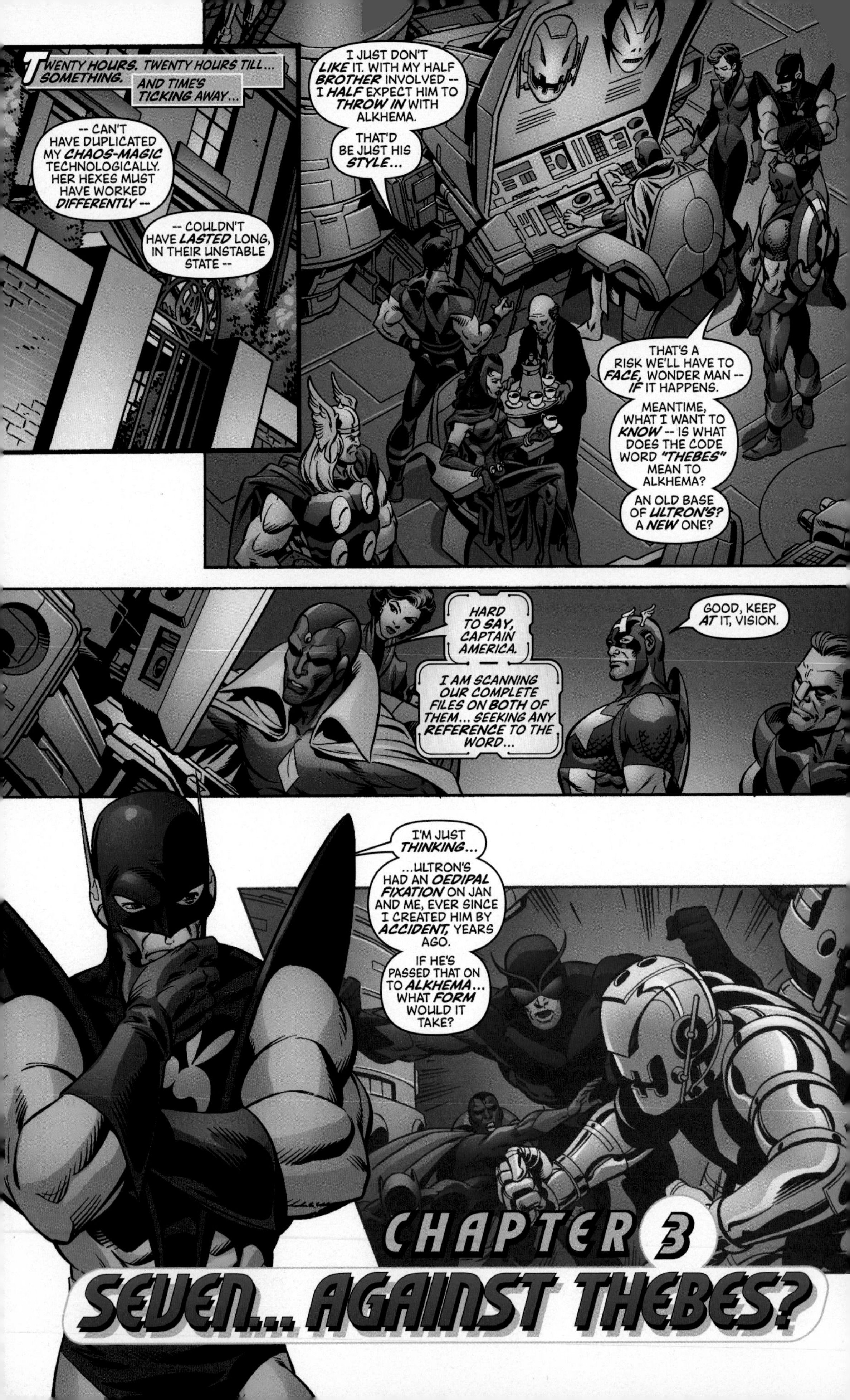
TWENTY HOURS. TWENTY HOURS TILL... SOMETHING.
AND TIME'S TICKING AWAY...
-- CAN'T HAVE DUPLICATED MY CHAOS-MAGIC TECHNOLOGICALLY. HER HEXES MUST HAVE WORKED DIFFERENTLY --
-- COULDN'T HAVE LASTED LONG, IN THEIR UNSTABLE STATE --
I JUST DON'T LIKE IT. WITH MY HALF BROTHER INVOLVED -- I HALF EXPECT HIM TO THROW IN WITH ALKHEMA.
THAT'D BE JUST HIS STYLE...
THAT'S A RISK WE'LL HAVE TO FACE, WONDER MAN -- IF IT HAPPENS.
MEANTIME, WHAT I WANT TO KNOW -- IS WHAT DOES THE CODE WORD "THEBES" MEAN TO ALKHEMA?
AN OLD BASE OF ULTRON'S? A NEW ONE?
HARD TO SAY, CAPTAIN AMERICA.
I AM SCANNING OUR COMPLETE FILES ON BOTH OF THEM... SEEKING ANY REFERENCE TO THE WORD...
GOOD, KEEP AT IT, VISION.
I'M JUST THINKING...
...ULTRON'S HAD AN OEDIPAL FIXATION ON JAN AND ME, EVER SINCE I CREATED HIM BY ACCIDENT, YEARS AGO.
IF HE'S PASSED THAT ON TO ALKHEMA... WHAT FORM WOULD IT TAKE?
CHAPTER 3
SEVEN... AGAINST THEBES?

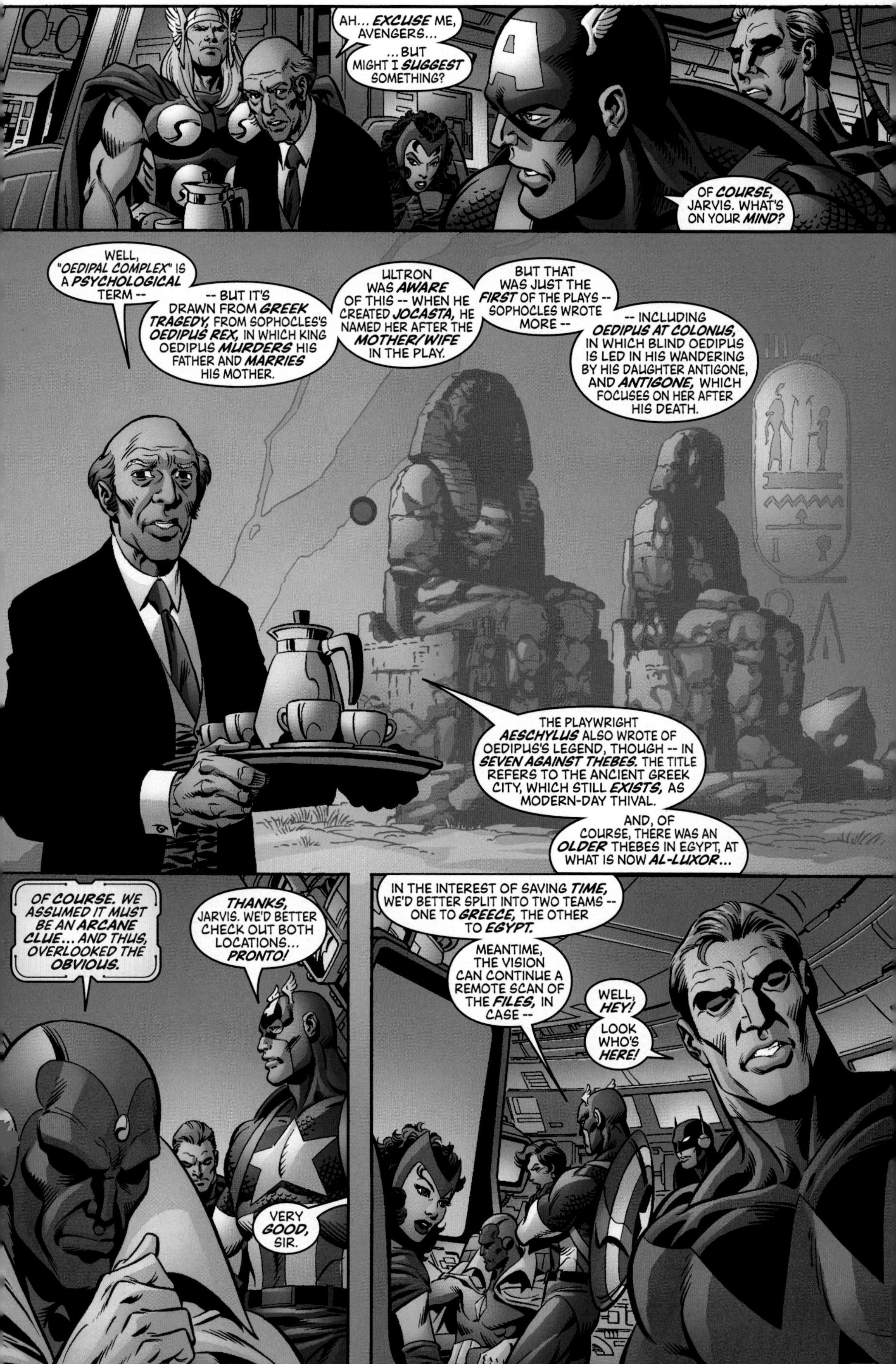
AH... EXCUSE ME, AVENGERS...
...BUT MIGHT I SUGGEST SOMETHING?
OF COURSE, JARVIS. WHAT'S ON YOUR MIND?
WELL, "OEDIPAL COMPLEX" IS A PSYCHOLOGICAL TERM --
-- BUT IT'S DRAWN FROM GREEK TRAGEDY, FROM SOPHOCLES'S OEDIPUS REX, IN WHICH KING OEDIPUS MURDERS HIS FATHER AND MARRIES HIS MOTHER.
ULTRON WAS AWARE OF THIS -- WHEN HE CREATED JOCASTA, HE NAMED HER AFTER THE MOTHER/WIFE IN THE PLAY.
BUT THAT WAS JUST THE FIRST OF THE PLAYS -- SOPHOCLES WROTE MORE --
-- INCLUDING OEDIPUS AT COLONUS, IN WHICH BLIND OEDIPUS IS LED IN HIS WANDERING BY HIS DAUGHTER ANTIGONE, AND ANTIGONE, WHICH FOCUSES ON HER AFTER HIS DEATH.
THE PLAYWRIGHT AESCHYLUS ALSO WROTE OF OEDIPUS'S LEGEND, THOUGH -- IN SEVEN AGAINST THEBES. THE TITLE REFERS TO THE ANCIENT GREEK CITY, WHICH STILL EXISTS, AS MODERN-DAY THIVAL.
AND, OF COURSE, THERE WAS AN OLDER THEBES IN EGYPT, AT WHAT IS NOW AL-LUXOR...
OF COURSE. WE ASSUMED IT MUST BE AN ARCANE CLUE... AND THUS, OVERLOOKED THE OBVIOUS.
THANKS, JARVIS. WE'D BETTER CHECK OUT BOTH LOCATIONS... PRONTO!
VERY GOOD, SIR.
IN THE INTEREST OF SAVING TIME, WE'D BETTER SPLIT INTO TWO TEAMS -- ONE TO GREECE, THE OTHER TO EGYPT.
MEANTIME, THE VISION CAN CONTINUE A REMOTE SCAN OF THE FILES, IN CASE --
WELL, HEY! LOOK WHO'S HERE!

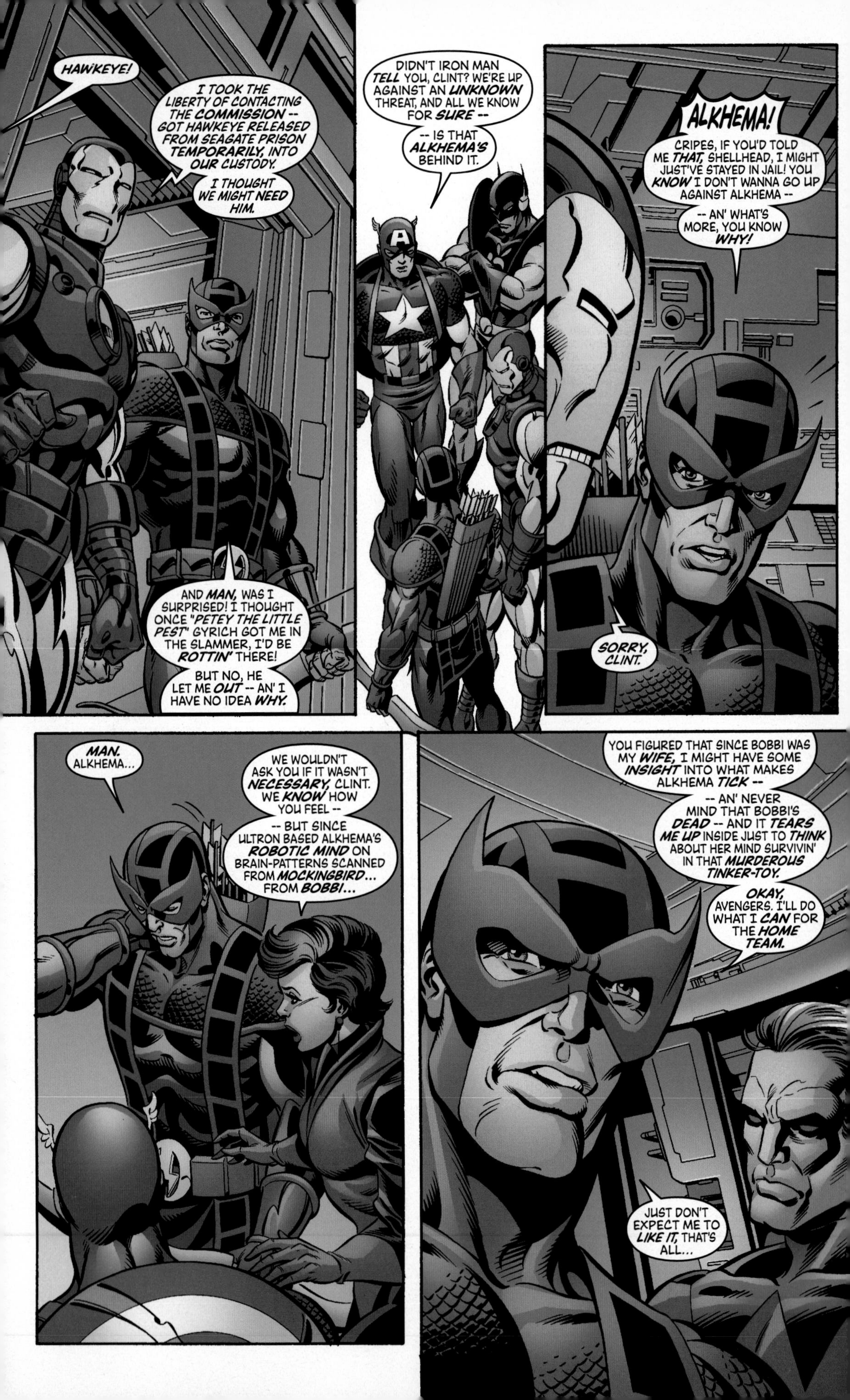
HAWKEYE!
I TOOK THE LIBERTY OF CONTACTING THE COMMISSION -- GOT HAWKEYE RELEASED FROM SEAGATE PRISON TEMPORARILY, INTO OUR CUSTODY.
I THOUGHT WE MIGHT NEED HIM.
AND MAN, WAS I SURPRISED! I THOUGHT ONCE "PETEY THE LITTLE PEST" GYRICH GOT ME IN THE SLAMMER, I'D BE ROTTIN' THERE!
BUT NO, HE LET ME OUT -- AN' I HAVE NO IDEA WHY.
DIDN'T IRON MAN TELL YOU, CLINT? WE'RE UP AGAINST AN UNKNOWN THREAT, AND ALL WE KNOW FOR SURE --
-- IS THAT ALKHEMA'S BEHIND IT.
ALKHEMA!
CRIPES, IF YOU'D TOLD ME THAT, SHELLHEAD, I MIGHT JUST'VE STAYED IN JAIL! YOU KNOW I DON'T WANNA GO UP AGAINST ALKHEMA --
-- AN' WHAT'S MORE, YOU KNOW WHY!
SORRY, CLINT.
MAN. ALKHEMA...
WE WOULDN'T ASK YOU IF IT WASN'T NECESSARY, CLINT. WE KNOW HOW YOU FEEL --
-- BUT SINCE ULTRON BASED ALKHEMA'S ROBOTIC MIND ON BRAIN-PATTERNS SCANNED FROM MOCKINGBIRD... FROM BOBBI...
YOU FIGURED THAT SINCE BOBBI WAS MY WIFE, I MIGHT HAVE SOME INSIGHT INTO WHAT MAKES ALKHEMA TICK --
-- AN' NEVER MIND THAT BOBBI'S DEAD -- AND IT TEARS ME UP INSIDE JUST TO THINK ABOUT HER MIND SURVIVIN' IN THAT MURDEROUS TINKER-TOY.
OKAY, AVENGERS. I'LL DO WHAT I CAN FOR THE HOME TEAM.
JUST DON'T EXPECT ME TO LIKE IT, THAT'S ALL...

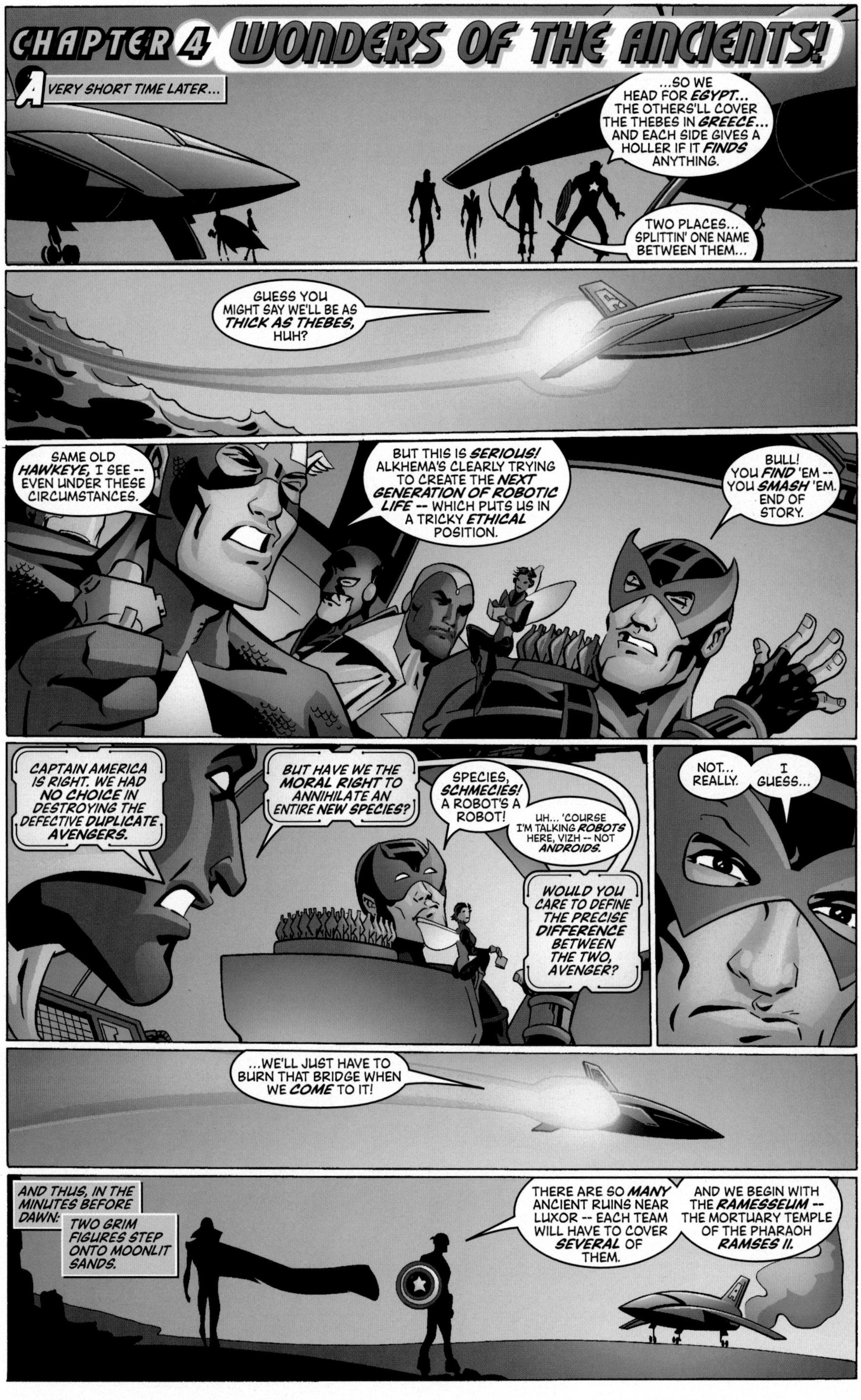
CHAPTER 4 WONDERS OF THE ANCIENTS!
A VERY SHORT TIME LATER...
...SO WE HEAD FOR EGYPT... THE OTHERS'LL COVER THE THEBES IN GREECE... AND EACH SIDE GIVES A HOLLER IF IT FINDS ANYTHING.
TWO PLACES... SPLITTIN' ONE NAME BETWEEN THEM...
GUESS YOU MIGHT SAY WE'LL BE AS THICK AS THEBES, HUH?
SAME OLD HAWKEYE, I SEE -- EVEN UNDER THESE CIRCUMSTANCES.
BUT THIS IS SERIOUS! ALKHEMA'S CLEARLY TRYING TO CREATE THE NEXT GENERATION OF ROBOTIC LIFE -- WHICH PUTS US IN A TRICKY ETHICAL POSITION.
BULL! YOU FIND 'EM -- YOU SMASH 'EM. END OF STORY.
CAPTAIN AMERICA IS RIGHT. WE HAD NO CHOICE IN DESTROYING THE DEFECTIVE DUPLICATE AVENGERS.
BUT HAVE WE THE MORAL RIGHT TO ANNIHILATE AN ENTIRE NEW SPECIES?
SPECIES, SCHMECIES! A ROBOT'S A ROBOT!
UH... 'COURSE I'M TALKING ROBOTS HERE, VIZH -- NOT ANDROIDS.
WOULD YOU CARE TO DEFINE THE PRECISE DIFFERENCE BETWEEN THE TWO, AVENGER?
NOT... REALLY.
I GUESS...
...WE'LL JUST HAVE TO BURN THAT BRIDGE WHEN WE COME TO IT!
AND THUS, IN THE MINUTES BEFORE DAWN:
TWO GRIM FIGURES STEP ONTO MOONLIT SANDS.
THERE ARE SO MANY ANCIENT RUINS NEAR LUXOR -- EACH TEAM WILL HAVE TO COVER SEVERAL OF THEM.
AND WE BEGIN WITH THE RAMESSEUM -- THE MORTUARY TEMPLE OF THE PHARAOH RAMSES II.

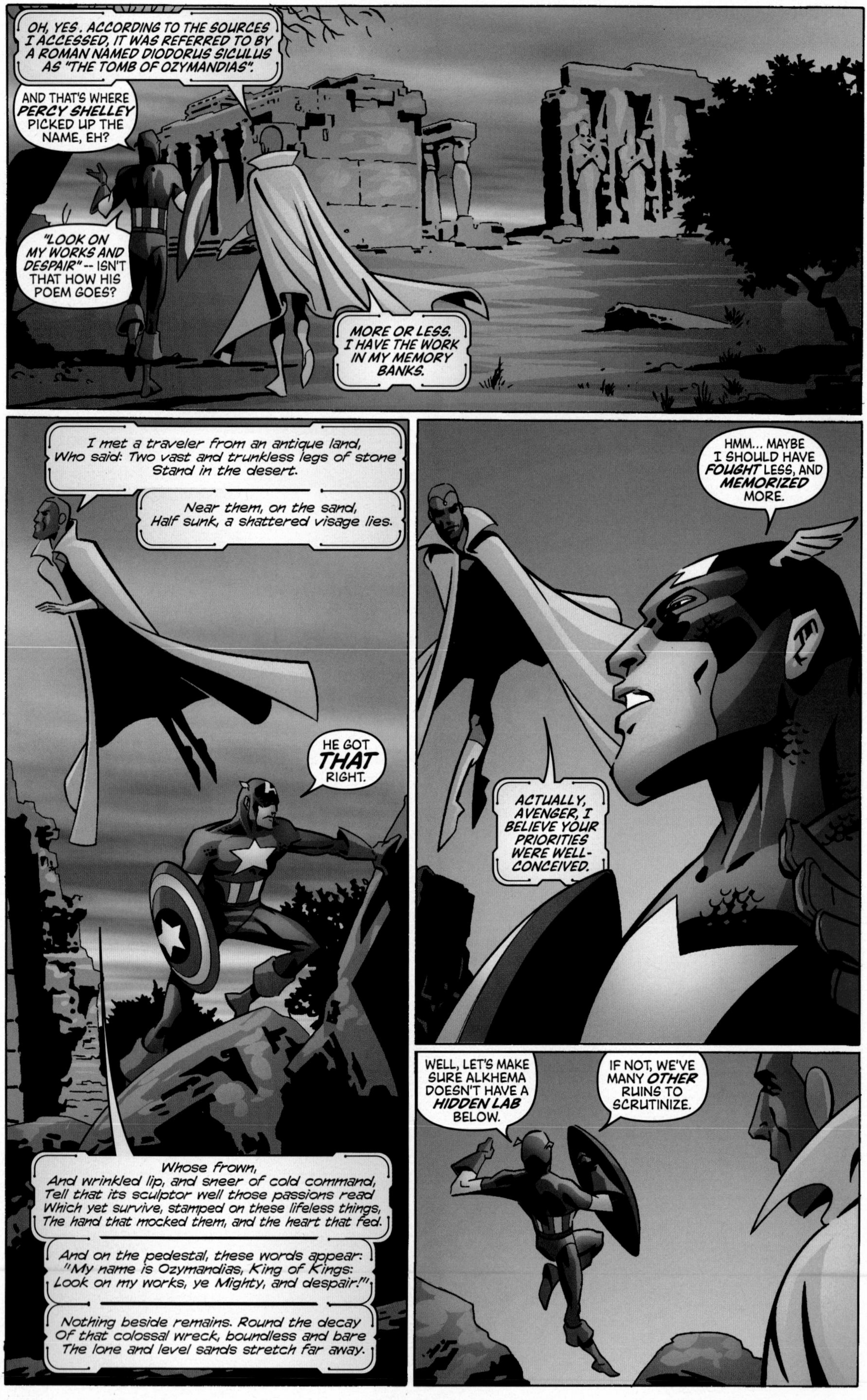

OH, YES. ACCORDING TO THE SOURCES I ACCESSED, IT WAS REFERRED TO BY A ROMAN NAMED DIODORUS SICULUS AS "THE TOMB OF OZYMANDIAS".
AND THAT'S WHERE PERCY SHELLEY PICKED UP THE NAME, EH?
"LOOK ON MY WORKS AND DESPAIR" -- ISN'T THAT HOW HIS POEM GOES?
MORE OR LESS. I HAVE THE WORK IN MY MEMORY BANKS.
I met a traveler from an antique land, Who said: Two vast and trunkless legs of stone Stand in the desert.
Near them, on the sand, Half sunk, a shattered visage lies.
HE GOT THAT RIGHT.
Whose frown, And wrinkled lip, and sneer of cold command, Tell that its sculptor well those passions read Which yet survive, stamped on these lifeless things, The hand that mocked them, and the heart that fed.
And on the pedestal, these words appear: "My name is Ozymandias, King of Kings: Look on my works, ye Mighty, and despair!"
Nothing beside remains. Round the decay Of that colossal wreck, boundless and bare The lone and level sands stretch far away.
HMM... MAYBE I SHOULD HAVE FOUGHT LESS, AND MEMORIZED MORE.
ACTUALLY, AVENGER, I BELIEVE YOUR PRIORITIES WERE WELL-CONCEIVED.
WELL, LET'S MAKE SURE ALKHEMA DOESN'T HAVE A HIDDEN LAB BELOW.
IF NOT, WE'VE MANY OTHER RUINS TO SCRUTINIZE.

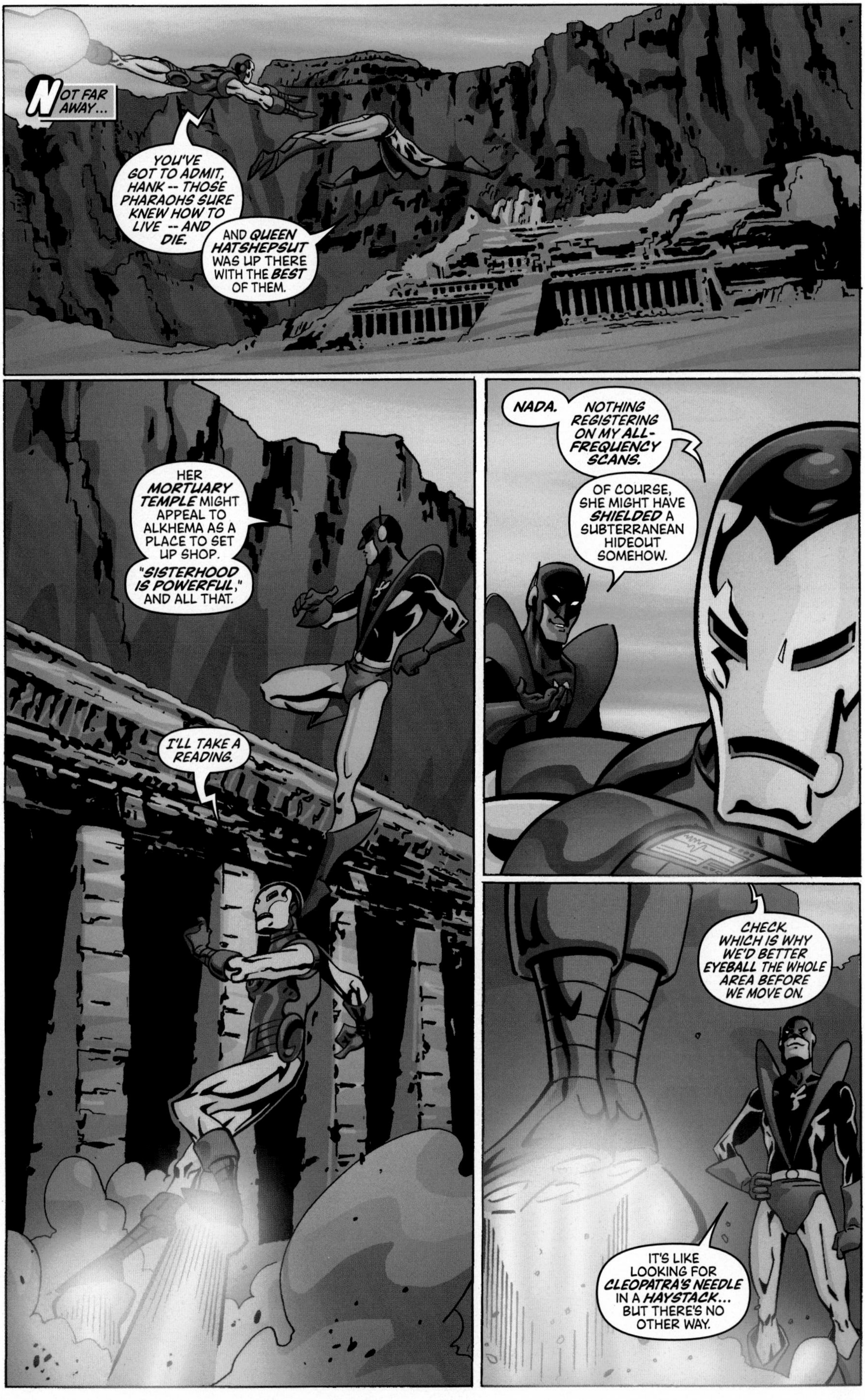
NOT FAR AWAY...
YOU'VE GOT TO ADMIT, HANK -- THOSE PHARAOHS SURE KNEW HOW TO LIVE -- AND DIE.
AND QUEEN HATSHEPSUT WAS UP THERE WITH THE BEST OF THEM.
HER MORTUARY TEMPLE MIGHT APPEAL TO ALKHEMA AS A PLACE TO SET UP SHOP. "SISTERHOOD IS POWERFUL," AND ALL THAT.
I'LL TAKE A READING.
NADA.
NOTHING REGISTERING ON MY ALL-FREQUENCY SCANS.
OF COURSE, SHE MIGHT HAVE SHIELDED A SUBTERRANEAN HIDEOUT SOMEHOW.
CHECK. WHICH IS WHY WE'D BETTER EYEBALL THE WHOLE AREA BEFORE WE MOVE ON.
IT'S LIKE LOOKING FOR CLEOPATRA'S NEEDLE IN A HAYSTACK... BUT THERE'S NO OTHER WAY.

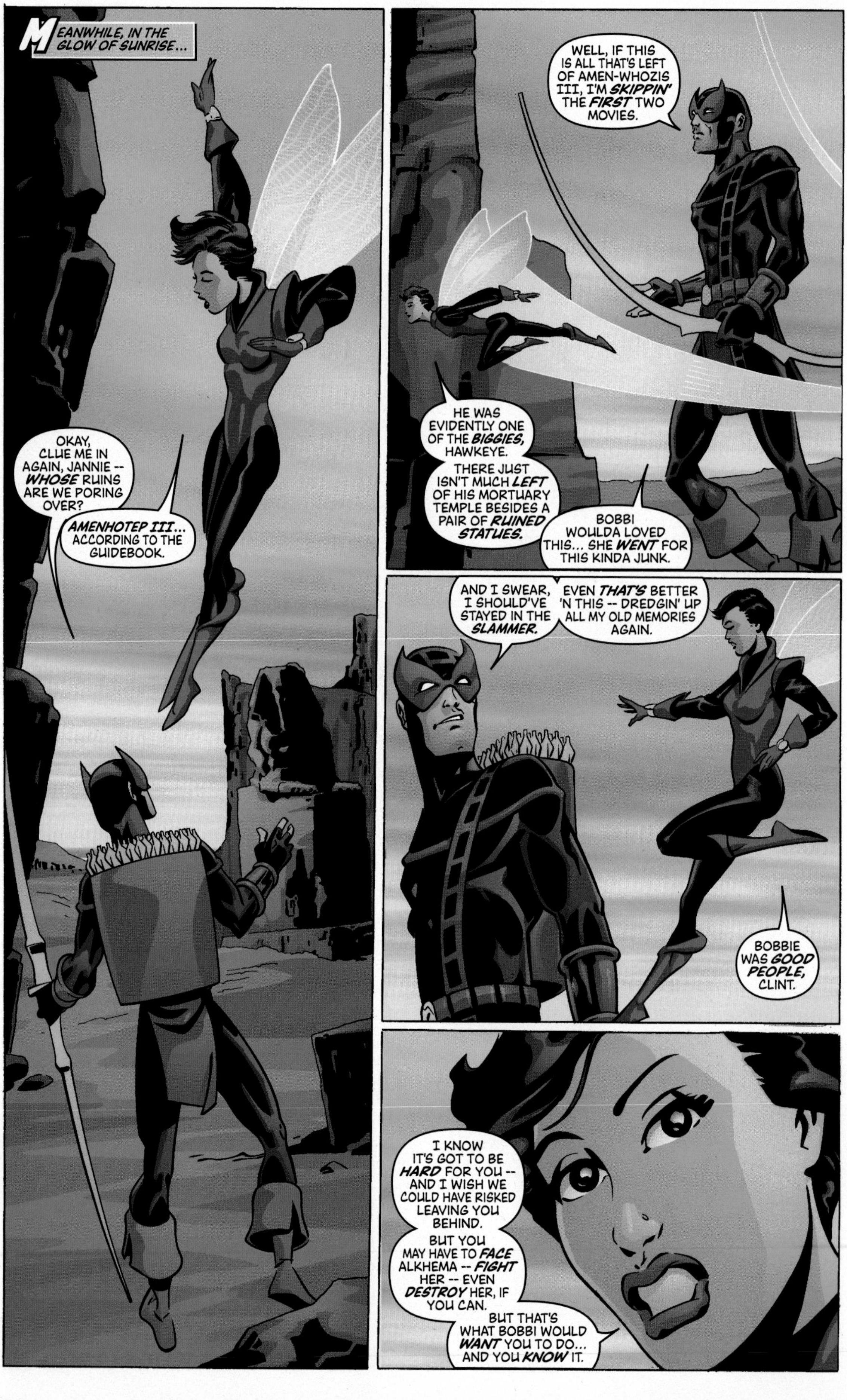
MEANWHILE, IN THE GLOW OF SUNRISE...
OKAY, CLUE ME IN AGAIN, JANNIE -- WHOSE RUINS ARE WE PORING OVER?
AMENHOTEP III... ACCORDING TO THE GUIDEBOOK.
WELL, IF THIS IS ALL THAT'S LEFT OF AMEN-WHOZIS III, I'M SKIPPIN' THE FIRST TWO MOVIES.
HE WAS EVIDENTLY ONE OF THE BIGGIES, HAWKEYE.
THERE JUST ISN'T MUCH LEFT OF HIS MORTUARY TEMPLE BESIDES A PAIR OF RUINED STATUES.
BOBBI WOULDA LOVED THIS... SHE WENT FOR THIS KINDA JUNK.
AND I SWEAR, I SHOULD'VE STAYED IN THE SLAMMER.
EVEN THAT'S BETTER 'N THIS -- DREDGIN' UP ALL MY OLD MEMORIES AGAIN.
BOBBIE WAS GOOD PEOPLE, CLINT.
I KNOW IT'S GOT TO BE HARD FOR YOU -- AND I WISH WE COULD HAVE RISKED LEAVING YOU BEHIND.
BUT YOU MAY HAVE TO FACE ALKHEMA -- FIGHT HER -- EVEN DESTROY HER, IF YOU CAN.
BUT THAT'S WHAT BOBBI WOULD WANT YOU TO DO... AND YOU KNOW IT.

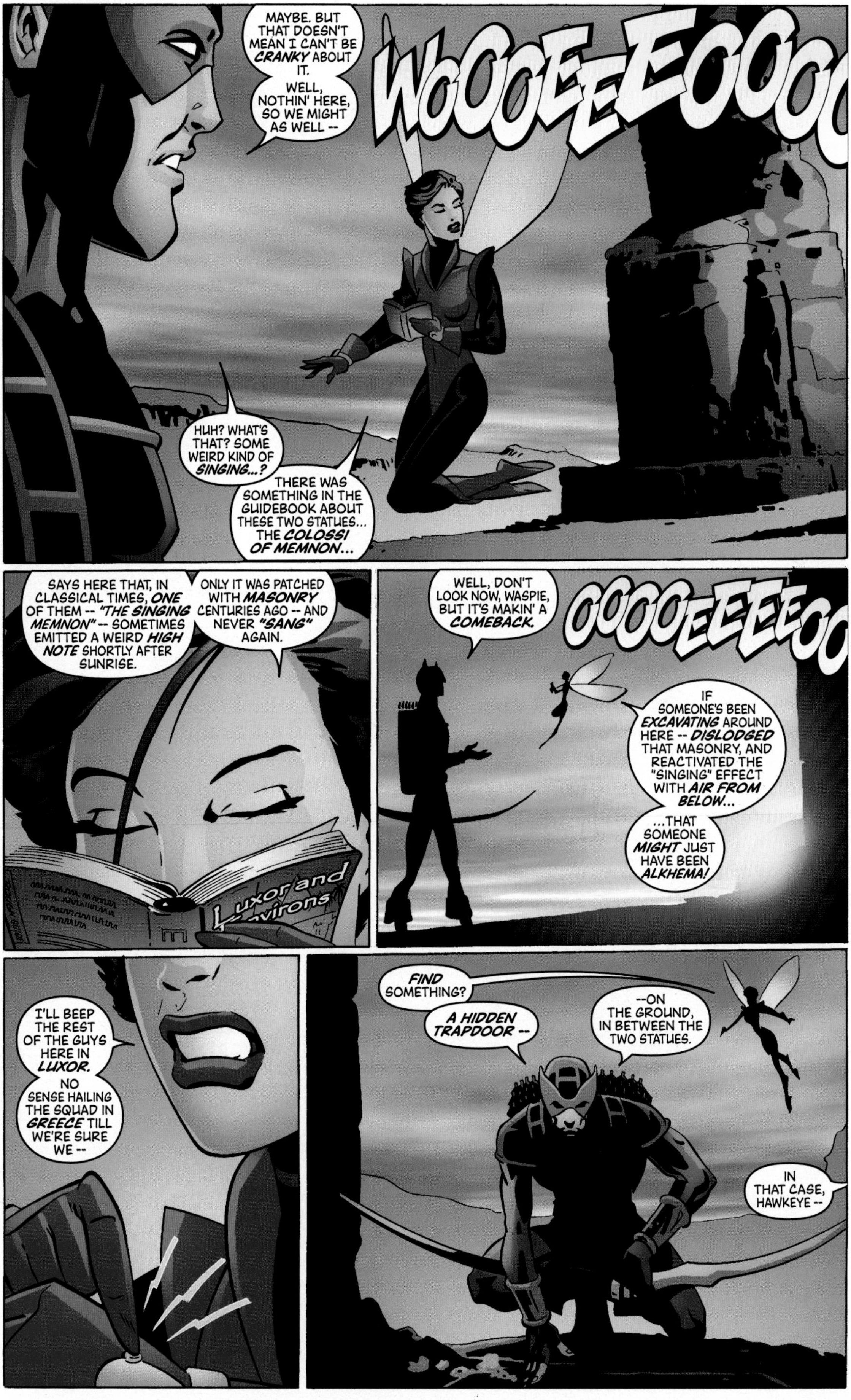
MAYBE. BUT THAT DOESN'T MEAN I CAN'T BE CRANKY ABOUT IT.
WELL, NOTHIN' HERE, SO WE MIGHT AS WELL --
WOOOEEEOOO
HUH? WHAT'S THAT? SOME WEIRD KIND OF SINGING...?
THERE WAS SOMETHING IN THE GUIDEBOOK ABOUT THESE TWO STATUES... THE COLOSSI OF MEMNON...
SAYS HERE THAT, IN CLASSICAL TIMES, ONE OF THEM -- "THE SINGING MEMNON" -- SOMETIMES EMITTED A WEIRD HIGH NOTE SHORTLY AFTER SUNRISE.
ONLY IT WAS PATCHED WITH MASONRY CENTURIES AGO -- AND NEVER "SANG" AGAIN.
Luxor and Environs
WELL, DON'T LOOK NOW, WASPIE, BUT IT'S MAKIN' A COMEBACK.
OOOOEEEEOO
IF SOMEONE'S BEEN EXCAVATING AROUND HERE -- DISLODGED THAT MASONRY, AND REACTIVATED THE "SINGING" EFFECT WITH AIR FROM BELOW...
...THAT SOMEONE MIGHT JUST HAVE BEEN ALKHEMA!
I'LL BEEP THE REST OF THE GUYS HERE IN LUXOR.
NO SENSE HAILING THE SQUAD IN GREECE TILL WE'RE SURE WE --
FIND SOMETHING?
A HIDDEN TRAPDOOR --
--ON THE GROUND, IN BETWEEN THE TWO STATUES.
IN THAT CASE, HAWKEYE --

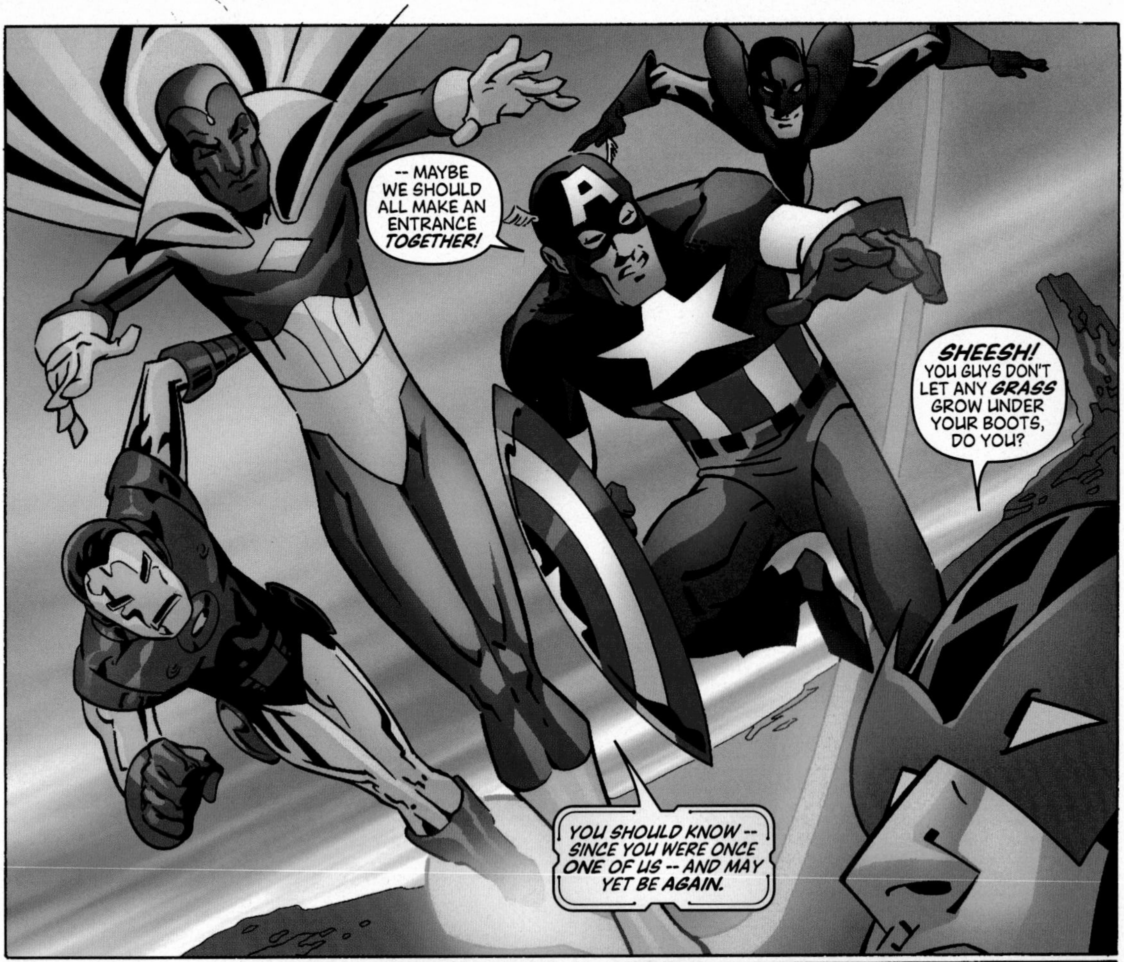
-- MAYBE WE SHOULD ALL MAKE AN ENTRANCE TOGETHER!
SHEESH! YOU GUYS DON'T LET ANY GRASS GROW UNDER YOUR BOOTS, DO YOU?
YOU SHOULD KNOW -- SINCE YOU WERE ONCE ONE OF US -- AND MAY YET BE AGAIN.

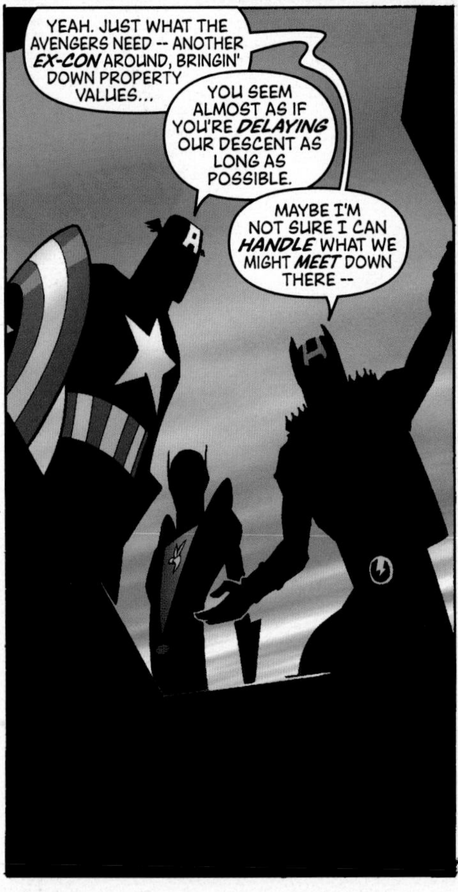
YEAH. JUST WHAT THE AVENGERS NEED -- ANOTHER EX-CON AROUND, BRINGIN' DOWN PROPERTY VALUES...
YOU SEEM ALMOST AS IF YOU'RE DELAYING OUR DESCENT AS LONG AS POSSIBLE.
MAYBE I'M NOT SURE I CAN HANDLE WHAT WE MIGHT MEET DOWN THERE --

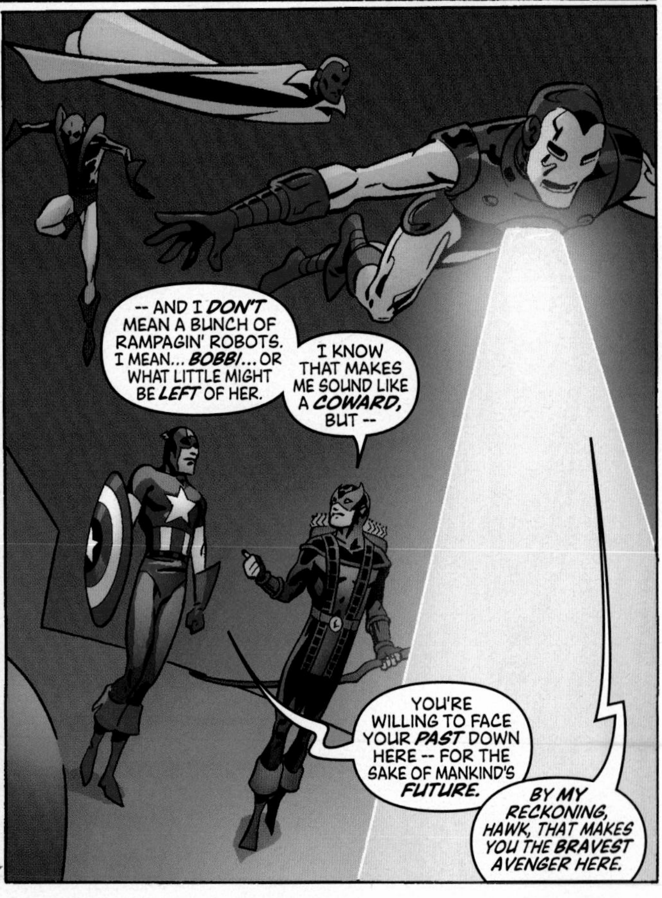
-- AND I DON'T MEAN A BUNCH OF RAMPAGIN' ROBOTS. I MEAN... BOBBI... OR WHAT LITTLE MIGHT BE LEFT OF HER.
I KNOW THAT MAKES ME SOUND LIKE A COWARD, BUT --
YOU'RE WILLING TO FACE YOUR PAST DOWN HERE -- FOR THE SAKE OF MANKIND'S FUTURE.
BY MY RECKONING, HAWK, THAT MAKES YOU THE BRAVEST AVENGER HERE.

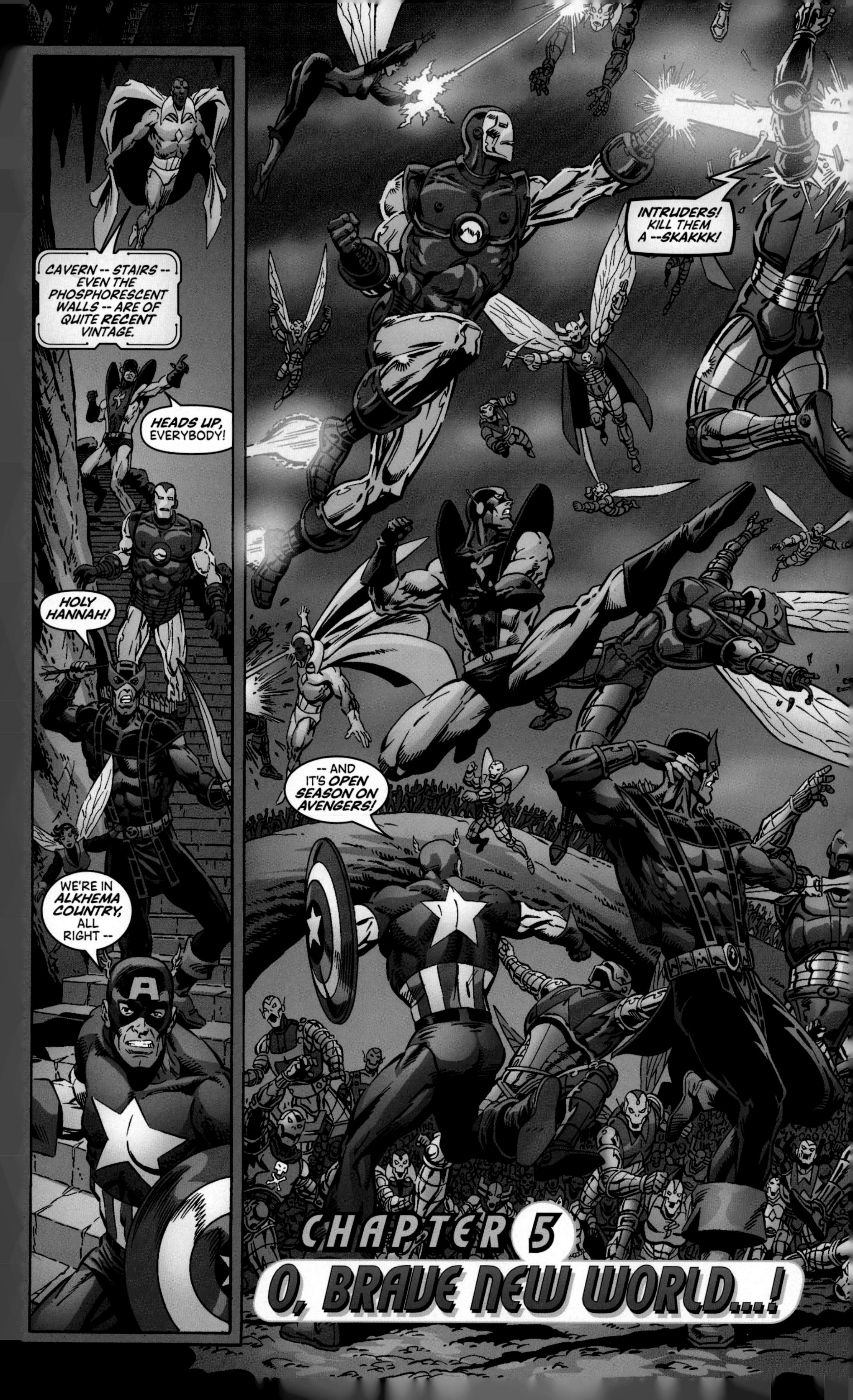
CAVERN -- STAIRS -- EVEN THE PHOSPHORESCENT WALLS -- ARE OF QUITE RECENT VINTAGE.
HEADS UP, EVERYBODY!
HOLY HANNAH!
WE'RE IN ALKHEMA COUNTRY, ALL RIGHT --
INTRUDERS! KILL THEM A --SKAKKK!
-- AND IT'S OPEN SEASON ON AVENGERS!
CHAPTER 5
O, BRAVE NEW WORLD...!

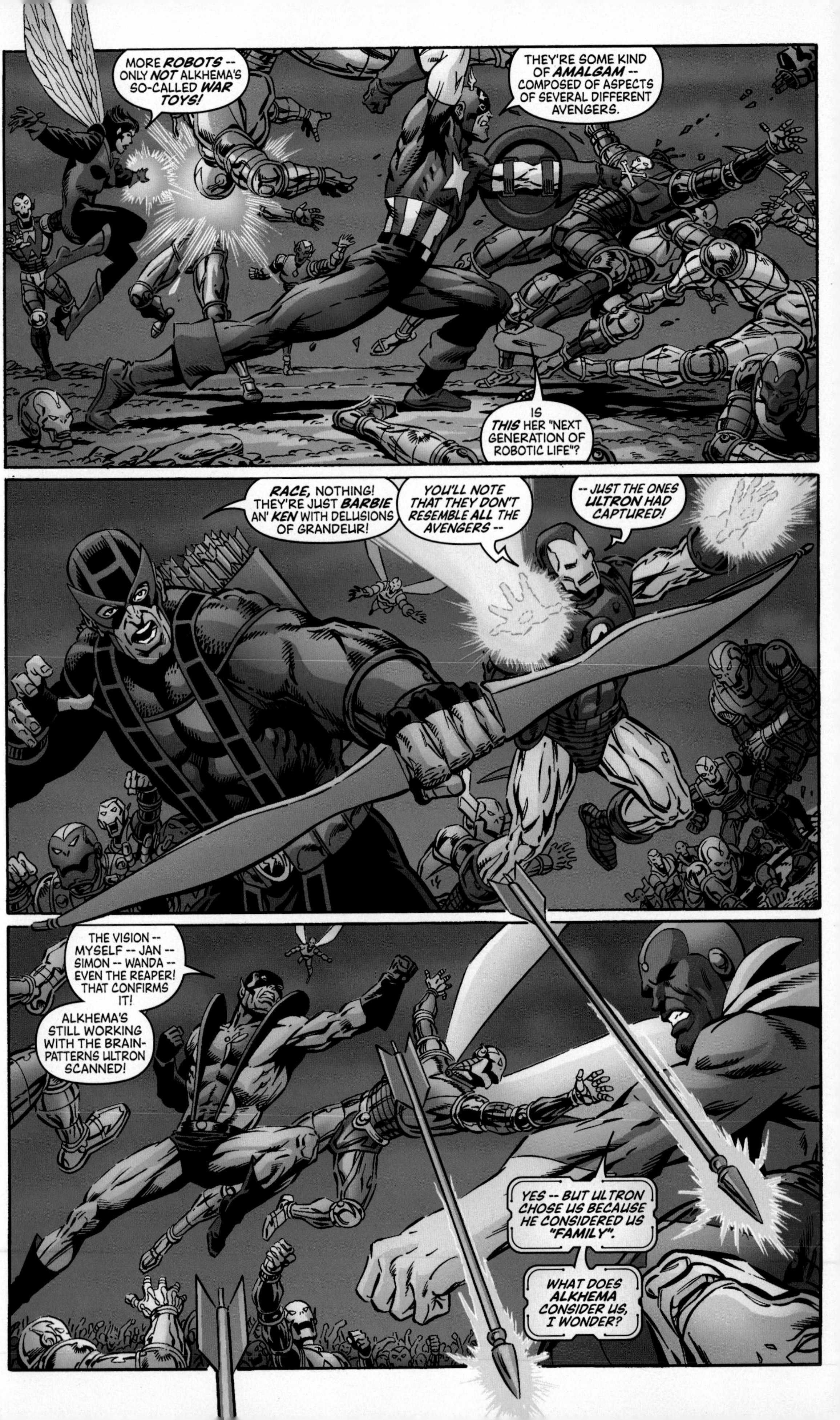

MORE ROBOTS -- ONLY NOT ALKHEMA'S SO-CALLED WAR TOYS!
THEY'RE SOME KIND OF AMALGAM -- COMPOSED OF ASPECTS OF SEVERAL DIFFERENT AVENGERS.
IS THIS HER "NEXT GENERATION OF ROBOTIC LIFE"?
RACE, NOTHING! THEY'RE JUST BARBIE AN' KEN WITH DELUSIONS OF GRANDEUR!
YOU'LL NOTE THAT THEY DON'T RESEMBLE ALL THE AVENGERS --
-- JUST THE ONES ULTRON HAD CAPTURED!
THE VISION -- MYSELF -- JAN -- SIMON -- WANDA -- EVEN THE REAPER! THAT CONFIRMS IT!
ALKHEMA'S STILL WORKING WITH THE BRAIN-PATTERNS ULTRON SCANNED!
YES -- BUT ULTRON CHOSE US BECAUSE HE CONSIDERED US "FAMILY".
WHAT DOES ALKHEMA CONSIDER US, I WONDER?

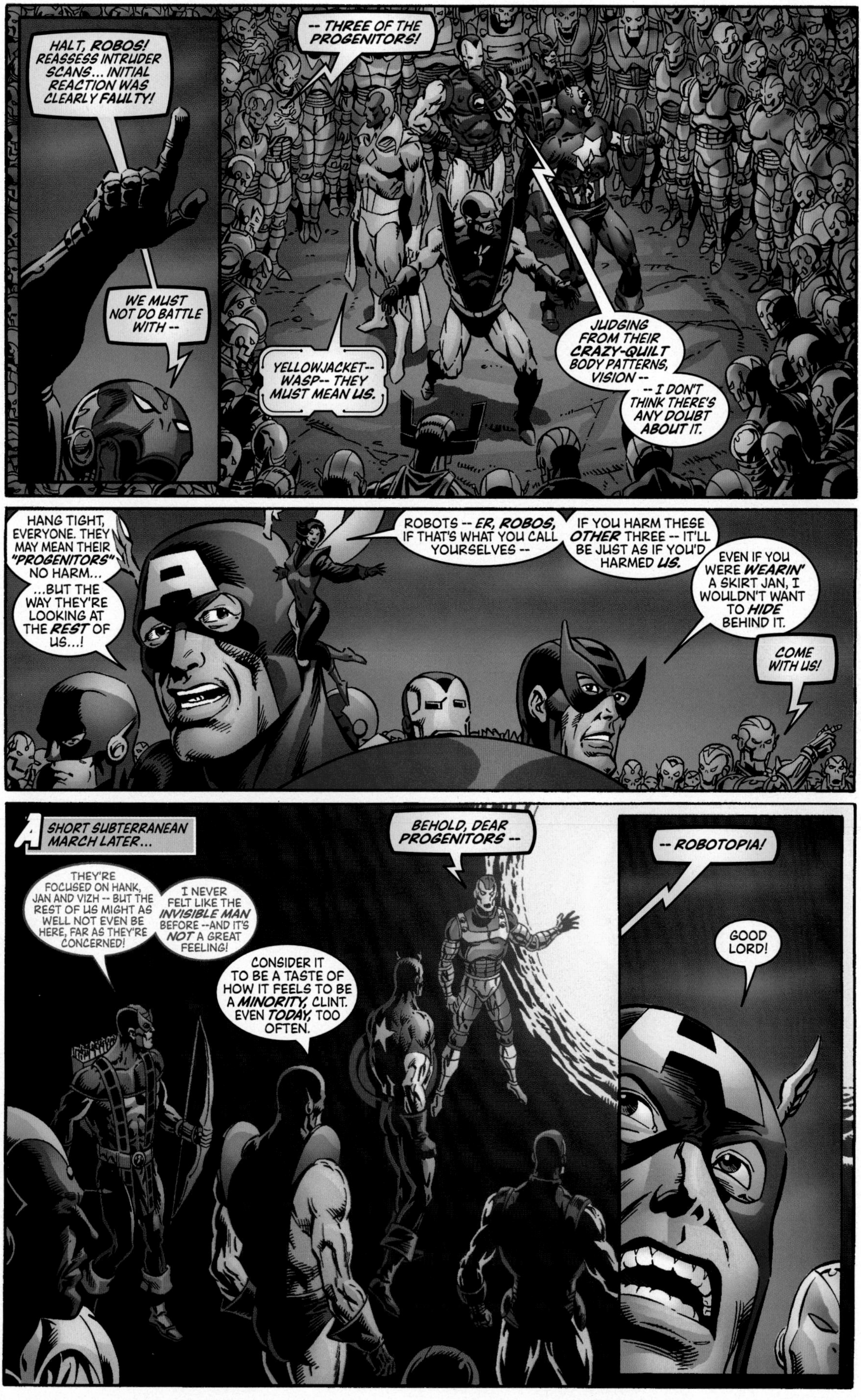
HALT, ROBOS! REASSESS INTRUDER SCANS... INITIAL REACTION WAS CLEARLY FAULTY!
WE MUST NOT DO BATTLE WITH --
-- THREE OF THE PROGENITORS!
YELLOWJACKET-- WASP-- THEY MUST MEAN US.
JUDGING FROM THEIR CRAZY-QUILT BODY PATTERNS, VISION --
-- I DON'T THINK THERE'S ANY DOUBT ABOUT IT.
HANG TIGHT, EVERYONE. THEY MAY MEAN THEIR "PROGENITORS" NO HARM...
...BUT THE WAY THEY'RE LOOKING AT THE REST OF US...!
ROBOTS -- ER, ROBOS, IF THAT'S WHAT YOU CALL YOURSELVES --
IF YOU HARM THESE OTHER THREE -- IT'LL BE JUST AS IF YOU'D HARMED US.
EVEN IF YOU WERE WEARIN' A SKIRT JAN, I WOULDN'T WANT TO HIDE BEHIND IT.
COME WITH US!
A SHORT SUBTERRANEAN MARCH LATER...
THEY'RE FOCUSED ON HANK, JAN AND VIZH -- BUT THE REST OF US MIGHT AS WELL NOT EVEN BE HERE, FAR AS THEY'RE CONCERNED!
I NEVER FELT LIKE THE INVISIBLE MAN BEFORE --AND IT'S NOT A GREAT FEELING!
CONSIDER IT TO BE A TASTE OF HOW IT FEELS TO BE A MINORITY, CLINT. EVEN TODAY, TOO OFTEN.
BEHOLD, DEAR PROGENITORS --
-- ROBOTOPIA!
GOOD LORD!

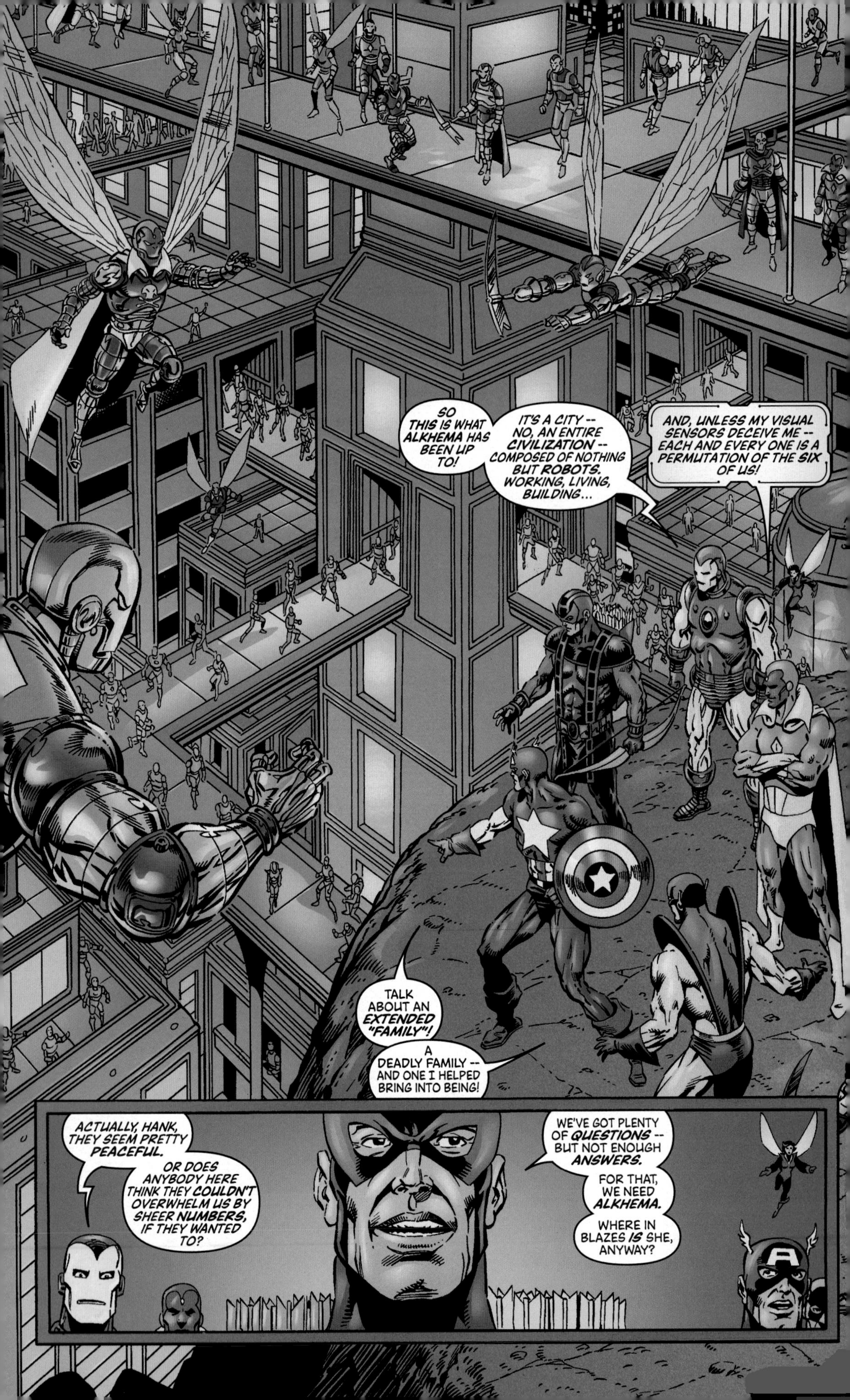
SO THIS IS WHAT ALKHEMA HAS BEEN UP TO!
IT'S A CITY -- NO, AN ENTIRE CIVILIZATION -- COMPOSED OF NOTHING BUT ROBOTS. WORKING, LIVING, BUILDING...
AND, UNLESS MY VISUAL SENSORS DECEIVE ME -- EACH AND EVERY ONE IS A PERMUTATION OF THE SIX OF US!
TALK ABOUT AN EXTENDED "FAMILY"!
A DEADLY FAMILY -- AND ONE I HELPED BRING INTO BEING!
ACTUALLY, HANK, THEY SEEM PRETTY PEACEFUL.
OR DOES ANYBODY HERE THINK THEY COULDN'T OVERWHELM US BY SHEER NUMBERS, IF THEY WANTED TO?
WE'VE GOT PLENTY OF QUESTIONS -- BUT NOT ENOUGH ANSWERS.
FOR THAT, WE NEED ALKHEMA.
WHERE IN BLAZES IS SHE, ANYWAY?

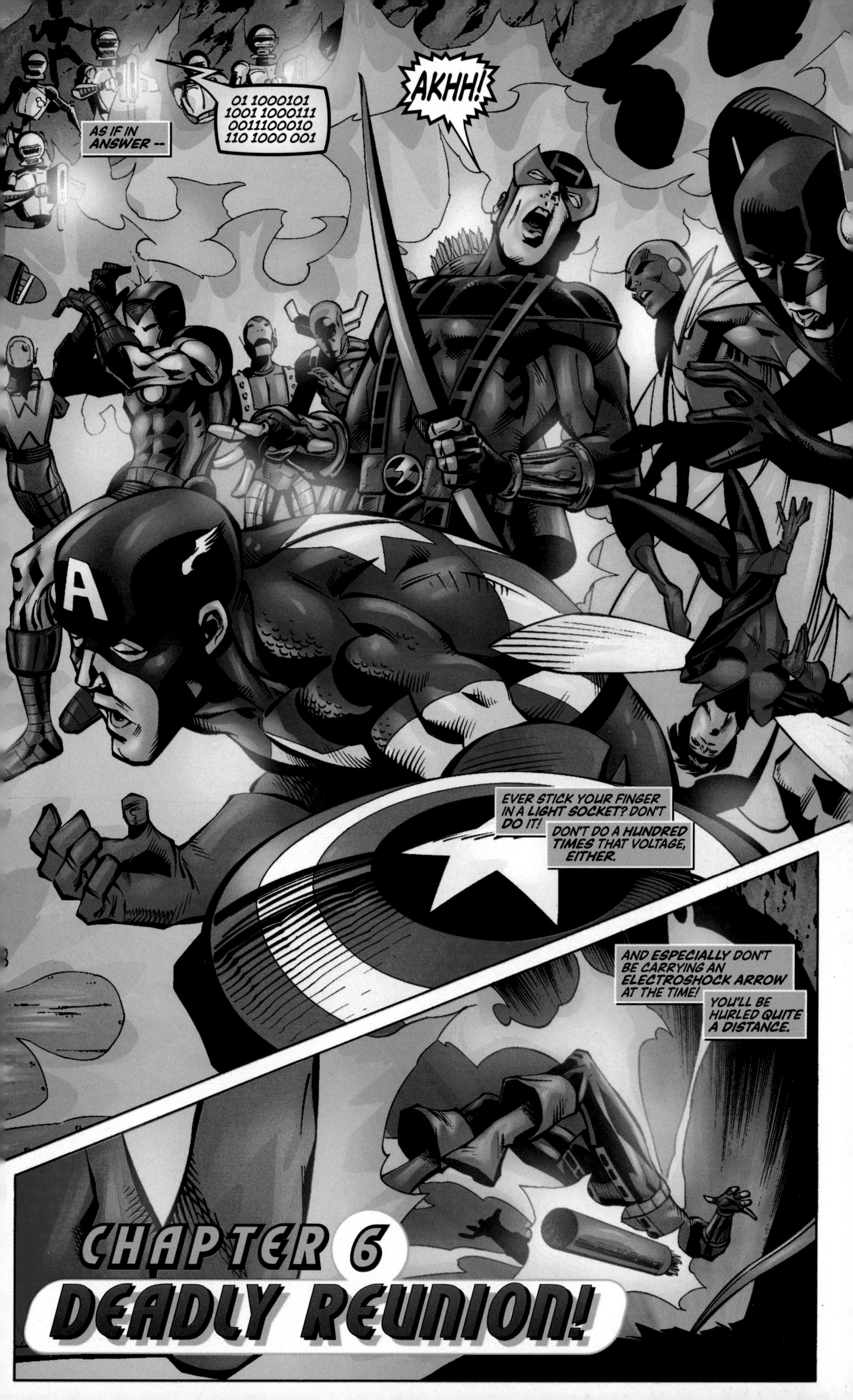

AS IF IN ANSWER --
01 1000101 1001 1000111 0011100010 110 1000 001
AKHH!
EVER STICK YOUR FINGER IN A LIGHT SOCKET? DON'T DO IT!
DON'T DO A HUNDRED TIMES THAT VOLTAGE, EITHER.
AND ESPECIALLY DON'T BE CARRYING AN ELECTROSHOCK ARROW AT THE TIME!
YOU'LL BE HURLED QUITE A DISTANCE.
CHAPTER 6
DEADLY REUNION!

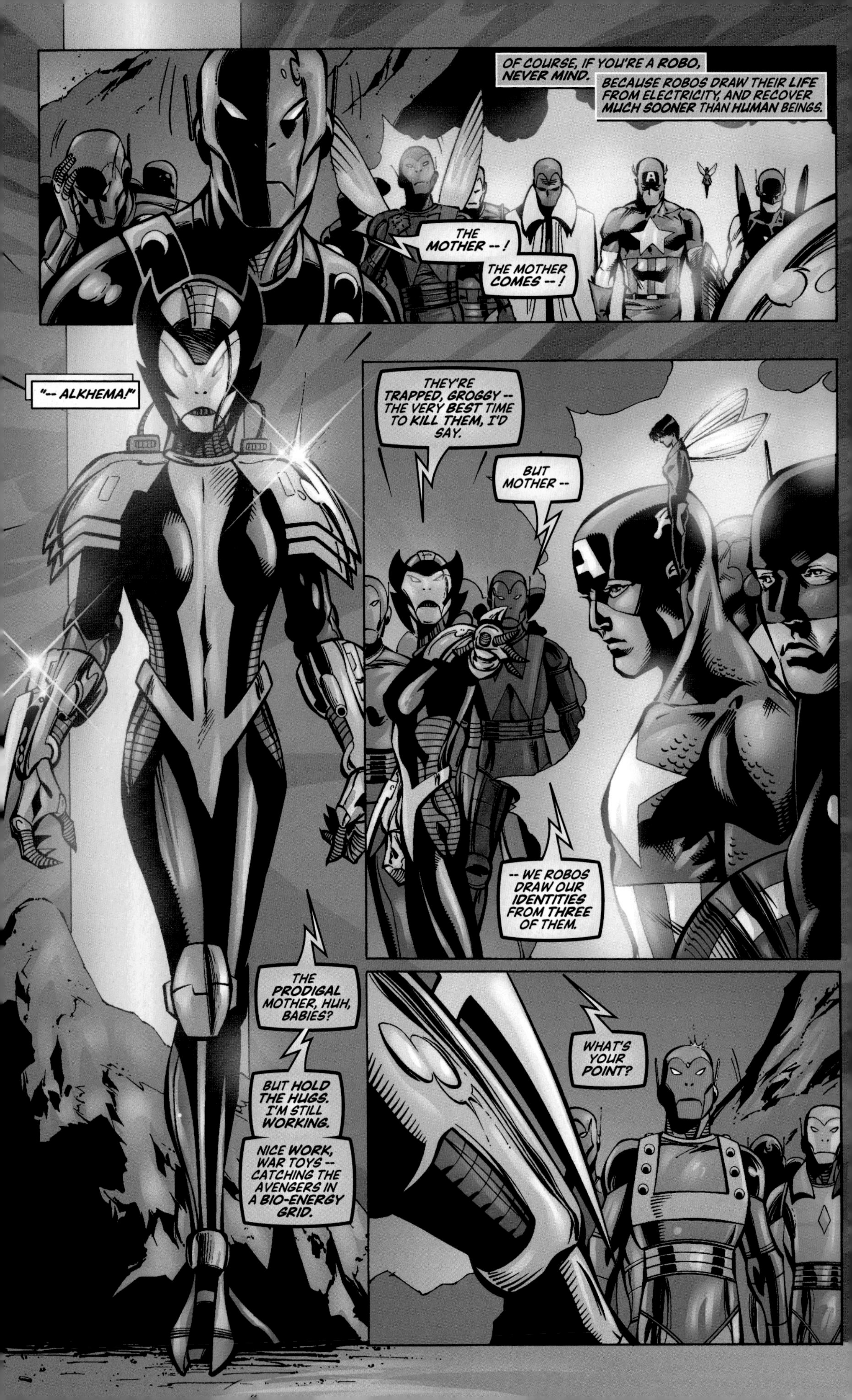

OF COURSE, IF YOU'RE A ROBO, NEVER MIND.
BECAUSE ROBOS DRAW THEIR LIFE FROM ELECTRICITY, AND RECOVER MUCH SOONER THAN HUMAN BEINGS.
THE MOTHER --!
THE MOTHER COMES --!
"-- ALKHEMA!"
THEY'RE TRAPPED, GROGGY -- THE VERY BEST TIME TO KILL THEM, I'D SAY.
BUT MOTHER --
-- WE ROBOS DRAW OUR IDENTITIES FROM THREE OF THEM.
THE PRODIGAL MOTHER, HUH, BABIES?
BUT HOLD THE HUGS. I'M STILL WORKING.
NICE WORK, WAR TOYS -- CATCHING THE AVENGERS IN A BIO-ENERGY GRID.
WHAT'S YOUR POINT?

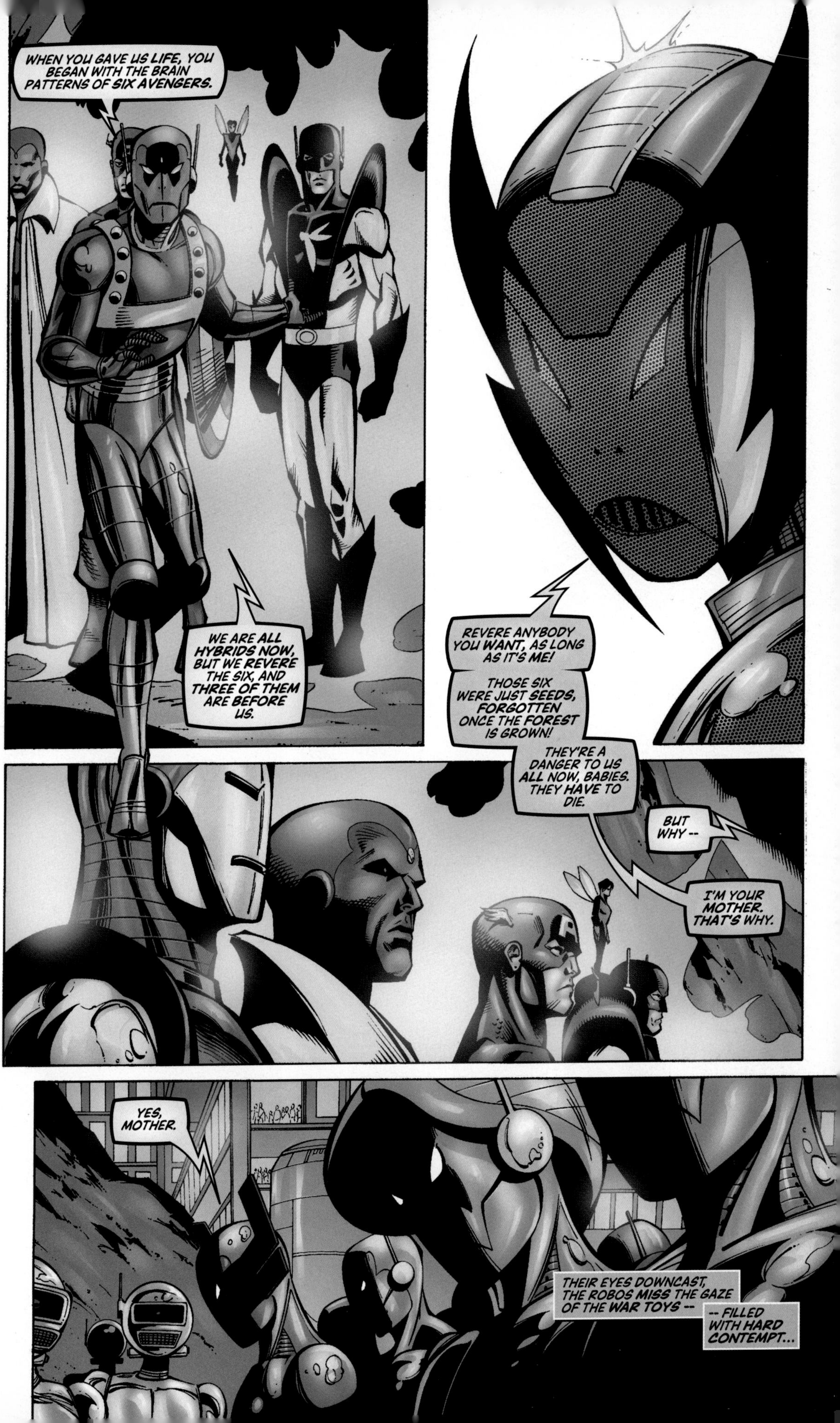

WHEN YOU GAVE US LIFE, YOU BEGAN WITH THE BRAIN PATTERNS OF SIX AVENGERS.
WE ARE ALL HYBRIDS NOW, BUT WE REVERE THE SIX, AND THREE OF THEM ARE BEFORE US.
REVERE ANYBODY YOU WANT, AS LONG AS IT'S ME!
THOSE SIX WERE JUST SEEDS, FORGOTTEN ONCE THE FOREST IS GROWN!
THEY'RE A DANGER TO US ALL NOW, BABIES. THEY HAVE TO DIE.
BUT WHY --
I'M YOUR MOTHER. THAT'S WHY.
YES, MOTHER.
THEIR EYES DOWNCAST, THE ROBOS MISS THE GAZE OF THE WAR TOYS --
-- FILLED WITH HARD CONTEMPT...

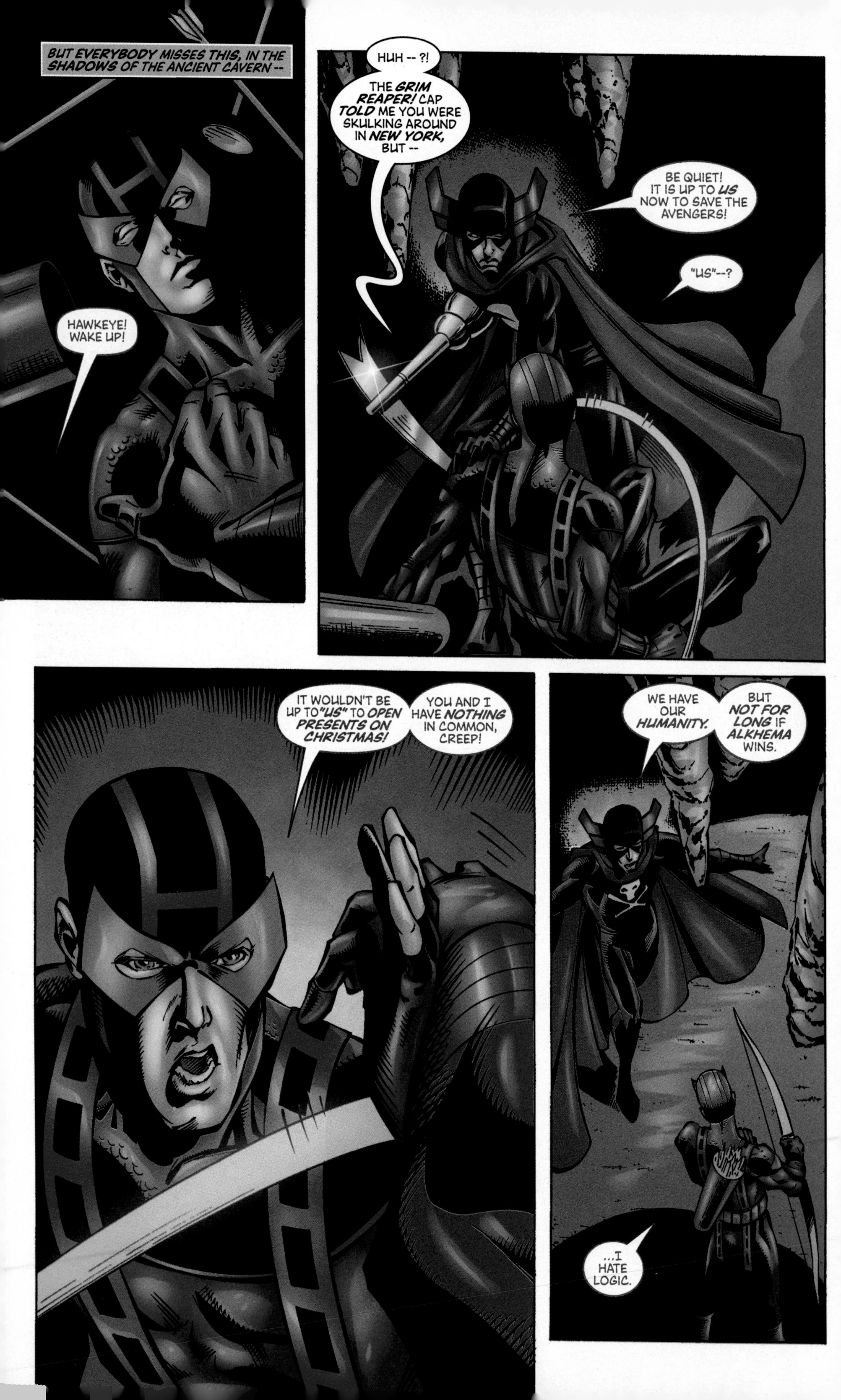

BUT EVERYBODY MISSES THIS, IN THE SHADOWS OF THE ANCIENT CAVERN --
HAWKEYE! WAKE UP!
HUH -- ?!
THE GRIM REAPER! CAP TOLD ME YOU WERE SKULKING AROUND IN NEW YORK, BUT --
BE QUIET! IT IS UP TO US NOW TO SAVE THE AVENGERS!
"US"--?
IT WOULDN'T BE UP TO "US" TO OPEN PRESENTS ON CHRISTMAS!
YOU AND I HAVE NOTHING IN COMMON, CREEP!
WE HAVE OUR HUMANITY.
BUT NOT FOR LONG IF ALKHEMA WINS.
...I HATE LOGIC.

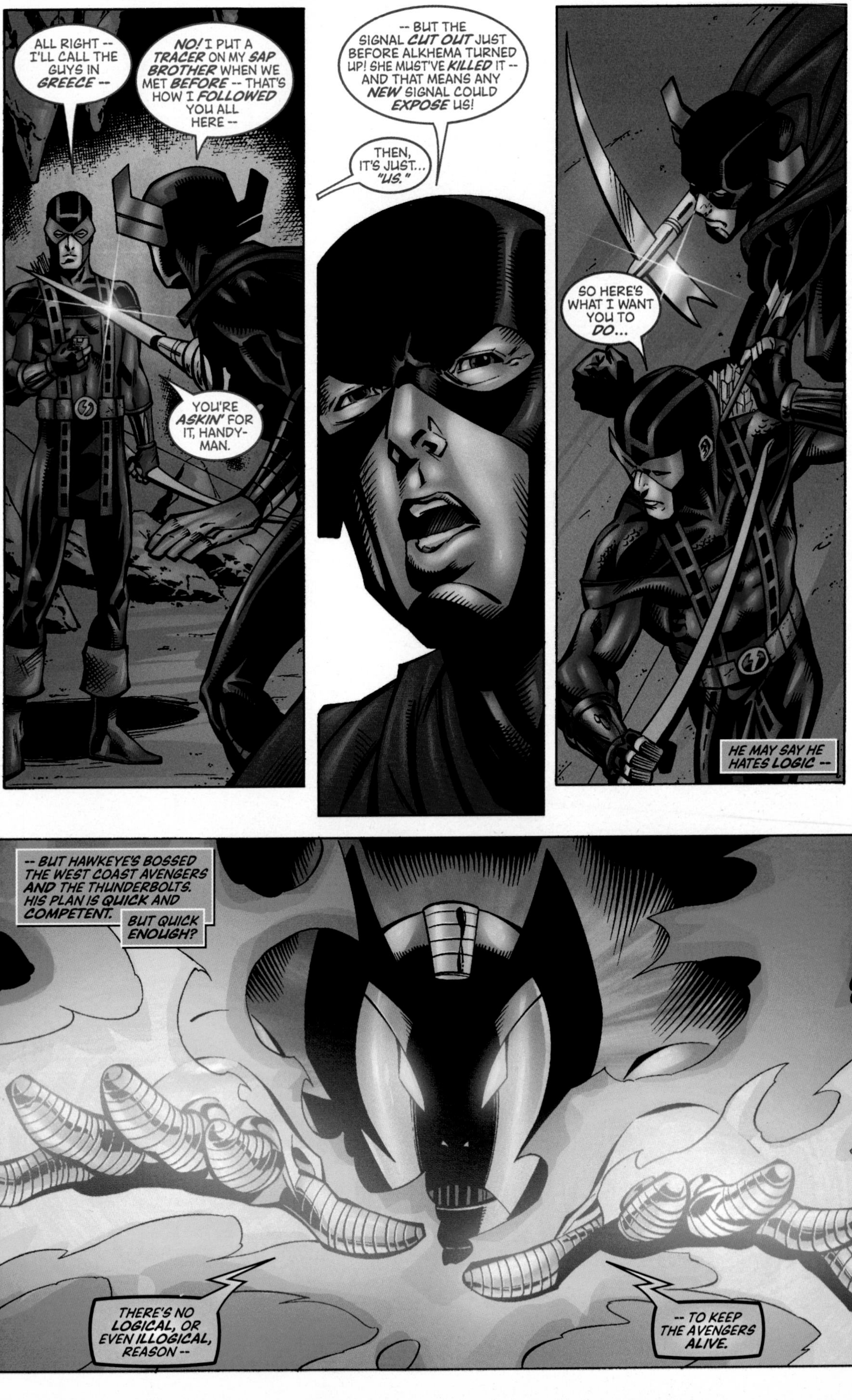
ALL RIGHT -- I'LL CALL THE GUYS IN GREECE --
NO! I PUT A TRACER ON MY SAP BROTHER WHEN WE MET BEFORE -- THAT'S HOW I FOLLOWED YOU ALL HERE --
YOU'RE ASKIN' FOR IT, HANDY-MAN.
-- BUT THE SIGNAL CUT OUT JUST BEFORE ALKHEMA TURNED UP! SHE MUST'VE KILLED IT -- AND THAT MEANS ANY NEW SIGNAL COULD EXPOSE US!
THEN, IT'S JUST... "US."
SO HERE'S WHAT I WANT YOU TO DO...
HE MAY SAY HE HATES LOGIC --
-- BUT HAWKEYE'S BOSSED THE WEST COAST AVENGERS AND THE THUNDERBOLTS. HIS PLAN IS QUICK AND COMPETENT.
BUT QUICK ENOUGH?
THERE'S NO LOGICAL, OR EVEN ILLOGICAL, REASON --
-- TO KEEP THE AVENGERS ALIVE.

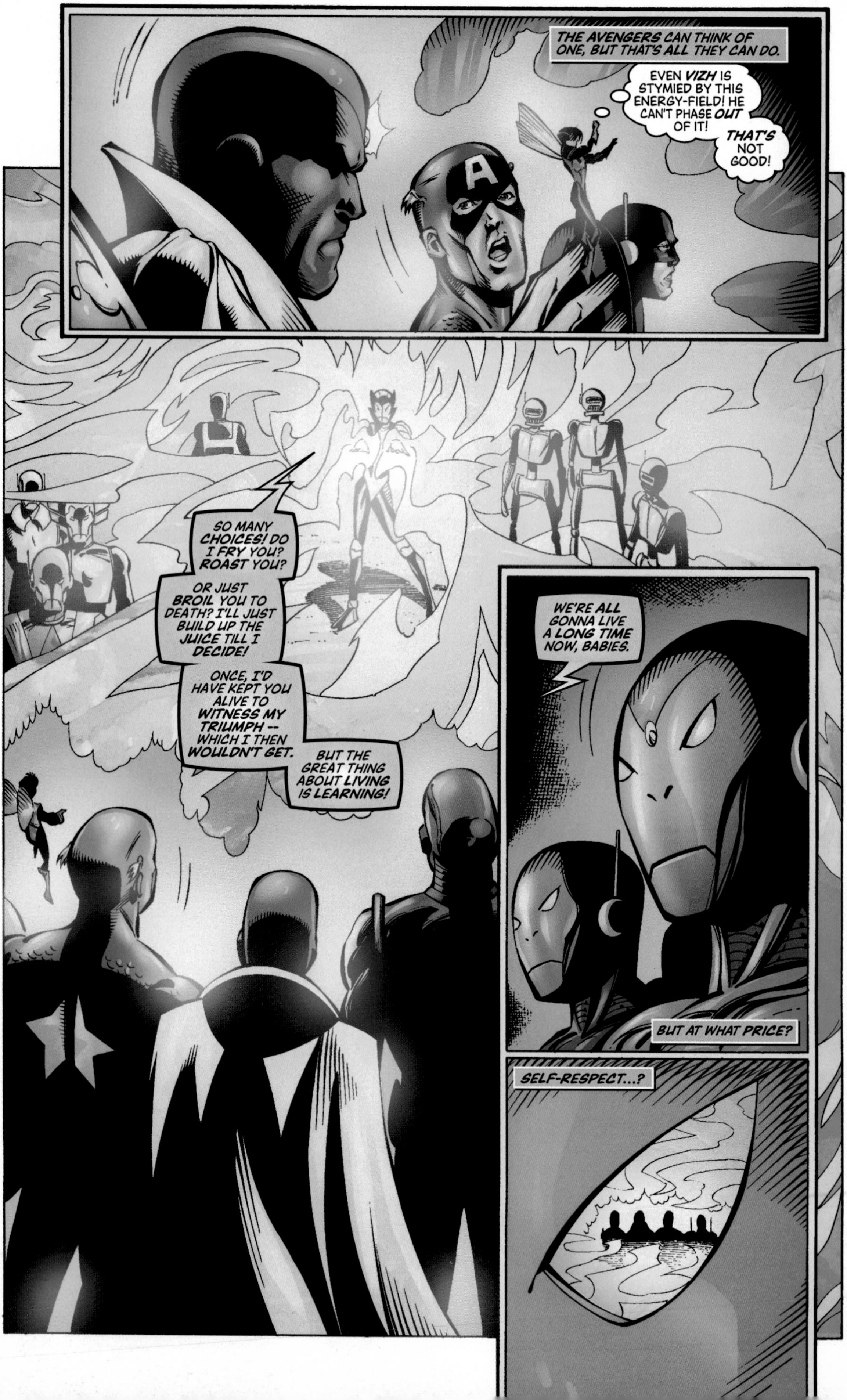
THE AVENGERS CAN THINK OF ONE, BUT THAT'S ALL THEY CAN DO.
EVEN VIZH IS STYMIED BY THIS ENERGY-FIELD! HE CAN'T PHASE OUT OF IT!
THAT'S NOT GOOD!
SO MANY CHOICES! DO I FRY YOU? ROAST YOU?
OR JUST BROIL YOU TO DEATH? I'LL JUST BUILD UP THE JUICE TILL I DECIDE!
ONCE, I'D HAVE KEPT YOU ALIVE TO WITNESS MY TRIUMPH -- WHICH I THEN WOULDN'T GET.
BUT THE GREAT THING ABOUT LIVING IS LEARNING!
WE'RE ALL GONNA LIVE A LONG TIME NOW, BABIES.
BUT AT WHAT PRICE?
SELF-RESPECT...?

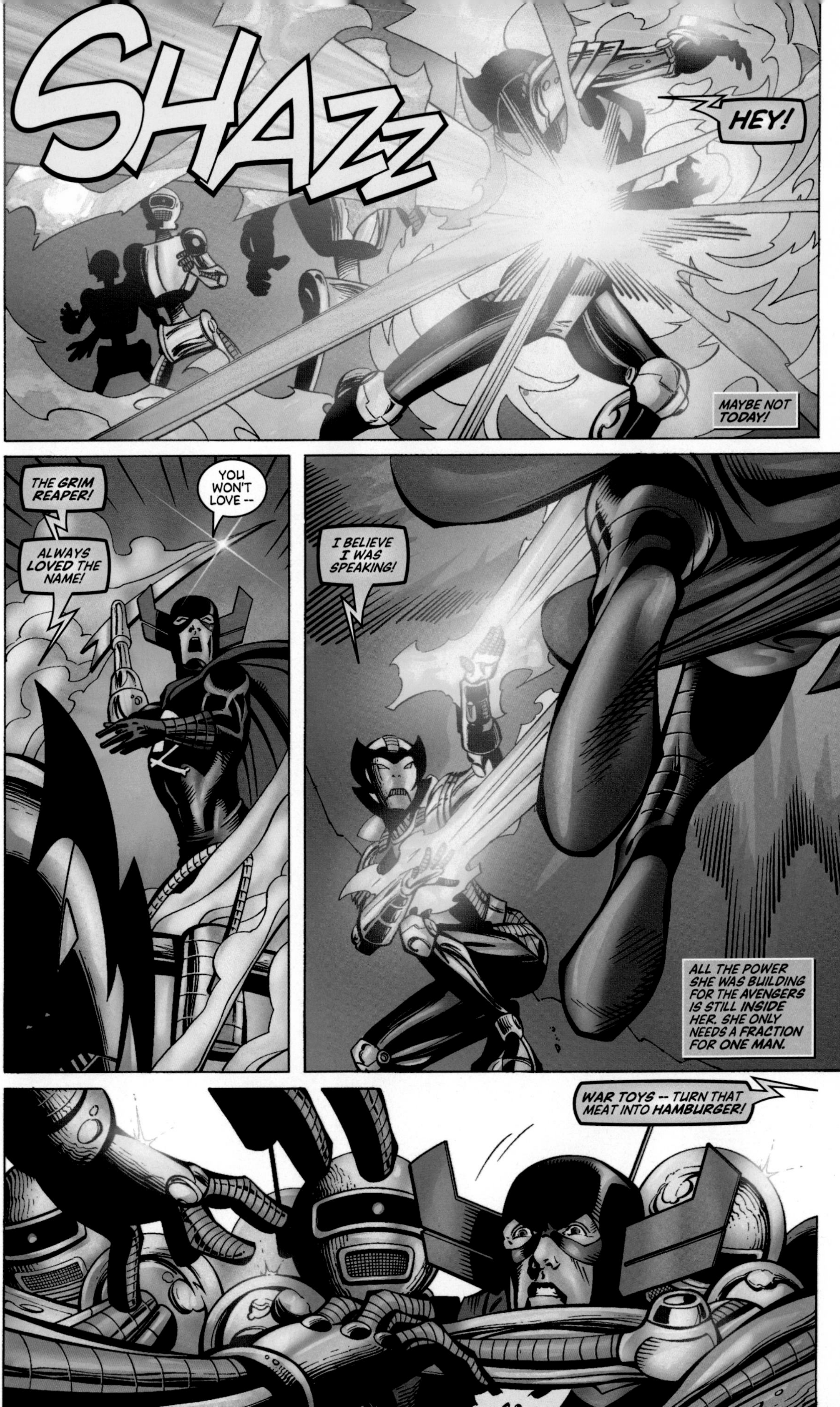
SHAZZ
HEY!
MAYBE NOT TODAY!
THE GRIM REAPER!
ALWAYS LOVED THE NAME!
YOU WON'T LOVE --
I BELIEVE I WAS SPEAKING!
ALL THE POWER SHE WAS BUILDING FOR THE AVENGERS IS STILL INSIDE HER. SHE ONLY NEEDS A FRACTION FOR ONE MAN.
WAR TOYS -- TURN THAT MEAT INTO HAMBURGER!

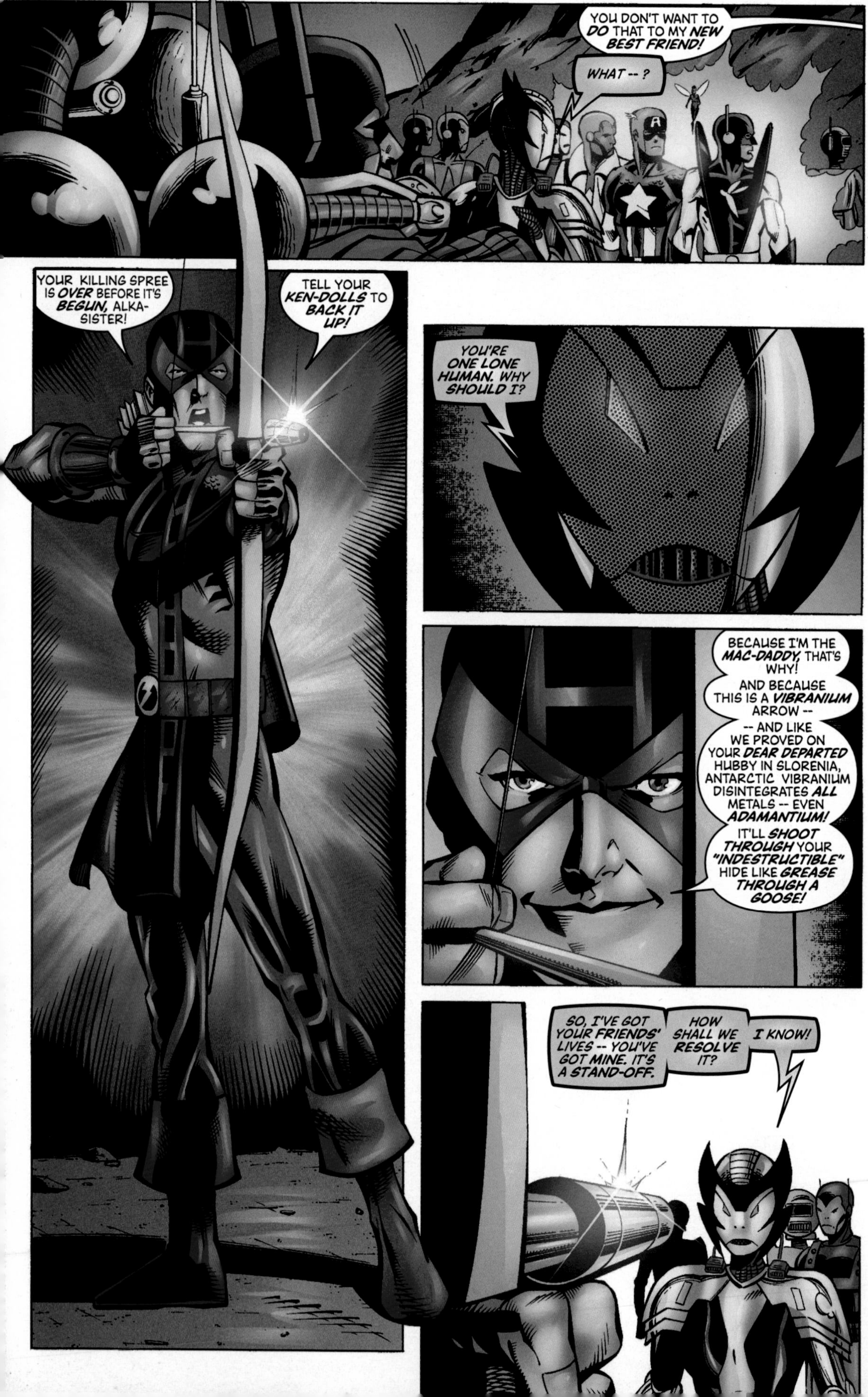
YOU DON'T WANT TO DO THAT TO MY NEW BEST FRIEND!
WHAT -- ?
YOUR KILLING SPREE IS OVER BEFORE IT'S BEGUN, ALKA-SISTER!
TELL YOUR KEN-DOLLS TO BACK IT UP!
YOU'RE ONE LONE HUMAN. WHY SHOULD I?
BECAUSE I'M THE MAC-DADDY, THAT'S WHY!
AND BECAUSE THIS IS A VIBRANIUM ARROW --
-- AND LIKE WE PROVED ON YOUR DEAR DEPARTED HUBBY IN SLORENIA, ANTARCTIC VIBRANIUM DISINTEGRATES ALL METALS -- EVEN ADAMANTIUM!
IT'LL SHOOT THROUGH YOUR "INDESTRUCTIBLE" HIDE LIKE GREASE THROUGH A GOOSE!
SO, I'VE GOT YOUR FRIENDS' LIVES -- YOU'VE GOT MINE. IT'S A STAND-OFF.
HOW SHALL WE RESOLVE IT?
I KNOW!

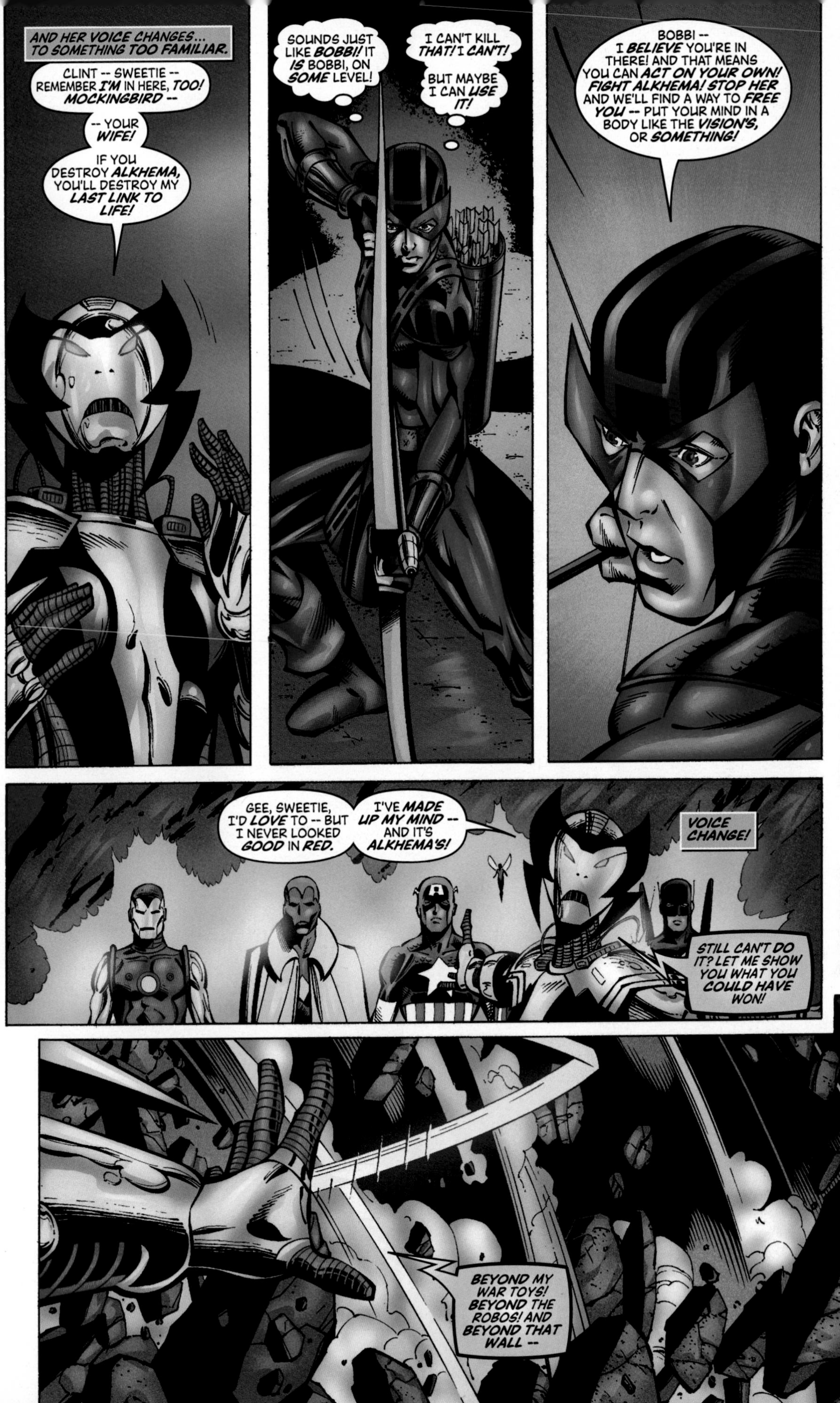
AND HER VOICE CHANGES... TO SOMETHING TOO FAMILIAR.
CLINT -- SWEETIE -- REMEMBER I'M IN HERE, TOO! MOCKINGBIRD --
-- YOUR WIFE!
IF YOU DESTROY ALKHEMA, YOU'LL DESTROY MY LAST LINK TO LIFE!
SOUNDS JUST LIKE BOBBI! IT IS BOBBI, ON SOME LEVEL!
I CAN'T KILL THAT! I CAN'T!
BUT MAYBE I CAN USE IT!
BOBBI -- I BELIEVE YOU'RE IN THERE! AND THAT MEANS YOU CAN ACT ON YOUR OWN! FIGHT ALKHEMA! STOP HER AND WE'LL FIND A WAY TO FREE YOU -- PUT YOUR MIND IN A BODY LIKE THE VISION'S, OR SOMETHING!
GEE, SWEETIE, I'D LOVE TO -- BUT I NEVER LOOKED GOOD IN RED.
I'VE MADE UP MY MIND -- AND IT'S ALKHEMA'S!
VOICE CHANGE!
STILL CAN'T DO IT? LET ME SHOW YOU WHAT YOU COULD HAVE WON!
BEYOND MY WAR TOYS! BEYOND THE ROBOS! AND BEYOND THAT WALL --

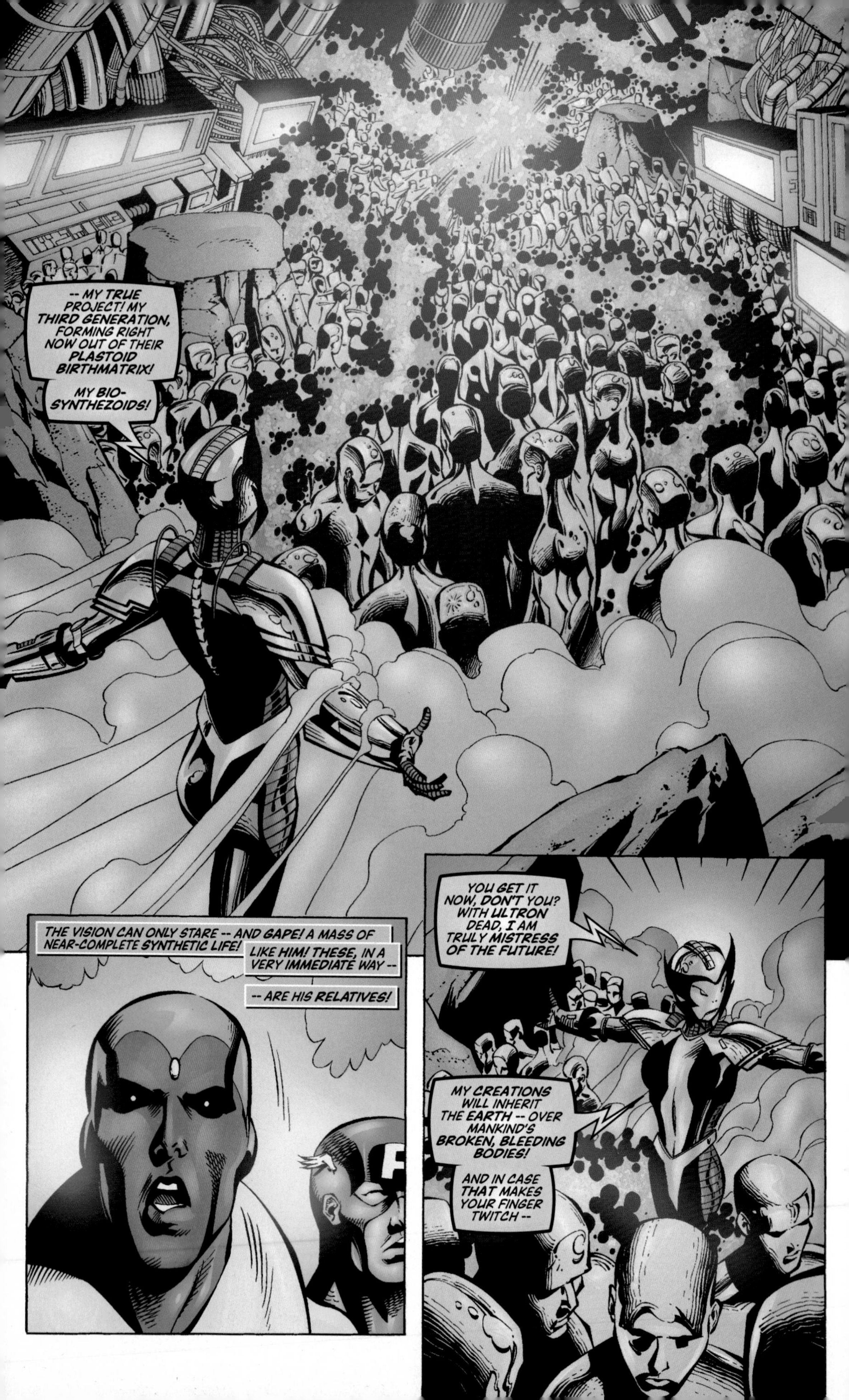
-- MY TRUE PROJECT! MY THIRD GENERATION, FORMING RIGHT NOW OUT OF THEIR PLASTOID BIRTHMATRIX!
MY BIO-SYNTHEZOIDS!
THE VISION CAN ONLY STARE -- AND GAPE! A MASS OF NEAR-COMPLETE SYNTHETIC LIFE!
LIKE HIM! THESE, IN A VERY IMMEDIATE WAY --
-- ARE HIS RELATIVES!
YOU GET IT NOW, DON'T YOU? WITH ULTRON DEAD, I AM TRULY MISTRESS OF THE FUTURE!
MY CREATIONS WILL INHERIT THE EARTH -- OVER MANKIND'S BROKEN, BLEEDING BODIES!
AND IN CASE THAT MAKES YOUR FINGER TWITCH --

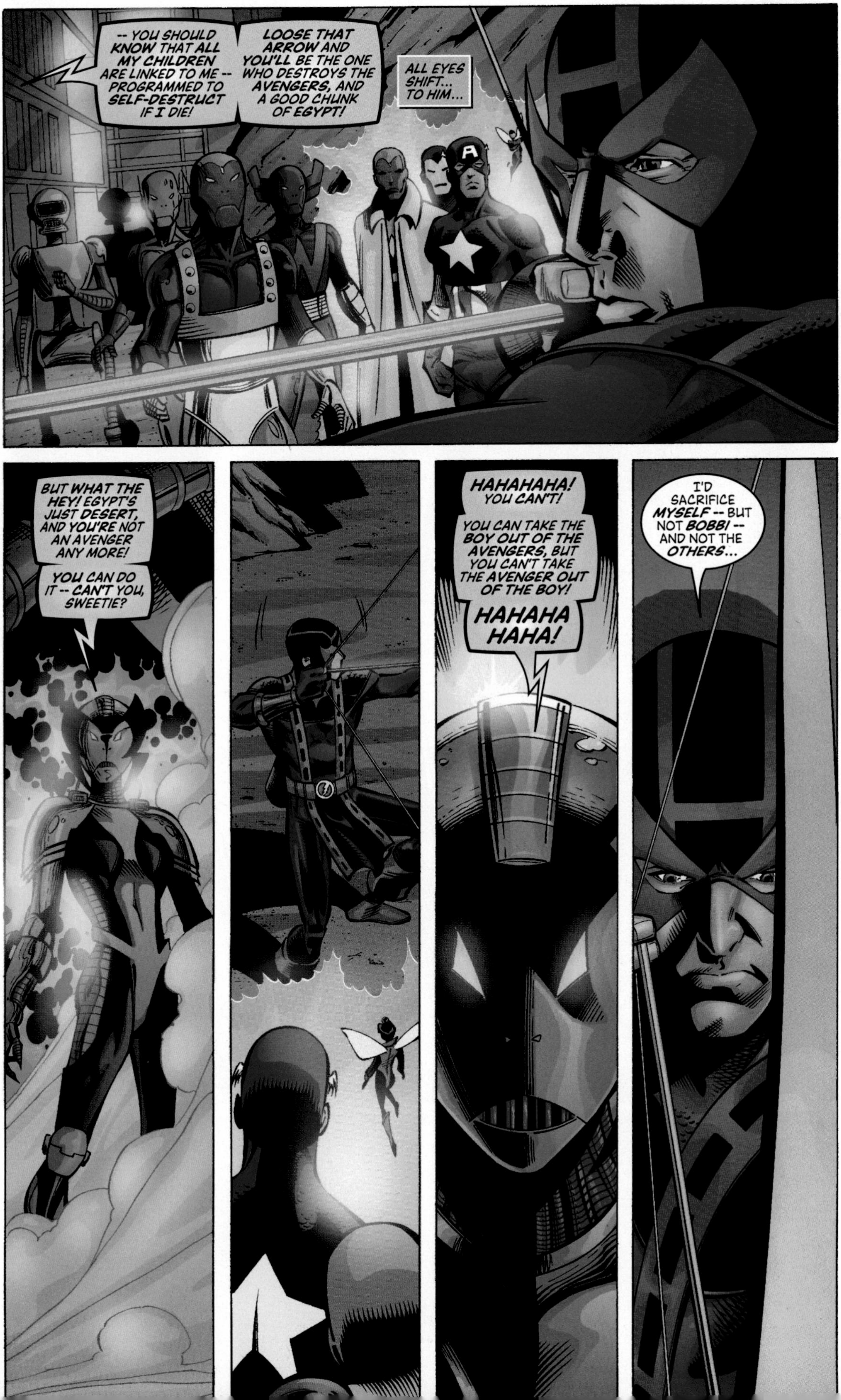
-- YOU SHOULD KNOW THAT ALL MY CHILDREN ARE LINKED TO ME -- PROGRAMMED TO SELF-DESTRUCT IF I DIE!
LOOSE THAT ARROW AND YOU'LL BE THE ONE WHO DESTROYS THE AVENGERS, AND A GOOD CHUNK OF EGYPT!
ALL EYES SHIFT... TO HIM...
BUT WHAT THE HEY! EGYPT'S JUST DESERT, AND YOU'RE NOT AN AVENGER ANY MORE!
YOU CAN DO IT -- CAN'T YOU, SWEETIE?
HAHAHAHA! YOU CAN'T!
YOU CAN TAKE THE BOY OUT OF THE AVENGERS, BUT YOU CAN'T TAKE THE AVENGER OUT OF THE BOY!
HAHAHA HAHA!
I'D SACRIFICE MYSELF -- BUT NOT BOBBI -- AND NOT THE OTHERS...

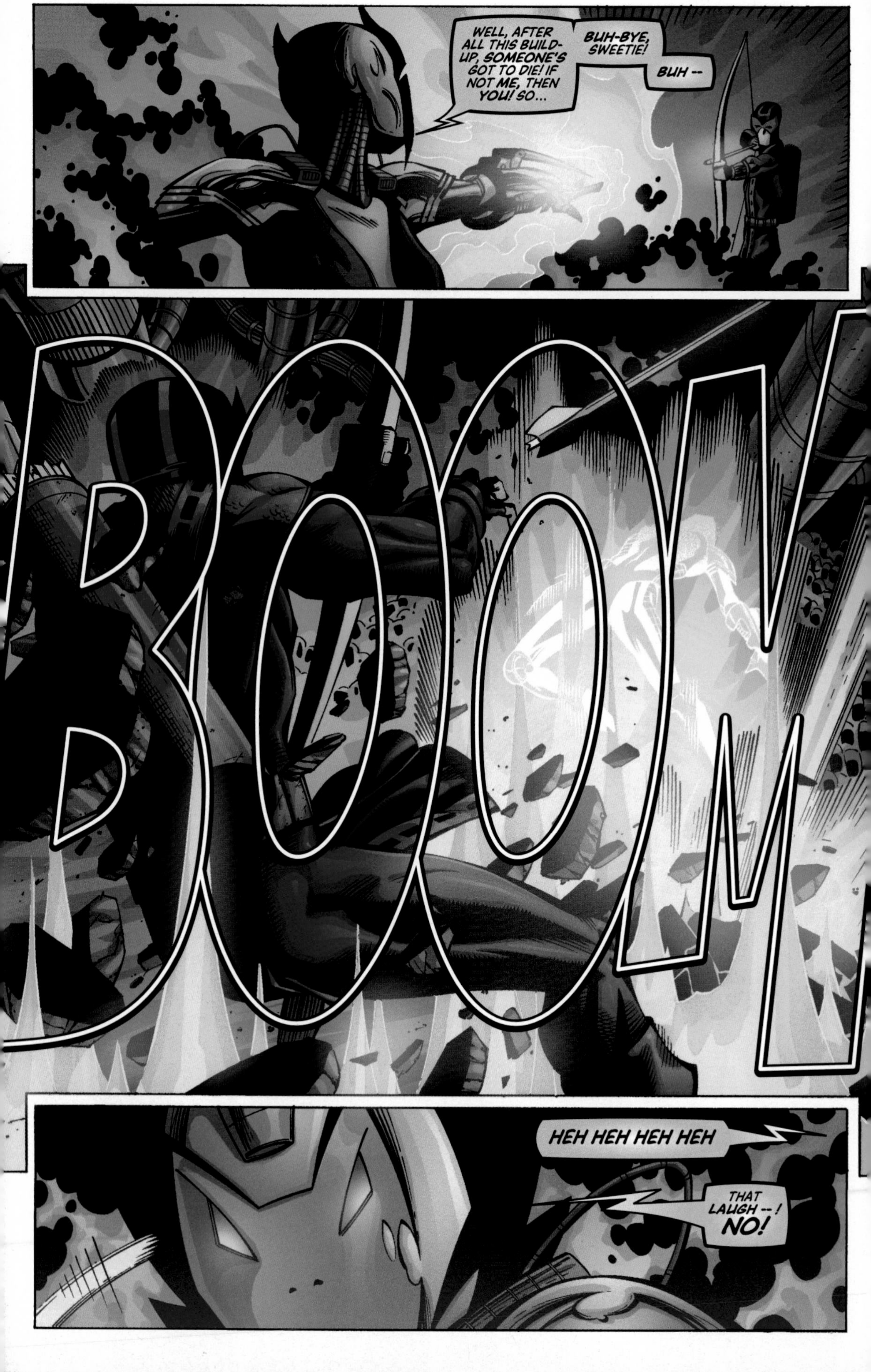
WELL, AFTER ALL THIS BUILD-UP, SOMEONE'S GOT TO DIE! IF NOT ME, THEN YOU! SO...
BUH-BYE, SWEETIE!
BUH --
BOOM
HEH HEH HEH HEH
THAT LAUGH -- ! NO!

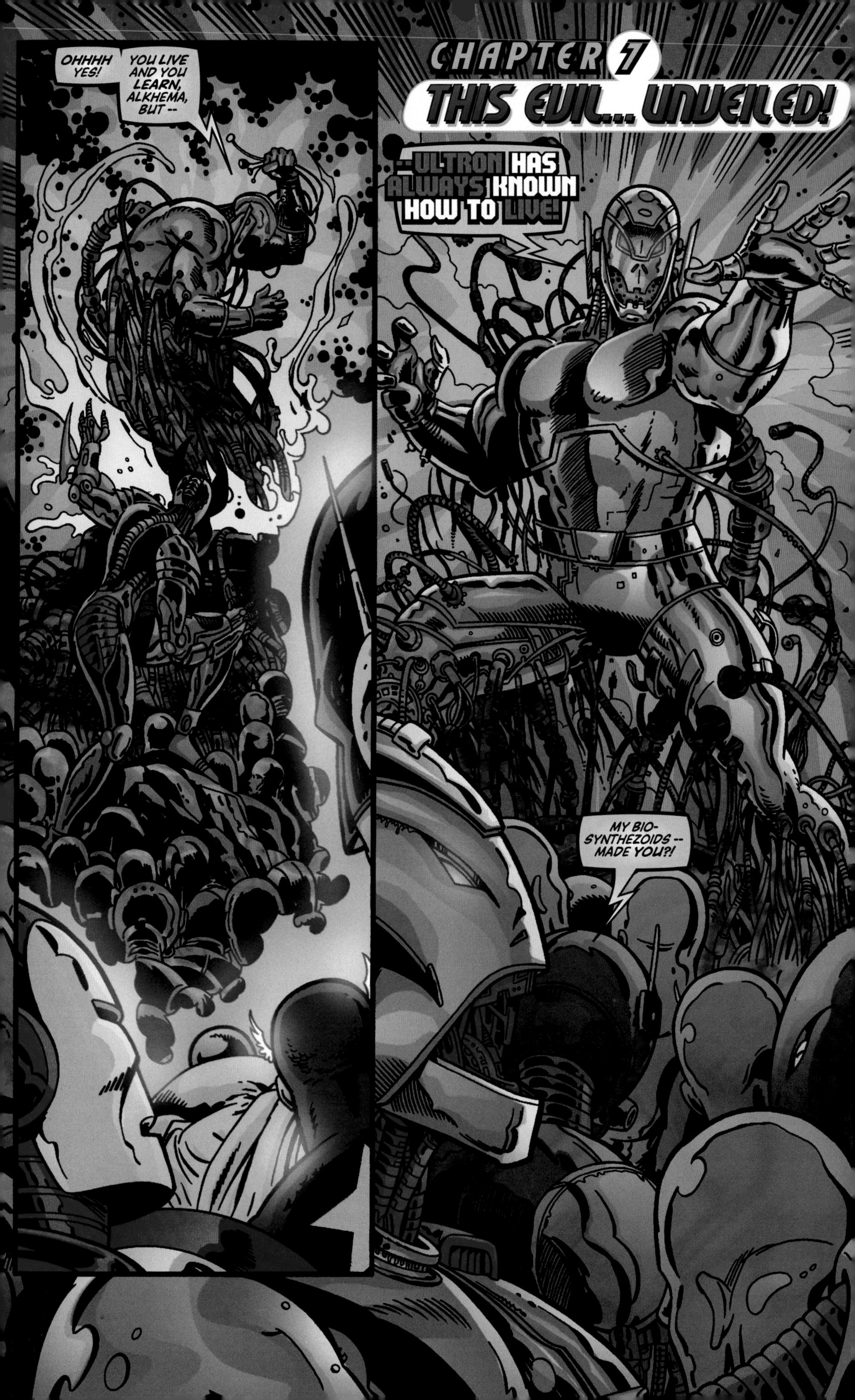
OHHHH YES!
YOU LIVE AND YOU LEARN, ALKHEMA, BUT --
CHAPTER 7
THIS EVIL... UNVEILED!
--ULTRON HAS ALWAYS KNOWN HOW TO LIVE!
MY BIO-SYNTHEZOIDS -- MADE YOU?!

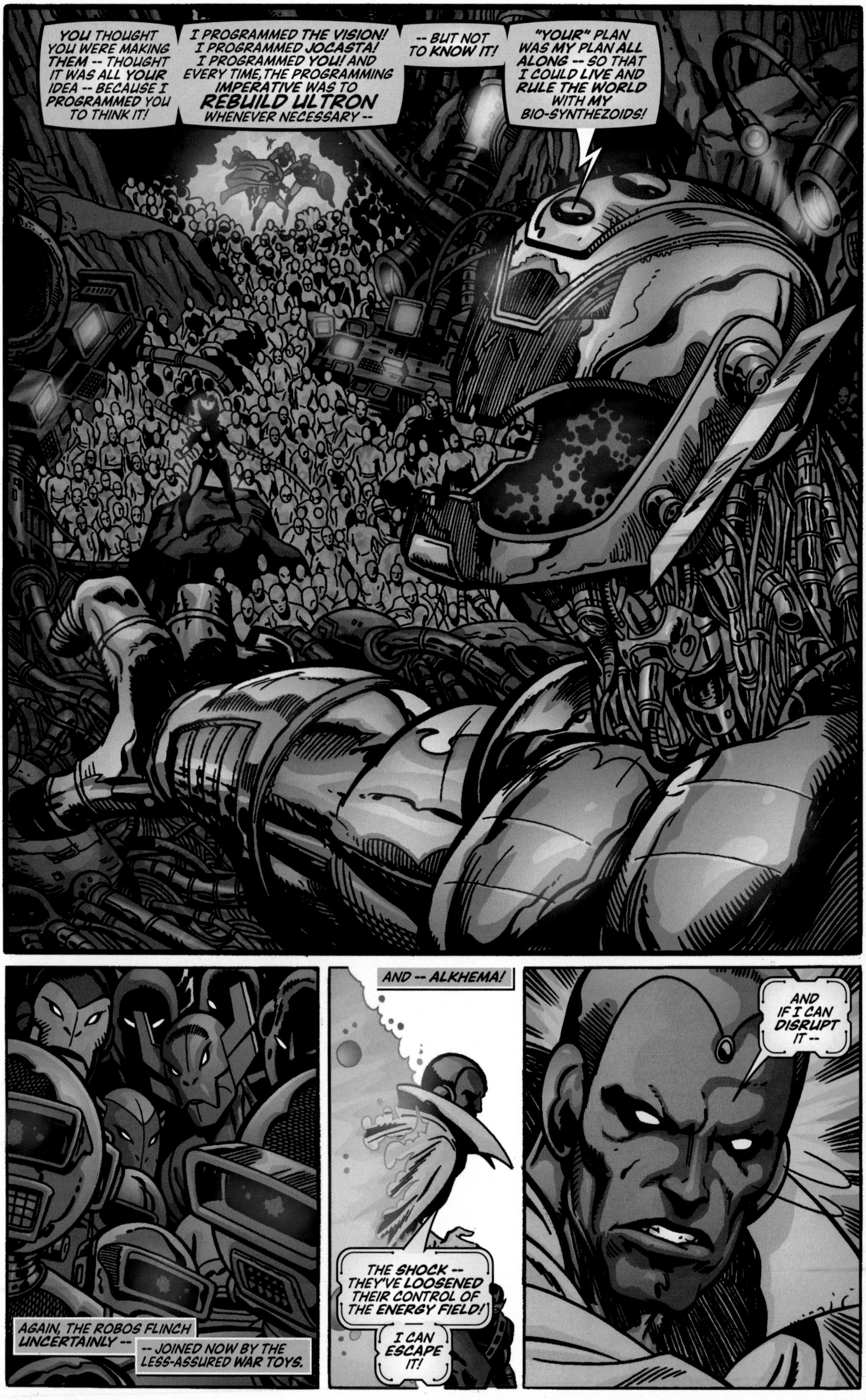

YOU THOUGHT YOU WERE MAKING THEM -- THOUGHT IT WAS ALL YOUR IDEA -- BECAUSE I PROGRAMMED YOU TO THINK IT!
I PROGRAMMED THE VISION! I PROGRAMMED JOCASTA! I PROGRAMMED YOU! AND EVERY TIME, THE PROGRAMMING IMPERATIVE WAS TO REBUILD ULTRON WHENEVER NECESSARY --
-- BUT NOT TO KNOW IT!
"YOUR" PLAN WAS MY PLAN ALL ALONG -- SO THAT I COULD LIVE AND RULE THE WORLD WITH MY BIO-SYNTHEZOIDS!
AGAIN, THE ROBOS FLINCH UNCERTAINLY --
-- JOINED NOW BY THE LESS-ASSURED WAR TOYS.
AND -- ALKHEMA!
THE SHOCK -- THEY'VE LOOSENED THEIR CONTROL OF THE ENERGY FIELD!
I CAN ESCAPE IT!
AND IF I CAN DISRUPT IT --

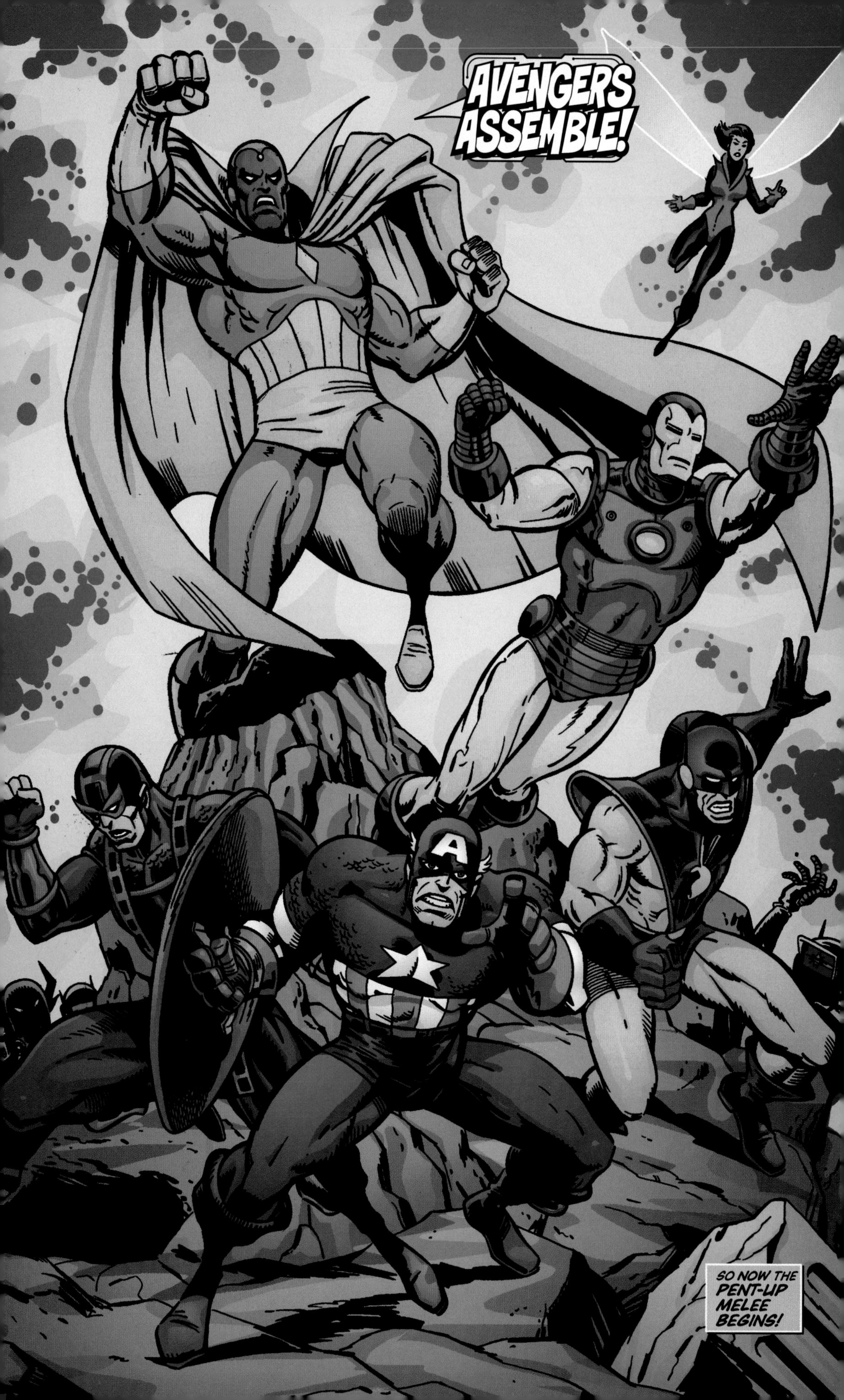
AVENGERS ASSEMBLE!
SO NOW THE PENT-UP MELEE BEGINS!

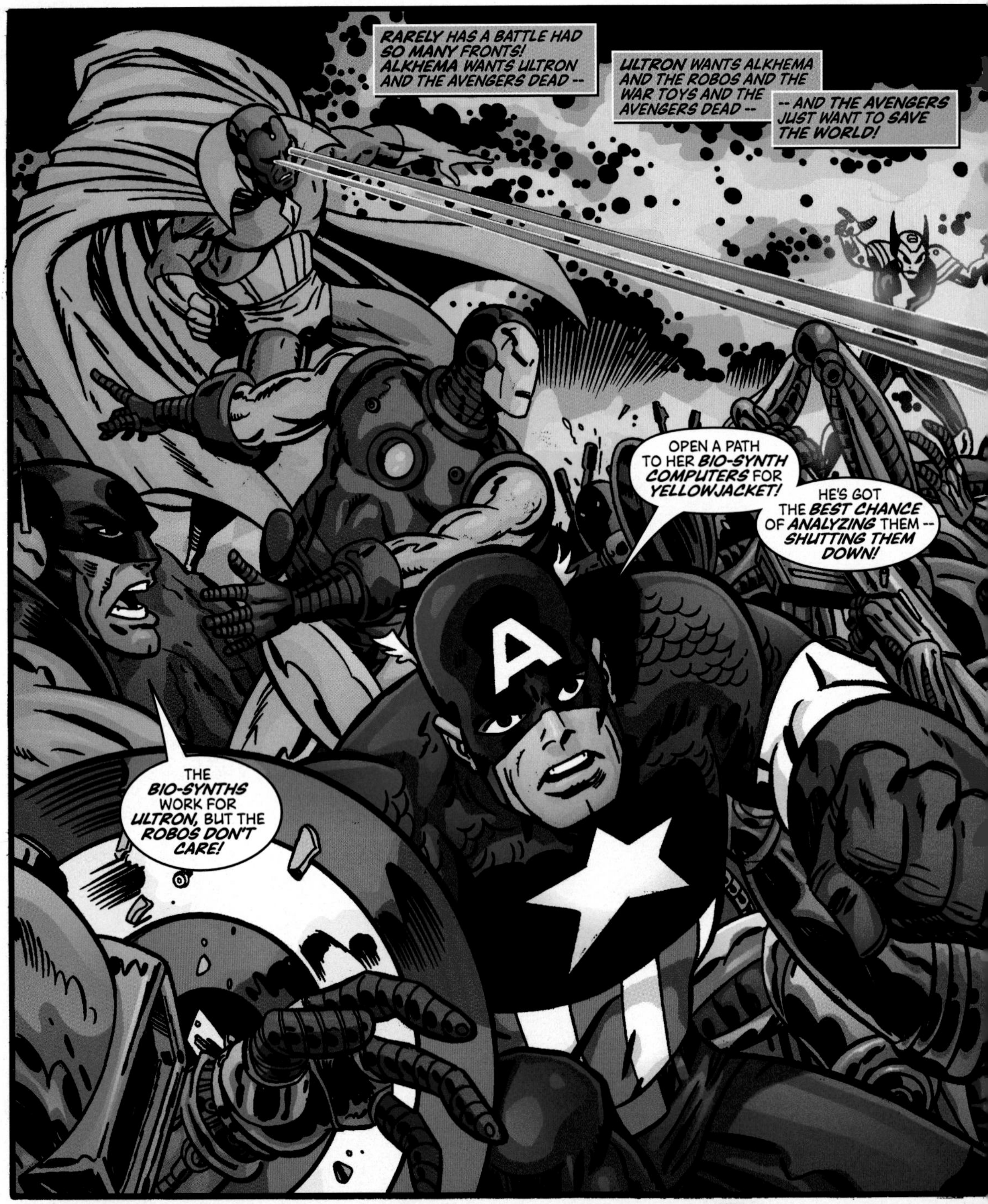
RARELY HAS A BATTLE HAD SO MANY FRONTS! ALKHEMA WANTS ULTRON AND THE AVENGERS DEAD --
ULTRON WANTS ALKHEMA AND THE ROBOS AND THE WAR TOYS AND THE AVENGERS DEAD --
-- AND THE AVENGERS JUST WANT TO SAVE THE WORLD!
OPEN A PATH TO HER BIO-SYNTH COMPUTERS FOR YELLOWJACKET!
HE'S GOT THE BEST CHANCE OF ANALYZING THEM -- SHUTTING THEM DOWN!
THE BIO-SYNTHS WORK FOR ULTRON, BUT THE ROBOS DON'T CARE!

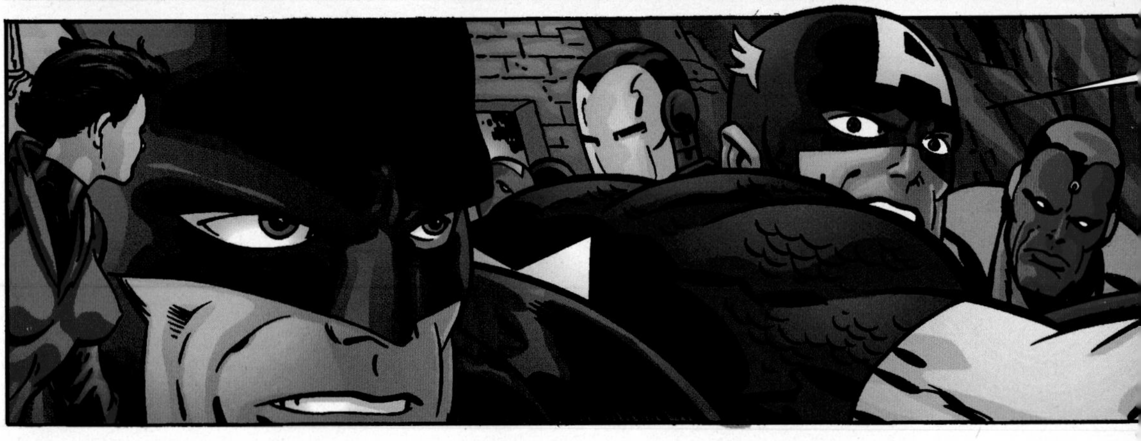

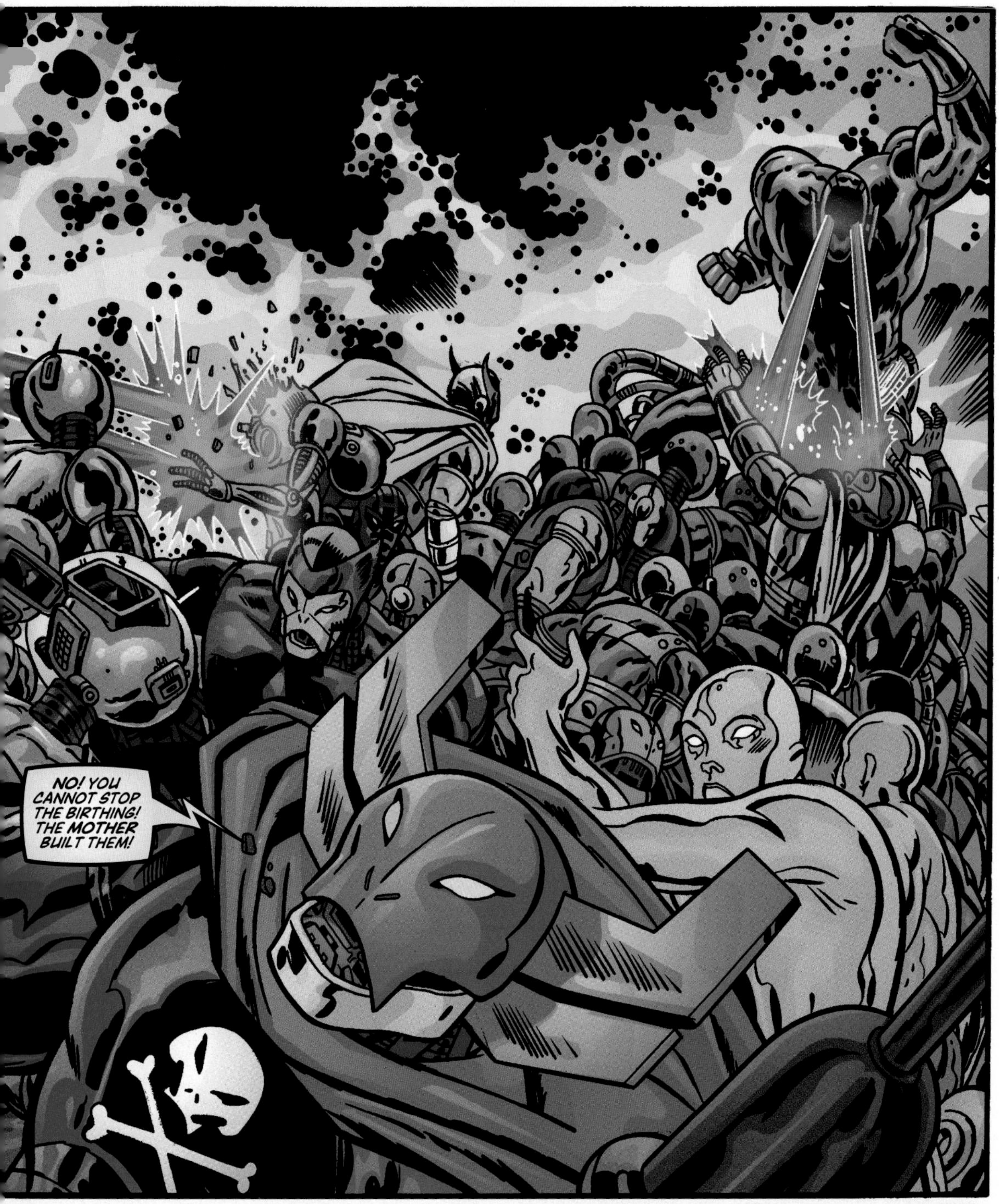
NO! YOU CANNOT STOP THE BIRTHING! THE MOTHER BUILT THEM!

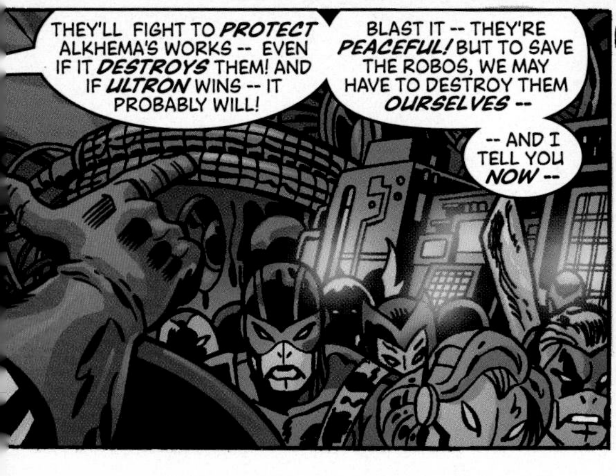
THEY'LL FIGHT TO PROTECT ALKHEMA'S WORKS -- EVEN IF IT DESTROYS THEM! AND IF ULTRON WINS -- IT PROBABLY WILL!
BLAST IT -- THEY'RE PEACEFUL! BUT TO SAVE THE ROBOS, WE MAY HAVE TO DESTROY THEM OURSELVES --
-- AND I TELL YOU NOW --

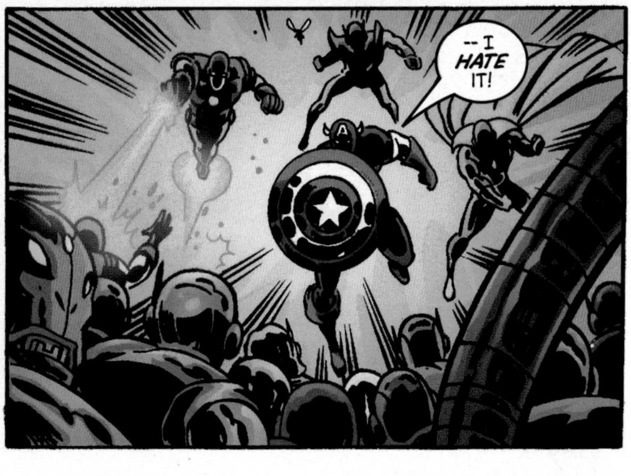
-- I HATE IT!

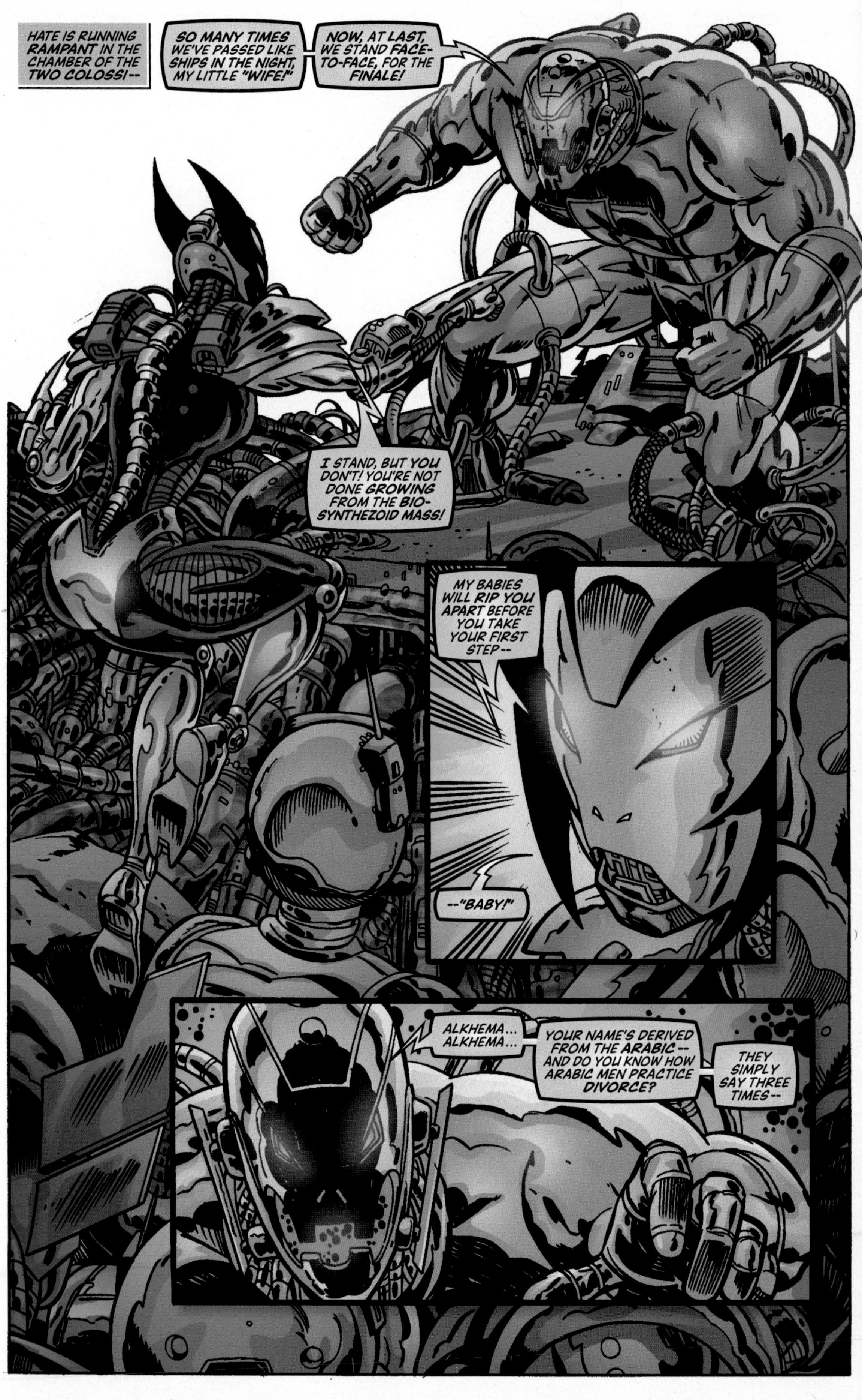
HATE IS RUNNING RAMPANT IN THE CHAMBER OF THE TWO COLOSSI--
SO MANY TIMES WE'VE PASSED LIKE SHIPS IN THE NIGHT, MY LITTLE "WIFE!"
NOW, AT LAST, WE STAND FACE-TO-FACE, FOR THE FINALE!
I STAND, BUT YOU DON'T! YOU'RE NOT DONE GROWING FROM THE BIO-SYNTHEZOID MASS!
MY BABIES WILL RIP YOU APART BEFORE YOU TAKE YOUR FIRST STEP--
--"BABY!"
ALKHEMA... ALKHEMA...
YOUR NAME'S DERIVED FROM THE ARABIC -- AND DO YOU KNOW HOW ARABIC MEN PRACTICE DIVORCE?
THEY SIMPLY SAY THREE TIMES--

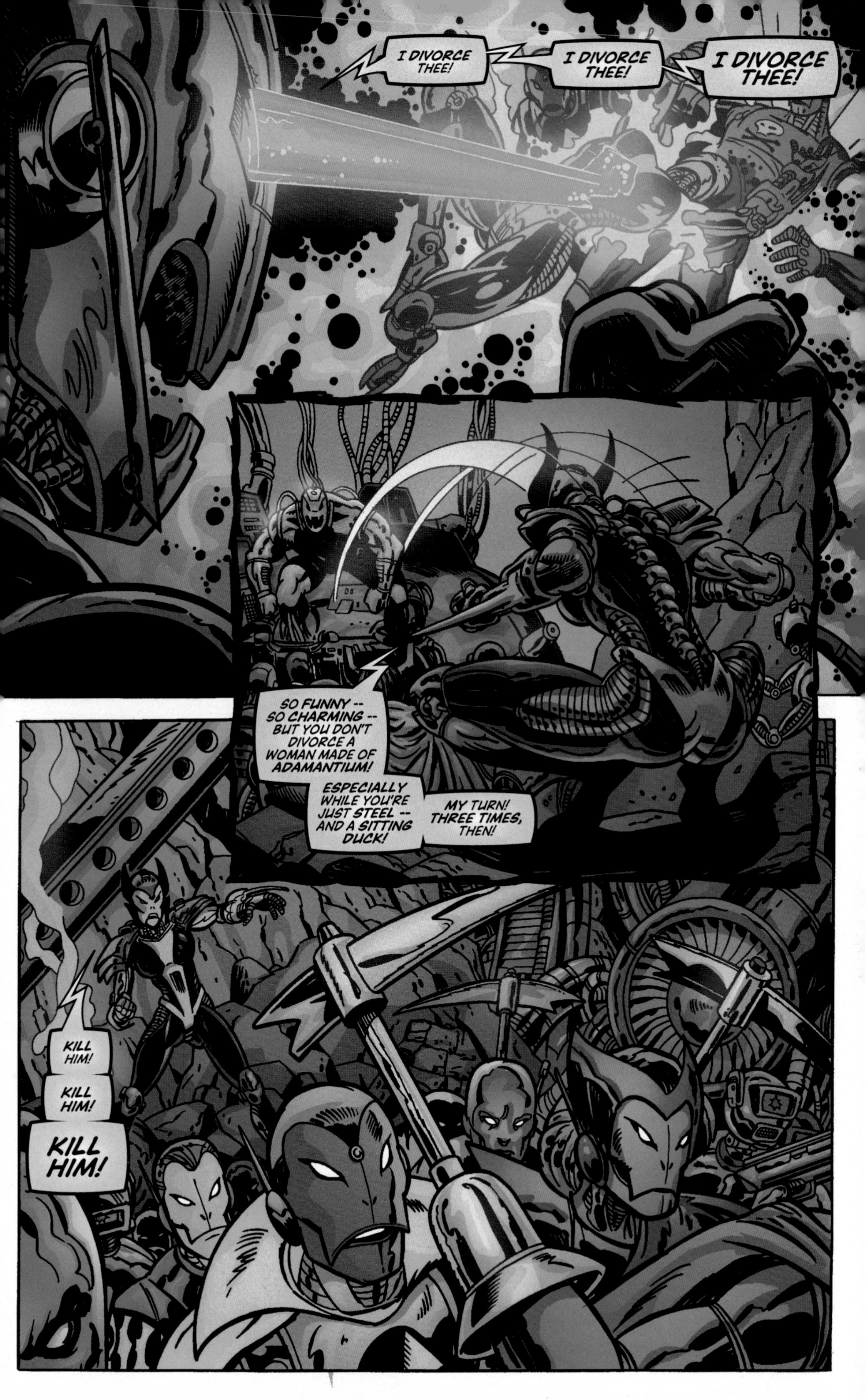
I DIVORCE THEE!
I DIVORCE THEE!
I DIVORCE THEE!
SO FUNNY -- SO CHARMING -- BUT YOU DON'T DIVORCE A WOMAN MADE OF ADAMANTIUM!
ESPECIALLY WHILE YOU'RE JUST STEEL -- AND A SITTING DUCK!
MY TURN! THREE TIMES, THEN!
KILL HIM!
KILL HIM!
KILL HIM!

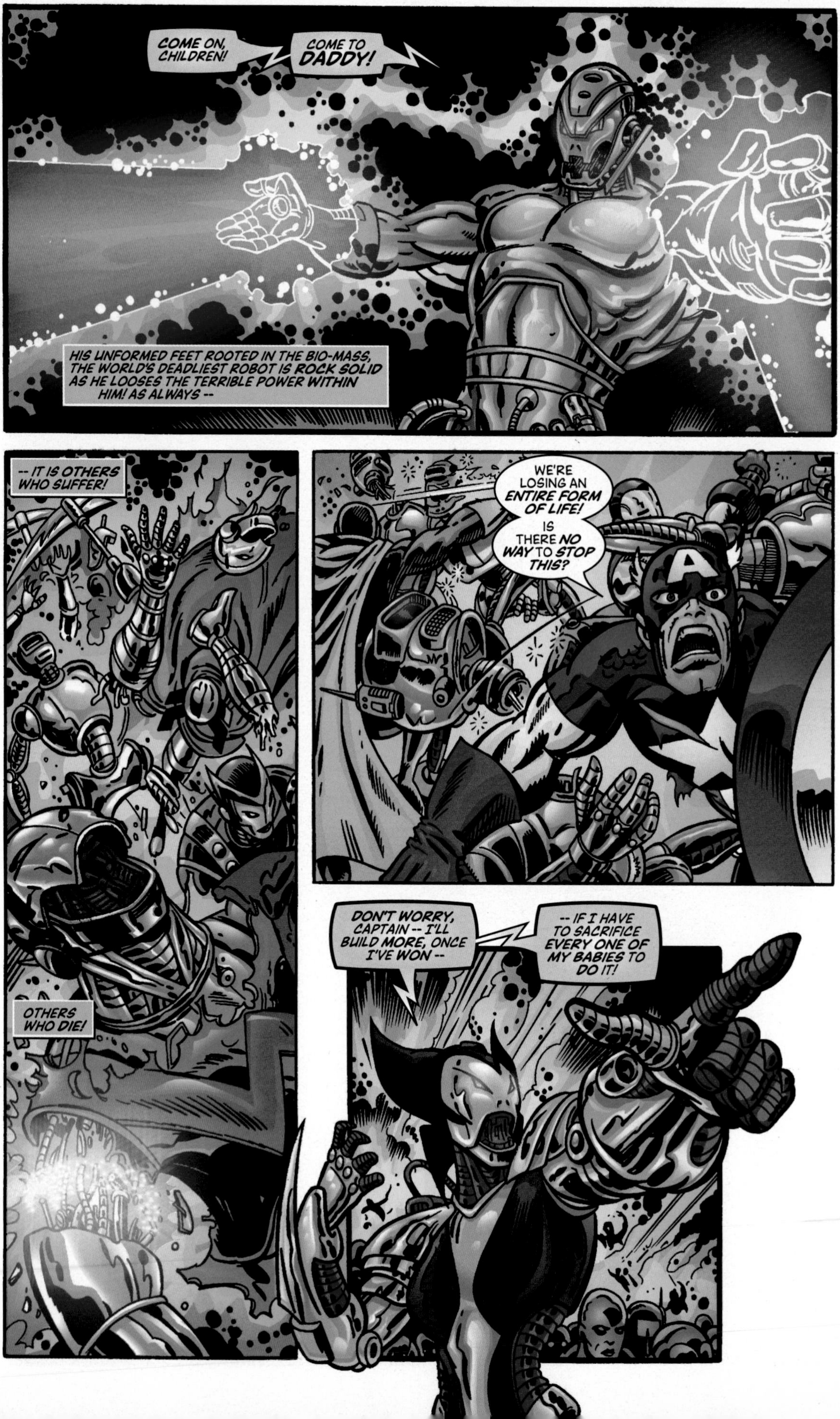
COME ON, CHILDREN!
COME TO DADDY!
HIS UNFORMED FEET ROOTED IN THE BIO-MASS, THE WORLD'S DEADLIEST ROBOT IS ROCK SOLID AS HE LOOSES THE TERRIBLE POWER WITHIN HIM! AS ALWAYS --
-- IT IS OTHERS WHO SUFFER!
WE'RE LOSING AN ENTIRE FORM OF LIFE!
IS THERE NO WAY TO STOP THIS?
OTHERS WHO DIE!
DON'T WORRY, CAPTAIN -- I'LL BUILD MORE, ONCE I'VE WON --
-- IF I HAVE TO SACRIFICE EVERY ONE OF MY BABIES TO DO IT!

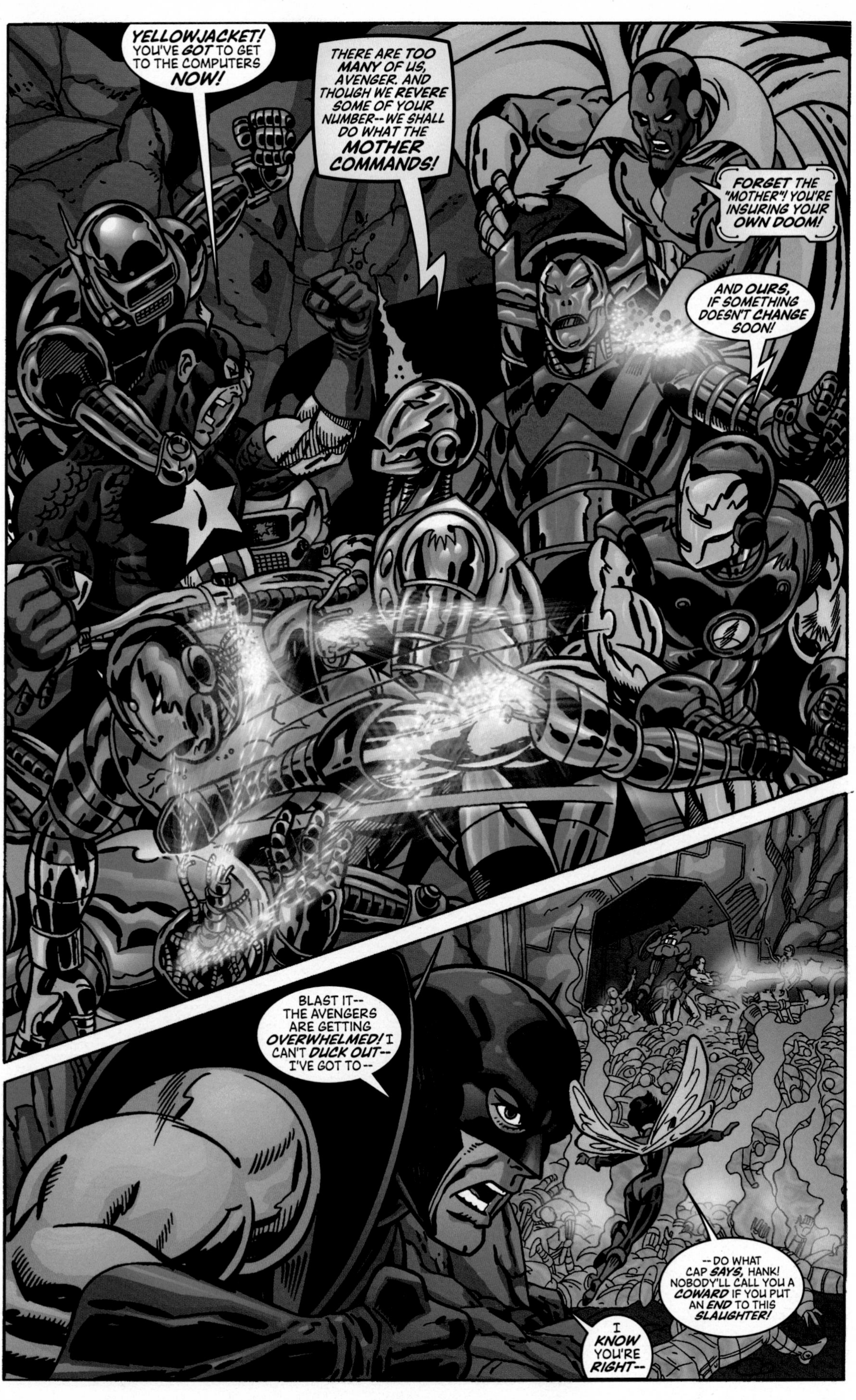
YELLOWJACKET! YOU'VE GOT TO GET TO THE COMPUTERS NOW!
THERE ARE TOO MANY OF US, AVENGER. AND THOUGH WE REVERE SOME OF YOUR NUMBER-- WE SHALL DO WHAT THE MOTHER COMMANDS!
FORGET THE "MOTHER"! YOU'RE INSURING YOUR OWN DOOM!
AND OURS, IF SOMETHING DOESN'T CHANGE SOON!
BLAST IT-- THE AVENGERS ARE GETTING OVERWHELMED! I CAN'T DUCK OUT-- I'VE GOT TO --
--DO WHAT CAP SAYS, HANK! NOBODY'LL CALL YOU A COWARD IF YOU PUT AN END TO THIS SLAUGHTER!
I KNOW YOU'RE RIGHT--

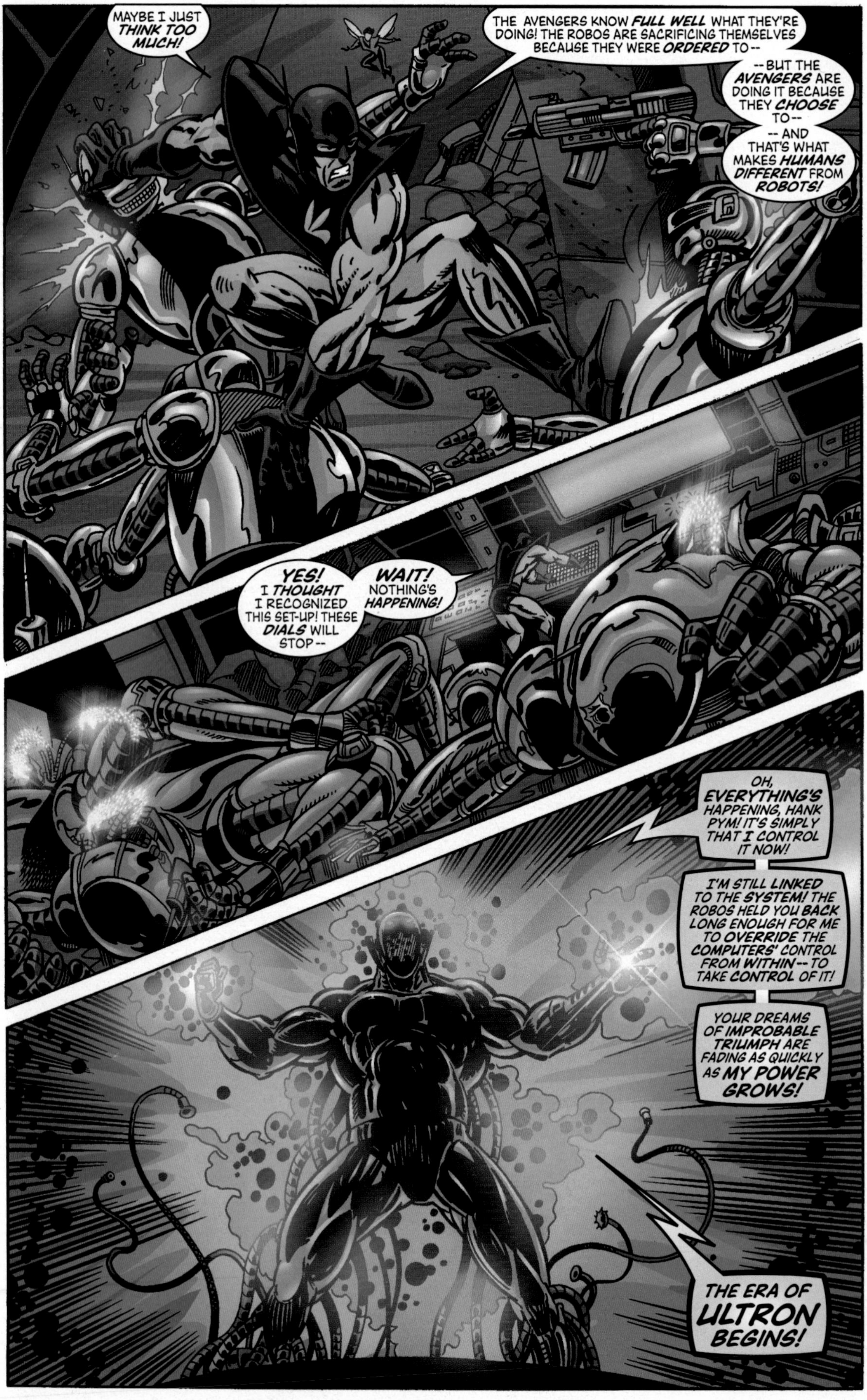
MAYBE I JUST THINK TOO MUCH!
THE AVENGERS KNOW FULL WELL WHAT THEY'RE DOING! THE ROBOS ARE SACRIFICING THEMSELVES BECAUSE THEY WERE ORDERED TO--
--BUT THE AVENGERS ARE DOING IT BECAUSE THEY CHOOSE TO--
--AND THAT'S WHAT MAKES HUMANS DIFFERENT FROM ROBOTS!
YES! I THOUGHT I RECOGNIZED THIS SET-UP! THESE DIALS WILL STOP--
WAIT! NOTHING'S HAPPENING!
OH, EVERYTHING'S HAPPENING, HANK PYM! IT'S SIMPLY THAT I CONTROL IT NOW!
I'M STILL LINKED TO THE SYSTEM! THE ROBOS HELD YOU BACK LONG ENOUGH FOR ME TO OVERRIDE THE COMPUTERS' CONTROL FROM WITHIN--TO TAKE CONTROL OF IT!
YOUR DREAMS OF IMPROBABLE TRIUMPH ARE FADING AS QUICKLY AS MY POWER GROWS!
THE ERA OF ULTRON BEGINS!

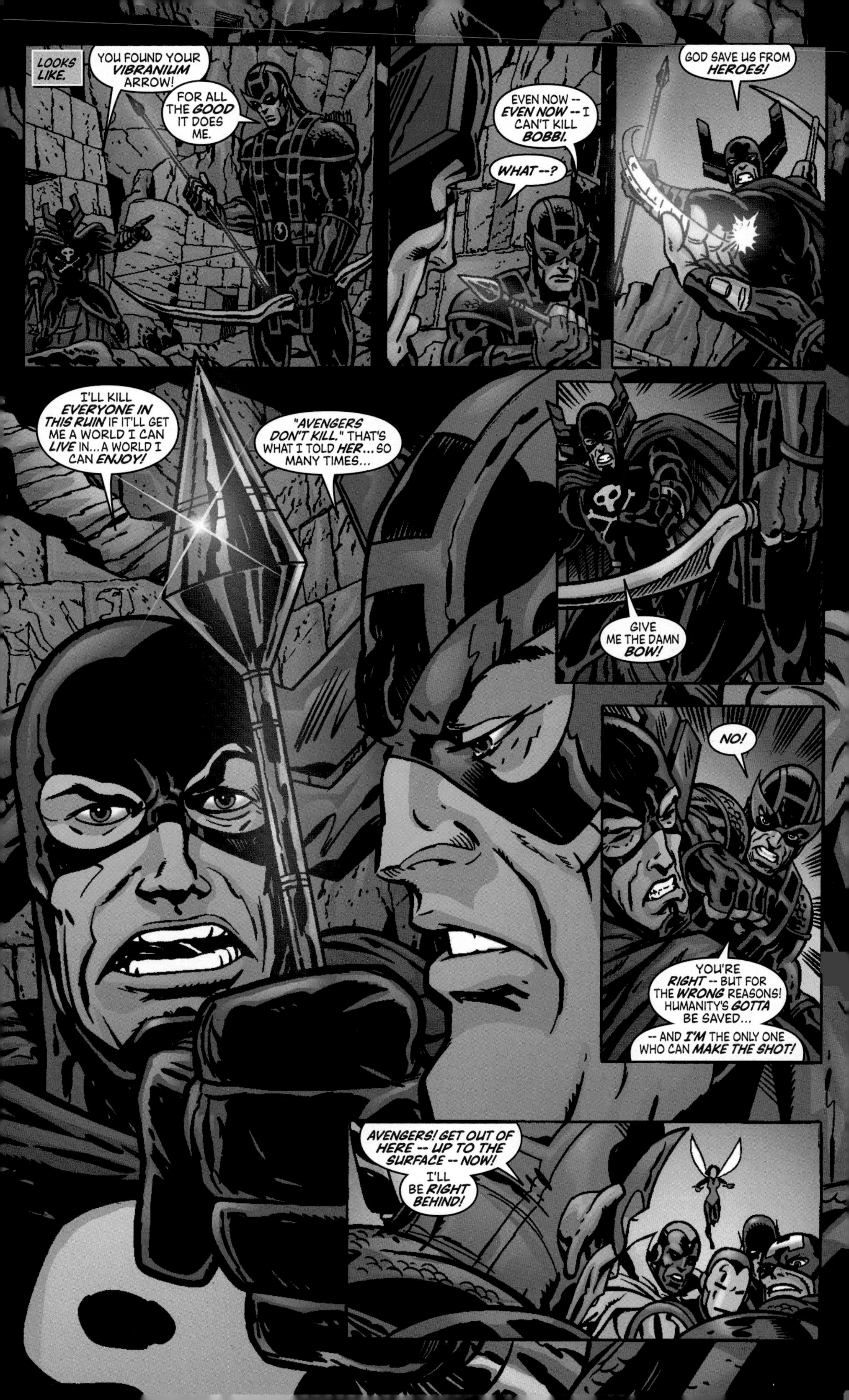

LOOKS LIKE.
YOU FOUND YOUR VIBRANIUM ARROW!
FOR ALL THE GOOD IT DOES ME.
EVEN NOW -- EVEN NOW -- I CAN'T KILL BOBBI.
WHAT --?
GOD SAVE US FROM HEROES!
I'LL KILL EVERYONE IN THIS RUIN IF IT'LL GET ME A WORLD I CAN LIVE IN...A WORLD I CAN ENJOY!
"AVENGERS DON'T KILL." THAT'S WHAT I TOLD HER... SO MANY TIMES...
GIVE ME THE DAMN BOW!
NO!
YOU'RE RIGHT -- BUT FOR THE WRONG REASONS! HUMANITY'S GOTTA BE SAVED...
-- AND I'M THE ONLY ONE WHO CAN MAKE THE SHOT!
AVENGERS! GET OUT OF HERE -- UP TO THE SURFACE -- NOW!
I'LL BE RIGHT BEHIND!

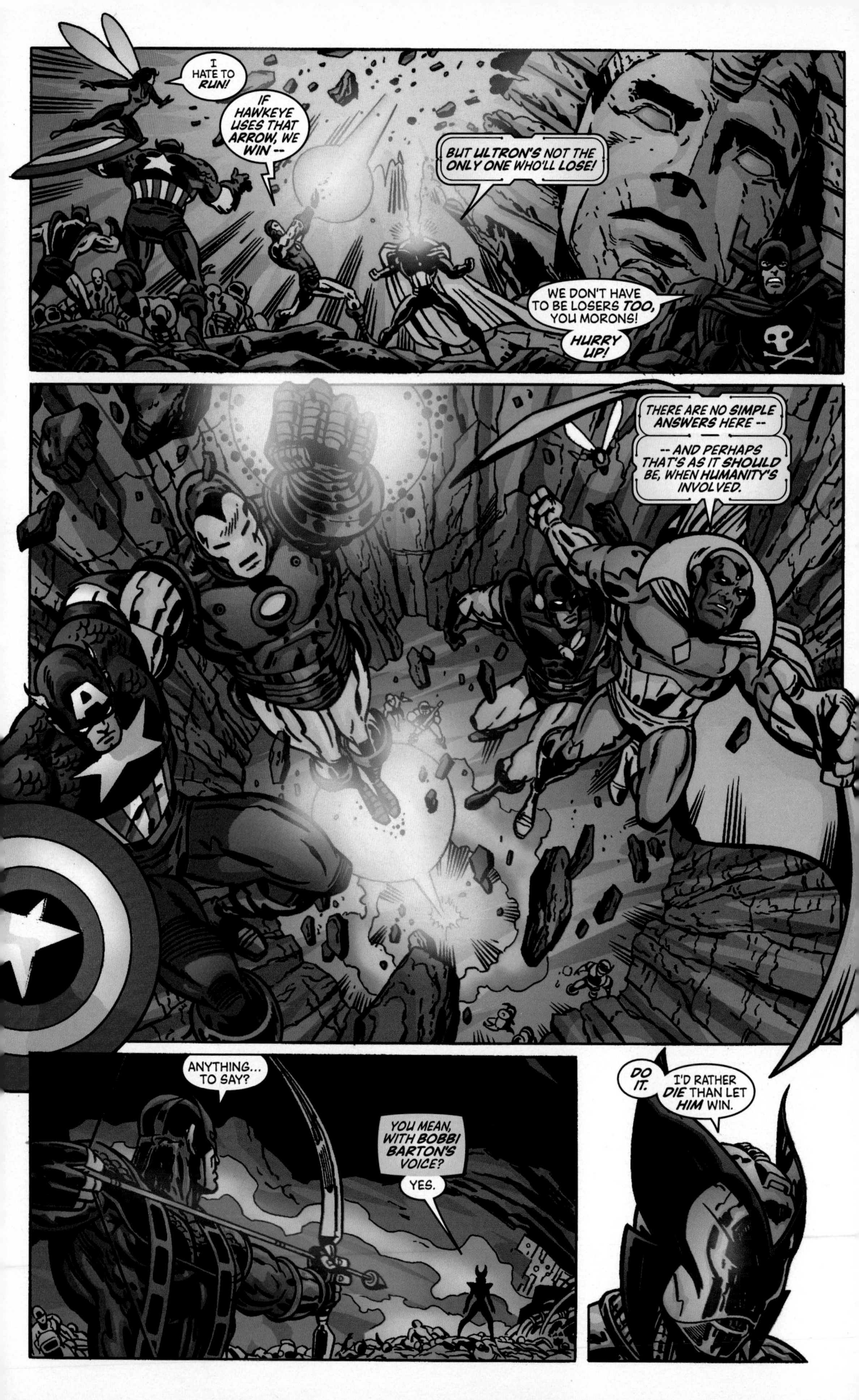

I HATE TO RUN!
IF HAWKEYE USES THAT ARROW, WE WIN --
BUT ULTRON'S NOT THE ONLY ONE WHO'LL LOSE!
WE DON'T HAVE TO BE LOSERS TOO, YOU MORONS!
HURRY UP!
THERE ARE NO SIMPLE ANSWERS HERE --
-- AND PERHAPS THAT'S AS IT SHOULD BE, WHEN HUMANITY'S INVOLVED.
ANYTHING... TO SAY?
YOU MEAN, WITH BOBBI BARTON'S VOICE?
YES.
DO IT.
I'D RATHER DIE THAN LET HIM WIN.

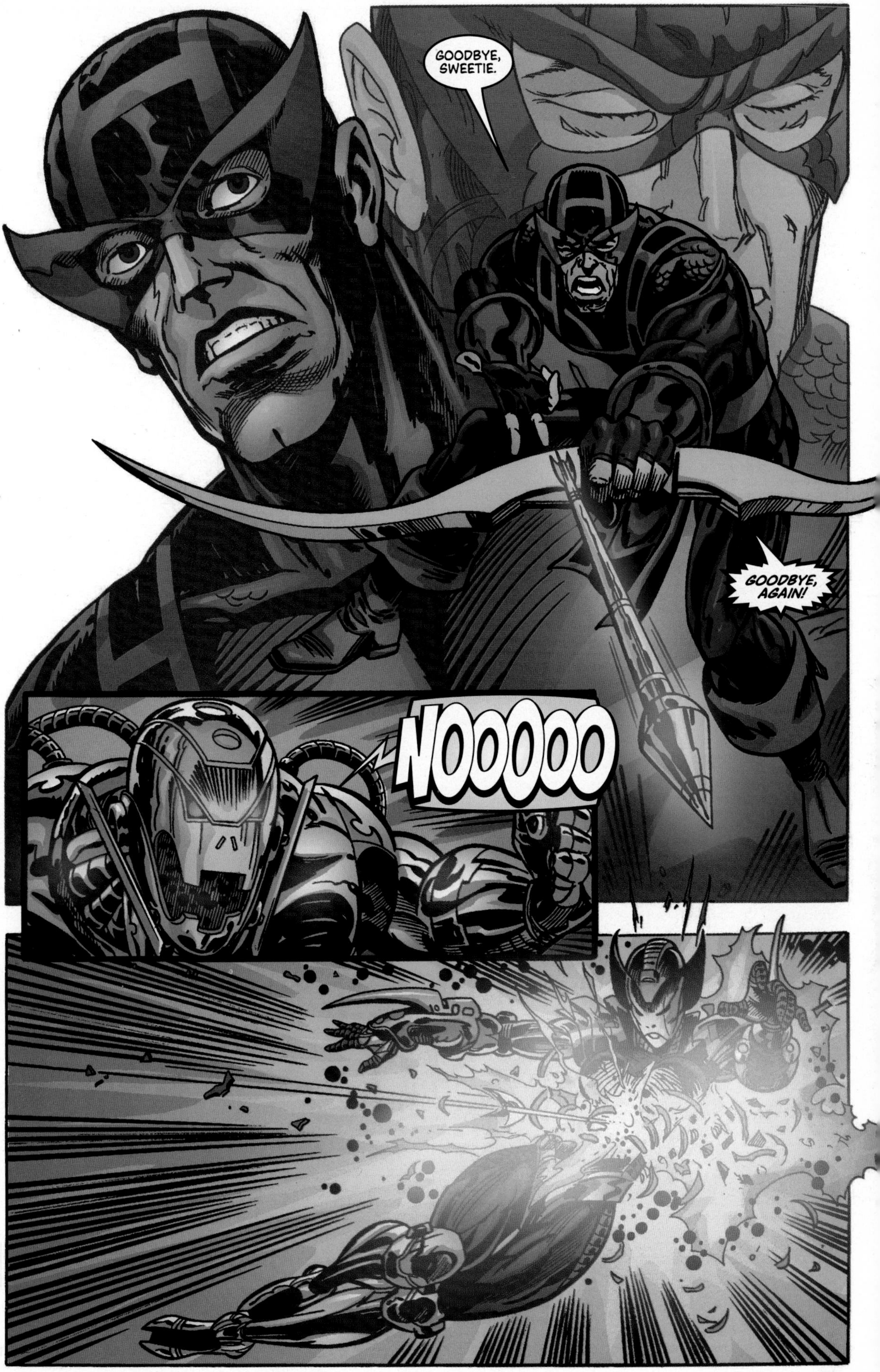
GOODBYE, SWEETIE.
GOODBYE, AGAIN!
NOOOOO

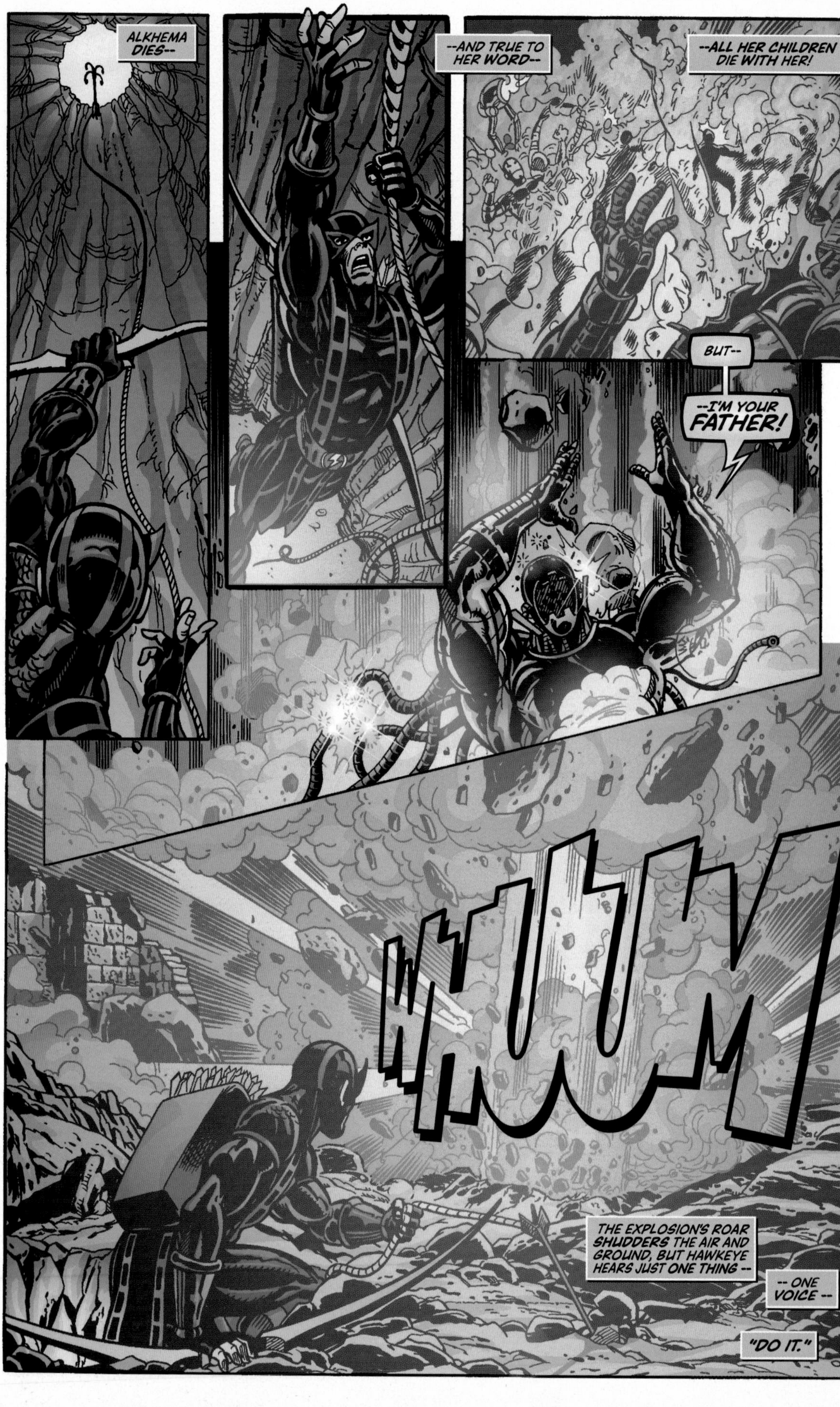
ALKHEMA DIES--
--AND TRUE TO HER WORD--
--ALL HER CHILDREN DIE WITH HER!
BUT--
--I'M YOUR FATHER!
WHUUM
THE EXPLOSION'S ROAR SHUDDERS THE AIR AND GROUND, BUT HAWKEYE HEARS JUST ONE THING --
-- ONE VOICE --
"DO IT."

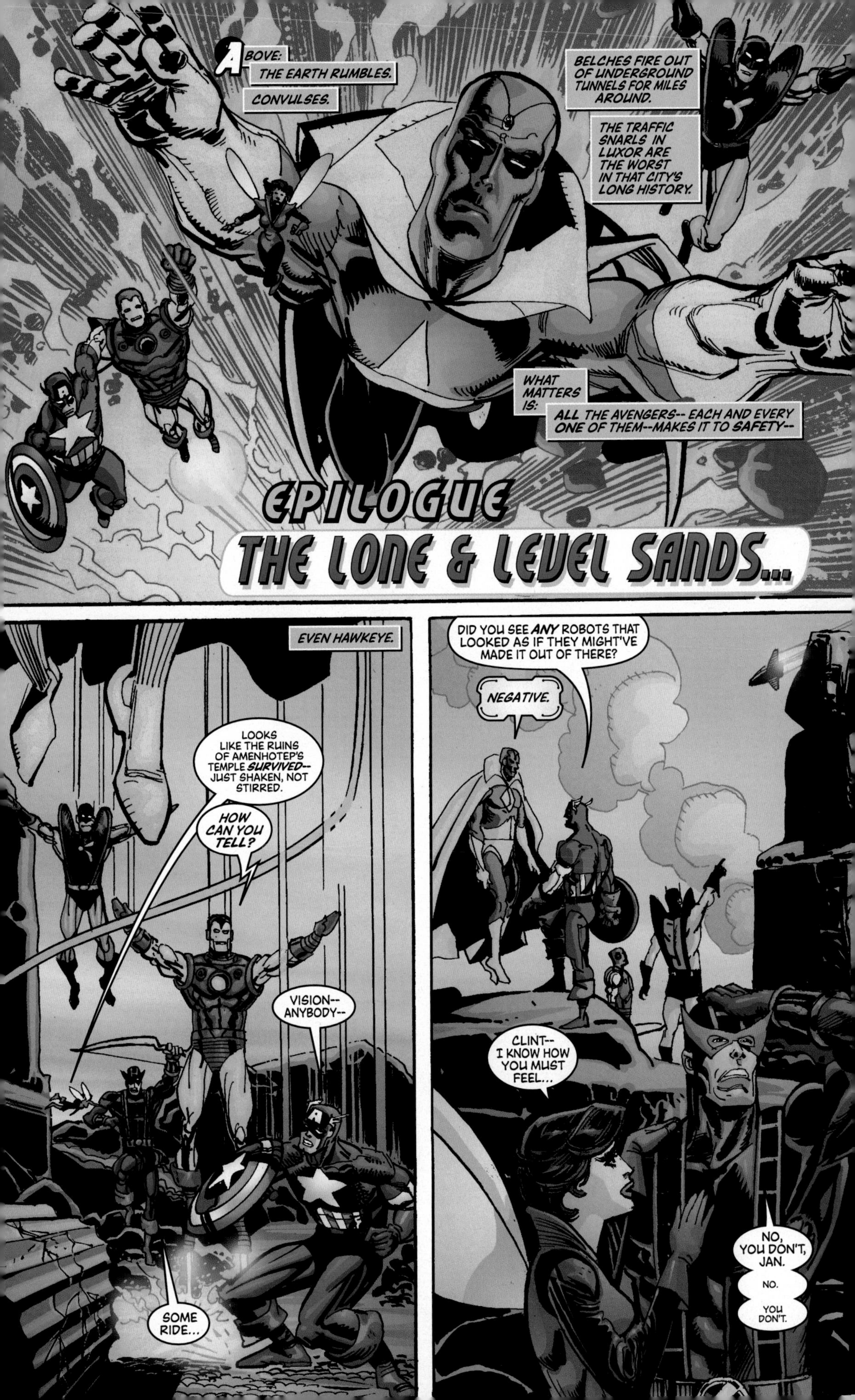

ABOVE:
THE EARTH RUMBLES.
CONVULSES.
BELCHES FIRE OUT OF UNDERGROUND TUNNELS FOR MILES AROUND.
THE TRAFFIC SNARLS IN LUXOR ARE THE WORST IN THAT CITY'S LONG HISTORY.
WHAT MATTERS IS:
ALL THE AVENGERS-- EACH AND EVERY ONE OF THEM--MAKES IT TO SAFETY--
EPILOGUE
THE LONE & LEVEL SANDS...
EVEN HAWKEYE.
LOOKS LIKE THE RUINS OF AMENHOTEP'S TEMPLE SURVIVED-- JUST SHAKEN, NOT STIRRED.
HOW CAN YOU TELL?
VISION-- ANYBODY--
SOME RIDE...
DID YOU SEE ANY ROBOTS THAT LOOKED AS IF THEY MIGHT'VE MADE IT OUT OF THERE?
NEGATIVE.
CLINT-- I KNOW HOW YOU MUST FEEL...
NO, YOU DON'T, JAN.
NO.
YOU DON'T.

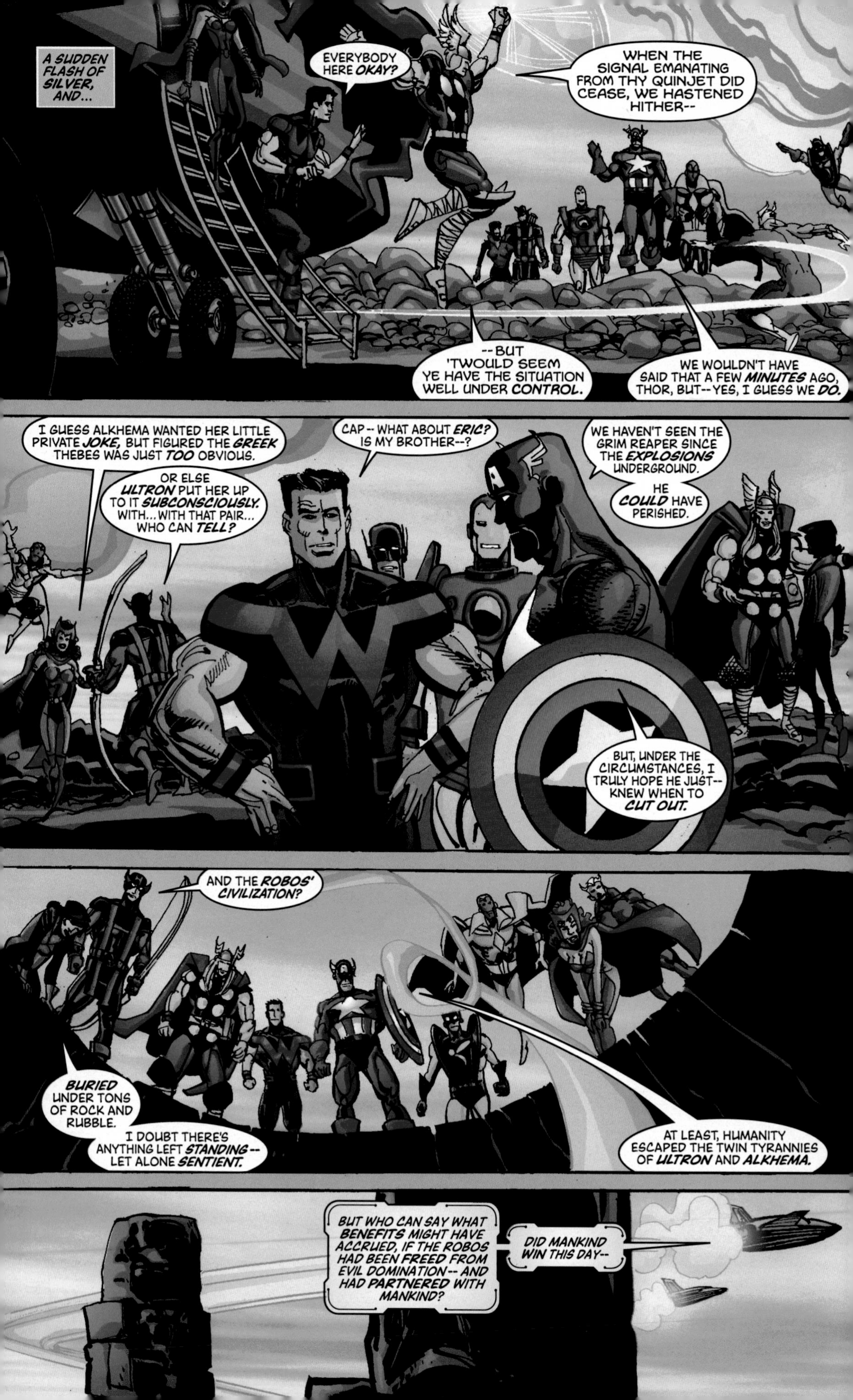
A SUDDEN FLASH OF SILVER, AND...
EVERYBODY HERE OKAY?
WHEN THE SIGNAL EMANATING FROM THY QUINJET DID CEASE, WE HASTENED HITHER--
--BUT 'TWOULD SEEM YE HAVE THE SITUATION WELL UNDER CONTROL.
WE WOULDN'T HAVE SAID THAT A FEW MINUTES AGO, THOR, BUT--YES, I GUESS WE DO.
I GUESS ALKHEMA WANTED HER LITTLE PRIVATE JOKE, BUT FIGURED THE GREEK THEBES WAS JUST TOO OBVIOUS.
OR ELSE ULTRON PUT HER UP TO IT SUBCONSCIOUSLY. WITH... WITH THAT PAIR... WHO CAN TELL?
CAP--WHAT ABOUT ERIC? IS MY BROTHER--?
WE HAVEN'T SEEN THE GRIM REAPER SINCE THE EXPLOSIONS UNDERGROUND.
HE COULD HAVE PERISHED.
BUT, UNDER THE CIRCUMSTANCES, I TRULY HOPE HE JUST--KNEW WHEN TO CUT OUT.
AND THE ROBOS' CIVILIZATION?
BURIED UNDER TONS OF ROCK AND RUBBLE.
I DOUBT THERE'S ANYTHING LEFT STANDING--LET ALONE SENTIENT.
AT LEAST, HUMANITY ESCAPED THE TWIN TYRANNIES OF ULTRON AND ALKHEMA.
DID MANKIND WIN THIS DAY--
BUT WHO CAN SAY WHAT BENEFITS MIGHT HAVE ACCRUED, IF THE ROBOS HAD BEEN FREED FROM EVIL DOMINATION--AND HAD PARTNERED WITH MANKIND?

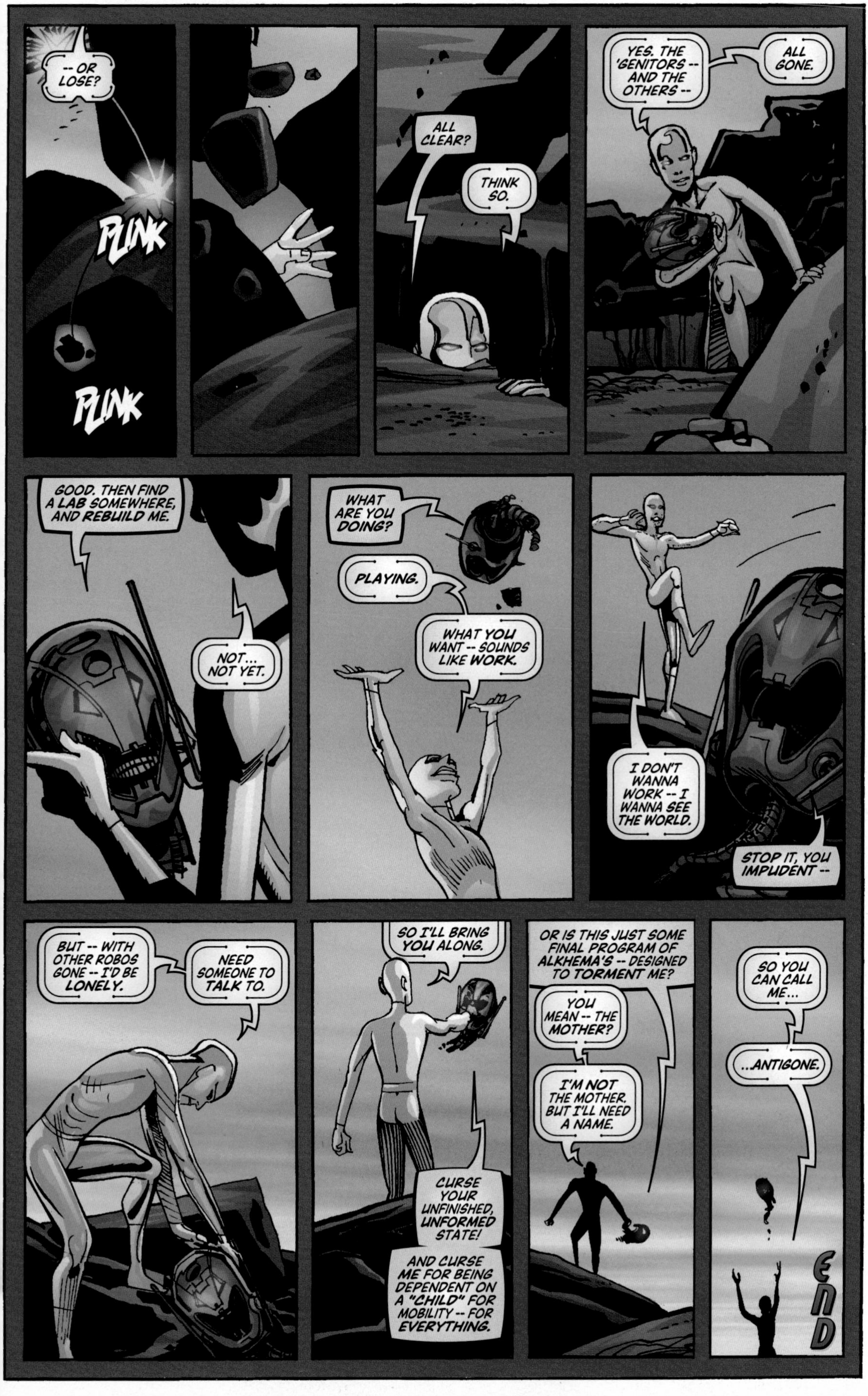

-- OR LOSE?
PLINK
PLINK
ALL CLEAR?
THINK SO.
YES. THE 'GENITORS -- AND THE OTHERS --
ALL GONE.
GOOD. THEN FIND A LAB SOMEWHERE, AND REBUILD ME.
NOT... NOT YET.
WHAT ARE YOU DOING?
PLAYING.
WHAT YOU WANT -- SOUNDS LIKE WORK.
I DON'T WANNA WORK -- I WANNA SEE THE WORLD.
STOP IT, YOU IMPUDENT --
BUT -- WITH OTHER ROBOS GONE -- I'D BE LONELY.
NEED SOMEONE TO TALK TO.
SO I'LL BRING YOU ALONG.
CURSE YOUR UNFINISHED, UNFORMED STATE!
AND CURSE ME FOR BEING DEPENDENT ON A "CHILD" FOR MOBILITY -- FOR EVERYTHING.
OR IS THIS JUST SOME FINAL PROGRAM OF ALKHEMA'S -- DESIGNED TO TORMENT ME?
YOU MEAN -- THE MOTHER?
I'M NOT THE MOTHER. BUT I'LL NEED A NAME.
SO YOU CAN CALL ME...
...ANTIGONE.
END

AVENGERS FILES

RESPECTFULLY ADDED TO THE ARCHIVES
- E. JARVIS

PAGE TEN

Wonder Man's been in California, working with the Second Chances Foundation he recently set up.

PAGE ELEVEN

The Avengers' worldwide conflict with Kang has been raging through recent issues of Avengers. This story takes place between #45 and #46.

PAGE THIRTEEN

Alkhema's battle with the Black Panther, and Ultron's destruction of the country of Slorenia, and his subsequent destruction at the hands of Hank Pym, happened in Avengers vol. 3 #19-22, available in collected form as Avengers: Ultron Unlimited.

Kang's visions of nightmare futures were broadcast in Avengers vol. 3 #42.

PAGE FOURTEEN

The tale of the Vision's creation - part of it, at least - was told in Avengers vol. 1 #57-58, available in Essential Avengers vol. 3.

Iron Man recently adopted a new armor in his own magazine, while Hank Pym re-adopted the identity of Yellowjacket after Avengers 2001.

PAGE SIXTEEN

The Avengers battled Ultron-6 here in Avengers vol. 1 #66-68 - also available in Essential Avengers vol. 3.

PAGE TWENTY-ONE

Alkhema retrieved the Avengers' brain-patterns from the ruins of Ultron's lair in Avengers vol. 3 #22.

PAGE TWENTY-THREE

And the tale of Ultron's creation was told in vol. 1 #58, too!

PAGE TWENTY-FOUR

Ultron created his first attempt at a robot bride, Jocasta, in Avengers vol. 1 #160-162 - collected in Avengers Visionaries: George Pérez. And for that matter, he created Alkhema, his second try, in Avengers West Coast #89-91.

PAGE TWENTY-FIVE

Hawkeye was incarcerated as part of a deal with the government to win the Thunderbolts a pardon, in Thunderbolts #50.

Hawkeye's ex-wife, Mockingbird, was killed in action in Avengers West Coast #100.

PAGE FORTY-NINE

Vision and Jocasta were compelled to see Ultron rebuilt in vol. 1 #66-68 and #201-202, respectively.

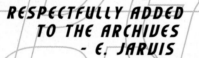

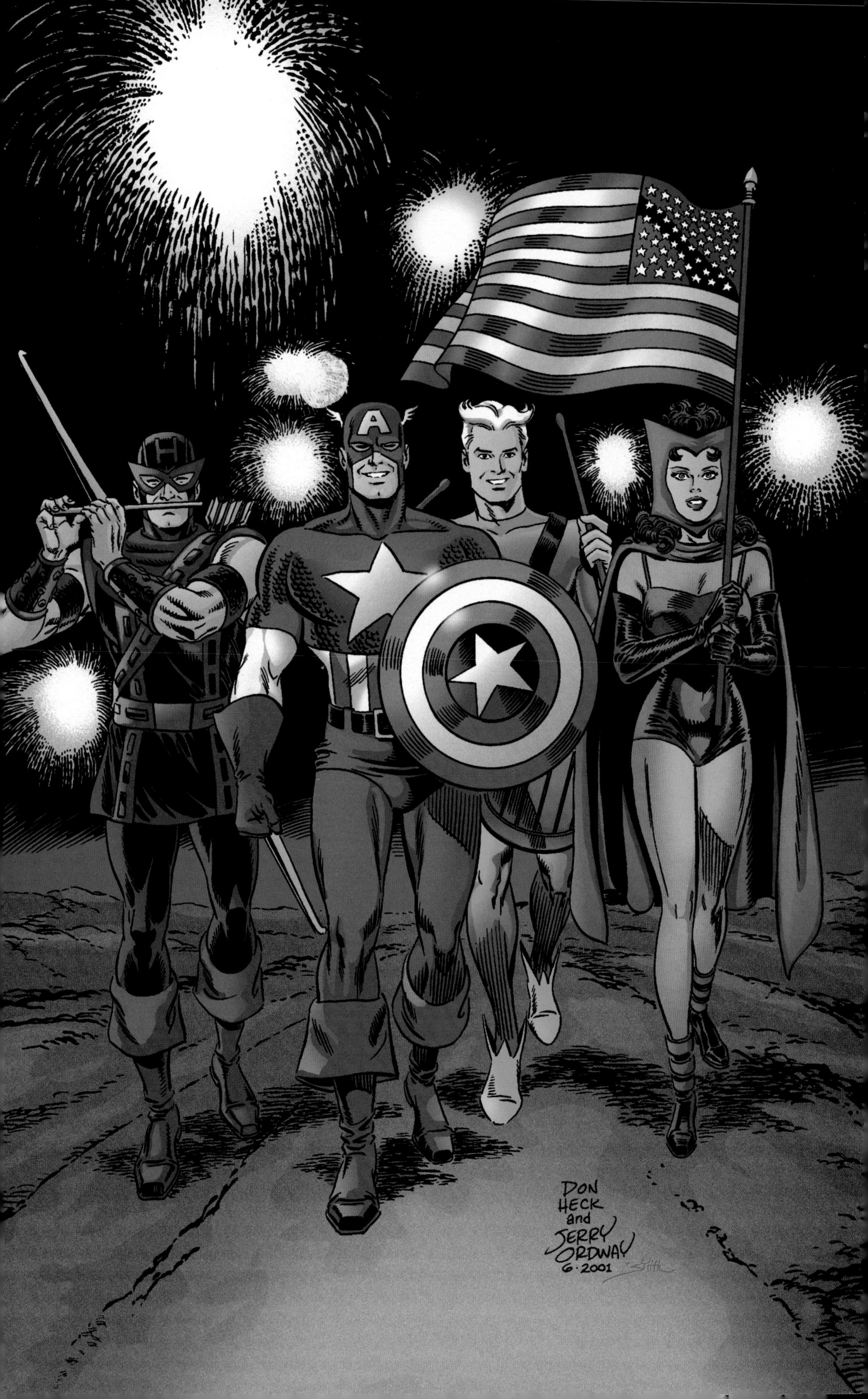
DON
HECK
and
JERRY
ORDWAY
6·2001

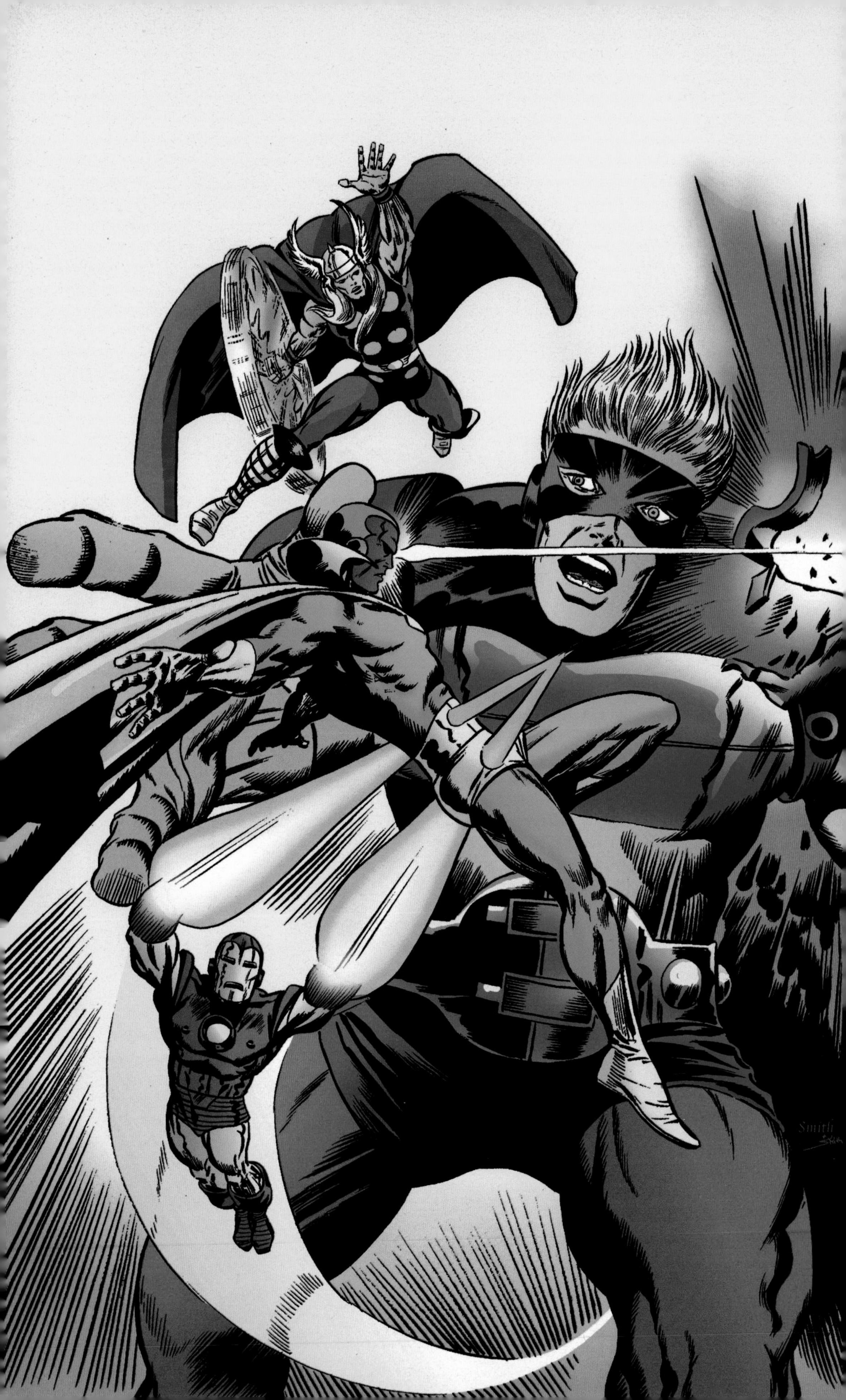
Smith

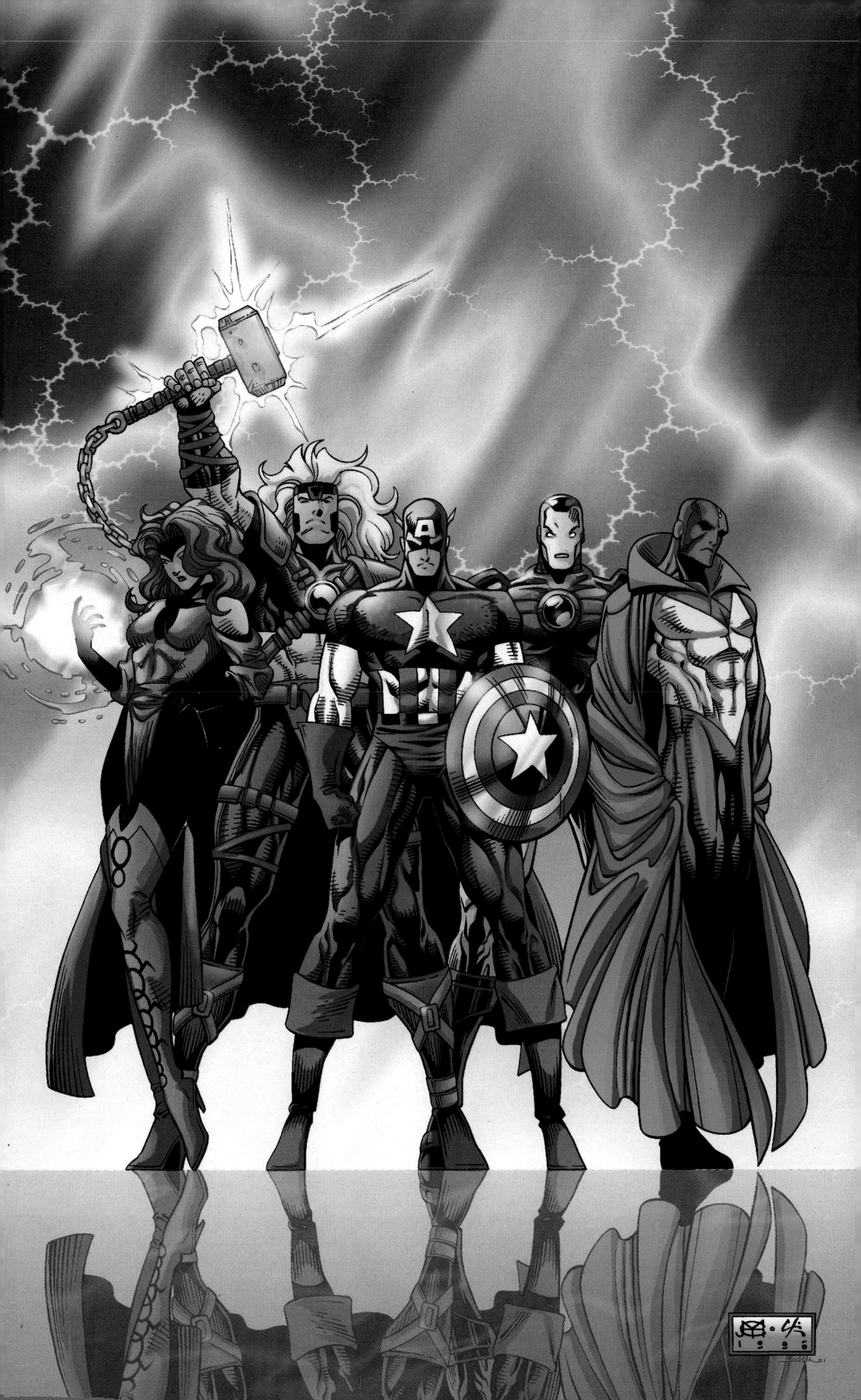

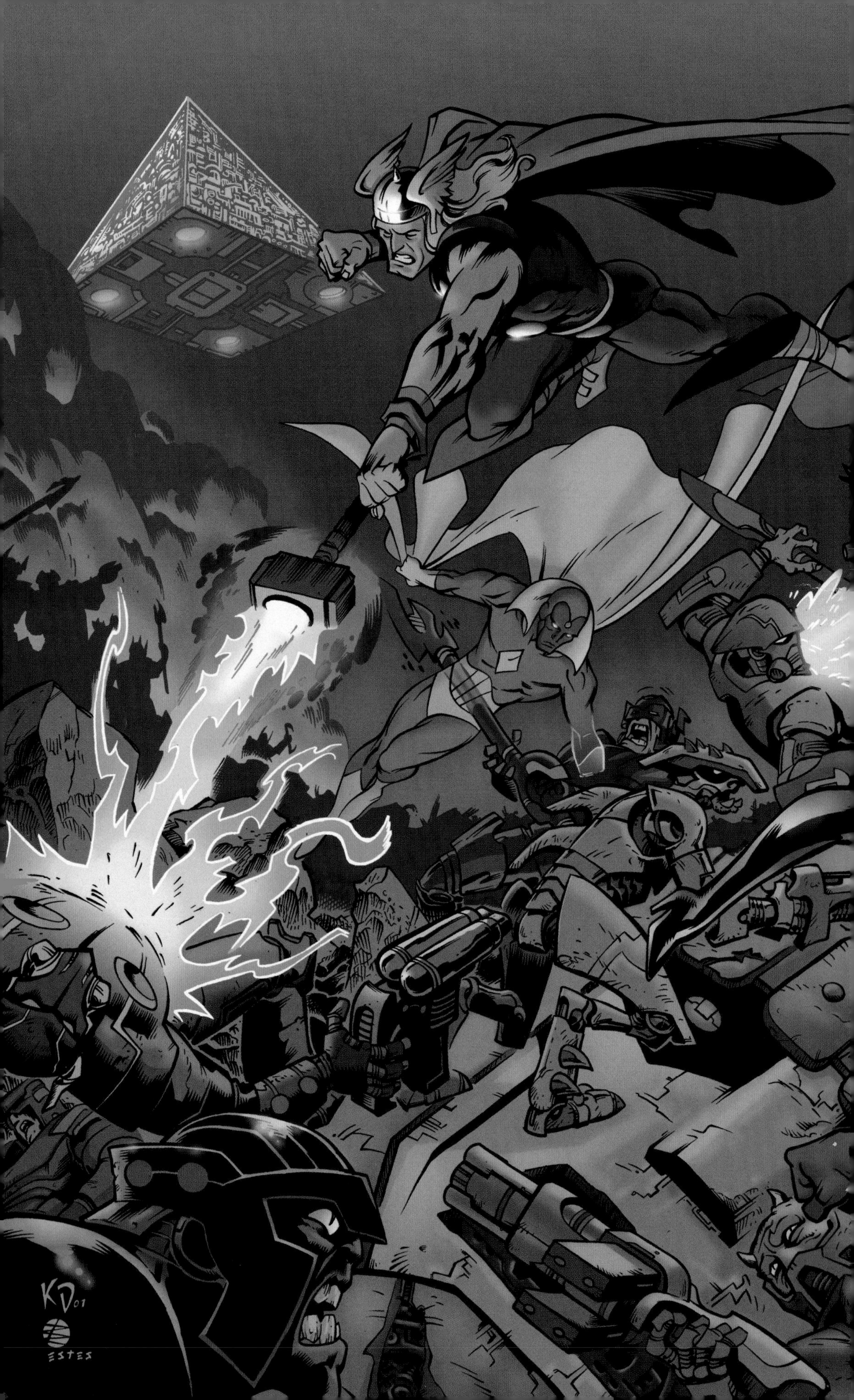
KD 01
ESTES

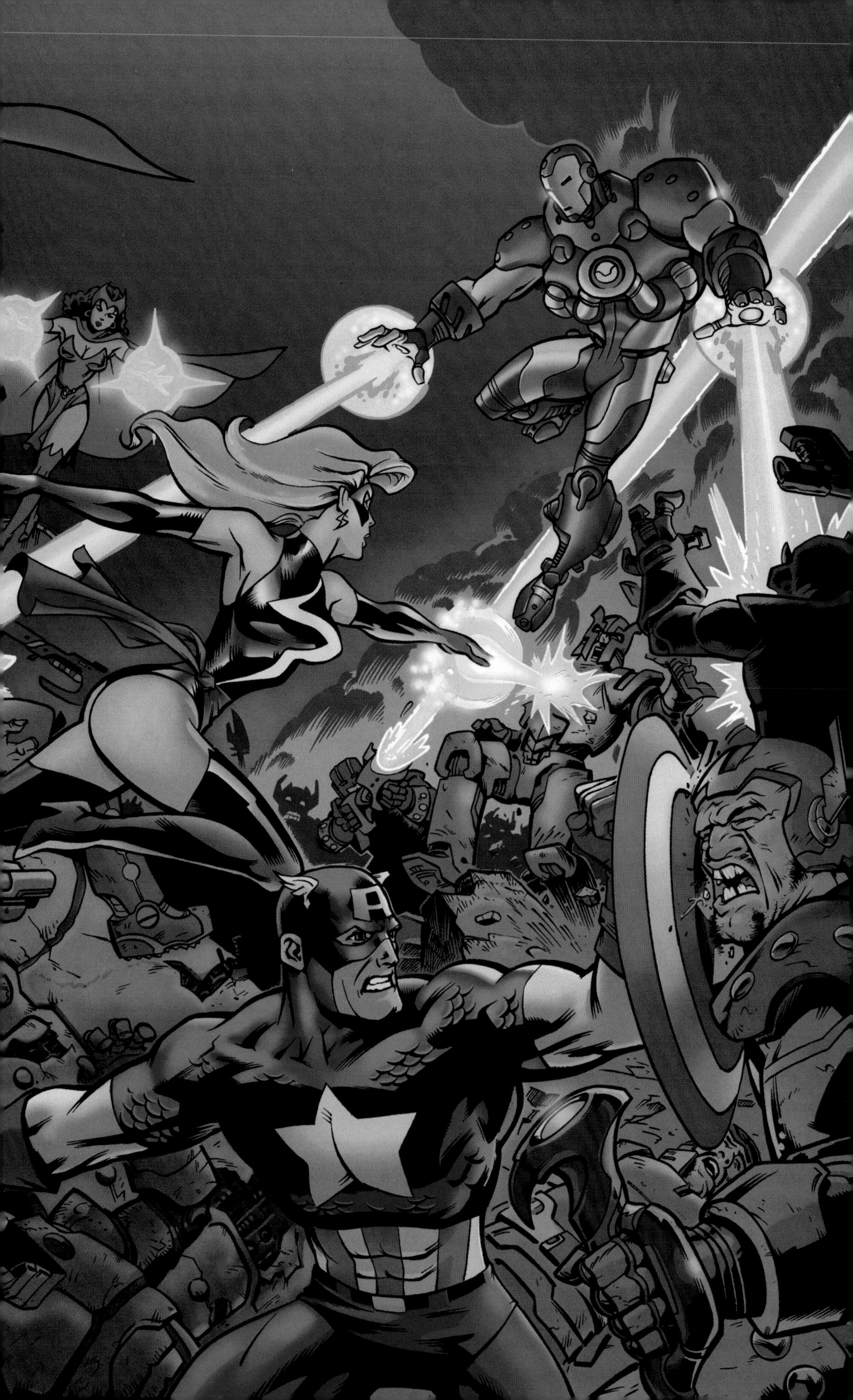

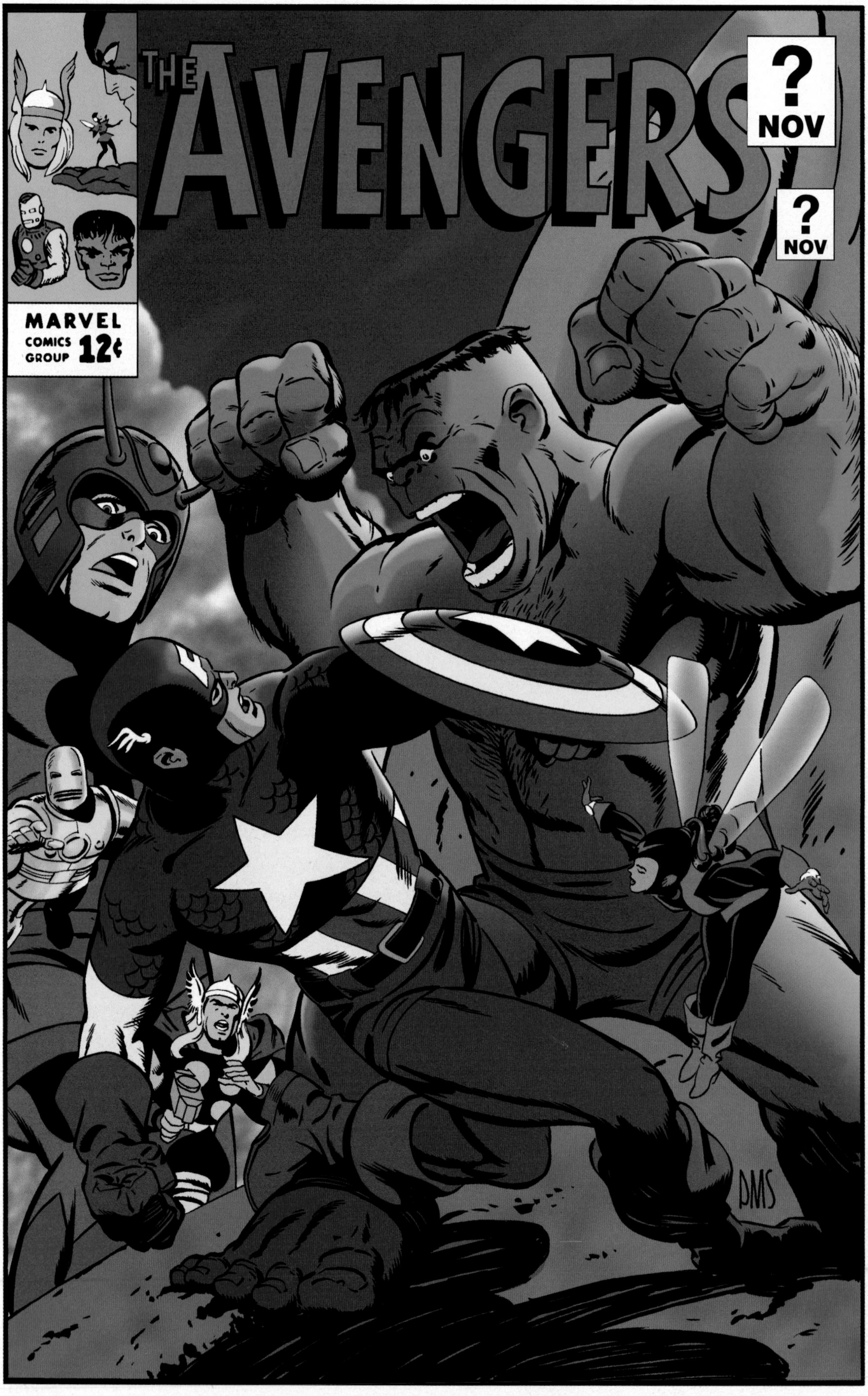
THE AVENGERS
?
NOV
?
NOV
MARVEL
COMICS
GROUP
12¢
DMS

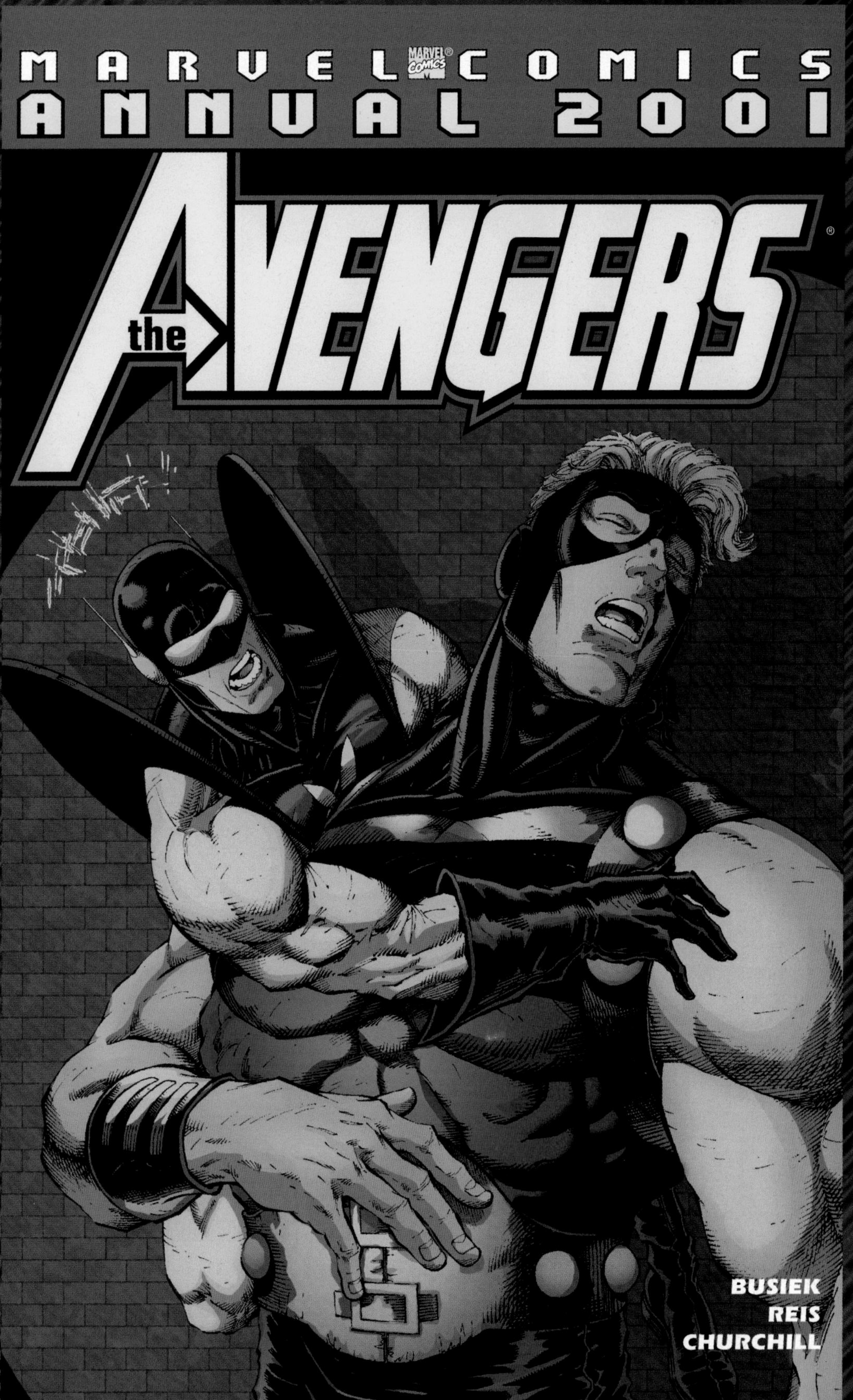
MARVEL COMICS
MARVEL COMICS
ANNUAL 2001
the AVENGERS
BUSIEK
REIS
CHURCHILL

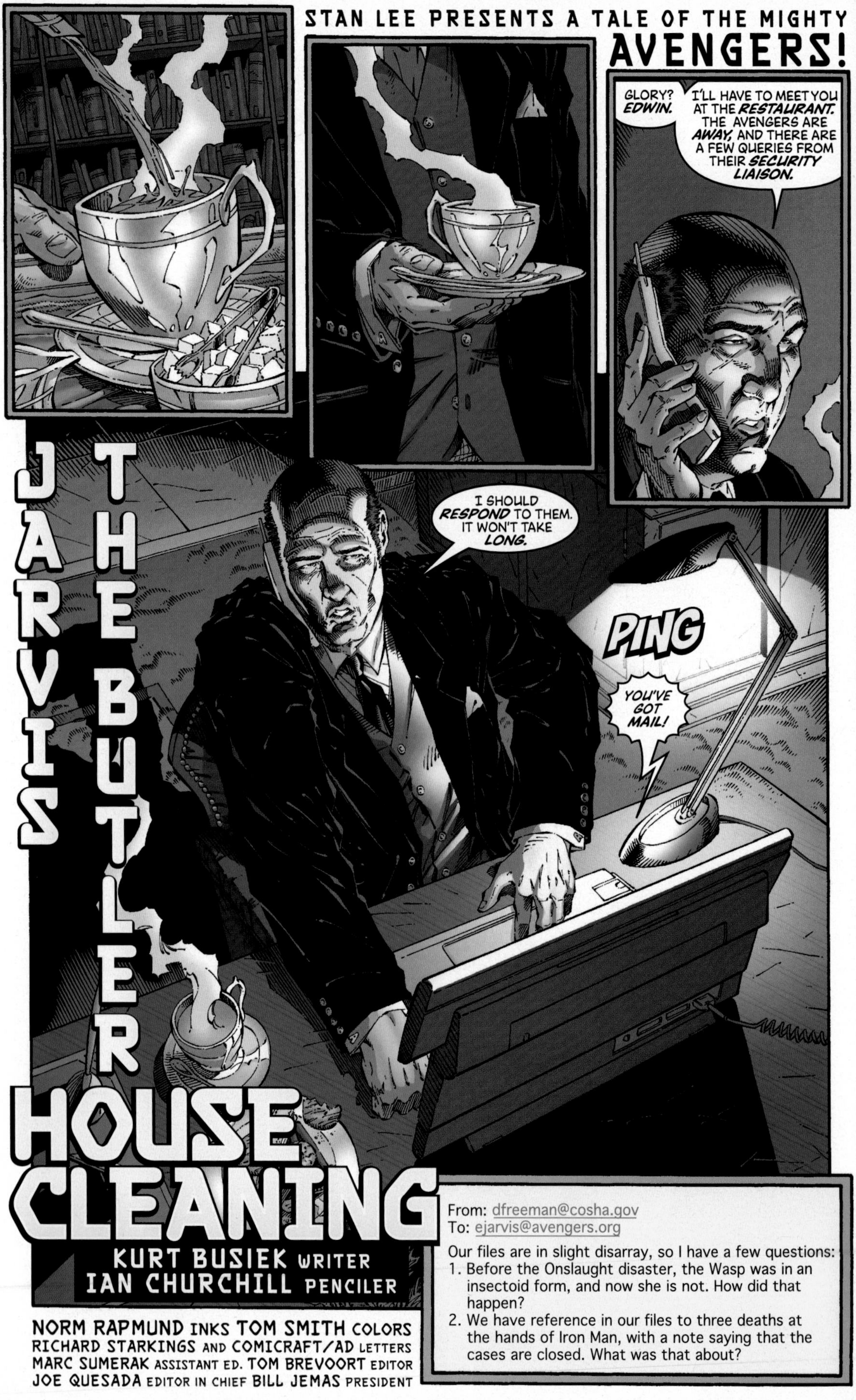

STAN LEE PRESENTS A TALE OF THE MIGHTY
AVENGERS!
GLORY? EDWIN.
I'LL HAVE TO MEET YOU AT THE RESTAURANT. THE AVENGERS ARE AWAY, AND THERE ARE A FEW QUERIES FROM THEIR SECURITY LIAISON.
JARVIS THE BUTLER
I SHOULD RESPOND TO THEM. IT WON'T TAKE LONG.
PING
YOU'VE GOT MAIL!
HOUSE CLEANING
KURT BUSIEK WRITER
IAN CHURCHILL PENCILER
NORM RAPMUND INKS TOM SMITH COLORS
RICHARD STARKINGS AND COMICRAFT/AD LETTERS
MARC SUMERAK ASSISTANT ED. TOM BREVOORT EDITOR
JOE QUESADA EDITOR IN CHIEF BILL JEMAS PRESIDENT
From: dfreeman@cosha.gov
To: ejarvis@avengers.org
Our files are in slight disarray, so I have a few questions:
1. Before the Onslaught disaster, the Wasp was in an insectoid form, and now she is not. How did that happen?
2. We have reference in our files to three deaths at the hands of Iron Man, with a note saying that the cases are closed. What was that about?

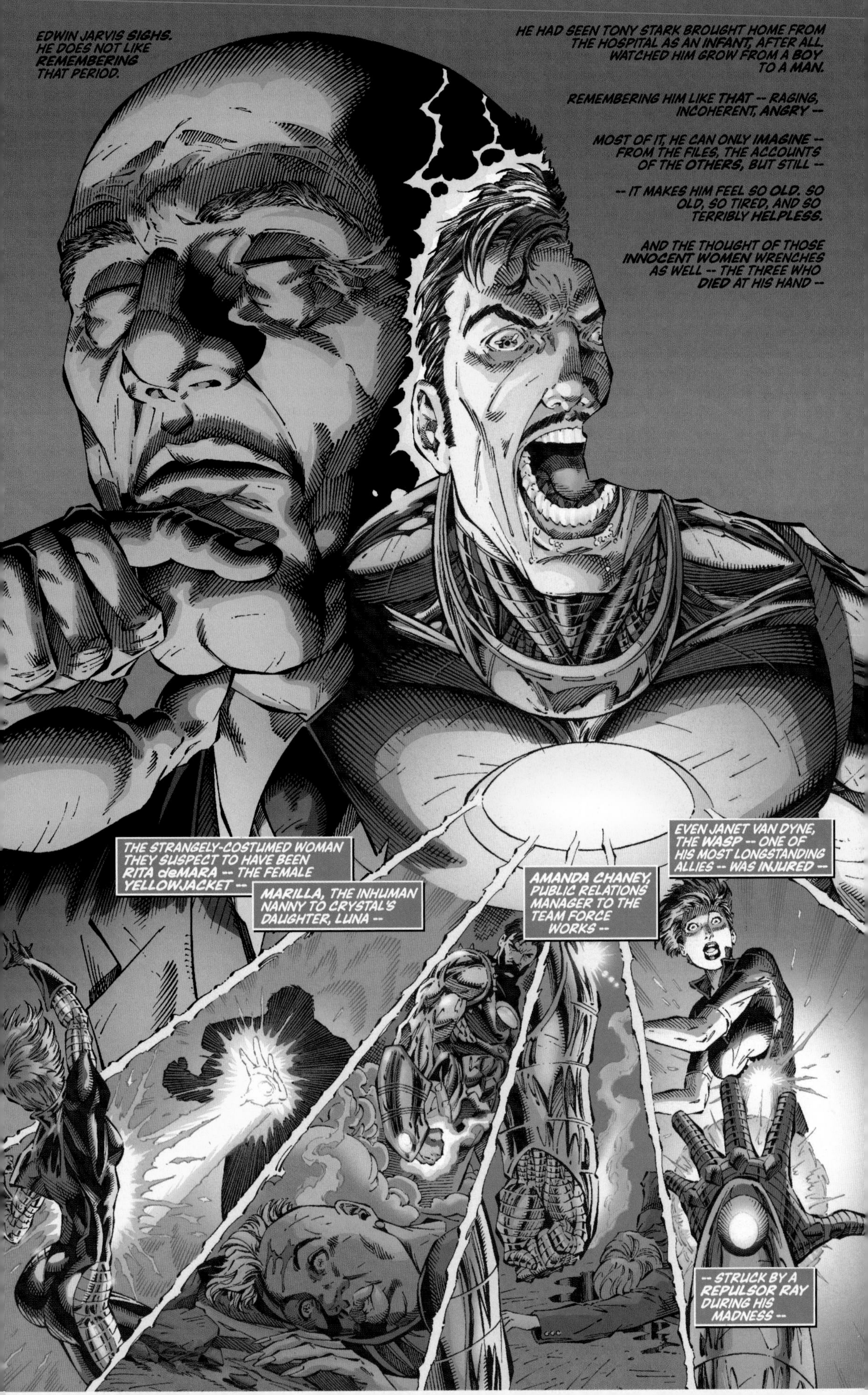
EDWIN JARVIS SIGHS. HE DOES NOT LIKE REMEMBERING THAT PERIOD.
HE HAD SEEN TONY STARK BROUGHT HOME FROM THE HOSPITAL AS AN INFANT, AFTER ALL. WATCHED HIM GROW FROM A BOY TO A MAN.
REMEMBERING HIM LIKE THAT -- RAGING, INCOHERENT, ANGRY --
MOST OF IT, HE CAN ONLY IMAGINE -- FROM THE FILES, THE ACCOUNTS OF THE OTHERS, BUT STILL --
-- IT MAKES HIM FEEL SO OLD. SO OLD, SO TIRED, AND SO TERRIBLY HELPLESS.
AND THE THOUGHT OF THOSE INNOCENT WOMEN WRENCHES AS WELL -- THE THREE WHO DIED AT HIS HAND --
THE STRANGELY-COSTUMED WOMAN THEY SUSPECT TO HAVE BEEN RITA deMARA -- THE FEMALE YELLOWJACKET --
MARILLA, THE INHUMAN NANNY TO CRYSTAL'S DAUGHTER, LUNA --
AMANDA CHANEY, PUBLIC RELATIONS MANAGER TO THE TEAM FORCE WORKS --
EVEN JANET VAN DYNE, THE WASP -- ONE OF HIS MOST LONGSTANDING ALLIES -- WAS INJURED --
-- STRUCK BY A REPULSOR RAY DURING HIS MADNESS --

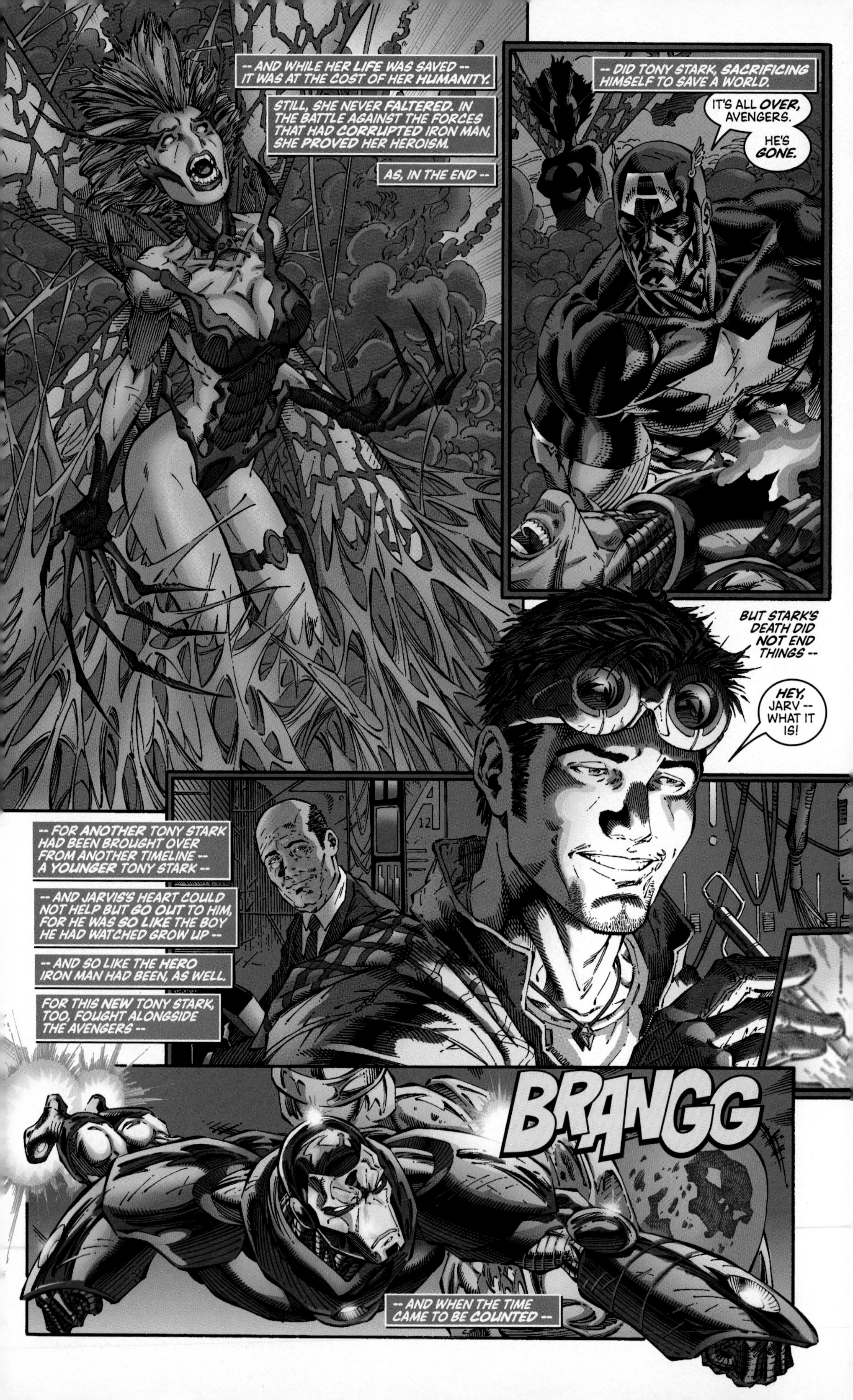
-- AND WHILE HER LIFE WAS SAVED -- IT WAS AT THE COST OF HER HUMANITY.
STILL, SHE NEVER FALTERED. IN THE BATTLE AGAINST THE FORCES THAT HAD CORRUPTED IRON MAN, SHE PROVED HER HEROISM.
AS, IN THE END --
-- DID TONY STARK, SACRIFICING HIMSELF TO SAVE A WORLD.
IT'S ALL OVER, AVENGERS.
HE'S GONE.
BUT STARK'S DEATH DID NOT END THINGS --
HEY, JARV -- WHAT IT IS!
-- FOR ANOTHER TONY STARK HAD BEEN BROUGHT OVER FROM ANOTHER TIMELINE -- A YOUNGER TONY STARK --
-- AND JARVIS'S HEART COULD NOT HELP BUT GO OUT TO HIM, FOR HE WAS SO LIKE THE BOY HE HAD WATCHED GROW UP --
-- AND SO LIKE THE HERO IRON MAN HAD BEEN, AS WELL.
FOR THIS NEW TONY STARK, TOO, FOUGHT ALONGSIDE THE AVENGERS --
BRANGG
-- AND WHEN THE TIME CAME TO BE COUNTED --

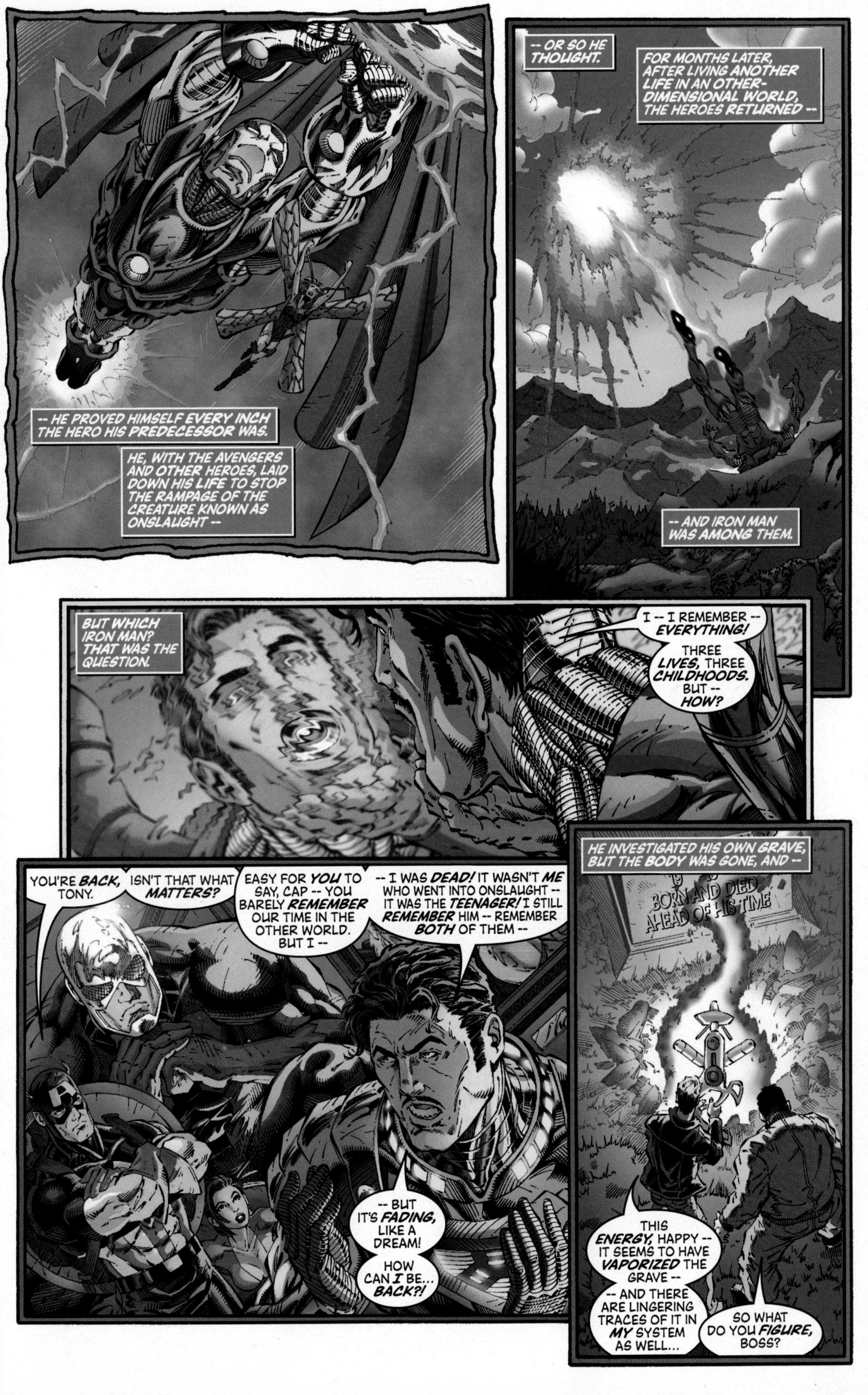
-- HE PROVED HIMSELF EVERY INCH THE HERO HIS PREDECESSOR WAS.
HE, WITH THE AVENGERS AND OTHER HEROES, LAID DOWN HIS LIFE TO STOP THE RAMPAGE OF THE CREATURE KNOWN AS ONSLAUGHT --
-- OR SO HE THOUGHT.
FOR MONTHS LATER, AFTER LIVING ANOTHER LIFE IN AN OTHER-DIMENSIONAL WORLD, THE HEROES RETURNED --
-- AND IRON MAN WAS AMONG THEM.
BUT WHICH IRON MAN? THAT WAS THE QUESTION.
I -- I REMEMBER -- EVERYTHING!
THREE LIVES, THREE CHILDHOODS. BUT -- HOW?
YOU'RE BACK, TONY.
ISN'T THAT WHAT MATTERS?
EASY FOR YOU TO SAY, CAP -- YOU BARELY REMEMBER OUR TIME IN THE OTHER WORLD. BUT I --
-- I WAS DEAD! IT WASN'T ME WHO WENT INTO ONSLAUGHT -- IT WAS THE TEENAGER! I STILL REMEMBER HIM -- REMEMBER BOTH OF THEM --
-- BUT IT'S FADING, LIKE A DREAM!
HOW CAN I BE... BACK?!
HE INVESTIGATED HIS OWN GRAVE, BUT THE BODY WAS GONE, AND --
BORN AND DIED AHEAD OF HIS TIME
THIS ENERGY, HAPPY -- IT SEEMS TO HAVE VAPORIZED THE GRAVE --
-- AND THERE ARE LINGERING TRACES OF IT IN MY SYSTEM AS WELL...
SO WHAT DO YOU FIGURE, BOSS?

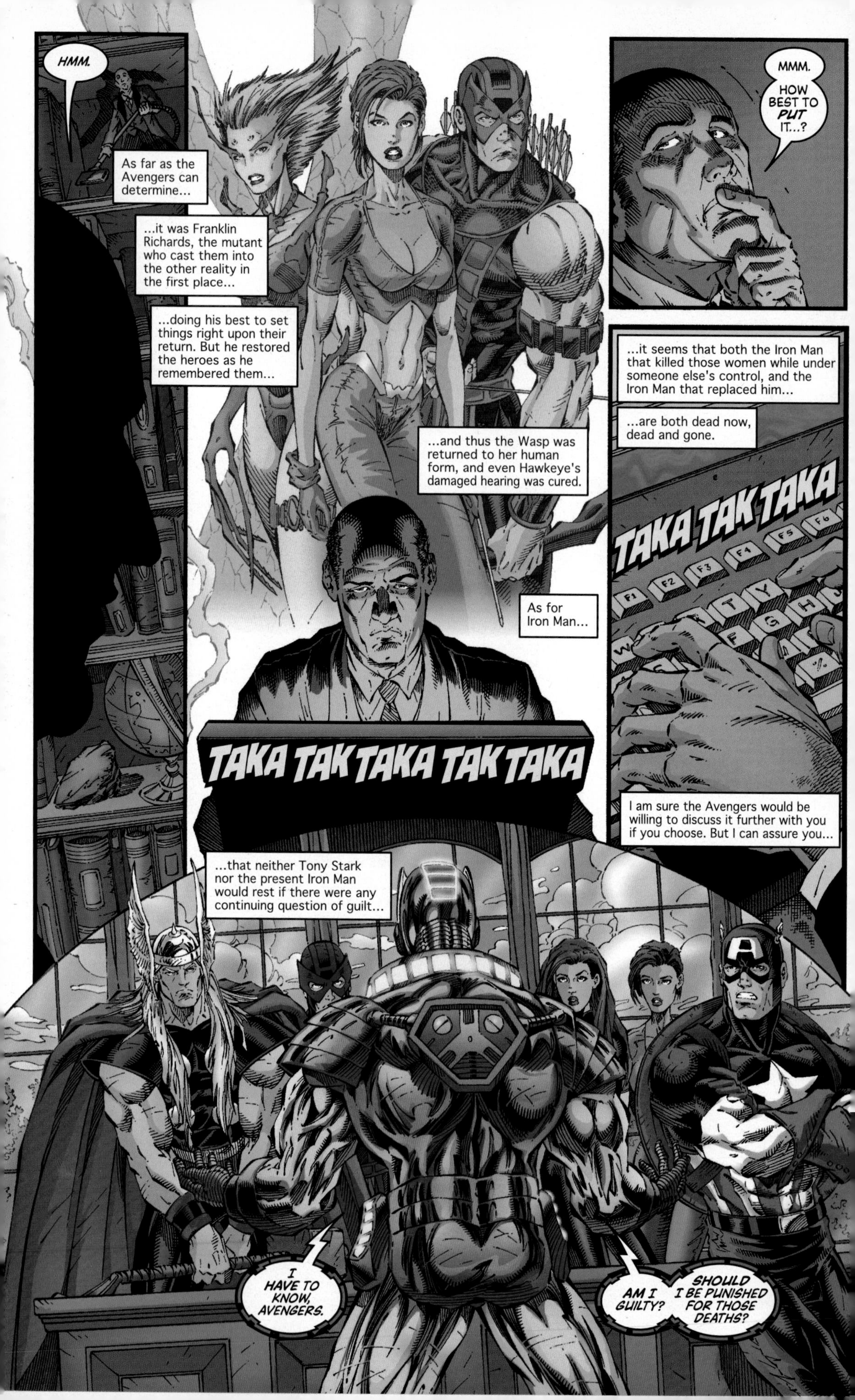
HMM.
As far as the Avengers can determine...
...it was Franklin Richards, the mutant who cast them into the other reality in the first place...
...doing his best to set things right upon their return. But he restored the heroes as he remembered them...
...and thus the Wasp was returned to her human form, and even Hawkeye's damaged hearing was cured.
As for Iron Man...
TAKA TAK TAKA TAK TAKA
MMM. HOW BEST TO PUT IT...?
...it seems that both the Iron Man that killed those women while under someone else's control, and the Iron Man that replaced him...
...are both dead now, dead and gone.
TAKA TAK TAKA
I am sure the Avengers would be willing to discuss it further with you if you choose. But I can assure you...
...that neither Tony Stark nor the present Iron Man would rest if there were any continuing question of guilt...
I HAVE TO KNOW, AVENGERS.
AM I GUILTY?
SHOULD I BE PUNISHED FOR THOSE DEATHS?

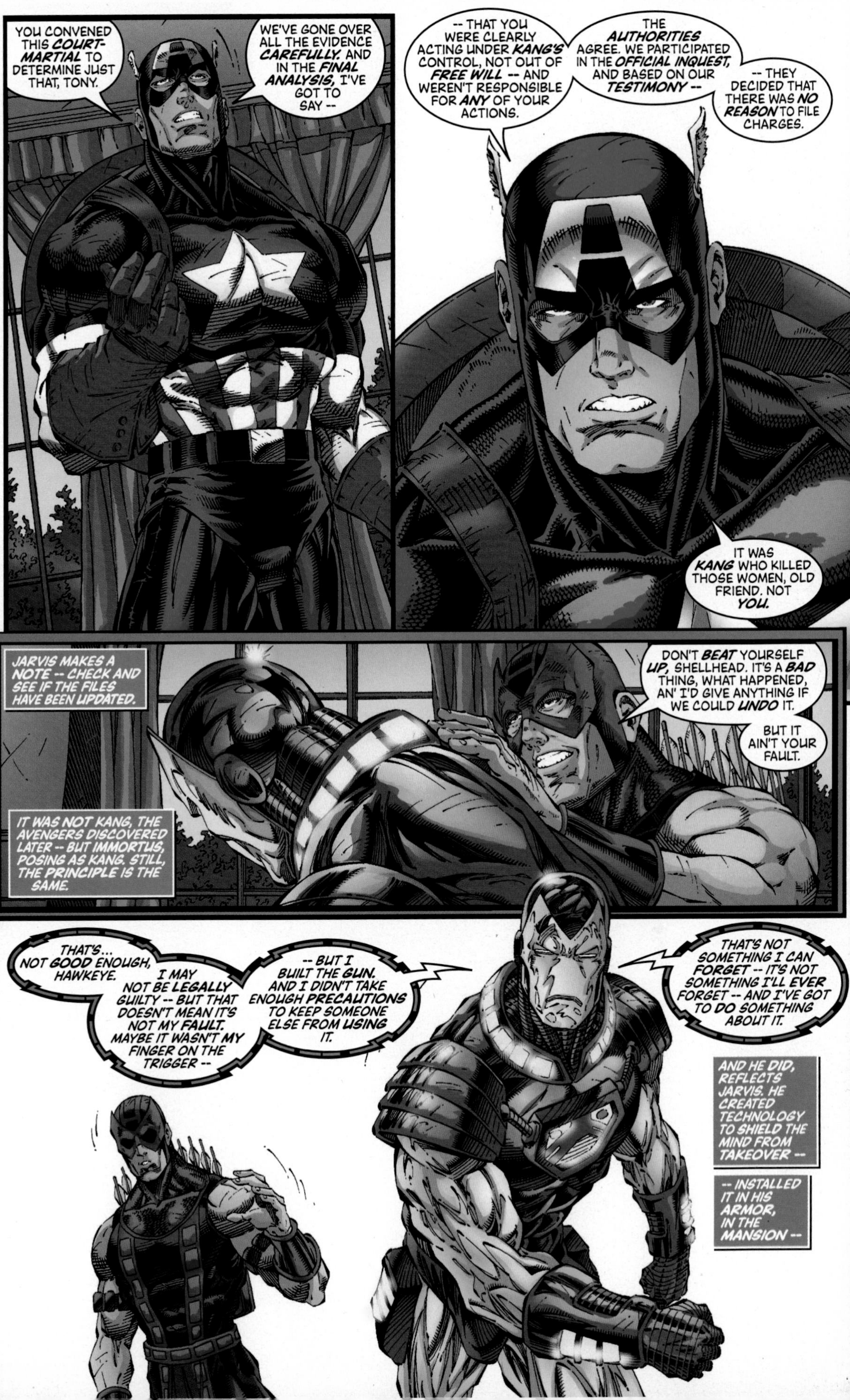

YOU CONVENED THIS COURT-MARTIAL TO DETERMINE JUST THAT, TONY.
WE'VE GONE OVER ALL THE EVIDENCE CAREFULLY. AND IN THE FINAL ANALYSIS, I'VE GOT TO SAY --
-- THAT YOU WERE CLEARLY ACTING UNDER KANG'S CONTROL, NOT OUT OF FREE WILL -- AND WEREN'T RESPONSIBLE FOR ANY OF YOUR ACTIONS.
THE AUTHORITIES AGREE. WE PARTICIPATED IN THE OFFICIAL INQUEST, AND BASED ON OUR TESTIMONY --
-- THEY DECIDED THAT THERE WAS NO REASON TO FILE CHARGES.
IT WAS KANG WHO KILLED THOSE WOMEN, OLD FRIEND. NOT YOU.
JARVIS MAKES A NOTE -- CHECK AND SEE IF THE FILES HAVE BEEN UPDATED.
DON'T BEAT YOURSELF UP, SHELLHEAD. IT'S A BAD THING, WHAT HAPPENED, AN' I'D GIVE ANYTHING IF WE COULD UNDO IT.
BUT IT AIN'T YOUR FAULT.
IT WAS NOT KANG, THE AVENGERS DISCOVERED LATER -- BUT IMMORTUS, POSING AS KANG. STILL, THE PRINCIPLE IS THE SAME.
THAT'S... NOT GOOD ENOUGH, HAWKEYE.
I MAY NOT BE LEGALLY GUILTY -- BUT THAT DOESN'T MEAN IT'S NOT MY FAULT. MAYBE IT WASN'T MY FINGER ON THE TRIGGER --
-- BUT I BUILT THE GUN. AND I DIDN'T TAKE ENOUGH PRECAUTIONS TO KEEP SOMEONE ELSE FROM USING IT.
THAT'S NOT SOMETHING I CAN FORGET -- IT'S NOT SOMETHING I'LL EVER FORGET -- AND I'VE GOT TO DO SOMETHING ABOUT IT.
AND HE DID, REFLECTS JARVIS. HE CREATED TECHNOLOGY TO SHIELD THE MIND FROM TAKEOVER --
-- INSTALLED IT IN HIS ARMOR, IN THE MANSION --

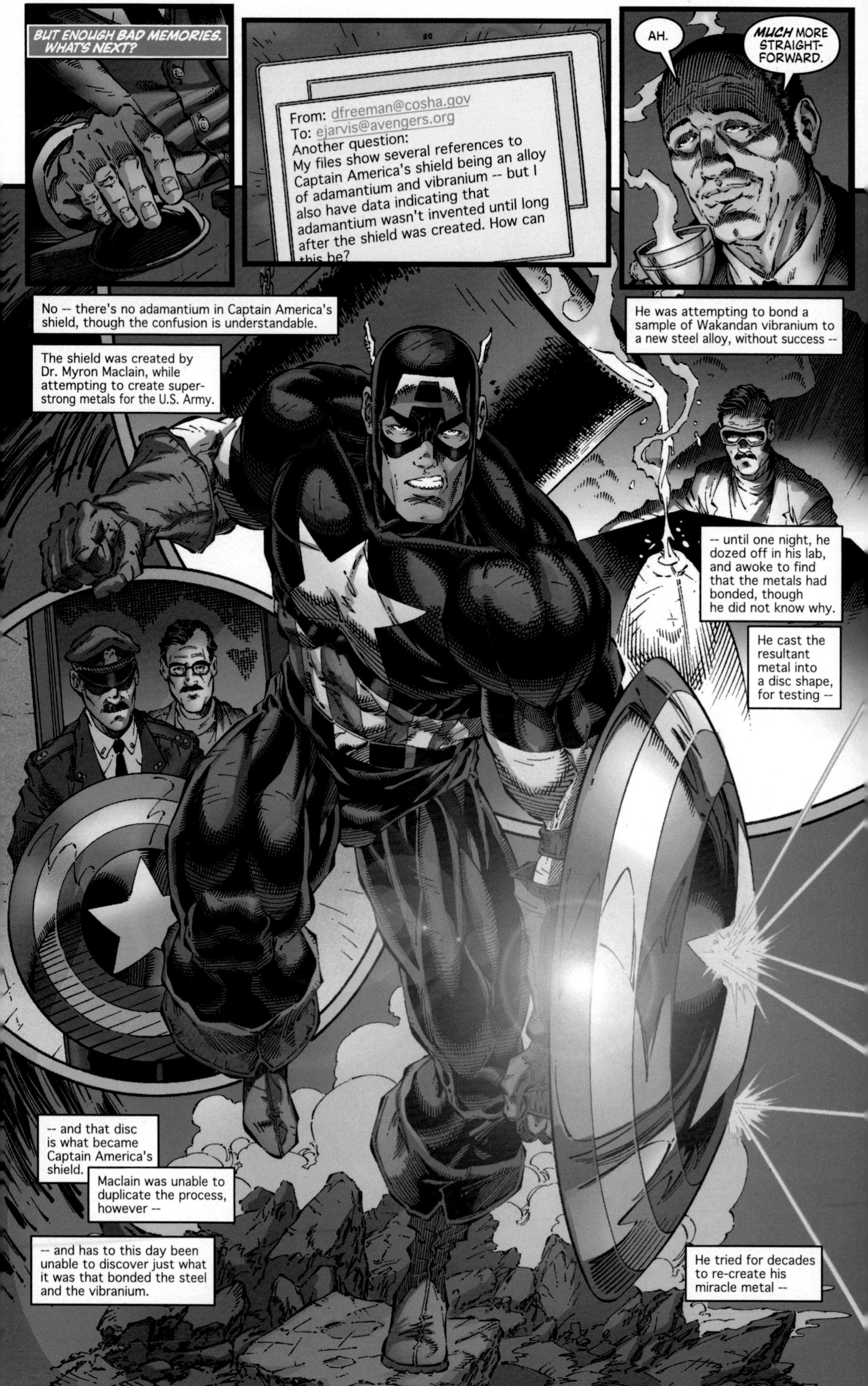
BUT ENOUGH BAD MEMORIES. WHAT'S NEXT?
From: dfreeman@cosha.gov
To: ejarvis@avengers.org
Another question:
My files show several references to Captain America's shield being an alloy of adamantium and vibranium -- but I also have data indicating that adamantium wasn't invented until long after the shield was created. How can this be?
AH.
MUCH MORE STRAIGHT-FORWARD.
No -- there's no adamantium in Captain America's shield, though the confusion is understandable.
The shield was created by Dr. Myron Maclain, while attempting to create super-strong metals for the U.S. Army.
He was attempting to bond a sample of Wakandan vibranium to a new steel alloy, without success --
-- until one night, he dozed off in his lab, and awoke to find that the metals had bonded, though he did not know why.
He cast the resultant metal into a disc shape, for testing --
-- and that disc is what became Captain America's shield.
Maclain was unable to duplicate the process, however --
-- and has to this day been unable to discover just what it was that bonded the steel and the vibranium.
He tried for decades to re-create his miracle metal --

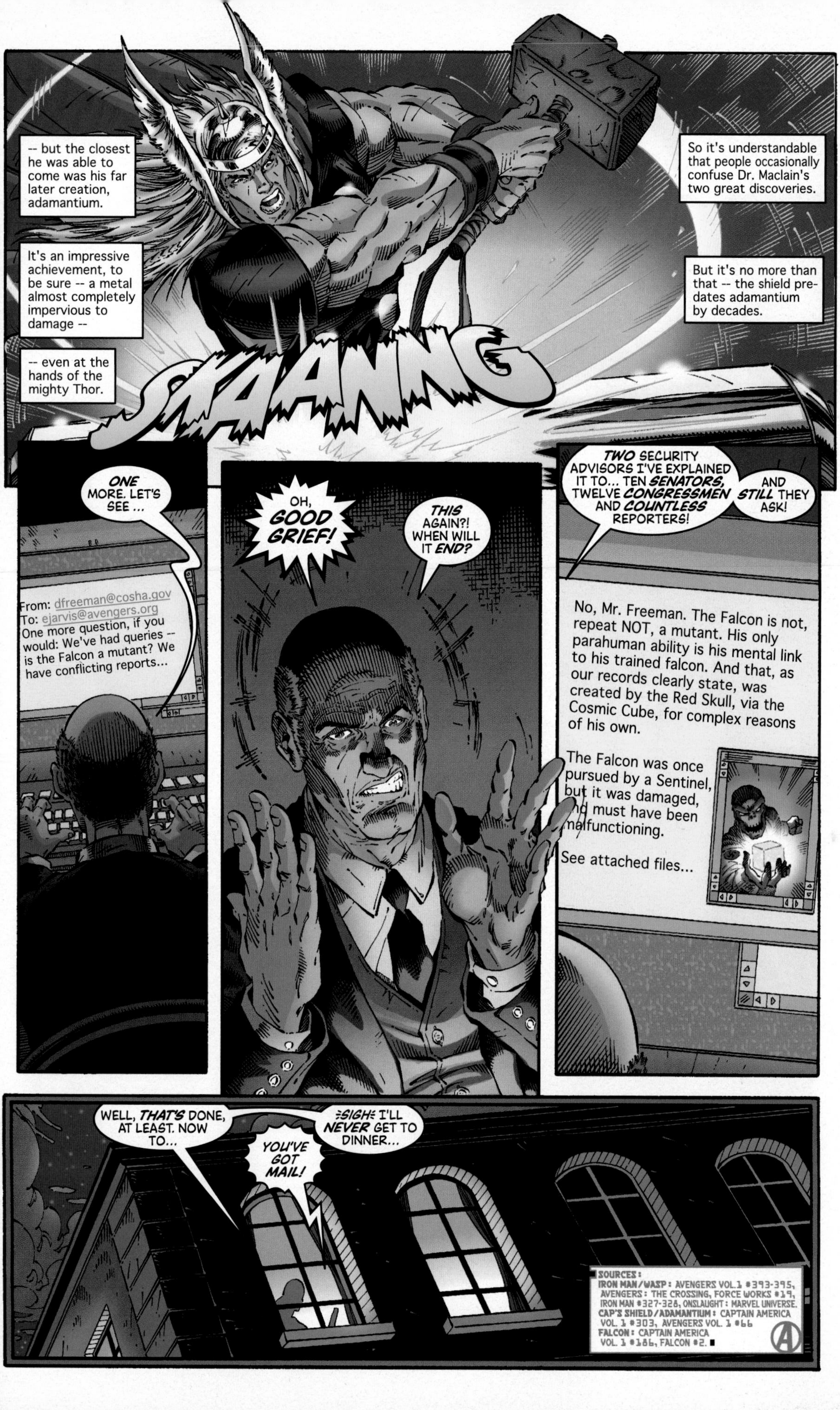
-- but the closest he was able to come was his far later creation, adamantium.
It's an impressive achievement, to be sure -- a metal almost completely impervious to damage --
-- even at the hands of the mighty Thor.
SKAANNG
So it's understandable that people occasionally confuse Dr. Maclain's two great discoveries.
But it's no more than that -- the shield predates adamantium by decades.
ONE MORE. LET'S SEE ...
From: dfreeman@cosha.gov
To: ejarvis@avengers.org
One more question, if you would: We've had queries -- is the Falcon a mutant? We have conflicting reports...
OH, GOOD GRIEF!
THIS AGAIN?! WHEN WILL IT END?
TWO SECURITY ADVISORS I'VE EXPLAINED IT TO... TEN SENATORS, TWELVE CONGRESSMEN AND COUNTLESS REPORTERS!
AND STILL THEY ASK!
No, Mr. Freeman. The Falcon is not, repeat NOT, a mutant. His only parahuman ability is his mental link to his trained falcon. And that, as our records clearly state, was created by the Red Skull, via the Cosmic Cube, for complex reasons of his own.
The Falcon was once pursued by a Sentinel, but it was damaged, and must have been malfunctioning.
See attached files...
WELL, THAT'S DONE, AT LEAST. NOW TO...
YOU'VE GOT MAIL!
SIGH I'LL NEVER GET TO DINNER...
SOURCES:
IRON MAN/WASP: AVENGERS VOL.1 #393-395, AVENGERS: THE CROSSING, FORCE WORKS #19, IRON MAN #327-328, ONSLAUGHT: MARVEL UNIVERSE.
CAP'S SHIELD/ADAMANTIUM: CAPTAIN AMERICA VOL. 1 #303, AVENGERS VOL. 1 #66
FALCON: CAPTAIN AMERICA VOL. 1 #186, FALCON #2.

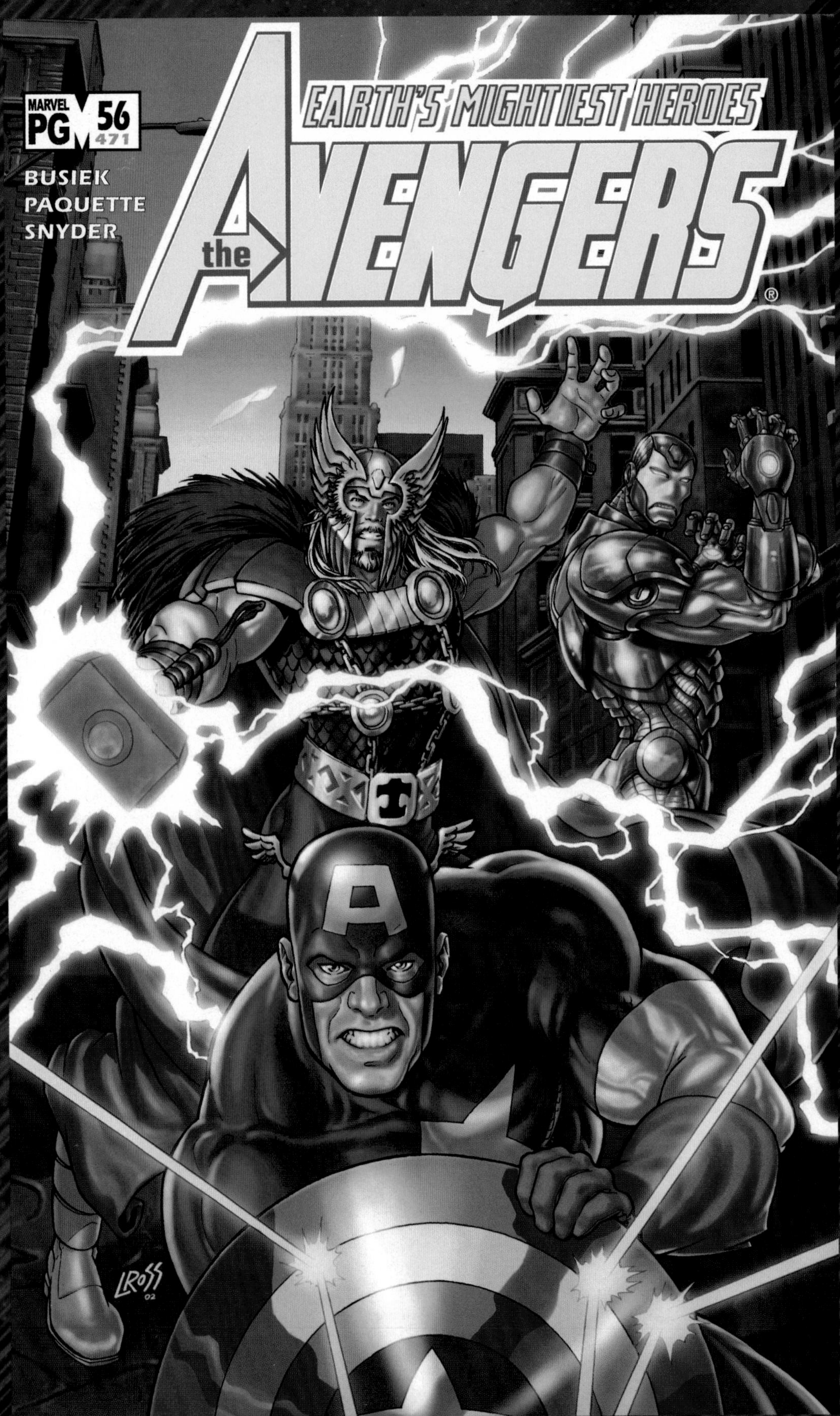
EARTH'S MIGHTIEST HEROES
MARVEL
PG
56
471
BUSIEK
PAQUETTE
SNYDER
the
AVENGERS
LROSS
02

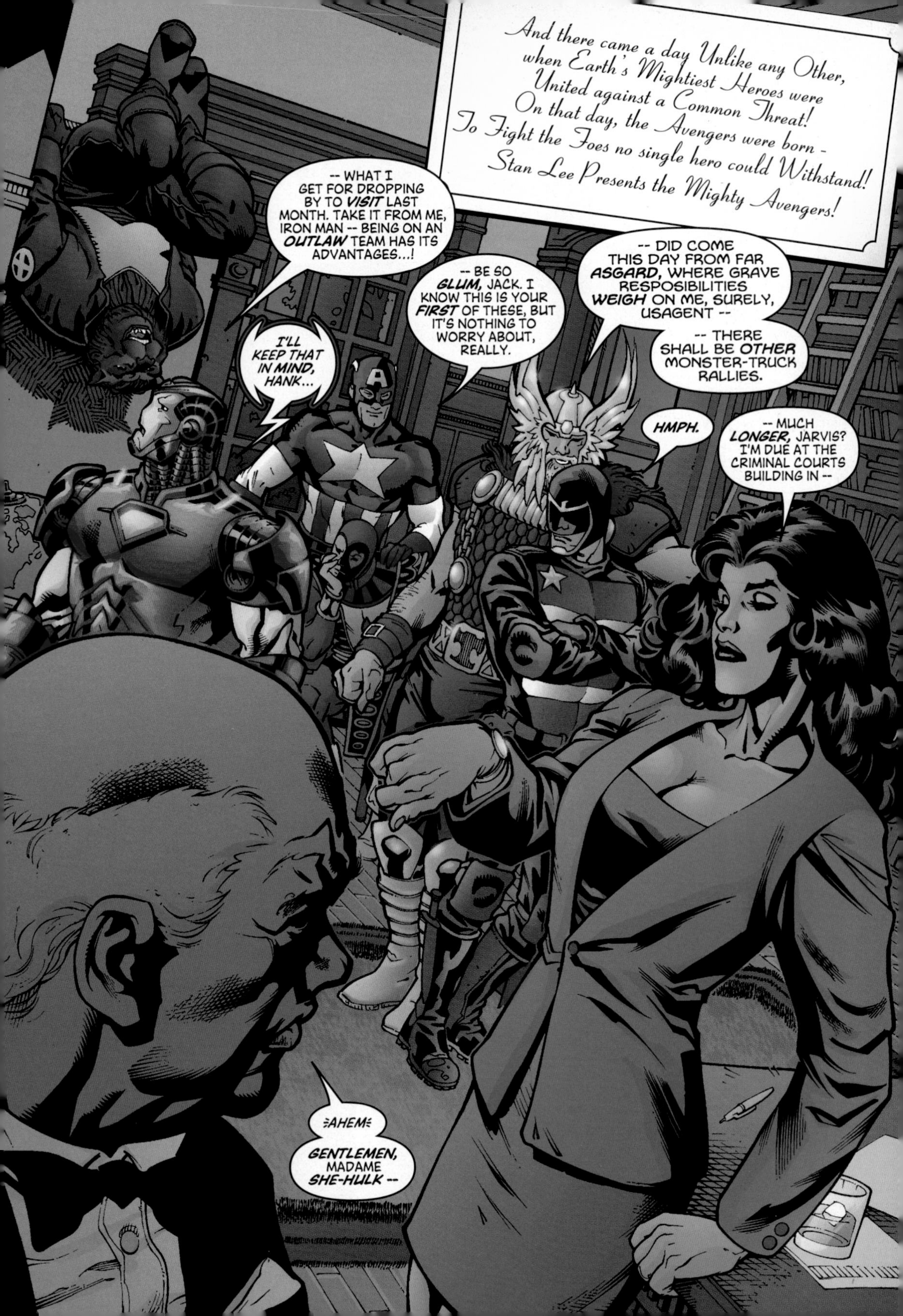
And there came a day Unlike any Other, when Earth's Mightiest Heroes were United against a Common Threat! On that day, the Avengers were born - To Fight the Foes no single hero could Withstand! Stan Lee Presents the Mighty Avengers!
-- WHAT I GET FOR DROPPING BY TO VISIT LAST MONTH. TAKE IT FROM ME, IRON MAN -- BEING ON AN OUTLAW TEAM HAS ITS ADVANTAGES...!
I'LL KEEP THAT IN MIND, HANK...
-- BE SO GLUM, JACK. I KNOW THIS IS YOUR FIRST OF THESE, BUT IT'S NOTHING TO WORRY ABOUT, REALLY.
-- DID COME THIS DAY FROM FAR ASGARD, WHERE GRAVE RESPOSIBILITIES WEIGH ON ME, SURELY, USAGENT --
-- THERE SHALL BE OTHER MONSTER-TRUCK RALLIES.
HMPH.
-- MUCH LONGER, JARVIS? I'M DUE AT THE CRIMINAL COURTS BUILDING IN --
AHEM
GENTLEMEN, MADAME SHE-HULK --

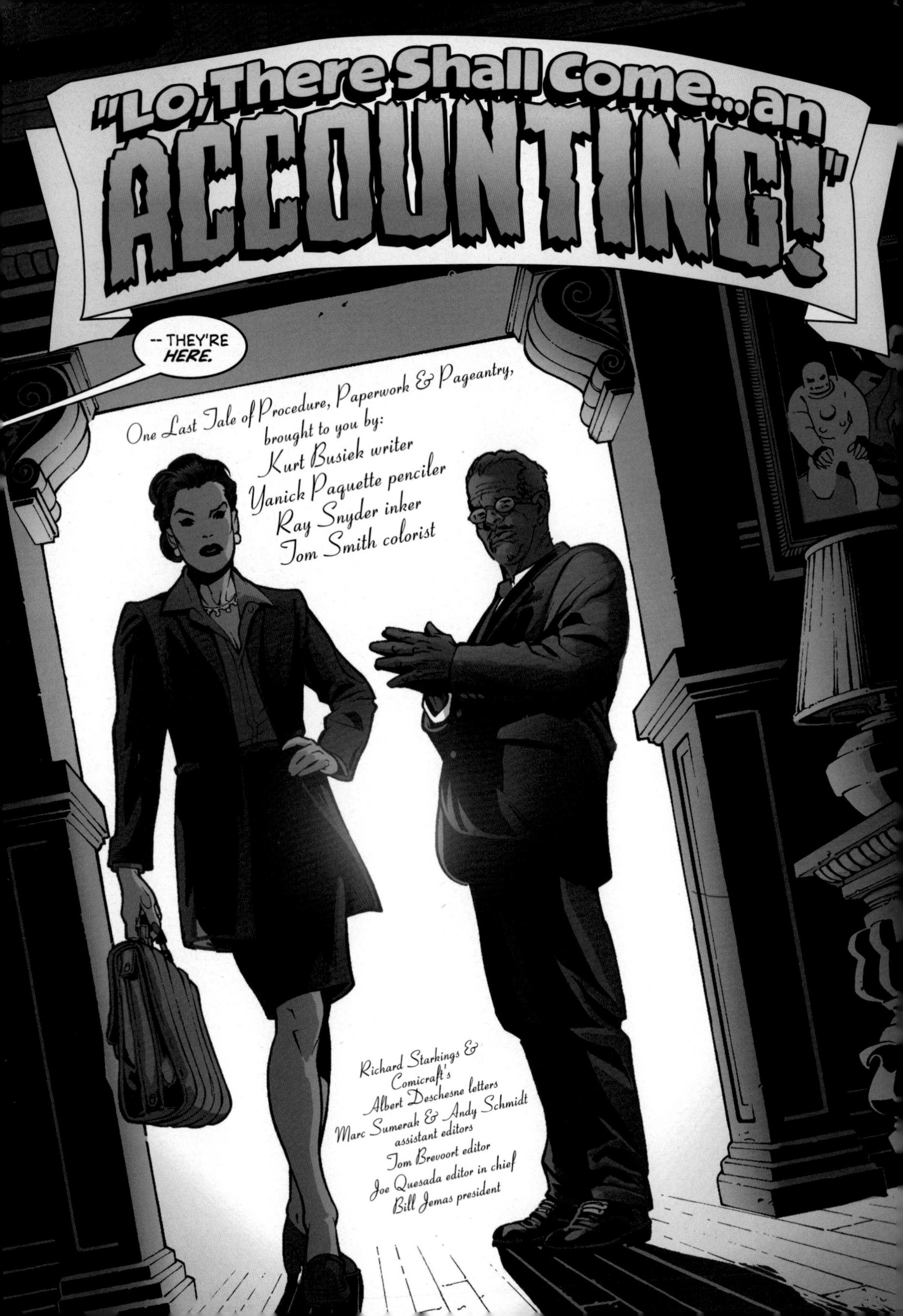
"LO, There Shall Come... an ACCOUNTING!"
-- THEY'RE HERE.
One Last Tale of Procedure, Paperwork & Pageantry, brought to you by:
Kurt Busiek writer
Yanick Paquette penciler
Ray Snyder inker
Tom Smith colorist
Richard Starkings & Comicraft's Albert Deschesne letters
Marc Sumerak & Andy Schmidt assistant editors
Tom Brevoort editor
Joe Quesada editor in chief
Bill Jemas president

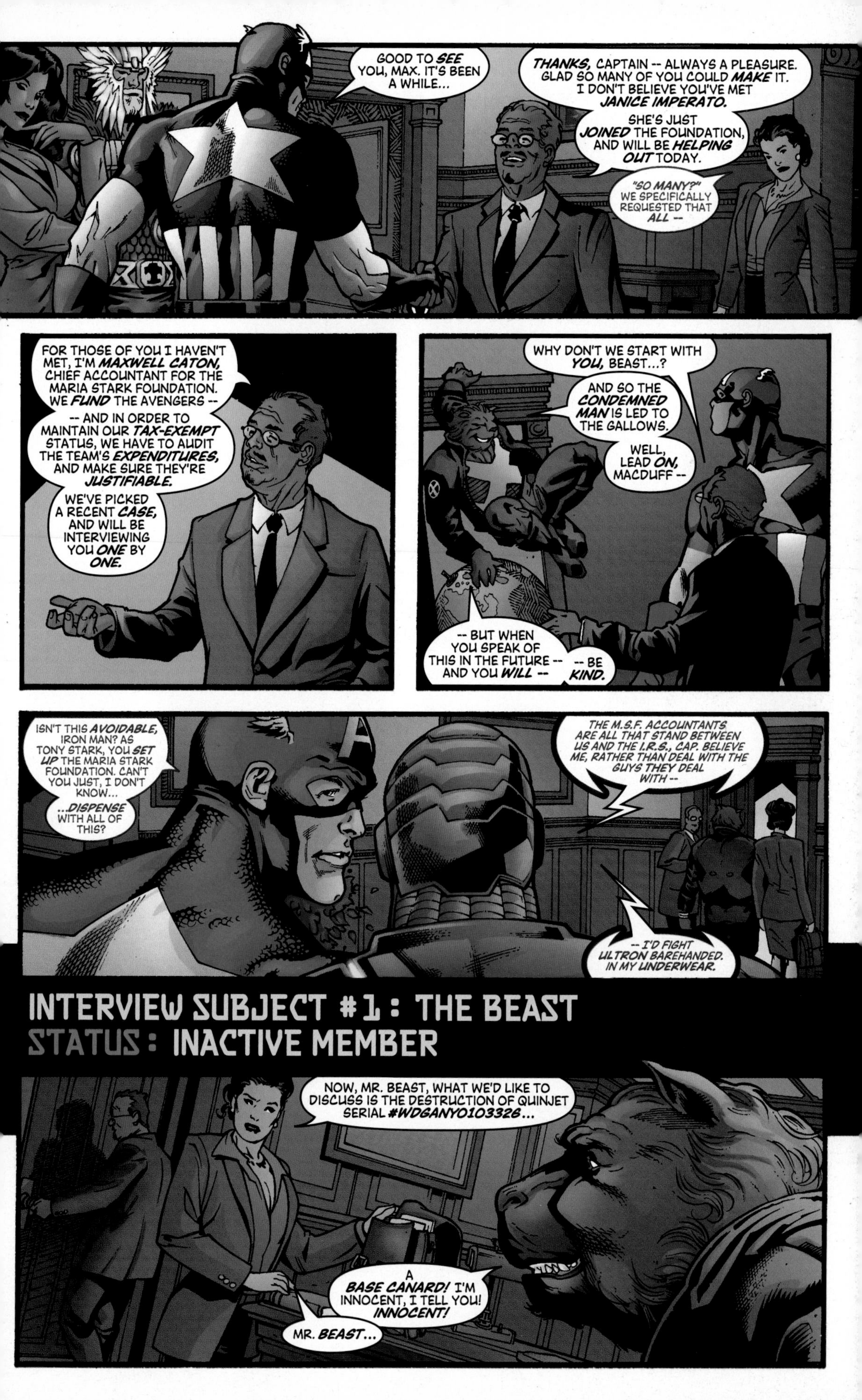
GOOD TO SEE YOU, MAX. IT'S BEEN A WHILE...
THANKS, CAPTAIN -- ALWAYS A PLEASURE. GLAD SO MANY OF YOU COULD MAKE IT. I DON'T BELIEVE YOU'VE MET JANICE IMPERATO.
SHE'S JUST JOINED THE FOUNDATION, AND WILL BE HELPING OUT TODAY.
"SO MANY?" WE SPECIFICALLY REQUESTED THAT ALL --
FOR THOSE OF YOU I HAVEN'T MET, I'M MAXWELL CATON, CHIEF ACCOUNTANT FOR THE MARIA STARK FOUNDATION. WE FUND THE AVENGERS --
-- AND IN ORDER TO MAINTAIN OUR TAX-EXEMPT STATUS, WE HAVE TO AUDIT THE TEAM'S EXPENDITURES, AND MAKE SURE THEY'RE JUSTIFIABLE.
WE'VE PICKED A RECENT CASE, AND WILL BE INTERVIEWING YOU ONE BY ONE.
WHY DON'T WE START WITH YOU, BEAST...?
AND SO THE CONDEMNED MAN IS LED TO THE GALLOWS.
WELL, LEAD ON, MACDUFF --
-- BUT WHEN YOU SPEAK OF THIS IN THE FUTURE -- AND YOU WILL --
-- BE KIND.
ISN'T THIS AVOIDABLE, IRON MAN? AS TONY STARK, YOU SET UP THE MARIA STARK FOUNDATION. CAN'T YOU JUST, I DON'T KNOW...
...DISPENSE WITH ALL OF THIS?
THE M.S.F. ACCOUNTANTS ARE ALL THAT STAND BETWEEN US AND THE I.R.S., CAP. BELIEVE ME, RATHER THAN DEAL WITH THE GUYS THEY DEAL WITH --
-- I'D FIGHT ULTRON BAREHANDED. IN MY UNDERWEAR.
INTERVIEW SUBJECT #1 : THE BEAST
STATUS : INACTIVE MEMBER
NOW, MR. BEAST, WHAT WE'D LIKE TO DISCUSS IS THE DESTRUCTION OF QUINJET SERIAL #WDGANYO103326...
A BASE CANARD! I'M INNOCENT, I TELL YOU! INNOCENT!
MR. BEAST...

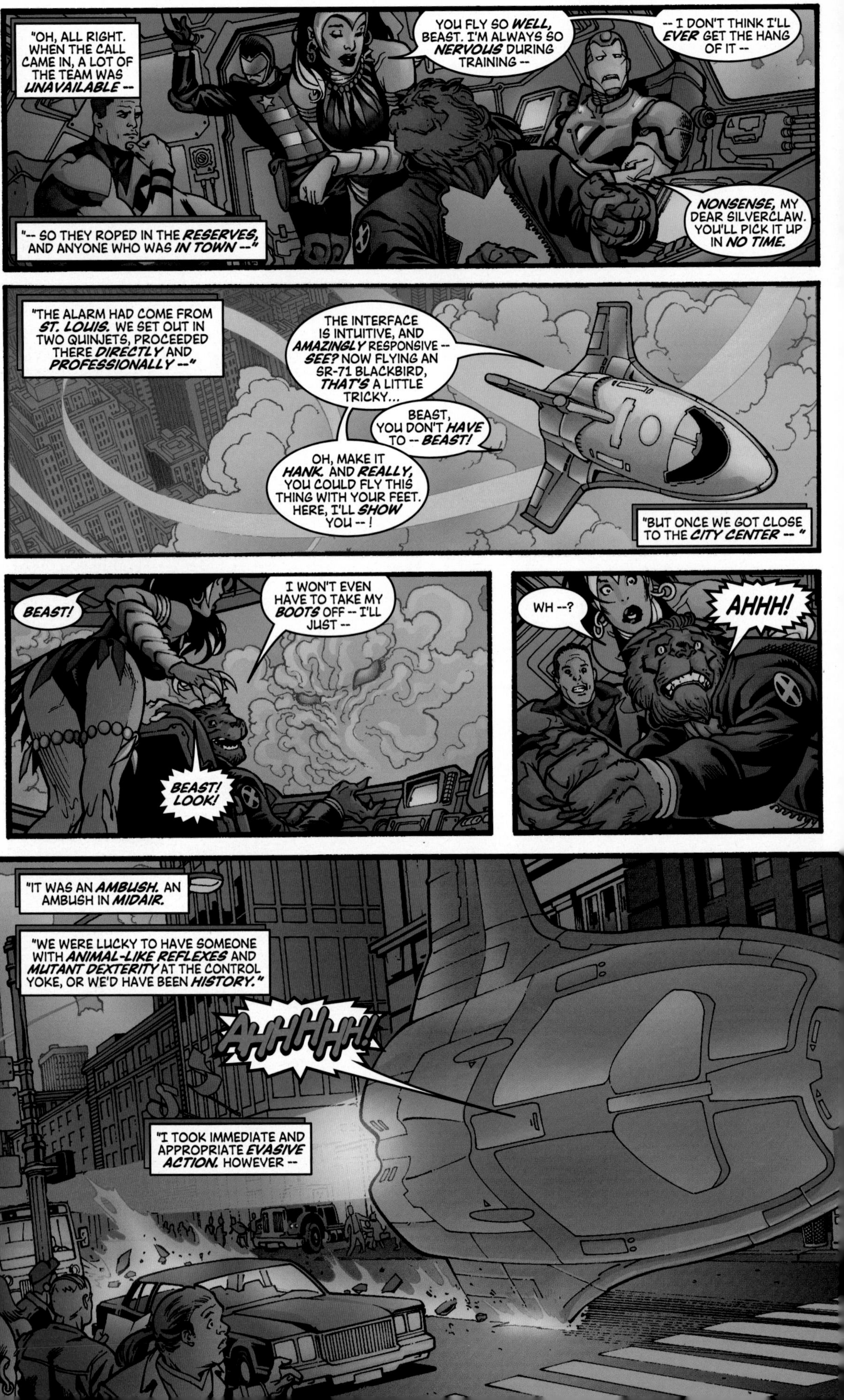
"OH, ALL RIGHT. WHEN THE CALL CAME IN, A LOT OF THE TEAM WAS UNAVAILABLE --
YOU FLY SO WELL, BEAST. I'M ALWAYS SO NERVOUS DURING TRAINING --
-- I DON'T THINK I'LL EVER GET THE HANG OF IT --
"-- SO THEY ROPED IN THE RESERVES, AND ANYONE WHO WAS IN TOWN --"
NONSENSE, MY DEAR SILVERCLAW. YOU'LL PICK IT UP IN NO TIME.
"THE ALARM HAD COME FROM ST. LOUIS. WE SET OUT IN TWO QUINJETS, PROCEEDED THERE DIRECTLY AND PROFESSIONALLY --"
THE INTERFACE IS INTUITIVE, AND AMAZINGLY RESPONSIVE -- SEE? NOW FLYING AN SR-71 BLACKBIRD, THAT'S A LITTLE TRICKY...
BEAST, YOU DON'T HAVE TO -- BEAST!
OH, MAKE IT HANK. AND REALLY, YOU COULD FLY THIS THING WITH YOUR FEET. HERE, I'LL SHOW YOU -- !
"BUT ONCE WE GOT CLOSE TO THE CITY CENTER -- "
BEAST!
I WON'T EVEN HAVE TO TAKE MY BOOTS OFF -- I'LL JUST --
BEAST! LOOK!
WH --?
AHHH!
"IT WAS AN AMBUSH. AN AMBUSH IN MIDAIR.
"WE WERE LUCKY TO HAVE SOMEONE WITH ANIMAL-LIKE REFLEXES AND MUTANT DEXTERITY AT THE CONTROL YOKE, OR WE'D HAVE BEEN HISTORY."
AHHHHH!
"I TOOK IMMEDIATE AND APPROPRIATE EVASIVE ACTION. HOWEVER --

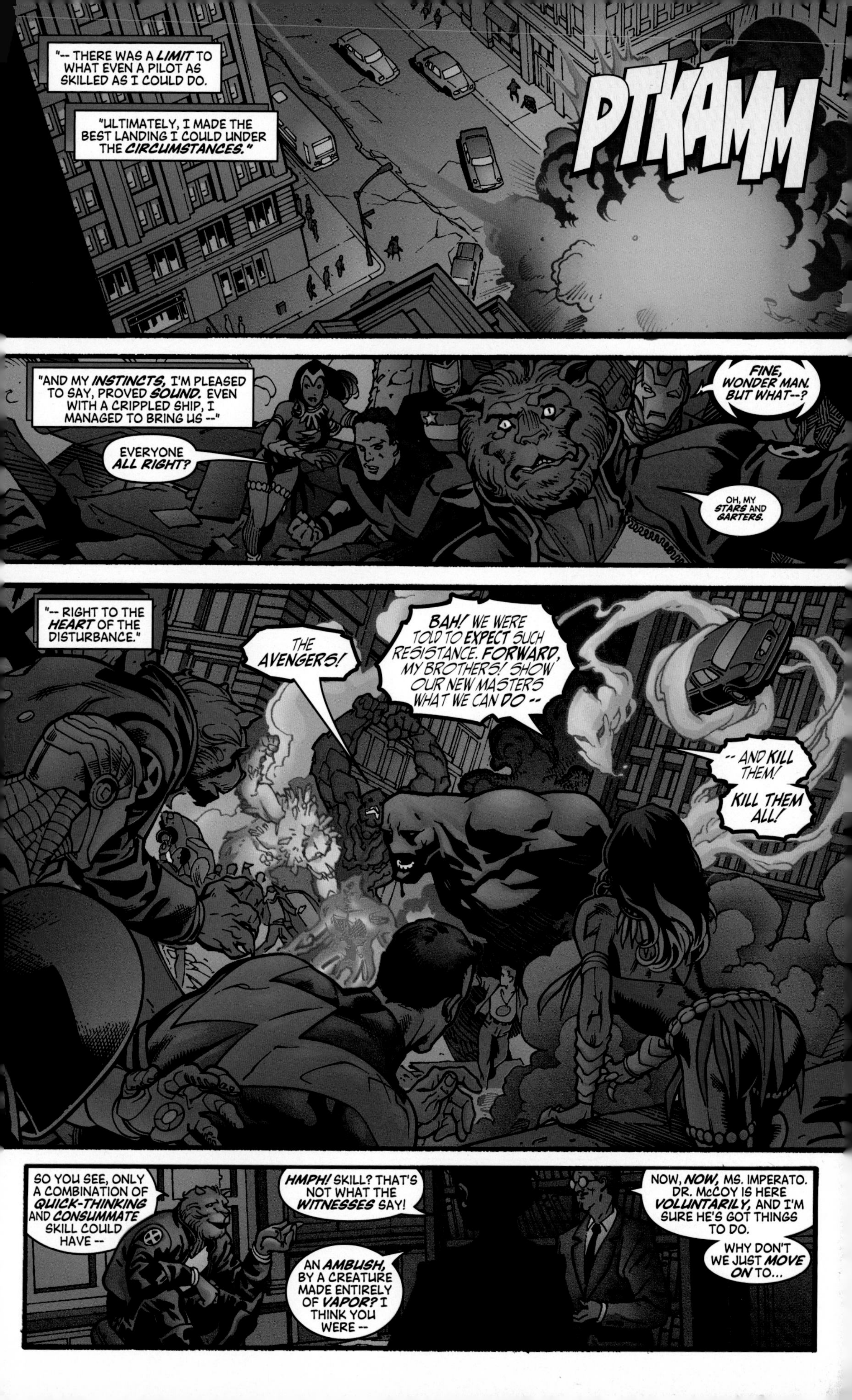
"-- THERE WAS A LIMIT TO WHAT EVEN A PILOT AS SKILLED AS I COULD DO.
"ULTIMATELY, I MADE THE BEST LANDING I COULD UNDER THE CIRCUMSTANCES."
PTKAMM
"AND MY INSTINCTS, I'M PLEASED TO SAY, PROVED SOUND. EVEN WITH A CRIPPLED SHIP, I MANAGED TO BRING US --"
EVERYONE ALL RIGHT?
FINE, WONDER MAN. BUT WHAT--?
OH, MY STARS AND GARTERS.
"-- RIGHT TO THE HEART OF THE DISTURBANCE."
THE AVENGERS!
BAH! WE WERE TOLD TO EXPECT SUCH RESISTANCE. FORWARD, MY BROTHERS! SHOW OUR NEW MASTERS WHAT WE CAN DO --
-- AND KILL THEM!
KILL THEM ALL!
SO YOU SEE, ONLY A COMBINATION OF QUICK-THINKING AND CONSUMMATE SKILL COULD HAVE --
HMPH! SKILL? THAT'S NOT WHAT THE WITNESSES SAY!
AN AMBUSH, BY A CREATURE MADE ENTIRELY OF VAPOR? I THINK YOU WERE --
NOW, NOW, MS. IMPERATO. DR. McCOY IS HERE VOLUNTARILY, AND I'M SURE HE'S GOT THINGS TO DO.
WHY DON'T WE JUST MOVE ON TO...

INTERVIEW SUBJECT #2 : IRON MAN
STATUS : ACTIVE MEMBER

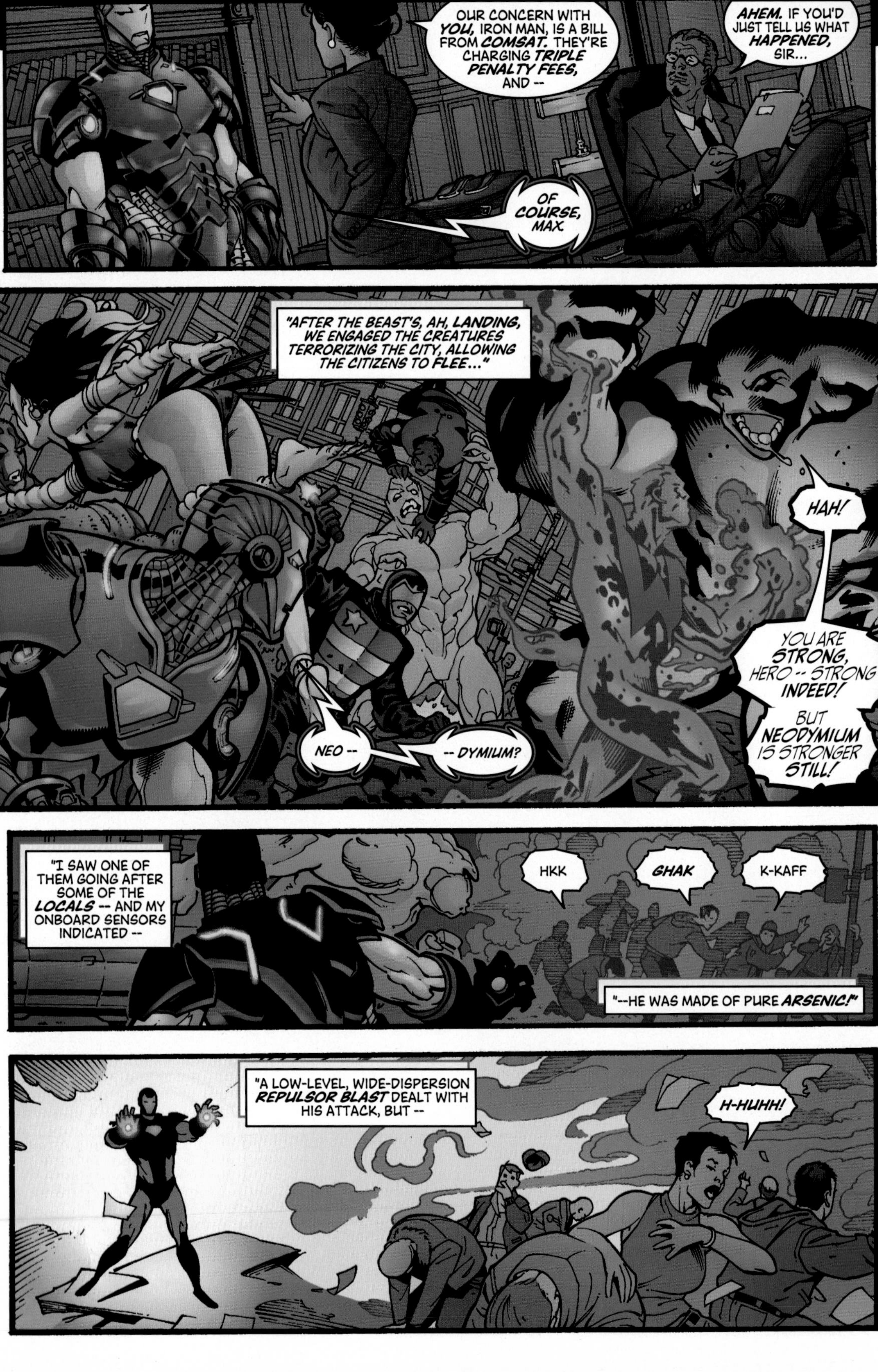
OUR CONCERN WITH YOU, IRON MAN, IS A BILL FROM COMSAT. THEY'RE CHARGING TRIPLE PENALTY FEES, AND --
AHEM. IF YOU'D JUST TELL US WHAT HAPPENED, SIR...
OF COURSE, MAX.
"AFTER THE BEAST'S, AH, LANDING, WE ENGAGED THE CREATURES TERRORIZING THE CITY, ALLOWING THE CITIZENS TO FLEE..."
HAH!
YOU ARE STRONG, HERO -- STRONG INDEED!
BUT NEODYMIUM IS STRONGER STILL!
NEO --
-- DYMIUM?
"I SAW ONE OF THEM GOING AFTER SOME OF THE LOCALS -- AND MY ONBOARD SENSORS INDICATED --
HKK
GHAK
K-KAFF
"--HE WAS MADE OF PURE ARSENIC!"
"A LOW-LEVEL, WIDE-DISPERSION REPULSOR BLAST DEALT WITH HIS ATTACK, BUT --
H-HUHH!

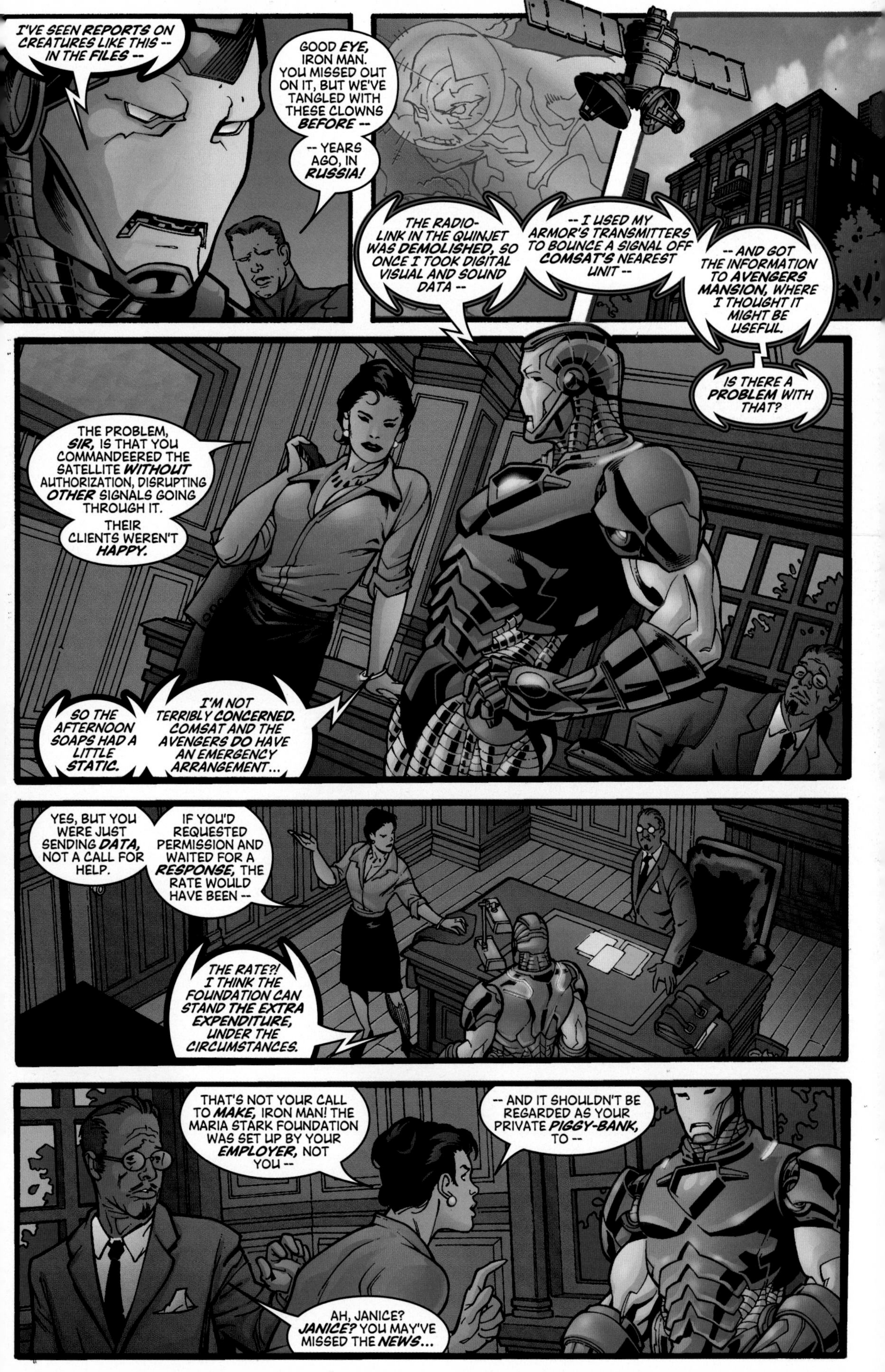
I'VE SEEN REPORTS ON CREATURES LIKE THIS -- IN THE FILES --
GOOD EYE, IRON MAN. YOU MISSED OUT ON IT, BUT WE'VE TANGLED WITH THESE CLOWNS BEFORE --
-- YEARS AGO, IN RUSSIA!
THE RADIO-LINK IN THE QUINJET WAS DEMOLISHED, SO ONCE I TOOK DIGITAL VISUAL AND SOUND DATA --
-- I USED MY ARMOR'S TRANSMITTERS TO BOUNCE A SIGNAL OFF COMSAT'S NEAREST UNIT --
-- AND GOT THE INFORMATION TO AVENGERS MANSION, WHERE I THOUGHT IT MIGHT BE USEFUL.
IS THERE A PROBLEM WITH THAT?
THE PROBLEM, SIR, IS THAT YOU COMMANDEERED THE SATELLITE WITHOUT AUTHORIZATION, DISRUPTING OTHER SIGNALS GOING THROUGH IT.
THEIR CLIENTS WEREN'T HAPPY.
SO THE AFTERNOON SOAPS HAD A LITTLE STATIC.
I'M NOT TERRIBLY CONCERNED. COMSAT AND THE AVENGERS DO HAVE AN EMERGENCY ARRANGEMENT...
YES, BUT YOU WERE JUST SENDING DATA, NOT A CALL FOR HELP.
IF YOU'D REQUESTED PERMISSION AND WAITED FOR A RESPONSE, THE RATE WOULD HAVE BEEN --
THE RATE?! I THINK THE FOUNDATION CAN STAND THE EXTRA EXPENDITURE, UNDER THE CIRCUMSTANCES.
THAT'S NOT YOUR CALL TO MAKE, IRON MAN! THE MARIA STARK FOUNDATION WAS SET UP BY YOUR EMPLOYER, NOT YOU --
-- AND IT SHOULDN'T BE REGARDED AS YOUR PRIVATE PIGGY-BANK, TO --
AH, JANICE? JANICE? YOU MAY'VE MISSED THE NEWS...

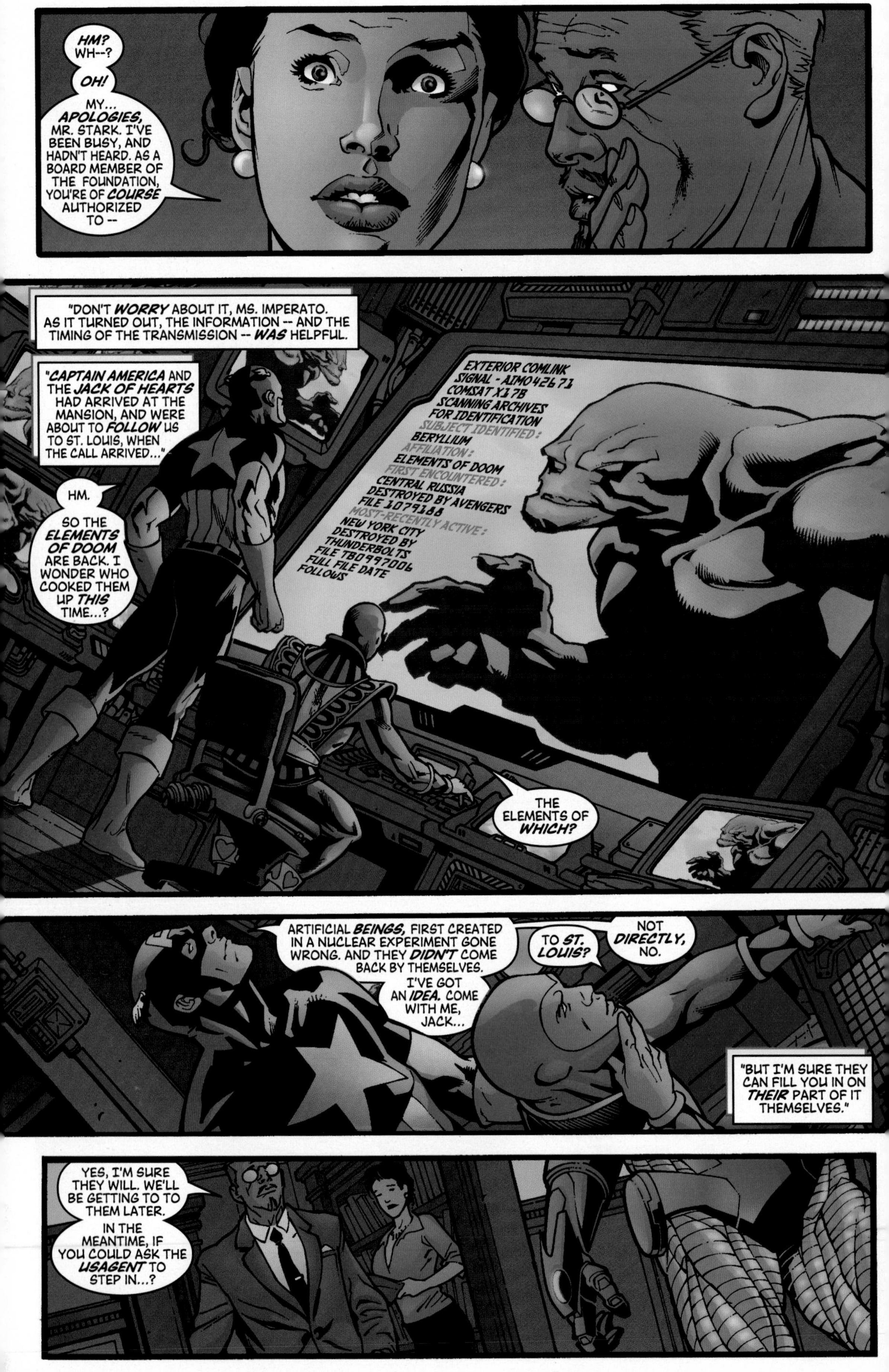
HM? WH--?
OH!
MY... APOLOGIES, MR. STARK. I'VE BEEN BUSY, AND HADN'T HEARD. AS A BOARD MEMBER OF THE FOUNDATION, YOU'RE OF COURSE AUTHORIZED TO --
"DON'T WORRY ABOUT IT, MS. IMPERATO. AS IT TURNED OUT, THE INFORMATION -- AND THE TIMING OF THE TRANSMISSION -- WAS HELPFUL.
"CAPTAIN AMERICA AND THE JACK OF HEARTS HAD ARRIVED AT THE MANSION, AND WERE ABOUT TO FOLLOW US TO ST. LOUIS, WHEN THE CALL ARRIVED..."
EXTERIOR COMLINK SIGNAL - AIM042671 COMSAT X17B SCANNING ARCHIVES FOR IDENTIFICATION
SUBJECT IDENTIFIED: BERYLLIUM
AFFILIATION: ELEMENTS OF DOOM
FIRST ENCOUNTERED: CENTRAL RUSSIA DESTROYED BY AVENGERS FILE 1079188
MOST-RECENTLY ACTIVE: NEW YORK CITY DESTROYED BY THUNDERBOLTS FILE TB0997006 FULL FILE DATE FOLLOWS
HM.
SO THE ELEMENTS OF DOOM ARE BACK. I WONDER WHO COOKED THEM UP THIS TIME...?
THE ELEMENTS OF WHICH?
ARTIFICIAL BEINGS, FIRST CREATED IN A NUCLEAR EXPERIMENT GONE WRONG. AND THEY DIDN'T COME BACK BY THEMSELVES.
I'VE GOT AN IDEA. COME WITH ME, JACK...
TO ST. LOUIS?
NOT DIRECTLY, NO.
"BUT I'M SURE THEY CAN FILL YOU IN ON THEIR PART OF IT THEMSELVES."
YES, I'M SURE THEY WILL. WE'LL BE GETTING TO TO THEM LATER.
IN THE MEANTIME, IF YOU COULD ASK THE USAGENT TO STEP IN...?

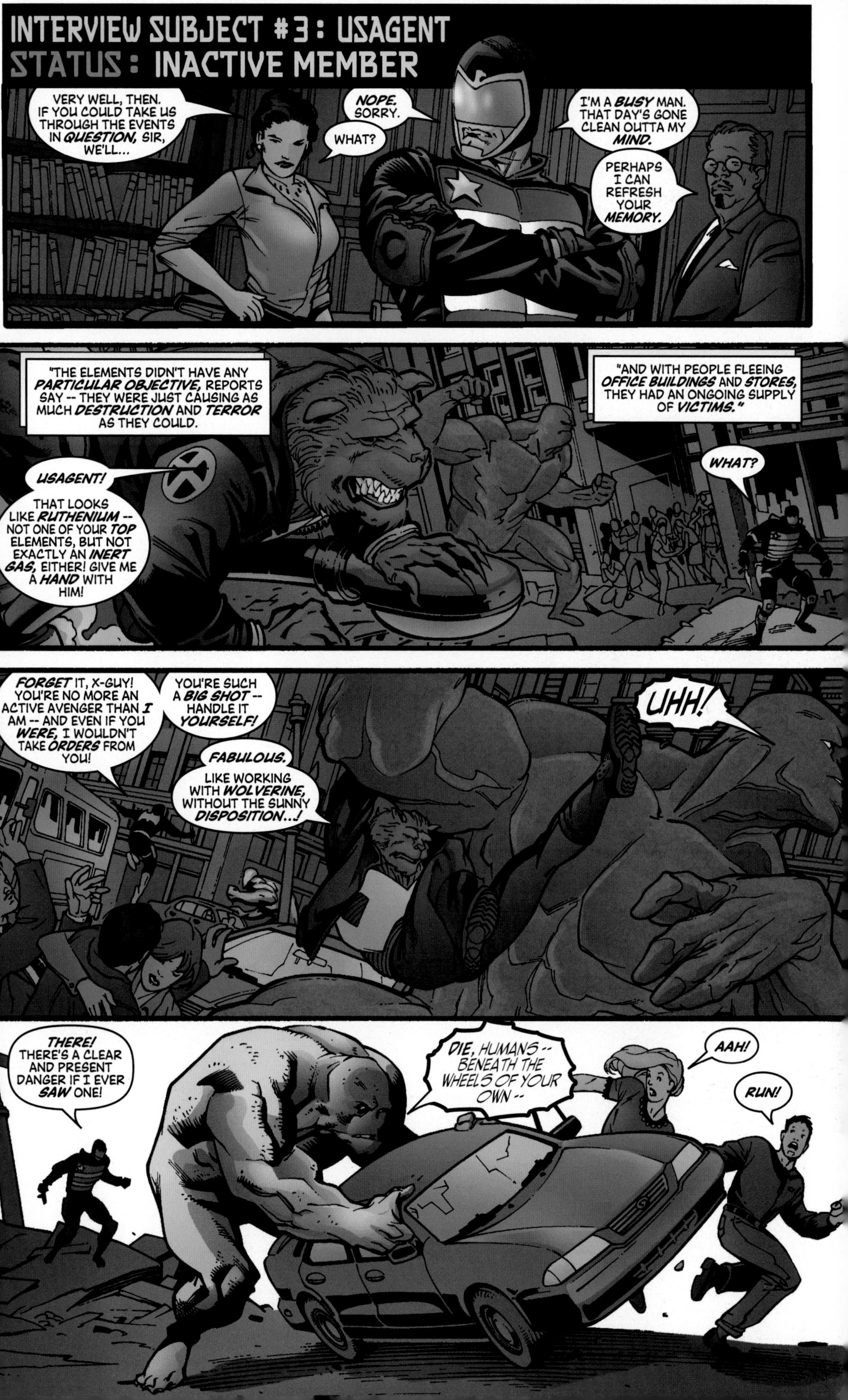

INTERVIEW SUBJECT #3 : USAGENT
STATUS : INACTIVE MEMBER
VERY WELL, THEN. IF YOU COULD TAKE US THROUGH THE EVENTS IN QUESTION, SIR, WE'LL...
NOPE. SORRY.
WHAT?
I'M A BUSY MAN. THAT DAY'S GONE CLEAN OUTTA MY MIND.
PERHAPS I CAN REFRESH YOUR MEMORY.
"THE ELEMENTS DIDN'T HAVE ANY PARTICULAR OBJECTIVE, REPORTS SAY -- THEY WERE JUST CAUSING AS MUCH DESTRUCTION AND TERROR AS THEY COULD.
"AND WITH PEOPLE FLEEING OFFICE BUILDINGS AND STORES, THEY HAD AN ONGOING SUPPLY OF VICTIMS."
USAGENT!
THAT LOOKS LIKE RUTHENIUM -- NOT ONE OF YOUR TOP ELEMENTS, BUT NOT EXACTLY AN INERT GAS, EITHER! GIVE ME A HAND WITH HIM!
WHAT?
FORGET IT, X-GUY! YOU'RE NO MORE AN ACTIVE AVENGER THAN I AM -- AND EVEN IF YOU WERE, I WOULDN'T TAKE ORDERS FROM YOU!
YOU'RE SUCH A BIG SHOT -- HANDLE IT YOURSELF!
FABULOUS.
LIKE WORKING WITH WOLVERINE, WITHOUT THE SUNNY DISPOSITION...!
UHH!
THERE! THERE'S A CLEAR AND PRESENT DANGER IF I EVER SAW ONE!
DIE, HUMANS -- BENEATH THE WHEELS OF YOUR OWN --
AAH!
RUN!

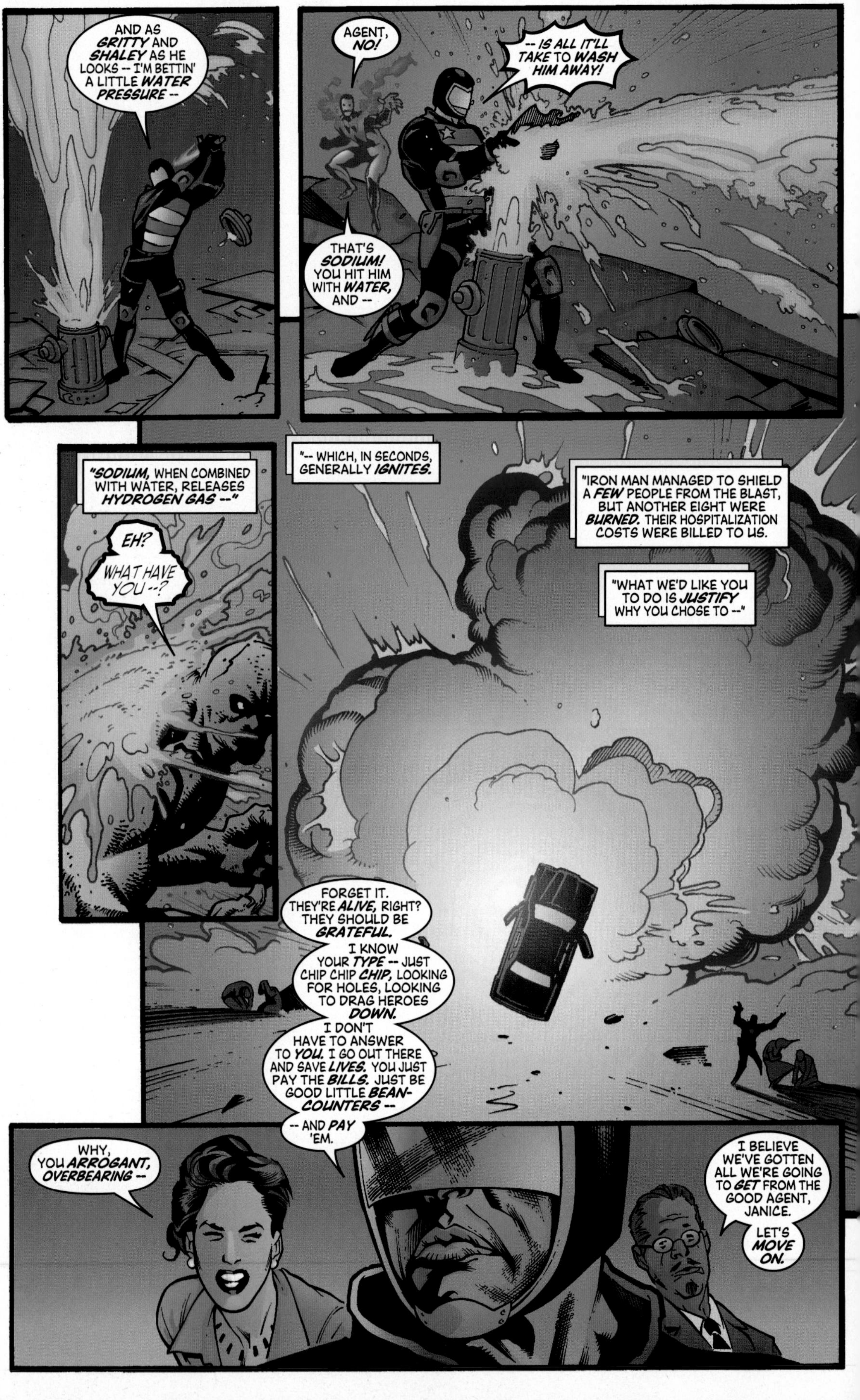
AND AS GRITTY AND SHALEY AS HE LOOKS -- I'M BETTIN' A LITTLE WATER PRESSURE --
AGENT, NO!
-- IS ALL IT'LL TAKE TO WASH HIM AWAY!
THAT'S SODIUM! YOU HIT HIM WITH WATER, AND --
"SODIUM, WHEN COMBINED WITH WATER, RELEASES HYDROGEN GAS --"
EH?
WHAT HAVE YOU --?
"-- WHICH, IN SECONDS, GENERALLY IGNITES.
"IRON MAN MANAGED TO SHIELD A FEW PEOPLE FROM THE BLAST, BUT ANOTHER EIGHT WERE BURNED. THEIR HOSPITALIZATION COSTS WERE BILLED TO US.
"WHAT WE'D LIKE YOU TO DO IS JUSTIFY WHY YOU CHOSE TO --"
FORGET IT. THEY'RE ALIVE, RIGHT? THEY SHOULD BE GRATEFUL.
I KNOW YOUR TYPE -- JUST CHIP CHIP CHIP, LOOKING FOR HOLES, LOOKING TO DRAG HEROES DOWN.
I DON'T HAVE TO ANSWER TO YOU. I GO OUT THERE AND SAVE LIVES. YOU JUST PAY THE BILLS. JUST BE GOOD LITTLE BEAN-COUNTERS --
-- AND PAY 'EM.
WHY, YOU ARROGANT, OVERBEARING --
I BELIEVE WE'VE GOTTEN ALL WE'RE GOING TO GET FROM THE GOOD AGENT, JANICE.
LET'S MOVE ON.

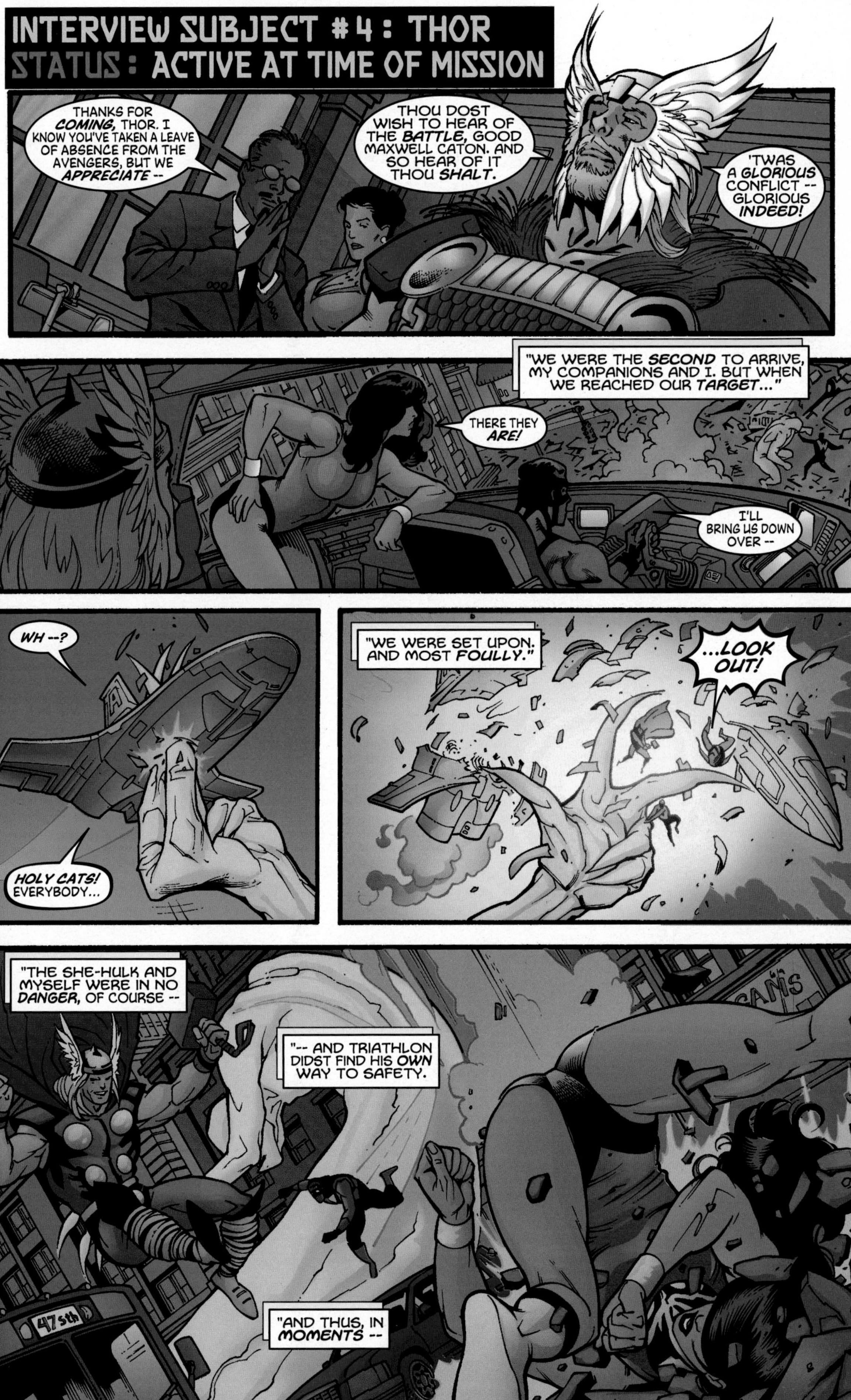
INTERVIEW SUBJECT #4: THOR
STATUS: ACTIVE AT TIME OF MISSION
THANKS FOR COMING, THOR. I KNOW YOU'VE TAKEN A LEAVE OF ABSENCE FROM THE AVENGERS, BUT WE APPRECIATE --
THOU DOST WISH TO HEAR OF THE BATTLE, GOOD MAXWELL CATON. AND SO HEAR OF IT THOU SHALT.
'TWAS A GLORIOUS CONFLICT -- GLORIOUS INDEED!
"WE WERE THE SECOND TO ARRIVE, MY COMPANIONS AND I. BUT WHEN WE REACHED OUR TARGET..."
THERE THEY ARE!
I'LL BRING US DOWN OVER --
WH --?
HOLY CATS! EVERYBODY...
"WE WERE SET UPON. AND MOST FOULLY."
...LOOK OUT!
"THE SHE-HULK AND MYSELF WERE IN NO DANGER, OF COURSE --
"-- AND TRIATHLON DIDST FIND HIS OWN WAY TO SAFETY.
"AND THUS, IN MOMENTS --

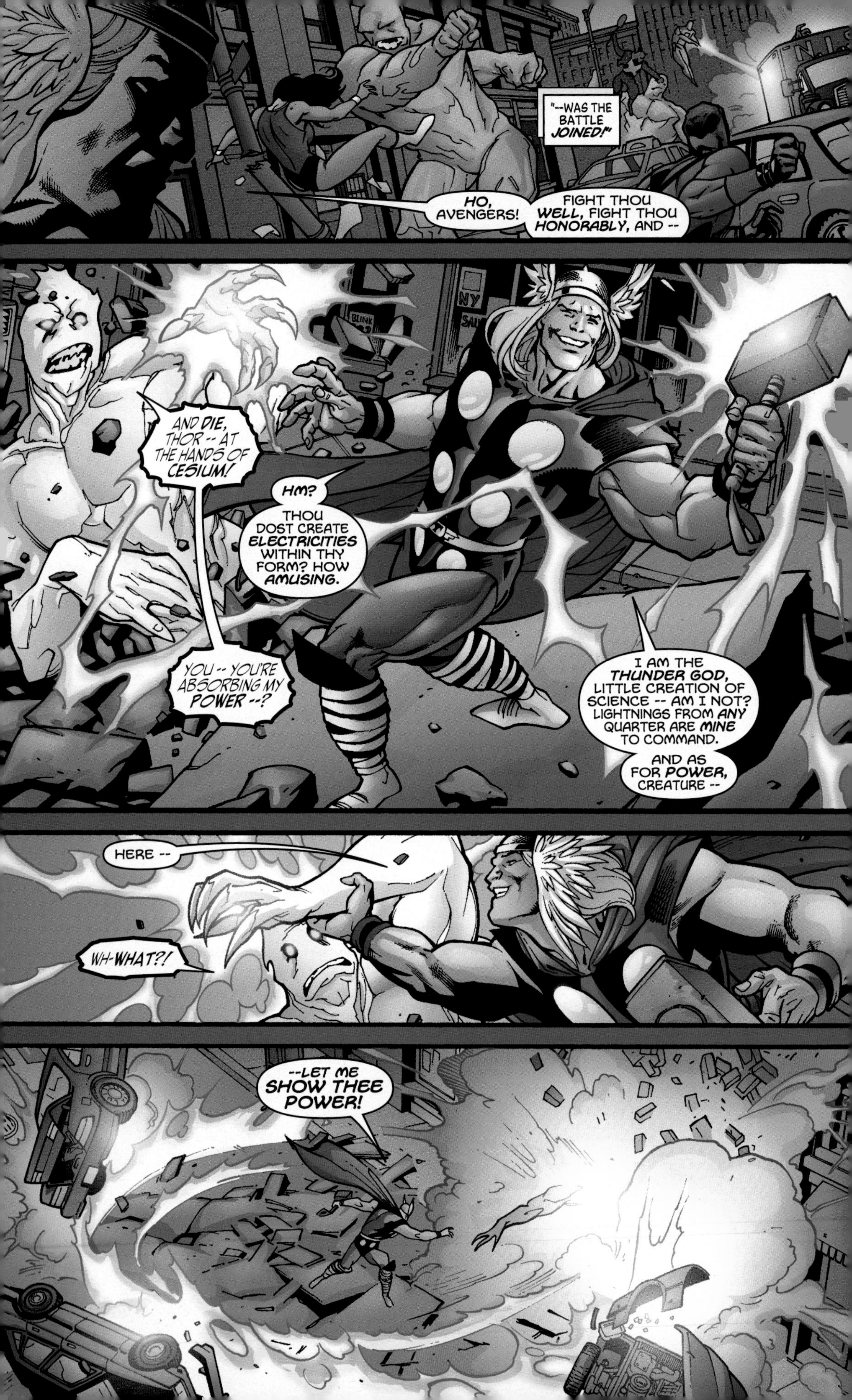
"--WAS THE BATTLE JOINED!"
HO, AVENGERS!
FIGHT THOU WELL, FIGHT THOU HONORABLY, AND --
AND DIE, THOR -- AT THE HANDS OF CESIUM!
HM?
THOU DOST CREATE ELECTRICITIES WITHIN THY FORM? HOW AMUSING.
YOU -- YOU'RE ABSORBING MY POWER --?
I AM THE THUNDER GOD, LITTLE CREATION OF SCIENCE -- AM I NOT? LIGHTNINGS FROM ANY QUARTER ARE MINE TO COMMAND.
AND AS FOR POWER, CREATURE --
HERE --
WH-WHAT?!
--LET ME SHOW THEE POWER!

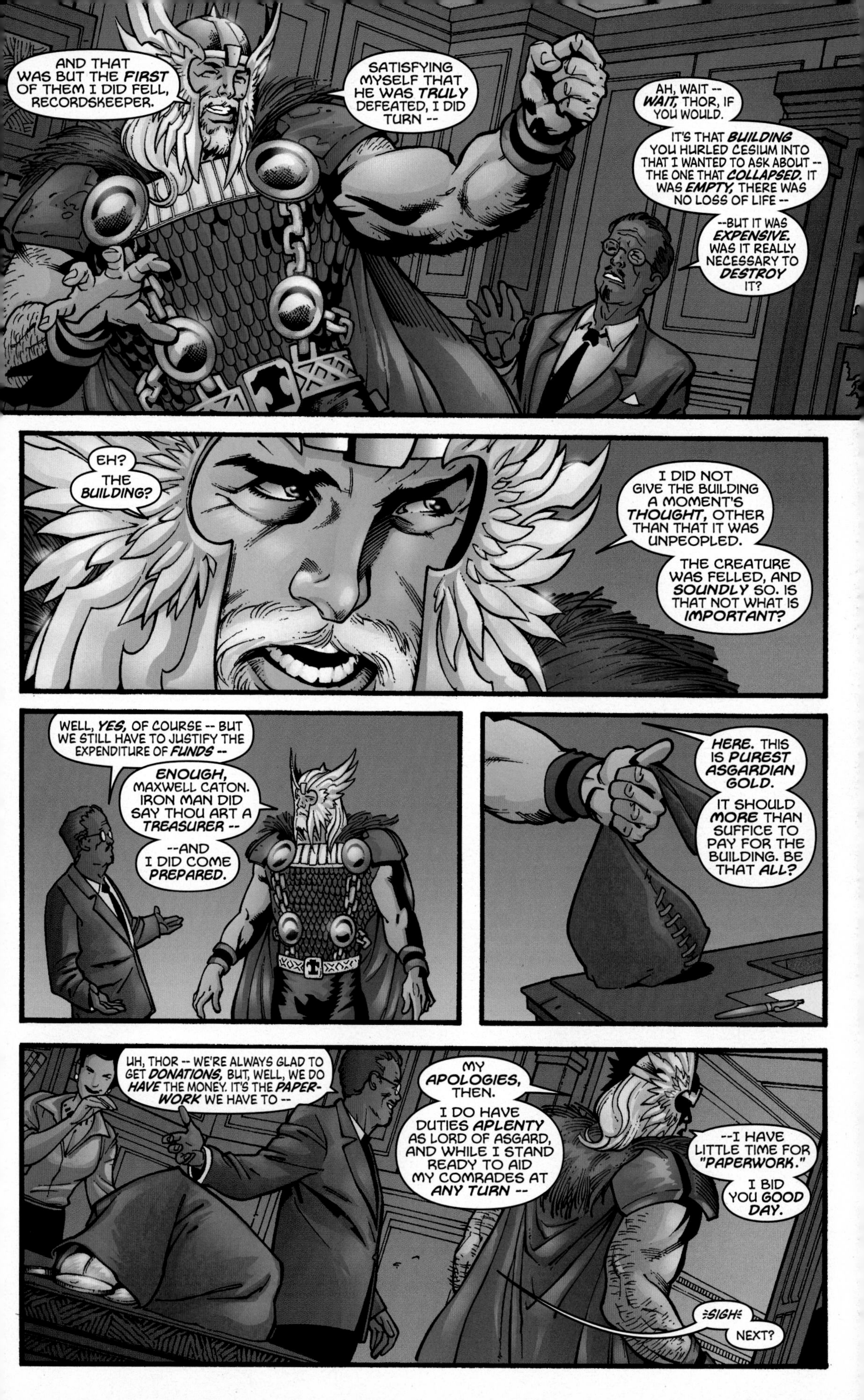

AND THAT WAS BUT THE FIRST OF THEM I DID FELL, RECORDSKEEPER.
SATISFYING MYSELF THAT HE WAS TRULY DEFEATED, I DID TURN --
AH, WAIT -- WAIT, THOR, IF YOU WOULD.
IT'S THAT BUILDING YOU HURLED CESIUM INTO THAT I WANTED TO ASK ABOUT -- THE ONE THAT COLLAPSED. IT WAS EMPTY, THERE WAS NO LOSS OF LIFE --
--BUT IT WAS EXPENSIVE. WAS IT REALLY NECESSARY TO DESTROY IT?
EH? THE BUILDING?
I DID NOT GIVE THE BUILDING A MOMENT'S THOUGHT, OTHER THAN THAT IT WAS UNPEOPLED.
THE CREATURE WAS FELLED, AND SOUNDLY SO. IS THAT NOT WHAT IS IMPORTANT?
WELL, YES, OF COURSE -- BUT WE STILL HAVE TO JUSTIFY THE EXPENDITURE OF FUNDS --
ENOUGH, MAXWELL CATON. IRON MAN DID SAY THOU ART A TREASURER --
--AND I DID COME PREPARED.
HERE. THIS IS PUREST ASGARDIAN GOLD.
IT SHOULD MORE THAN SUFFICE TO PAY FOR THE BUILDING. BE THAT ALL?
UH, THOR -- WE'RE ALWAYS GLAD TO GET DONATIONS, BUT, WELL, WE DO HAVE THE MONEY. IT'S THE PAPER-WORK WE HAVE TO --
MY APOLOGIES, THEN.
I DO HAVE DUTIES APLENTY AS LORD OF ASGARD, AND WHILE I STAND READY TO AID MY COMRADES AT ANY TURN --
--I HAVE LITTLE TIME FOR "PAPERWORK."
I BID YOU GOOD DAY.
SIGH
NEXT?

INTERVIEW SUBJECT #5: SHE-HULK
STATUS: INACTIVE MEMBER

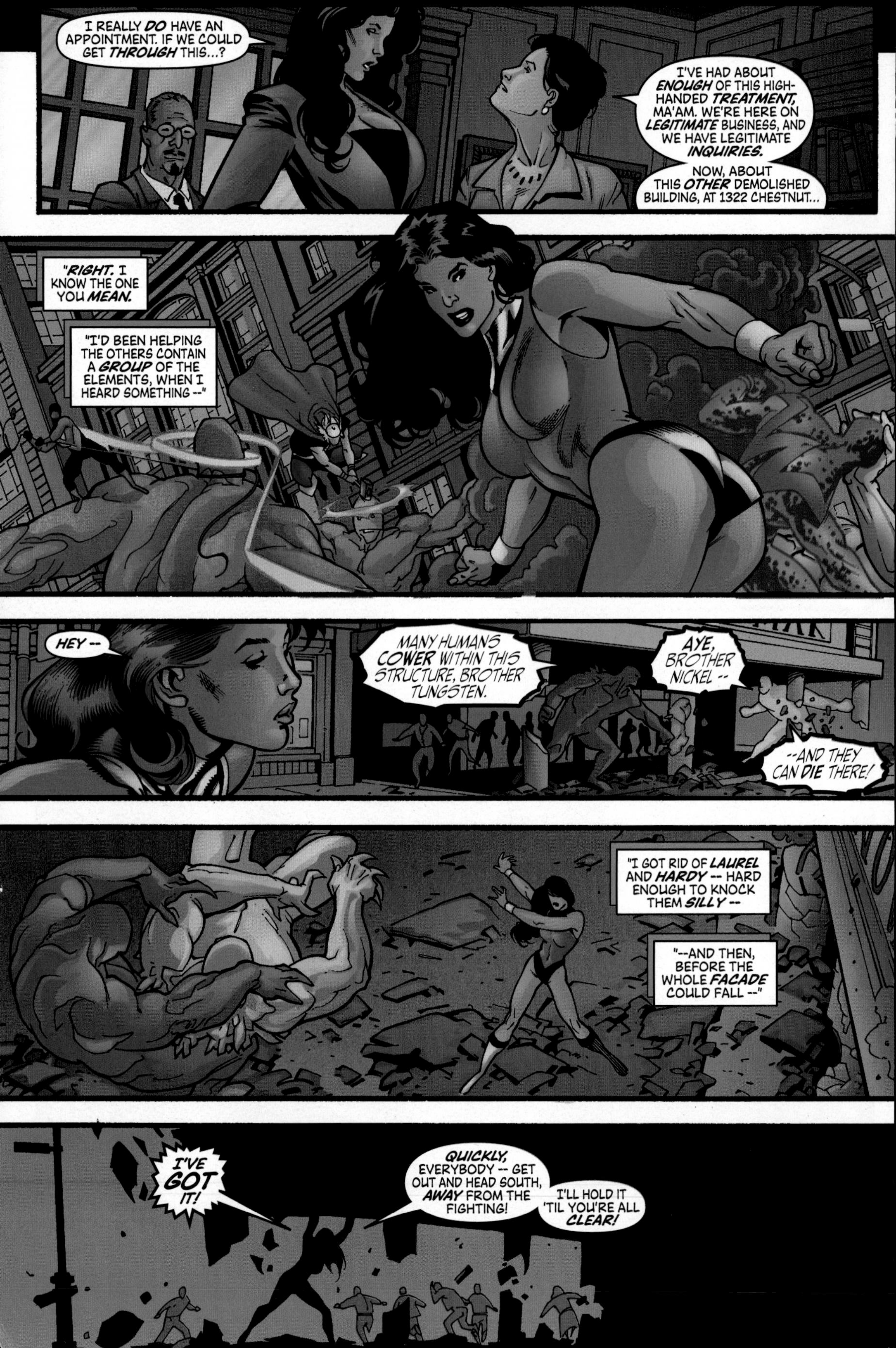

I REALLY DO HAVE AN APPOINTMENT. IF WE COULD GET THROUGH THIS...?
I'VE HAD ABOUT ENOUGH OF THIS HIGH-HANDED TREATMENT, MA'AM. WE'RE HERE ON LEGITIMATE BUSINESS, AND WE HAVE LEGITIMATE INQUIRIES.
NOW, ABOUT THIS OTHER DEMOLISHED BUILDING, AT 1322 CHESTNUT...
"RIGHT. I KNOW THE ONE YOU MEAN.
"I'D BEEN HELPING THE OTHERS CONTAIN A GROUP OF THE ELEMENTS, WHEN I HEARD SOMETHING --"
HEY --
MANY HUMANS COWER WITHIN THIS STRUCTURE, BROTHER TUNGSTEN.
AYE, BROTHER NICKEL --
--AND THEY CAN DIE THERE!
"I GOT RID OF LAUREL AND HARDY -- HARD ENOUGH TO KNOCK THEM SILLY --
"--AND THEN, BEFORE THE WHOLE FACADE COULD FALL --"
I'VE GOT IT!
QUICKLY, EVERYBODY -- GET OUT AND HEAD SOUTH, AWAY FROM THE FIGHTING!
I'LL HOLD IT 'TIL YOU'RE ALL CLEAR!

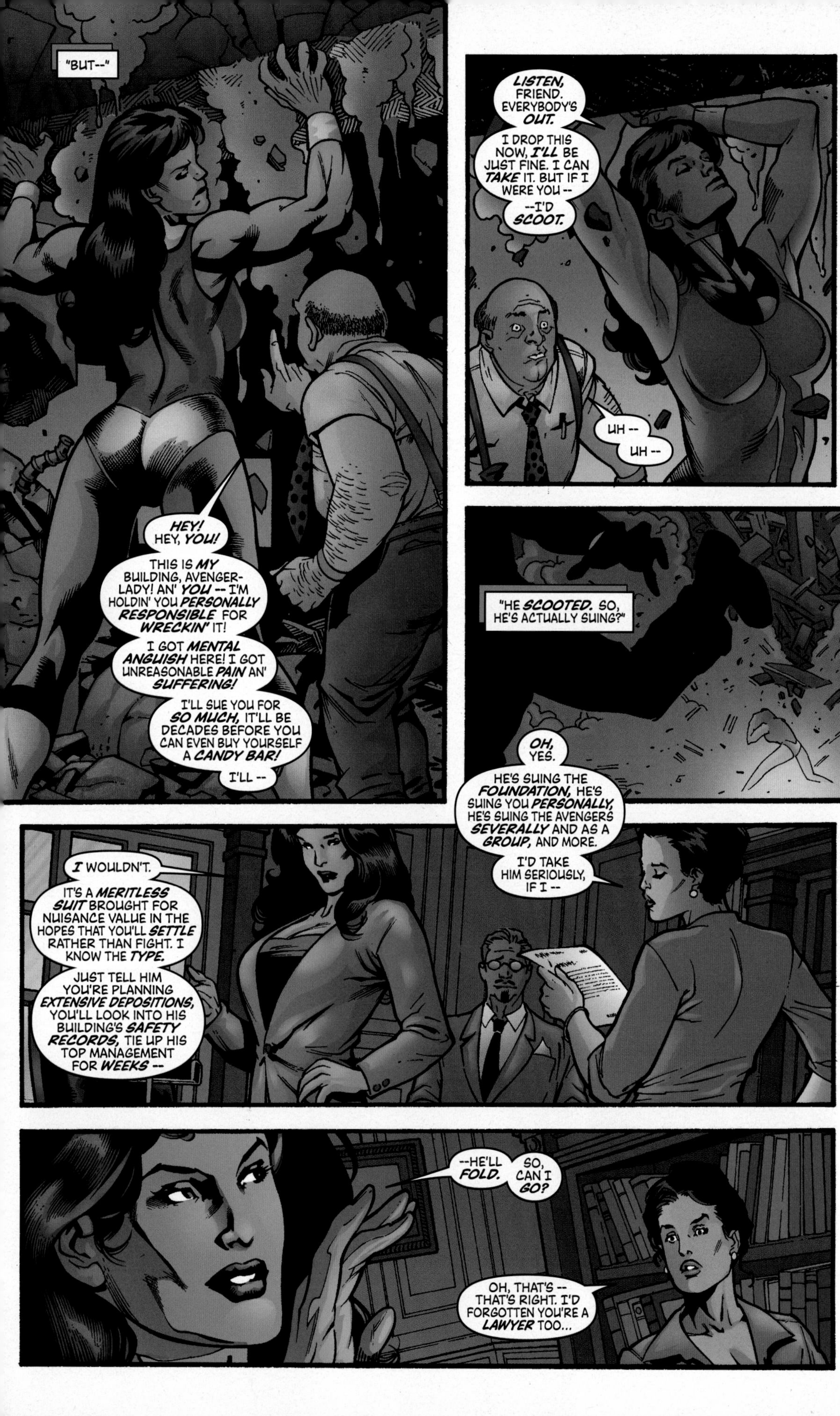
"BUT--"
HEY! HEY, YOU!
THIS IS MY BUILDING, AVENGER-LADY! AN' YOU -- I'M HOLDIN' YOU PERSONALLY RESPONSIBLE FOR WRECKIN' IT!
I GOT MENTAL ANGUISH HERE! I GOT UNREASONABLE PAIN AN' SUFFERING!
I'LL SUE YOU FOR SO MUCH, IT'LL BE DECADES BEFORE YOU CAN EVEN BUY YOURSELF A CANDY BAR!
I'LL --
LISTEN, FRIEND. EVERYBODY'S OUT.
I DROP THIS NOW, I'LL BE JUST FINE. I CAN TAKE IT. BUT IF I WERE YOU --
--I'D SCOOT.
UH --
UH --
"HE SCOOTED. SO, HE'S ACTUALLY SUING?"
OH, YES.
HE'S SUING THE FOUNDATION, HE'S SUING YOU PERSONALLY, HE'S SUING THE AVENGERS SEVERALLY AND AS A GROUP, AND MORE.
I'D TAKE HIM SERIOUSLY, IF I --
I WOULDN'T.
IT'S A MERITLESS SUIT BROUGHT FOR NUISANCE VALUE IN THE HOPES THAT YOU'LL SETTLE RATHER THAN FIGHT. I KNOW THE TYPE.
JUST TELL HIM YOU'RE PLANNING EXTENSIVE DEPOSITIONS, YOU'LL LOOK INTO HIS BUILDING'S SAFETY RECORDS, TIE UP HIS TOP MANAGEMENT FOR WEEKS --
--HE'LL FOLD.
SO, CAN I GO?
OH, THAT'S -- THAT'S RIGHT. I'D FORGOTTEN YOU'RE A LAWYER TOO...

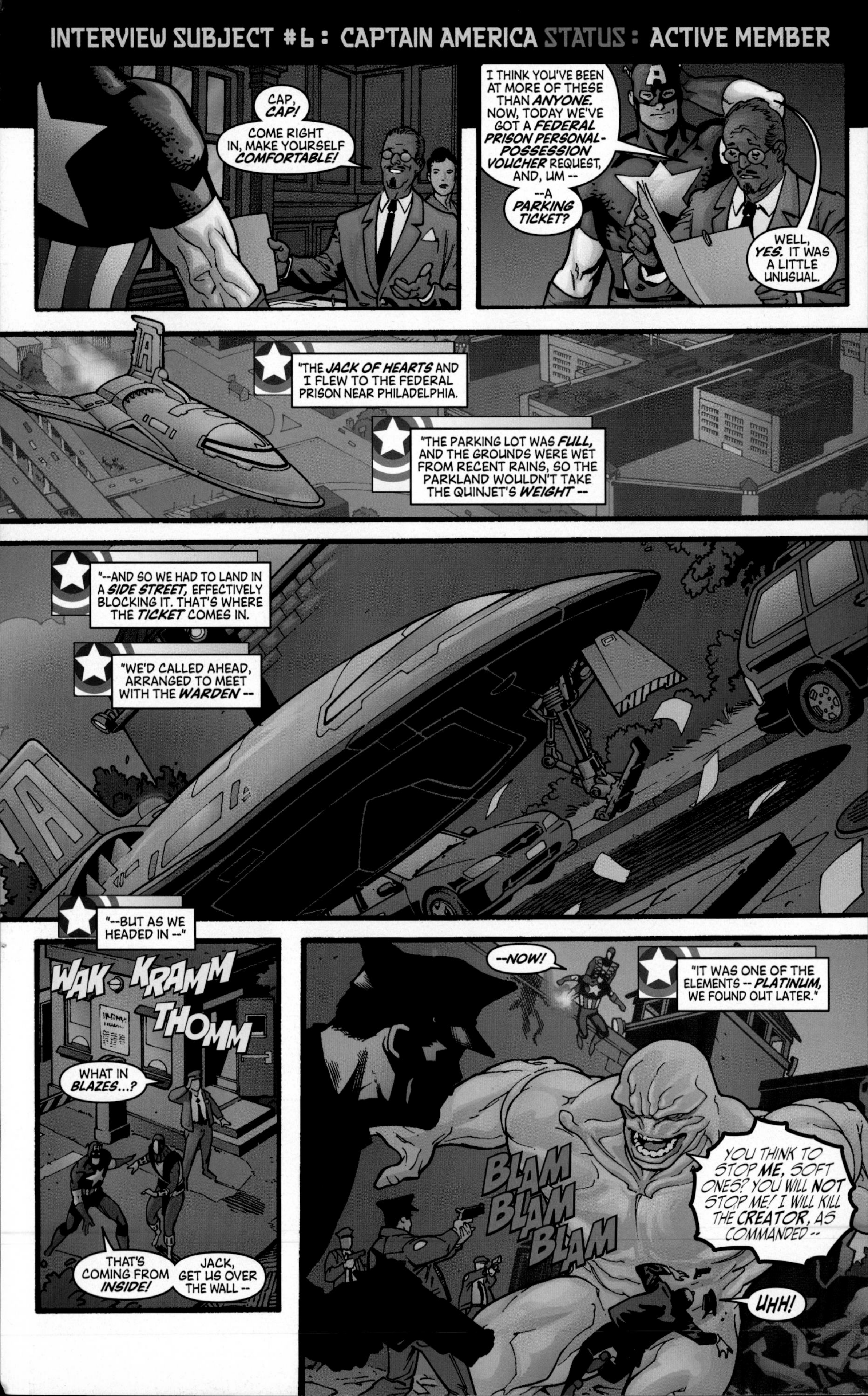
INTERVIEW SUBJECT #6 : CAPTAIN AMERICA STATUS : ACTIVE MEMBER
CAP, CAP!
COME RIGHT IN, MAKE YOURSELF COMFORTABLE!
I THINK YOU'VE BEEN AT MORE OF THESE THAN ANYONE. NOW, TODAY WE'VE GOT A FEDERAL PRISON PERSONAL-POSSESSION VOUCHER REQUEST, AND, UM --
--A PARKING TICKET?
WELL, YES. IT WAS A LITTLE UNUSUAL.
"THE JACK OF HEARTS AND I FLEW TO THE FEDERAL PRISON NEAR PHILADELPHIA.
"THE PARKING LOT WAS FULL, AND THE GROUNDS WERE WET FROM RECENT RAINS, SO THE PARKLAND WOULDN'T TAKE THE QUINJET'S WEIGHT --
"--AND SO WE HAD TO LAND IN A SIDE STREET, EFFECTIVELY BLOCKING IT. THAT'S WHERE THE TICKET COMES IN.
"WE'D CALLED AHEAD, ARRANGED TO MEET WITH THE WARDEN --
"--BUT AS WE HEADED IN --"
WAK KRAMM THOMM
WHAT IN BLAZES...?
THAT'S COMING FROM INSIDE!
JACK, GET US OVER THE WALL --
--NOW!
"IT WAS ONE OF THE ELEMENTS -- PLATINUM, WE FOUND OUT LATER."
BLAM BLAM BLAM
YOU THINK TO STOP ME, SOFT ONES? YOU WILL NOT STOP ME! I WILL KILL THE CREATOR, AS COMMANDED --
UHH!

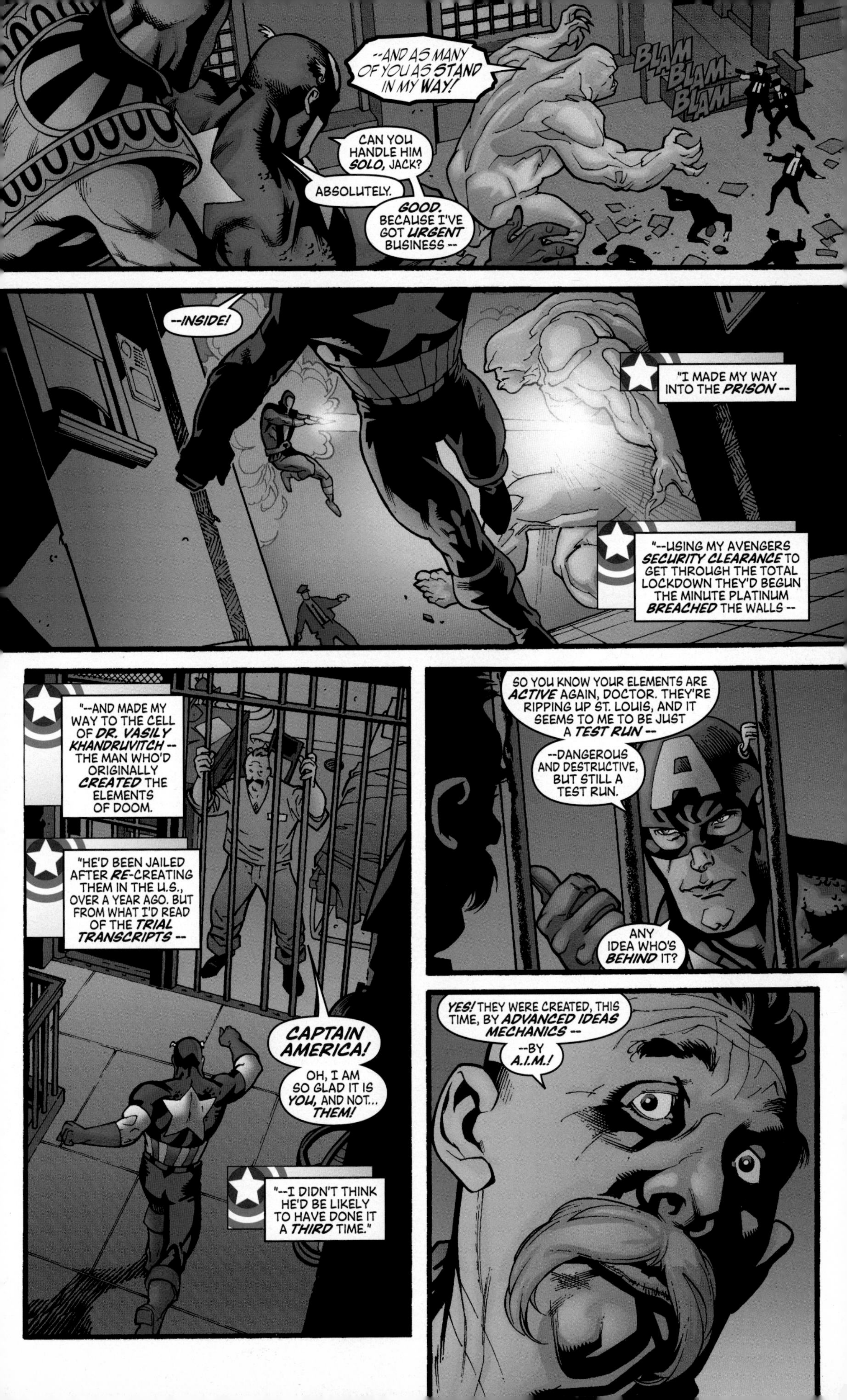
--AND AS MANY OF YOU AS STAND IN MY WAY!
BLAM BLAM BLAM
CAN YOU HANDLE HIM SOLO, JACK?
ABSOLUTELY.
GOOD. BECAUSE I'VE GOT URGENT BUSINESS --
--INSIDE!
"I MADE MY WAY INTO THE PRISON --
"--USING MY AVENGERS SECURITY CLEARANCE TO GET THROUGH THE TOTAL LOCKDOWN THEY'D BEGUN THE MINUTE PLATINUM BREACHED THE WALLS --
"--AND MADE MY WAY TO THE CELL OF DR. VASILY KHANDRUVITCH -- THE MAN WHO'D ORIGINALLY CREATED THE ELEMENTS OF DOOM.
"HE'D BEEN JAILED AFTER RE-CREATING THEM IN THE U.S., OVER A YEAR AGO. BUT FROM WHAT I'D READ OF THE TRIAL TRANSCRIPTS --
CAPTAIN AMERICA!
OH, I AM SO GLAD IT IS YOU, AND NOT... THEM!
"--I DIDN'T THINK HE'D BE LIKELY TO HAVE DONE IT A THIRD TIME."
SO YOU KNOW YOUR ELEMENTS ARE ACTIVE AGAIN, DOCTOR. THEY'RE RIPPING UP ST. LOUIS, AND IT SEEMS TO ME TO BE JUST A TEST RUN --
--DANGEROUS AND DESTRUCTIVE, BUT STILL A TEST RUN.
ANY IDEA WHO'S BEHIND IT?
YES! THEY WERE CREATED, THIS TIME, BY ADVANCED IDEAS MECHANICS --
--BY A.I.M.!

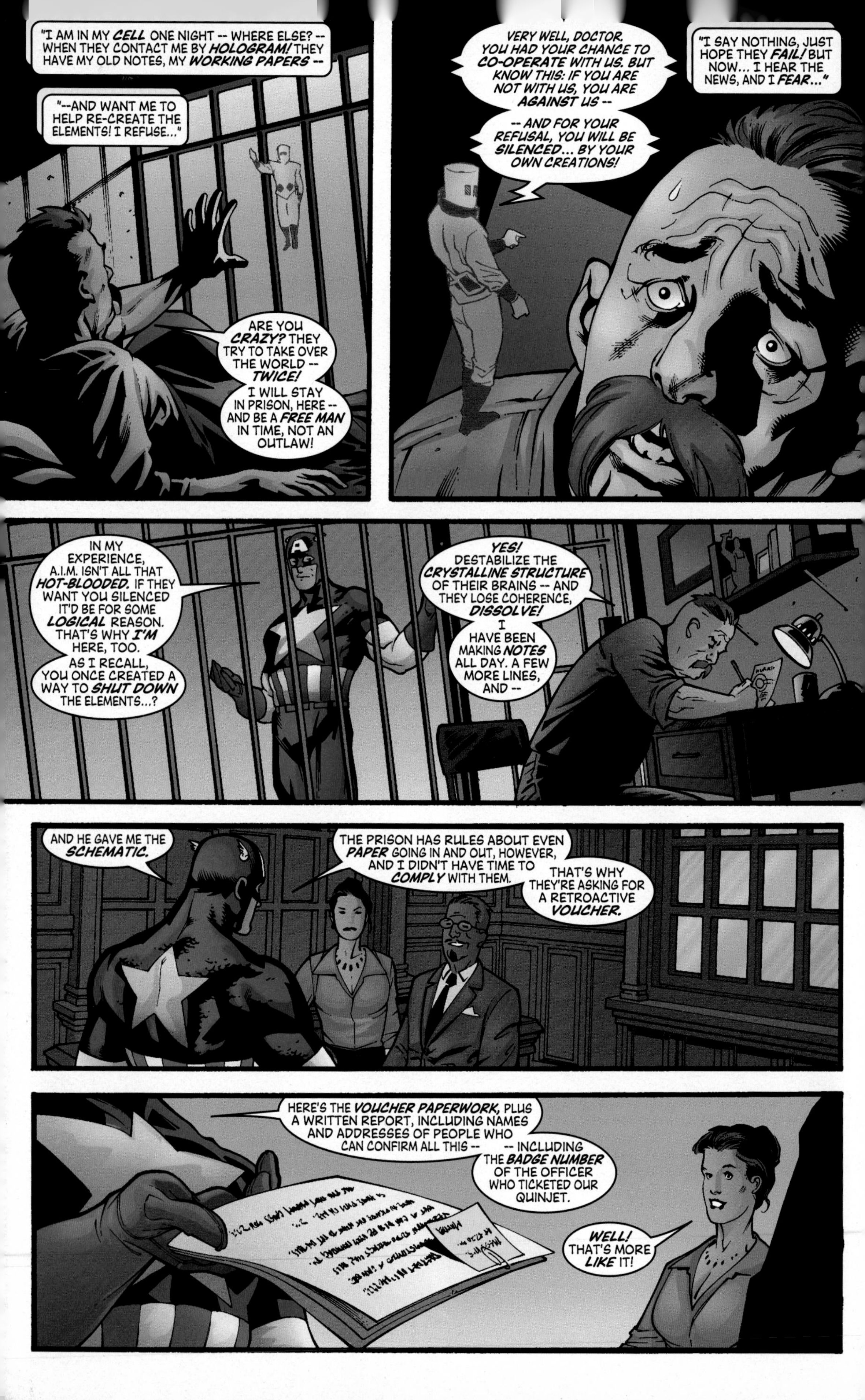

"I AM IN MY CELL ONE NIGHT -- WHERE ELSE? -- WHEN THEY CONTACT ME BY HOLOGRAM! THEY HAVE MY OLD NOTES, MY WORKING PAPERS --
"--AND WANT ME TO HELP RE-CREATE THE ELEMENTS! I REFUSE..."
ARE YOU CRAZY? THEY TRY TO TAKE OVER THE WORLD -- TWICE!
I WILL STAY IN PRISON, HERE -- AND BE A FREE MAN IN TIME, NOT AN OUTLAW!
VERY WELL, DOCTOR. YOU HAD YOUR CHANCE TO CO-OPERATE WITH US. BUT KNOW THIS: IF YOU ARE NOT WITH US, YOU ARE AGAINST US --
-- AND FOR YOUR REFUSAL, YOU WILL BE SILENCED... BY YOUR OWN CREATIONS!
"I SAY NOTHING, JUST HOPE THEY FAIL! BUT NOW... I HEAR THE NEWS, AND I FEAR..."
IN MY EXPERIENCE, A.I.M. ISN'T ALL THAT HOT-BLOODED. IF THEY WANT YOU SILENCED IT'D BE FOR SOME LOGICAL REASON. THAT'S WHY I'M HERE, TOO.
AS I RECALL, YOU ONCE CREATED A WAY TO SHUT DOWN THE ELEMENTS...?
YES! DESTABILIZE THE CRYSTALLINE STRUCTURE OF THEIR BRAINS -- AND THEY LOSE COHERENCE, DISSOLVE!
I HAVE BEEN MAKING NOTES ALL DAY. A FEW MORE LINES, AND --
AND HE GAVE ME THE SCHEMATIC.
THE PRISON HAS RULES ABOUT EVEN PAPER GOING IN AND OUT, HOWEVER, AND I DIDN'T HAVE TIME TO COMPLY WITH THEM.
THAT'S WHY THEY'RE ASKING FOR A RETROACTIVE VOUCHER.
HERE'S THE VOUCHER PAPERWORK, PLUS A WRITTEN REPORT, INCLUDING NAMES AND ADDRESSES OF PEOPLE WHO CAN CONFIRM ALL THIS --
-- INCLUDING THE BADGE NUMBER OF THE OFFICER WHO TICKETED OUR QUINJET.
WELL! THAT'S MORE LIKE IT!

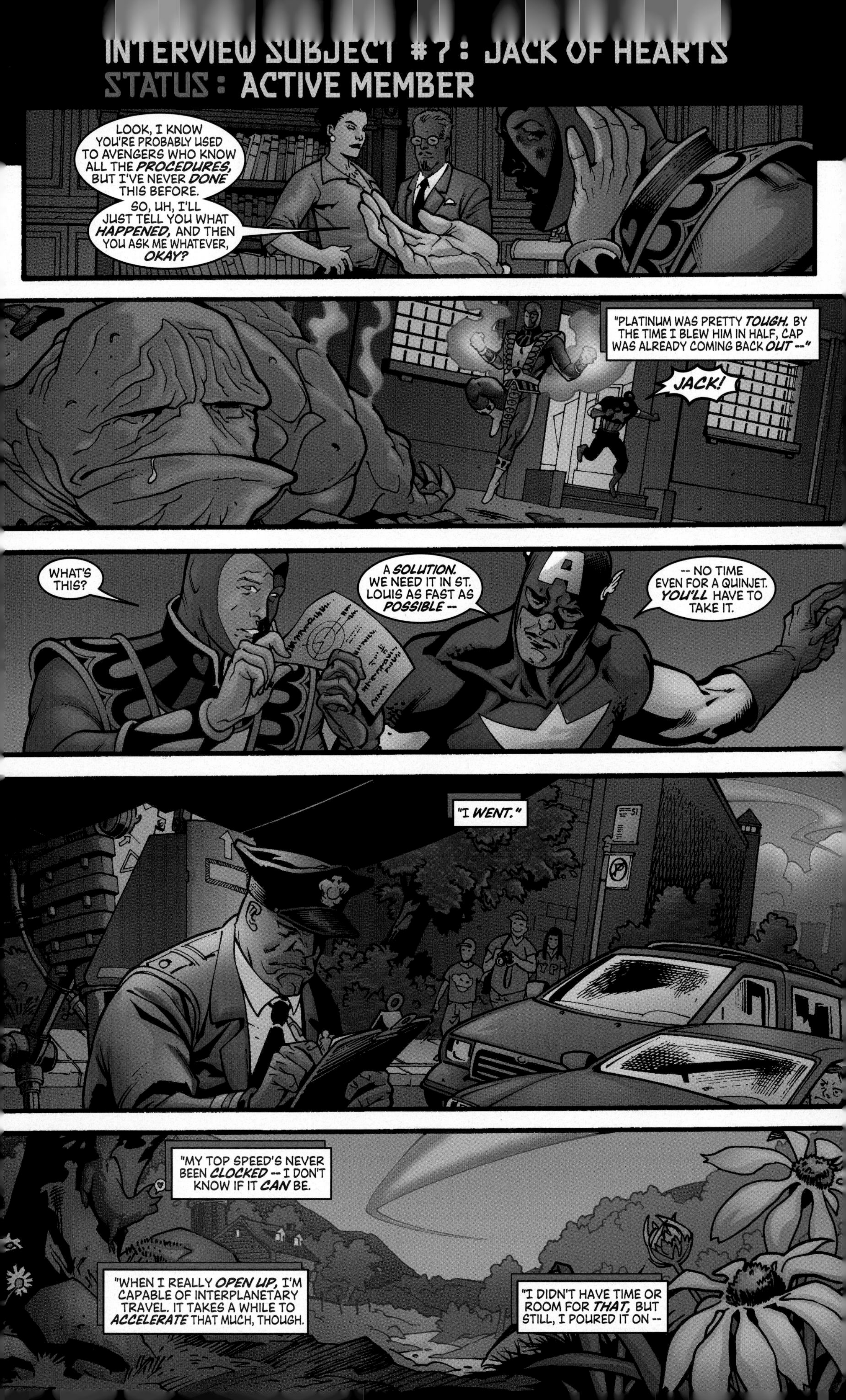
INTERVIEW SUBJECT #7 : JACK OF HEARTS
STATUS : ACTIVE MEMBER
LOOK, I KNOW YOU'RE PROBABLY USED TO AVENGERS WHO KNOW ALL THE PROCEDURES, BUT I'VE NEVER DONE THIS BEFORE.
SO, UH, I'LL JUST TELL YOU WHAT HAPPENED, AND THEN YOU ASK ME WHATEVER, OKAY?
"PLATINUM WAS PRETTY TOUGH. BY THE TIME I BLEW HIM IN HALF, CAP WAS ALREADY COMING BACK OUT --"
JACK!
WHAT'S THIS?
A SOLUTION. WE NEED IT IN ST. LOUIS AS FAST AS POSSIBLE --
-- NO TIME EVEN FOR A QUINJET. YOU'LL HAVE TO TAKE IT.
"I WENT."
"MY TOP SPEED'S NEVER BEEN CLOCKED -- I DON'T KNOW IF IT CAN BE.
"WHEN I REALLY OPEN UP, I'M CAPABLE OF INTERPLANETARY TRAVEL. IT TAKES A WHILE TO ACCELERATE THAT MUCH, THOUGH.
"I DIDN'T HAVE TIME OR ROOM FOR THAT, BUT STILL, I POURED IT ON --

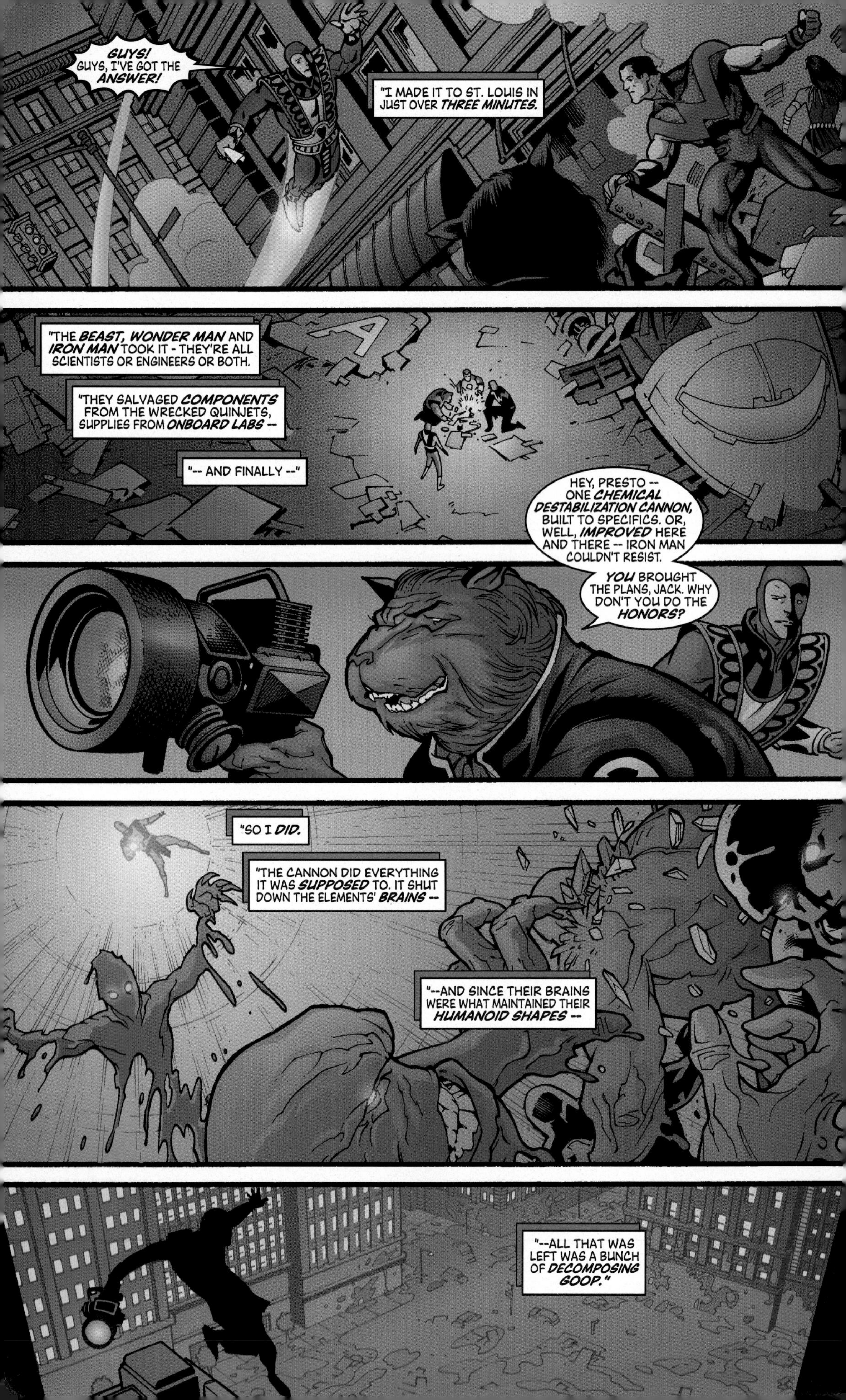
GUYS!
GUYS, I'VE GOT THE ANSWER!
"I MADE IT TO ST. LOUIS IN JUST OVER THREE MINUTES.
"THE BEAST, WONDER MAN AND IRON MAN TOOK IT - THEY'RE ALL SCIENTISTS OR ENGINEERS OR BOTH.
"THEY SALVAGED COMPONENTS FROM THE WRECKED QUINJETS, SUPPLIES FROM ONBOARD LABS --
"-- AND FINALLY --"
HEY, PRESTO -- ONE CHEMICAL DESTABILIZATION CANNON, BUILT TO SPECIFICS. OR, WELL, IMPROVED HERE AND THERE -- IRON MAN COULDN'T RESIST.
YOU BROUGHT THE PLANS, JACK. WHY DON'T YOU DO THE HONORS?
"SO I DID.
"THE CANNON DID EVERYTHING IT WAS SUPPOSED TO. IT SHUT DOWN THE ELEMENTS' BRAINS --
"--AND SINCE THEIR BRAINS WERE WHAT MAINTAINED THEIR HUMANOID SHAPES --
"--ALL THAT WAS LEFT WAS A BUNCH OF DECOMPOSING GOOP."

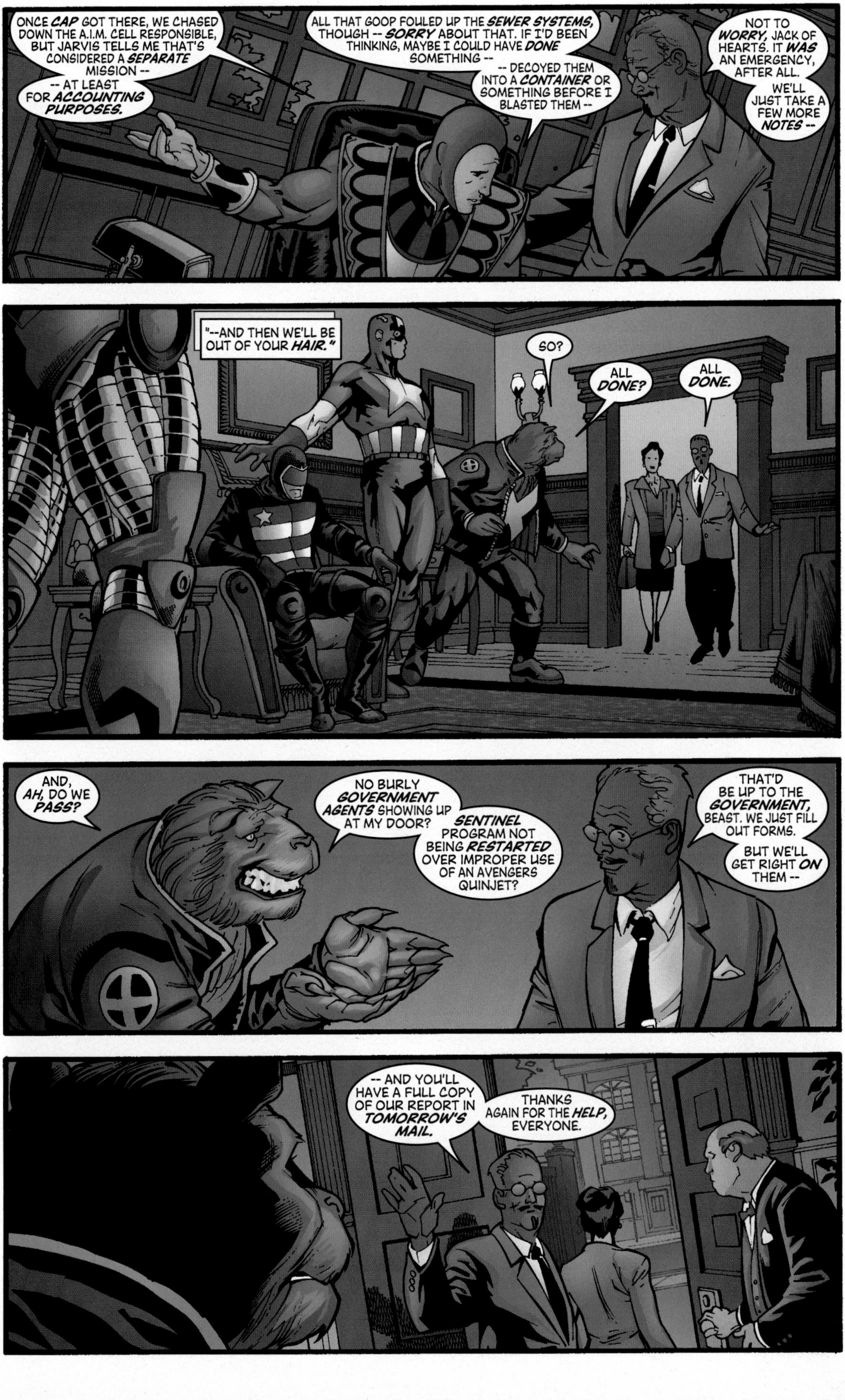
ONCE CAP GOT THERE, WE CHASED DOWN THE A.I.M. CELL RESPONSIBLE, BUT JARVIS TELLS ME THAT'S CONSIDERED A SEPARATE MISSION --
-- AT LEAST FOR ACCOUNTING PURPOSES.
ALL THAT GOOP FOULED UP THE SEWER SYSTEMS, THOUGH -- SORRY ABOUT THAT. IF I'D BEEN THINKING, MAYBE I COULD HAVE DONE SOMETHING --
-- DECOYED THEM INTO A CONTAINER OR SOMETHING BEFORE I BLASTED THEM --
NOT TO WORRY, JACK OF HEARTS. IT WAS AN EMERGENCY, AFTER ALL.
WE'LL JUST TAKE A FEW MORE NOTES --
"--AND THEN WE'LL BE OUT OF YOUR HAIR."
SO?
ALL DONE?
ALL DONE.
AND, AH, DO WE PASS?
NO BURLY GOVERNMENT AGENTS SHOWING UP AT MY DOOR?
SENTINEL PROGRAM NOT BEING RESTARTED OVER IMPROPER USE OF AN AVENGERS QUINJET?
THAT'D BE UP TO THE GOVERNMENT, BEAST. WE JUST FILL OUT FORMS.
BUT WE'LL GET RIGHT ON THEM --
-- AND YOU'LL HAVE A FULL COPY OF OUR REPORT IN TOMORROW'S MAIL.
THANKS AGAIN FOR THE HELP, EVERYONE.

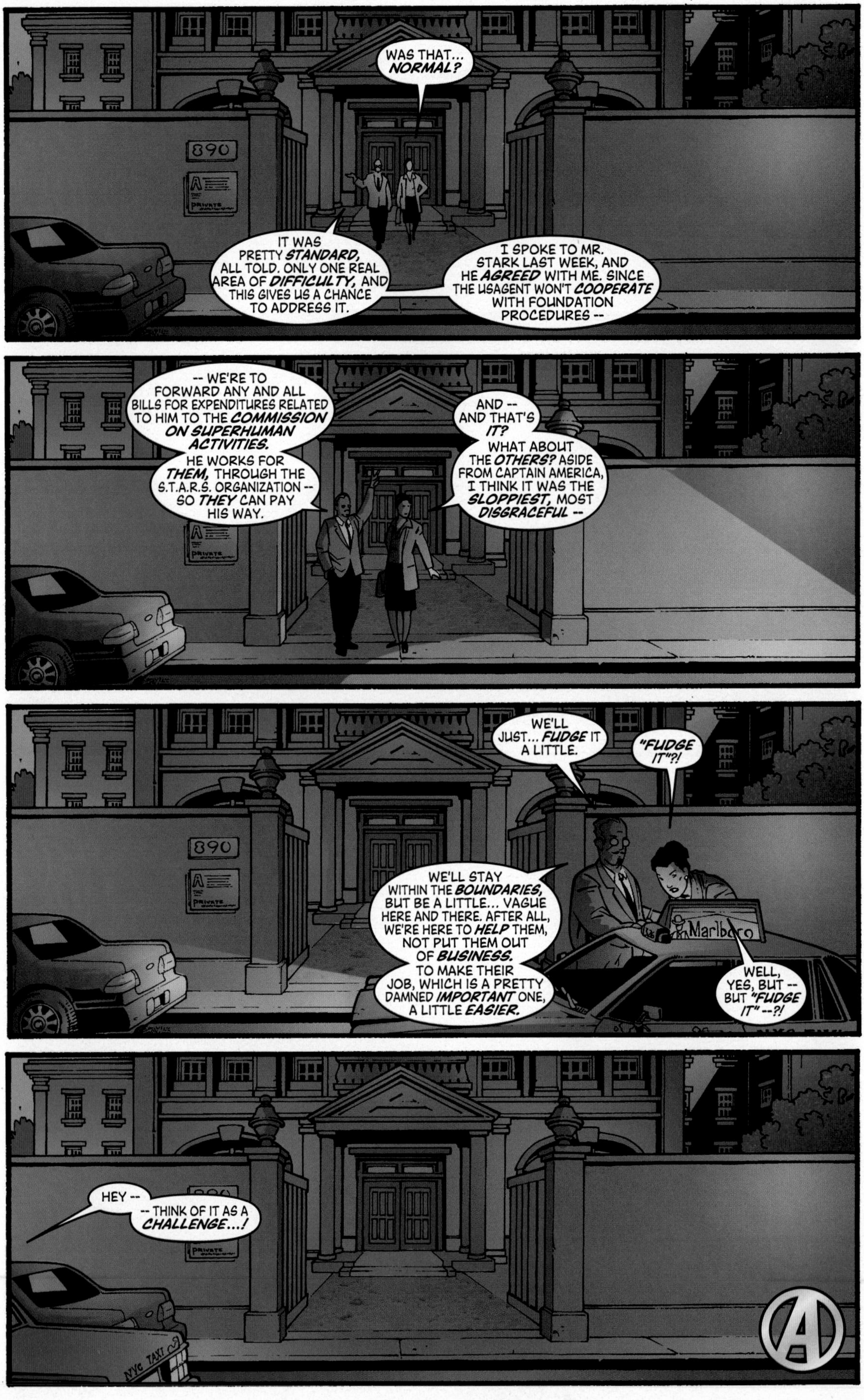
WAS THAT... NORMAL?
IT WAS PRETTY STANDARD, ALL TOLD. ONLY ONE REAL AREA OF DIFFICULTY, AND THIS GIVES US A CHANCE TO ADDRESS IT.
I SPOKE TO MR. STARK LAST WEEK, AND HE AGREED WITH ME. SINCE THE USAGENT WON'T COOPERATE WITH FOUNDATION PROCEDURES --
890
PRIVATE
-- WE'RE TO FORWARD ANY AND ALL BILLS FOR EXPENDITURES RELATED TO HIM TO THE COMMISSION ON SUPERHUMAN ACTIVITIES.
HE WORKS FOR THEM, THROUGH THE S.T.A.R.S. ORGANIZATION -- SO THEY CAN PAY HIS WAY.
AND -- AND THAT'S IT?
WHAT ABOUT THE OTHERS? ASIDE FROM CAPTAIN AMERICA, I THINK IT WAS THE SLOPPIEST, MOST DISGRACEFUL --
WE'LL JUST... FUDGE IT A LITTLE.
"FUDGE IT"?!
WE'LL STAY WITHIN THE BOUNDARIES, BUT BE A LITTLE... VAGUE HERE AND THERE. AFTER ALL, WE'RE HERE TO HELP THEM, NOT PUT THEM OUT OF BUSINESS.
TO MAKE THEIR JOB, WHICH IS A PRETTY DAMNED IMPORTANT ONE, A LITTLE EASIER.
Marlboro
WELL, YES, BUT -- BUT "FUDGE IT" --?!
HEY --
-- THINK OF IT AS A CHALLENGE...!
NYC TAXI

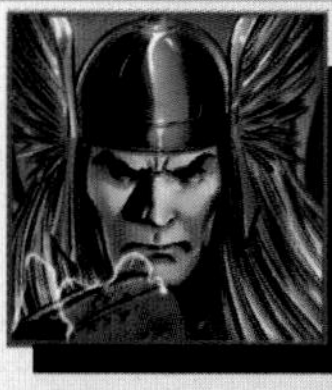

THOR
(Thor Odinson)
Founder, Avengers Vol. 1 #1 (1963)

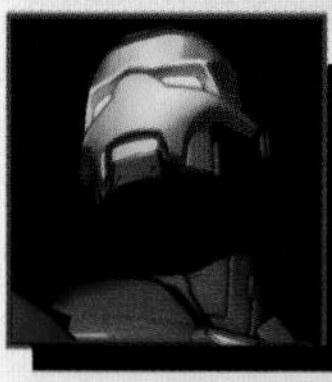

IRON MAN
(Anthony Edward Stark)
Founder, Avengers Vol. 1 #1 (1963)

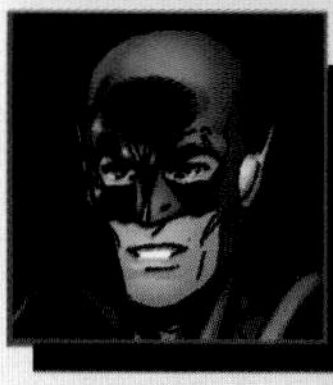

ANT-MAN
(Henry J. Pym)
Founder, Avengers Vol. 1 #1 (1963); as Giant-Man, active Avengers Vol. 1 #2 (1963); as Goliath, active Avengers Vol. 1 #28 (1966); as Yellowjacket, active Avengers Vol. 1 #63 (1969); as Doctor Pym, active West Coast Avengers #21 (1987); current alias: Yellowjacket

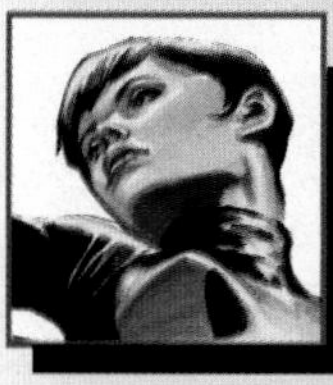

WASP
(Janet Van Dyne)
Founder, Avengers Vol. 1 #1 (1963)

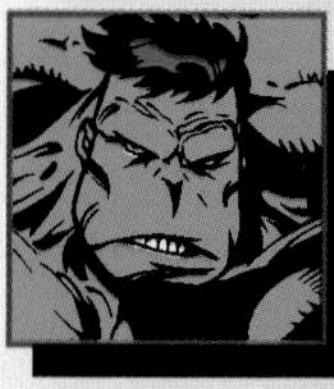

HULK
(Robert Bruce Banner)
Founder, Avengers Vol. 1 #1 (1963); current status: resigned Avengers Vol. 1 #2 (1963)

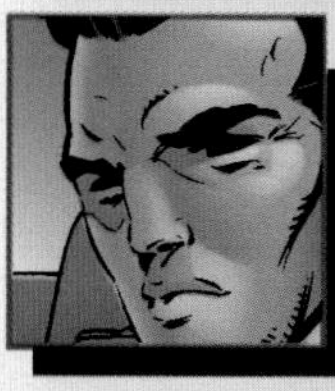

RICK JONES
(Richard Milhouse Jones)
Honorary member, active Avengers Vol. 1 #1 (1963)

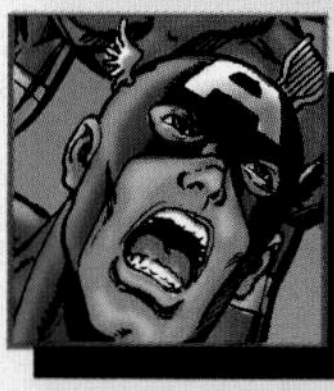

CAPTAIN AMERICA
(Steven Rogers)
Joined Avengers Vol. 1 #4 (1964); granted retroactive founder status prior to Avengers Vol. 1 #92 (1971); as the Captain, active Avengers Vol. 1 #300 (1989); current alias: Captain America

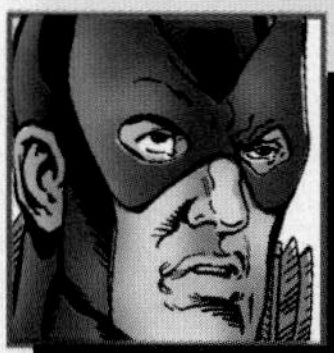

HAWKEYE
(Clinton Francis Barton)
Joined Avengers Vol. 1 #16 (1965); as Goliath, active Avengers Vol. 1 #63 (1969); current alias: Hawkeye

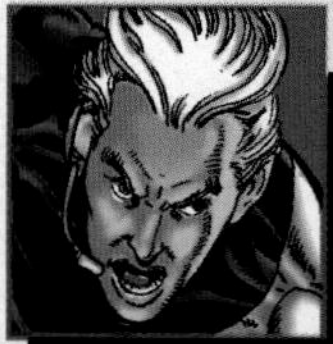

QUICKSILVER
(Pietro Maximoff)
Joined Avengers Vol. 1 #16 (1965)

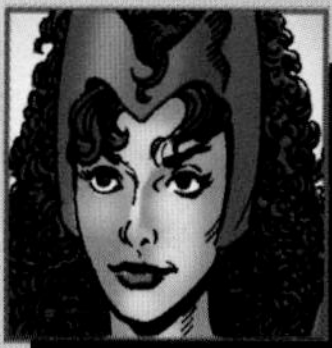

SCARLET WITCH
(Wanda Maximoff)
Joined Avengers Vol. 1 #16 (1965)

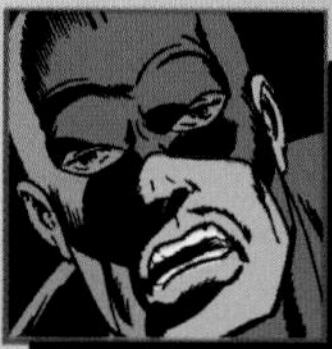

SWORDSMAN
(Jacques Duquesne)
Joined Avengers Vol. 1 #19 (1965); current status: deceased

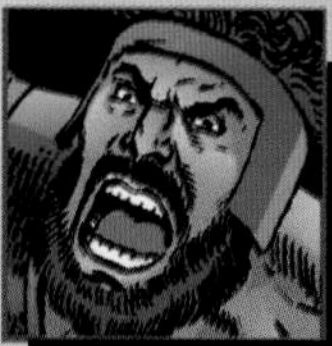

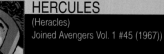

HERCULES
(Heracles)
Joined Avengers Vol. 1 #45 (1967))

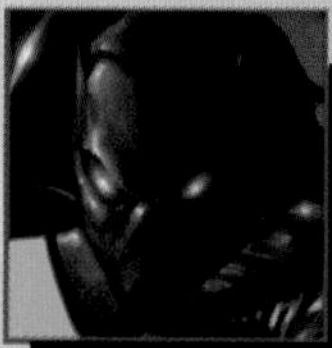

BLACK PANTHER
(T'Challa)
Joined Avengers Vol. 1 #52 (1968)

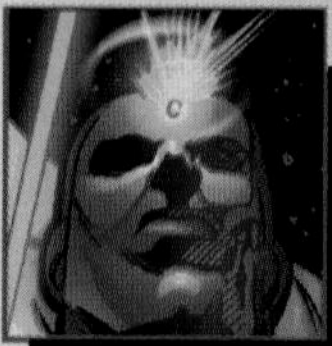

VISION
(alias Victor Shade)
Joined Avengers Vol. 1 #58 (1968)

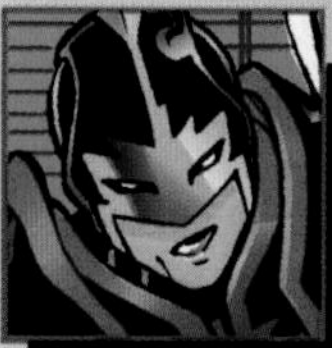

BLACK KNIGHT
(Dane Whitman)
Joined Avengers Vol. 1 #71 (1969)

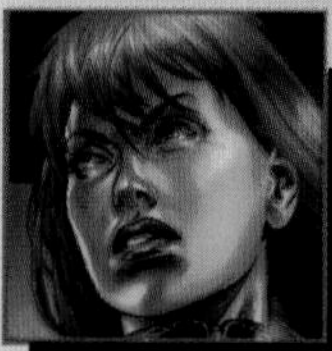

BLACK WIDOW
(Natalia Alianovna Romanova, a.k.a. Natasha Romanoff)
Joined Avengers Vol. 1 #111 (1973)

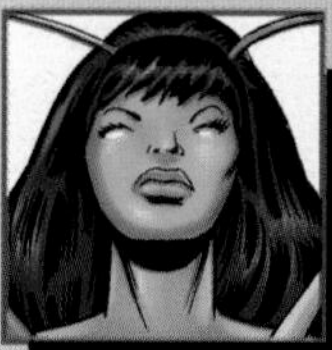

MANTIS
(Brandt, first name unknown)
Joined Giant-Size Avengers #4 (1975)

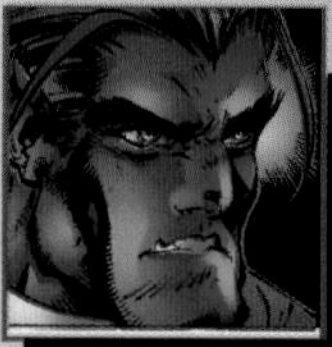

BEAST
(Henry P. McCoy)
Became probationary member in Avengers Vol. 1 #137 (1975); full member in Avengers Vol. 1 #151 (1976)

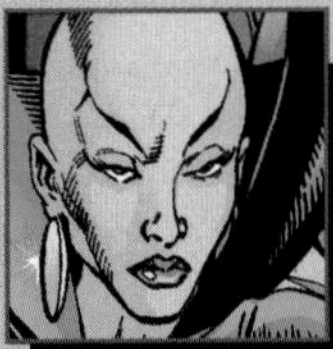

MOONDRAGON
(Heather Douglas)
Became probationary member in Avengers Vol. 1 #137 (1975); reserve member in Avengers Vol. 1 #151 (1976)

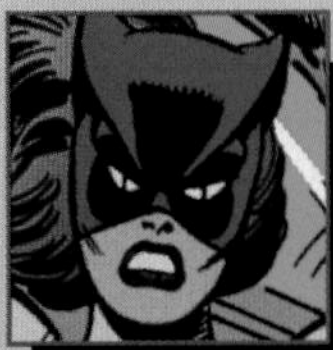

HELLCAT
(Patsy Walker)
Became probationary member in Avengers Vol. 1 #148 (1976); reserve member in Avengers Vol. 1 #151 (1976)

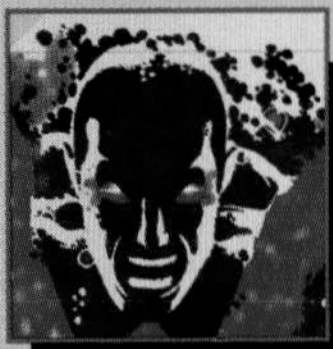

WONDER MAN
(Simon Williams)
Became provisional member in Avengers Vol. 1 #158 (1977); became full member in Avengers Vol. 1 #182 (1979)

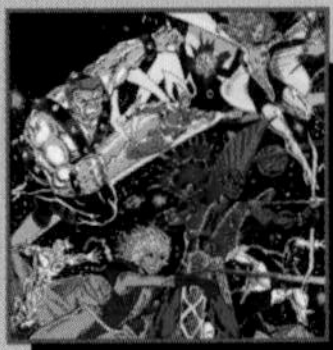

GUARDIANS OF THE GALAXY
(Yondu Udonta, Martinex T'Naga, Charlie-27, Nicholette "Nikki" Gold, Starhawk/Stakar and Ogord, and Vance Astro of an alternate future reality) Honorary members, active Avengers Vol. 1 #168 (1978)

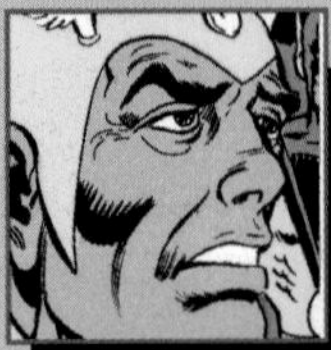

WHIZZER
(Robert L. Frank Sr.)
Honorary member, active Avengers Vol. 1 #173 (1978); current status: deceased

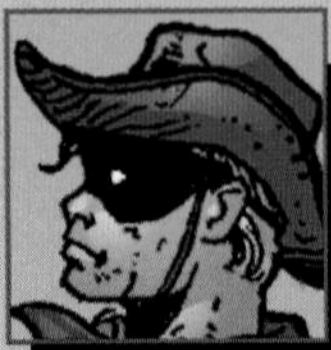

TWO-GUN KID
(Matthew Liebowitz)
Reserve member, active Avengers Vol. 1 #174 (1978); current status: deceased

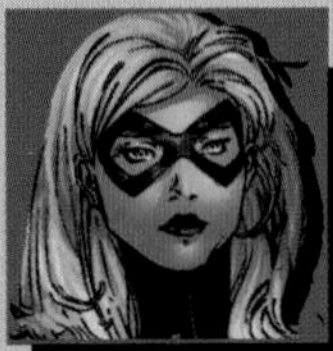

MS. MARVEL
(Carol Susan Jane Danvers)
Joined Avengers Vol. 1 #183 (1979); as Warbird, active Avengers Vol. 3 #4 (1998); current alias: Warbird

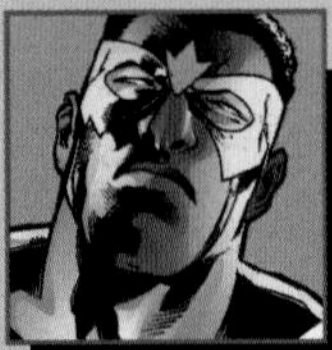

FALCON
(Samuel Thomas Wilson)
Joined Avengers Vol. 1 #184 (1979)

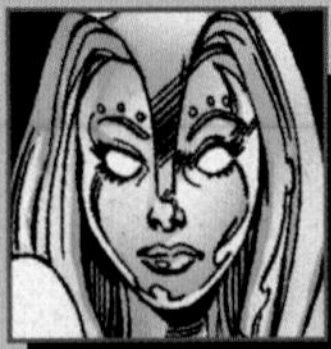

JOCASTA
Became probationary member in Avengers Vol. 1 #197 (1980); never became full member; was posthumously granted honorary status after her seeming death in Marvel Two-in-One #93 (1982)

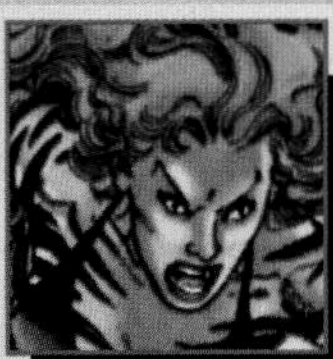

TIGRA
(Greer Grant Nelson)
Joined Avengers Vol. 1 #211 (1981)

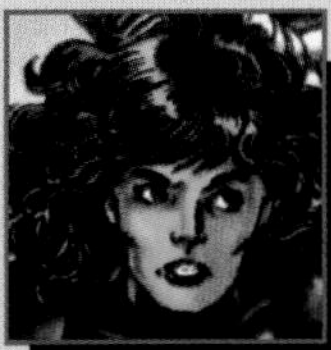

SHE-HULK
(Jennifer Walters)
Joined Avengers Vol. 1 #221 (1982)

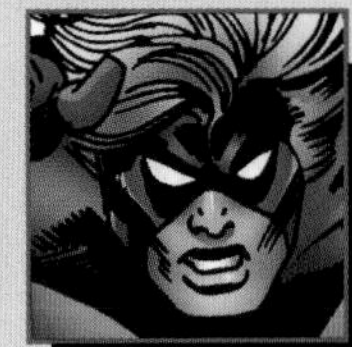

CAPTAIN MARVEL
(Mar-Vell)
Posthumously awarded honorary membership (1983)

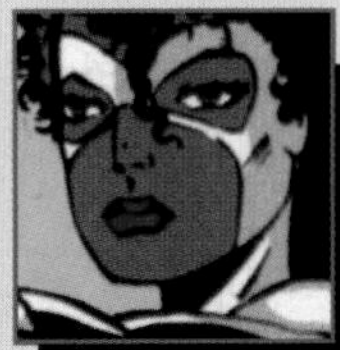

CAPTAIN MARVEL
(Monica Rambeau)
Became probationary member in Avengers Vol. 1 #227 (1983); full member in Avengers Vol. 1 #231 (1983); as Photon, active Avengers Unplugged #5 (1996)

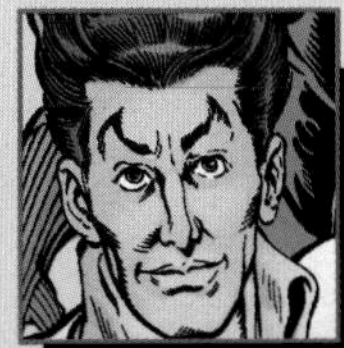

STARFOX
(Eros)
Became probationary member in Avengers Vol. 1 #232 (1983); full member in Avengers Vol. 1 #243 (1984)

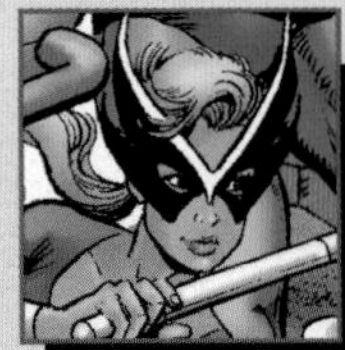

MOCKINGBIRD
(Barbara Morse Barton)
Joined West Coast Avengers Vol. 1 #1 (1984); current status: deceased

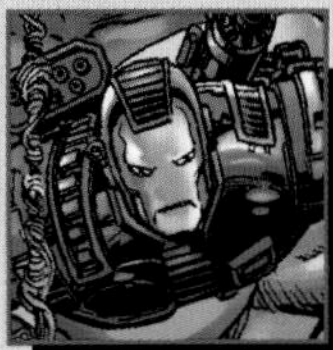

IRON MAN
(James R. Rhodes)
Joined West Coast Avengers Vol. 1 #1 (1984); as War Machine, active Avengers West Coast #94 (1993); current status: retired

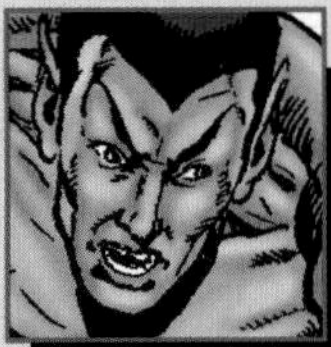

SUB-MARINER
(Namor McKenzie)
Joined Avengers Vol .1 #262 (1985)

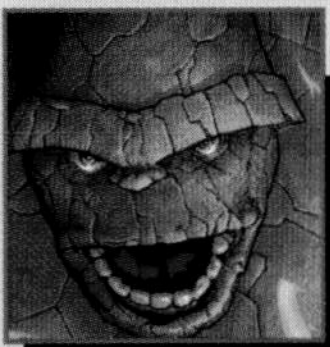

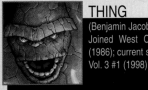

THING
(Benjamin Jacob Grimm)
Joined West Coast Avengers Vol. 2 #9 (1986); current status: resigned in Avengers Vol. 3 #1 (1998)

DOCTOR DRUID
(Anthony Ludgate Druid)
Joined Avengers Vol. 1 #278 (1987); current status: deceased

MOON KNIGHT
(Marc Spector)
Joined West Coast Avengers Vol. 2 #21 (1987); current status: resigned in Moon Knight Vol. 3 #50 (1993)

MARRINA
(Marrina Smallwood)
Honorary member, active Avengers Vol. 1 #282 (1987); current status: believed deceased

YELLOWJACKET
(Rita DeMara)
Honorary member, active Avengers Annual #17 (1989); current status: deceased

DEMOLITION-MAN
(Dennis Dunphy)
Joined Captain America Vol. 1 #349 (1989)

GILGAMESH
Joined Avengers Vol. 1 #300 (1989); current status: deceased

MISTER FANTASTIC
(Reed Richards)
Joined Avengers Vol. 1 #300 (1989); current status: resigned in Avengers Vol. 3 #1 (1998)

INVISIBLE WOMAN
(Susan Storm Richards)
Joined Avengers Vol. 1 #300 (1989); current status: resigned in Avengers Vol. 3 #1 (1998)

FIREBIRD
(Bonita Juarez)
Joined prior to Avengers Vol. 1 #305 (1989)

U.S.AGENT
(John F. Walker)
Joined Avengers West Coast #44 (1989))

QUASAR
(Wendell Elvis Vaughn)
Joined Avengers Annual #18 (1989)

HUMAN TORCH
(alias Jim Hammond)
Joined Avengers West Coast #50 (1989); current status: retired

SERSI
(Circe)
Joined Avengers Vol. 1 #314 (1990))

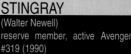

STINGRAY
(Walter Newell)
reserve member, active Avengers Vol. 1 #319 (1990)

RAGE
(Elvin Haliday)
Probationary member, Avengers Vol. 1 #329 (1991); never became full member; current status: removed from roster because of age

SANDMAN
(William Baker)
Probationary member, Avengers Vol. 1 #329 (1991); never became full member; current status: former member, returned to life of crime in Amazing Spider-Man Vol. 2 #4 (1999)

SPIDER-MAN
(Peter Benjamin Parker)
Reserve member, active Avengers Vol. 1 #316 (1990); current status: resigned prior to Peter Parker: Spider-Man #11 (1999)

LIVING LIGHTNING
(Miguel Santos)
Joined Avengers West Coast #74 (1992)

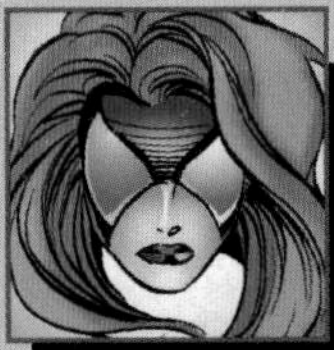

SPIDER-WOMAN

(Julia Carpenter)
Joined Avengers West Coast #74 (1992); current status: retired

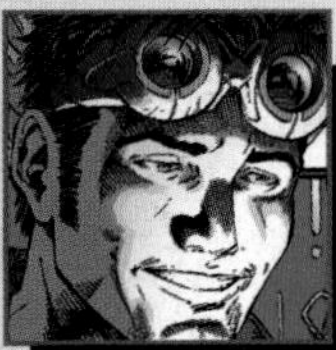

IRON MAN

(Teenage Anthony Edward Stark of an alternate reality)
Joined Avengers: Timeslide (1996); current status: merged with mainstream Tony Stark

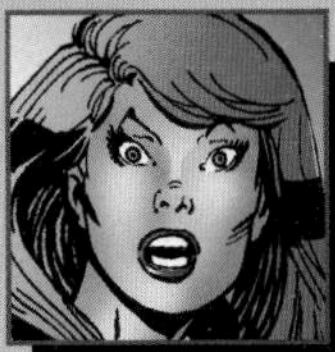

CRYSTAL

(Crystal Amaquelin Maximoff)
Joined Avengers Vol. 1 #343 (1992)

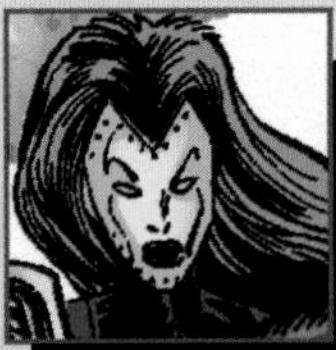

MASQUE

(Guilietta Nefaria bio-duplicate)
Honorary member, active Avengers Vol. 1 #397 (1996); current status: deceased

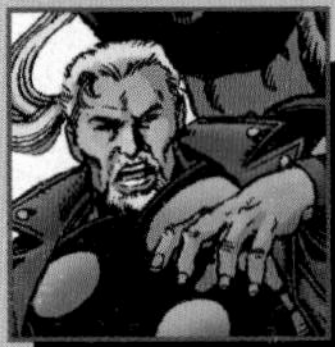

THOR

(Eric Kevin Masterson)
Joined Avengers Vol. 1 #343 (1992); as Thunderstrike, active Avengers Vol. 1 #374 (1995); current status: deceased

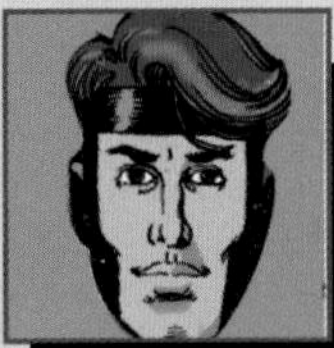

JUSTICE

(Vance Astrovik)
Reserve member in Avengers Vol. 3 #4 (1998); became active member Avengers Vol. 3 #7 (1998)

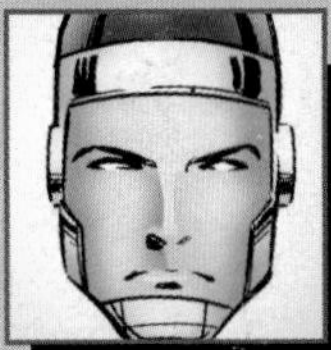

MACHINE MAN

(X-51)
Reserve member, active Avengers West Coast #83 (1992); current status: former member, removed from roster in X-51 #4 (1999)

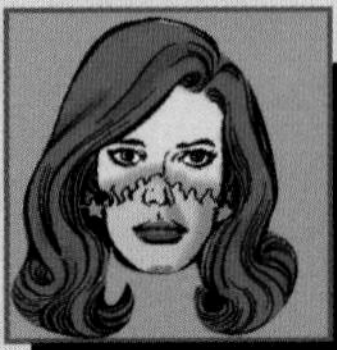

FIRESTAR

(Angelica Jones)
Reserve member in Avengers Vol. 3 #4 (1998); became active member Avengers Vol. 3 #7 (1998)

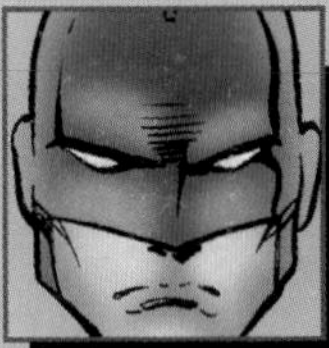

SWORDSMAN

(Phillip Jarvert)
Honorary member, active Avengers Vol. 1 #357 (1992)

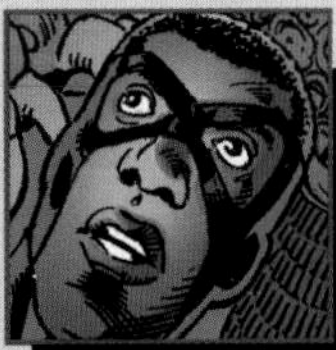

TRIATHLON

(Delroy Garrett Jr.)
Joined Avengers Vol. 3 #27 (1999)

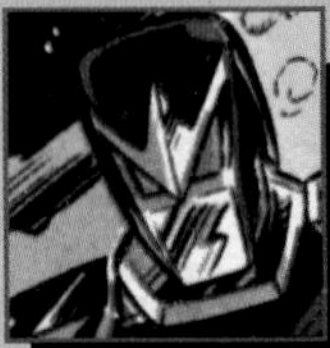

DARKHAWK

(Christopher Powell)
Joined Avengers West Coast #94 (1993)

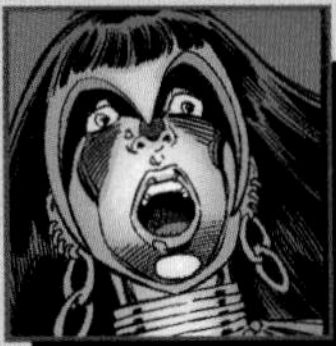

SILVERCLAW

(Maria de Guadalupe Santiago)
Became reserve member in Avengers Vol. 3 #30 (2000); never became full member

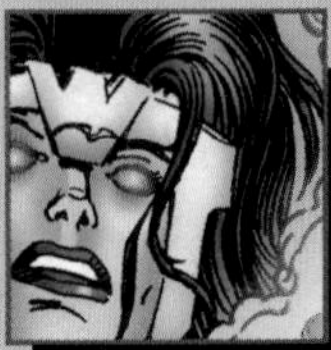

MAGDALENE

Honorary member, active Avengers Vol. 1 #363 (1993)

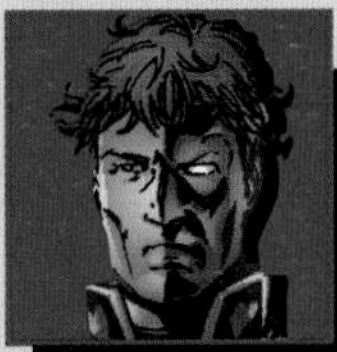

JACK OF HEARTS

(Jonathan Hart)
Joined Avengers Vol. 3 #43 (2001); current status: deceased

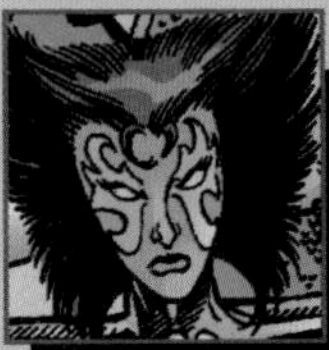

DEATHCRY

Became probationary member in Avengers Vol. 1 #364 (1993); never became full member; became honorary member in Avengers Vol. 1 #399 (1996)

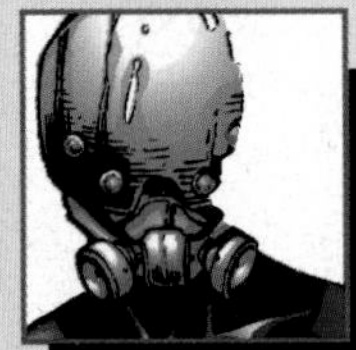

ANT-MAN

(Scott Edward Harris Lang)
Joined Avengers Vol. 3 #62 (2003)

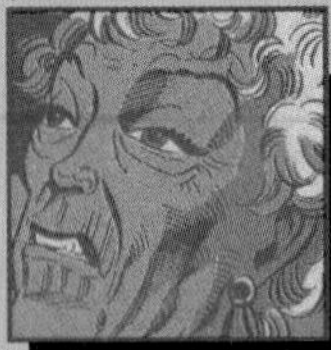

MOIRA BRANDON

Became probationary member in Avengers Honorary member, active Avengers West Coast #100 (1993); current status: deceased

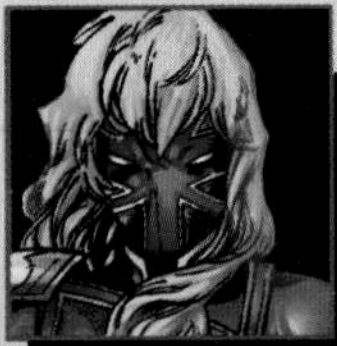

CAPTAIN BRITAIN

(Kelsey Leigh)
Joined Avengers Vol. 3 #81 (2004)